Hearts in Conflict

Hearts in Conflict

A One-Volume History of the Civil War

CURT ANDERS

A Birch Lane Press Book
Published by Carol Publishing Group

A Birch Lane Press Book
Published by Carol Publishing Group
Birch Lane Press is a registered trademark of Carol Communications, Inc.
Editorial Offices: 600 Madison Avenue, New York, N.Y. 10022
Sales & Distribution Offices: 120 Enterprise Avenue, Secaucus, N.J. 07094
In Canada: Canadian Manda Group, P.O. Box 920 Station U, Toronto, Ontario M8Z 5P9
Queries regarding rights and permissions should be addressed to Carol Publishing Group, 600 Madison Avenue, New York, N.Y. 10022

Carol Publishing Group books are available at special discounts for bulk purchases, for sales promotions, fund-raising, or educational purposes. Special editions can be created to specifications. For details, contact Special Sales Department, Carol Publishing Group, 120 Enterprise Avenue, Secaucus, N.J. 07094

Manufactured in the United States of America
10 9 8 7 6 5 4 3 2 1

Library of Congress Cataloging-in-Publication Data

Anders, Curt, 1927–
    Hearts in conflict : a one volume history of the Civil War / by Curt Anders.
        p.   cm.
    "A Birch Lane Press book."
    ISBN 1-55972-184-7
    1. United States—History—Civil war, 1861–1865. I. Title.
E468.A54   1994
973.7—dc20   92-39497
                                                                  CIP

Contents

Part Three: Only the Heroes Are Left

Part Four: Hurry, This Is the Last!

Introduction

"I know something about the Civil War," a friend said to me several years ago, "but I don't understand *how* and *why* such disasters as Shiloh or Sherman's march through Georgia could have happened. Why don't you write a book that *explains* the war to people like me?"

Hadn't that been done? Well, no, except in multivolume works, mainly those by Shelby Foote and Bruce Catton. Of course there were single-volume histories. But they were either coffee-table decorations whose profuse illustrations left little room for text or heavy scholarly works burdened by more facts than most of us ever craved. True, new biographies and studies of campaigns and battles appear every year. But many readers postpone trying such books, knowing they will derive much more benefit from them *after* they have the perspective which a one-volume history that is neither too basic nor too ponderous can provide.

Whether I was qualified to write the kind of book my friend (and others, I discovered) wanted but had not found depended in large part on the approach I would take. My goal was to share my perspective, to act as an unobtrusive guide—not to encroach on academicians' turf by discovering and presenting long-overlooked information or challenging prevailing "myths." What did I bring to reader-guiding that might be significant?

A clue may be found on page one, where I began writing about East Texans who were troubled by mysterious omens and portents. That was natural for me. I am an East Texan; I might have been among them had I been born six decades earlier. Indeed, many of my experiences have paralleled those of some of the men whose ideas and actions drive the events I describe. And my focus on people would remain steady for six hundred more pages.

Always in my mind were the questions you may be asking. How could people such as ourselves have been swept into the most devastating calamity our nation has ever endured? How did our predecessors cope with it? And what results did their enormous sacrifices produce?

In my view, the politicians and generals of the Civil War era were as ordinary as we are, but they faced extraordinary challenges. Some became heroes the old-fashioned way—they *earned* respect—while others failed, lacking the characteristics required to deal with situations utterly unforeseen before Fort Sumter.

This is why I have used the Civil War's participants' own words wherever possible, mainly drawn from messages they sent or letters they wrote. In addition, I have attempted to place us behind both the Northern and Southern lines as events were developing and also to keep you watching what was happening (again, on both sides) in different parts of the vast, embattled country within roughly the same time frames. I hope you do not find this bewildering. But if you do, consider the plight of Major General Henry Wager Halleck, the Union armies' general-in-chief, who was often trying to help his forces win three or more battles at once, however distant they were from each other, by telegraph from a small office in Washington.

General Halleck would be listed among the war's failures, but I see him mainly as (in William Faulkner's phrase) a man whose heart was in conflict with itself. And so I would have us look upon even "saints," such as Abraham Lincoln and Robert E. Lee, as men well aware of what duty demanded of them but who were often as perplexed as we are over the next step to take.

So this book is as much a search for values as it is the story of how people responded. It is the kind of book I wish I could have read in 1950 as I sat in a C-54 flying over the Pacific on my way to the Korean War, mindful of how little I knew about how those before me, facing combat for the first time, had transcended their inadequacies.

One who felt them earlier was the late Reverend William S. Reisman, an infantry company commander in World War II, who anticipated my feelings in a poem he called, simply, "Fear."

> Two fears appear when battle's near;
> Fear of death and fear of fear.
> When battle's won, there's another one;
> Fear of what you might have done.

Our fate, it often seems, is to bungle no matter how much enlightened guidance we have been given. Whether or not history repeats itself, some things do not change: Presidents appear incompetent, Congress still has a radical element, we enter wars unprepared and without agreement as to our goals, military commanders must prove their abilities to lead troops under fire. But no matter what kind of disaster we face, we can probably find a time during the Civil War when conditions were far worse and the outlook much more dismal. Maybe this is what my friend William W. Wallace had in mind; he prodded me almost to the day his heart quit to put whatever I had on paper so that we might have a better understanding of events both awesome and distant, examples from which we may draw enough of whatever it takes to face our futures.

Such have been my motivations, to which one more must be added—the challenge William Faulkner posed in 1950 when he accepted the Nobel Prize in literature and declared:

> I believe that man will not only endure: he will prevail. He is immortal, not because he alone among creatures has an inexhaustible voice, but because he has a soul, a spirit capable of compassion and sacrifice and endurance. The poet's, the writer's, duty is to write about these things. It is his privilege to help man endure by lifting his heart, by reminding him of the courage and honor and hope and pride and compassion and pity and sacrifice which have been the glory of his past.

Unfortunately, wars highlight these values more than any other human experiences. Where other than in the Civil War have they been displayed so abundantly? And when, in America, have so many millions of hearts been in conflict?

PART ONE

As They Were in the Beginning

Chapter 1

"Coercion!" Versus "States' Rights!"

"Comets always come to foretell fearful wars."

This was what A. W. Sparks remembered hearing old men and women say during the summer of 1860 as they watched the Comet of Charles V streaking across the East Texas skies night after night for three months—so bright, "we could almost see to read by its light."

That comet, however, was only one of the omens of change disturbing Sparks in the last year of his youth. "War was in the air," he recalled several decades later. "It was war from the plowhandles to the pulpit; war from the head of the family who talked and read it to his children; war that was sung by our sisters and sweethearts, and it was war in our hearts."

The cause: politics, "red with heat," wrote Sparks, "hot times in the United States Senate, hot in Congress, hot at the State capitols, hot with threats both North and South."

And, nearer Sparks's home:

> That summer numbers of villages throughout Texas were burned, probably from spontaneous combustion, as the thermometer reached 114 degrees Fahrenheit in the shade at my father's house, and sulphur matches caught fire and burned their heads off in the little wooden boxes in which they were kept. Our house would have been burned had the fire not been discovered in time. So hot was politics that it was generally agreed that the burning was the work of incendiaries sent from the North to burn us out so that we could not resist invasion. Such were the conclusions of a mad people.

But the madness was not confined to the people of Texas. Indeed, it is remarkable that it extended that far, to the Southwest, for most of the political heat of which Sparks wrote was being generated a thousand miles or more to the east and to the north of where he was in 1860.

Everyone could sense the danger, but hardly anyone seemed capable of doing anything to prevent emotions from obliterating cool, dispassionate logic. Sparks and millions of other Americans had good reason to expect the political processes that had served the nation so well for so long to dampen or at least moderate the fires. Election-year heat, after all, was nothing new. Nor were the problems the nation faced in the summer of 1860.

But apart from an ominous comet's visit, there were some important differences between that year's election and all the earlier ones, and not merely because of the war talk it was stimulating. This time around it was as though an ancient idea were working its way into evidence, something to this effect: The gods visit the sins of the fathers upon the children. And the children, who had been brought up to look upon politicians as fathers of a sort, were bewildered.

Whatever role the gods may have played in what happened, men did the original sinning, which was to bring slaves from Africa to the British colonies in North America in the early 1600s. Legal importation ended after 1807, but there were about 4 million slaves in the United States in 1860, and this number seemed likely to double in another twenty-six years.

More sinning occurred, by omission, in 1787, when the Founding Fathers met in Philadelphia to frame a Constitution intended to unite thirteen states. Admirable though it proved in so many other respects, their product left two key questions unanswered: Were slaves property, equivalent to land or cattle? And: Did states have the right to withdraw from the Union?

Soon thereafter some of the "several states," having retained all the powers not specifically granted to the federal government when they ratified the Constitution, remedied the Fathers' lapse by passing laws making ownership of slaves legal within their borders—in effect, creating a North and a South. Federal lawmakers respected the distinction, including in the Compromise of 1850 a provision requiring residents in "free" states to return runaway slaves to their owners in the South. And in national census taking, a slave was counted as three-fifths of a person.

Moral opposition to slavery in America began in the 1600s—almost as soon as the "peculiar institution" took root—and in the 1830s the abolitionist movement, centering in Boston, became militant in demanding correction of the error. Enforcement of the

Fugitive Slave Act was so obnoxious to New Englanders in particular that thousands cheered on July 4, 1854, when William Lloyd Garrison burned a copy of the Constitution to protest a runaway slave's return to his owner in Virginia.

Also powering expansion of the abolitionist movement was the popularity of stories, such as *Uncle Tom's Cabin*, describing the plight of slaves seeking freedom. Even in the Deep South people bought the book, for many whites in that region agreed that it was wrong for one human being to own another.

Roger Taney, chief justice of the United States, disagreed, holding—in *Dred Scott v. Sandford*, decided by the Supreme Court in 1857—that slaves were indeed property and did not enjoy the rights granted other Americans by the Constitution. This ignited a firestorm of controversy, appalling Northerners but enabling jubilant Southern extremists to claim that slavery "is now the supreme law of the land."

Not so, argued some legal scholars, citing many flaws in Taney's reasoning. Particularly suspect was his finding that Congress had no right to authorize a territorial government to prohibit slavery within its borders—a subject beyond the scope of the case before the Court and one still being debated with considerable heat in 1860.

Actually, the existence of the new territories west of Missouri and Iowa and east of California and Oregon was a very mixed blessing at the time. The economic opportunities they afforded were enormous, beyond calculation; but to obtain those benefits the nation had to settle the question of whether the rights of slave owners should be protected if they took their human property into those regions. This dispute focused the attention of political leaders on containment of slavery versus its expansion more clearly than did any other single issue, and eventually it would prove too hot for them to handle.

They might have; they were able men, patriots, some of them veterans of the war with Mexico in 1846–47, which, sinful though it may have been, had added vast amounts of land to the United States. But a dramatic incident triggered by the actions of an ordinary individual can have an inordinate impact on the course of events, as one John Brown demonstrated in 1859.

Almost anything that can be said about John Brown may be true, at least in part. In his fifty-nine years he sired twenty children, failed in every business he tried to enter, and reaped the scorn of some people for his suspected dishonesty and the respect and support of others who sensed in him the power of a born leader.

John Brown's hanging—following his conviction for the crimes of insurrection, murder, and treason—was, ironically, his only moment of true success. He died knowing that his acts of violence and his condemnation were polarizing public opinion North and South, hardening concern into antagonism and hatred. And this was as it must be, he believed: His favorite passage in the Bible had been, "Without the shedding of blood there is no remission of sins."

Roughly seven weeks earlier, on a Sunday night in mid-October 1859, Brown had led his 21 recruits in the seizure of an undefended federal arsenal, armory, and rifle works at Harpers Ferry, a tiny village in northern Virginia where the waters of the Shenandoah River meet those of the Potomac. This was the first stage in a campaign, financed secretly by six abolitionists in New England, during which Brown expected slaves to flee from their masters and join his force; he would arm the blacks and teach them how to defend themselves as he led them along the Appalachians into the heart of the South.

Initially, all went as Brown had planned, including the taking of hostages, three white and fourteen black. But during the night his men had killed a free Negro baggagemaster while they were detaining a Baltimore-bound train, and at dawn they shot a white citizen of the village. By midmorning even the nation's president knew there was serious trouble at Harpers Ferry.

Militiamen from nearby Charles Town were among the first to respond. Later came a detachment of U.S. Marines commanded by Colonel Robert E. Lee, on leave from the army's Second Cavalry, with Lieutenant J. E. B. Stuart acting as his aide. In a sharp but brief fight Brown was wounded by a marine officer; two of his sons had already been killed.

Again John Brown had failed. Not one slave had joined him voluntarily; he had done nothing to let any of them know of his intent to enlist them. Of the twenty-one men he led into Harpers Ferry, ten were dead or dying, five were under arrest, and six were fugitives.

Even so, Brown sensed victory and went on to make the most of it. At his trial one of his five lawyers argued that other members of Brown's family were insane; Brown protested that he was of sound mind and responsible for his actions.

Convicted as charged, speaking just before his sentence was to be pronounced, John Brown told the court:

> I say I am yet too young to understand that God is any respecter of persons. I believe that to have interfered as I have done, as I have always freely admitted I have done, in behalf of His despised poor, I did no wrong, but right. Now, if it is deemed necessary that I should forfeit my life for the

furtherance of the ends of justice, and mingle my blood further with the blood of my children and with the blood of millions in this slave country whose rights are disregarded by wicked, cruel, and unjust enactments, I say, let it be done.

John Brown's body became a symbol as soon as it was cut down from the scaffold in Charles Town on December 2, 1859, with a detachment of Virginia Military Institute cadets accompanied by Professor Thomas J. Jackson looking on. In the North on that day church bells tolled, and cannons fired at one-minute intervals; at meetings of mourners from New England to Iowa, John Brown was proclaimed a martyr. And many Southerners took this vast outpouring of lament for a convicted felon, madman though he may have been, as proof that their countrymen above the Potomac intended to launch more invasions of their region.

"His soul goes marching on," sang Union soldiers two years later, but agitation was afoot soon after John Brown's body was lying "a-mould'ring in the grave." The hanged man's spirit spread throughout the halls of Congress, where differences of opinion were so much more acrimonious than usual that a senator remarked, "The only persons who do not have a revolver and a knife are those who have two revolvers." And with Congress paralyzed by partisan maneuvering and James Buchanan's administration inert, hopes turned first toward the political parties' presidential-candidate selection process and ultimately to the election of a man who could, somehow, prevent a ghastly national disaster.

Democrats were dominant in the South and strong throughout the North; the Republicans had made considerable progress since 1854, when the party was created by Whigs and survivors of splinter movements, but only in the North, especially in New England. Although leaders of both parties condemned John Brown's "interference," Democratic extremists in the South linked the convicted felon's near canonization in the North to the "Black Republicans" and advocated immediate secession if any man they nominated won in November. Such ravings crowded out moderate voices; they also made the Republicans realize that there was no point in expecting their candidate's name to appear on Southern ballots in November.

Unusually intense, then, was the national attention given to the Democrats' convention when it opened in Charleston, South Carolina on April 23, 1860. Northern delegates favored Senator Stephen A. Douglas of Illinois, the "Little Giant," who was also popular enough among Southern moderates to have an excellent chance of winning the nomination. Extremists, however, many of whom were called "fire-eaters," succeeded in placing the platform ahead of candidate selection on the agenda, their intent being to secure the party's support for a key Southern demand: federal protection of slave owners' rights in the territories, or the "slave code."

For days the delegates argued. On April 30 the walkouts began, led by Alabama's delegation, splitting the Democratic party and dooming its lengthy and acrimonious Charleston convention to utter failure.

The Republicans who assembled in Chicago's "Wigwam" in the middle of May knew that their party's candidate had to be the winner in virtually all of the Northern and "border" states (such as Missouri, Kentucky, and Maryland) in November. Most likely to be nominated was New York's William H. Seward; worrying the senator's many supporters, however, was a man whose strength was thought to be mainly in the west: Abraham Lincoln.

"Old Irrepressible" Seward had gained that nickname in 1858 after a speech in which he warned that the nation faced "an irrepressible conflict between opposing and enduring forces and it means that the United States must and will, sooner or later, become either entirely a slave holding nation or entirely a free-labor nation."

Earlier in 1858, shortly before running for the Senate against Stephen Douglas, Abraham Lincoln—a Springfield lawyer again after having served a term in Congress—had also faced the slavery question:

"A house divided against itself cannot stand." I believe this government cannot endure half slave and half free. I do not expect the Union to be dissolved—I do not expect the house to fall—but I do expect it will cease to be divided. It will become all one thing, or all the other.

And at New York City's Cooper Union, in February 1859, Lincoln, speaking of Southern extremists' demands, told a distinguished and discerning audience:

Wrong as we think slavery is, we can yet afford to let it alone where it is, because that much is due to the necessity arising from its actual presence in the nation; but can we, while our votes will prevent it, allow it to spread to our national Territories, and to overrun us here in these free states?

Unlike Seward, "Honest Abe," once a humble splitter of fence rails, had few controversial political ties. But could the rough-hewn country lawyer win more states than the urbane, better-known senator? Yes, the delegates in the Wigwam decided; after three ballots Lincoln was declared the Republican party's nominee for president.

The Democrats met again in Baltimore on June 18, but the second attempt proved almost as futile as the first. After another fire-eaters' walkout, the remaining delegates nominated Stephen Douglas. When told of his nomination, he wondered:

> Can the seceders [from the convention] fail to perceive
> that their efforts to divide and defeat the Democratic party,
> if successful, must lead directly to the secession of the
> Southern States?

Whether the bolting extremists meant to achieve such dire results or not, before leaving Baltimore the Southern Democrats assembled, chose John C. Breckinridge of Kentucky as their candidate, and made the slave code part of their platform. Ironically, Breckinridge, then vice president of the United States, was a man sworn to defend the Union against all enemies, foreign and domestic.

Earlier, some Southern moderates had selected John Bell of Tennessee to run as the Constitutional Union party's candidate. So now there were four nominees; none favored secession; yet by splitting the Southern vote, the fire-eaters had made it all but certain that the next president would be Abraham Lincoln.

Of the quartet of contenders only Stephen Douglas broke with tradition and campaigned himself, and then mainly to cool secessionist fever. "I hold that the election of any man on earth by the American people, according to the Constitution," he told Southerners, "is no justification for breaking up this government." Lincoln turned down appeals even for a fresh statement, asking:

> What is it I could say which would quiet alarm? Is it that
> no interference by the government, with slaves or slavery
> within the states, is intended? I have said this so often
> already, that a repetition is but mockery, bearing an ap-
> pearance of weakness.

The candidates' supporters showed no such restraint, at times letting the mud fly. Newspapers were avidly partisan. Yet for all the parades and speeches and frothy editorials, the 1860 campaign had a sobering dimension: disunion.

If Southerners were unduly alarmed by fears of "Coercion!" or too entranced by "States' Rights!" to prevent their emotions from prevailing over reason, Northerners may have been equally at fault by failing to realize how serious threats of secession actually were. Ignorance also contributed to miscalculation, for vast numbers of Northerners had no firsthand knowledge of what W. J. Cash later called "the mind of the South," and vice versa. Nor was either region as uniform as stereotypes, widely accepted at the time, suggested.

Many Republicans, but not the silent Lincoln, said they thought warnings of secession were mostly bluff. The *New York Tribune* declared that Southern threats would appall only fools and that the diabolical mask did not frighten men who knew at what toy shop it was bought.

Such reactions reflected a dangerous overestimation of the appeal of "union" to masses of ordinary Southerners. They were patriots, wrote W. J. Cash, but only to their communities and states:

> So little had they been aware of any common bond of affection and pride, indeed, that often the hallmark of their patriotism had been an implacable antagonism toward the states which immediately adjoined their own....

So pervasive had been John Brown's posthumous success that Southerners who owned no slaves were deeply disturbed by the possibility of servile uprisings. Many Northerners were looked upon with suspicion and in some cases driven out. Southerners, especially those in rural areas, wanted most of all to be left alone, knowing that coping with the uncertainties of weather and crop prices provided worries enough to take a man under before his time. No one really wanted a war. But nobody liked feeling coerced, particularly by holier-than-thou zealots. If it took secession to keep the Yankees from stirring up trouble hundreds of miles from where they had any business being, let it happen. And if it took a war to preserve independence—well, it might be worth it.

Most Northerners, however, had no real desire to bother anybody in the South. If the people down there were in the wrong, that was their problem. Hadn't Lincoln said he'd leave slavery in the South alone, and Douglas, that he'd allow the settlers in the territories to make up their own minds about it?

Breaking up the Union made no sense from the Northern point of view, especially given all the benefits that might come from free homesteads carved out of vacant public lands in the West, tariff revisions that could create jobs, internal improvements, such as railroads to the Pacific coast, and more telegraph lines everywhere.

How could anyone be power mad enough to ignore the future's appeal, and seek to perpetuate the sins of the distant past, at a time when unity of effort could create such a powerful and wealthy nation? Secession and war now would be insanity compounded!

But the question of prosperity versus war was not put to the voters in such stark terms. What they saw on their ballots were candidates' names, and not all of them at that: The range of choices was limited, usually to two of the four—in the North, generally to Lincoln versus Douglas; in most of the South, to Breckinridge versus Bell, with Douglas also "available" in some border states.

Soon after all the polls closed on November 6, 1860, it was clear that Abraham Lincoln had won more electoral votes than he needed in order to be declared the next president of the United States. Stephen Douglas was the victor only in New Jersey and a border state, Missouri. Breckinridge swept the Southern tier of states plus Maryland and Delaware; John Bell took Tennessee, Kentucky, and Virginia.

Combined, and nationwide, Lincoln's three opponents outdrew him six to four. Another quirk: John Breckinridge's popular total was not a clear indication that a majority of Southern voters wanted to secede, for in the "slave" states the ballots cast for pro-Union Bell and Douglas, combined, exceeded those the fire-eaters' candidate received.

That Abraham Lincoln had indeed been elected was all South Carolina's planter-dominated legislature needed to know before it began the formal process of withdrawing from the Union. The people of the state—particularly in Charleston—could not wait, replacing the Stars and Stripes with their Palmetto State flag and cheering the parading patriots who had long since joined military units dedicated to resist "Coercion!"

And so it was in Alabama and Mississippi and would be in Georgia and Florida, each state acting in the belief it had the right within the Constitution to withdraw from the Union and arm its troops for the defense of its borders. There was some opposition, but most of it came from men who thought it best to avoid taking such a grave step until passions cooled. Moreover, it seemed worth asking what benefit, other than emotional satisfaction, would accrue from creating so many small new "republics." But, as before, the fire-eaters prevailed. "You might as well attempt to control a tornado as to attempt to stop them," warned one Southerner. Louisiana went along with the rest of the cotton states, and Texas, too.

What politicians believed and did, however, would require— ultimately—popular support. Alone among the initial seven, Texas gave its voters the opportunity to ratify its convention's recommendation that the state withdraw from the Union. Confirm it they did, and by a wide margin, although two-thirds of Texas's farms had no slaves on them and the remote Lone Star State had little else beyond ancestral ties to link it to the secession surge.

This is how the comet watcher A. W. Sparks explained his reaction to the ratification vote and its aftermath:

> Under the laws of Texas it would have been treason for her people to have refused to respond to this legal calling, for the legislative and executive bodies had declared us no longer connected with the United States, and that government had been formally notified to remove all her possessions from Texas soil. United States mails had been discontinued and the Texas papers gave the news from sister States under the heading "Foreign News." In short, Texas was out of the Union to my mind and I must go and fight for Texas or "pull my freight" as a traitor to a foreign country—a thought I could never entertain for a moment.

Neither could many thousands of other ordinary young men well to the east of him, many of them better educated and more deeply immersed in what some have called the Southern tradition— a romantic illusion of masculine dashing and gallantry, much of it displayed to impress blushing belles whirling their tiny parasols beneath trees laden with magnolia blossoms. Whatever their reasons, wherever in the Deep South they were, men of military age rushed to express their loyalties to their states.

So did Jefferson Davis, until Mississippi's secession a U.S. senator, a Democrat but not a fire-eater, who—at home again in early 1861—accepted a commission as major general of his state's volunteers. Amply qualified for such a command, even at fifty-three, Davis was a West Point graduate, a wounded veteran of hard-fought battles in Mexico, and secretary of war in the early 1850s in President Franklin Pierce's administration.

But field command was not to be this man's destiny. While Davis enjoyed a peaceful interlude on his plantation, delegates from the seven seceded states met in Montgomery, Alabama, early in February 1861 to decide what to do next. Within an astonishingly short time they modified the old Constitution into one for the Confederate States of America and elected Jefferson Davis its provisional president.

Instead of eight separate republics—possibly more—on the American continent, there would be two. But the newer one was hardly a match for its Northern neighbor in any respect. To survive, it would have to attract strength from states in the still-uncommitted border belt: Arkansas, Missouri (if possible), Tennessee, Kentucky, North Carolina, Maryland, and Virginia.

High, though, were the hopes of William Lowndes Yancey—prominent if not foremost among the fire-eaters earlier—when he presented President Davis, just arrived, to the cheering throngs in Montgomery's Fountain Square on February 16, 1861. Declared Yancey: "The man and the hour have met!"

All of this was more bewildering than cause for much alarm to the people in the Northern states, many of whom agreed with old Winfield Scott, general-in-chief of the 17,000-man Union army and a Virginian, and the *New York Tribune's* Horace Greeley, who advised President Buchanan to "let the erring sisters depart in peace."

And so Democrat Buchanan might have done, for he had been Southern inclined throughout his presidency. But his term would end on March 4. Since the Republicans appeared to have brought on the crisis, he preferred to leave it for Abraham Lincoln to cope with.

For all his faults, though, James Buchanan was among the first to realize that the nature of the crisis had changed. Failure to resolve disputes related to slavery had resulted in secession; now secession, and not slavery, was the question to be settled. Others in the North were not as quick either to perceive the difference or to see how important it was. Many of them had dismissed threats of secession as meaningless Southern blustering; now they were unprepared to deal with the breaking up of the old Union. And when reality dawned, belatedly, they found that there were only three possible responses: letting the "erring sisters" depart in peace, compromise, and war.

Actually, there were only two. Compromise would require the North to make most of the concessions—in effect, to reverse nearly all of the positions it had taken earlier.

"Let there be no compromise on the question of *extending* slavery," said Lincoln, still a private citizen in Springfield, Illinois, in early December 1860. He also refused all requests to issue a conciliatory statement. "It would make me appear as if I repented for the crime of having been elected," he replied, "and was anxious to apologize and beg forgiveness."

The general feeling in Washington was that an effort to find common ground had to be made. But could men who had been unable to prevent the rupture now—suddenly—mend it?

Buchanan doubted it, and in his message to Congress on December 4 he suggested the calling of a constitutional convention to amend the document. Southern fears of servile insurrection were the problem, in his view, destroying the "sense of security around the family altar." And he warned:

> Should this apprehension of domestic danger, whether real or imaginary, extend and intensify itself until it shall pervade the masses of the Southern people, then disunion will become inevitable.

Correct though Buchanan's analysis may have been, however, his remedy seemed impractical. He enraged many of his critics by appearing to blame Northern agitation for the crisis; some thought his message could only encourage secession. And pity was perhaps the most generous reaction he could have expected when he maintained that under the laws as he saw them, secession could neither be carried out by a state nor prevented by the federal government.

Having put the address to Congress behind him, Buchanan returned to executive matters. Secession meant, among lesser things, that he would have to replace the Southerners in his cabinet—four, including Secretary of War John Floyd of Virginia, who was suspected of fraud and possibly treasonable shifting of weapons from Northern arsenals to destinations in the South. Far more pressing, however, was the situation at Fort Sumter in Charleston's harbor: a Union bone in South Carolina's throat and one too vexing to that "erring sister" for Buchanan, lame duck though he was, to ignore.

In late 1860 most of General-in-Chief Scott's small Union army was in the West guarding settlers from Indian raids, but there were a few detachments manning defensive posts designed to keep a foreign enemy's ships from entering coastal waters. Units such as these were about all that remained of federal military force in the South after secession-bent mobs seized Union arsenals and camps—in some instances promising to pay for the weapons, ammunition, and equipment they captured.

Still under the Stars and Stripes in the South were Fort Pickens, on Santa Rosa Island near Pensacola, Florida, and two federal posts guarding Charleston's harbor: Fort Moultrie, on its northeastern shore, and Fort Sumter—in early December occupied primarily by civilians building a massive red brick emplacement for hundreds of guns on an outcropping of rock in the middle of the bay, covering its entrances. Ashore at Fort Moultrie, awaiting the completion of the island fortress, were roughly sixty men under the command of Major Robert Anderson, a Kentuckian sent there after Lincoln's election in the hope an officer with a border-state background might ease the anxieties of sensitive South Carolinians regarding federal intentions.

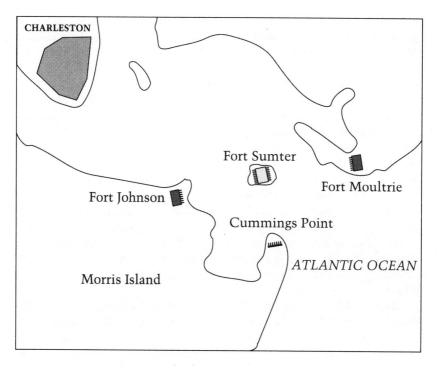

Charleston Harbor

Anderson quickly discovered that Fort Moultrie, built to repel waterborne invaders, was indefensible against attack by South Carolina troops controlling its landward approaches. He asked the War Department for reinforcements as well as fresh instructions. On December 11, Major Don Carlos Buell arrived at Fort Moultrie with Washington's reply, which was for Anderson to do nothing provocative but to defend himself vigorously if attacked. On his own responsibility Buell, having seen how vulnerable Anderson's tiny garrison was, added permission for its commander to withdraw to Fort Sumter for greater security whenever he had "tangible evidence of a design [by the South Carolinians] to proceed to a hostile act."

Following South Carolina's formal secession from the Union on December 20, Major Anderson received more guidance from the secretary of war, controversial Virginian John Floyd, telling him to "exercise a sound military discretion," defending his post if attacked, but to make no "useless sacrifice" of lives. If compelled by superior forces to surrender, Anderson should obtain the best terms he could negotiate.

Nothing in Floyd's directive, however, countermanded Major Buell's authorization of Anderson's withdrawal to Fort Sumter whenever he had sufficient evidence of hostility. And military discretion was a very broad term. Influenced by rumors and not wanting either to be obliged to surrender or to start a war in defense of an untenable position, Major Anderson, on the night of December 26, quietly and skillfully spiked Fort Moultrie's guns and moved his small force in boats to Fort Sumter.

Charlestonians were furious when they found Fort Moultrie abandoned. So was South Carolina's governor, Francis W. Pickens, who had sent three commissioners to Washington to negotiate the transfer of the forts to the seceded state; angrily he demanded that Buchanan order Anderson to return to Fort Moultrie. This, after some vacillation and several tumultuous meetings with his cabinet, Buchanan refused to do. Major Anderson would remain where he was and Fort Sumter would be defended, Buchanan told the commissioners, "against hostile attacks from whatever quarter they come." And Buchanan went beyond that, on the last day in 1860, by ordering the War and Navy departments to send the sloop of war *Brooklyn* to Fort Sumter with reinforcements, ammunition, and stores.

Ironically, also on December 31, Major Anderson sent Washington a dispatch in which he reported shortages only of soap, coal, and candles and said his men could "command this harbor as long as our Government wishes to keep it." While this message was en route to Washington, General Scott, knowing the *Brooklyn* might not clear a barrier of sunken boats in Charleston Harbor's entrance and thinking a merchant steamer would appear less provocative, chartered the shallow-draft *Star of the West*. Anderson's reassuring words reached Buchanan on January 5 and convinced him the risk-laden rescue voyage was unnecessary. To his dismay, however, Buchanan was told that the *Star of the West* had just left New York and could not be recalled.

Southern politicians in Washington warned Governor Pickens a ship was coming, and the militiamen got their guns ready; but no one had given Major Anderson official notice or orders. From Fort Sumter on January 9 he watched the *Star of the West* approach the harbor's entrance, draw fire from South Carolinian batteries, and then turn back unharmed toward New York.

First by putting a mile of water between his command and the South Carolina militiamen and then by keeping Fort Sumter's guns silent on January 9, Robert Anderson had done all he could for the time being to prolong peace. The next moves were up to the politicians.

Governor Pickens ordered gun positions built on shore points so that Fort Sumter would become the center of "a ring of fire," and he gradually turned the problem of removing the Stars and Stripes from his state over to the new Confederate government. James Buchanan recovered from humiliation over the *Star of the West* fiasco, resisted pressure to attempt another expedition, and counted down the days to March 4. And out in Springfield, Illinois, the president-elect received visitors, made decisions regarding the composition of his cabinet, and began packing large boxes marked for shipment to A. Lincoln, Executive Mansion, Washington.

As late as February 11, when Lincoln bade an affectionate farewell to his friends and neighbors and boarded an eastbound train, he had announced only two of his selections for cabinet posts: Edward Bates of Missouri as attorney general and New York's senator William Seward as secretary of state. Both had been his rivals for nomination in Chicago, and so had been two others under consideration—Salmon P. Chase of Ohio and Simon Cameron of Pennsylvania.

Cameron had been a problem. "Make no deals," Lincoln had told his campaign managers in Chicago, but whether they had or not mattered less than Cameron's insistence on being rewarded for his support at the convention and afterward. Reluctantly, Lincoln decided to make Cameron secretary of war, a post in which he might do less damage than he could as secretary of the treasury: Cameron had been suspected, earlier, of fraud while acting as an agent for the settlement of claims by the Winnebago Indians. This left Chase, who would be treasury secretary if Lincoln could persuade Seward to remain in a cabinet that included a man he loathed.

For the most part the prairie lawyer's preliminary cabinet selections showed remarkable political sophistication. Lincoln seemed to be seeking men whose points of view were uncommonly diverse, ranging from abolitionist Chase to moderates Seward and Bates. The South would not be represented, of course, and finding a border-state man seemed hopeless; even so, Lincoln extended his coverage of geographic regions by selecting Gideon Welles, a Connecticut newspaper editor, as secretary of the navy; Montgomery Blair of Maryland, son of powerful old Frank Blair (an adviser to presidents since Andrew Jackson's time), a lawyer who had argued Dred Scott's case before the Supreme Court, and a West Point graduate, as postmaster general; and Caleb Smith of Indiana as secretary of the interior.

Tedious though matching all these names, states, shadings of political leanings, integrity, ability, and expedience with positions may have been—Lincoln remarked that he was sick of his office before he got into it—he stayed at the task until he had what he wanted, or most of it. And along the way the exercise had obliged him to formulate some of the policies he felt he should adopt and announce to the nation in the address he would deliver at his inaugural in Washington on March 4.

That nation would be a house divided against itself, and the crisis Lincoln had expected had come. Yet if Unionists in the South had failed to prevent seven states from seceding, it was also true that they had been strong enough in the border states to halt the Confederacy's expansion. His appeal, then, would be directed to the hearts and minds of reasonable people everywhere, but especially to those still uncommitted.

Buchanan, of course, might blunder anew. As a precaution, Lincoln instructed General Scott to be prepared on March 4 to recapture any federal posts that might have been seized by secessionists in the meantime.

Winfield Scott, seventy-four, a soldier since 1807, hero of the War of 1812 and conqueror of Mexico in 1847, was already acting to protect the interests of the president-elect as well as those of the Union. To prevent secessionists from denying members of the Electoral College the opportunity to meet in Washington and declare Lincoln the winner of the November election, Scott had "flying" artillery units and other troops positioned near the Capitol. And later in February, as the special train bearing the Lincoln family from Springfield neared its destination, General Scott joined Seward and railroad detective Allan Pinkerton in warning the president-elect that he might be assassinated while making a transfer from one railroad line to another in Baltimore.

Wisely, Lincoln heeded such advice, changing his schedule and reaching Washington alone, as any citizen might, though the newspapers subsequently made it seem as though his arrival resembled that of a fugitive slave. Once there, the president-elect quickly perceived serious differences between the free and open life he had enjoyed in Springfield and Washington's politically charged atmosphere. As he unpacked his bag in a Willard's Hotel suite, he may well have wondered if even a log cabin–born man who had been pretty good at splitting rails could long endure amid this strange city's tensions, given a nation so vastly different now from what it had been in May 1860, in his—and the country's—noonday of innocence.

Abraham Lincoln and Jefferson Davis were both natives of Kentucky, born less than a year apart at places within a hundred miles of each other, and twice their paths crossed—during the Black Hawk War in 1832, when Davis swore in Captain Lincoln and his company of volunteers, and in Congress from 1847 to 1849. There, however, the similarities ended until early 1861, when both men, now leaders of their regions, knew that the chances for war depended in large part on whether Kentuckians and the people in other border states decided to heed Davis's appeal and join the Confederacy or to remain in Lincoln's Union.

Senator John J. Crittenden of Kentucky, who was doing as much as any man could to find a basis for compromise, was in many ways typical of Southern conservatives. In 1859 he had led in the formation of the Constitutional Union party, which drew support from Northern moderates who deplored the excesses of extremists on both sides. Significantly, the three states the conservatives' party carried in 1860—Kentucky, Tennessee, and Virginia—had not joined the lower South in its rush to secession and were still reserving their decision in early 1861.

So the question both Lincoln and Davis pondered as they saw Crittenden's gallant compromise effort failing was how to get the border states to make a commitment one way or the other. Lincoln's hopes remained tied to his belief in the strength of Unionists in all three states, particularly in mountainous sections in which slavery was virtually nonexistent. Davis, whose infant Confederacy had nothing much to offer the fence sitters—which also included Arkansas, Missouri, North Carolina, Delaware, and Maryland— could only wait for some Northern blunder to jolt them in his direction.

In strategic terms Virginia was the most important prize, followed by Maryland. Together they sandwiched Washington. If Virginia remained in the Union, so might Maryland and North Carolina and the rest of the states in the undecided buffer zone. Conversely, geographic considerations alone suggested that Virginia's joining the Confederacy would oblige most of the other border states to follow her lead.

President-elect Lincoln's main problem as he awaited his inauguration was to keep from making the kind of a mistake that might give Davis the states his emissaries had not yet been able to attract through persuasion. Lincoln understood both the precariousness of the geopolitical balance and the need to consolidate his support in the North, both of which required a show of strength on his part.

Secretary of State (designate) Seward, however, threatened to weaken Lincoln's preparations just before the inauguration by demanding that Salmon Chase's name be dropped from the list of proposed cabinet members. Lincoln stood firm against the "Premier," a new nickname some had given Seward on the theory he would wrest power from the inexperienced westerner and run the government, but he did accept several of Seward's proposed softenings in the wording of his inaugural address.

On March 4, 1861 General Scott's troops—their bayonets

fixed—were in ranks in case secessionists attempted to keep a Black Republican from being duly sworn in as president of the United States. Scott also had his "flying" artillery near the platform on the unfinished Capitol's east side. But "Old Fuss and Feathers" was not among the 25,000 or so who assembled to hear what Abraham Lincoln would say, thinking it best to remain in a carriage from which he could direct his men if the rumored attempt at disruption was made.

Lincoln began his address by telling the nation he did not consider the Union broken and that he meant to see its laws executed in all of the states. This, he said, he saw as his simple duty—one he would perform unless the American people should withhold the means or direct him to the contrary:

> In doing this there needs to be no bloodshed or violence; and there shall be none, unless it be forced upon the national authority. The power confided to me will be used to hold, occupy, and possess the property and places belonging to the government, and to collect the duties and imposts; but beyond what may be necessary for these objects, there will be no invasion, no using of force against or among the people anywhere.

Remembering, perhaps, that his power could no longer be applied in seven states, Lincoln faced that fact:

> Where hostility to the United States, in any interior locality, shall be so great and universal as to prevent competent resident citizens from holding the Federal offices, there will be no attempt to force obnoxious strangers among the people for that object.

But Lincoln recognized that conditions might change. He would exercise his best discretion, he warned,

> according to circumstances actually existing, and a view and a hope of a peaceful solution of the national troubles and the restoration of fraternal sympathies and affections.

Speaking directly to his "dissatisfied fellow-countrymen," the new president said, "You can have no conflict without being yourselves the aggressors." They had taken no oath to destroy the government, he reminded them, "while I shall have the most solemn one to 'preserve, protect, and defend' it."

Yet conciliation had been his main theme, and he returned to it in closing:

> We are not enemies, but friends. We must not be enemies. Though passion may have strained, it must not break our bonds of affection. The mystic chords of memory, stretching from every battlefield and patriot grave to every living heart and hearthstone all over this broad land, will yet swell the chorus of the Union when again touched, as surely they will be, by the better angels of our nature.

Chapter 2

Fort Sumter: *The Guns of April*

On the day before Lincoln invoked the mystic chords of memory in Washington, Pierre Gustave Toutant Beauregard took command of the South's troops in Charleston. Until February 20, Major Beauregard had been—briefly—superintendent of the United States Military Academy at West Point, where as a cadet he had learned the art of employing artillery from Major Robert Anderson. Now, suddenly, Beauregard was a brigadier general in the new Confederate army, with the mission of sending his former instructor northward, using artillery fire if necessary to persuade Anderson to depart.

"CSA" linked to Beauregard's rank, and also the fact that he had been sent from Montgomery, indicated how rapidly the three-week-old government was moving. In secession's initial wake, many Southern-born officers resigned from the "Old Army" to offer their services to their native states. Davis, having been secretary of war as recently as 1856, was aware of their careers and merits; now, as constitutional commander-in-chief of the Confederate army and navy, he selected men such as Louisiana's Beauregard to give cohesion as well as leadership to the military forces the seven states were building.

Beauregard—a twice-wounded veteran of Winfield Scott's Mexico City campaign, erect, punctilious in his courtesy—was a superb choice for the Charleston assignment. Apart from his charm and ability, the South Carolinians welcomed him as a sign they would no longer be alone in asserting their sovereignty, and they matched his energy in strengthening the "ring of fire" on shore points from which their guns and mortars could reduce Fort Sumter to smoldering rubble.

General Beauregard arrived on March 3, Lincoln swore to "preserve, protect, and defend" on the fourth, and the next day the new president of the United States learned that Major Anderson had enough food to remain at Fort Sumter only until about April 15. So it was that hunger—a simple fact of life —earned its place on the long list of proximate causes of all that happened after this deadline for decisions reached the Executive Mansion in Washington.

Montgomery Blair recalled that his brother-in-law, former naval officer Gustavus V. Fox, had been working since January on a plan to deliver supplies and several companies of troops to Fort Sumter, at night and on tugboats. The new postmaster general summoned Fox to Washington and took him to see Lincoln. The president quickly grasped the idea's subtlety: Sumter's food stocks might be replenished without bringing on a test of gunners' skills. Landing reinforcements, however, was a step Lincoln was not yet ready to consider.

With Fox's plan in mind, the president assembled his seven cabinet members and asked for their opinions on whether it was wise to send a provisioning expedition to Fort Sumter, given General Scott's warning that indeed the task would require a large fleet and 25,000 troops, more forces than the Union had, to reach Anderson's garrison.

If diversity was what Lincoln had sought in selecting his cabinet, that he had obtained it was soon apparent. Blair was alone in advocating that Lincoln keep the flag flying over Fort Sumter whatever the risk. Five of the remaining six advised giving up the post; Salmon Chase said (in effect), go ahead and try resupplying Anderson, but only if it will not cause a war.

That Secretary of War Cameron and Secretary of the Navy Welles favored letting the secessionists have Fort Sumter was not surprising. They respected General Scott's judgment of the requirements, and they were aware of how ill prepared the Union was militarily. Secretary of State Seward agreed; he and Scott had long been allies, and Seward sincerely believed that if the Union employed restraint and conciliation, avoiding all actions that might spread secession, eventually the "erring sisters" would repent and return. But the ambition to be "premier" in the new administration still motivated Seward, and the Sumter question gave him an opportunity to advance his hopes.

As secretary of state, Seward could not receive the three Confederate commissioners President Jefferson Davis had sent to Washington without implying recognition of their government. Through an intermediary, however, surreptitiously, without any authority whatsoever, behaving as though whatever policies and plans Lincoln was pursuing mattered not at all, Seward gave the Southerners his word that within a short time the Union would abandon both Fort Sumter and Fort Pickens.

"At all hazards and under all circumstances during this stage of proceedings any Fortress accessible by the Sea, over which we still have dominion, should be held. If war comes, let it."

So Stephen Hurlbut had advised Abraham Lincoln after a visit to his native Charleston. Hurlbut, an old friend from the Illinois years, was only one of three men Lincoln had sent there to make fresh estimates of the situation. Gustavus Fox returned more confident than ever that his plan for resupplying Sumter would succeed. The third scout, Ward Lamon, was lucky to have escaped—a mob had offered to stretch his neck—but he did bring back a warning from South Carolina's governor: "Nothing can prevent war except the acquiescence of the President of the United States in secession, and his unalterable resolve not to attempt any reinforcement of the Southern forts."

All of what Fox, Lamon, and Hurlbut had told the president must have been running through his mind on the night of March 28, when General Scott astonished Lincoln and the cabinet—except Seward—by sending Lincoln a message in which he declared that the time had come to surrender both Fort Sumter and Fort Pickens. Montgomery Blair, looking straight at Seward, charged that Scott had been governed by political considerations, implying that he believed Scott's words had been inspired, if not dictated, by the secretary of state.

Lincoln got no sleep that night, but he set Gustavus Fox's plan in motion the next morning by sending this order to Secretary of War Simon Cameron:

> I desire that an expedition, to move by sea, be got ready to sail as early as the 6th of April next, the whole according to memorandum attached, and that you cooperate with the Secretary of the Navy for that object.

For the ambitious secretary of state everything had gone wrong since he had made his pledge to the visiting Confederate commissioners. But the Southerners were in no hurry. "We are playing a game in which time is our best advocate," said one in a letter to Jefferson Davis. "There is a terrific fight in the Cabinet. Our policy is to encourage the peace element in the fight, and at least blow up the Cabinet on the question."

Seward, seeing the game going against him, grew more and more evasive when the Confederates' intermediary pressed him for the often-promised results. He devised two schemes. In carrying out the first he won Lincoln's approval to manage a secret force intended to *reinforce* Fort Pickens, on Santa Rosa Island in the Gulf of Mexico, near Pensacola, Florida, then used this authority—covertly—to take critical strength away from Gustavus Fox's Fort Sumter expedition without its leader realizing he had been undercut. Seward's second response was nothing less than an attempt to take control of the government. On April 1 the would-be premier sent the president a memo in which he demanded, in effect, that Lincoln abdicate and give all but ceremonial powers to him.

Seward was not alone in thinking that Abraham Lincoln had been slow to become "presidential." Among other deficiencies, the former rail-splitter seemed hamstrung by lack of troops and plagued by hordes of men seeking jobs in his administration. This inspired the *New York Herald* to suggest a remedy:

> Major Anderson says twenty thousand men can relieve him and reinforce Fort Sumter. There are over fifty thousand patriots now at the command of Mr. Lincoln, waiting for office. Send them along.

Seward, though, was serious. In his April 1 memo to the president—after alleging absence of policies for dealing with the domestic crisis—he turned to foreign matters and suggested steps that could generate war with Spain and France, the idea being that Southerners would forget secession and rally round the flag if there was a foreign foe to fight. But lest country lawyer Lincoln miss his basic point, Seward closed with these passages:

> But whatever policy we adopt there must be energetic prosecution of it.

> For this purpose it must be somebody's business to pursue it and direct it incessantly.

> Either the President must do it himself, and be all the while active in it, or

> Devolve it on some member of the cabinet. Once adopted, debates on it must end, and all agree and abide.

> It is not my especial province.

> But I neither seek to evade nor assume responsibility.

Disingenuous, astonishing, insulting, insubordinate—an appalled Lincoln must have found all these qualities and more in Secretary of State Seward's words. But having read them, on the same day the president replied in a polite letter in which he demolished every argument the would-be dictator had made.

Although the president may well have considered the case closed, the "premier" did not concur. Seward had long shared Lincoln's faith in the Unionists' influence in Virginia, of all uncommitted states the most important strategically, and he may have engineered contact between the Union's president and John B. Baldwin. The purpose: a deal.

"If you will guarantee to me the state of Virginia," said Lincoln, reportedly, to Baldwin, "I shall remove the troops [from Fort Sumter]. A state for a fort is no bad business."

But nothing came of that. And in the wake of this failure Seward was running out of excuses to give the three Confederate commissioners who were waiting, knowing that time was on their side, for him to live up to his word.

Though Major Robert Anderson had been starving for instructions while James Buchanan was president, his pangs grew even more acute in the days after Abraham Lincoln became commander-in-chief. Not a word came from Secretary of War Simon Cameron. Anderson learned of the fate Seward intended for his fort from the *New York Courier*: "EVACUATION OF FORT SUMTER DETERMINED ON," its headline proclaimed; "ANDERSON TO GO TO FORT MONROE."

Beauregard proved firm in employing the hunger weapon, but he relented a little when Governor Pickens's aide returned from an errand to the fort one day with a report that some of the federal officers were suffering from a lack of cigars. On his next trip, the Confederate colonel took along several cases of claret—courtesy of the general—as well as cigars.

All the while, Major Anderson and Captain John Foster had been guiding the efforts of the soldiers and civilian workmen marooned with them to prepare the fort for battle. Actually, Fort Sumter was a brick pentagon, with walls five feet thick, enclosing an open parade area in the center and a barracks designed to house 650 men, of which Anderson had roughly one-tenth, not counting the civilian workmen. Studded along the walls were openings in two tiers for guns on the lower casemate and the intermediate barbette platforms. Guns whose muzzles had to be elevated considerably for their powerful explosives to reach distant targets were on a top deck or down in the parade area. Sumter's design called for 146 guns: Anderson had 51, ranging from light twenty-two-pounders to ten-inch columbiads. But the island fortress's guns could reach Beauregard's onshore batteries, while the Confederates had little chance of hitting Anderson's well-protected artillery pieces and crews.

Fort Sumter's most significant feature, however, may have been its flagpole. The Stars and Stripes whipping out proudly in the harbor breeze reminded Charlestonians that the Palmetto State's sovereignty was limited. And Anderson and his men saw their flag as the symbol of all the values they had dedicated their lives to defend.

Back in January, Robert Anderson had restrained his gunners while they watched South Carolinian batteries fire at the star-spangled banner flying over the unarmed *Star of the West*—not learning until much later that General Scott had instructed his staff to advise the major, in advance and in writing, that "the guns of Fort Sumter may be employed to silence such fire, and the same in case of like firing upon Fort Sumter itself." And in late February, the last time he had heard anything at all from the War Department, he had been told to remain on the defensive and act with the "forebearance that has distinguished you heretofore."

Remembering, perhaps, both the January permission he had not received in time and the February prohibition, Anderson was understandably confused on April 3 as he watched Beauregard's gunners open fire on a little schooner, its Union flag clearly visible, attempting to enter the harbor. Again the major held his fire, setting aside the pleas of most of his officers to let them avenge this fresh insult.

An investigation showed that the schooner had merely been blown off course, and Governor Pickens expressed his regrets. But Anderson knew his "forebearance" was causing his officers and men to lose their respect for him. To Washington he wrote:

> The truth is that the sooner we are out of this harbor the better. Our flag runs an hourly risk of being insulted, and my hands are tied by my orders, and if that was not the case, I have not the power to protect it. God grant that neither I nor any other officer in our Army may be again placed in a position of such mortification and humiliation.

More mortification came to Anderson when one of his junior officers returned from a session with Pickens during which the lieutenant read a dispatch one of the Confederate commissioners in Washington had sent the governor. The message's thrust, Anderson learned, was that the president lacked the courage to withdraw Sumter's garrison but intended, instead, to shift the responsibility to the fort's commander by allowing him to be starved out.

Next to buffet Robert Anderson was a letter he received from

Washington on April 7, one written on April 4, signed by Secretary of War Simon Cameron. It said:

> Your letter of the 1st instant occasions some anxiety to the President. On the information of Captain Fox he had supposed you could hold out until the 15th instant without any great inconvenience; and had prepared an expedition to relieve you before that period. Hoping still that you will be able to sustain yourself till the 11th or 12th instant, the expedition will go forward; and, finding your flag still flying, will attempt to provision you, and, in case the effort is resisted, will endeavor also to reinforce you.
>
> You will therefore hold out, if possible, till the arrival of the expedition.
>
> It is not, however, the intention of the President to subject your command to any danger or hardship beyond what, in your judgment, would be usual in military life; and he has entire confidence that you will act as becomes a patriot and soldier, under all circumstances. Whenever, if at all, in your judgment, to save yourself and command, a capitulation becomes necessary, you are authorized to make it.

Anderson was stunned. As he interpreted Cameron's words (actually, Lincoln's, though the major had no way of knowing that), the government was committed to risking war, the very thing Anderson had sacrificed so much to avoid—and thought he had avoided.

In a restrained reply Anderson confessed his surprise, coming as the message had in the wake of assurances given the Confederates that the government would evacuate Fort Sumter. He continued:

> It is, of course, now too late for me to give any advice in reference to the proposed scheme of Captain Fox. I fear that its result cannot fail to be disastrous to all concerned....
>
> We have not enough oil to keep a light in the lantern for one night. The boats will have, therefore, to rely at night entirely on other marks. I ought to have been informed that this expedition was to come. Colonel Lamon's remark convinced me that the idea, merely hinted at to me by Captain Fox, would not be carried out. We shall strive to do our duty, though I frankly say that my heart is not in the war which I see is to be thus commenced. That God will still avert it, and cause us to resort to pacific measures to maintain our rights, is my ardent prayer....

Off on the mail boat went Anderson's response, but what he had said would not reach Washington. Later that day the major learned that the Confederate government had directed General Beauregard to intercept all official mail to and from Sumter and send it to Montgomery.

It might have relieved Robert Anderson's anguish a little if he could have known that the Confederates had already picked up reports of Gustavus Fox's preparations. On April 7, the same day Anderson's letter was seized, Governor Pickens admitted his confusion in a wire to Davis's commissioners in Washington:

> We have so many extraordinary telegrams, I would be glad to know from you if it is true that they have determined to reinforce Sumter, and if a naval force is sent to our harbor.

The next day, April 8, Pickens received this reply: "We are assured that you will not be disturbed without notice, and we think Sumter is to be evacuated and [Fort] Pickens provisioned."

Notice arrived in Charleston that evening, brought by two emissaries from the president of the United States to Governor Pickens. One was Robert Chew, a State Department official, who first recited lines he had memorized and then handed Pickens a copy of what he had just said:

> I am directed by the President of the United States to notify you to expect an attempt will be made to supply Fort Sumter with provisions only, and that if such attempt be not resisted, no effort to throw in men, arms or ammunition, will be made, without further notice, or in case of attack.

If Pickens was offended by the irregular and undiplomatic means Lincoln had employed in communicating with the head of another sovereign government, he received a second jolt when Chew told Pickens that he was not authorized to take a reply back to Washington. Apparently, nothing the governor had to say was of any interest to the president.

In any case, Abraham Lincoln was busy. He had been even busier on April 1, the day William Seward had offered to take charge of the government, and in haste the president signed an order—apparently without first reading it—that Seward put among a mass of other papers awaiting Lincoln's signature.

Addressed to Captain Andrew H. Foote, the commandant of the Brooklyn Navy Yard, the order said:

> You will fit out the *Powhatan* without delay. Lieutenant Porter will relieve Captain Mercer in command of her. She is bound on secret service, and you will under no circumstances communicate to the Navy Department that she is fitting out.

Captain Foote was already fitting out the *Powhatan* by order of Secretary of the Navy Gideon Welles—why, he knew not, for Gustavus Fox was employing as much secrecy as he could as he assembled his fleet of warships, steamers, and three tugboats for the Fort Sumter expedition. Understandably, then, Foote was confused on April 5 when Lieutenant David Dixon Porter presented him with a presidential order to place the eleven-gun frigate under his command.

Foote, a by-the-book naval officer, insisted on Secretary Welles's approval before complying with the order. A telegram to Washington set in motion a midnight flurry of activity, but in the end the *Powhatan* was at sea, under Porter's command, bound for the Gulf of Mexico and Fort Pickens.

It might have been otherwise. The conclusion President Lincoln reached in a conference with Welles and Seward was that command of the *Powhatan* should be returned to Captain Mercer, who — presumably—would take the frigate to Charleston as Gustavus Fox had planned. Seward volunteered to send a message to Porter. This he did, the next day, signing it himself and thus giving Porter a reason to refuse to turn back.

Fox, unaware of any of this, sailed from Brooklyn on the steamer *Baltic* on April 10 with 200 troops and enough food to keep Major Anderson's men alive for another year. His fleet, Fox expected, would rendezvous off Charleston Harbor—with the *Powhatan* and her firepower there, too.

Another thing Captain Fox did not know was what Seward had told the intermediary he had been using for communication with the Confederate commissioners: "Faith as to Sumter fully kept; wait and see."

A day before Fox sailed, on April 9, President Jefferson Davis assembled his cabinet to consider the notice Robert Chew had given Governor Pickens the night before, along with all the other reports from the North suggesting that "Coercion!" was no longer merely a slogan.

Davis saw coercion first in the *Star of the West* intrusion and declared this new expedition aggressive enough to justify the Confederate government's ordering Fort Sumter to be taken, even if this meant the South would have to fire the first shot. But did the cabinet agree?

No, said Georgia's Robert Toombs, a fire-eater in 1860, now the Confederate secretary of state. "The firing on that fort will inaugurate a civil war greater than any the world has yet seen," he argued. "You will wantonly strike a hornet's nest which extends from mountains to ocean, and legions now quiet will swarm out and sting us to death. It is unnecessary; it puts us in the wrong; it is fatal."

Perhaps, but what would people in the uncommitted border states think if the Confederacy ignored both Seward's false and misleading assurances and this new threat to sovereignty? How could the new nation hope to survive if it left it to South Carolinians alone to repel the invasion?

"Unless you sprinkle blood in the face of the Southern people," warned an Alabamian, "they will be back in the old Union in less than ten days."

Again, maybe. Who really knew? But a decision had to be made, and Secretary of War Leroy P. Walker telegraphed it to General Beauregard in Charleston the next morning:

> If you have no doubt of the authorized character of the agent who communicated to you the intention of the Washington Government to supply Fort Sumter by force you will at once demand its evacuation, and if this is refused proceed, in such manner as you may determine, to reduce it.

Lincoln had placed his faith in Gustavus Fox to reach Robert Anderson; now Davis had entrusted to Beauregard the task of preventing the resupply of Fort Sumter—if possible, through negotiation; if not, by gunfire.

Pierre Beauregard knew what to do, and Robert Anderson knew what to expect. Duty, Honor, Country would not become West Point's terse but enormously powerful motto for a generation, yet those beacons had guided them since they were cadets. They still did, though their countries were no longer the same.

On the afternoon of April 11 a small boat carried Lieutenant Colonel A. R. Chisholm (who had, earlier, brought wine and cigars) to Fort Sumter; James Chesnut, former senator from South Carolina and now colonel; and Captain Stephen D. Lee. Anderson greeted them, then read the message Beauregard had sent them to present:

> I am ordered by the Government of the Confederate States to demand the evacuation of Fort Sumter.... All proper facilities will be afforded for the removal of yourself and

command, together with company arms and property, to any post in the United States which you may select. The flag which you have upheld so long and with so much fortitude, under the most trying circumstances, may be saluted by you on taking it down.

Anderson conferred with his officers. Not even young Lieutenant R. K. Meade, from Virginia, favored surrender.
Anderson wrote to General Beauregard:

I have the honor to acknowledge the receipt of your communication demanding the evacuation of this fort, and to say, in reply thereto, that it is a demand with which I regret that my sense of honor, and of my obligations to my Government, prevent my compliance.

Anderson escorted Beauregard's aides to the wharf where the boatmen were waiting. "Will General Beauregard open his batteries," he asked, "without further notice to me?"
"I think not," Colonel Chesnut replied.
"I shall await the first shot, and if you do not batter us to pieces, we shall be starved out in a few days."
Gentleman that he was, Chesnut asked if he might pass that remark on to General Beauregard. Anderson, noting only that it was true, did not object.
Night came, during which Beauregard reported the day's progress and Anderson's remark to Montgomery. And, shortly after midnight on April 12, back to Fort Sumter came the three aides with a question: When, precisely, would starvation compel Anderson to surrender?
Not earlier than at noon on April 15, the major's officers agreed, having in mind the status of food supplies remaining and the lack of any sign of Fox's ships—and then only if the Confederates made no hostile moves, if no new instructions came from Washington, and if no fresh supplies arrived.
Too many "ifs," Colonel Chesnut decided, shaking his head. Observing ritual to the last, he wrote a reply and handed it to Major Anderson, who read:

By authority of Brigadier-General Beauregard, commanding the provisional forces of the Confederate States, we have the honor to notify you that he will open the fire of his batteries on Fort Sumter in one hour from this time.

Edmund Ruffin was among the 4,000 or so soldiers waiting on

shore points for orders. At sixty-seven years of age, this white-haired man had come a long way to see a dream come true, for he was a Virginian fire-eater too impatient with his own state's reticence to be anywhere but in Charleston, where secession was a fact. He had watched John Brown hanged back in 1859; now he was with the Palmetto Guards on Morris Island, south of Fort Sumter, scanning the dark skies for the burst of a mortar round that would be the signal for him to fire the Confederacy's first shot.

Born in 1794, sickly as a child, regarded as an eccentric by his neighbor, who thought he was crazy to use marl to restore fertility to his Virginia farm's depleted soil until he proved it did, Ruffin had witnessed almost the entire span of politicians' futile attempts to settle disputes rooted in the initial sin. Now two hundred years of failure to agree would close with the signal burst over that dark mass out in the harbor's entrance. The power to end that era was in Ruffin's hand—to him, an honor—and when the fireball exploded directly over the fort at four-thirty A.M., he sent a columbiad's round arching into the kind of future a comet, the year before, had foretold.

For the first few hours the fireworks were disappointing, the war entirely one-sided, and thousands of spectators along the waterfront and on rooftops in Charleston wondered why. So did Beauregard's gunners. Had the Yankees gone to sleep?

Those not on guard had. Captain Abner Doubleday was on his cot when the signal shot brightened the night sky and he heard the thud of the first round as it hit the parapet, but he knew there would be no return firing until after reveille and a breakfast of fat pork and water. Only then did Anderson give Doubleday the honor of firing the first shot toward quelling the rebellion. Aimed at the Confederate batteries south of Sumter at Cummings Point on Morris Island, the round was well placed but did no damage beyond, perhaps, destroying a little more of old Edmund Ruffin's hearing.

That set the pattern for the day's dueling. Beauregard's rounds converged on a single point, Sumter; Anderson resembled a farmer scattering grain to honking geese surrounding him. Neither side could do the other much harm, so well shielded were the men and guns around the "ring of fire" as well as inside the fort. Yet this wearying exchange of metal had a purpose, for Fox's fleet might arrive at any moment and change the odd battle's geometry dramatically and perhaps decisively.

Both Anderson and Beauregard watched the harbor's entrance with increasing anxiety as the hours passed. Then, early in the afternoon, two ships appeared; soon, a third.

The *Harriet Lane* was the first in Gustavus Fox's flotilla to reach the rendezvous point ten miles outside Charleston Harbor. The five-gun paddle wheeler was waiting there at three A.M. on April 12—as Colonel Chesnut was informing Major Anderson that the firing would begin in one hour—when the unarmed *Baltic*, bearing Fox and 200 troops, steamed alongside.

A fierce spring storm had made the *Baltic*'s trip from New York a miserable one. Seas were rough and skies still angry at dawn when the *Pawnee* came in sight and dropped anchor near the *Baltic*.

Relieved somewhat but surely wondering where his other five ships might be, Fox went over to the *Pawnee* to confer with her master, Captain Stephen C. Rowan. Fox's intention was to make a run for Sumter with the three vessels he now had, but Rowan wanted no part of triggering a civil war. His orders were, he told Fox, to stay where he was and await the *Powhatan*'s arrival.

Fox left Rowan and took the *Baltic* and the *Harriet Lane* toward the bar at Charleston Harbor's entrance. Smoke covered the water in the distance, and Fox could hear guns booming. Fox went back to Rowan with the news that the war had already begun. Now Rowan was ready to fight, but Fox thought it best to wait for the *Powhatan*'s guns and the three tugs.

Having three ships in sight beyond the bar, even though they showed no sign of moving in, encouraged Robert Anderson and his men. All day the major had been conserving everything, especially powder-bag cartridges, thinking that he might need to concentrate his fire on the Confederate batteries flanking the channel as the ships started toward the fort.

Anderson ordered the colors dipped, a signal that he knew the sailors were there. Suddenly a Confederate shot cut the halyard. Raising the flag to the top of the pole, however, would have to be done later: Rebel hot-shot rounds had set the barracks on fire.

With sundown came rain and some respite from the chipping away the Confederates had been doing along Fort Sumter's walls. With Sumter's firing suspended, Lieutenant Meade put a detail of men to work making new cartridge bags, a task now limited both by the few scraps of fabric remaining and needles, of which there were only six.

Darkness and foul weather presented another problem: How could Anderson's lookouts tell the difference between boats sent from the ships outside the harbor, which would be most welcome, and any filled with Confederates bent on fighting their way inside the walls?

Vigilance was the only remedy. But all that the keepers of the nightlong watches saw were rowboats moving out from Charleston, each bearing a torch to light the harbor's entrance so that batteries at Fort Moultrie and on Cummings Point could fire on any ship heading up the channel toward Sumter.

As disappointed as Beauregard's gunners were the thousands of spectators still lining Charleston's wharves and rooftops when morning came on April 13, bringing more rain. And out beyond the bar Gustavus Fox had spent a discouraging night scanning seaward for the *Powhatan's* lights—in vain.

Anderson's tired men faced fat pork and water again for breakfast. Soon afterward, Fort Moultrie's batteries sent more hot shot into the barracks' smoldering ruin, igniting fresh fires too wind whipped to fight. Now it was a matter of keeping the fort from being blown off its rock outcropping, for stored inside the magazine were more than three hundred barrels of gunpowder, and the flames were not far from the magazine's door. Anderson's men removed fifty barrels, perhaps more, then had to quit because the air was filled with sparks. With no safe place for the powder barrels, the men rolled all but five into the harbor—but five would be enough, since there was no more cloth for making cartridge bags.

Dense smoke and fumes from the burning barracks almost suffocated Sumter's defenders, reduced now to firing only one gun at ten-minute intervals. Beauregard's gunners, watching the black plume thicken, cheered the bravery of men who could keep fighting with an inferno at their backs, then sent more hot shot flying toward the fort.

Honor fully satisfied, how much longer would Anderson hold out? Louis T. Wigfall, over on Cummings Point, pondered that question as the ships outside the harbor remained motionless and the fort they had come to save fought on.

Like old Edmund Ruffin, fire-eater Wigfall was there by choice. He had returned to his native state from Washington, where he had been serving as a senator from Texas; now he was a colonel, but one without a command, and his patience was running low.

Around one o'clock that afternoon a Confederate round hit Fort Sumter's flagpole: Lieutenant Norman Hall rushed across the parade area, ignoring the heat and flames, and picked up the flag before more than its fringes got burned. Hall and three other men found a spar, attached the flag to it, took the improvised flagpole up to the parapet, and raised it.

Colonel Wigfall saw the flag go down, and that was enough. Cummings Point's guns held their fire while a rowboat carried Wigfall to Sumter. Once there, he tied a white handkerchief to the tip of his sword, jumped through an embrasure, and told Major Anderson: "You have defended your flag nobly, sir. It's madness to persevere in such useless resistance."

Anderson, under the impression Wigfall represented General Beauregard, agreed. Down came the flag, up went a white one; Sumter ceased firing; Wigfall departed.

Then, sent by Beauregard, Captain Stephen Lee and two other aides came to the fort to offer Southern assistance in putting out the fires. Confusion prevailed until Lee told Anderson that Wigfall had been at Cummings Point for the past two days and had no authority to negotiate a surrender. Major Anderson ordered his flag raised again and sent his men back to their guns. But Captain Lee persuaded Anderson first to extend the accidental truce, then to surrender—again—the terms being the same as those Beauregard had proposed on the day before the firing had begun.

Weary, his face smudged, the weight of defeat as well as advancing age upon him, Anderson still had the satisfaction of duty well performed and honor unblemished. Not so fortunate was Gustavus Fox.

While the impetuous Wigfall and Major Anderson had been reaching the first agreement, at around two o'clock on the afternoon of April 13, the *Pocahontas* reached the *Baltic*, the *Harriet Lane*, and the *Pawnee* outside the harbor's entrance. The *Pocahontas* arrived too late, of course, but the information her master gave Fox was even more devastating: The *Powhatan* could never have supported his effort, for she was Florida-bound—and had been since before Fox sailed from New York into the storm that had also denied him the three vital tugboats.

Calm restored, there remained the adding up. During the thirty-three hours of Sumter's resistance not a man had been killed. On each side four were wounded, none seriously. Confederate guns sent 3,341 rounds toward the fort and ruined it. Damage done by Sumter's batteries was insignificant.

The next morning, Sunday, April 14, 1861, in accordance with the terms General Beauregard had set forth, Major Anderson assembled his men to give their tattered, flame-singed flag a 100-gun salute before lowering it and leaving the fort. When the count reached fifty, however, an accident killed one of the gunners: Private Daniel Hough, the first of more than 620,000 American soldiers who would not live to see the war's end.

Anderson delayed his garrison's departure to bury Private Hough at Fort Sumter with all military honors. A company of Confederate infantrymen stood at present arms as a Confederate chaplain conducted the service.

Soon thereafter, Anderson's men marched out of the fort to the wharf, the strains of "Yankee Doodle" in their ears, to board the

Isabel, the ship Beauregard had sent to take them out to the *Baltic*. Anderson brought with him the flag.

As the *Isabel* steamed past Fort Moultrie, the gunners lined up along the shore removed their hats in salute. No one cheered.

Chapter 3

The Clanking of the War Chariots

F or Robert Anderson's soldiers, boarding the *Baltic* had been a strange way to leave a battle. Crewmen, sensing this, did all they could to make the discouraged men comfortable. Even so, Sumter's defeated defenders crowded the rail as the *Baltic* began to move. They watched their fort recede in the west until they could see it no more.

Anderson, duty still foremost in his mind, felt compelled to write a report. But he was too tired to hold a pen, so he dictated a message to Gustavus Fox, to be sent to Secretary of War Cameron once they reached New York: one long sentence. He might have said much more—mentioned five months of strain, neglect, frustration, anger, confusion, fatigue, the quenching of his hopes for peace. But he was reporting to a faceless government, not to a man.

Fox then wrote his own report. He recited the sequence of dates and events in the terse way naval officers do in ships' logs, but at the close he added: "In justice to itself I trust the Government has sufficient reasons for putting me in the position they have placed me."

Major Anderson might well have said the same thing.

When the *Baltic* reached New York on April 18, the tattered Fort Sumter flag flying from her foremast, she was greeted by whistles and bells from every vessel in the harbor. Cheering crowds at dockside welcomed the soldiers; the men, astonished to find themselves hailed as heroes, were bewildered even more by the jubilant cries filling the air.

Virginia had started its secession process while the *Baltic* was steaming northward, and war fever had spread all over the Union. On Sunday, April 14, while Major Anderson was lowering the flag at Fort

Sumter, Lincoln and his cabinet—of one mind now—took up a host of vexing questions; the next day, the president issued a proclamation in which he called upon the states to provide 75,000 militiamen for ninety days to resist "combinations too powerful to be suppressed" by ordinary means and set July 4 as the date for a special session of Congress to convene. Virginians, appalled at the idea of fighting fellow Southerners, responded on April 17 by passing an ordinance of secession that was to be ratified by voters on May 23.

Lincoln's action had been bold indeed. Lacking any other authority to deal with armed rebellion, he had relied on a 1795 statute dealing with the militia in making the call for troops. He assumed other broad war powers as well, trusting that Congress would approve his decisions when it met in July. And by giving the border states a clear signal that conciliation efforts had ended, that coercion was now federal policy, he risked losing all of them to the Confederacy.

None of that mattered to the people of the North. From Boston westward city streets filled with parading patriots chanting belligerent slogans—as Anderson's men discovered when they left the *Baltic* in New York. John Andrew, the governor of Massachusetts, responded to the call for troops by telegraphing Secretary of War Simon Cameron: "By what route shall we send?" Offers of regiments by other Northern governors soon caused the overwhelmed Cameron to ask them to cease recruiting while he absorbed the units he had already accepted.

This sudden outpouring of support was both emotional and practical. Fort Sumter's fall incited shame and anger, fueling desire for revenge. Abolitionists in New England, overlooking the fact that Lincoln's stated intent was limited to restoring enforcement of the laws, were delighted. Citizens of the states along the upper Mississippi wanted the "foreign" power removed from control of the river's mouth. Similarly, Pennsylvanians and their neighbors in Ohio and New York saw militant response as the best means of protecting East-West railroad lines and access to Chesapeake Bay.

Mixed with the enthusiasm, however, and perhaps spread by it were delusions. The war would be short, the chances for glory high, the cost negligible.

The men of the 6th Massachusetts may have thought that on April 19 when their Washington-bound train reached Baltimore. At the time, there was no through rail line connecting the two cities; it was necessary for the cars to be uncoupled and drawn by horses along a street for about a mile to another station. By noon word of the regiment's approach had attracted an angry secessionist mob. At first, the crowd's jeers and stones thrown at the cars were all the soldiers had to endure, but the last four companies were obliged to march the rest of the way—and when a shot was fired, some of the troops fired back. Police belatedly got the soldiers to the Washington rail line, but in the regiment's wake four militiamen were dead and thirty-six wounded; the Baltimoreans' casualties were twelve killed, scores injured.

Never again, decreed Maryland's authorities and those in Baltimore. They ordered railroad bridges connecting the city with Philadelphia and Harrisburg burned; then secessionists cut telegraph lines, isolating Washington from the rest of the Union for several days.

While General-in-Chief Winfield Scott and his tiny staff made plans to use the Treasury building as Washington's citadel if rebels attacked, Major General John Wool—another veteran of the War of 1812—voluntarily set up temporary headquarters in New York and expedited movements of troops and supplies. Railroad officials and Brigadier General Benjamin F. Butler worked out a scheme for shipping militia units to Annapolis, bypassing Baltimore. After a few days, Washington's anxieties eased as more regiments arrived and contact with the outside world was restored. One sign that conditions in the Union capital were normal again was a sharp rebuke Secretary of War Cameron sent General Wool for exceeding his authority.

Discouraging to President Lincoln though the Baltimore riots and their aftermath surely were, he remained calm and kept busy. On April 19, the day the 6th Massachusetts had fought its way through Baltimore, he proclaimed a blockade of Southern ports. Also on his agenda was the question of what could be done in response to Virginians' seizures of Harpers Ferry's arsenal and the Norfolk navy yard, having in mind that not until May 23 would Virginia's secession be voted upon by the people of the state just across the Potomac.

And in the days ahead more questions would demand answers. Curiously, however, moving the Union's seat of government to a less vulnerable place was not among them. But the war was not yet a month old, and perhaps it would not take many more weeks to dispose of what Lincoln had called "combinations too powerful to be suppressed by the ordinary course of judicial proceedings."

Northern governors had been prompt and enthusiastic in responding to Lincoln's call for troops; impassioned refusals of chief executives of border states to comply were almost as quick in coming. Beyond rhetoric came action. In Virginia's wake North Carolina, Tennessee, and Arkansas seceded, greatly expanding the

Confederacy's territorial coverage, population, and industrial potential and making the infant nation a viable entity. Missouri appeared pro-Confederate. Kentucky declared neutrality. Federal intimidation following the Baltimore riots prevented Maryland from becoming another "erring sister."

Clearly, Lincoln's proclamation had cost the Union almost the entire border tier. Seldom in history had the strokes of a pen given an adversary such enormous advantages.

Still, this was a mixed blessing. People in mountainous western Virginia and East Tennessee remained staunch Unionists. What Jefferson Davis really had, along with more stars in the Confederate flag, was an alliance of states: a nation in form but not much else. "All we want is to be left alone," said Davis, speaking as president. Any Southern governor might have used the same words—with Montgomery in mind now instead of Washington—except for the common need for defense of the region against Yankee invasion.

Davis's first challenge, then, was to combine the assets of eleven states, plus contributions from Kentucky and Maryland, into an army. Among the Confederate Congress's earliest acts was authorization of a 100,000-man force, and as in the North, governors had proved more eager to send state militia units than the secretary of war was to accept them. Congress also made provision for three-year enlistments and gave Davis authority for organizing and deploying the Confederate States army. But Congress could do little more, leaving it to Davis and his cabinet to cope with shortages of everything fighting men needed. Seizures of federal arsenals yielded little in the way of modernized muskets and cannon. Militiamen would bring with them a bewildering variety of weapons, complicating the resupply of ammunition, for which sources had to be created. Cavalrymen would ride their own horses, but the government must find and deliver fodder in wagons it did not yet have.

As Davis was struggling to create something, including a navy, out of next to nothing, his Congress voted to accept an invitation from Virginia to move the Confederacy's capital from Montgomery to Richmond. Davis vetoed that act, mindful perhaps that Richmond was only about 100 miles south of Washington and could prove just as vulnerable. But the legislators—less tolerant than Davis of Montgomery's mosquitoes, humid climate, and overcrowded hotels—overrode his veto, in part on the theory that proximity to the fighting would enable them to be more responsive to their troops' actual needs.

One resource abundantly available to the Confederate army was leadership. The Virginia Military Institute and The Citadel in Charleston had long been models for other academies throughout the South, and in the Old Army General-in-Chief Scott, Virginia-born, had given West Point graduates whose roots were Southern many opportunities to gain experience.

Scott, recognizing that he was too old and too plagued by illness to see a long war through, hoped that Virginian Robert E. Lee would succeed him in command of the Union forces. Lee had served under Scott in the Mexico City campaign back in 1847, and his brilliance, coupled with audacity, had made an indelible impression. Scott recommended Lee's appointment to President Lincoln, who asked Francis Blair, Sr., to interview the colonel as a preliminary step. Blair did so on April 18, only to be told by Lee that while he was opposed to secession, he could take no part in an invasion of the Southern states.

Immediately after leaving Blair, Lee spent several hours with General Scott, announcing, finally, that he could not draw his sword against his native state.

"Lee, you have made the greatest mistake of your life," said Scott sadly. "But I feared it would be so."

On the night of April 19, Colonel Lee wrote his letter of resignation to General Scott. And though Lee accepted Virginia governor John Letcher's offer of command of the state's forces as a major general, on May 5 he said this in a letter to a Northern girl who had requested his photograph:

> I should like, above all things, that our difficulties might be peaceably arranged, and still trust that a merciful God, who I know will not unnecessarily afflict us, may yet allay the fury for war. Whatever may be the result of the contest, I foresee that the country will have to pass through a terrible ordeal, a necessary expiation perhaps for our national sins.

Ahead of Lee in resigning were Floridian Edmund Kirby Smith and Louisiana's Pierre Beauregard. Joseph Eggleston Johnston, a Virginian who had been quartermaster general in the Old Army, followed Lee in a few days. In all, roughly 300—about a third of the Old Army's commissioned officers—went home to offer their swords to their native states.

Edward Porter Alexander, in early 1861 a young lieutenant three years out of West Point and Georgia-born, wrote James B. McPherson—from Ohio, four years ahead of him at the U.S. Military Academy—of his anguish. McPherson replied:

> Aleck if you must go I will do all I can to facilitate your going. But don't go....

Now this is not going to be any 90 days or six months affair as some of the politicians are predicting. Both sides are in deadly earnest, & it is long & desperate & fought out to the bitter end.

If you go as an educated soldier you are sure to be put in the front rank & where the fighting will be hardest. God only knows what may happen to you individually, but for your cause there can be only one possible result. It must be lost.

The population of the seceding states is only 8 million while the North has twenty million. Of your 8 million over 3 million are slaves & may prove a dangerous element. You have no army, no navy, no treasury, no organisation & practically none of the manufacturers—the machine shops, coal & iron mines & such things—which are necessary for the support of armies & carrying on war on a large scale. You are but scattered agricultural communities & will be isolated from the world by blockades. It is not possible for your cause to succeed in the end & the individual risks you must run meanwhile are very great.

But Alexander went home to Georgia, feeling the tug of roots too strong to suppress, and so it was with others like him, enough to leave Abraham Lincoln with a problem he would not be able to solve for nearly three more years.

"All we want is to be left alone," Jefferson Davis had said, and that pretty well summed up the Confederacy's main war goal. Survival would be victory enough, as George Washington—in some ways the model for Davis as he contemplated grand strategy—had concluded during the Revolutionary War.

But, like other West Pointers, Davis was also familiar with Napoleon's campaigns, and he had his own experience in the Mexican War to rely upon. Sooner or later, he knew, the South would have to destroy the invading Union armies even if this meant giving up ground—as had General Washington—until the decisive blow could be dealt. But how much territory could be put at risk before other landowners rose up against him and demanded that the Confederacy declare "the Cause" lost?

The Cause, of course, was almost the only thread holding the new nation together. And to prevent that critical tie from breaking there must be enough victories among the defeats to maintain hopes of eventually being "left alone."

For the time being, at least, all Davis could do was place such troops as he had where invasion from the North seemed most likely to occur: northern Virginia. Railroads were already moving troops from points as far away as Texas toward Richmond, evidence that Davis was taking advantage of "interior lines"—a central position from which it was easier for him to shift forces along his defensive perimeter than it was for General-in-Chief Scott, who faced much longer distances in making any changes in his deployment of troop units.

Scott had already upset Union officials, such as Secretary of State Seward, by predicting that the war might take three years to win, perhaps longer. The old general-in-chief gave complacent civilian authorities a more severe jolt when he proposed what soon came to be called his Anaconda strategy.

Triggering Scott's thinking was a letter he had received from Major General George Brinton McClellan, who had—like Robert E. Lee—served on Scott's staff during the Mexico City campaign. In 1855 then secretary of war Jefferson Davis sent Captain McClellan as an observer to the Crimean War, causing some to consider the brash young West Pointer Davis's protégé. After writing a report on what he had seen of how European armies fought, however, McClellan resigned from the army and became a railroad executive. Soon after Fort Sumter, Ohio's governor William Dennison outbid his opposite numbers in two other states and placed McClellan in charge of Ohio's militia, with the rank of major general. It was in this capacity that McClellan, less than half Scott's age in 1861, presumed to suggest two drives southward to sever the Confederacy.

Immature, thought Scott when he read McClellan's letter, but he passed it along to President Lincoln with an endorsement in which he set forth the main features of his Anaconda plan. That term was given the strategy by newspapers, but it was an apt one, for Scott proposed strangling the Confederacy by the naval blockade, applying pressure along the Mississippi River's course, and use of "the best regulars" to squeeze from the North until Union sympathizers in the South prevailed upon the fire-eaters to abandon the war and allow the "erring sisters" to return to the family's bosom.

Winfield Scott was a remarkable man in many respects—huge in size, six feet five, 350 pounds; a soldier with no peer in American military experience; a gourmand whose table and wines were unmatched in Washington; politically a survivor—but he had the unfortunate habit of blundering whenever he took pen in hand. So it was in this instance. Scott's Anaconda strategy was not only criticized but ridiculed unmercifully as being too timid, too demanding in terms of training and logistic preparation, too time consuming.

"Onward to Richmond!" was the battle cry newspaper editors and those who agreed were chanting. So were politicians, offended by Scott's implication that volunteers were unreliable. Scott made no more proposals, turning instead to the problems of housing and feeding the troops the governors had sent him.

Acting as the swelling Washington garrison's quartermaster turned out to be a heavy burden for Scott and his small staff; Secretary of War Cameron was deeply immersed in the political aspects of war-matériel procurement; very little planning was being done. But time was passing, the masses of units in and around the capital at least resembled an army, and pressure to do something with these resources was rising.

An order from President Lincoln eased that pressure soon after it became official that Virginia was Confederate. At one o'clock on the morning of May 24, by the light of a full moon, the first of eight regiments crossed the Long Bridge over the Potomac and seized the high ground near the stately old Custis Mansion: Arlington, owned by the departed Robert E. Lee and his wife (Martha Custis Washington's great-granddaughter). Scott's columns spread west and southeast of Arlington and were in their assigned locations in time for breakfast.

Among the regiments in this 8,000-man force was one called the New York Fire Zouaves, commanded by Colonel Elmer Ellsworth, once a law student in Lincoln's office in Springfield and still a close friend. Ellsworth's men were volunteer firemen he had recruited in New York City, trained, and provided with uniforms consisting of baggy red knickers, russet leather gaiters, short blue jackets over big sashes, and red fezzes.

Ellsworth, only twenty-four, hoped his taking of Alexandria would give his Zouaves an opportunity to prove they were as ferocious as they looked. In this he was disappointed; no rebels opposed the regiment's occupation of the sleeping town. But there was an opportunity to display some spirit, and Ellsworth seized it.

Spotting a Confederate flag atop the Marshall House, the young colonel dashed inside, went up to the roof, and took down the banner. He was in a hallway, on his way out of the hotel, when the proprietor aimed a shotgun at Ellsworth's belly and fired, only to be shot and killed a moment later by a Zouave. Ellsworth's body was taken to lie in state in the East Room of the Executive Mansion; Abraham Lincoln and his family led the Union in mourning him.

Scott's seizure of even a few square miles of Confederate territory encouraged people in the North and eased concerns over Washington's vulnerability. Federal initiatives elsewhere also suggested that the Union's war machine was clanking into motion.

Aware that Confederates in western Virginia were burning bridges along the Baltimore & Ohio Railroad, Scott, on May 24, asked General McClellan what counteraction he could take. This prompted McClellan to send a small force of Ohio militia to a B & O junction at Grafton and also to issue a proclamation to the people of western Virginia in which he promised to respect private property rights—and more:

> Notwithstanding all that has been said by the traitors to induce you to believe that our advent among you will be signalized by interference with your slaves, understand one thing clearly—not only will we abstain from all such interference but we will on the contrary with an iron hand, crush any attempt at insurrection on their part.

McClellan remained in Cincinnati, writing the president that there had been no time in which to obtain his approval of the statement before issuing it, while the Ohio units moved a few miles southward from Grafton. On the morning of June 3 they surprised a Confederate detachment at Philippi and, after a brief fight, sent it running in all directions, inspiring newspapers to call the incident the "Philippi Races."

Over in eastern Virginia, General Scott had reinforced the federal garrison at Fort Monroe, on the end of the peninsula flanked by the James River to the south and the York River to the north. On June 10, Brigadier General Ben Butler took seven Federal regiments westward from the fort to seize a rebel artillery battery near Big Bethel. Butler's brigade collided with a Confederate force half its size, then fled.

Concurrently, worse was going to worst out in Missouri, the richest and strongest state west of the Mississippi River and one not committed to either side. On the night of April 25, Captain Nathaniel Lyon and Congressman Francis Blair, Jr., both semifanatical Unionists, stripped the St. Louis arsenal and moved its huge quantities of weapons and ammunition across and up the river to Alton. This action, made possible through the cooperation of Illinois' governor Richard Yates, infuriated moderates as well as pro-Confederates.

Next, on May 10, Lyon's federal forces surrounded the 700 militiamen encamped at Lindell's Grove, on St. Louis's western fringe. Surrender was the militia commander's only option, and Lyon might have been content with it. Instead, he ordered the disarmed prisoners paraded through the streets of St. Louis, thus attracting an angry mob and inciting a riot that killed twenty-eight or more people and injured many others.

"In for a fight, in for a funeral" was the Blairs' motto. Missouri's secessionists and many moderates may have felt the same way, for Lyon and Blair had polarized opinion in the state beyond all hope of compromise. Former governor Sterling Price, a moderate earlier, accepted command of the militia, which was growing as Missourians responded to Claiborne Jackson's call for 50,000 volunteers. But Price could do nothing to block Lyon's forces; in mid-June they chased the militiamen to the state's capital, Jefferson City, then beyond it. Guerrilla warfare broke out in areas Lyon could not control. Governor Jackson went on driving pro-Confederate measures through a fugitive legislature its own troops could not defend.

Concurrently, George McClellan, preparing to join his troops in western Virginia, made certain a portable printing press would be taken along. It was, and at Grafton on June 25 it helped the general proclaim:

> Soldiers! I have heard that there was danger here. I have come to place myself at your head and to share it with you. I fear now but one thing—that you will not find foemen worthy of your steel.

And while McClellan waited for supplies to arrive, he wrote Scott's adjutant, urging him to tell the general-in-chief he intended to win "by manoeuvering rather than by fighting; I will not throw these men of mine into the teeth of artillery & intrenchments, if it is possible to avoid it." In fact, western Virginia's rugged terrain restricted McClellan's opportunities for maneuvering; if he ever meant to reach Staunton, gateway both to the Shenandoah Valley and to Richmond, he would have to use the turnpike extending southeastward from Parkersburg. And Confederates held Beverly, where the road from Philippi to the north met the turnpike.

Virginian Brigadier General Robert S. Garnett had about 4,000 of his men in a pass on Laurel Mountain, blocking the road from Philippi to Beverly, and another 1,300 west of the town astride the turnpike at the base of Rich Mountain. Given this situation, McClellan employed military art on a small scale. He ordered Brigadier General T. A. Morris to move southward from Philippi with 4,000 troops to Laurel Hill and hold Garnett in place while he took another 4,000 men along the turnpike to dispose of the smaller rebel force, enter Beverly, and cut off Garnett's escape route.

Confederates blocking the turnpike presented McClellan with

more of a problem than he may have expected. Unwilling to throw his men "into the teeth of artillery & intrenchments," he paused, seeking a way around the rebels. Then, in the middle of the night of July 10–11, luck intervened: David Hart, a farmer who lived at the top of Rich Mountain, found Brigadier General William Starke Rosecrans and offered to guide a maneuvering force along a little-used pathway that led up the slope and to the rear of the Confederate line. Rosecrans brought Hart to McClellan, who then told Rosecrans to follow Hart with 2,000 men first thing in the morning. Once he heard Rosecrans's men firing, McClellan added, he would assault the rebel line.

Rosecrans's column moved out. All morning and past noon McClellan waited, listening. What happened next is best told by Lieutenant Colonel John Beatty of the 3d Ohio, who wrote:

> Between two and three o'clock we heard shots in the rear of the fortifications; then volleys of musketry, and the roar of artillery. Every man sprang to his feet, assured that the moment for making the attack had arrived. General Mc-Clellan and staff came galloping up, and a thousand faces turned to hear the order to advance; but no order was given. The general halted a few paces from our line and sat on his horse listening to the guns, apparently in doubt as to what to do; and as he sat there with indecision stamped on every line of his countenance, the battle grew fiercer in the enemy's rear. Every volley could be heard distinctly. There would occasionally be a lull for a moment, and then the uproar would break out again with increased violence. If the enemy is too strong for us to attack, what must be the fate of Rosecrans' four regiments, cut off from us and struggling against such odds?

McClellan finally rode away. Beatty added: "The belief grew strong that Rosecrans had been defeated and his brigade cut to pieces or captured." At day's end McClellan was planning to place artillery fire on the rebel position—the next morning.

Actually, Rosecrans had encountered and whipped a small detachment sent to intercept him. His flank march succeeded in forcing the Confederates to withdraw during the night, giving General McClellan his first victory as a field commander.

With McClellan in Beverly, General Garnett was obliged to abandon his position on Laurel Mountain. While commanding the rear guard, he was killed, the first general officer on either side to die in the war.

Now the turnpike to Staunton was open, but McClellan remained near Beverly, writing reports in which he minimized the contributions Rosecrans had made at Rich Mountain. And from the portable printing press came another proclamation:

> Soldiers of the Army of the West!
> I am more than satisfied with you.
> You have annihilated two armies, commanded by educated and experienced soldiers, and entrenched in mountain fastnesses fortified at their leisure....

There was more, much of it in the same enriched manner. But no matter how puzzled eyewitnesses such as Colonel Beatty may have been as they read the florid prose, at least McClellan had given the Union a victory to celebrate.

Within a few days newspapers began to arrive. At the top of a column of praise in the *New York Herald* was the headline "GEN. McCLELLAN, THE NAPOLEON OF THE PRESENT WAR." In Louisville the *Journal* said, "There is something extremely satisfactory in contemplating what might be called a piece of finished military workmanship by a master hand." And from General Scott came a telegram: "The General-in-Chief, and what is more, the Cabinet, including the President are charmed with your activity, valor and consequent success...."

Ironies abounded when the federal Congress convened in Washington on July 4. The legislators' principal task was to drape the veil of legality over actions Abraham Lincoln had taken, many of which were contrary to the basic law of the land: the Constitution. And from this circumstance many unusual and unsettling questions soon emerged.

An example: If the president had done something illegal, even for the best of reasons, could an act of Congress really wipe away the stain? Or would Congress, merely by attempting to do so, actually confirm the president's guilt? Another: Should the government, fighting as it was for the survival of constitutional guarantees, always restrict its actions to those clearly lawful?

Did these questions matter? Well, yes: Congress had to face them or let the world assume that the United States of America had become a dictatorship by default. And there was no doubt that Lincoln had warped the Constitution. In his message to Congress on July 5 the president admitted he had (among many other things) blockaded Southern ports while maintaining that the "erring sisters" still belonged to the Union; suspended the writ of habeas corpus and violated various other civil rights in Maryland to keep that key state from seceding; and committed the government to expenditures of millions of dollars to obtain war matériel.

Lincoln had done nothing to stop young Frank Blair and Lyon from interfering with Missouri's duly elected government, though that state had not seceded. While insisting secession was fundamentally illegal, he was actively encouraging western Virginians to secede from their state. Moreover, fugitive slave laws still on the books notwithstanding, the president had authorized General Butler down at Fort Monroe to protect runaway blacks on the theory they were "contraband," the equivalent of weapons seized from persons engaged in felonies.

Everyone understood why Lincoln and others had done what they had, and eventually Congress approved. Along the way the legislators also accepted a statement of war aims proposed by Senator Crittenden:

> ...that this war is not waged, upon our part, in any spirit of oppression, nor for any purpose of conquest or subjugation, nor purpose of overthrowing or interfering with the rights or established institutions of these States, but to defend the supremacy of the Constitution and to preserve the Union, with all the dignity, equality, and rights of the several States unimpaired; that as soon as these objects are accomplished, the war ought to cease.

Lest anyone think the Union meant to fight a "soft" war, however, Lincoln also asked for—and got—authority to spend $400 million. Instead of the minimum 400,000 volunteers the president wanted, Congress raised the number to 500,000.

"One of the greatest perplexities of the Government," Lincoln had said, "is to avoid receiving troops faster than it can provide for them." Congressmen could agree with that, for in their absence Washington had become one huge camp, and they had heard that in the war's early days the first regiments to arrive had been quartered in the Capitol.

In fact, the Union buildup in troop strength had occurred with breathtaking speed. When Fort Sumter was surrendered, the regular army had only 17,000 men, perhaps fewer, all but about 3,000 of them scattered throughout the West. The militia call-up added roughly 80,000, and additional volunteers brought the total to 310,000 by July 1. Even after the militia units' ninety-day terms expired, the Union armies would have 230,000 men in uniform—

nearly half as many as Congress had authorized.

Those 80,000 militiamen were a problem, and had been since late in June, when the post-Sumter enthusiasm began turning into boredom. Pressure from politicians grew to use them or lose them. General McClellan had moved troops under his command from Ohio into western Virginia; why was old General Scott so reluctant to send his men "Forward to Richmond!" as the *New York Tribune* was urging, daily, with the slogan now emblazoned above the newspaper's masthead?

Manassas Battle Area

Tribune editor Horace Greeley was no strategist, but he did understand the power of symbols. Richmond served his purpose admirably, focusing his readers' attention on a precise goal at a time when Union war aims seemed vague, sensing perhaps that "Forward to the Shenandoah Valley!" or "Crush the Confederacy!" would neither get much effort moving nor sell many newspapers.

Richmond had some strategic importance. Its Tredegar Iron Works was then the only facility in the South capable of making cannon, and the city was a railroad hub.

Greeley's error, shared widely in the North, was to place too much emphasis on the presence of the Confederate government in Richmond, the implication being that if the monster's head were lopped off, the beast would die and the war would end very quickly. Moreover, Jefferson Davis and his associates had recently demonstrated how portable their organization was by moving it from overcrowded Montgomery to overcrowded Richmond in a matter of only a few days.

Virginia itself was the prize, and the state's governor and General Lee had acted quickly to reduce its vulnerability by placing militia units at four key points to block invasion: Philippi; Harpers Ferry; Manassas Junction, west of Washington; and Aquia Landing, on the Potomac north of Fredericksburg. This had been a scattering of shortages, mostly, until late May, when Virginia's secession became official and volunteers from other Confederate states began arriving in Richmond, bringing with them cause for a shift from Virginia's control to "national."

Jefferson Davis took his additional title as commander-in-chief seriously, as well he might, given his background: West Point, the Mexican War, his service as secretary of war. He knew Lee and admired him, but Beauregard and Joe Johnston were Confederate generals, and to them went the choice assignments. Davis ordered Beauregard to take command at Manassas Junction, the point nearest the Union forces massing around Washington. Johnston replaced Colonel Thomas J. Jackson at Harpers Ferry. Lee accepted being eclipsed with good grace, waiting patiently for his appointment as a Confederate general to be confirmed and for the president to give him something useful to do.

In fact, Davis built upon the beginning Lee had made. To Beauregard he sent most of the incoming troop units, having in mind that the railroad from Manassas Junction westward through the Blue Ridge Mountains enabled Beauregard to shift brigades sixty miles to support Johnston in the Shenandoah Valley if necessary— and vice versa. By mid-July General Beauregard had about 24,000 men and twenty-nine artillery pieces north of Manassas Junction, along the steep banks of Bull Run.

Over in the Shenandoah Valley, Johnston had abandoned Harpers Ferry—an indefensible position, one Lee had ordered held only until its armory's rifle-making machines were moved to Richmond—and had withdrawn his 15,000 men to Winchester, about a day's march north of the railroad line that linked the Valley to

Manassas Junction. And for a time Johnston's forces seemed in greater peril than Beauregard's.

Southward from Chambersburg, Pennsylvania, came about 14,000 Union militiamen commanded by Major General Robert Patterson, sixty-nine, a veteran of the War of 1812 and Mexico, who was also a ninety-day volunteer. Patterson took Martinsburg, Virginia, and moved into Harpers Ferry when Johnston left. Attempting to carry out confusing orders sent by General Scott, Patterson was hoping to keep Johnston at Winchester in mid-July while Major General Irvin McDowell destroyed Beauregard at Manassas.

Like a comet McDowell had streaked from major to general officer since Fort Sumter, in part because he was on Scott's staff but also with help from fellow Ohioan Secretary of the Treasury Salmon Chase. McDowell, forty-two, West Pointer, Mexican War veteran, was best known for his appetite—he once concluded an otherwise gargantuan meal by eating an entire watermelon—but he was also more willing than Scott to heed pressure from politicians to do something with the ninety-day volunteers under his command near Washington. By late June President Lincoln had approved his plan to rid the Union capital of the Confederate presence less than thirty miles to the west at Manassas Junction.

His men were green, McDowell had pointed out. Yes, the president conceded, but the Confederates were "green alike." Irvin McDowell, too, was green. But he was far from alone in that respect: No officer on either side, except Scott, had ever maneuvered more than a few thousand men.

Chapter 4

First Manassas:
Blundering Accelerates

McDowell's lack of experience in leading troops became apparent soon after his advance to contact began. March and stop—stop, mostly—was the manner of the volunteers' first two days on the Warrenton Turnpike west of Washington. In the fields along the road berries were ripe; regiments' officers let their men harvest them. Unit commanders also allowed the home-minded soldiers to consume the two days' rations in their knapsacks in one. Then, with delay being measured in days, McDowell discovered how little he knew about the terrain along Bull Run or the road net or the locations and suitabilities of the few fords across the stream.

So it was that McDowell inadvertently gave his West Point classmate Beauregard time in which to detect the movement toward him and to telegraph pleas to Richmond for reinforcements—and Davis time in which to order Joe Johnston to rush his brigades from Winchester to Manassas by railroad. Davis also got troops at Aquia Landing moving toward Beauregard's position. And when the commander-in-chief could do no more from Richmond, he boarded a special northbound train.

For all his Virginia-bred dignity, Joe Johnston was a fighter and had been since his cadet days, when he may (or may not) have tangled with Jefferson Davis over the affections of a tavern keeper's daughter. Serving under Scott, Johnston fought Seminole Indians in Florida in the 1830s. In Mexico he was among Scott's engineers, a group including his classmate Lee, Beauregard, and George McClellan. But, as though that duty were too tame, he won command of a special skirmishing regiment known as the *voltigeurs* and led them in every battle on the way to Mexico City. Wounded twice earlier, Johnston was hit three times while leading his *voltigeurs* up Chapultepec's slope in the campaign's climactic fight.

"Johnston is a great soldier," said Scott afterward, "but he has an unfortunate knack of getting himself shot in nearly every engagement."

Now fifty-four, Joe Johnston proved as eager as ever to get where the fight was most likely to occur. On July 20, while McDowell was still prodding his columns and sending out scouts in search of ways to cross Bull Run, Johnston reached Manassas in time to greet Colonel Thomas Jonathan Jackson's men as they got out of the rail cars and to place that brigade, the first to arrive, at the disposal of General Beauregard.

On that Saturday Irvin McDowell realized that his forces could not use the Warrenton Turnpike's stone bridge to cross Bull Run; the Confederates were bound to mass artillery fire on the span. Downstream from the bridge, probes of known fords drew enough rebel opposition to send McDowell's scouts hurrying northeastward. Upstream, however, they found places where his brigades and teams of horses pulling guns and wagons could dash through low water.

Now Irvin McDowell abandoned his original idea, attacking across Bull Run downstream from the stone bridge, and decided to move northeastward, upstream to his right, far enough to get around and behind the rebels' defenses. Ironically, at about the same time, Beauregard intended to throw a right envelopment at McDowell that—had both plans been carried out—would have produced a pinwheel battle, one resembling two snakes, each gobbling up the other's tail.

No fight is ever as neat as the image of the two hungry snakes suggests; certainly this one would not be. Given the bewildering variety of blue, gray, and Zouave uniforms on both sides, confusion was inevitable. There was too much slack in the chains of command. A private might know who his company's officers were or maybe a few of those in the regiment to which his company belonged, but brigades were still too new to be cohesive. Neither army's commander had any assurance that orders sent to brigades would cause them to move, much less fight, as units. And while McDowell's idea of batching two or three brigades into divisions made sense, a battleground was a poor place on which to test it.

A partial offset was the presence of regular-army officers and West Point graduates with Mexican War experience among the commanders of most of the Union's brigades and divisions. But these officers barely knew the names of their regiments' senior leaders and were still ignorant regarding their capabilities at two o'clock on Sunday morning, July 21, when the first company in the federal force began moving northwestward in moonlight on roads leading to the fords several miles up Bull Run.

Two of McDowell's five divisions, about 14,000 men, were in that enveloping wing of his army. Another two divisions moved along the Warrenton Turnpike to the stone bridge and halted to wait for the others to make the long march upstream, sweep down Bull Run's southern banks, and drive the defenders off the hills beyond them; then they would rush across the bridge and join in winning the victory.

Such in brief was the federal plan, the point of the early start being to have the maneuvering wing over the fords near Sudley Springs soon after sunrise. In theory, this should have presented no problems: Confederate defenders at the ford were few, for nearly all of Beauregard's brigades were well to the southeast of the stone bridge, six miles or so from Sudley Springs. But the federals' moonlit march northwestward turned into another stop-and-go fiasco, and not until midmorning did the column finally cross Bull Run.

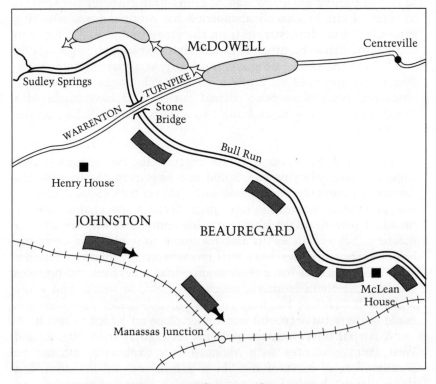

Manassas—Advance to Contact

During that delay several curious things happened. After sunrise, thinking that the envelopers were at Sudley Springs, Union artillery opened fire on Confederate lines downstream from the stone bridge; one gun put a solid shot into Wilbur McLean's kitchen, spoiling General Beauregard's breakfast and also his plan for the attack that would have set the pinwheel spinning. Another odd event early on that Sunday morning was the departure from Washington of a stream of carriages bringing civilians, among them congressmen and ladies eager to witness a historic spectacle while having a pleasant picnic.

Unplanned as well was the response Confederate Colonel Nathan G. Evans made to wigwag flag signals warning him that McDowell's enveloping wing was near Sudley Springs. Ignoring the Union force north of the stone bridge, "Shanks" Evans promptly led his 1,100 or so men upstream.

Thus began a "meeting engagement," an apt term for leading elements of opposing armies colliding and not moving much while units behind them build lines and get to work. Union Colonel Ambrose E. Burnside's Rhode Islanders ran into Shanks Evans's South Carolinians and Louisianans and were thrown back. But Evans's rebels could not stay where they were for long: McDowell could strengthen his line faster than could Beauregard.

Sunday morning was getting on toward noon when the noise of the Evans-Burnside collision reached Joe Johnston's ears, miles to the southeast. "The battle is there," said Johnston to Beauregard. "I am going."

Beauregard had already started brigades northwestward: T. J. Jackson's Virginians, Barnard Bee's Mississippians and Georgians, Wade Hampton's South Carolinians. He sent more, then followed Johnston at a gallop toward the hills south of the stone bridge and overlooking the Warrenton Turnpike.

On the hill nearest the turnpike was a white farmhouse in which Judith Henry, eighty-nine, was dying. She had insisted on staying in her home to the end. It came in the afternoon as her hill became the place on which, as General Beauregard later put it, "the political hostilities of a generation were now face to face with weapons instead of words."

Union artillery bursts set fire to Judith Henry's house; volleys fired by the gunners' supporters thinned the line of Confederate defenders and drove them off her hill's western slope. Evans's remnants retreated over it, as did Francis Bartow's Georgians and Barnard Bee's brigade. Beauregard tried to rally them—only to be blown from his saddle to the ground when a federal artillery round exploded under his horse, killing the animal but sparing the general.

Waiting on Henry House Hill's southeastern slope, watching fugitives from the Union onslaught stream through his brigade's line, was Colonel T. J. Jackson. Near him was Wade Hampton's brigade. Their men and a few guns were all that stood between McDowell's onrushing Union troops and the Confederacy's ruin.

Barnard Bee rode up to Jackson. "General," he said, "they are beating us back."

"Sir," replied Jackson, "we will give them the bayonet."

Off rode Bee, trying once more to stop the shameful flow of his men to the rear. "Look!" he cried. "There is Jackson standing like a stone wall! Rally behind the Virginians!"

Then a Union bullet hit Bee in the belly, knocking him to the ground, killing him, but some of his men had heard him. Still Jackson waited, watching the smoke rise from the burning house on the hill's crest, scanning the horizon for Yankees.

Had Jackson gone to the top of Henry House Hill, he would have seen enough Yankee soldiers to chill his heart, even on such a hot and sultry day, for McDowell's entire maneuvering wing was approaching. And beyond the stone bridge, north of Bull Run, federal masses were ready to cross. Still Jackson remained where he was, brushing off alarming reports, while McDowell aligned his brigades for a win-the-battle assault.

Now the hillcrest Colonel Jackson had long been scanning was filled with advancing Yankees. Jackson raised his hand, a minié ball hit it, then his men fired. Volley after volley they sent into the federal regiments surging toward them.

Southwest of Henry House Hill, on the Warrenton Turnpike, young Colonel J. E. B. Stuart—"Jeb" to his cavalrymen because of his three initials—saw the New York Fire Zouaves and other Union troops rushing up the slope. Stuart charged, driving the Zouaves in near panic toward the stone bridge.

Some of Jackson's Virginians, in blue uniforms, spotted two Union batteries moving into position to fire on their line. At first, the federal artillerymen thought the troops advancing toward their guns were coming to support them. The Virginians fired a volley at close range, killing or wounding almost every man and horse in those batteries.

Joe Johnston, Confederate general-in-command, had left the tactical control of the battle to Beauregard. But the senior soldier was in the right place when a brigade led by Floridian Edmund Kirby Smith, just arrived by train from the Shenandoah Valley, marched toward him from the south. Johnston hurried the troops to Henry House Hill. They got there just in time to join Brigadier General

Jubal A. Early's brigade in striking the flank of the Union forces McDowell had sent to overrun Jackson's line.

Then came the moment for Jackson to counterattack. "Yell like furies!" he shouted. Some soldier emitted a high-pitched half scream; others picked it up, filling the humid air with sounds unlike any the Yankees or anyone else had ever heard.

From that moment on there was nothing McDowell or any of his officers could do to stop the panicked federal troops' rush to get back over on the far side of Bull Run. They left behind their artillery and their dead and wounded; dropping rifles and everything else they carried, they headed up the turnpike for Washington—and their homes.

Blocking the fleeing blue-clad mob's way were the civilian picnickers' carriages. One congressman who had tarried too long was captured by a fierce-looking, hard-cussing Confederate colonel. Porter Alexander, the signal officer who had warned Shanks Evans of the Yankees' movements many hours earlier, rescued the politician. "You keep out of his way," Alexander told him, for "he would as soon cut your ears off as not."

A few miles to the south, above Manassas Junction, the sight of the walking wounded had disturbed President Davis, who had just arrived from Richmond. The fight was lost, he was told, yet—riding a horse someone loaned him—he tried to rally stragglers. "Battles are not won where men leave their ranks in such numbers as this," he remarked, then he led those who would follow him northward.

Davis reached Henry House Hill at about the same time old Edmund Ruffin did. Ruffin, carrying a musket, had hitched a ride on an artillery battery's caisson. After unlimbering, the unit's commander offered the honor of firing the first gun to Ruffin, who sent a round crashing into the mass of Washington-bound Yankees beyond the stone bridge.

Both civilians arrived too late to do anything decisive, though Davis conferred with Johnston and Beauregard until long after moonrise about the wisdom of pursuing McDowell's routed army all the way into Washington. Jackson, his hand bandaged, joined them and declared that with enough men he could get there. For a moment it seemed Davis was ready to write such an order. But he did not, sending instead a message to Richmond in which he reported "a glorious victory."

Some of McDowell's men had streaked the same distance in one rainy night that they had spent four days covering outward bound. Early the next morning many Washingtonians found them sleeping on their doorsteps. Yet the impression distressed citizens got from the sight of a broken and defeated rabble in their midst was wrong.

McDowell had lost a battle but not his army; it was dispersed, fragmented, for the time being useless; but his rear guard, regular-army troops mostly, was intact, and Washington was safe.

Lincoln took the defeat calmly. But a message he sent to Major General George McClellan in western Virginia reflected what was running through his mind: "Circumstances make your presence here necessary. Charge Rosecrans or some other general with your present department and come hither without delay."

Reaction to news from Manassas was curiously restrained in Richmond, the initial mood reverent. In the North deep gloom prevailed. Horace Greeley removed the "Forward to Richmond!" banner from his *New York Tribune's* masthead and wrote Lincoln:

> On every brow sits sullen, scorching, black despair. If it is best for the country and for mankind that we make peace with the rebels at once and on their own terms, do not shrink even from that.

Governors of Union states thought otherwise, some of them offering fresh regiments. And once the facts emerged from the nonsense, Bull Run had much the same invigorating effect on the North the people had felt after Fort Sumter.

Actually, McDowell had come within a few heartbeats of winning the fight that Sunday afternoon on Henry House Hill. Old General Scott knew that, and he tried to shield McDowell by taking the blame himself. To President Lincoln and several congressmen, Scott declared:

> I am the greatest coward in America! I will prove it. I have fought this battle, sir, against my judgment; I think the President of the United States ought to remove me for doing it.

There remained the counting of casualties, a task doomed to imprecision. McDowell lost roughly 2,775 men: about 625 killed, 950 wounded, and 1,200 captured. On the same highly approximate basis the Confederate total was 2,000: 400 dead, 1,600 wounded. Each side had about 30,000 men on the field at Manassas (or Bull Run, as the battle would be called in the North), and for the federals and Confederates alike the number of troops actually engaged in the fighting was about 18,000.

McDowell, of course, had to give way to McClellan. When the "Young Napoleon" reached Washington, Scott gave the newcomer the task of getting Bull Run's veterans off Washingtonians' doorsteps. McClellan did that and more. Soon he had the men in camps undergoing rigorous training under his careful eye, riding at a gallop from one point to another, plunging also into the Union capital's social life, and somehow finding the time to write his wife:

I find myself in a new & strange position here—Presdt, Cabinet, Genl Scott & all deferring to me—by some strange operation of magic I seem to have become *the* power of the land. I almost think that were I to win some small success now I could become Dictator or anything else that might please me—but nothing of that kind would please me— *therefore* I *won't* be Dictator. Admirable self-denial!...

Indeed, Lincoln deferred to McClellan, asking him behind General Scott's back for a war plan. Responding, McClellan brushed aside the Anaconda strategy and proposed creation of a Napoleonic grand army, 273,000 men strong and with 600 guns. Richmond would be his first goal, then Charleston, Savannah, Montgomery, Mobile, and finally, New Orleans. He also suggested efforts in the West. But McClellan had been in Washington only a little over a week, and no more than Lincoln could he foresee distressing events in Missouri.

Earlier, and partly at the urging of the powerful Blairs, the president had sent Major General John Charles Frémont to St. Louis in the hope that the "Pathfinder"—the nickname Frémont had gained while winning fame as an explorer in the West—could bring Missouri under firm Union control. Politically, the appointment seemed a masterstroke. Frémont's wife was the daughter of Missouri's late but still widely admired senator Thomas Hart Benton. The Pathfinder had been the Republican party's first candidate for president in 1856, and although losing to the Democrats' James Buchanan, he had gained the respect of New England's abolitionists. And, presumably, a frontiersman could best deal with frontier threats.

Frémont had been in command in Missouri for little over a month on August 10 when Brigadier General Nathaniel Lyon fought a Confederate force at Wilson's Creek, near Springfield in the state's southwestern corner. Lyon lost his life as well as the bloody standup battle. And mixed with Union-wide mourning for the gallant but rash Lyon were allegations that Frémont had not given the fallen hero enough support.

For Frémont to be the center of controversy was nothing new. He generated some of it by renting a mansion for his headquarters and acquiring a huge staff—many of his officers Europeans—to screen him from visitors. On gallops through the city's streets he was escorted by a clattering squadron of cavalry. But in some ways he was a victim of circumstances, or so it seemed in his "sacrificing" of General Lyon.

Before Lyon marched toward Wilson's Creek, the question facing Frémont was whether to reinforce him or to send 4,000 men—all he had available—to hold strategically important Cairo, Illinois, near the junction of the Mississippi and Ohio rivers. Cairo's Union garrison had been depleted by disease, departures of ninety-day volunteers, and desertions. Lyon, on the other hand, could hold his highly mobile troops away from the Confederates in southwestern Missouri. Frémont secured Cairo; Lyon disregarded his instructions, fought, and lost.

If Frémont's critics were correct in arguing that he ought to have sent the troops to Lyon, the Pathfinder could claim with equal vehemence that Washington should have provided him with more support instead of stripping the West of men and supplies to build up George McClellan's Army of the Potomac. But Missouri was a sideshow in the larger carnival, as was the seizure in late August of Cape Hatteras, North Carolina—barrier islands, mostly, but points facilitating the Union's blockade of the Confederacy's coastline. Driving Johnston's rebel army away from its lines within sight of the unfinished dome of the Capitol would be the main event, once the Young Napoleon was ready to attack.

As the summer of 1861 dragged on, Kentuckians maintained their precarious official aloofness but split internally into opposing political factions. Families, too, divided: Senator Crittenden's sons were typical—one remaining with the Union, the other "going South." It seemed inevitable that one side or the other would violate the state's professed neutrality. The only questions were which would move first and how soon.

Lincoln respected his native Kentucky's desire to stand aside, as did the Kentucky-born soldier he sent west late in August to command that "department"—Brigadier General Robert Anderson. Fort Sumter's hero established his headquarters in Cincinnati and awaited developments south of the Ohio River.

Also watching Kentucky from the discreet distance Richmond afforded was a third native of the Bluegrass State, Jefferson Davis. He remembered Louisiana's Episcopal bishop Leonidas Polk from their days as cadets at West Point, commissioned Polk—then fifty-five — a major general in the Confederate army, and sent him to Memphis with orders to seize Columbus, a key Kentucky town overlooking the Mississippi River, the moment "How soon?" ceased to be a question.

Pathfinder John Frémont had already acted to keep the Ohio River, Kentucky's northern border, a Union-controlled artery by reinforcing Cairo. This enabled him to seize Paducah and other key points east and northward on Kentucky's shore, but Cairo was also a base for an eventual drive southward to clear the Mississippi of rebels all the way to the Gulf of Mexico.

Commanding Frémont's troops in Cairo was Brigadier General Ulysses S. Grant, thirty-nine, whose record no one could envy. At West Point, Grant had excelled mainly in riding horses; in Mexico his gallantry was eclipsed by that of others; in the postwar army he turned to whiskey to alleviate his boredom, leaving open the question of whether his resignation was voluntary or forced; and in every civilian venture he undertook, he had failed. But Illinois congressman Elihu Washburne thought Grant deserved one more chance, which is why he was at Cairo watching Columbus.

On the west, then, both sides were preparing to demolish the myth of Kentucky's neutrality. Eastward, nearly 400 miles across the state, federal troops controlled points along the border with western Virginia. North of the Ohio River, Robert Anderson was waiting to move in and take charge. And to complete Kentucky's encirclement, Jefferson Davis sent another native of the Bluegrass State, General Albert Sidney Johnston, to assume command of Confederate forces gathering south of there on the long Kentucky-Tennessee border.

Sidney Johnston was a soldier's soldier, a graduate of West Point two years ahead of Davis and three of Virginian Joe Johnston, a veteran of the Black Hawk War. After resigning, he entered Texas's army as a private in 1836 and fought there to win the Lone Star Republic's independence from Mexico, serving later as Texas's secretary of war. Sidney Johnston was back in a federal uniform for the Mexican War in 1846–48, and he led the Utah Expedition against the Mormons in 1857. By early 1861 he was in California command-ing the Department of the Pacific. He waited first for Texas to secede and then for a Union army replacement to arrive, refusing an offer from Washington to become second in command to Winfield Scott but accepting from Davis in late August a Confederate commission as a full general.

But leaders' reputations, exemplary and otherwise, meant less in Kentucky's case than an internal action. It came in the form of a petition from Columbus's citizens asking General Polk to save them from a Frémont-ordered invasion by Grant; the bishop set his troops in motion, and by September 4 they held the threatened town. Grant responded by seizing Paducah.

Kentucky's veil, once pierced, quickly became a memory. Anderson crossed the Ohio and began recruiting; from Tennessee Sidney Johnston moved northward to Bowling Green and did the same thing, proving anew that wars—like nature—abhor vacuums.

As September 1861 neared its close, Jefferson Davis went to Manassas to hear Generals Joe Johnston and Pierre Beauregard explain their plan to carry the war into the North. They had 40,000 men defending the ground they had held on July 21. With another 20,000 they felt they could cross the Potomac and cut Washington's lines of communication with the rest of the Union—provided they acted before George McClellan got his 100,000 troops trained and equipped and attacked them.

At a minimum, a preemptive strike would greatly improve Confederate morale. Nothing good had happened since Manassas. True, Wilson's Creek had been a victory; but Southern forces in southwest Missouri had been too weak to follow Nathaniel Lyon's beaten troops as they retreated to Rolla. Then the federals seized Cape Hatteras and started using the region as a base supporting the blockade. Many Kentuckians, indignant over Polk's occupation of Columbus, had turned pro-Union. And in western Virginia, General Robert E. Lee had proved unable to defeat stronger federal units in the Alleghenies.

From such a review of the Confederate situation Davis had to conclude that he could not reinforce the army at Manassas without "a total disregard for the safety of other threatened positions." Joe Johnston's 40,000 men would remain where they were, build huts before winter set in, and watch McClellan's Army of the Potomac grow more powerful day by day. And it would be much the same for Davis's other commanders spotted along the thousand miles stretching from Manassas out to Missouri's southwestern corner— that is, if growing Union forces left them alone.

Abraham Lincoln had more troops than his secretary of war could equip, but he also had a problem Davis was spared: John Charles Frémont. Fearing guerrilla uprisings in the wake of Lyon's defeat at Wilson's Creek, General Frémont on August 30 abruptly issued a proclamation extending martial law throughout Missouri. In it he also threatened death by firing squad and confiscation of all property of citizens found guilty of pro-Confederate acts. This much, military necessity may well have justified. But Frémont added: "And their slaves, if any they have, are hereby declared freemen."

Abolitionists were as delighted as Lincoln, learning of it no sooner, was appalled. Congress had just produced a law covering confiscation of property, one to which commanders such as Frémont were expected to conform. In any event, emancipation was a political matter the president reserved to himself. And, understandably, Abraham Lincoln did not relish being surprised.

The president wrote Frémont a letter—one calm in tone, careful in its reasoning—in which he asked the Pathfinder to modify his proclamation in line with Congress's recent confiscation act, a copy of which he enclosed. In his belated rebuttal Frémont refused to comply, in effect daring Lincoln to order him to do so publicly. And in case the president had any questions, the defiant general sent his letter to Washington in the hands of his devoted wife, Jessie Benton Frémont.

So devoted was Mrs. Frémont, indeed, that after two days and nights in an eastbound train's chair car, the first thing she did after checking into Willard's Hotel was to send a card to the Executive Mansion announcing her arrival and asking for an appointment with the president. Minutes later she read his reply: "Now, at once. A. Lincoln."

Late in the evening though it was and dressed as she had been while en route, Jessie Frémont hurried to the White House. According to later reports—hers, mostly—their meeting was an utter disaster from the moment the president greeted her by snapping: "Well?"

Intimidated neither by the stubborn general's letter nor the formidable Jessie's blending of arguments with threats, Lincoln wrote Frémont the next day:

> I wrote you expressing my wish that the clause [in relation
> to the confiscation of property and the liberation of slaves]
> should be modified accordingly. Your answer, just received,
> expresses the preference on your part, that I should make an
> open order for the modification, which I very cheerfully do.

That letter, however, the president did not entrust to "General Jessie" to take back to St. Louis with her. And if Lincoln had been less than gracious to her, the next day she found old Francis Blair even more brusque: "Madam, I made your husband what he is," he reminded her, "and I will unmake him."

But Frémont had pretty well unmade himself, tangling with young Frank Blair out in Missouri, imprisoning the congressman, charging him with insubordination. Then there was the money Frémont had spent without War Department authorization; Lincoln had sent officers west to investigate that matter before Mrs. Frémont reached Washington. And, since Wilson's Creek, the Pathfinder had done nothing much to enhance his already precarious reputation as a military leader.

It took Lincoln until the third week in October to do it, but he finally relieved Frémont of command. In attempting to solve his Missouri problem, however, the Union's president inadvertently created another one in Kentucky.

Among the people Lincoln sent west to investigate Frémont was Secretary of War Simon Cameron, himself suspected by many of being at best an incompetent administrator and at worst "a man who would not steal a hot kitchen stove." Returning from Missouri, Cameron paused in Louisville to confer with Brigadier General William Tecumseh Sherman, commander of what was now called the Department of the Cumberland, the man who replaced Robert Anderson when deteriorating health forced Fort Sumter's hero into semiretirement.

Cameron's room in Louisville's Galt House was the scene of his meeting with Sherman. All might have been well if only the two of them had been there, but reporters were also present. Assuring Sherman the newsmen were friendly, the secretary of war encouraged the fatigued and suspicious general to speak freely. Sherman did, telling Cameron the rebels were closing in on his scattered units from three directions and that saving Kentucky would require an army of 200,000 men.

Insanity, concluded the journalists, awed by that figure but overlooking Sherman's reasons for suggesting it. General Sherman, they told newspaper readers all over the North, was crazy; in time, even their victim would come to believe them. Before then, though, enough Kentuckians did to impair Sherman's effectiveness; in November he would be removed from command and replaced by Brigadier General Don Carlos Buell, the former major who had nudged history a little in December 1860 by suggesting to Anderson that certain circumstances might make withdrawing from Fort Moultrie to Fort Sumter advisable.

But October 1861 contained more mischief destined to plague Lincoln. Some of it was harmless, more of it tragic, all of it related to his hasty decision late on the night of McDowell's defeat at Bull Run to send for the Young Napoleon.

When given an opportunity, George McClellan usually made the most of it. West Point bent the rules by admitting him at sixteen. Cadet McClellan not only survived but finished second in the class of 1846. In the Mexican War he won the approval of a soldier then old enough to be his grandfather: Winfield Scott. And in civilian life, too, McClellan advanced rapidly; within three years he had become a senior railroad executive whose circle of friends included some of the most powerful business leaders in the North.

"He was well educated," recalled McClellan's rival for top academic honors at West Point, "and, when he chose to be, brilliant."

In Washington in the early fall of 1861, a major general at thirty-four, McClellan chose to be brilliant in building the Army of the Potomac and in shoving Scott aside so he could be general-in-chief of the Union armies. He did not choose to lead his huge army out to Manassas and drive Joe Johnston's forces away.

McClellan explained to all those who were pressing him to do something—Lincoln, many congressmen, newspaper editorial writers—that Johnston had at least 100,000 troops defending the hills just west of Washington. So said the reports of railroad detective Allan Pinkerton, which the army commander accepted.

Then Johnston, who in Old Army years began his letters to McClellan with "Beloved Mac," withdrew the token force he had been keeping on Munson's Hill, an apparently formidable outpost less than ten miles from the Capitol's unfinished dome. In late September a Union probe of the abandoned position was accompanied by a *New York Tribune* correspondent, who reported:

> Munson's Hill will hereafter be the expression and measure of military false pretensions. There were no intrenchments there; there had been no cannon there. In the terrible batteries behind the hill there is but a derisive log, painted black.

According to General McClellan, however, by mid-October his old friend's army had swelled to 150,000. In fact, at best Johnston had 41,000, including units posted near Leesburg, well up the Potomac from Manassas, guarding against a federal flanking maneuver launched from the northwest.

General McClellan shrugged off Munson's Hill, decided to verify rumors that Johnston was giving up Leesburg, and led Brigadier General George McCall's regulars northwestward along the Potomac's southern bank to within about ten miles of the town. Halting, he sent an order over to Brigadier General Charles P. Stone, on the Potomac's northern bank a little above Leesburg, to make a demonstration to hasten the Confederates' departure.

Having encountered no rebels, McClellan left the rest to Stone and returned to Washington—followed by McCall's force—without advising General Stone of his or McCall's departure. The next day, October 21, Stone ordered his regiments across the Potomac to make a reconnaissance in force. But Stone did not lead it himself, entrusting the "demonstration" first to the commander of a Massachusetts regiment and later to Colonel Edward D. Baker, who was also a senator from Oregon and perhaps the dearest of Abraham Lincoln's friends.

Ball's Bluff, as the battle would later be called, was a federal fiasco in which Baker was shot dead. To reach the Confederate sniper's bullet the senator had crossed the Potomac's rushing waters in a small boat, as had the Massachusetts regiments before him in similar ones, and climbed the now-worn cow path up the steep embankment a hundred feet to the plateau.

Colonel Shanks Evans was not there that day, but his Manassas veterans were. They waited on the plateau until almost all the Union force had struggled up Ball's Bluff, then let loose their terrifying, demonic yell and charged, driving the Yankees back to the edge of the cliff and over it.

Below them the Confederates saw blue-clad men sliding down the slope in panic, some slipping and screaming as their bodies fell onto the bayonet tips of federal soldiers massed below on the foaming Potomac's bank. For the rebels it was a turkey shoot. The river killed many of the targets they missed, for Yankees surged into boats already overloaded with wounded men, dooming all aboard to death by drowning.

For several days afterward bodies floated slowly down the Potomac, finally reaching Washington, providing mute evidence of a Union defeat almost as devastating as Bull Run. The North had lost roughly a thousand men, the Confederates hardly any.

One by one, the drowned and shot and bayonet-speared dead were buried by their families and friends in their hometowns throughout Massachusetts, New York, and Pennsylvania. Senator-Colonel Edward Baker's death—like Colonel Elmer Ellsworth's at Alexandria five months earlier—was a devastating personal loss to the president, one of whose sons bore Baker's name, and this gave national significance to what might otherwise have been treated as a badly mismanaged skirmish.

Congressmen, ignoring reports suggesting that Baker's rash and amateurish actions contributed to the calamity, mourned the senator by creating a Joint Committee on the Conduct of the War and filling it with "Jacobins," frustrated Radical Republicans who deemed Lincoln's efforts to quell the rebellion too timid. And among its first actions the committee made General Stone the scapegoat for the Ball's Bluff fiasco.

For months stretching midway into 1862, Stone would sit in prison not knowing why he was there, denied all civil rights a common thief could claim, the victim of McClellan's ineptness as well as a blatantly unconstitutional congressional drive for power. Extremism, a proximate cause of the war, now seemed poised to prosecute it.

If George McClellan sensed that he was the committee's actual target—as he may well have been—he shrugged off congressional pressure as casually as he had rejected Lincoln's repeated suggestions that he take his huge Army of the Potomac and drive Johnston's little force away from Manassas. He wanted control first, which meant that he would have to become the Union armies' general-in-chief.

This was possible, or so McClellan wrote his wife on August 2, only about a week after his arrival in Washington:

> Genl Scott...is fast becoming very slow & very old. He cannot long retain command I think—when he retires I am sure to succeed him, unless in the mean time I lose a battle—which I do not expect to do....

And after another week, on August 8:

> Rose early today (having retired at 3 am) & was pestered to death with Senators etc & a row with Genl Scott....I do not know whether he is a *dotard* or a *traitor*! I can't tell which. He *cannot* or *will* not comprehend the condition in which we are placed & is entirely unequal to the emergency. If he cannot be taken out of my path I will not retain my position but will resign & let the admn take care of itself.... Every day strengthens me—I am leaving nothing undone to increase our force—but that confounded old Genl always comes in the way—he is a perfect imbecile. He understands nothing, appreciates nothing & is ever in my way.

Winfield Scott understood insubordination. He also knew he was in a fight he could not win. On the next day, August 9, the general-in-chief wrote Secretary of War Simon Cameron:

> Having now been long unable to mount a horse, or to walk more than a few paces at a time, and consequently being unable to review troops, much less direct them in battle—in short, being broken down by many particular hurts, besides the general infirmities of age—I feel that I have become an incumbrance to the Army as well as to myself, and that I

ought, giving way to a younger commander, to seek the palliatives of physical pain and exhaustion.

Not yet, said President Lincoln, so Scott provided some specifics:

> The original offense given to me by Major-General McClellan...seems to have been the result of deliberation between him and some of the members of the Cabinet, by whom all the greater war questions are to be settled, without resort to or consultation with me, the nominal General-in-Chief of the Army. In further proof of this neglect,—although...many regiments have arrived and others have changed their positions; some to a considerable distance,—not one of these movements has been reported to me (or anything else) by Major-General McClellan; while it is believed, and, I may add, known, that he is in frequent communication with portions of the Cabinet and on matters appertaining to me. That freedom of access and consultation have, very naturally, deluded the junior officer into a feeling of indifference toward his superior.

Thinking, perhaps, that a general order reminding all army officers of the need for communicating through the prescribed chain of command might cause McClellan to repent and sin no more, Scott issued one in mid-September, noting that "the same rule applies to correspondence with the President direct, or with him through the Secretary of War, unless it be by the special invitation or request of the President."

McClellan ignored the warning. On October 4, Scott wrote Secretary of War Cameron:

> Eighteen days have now elapsed, and not the slightest response has been shown...by Major-General McClellan.... Has, then, a senior no corrective power over a junior officer in a case of such persistent neglect and disobedience?
> The remedy by arrest and trial before a court-martial would probably soon cure the evil. But it has been feared that a conflict of authority near the head of the Army would be highly encouraging to the enemies and depressing to the friends of the Union. Hence my long forebearance;...

Two more weeks passed. Then, sensing victory, McClellan wrote his wife, Ellen, on October 19:

It seems to be pretty well settled that I will become Comdr in Chf within a week. Genl Scott proposes to retire in favor of [Henry W.] Halleck. The Presdt & Cabinet have determined to accept his retirement, but *not* in favor of Halleck.

These communications, of course, were private. But the plight of the lieutenant general, now seventy-five, was known throughout the Union, and it was obvious to Washingtonians. "Hard is the fate of those who serve republics," wrote British newspaperman William Howard Russell, adding:

The officers who met the old man in the street today passed him by without a salute or mark of recognition, although he wore his uniform coat, with yellow lapels and yellow sash; and one of the group which came out of a restaurant close to the General's house exclaimed, almost within his hearing, "Old fuss and feathers don't look first rate today."

On October 31 General Scott sent Secretary Cameron a final letter in which he cited only his infirmities as reasons for his request that he be placed on the retired list. His plea was granted the next day, and McClellan, not Halleck, would replace him.

But the president must have had misgivings regarding the appointment he had just made, for when he visited McClellan that evening, he said: "In addition to your present command, the supreme command of the Army will entail a vast labor on you."

And McClellan replied: "I can do it all."

Thus, the torch was passed, not directly but by the man who led his cabinet to Scott's house the next afternoon to pay a farewell call on the nation's most distinguished soldier, the only one since George Washington to hold the rank of lieutenant general. Afterward, presumably, Winfield Scott enjoyed his usual gourmet dinner, enhanced by his excellent wines.

At four o'clock the next morning, with early November rain making an otherwise sad occasion all the more funereal, aides of old General Scott helped him get from his carriage to the waiting room of the railroad station. All the New York bound passengers rose as he entered—and tensed when, rain dripping from his cloak, in came the Young Napoleon.

Afterward, McClellan wrote his wife:

The old man said that his sensations were very peculiar in leaving Washn & active life—I can easily understand them—& it may be that at some distant day I too shall totter away from Washn—a worn out soldier, with naught to do but make my peace with God. This sight of this morning was a lesson to me which I hope not soon to forget. I saw there the end of a long, active & ambitious life—the end of the career of the first soldier of his nation—& it was a feeble old man scarce able to walk—hardly anyone there to see him off but his successor. Should I ever become vainglorious & ambitious remind me of that spectacle.

Chapter 5

War on the Waters—and the Land

So General Scott departed, destined to spend the rest of his years watching his successors, nudged by Abraham Lincoln, carry out his ridiculed and set-aside Anaconda strategy as though its elements had occurred only to them. Meanwhile, Old Fuss and Feathers could take some satisfaction from two Union actions, both in early November, directly in line with his thinking: one in Missouri, the other on South Carolina's seacoast.

Imposing a blockade of more than 3,500 miles of Southern shoreline, from Chesapeake Bay and around Florida to the Rio Grande's mouth in the Gulf of Mexico, had been among Abraham Lincoln's first responses after the surrender of Fort Sumter. But enforcing this aspect of Scott's Anaconda strategy proved difficult; the Union navy had few ships, and those available spent almost as much time on trips back to bases to refuel and restock their stores as they did on station off ports such as Charleston.

Secretary of the Navy Gideon Welles, by profession the editor of a newspaper, ordered more ships. That much done, the prudent Connecticut Yankee appointed three experts to a board to decide what to do with the assets he had: Cape Hatteras was the first target the navy's strategists selected. Following that seizure in September and the establishment there of a new supply base, the board sent a force to take Ship Island, in the Gulf of Mexico near the mouth of the Mississippi River. Next on the federal naval strategists' target list was Port Royal, South Carolina. This harbor was large enough for any number of ships to use as a refueling and resupply base, and its location between Savannah and Charleston would enable Union warships to tighten the blockade of both key ports.

Welles gave the responsibility for assembling a flotilla of sev-

73

enty-four ships and borrowing 15,000 army troops to a member of the board, Flag Officer Samuel F. Du Pont. Near the end of October he led his fleet from Hampton Roads out of Chesapeake Bay and into a severe storm. Adding to his distress over the pro-Confederate weather was his anxiety over whether his innovative plan would work. Naval battle tactics had always been based primarily on wind conditions at the scene. With steam powering his ships, however, Du Pont saw the opportunity to render obsolete much of 2,000 years of seaborne warriors' experience.

Guarding the two-mile-wide entrance to Port Royal's huge harbor, Du Pont knew, were two Confederate forts—Walker, on Hilton Head, and Beauregard, on Bay Point to the northeast. He might have planned on landing army troops and leaving it to them to attack the rebel defenses from the rear while his ships covered the objectives with gunfire from offshore. Instead, he meant for his column to steam past Fort Beauregard, shelling it as they did, then turn about and move downchannel, blasting away at Fort Walker, turning again for as many circuits along the elliptical course as might be required for his gunners to demolish both Confederate obstacles to the Union navy's control on the waters of Port Royal Sound.

Early on the morning of November 7, Du Pont executed his plan. It worked perfectly. By early in the afternoon the Union flag waved over Fort Walker on Hilton Head, and overnight the Confederates abandoned Fort Beauregard.

Now the navy's strategic board began thinking about moving up the Mississippi to seize New Orleans. Upstream near Cairo, however, another aspect of Scott's Anaconda plan had been put to a test on a very small scale.

In early November, Brigadier General U. S. Grant acted to prevent Confederates at Columbus, Kentucky, from sending units westward across the Mississippi into Missouri to reinforce rebel Sterling Price's little force of militiamen. First he ordered Brigadier General C. F. Smith to lead a column from Paducah southward toward Columbus; then he took about 3,000 men, a few guns, and some cavalry on steamboats down the river, with two gunboats as escorts.

"I had no orders which contemplated an attack by [Union] troops," wrote Grant years later, "nor did I intend anything of the kind when I started out from Cairo...." But there was a Confederate camp at Belmont, Missouri, directly across from Columbus, and Grant thought it would improve the morale of his men even if they did no more than raid it while Smith, over in Kentucky, demonstrated near Bishop Polk's fortress.

At about eight o'clock on the morning of November 7—the same day Du Pont bombarded Port Royal, a thousand miles to the east—Grant led his force ashore a few miles above Belmont. Skirmishing soon turned into heavier fighting. After four hours of it the Confederates retreated, abandoning their camp, scurrying down the bluff, seeking shelter from federal fire.

To that point Grant had been pleased by the conduct of his men, all of whom were in a fight for the first time. But the urge to loot the rebel camp was too strong; discipline vanished as quickly as had the enemy.

In the interval Polk sent reinforcements across the river. Confederates below the bluff moved upstream to prevent Grant's force from returning to their steamboats. And once there was no danger of hitting his own men, Polk opened fire on Belmont with Columbus's heavy guns.

"I announced that we had cut our way in," Grant said in his *Memoirs*, "and could cut our way out just as well." They did. Grant was the last man to reboard, riding his horse up a single gangplank to the steamer's deck.

In the fight Grant's casualties were about 500, those of the defenders, over 600—heavy, considering the small numbers of troops on both sides. An unnecessary battle, one barren of results, declared critics in the North. But Grant returned to Cairo with something he needed desperately: confidence. And in time to come, that gain alone would give the fight at Belmont significance far beyond the event itself.

Mixed with the depressing reports from South Carolina and Kentucky in early November 1861 was news of a different kind: Jefferson Davis was elected president of the Confederate States of America. Actually, this was merely the conversion of that government and his role in it from provisional status to one in accordance with the Constitution. There had been no opponent, no serious controversy, only ratification.

If Davis had little cause for celebrating the prospect of six years as president, he could at least take pleasure from a gift of sorts. It took the form of a report that the USS *San Jacinto*, an armed sloop, had stopped the British steamer *Trent* and seized four Southerners: John Slidell of Louisiana, James M. Mason of Virginia, and their two male secretaries.

Earlier, Davis had appointed Slidell as commissioner to France, Mason to Great Britain, and a blockade runner had taken them to Havana, where they boarded the *Trent* for the voyage across the Atlantic to Southampton. Now, thanks to Captain Charles Wilkes of the *San Jacinto*, Mason and Slidell were providing the Confederacy with greater benefits than Jefferson Davis may have hoped for when he selected them to be his ambassadors. Indeed, so outrageous was Wilkes' action that this offense against an unarmed mail steamer on the high seas might well anger the British enough to declare war on the Union.

Abraham Lincoln saw the threat and worried about it, but his supply of problems was already ample. Secretary of War Cameron was one. Lincoln had appointed him with misgivings, mainly to honor a pledge made without his knowledge at the Chicago convention. That Cameron was unfit as an administrator was obvious; less clear was his honesty, and a congressional committee was looking into allegations of fraud.

Perhaps to curry favor with the abolitionists in Congress, the secretary of war included in his annual report to that body a long passage advocating the employment of freed slaves as Union soldiers. Cameron not only neglected to clear this with the president, but—before Lincoln saw the document—mailed copies of his report to postmasters throughout the Union for distribution to newspapers in their cities.

Lincoln ordered the recall of copies already mailed and the substitution of a version omitting the controversial passage, but some newspapers printed both texts side by side. As a result, many persons who would never have read such a document were drawn to do so by the spectacle of a president unable to control even one of his closest associates.

And then there was General McClellan. In time he might be able to "do it all," but in his first few weeks as general-in-chief the Young Napoleon's performance disappointed not only Lincoln but the Radicals in Congress. Instead of using his huge Army of the Potomac to drive Joe Johnston's forces away from nearby Manassas, McClellan held more and more parades.

As the late autumn's good fighting weather passed into December's threatening variety, congressional pressure on the president intensified. Now, ironically, he was discovering what old General Scott may have meant in a letter to Cameron by alluding to "hurts." One evening Lincoln went by McClellan's house to talk to him. A servant said the general was out; the president replied he would wait. He did. Long afterward, the servant told Lincoln the general had returned but had retired for the night. On the way back to the White House, Lincoln's secretary, John Hay, was indignant over the apparently intentional discourtesy. "I will hold McClellan's horse," said the president, "if he will only bring us success."

But Lincoln did more than wait; he studied. Among the books he read was *Elements of Military Art and Science* by Henry W. Halleck, the man Winfield Scott had recommended as his successor, now the major general in St. Louis cleaning up the mess Pathfinder Frémont had left behind. And late in December, on learning that General-in-Chief McClellan was seriously ill with typhoid fever, Lincoln acted.

Were they cooperating, he asked Halleck in St. Louis and Buell in Louisville by telegraph. No, they replied. Lincoln sent for Quartermaster General Montgomery Meigs. "The people are impatient," he said. "Chase has no money, and tells me he can raise no more; the General of the Army has typhoid fever. The bottom is out of the tub. What shall I do?"

Meigs was of no help, nor were McClellan's subordinates able to tell him much about the secret plan the general had said he was developing. Once McClellan heard about Lincoln's inquiries, however, he had an amazingly fast recovery.

While Lincoln had been delving into military matters, the Trent Affair, as the newspapers called Captain Wilkes's seizure of the Confederate diplomats, strained Union-British relations almost to the point Jefferson Davis desired. But in the time it took for ships to carry notes from one government to the other, British outrage receded, and at the last moment Lincoln released Mason and Slidell.

Once Davis's emissaries had sailed for Europe, the Union's president also sent Simon Cameron across the Atlantic as ambassador to Russia. To replace him as secretary of war, Lincoln selected Edwin McMasters Stanton, pleasing Congress and the public generally. But those who knew both the president and Stanton may well have thought either that Lincoln had lost his mind or that Stanton was falling into a trap.

Born in Ohio, troubled in his early life by depression, Stanton won a nationwide reputation as an able but extremely aggressive lawyer in the 1850s. In a California case he came close to accusing Henry Halleck of perjury; and in another he rudely snubbed an associate counsel, Abraham Lincoln.

Stanton was a lifelong Democrat and an abolitionist. In the last months of James Buchanan's presidency he served as attorney general, but he also nurtured friendships among Radical Republicans before and after Lincoln's inauguration. General McClellan found Stanton a willing and congenial ally in his campaign to become general-in-chief; and both men held a low opinion of Lincoln, referring to him as "the original gorilla."

An honest, energetic, and ruthlessly efficient manager was what the president wanted, however, and Edwin Stanton appeared to meet these specifications. The new secretary quickly began clearing the

War Department of incompetent Cameron-appointed officials and establishing strict operating procedures.

But Stanton was hardly the man to spur General McClellan. That task belonged to the president; and while Lincoln deplored certain Radical Republicans' opinions that the Young Napoleon's stubborn silence regarding his plans reeked of treason, he grew increasingly impatient for someone, somewhere, to do something.

Confederate Thomas J. Jackson, a major general now and in command of a small force at Winchester in the Shenandoah Valley of Virginia, needed no prompting. Recalling one of the real Napoleon's maxims—that troops will be healthier if they are campaigning during the winter than they are likely to be if kept in damp huts or sitting around campfires—Jackson took his brigade and one he borrowed northwestward to chase Yankee detachments from Romney and Bath to the Union side of the Potomac River.

On New Year's Day the march began in pleasant weather, and at first the going was easy, but before sundown the column was climbing mountain roads in the midst of a fierce snowstorm with hail mixed in. Ice on the steep inclines prevented the supply wagons from reaching the bivouac area. The tired and hungry men, without overcoats or blankets, spent the cold and windy night huddled around campfires.

Harsh winter weather persisted throughout the campaign. Jackson's borrowed troops, commanded by Brigadier General William W. Loring, suffered even more than the veterans of the Stonewall Brigade. Loring's men, not accustomed to stern discipline, thought Jackson was crazy. They became even more disaffected when, after federal units retreated, Jackson ordered Loring to occupy Romney and patrol the Potomac line, then took the Stonewall Brigade back to Winchester.

Although very few people knew it, Jackson's real purpose in undertaking the Romney campaign was to seize and hold ground from which a larger Confederate army could invade Maryland and Pennsylvania. True, the authorities in Richmond were hardly in a position to exploit this strategic opportunity; but he had made it possible, and for the time being he could take some satisfaction from the quantities of weapons and supplies his men captured and the seasoning he and they had undergone.

Then, in early February, Virginia's governor John Letcher received this letter from his Lexington neighbor, Jackson:

> This morning I received an order from the Secretary of
> War to order General Loring and his command to fall back to

[Winchester] immediately. The order was promptly complied with, but as the order was given without consulting me, and is abandoning to the enemy what has cost much preparation, expense and exposure to secure, and is in direct conflict with my military plans, and implies a want of confidence in my ability to judge when General Loring's troops should fall back, and is an attempt to control military operations in detail from the Secretary's desk at a distance, I have...requested to be ordered back to the [Virginia Military] Institute, and if this is denied me, then to have my resignation accepted....

I desire to say nothing against the Secretary of War. I take it for granted that he has done what he believed to be best, but I regard such a policy as ruinous.

Jefferson Davis's secretary of war, former U.S. senator Judah P. Benjamin of Louisiana, was noted for his rapid grasp of complex situations. But in this one Benjamin had acted too quickly, relying on vague reports of a federal advance toward Romney, unaware that Jackson had developed a broad network of information sources throughout his zone of responsibility or that these scouts had told him the Yankees were not moving. Moreover, some of Loring's officers had visited Richmond and filled the ears of Benjamin and newspaper editors with vivid descriptions of the misery their troops endured in the frigid weather and almost impassable terrain.

General Jackson's reaction to the withdrawal order shocked the Confederate government enough to drive home a critically important lesson: No official should try to control military operations in detail from a desk, at a distance. Much later, General Halleck would say, bluntly, to his president what Jackson was implying: "I hold that a General in command of any army in the field is the best judge of existing conditions."

This was common sense, and no more; yet it took someone as bold as Jackson to stop a practice that might have enfeebled all Confederate army commanders eventually. To their credit, his civilian superiors not only backed down and refused even to consider his resignation but abstained from meddling—for a time. And this, perhaps, was the most significant result of the campaign Jackson won and Secretary Benjamin blighted.

Meanwhile, out in northwestern Kentucky, another campaign was about to begin—this one a Union initiative. Whose idea it was would remain controversial, although anyone who looked at a map could figure out the best way to attack the two Confederate forts just south of the Kentucky-Tennessee border.

Rebels started building Fort Henry on the Tennessee River and Fort Donelson on the Cumberland in 1861 because those northward-flowing tributaries of the Ohio were natural Yankee invasion routes and Kentucky had been neutral. That neither fort had been completed by early 1862 made them all the more attractive to senior federal officers.

Forts Henry and Donelson

One was Major General Henry Halleck. He had been nicknamed "Old Brains" long before, and he could read a map better than most soldiers. That, the Missouri Department commander did one January night in a St. Louis hotel room, with William Tecumseh Sherman looking on.

Afterward it would be clear that Halleck was driven by ambition to become supreme commander in the west, meaning that he meant to make a subordinate of Major General Don Carlos Buell, who commanded Union forces in Kentucky east of both the Tennessee and Cumberland rivers. And Old Brains may have been goaded by Buell's response to goading from President Lincoln: In mid-January Buell's lieutenant, Brigadier General George Henry Thomas, had whipped the rebels in a sharp fight at Mill Springs in eastern Kentucky—a step toward liberating Unionists in East Tennessee. In any event, Halleck was receptive when Grant asked for permission to seize Forts Henry and Donelson. Do it, in effect, Old Brains replied.

Southward up the flooded Tennessee River on February 6, 1862, Grant sent seven gunboats, manned by his soldiers but commanded by Commodore Andrew H. Foote, an aging naval warrior who conducted Bible school every Sunday wherever in the world duty took him. After the gunboats came nine transports packed with roughly 8,000 troops. Grant meant to land his brigades on both banks of the river a short distance downstream from Fort Henry; these would advance southward and strike the rebels by land as the gunboats steamed up, their guns firing.

And so they would, but there were surprises. Confederate Brigadier General Lloyd Tilghman, recognizing that his fort would have to be abandoned, sent his infantry twelve miles eastward to Fort Donelson and defended his partially flooded position by concentrating artillery fire on the approaching Union gunboats. Soon, though, rising water silenced some of Tilghman's guns, and others were blown away or ran out of ammunition. About an hour before Grant arrived, Tilghman surrendered Fort Henry to Commodore Foote.

While Grant's men went into camp, Foote sent three of his gunboats up the Tennessee to destroy a railroad bridge fifteen miles south of Fort Henry. Having cut the Confederacy's main East-West rail line the gunboats steamed on, eventually reaching the river's head of navigation at Muscle Shoals in northern Alabama.

As Confederate General Albert Sidney Johnston viewed the situation, Grant and Foote had broken the center of his almost theoretical line, which had stretched from Columbus eastward across Kentucky to Bowling Green; now his challenge was to keep the Yankees from taking Nashville, his main supply and communications base and Tennessee's capital. Grant could seize the city by capturing Fort Donelson, loading his army on transports, and following Foote's gunboats up the Cumberland River to within a few miles of their goal. But even if Grant remained at Fort Henry, which seemed unlikely, the 40,000 men Don Carlos Buell had started toward Bowling Green could keep marching until they reached Nashville.

Johnston knew more, all of it discouraging: Richmond could provide no reinforcements, his forces were scattered, Yankee gunboats on the Tennessee had cut his railroad link to Memphis, Columbus would have to be abandoned. Was it time to order a general retreat to some point south of the Cumberland? Or should he fight first Grant, then Buell, though each Union army was larger than his would be if he could get it together?

To Sidney Johnston, withdrawing seemed the lesser of two evils. That was what he told Richmond he intended to do, and he ordered pullbacks from Bowling Green and Columbus. But he changed his mind about Fort Donelson. To its small garrison he added troops until the little fort's strength reached 17,500. And on February 13, Johnston sent orders to John Floyd, the senior of the four brigadier generals then at Donelson, to hold out for as long as possible.

While Sidney Johnston got part of his army retreating and part preparing to fight, Commodore Foote removed his gunboat flotilla from the Tennessee River and sent it up the Ohio a few miles to the Cumberland's mouth. Grant made a reconnaissance near Donelson, saw that it was much stronger than Fort Henry, watched Confederate reinforcements arrive, and waited for the brigades General Halleck was sending him from Missouri.

Fort Donelson itself was nothing more than an uncompleted redoubt on a bluff a hundred feet or so above the Cumberland's flooded waters, its purpose being to pour fire from heavy guns on any enemy ships approaching from the north before they could follow the river's course upstream around a bend to the east. Protecting the guns, then, was General Floyd's main concern. To do this he deployed his brigades in a crescent resembling a horseshoe, westward, then southward, and finally eastward, roughly two miles long.

Ulysses Grant led his men from Fort Henry eastward on February 12 in weather so pleasant the troops littered the crude road through the forest with blankets and overcoats. Soon the route turned hilly, and so it remained for about ten miles; then the leading elements drew the fire of rebel snipers. Ignoring that, Grant closed all the routes Floyd might take if he decided to abandon Fort Donelson.

On the Cumberland the USS *Carondelet* steamed toward the rebel batteries. Not a creature was in sight. Captain Henry Walke moved the little ironclad closer and ordered the *Carondelet*'s bow guns to open fire. No response; but at least Walke got a good look at the Confederates' batteries on the bluff, and he had let General Grant know he was there, and that was enough.

"We are doing well on the land side," said Grant in a message to Walke, and he also asked for "a diversion in our favor" the next day.

As things turned out, Grant needed it. Early on Thursday morning, the thirteenth, Brigadier General John A. McClernand—veteran of Grant's raid at Belmont but still more of a politician than a soldier—sent a brigade forward to attack a rebel artillery battery, only to see his men cut down in a murderous crossfire.

The *Carondelet* provided the desired diversion, in the process drawing hell's own fire from the Confederate guns on the bluff and taking hits that sent arrowlike splinters flying through confined spaces such as the badly damaged engine room. Some of Walke's men were so surprised that they were unaware of their wounds until blood filled their shoes. Except for a brief fallback to repair damage and put the wounded on another vessel, though, the *Carondelet* fought the shore batteries until dusk, enabling old C. F. Smith to engage Floyd's defenders on the northwestern segment of Grant's long arc while McClernand extricated most of his men from the disaster his rashness had triggered.

Near sundown that Thursday rain began, and overnight the temperature plunged into the teens, turning the drizzle into wind-blown sleet and snow, freezing some of the unrecovered Union wounded to death, dooming all the men on both sides to hours of misery hardly any amount of patriotism could offset. And as they suffered—Grant's men especially, because they had thrown away their overcoats and blankets during the false spring—they knew that dawn might bring something even worse.

But with the bone-chilling storm also came, near midnight, the rest of Commodore Foote's gunboat flotilla: the flag steamer *St. Louis*, the ironclads *Louisville* and *Pittsburgh*, and the wooden *Tyler* and *Conestoga*. And on transports Foote brought enough troops for General Grant to place a third division between Smith and McClernand, which he did first thing the next morning, Friday, February 14.

Apparently, what Grant and Foote envisioned was the kind of attack that had been so successful at Fort Henry. Foote, however, had seen the damage Donelson's batteries had done to the *Carondelet*, and he took the time to have all his vessels place chains, lumber, and bags of coal on their decks to protect them from plunging fire. Ashore, commanders on both sides waited.

Finally, around three o'clock that Friday afternoon, Foote got his four ironclad gunboats abreast and moving upstream to engage the Confederate guns. At a range of one mile, the *St. Louis* opened fire.

On Fort Donelson's high ground General Floyd watched the Union flotilla steaming toward him. "This fort cannot hold out twenty minutes," he wired Sidney Johnston.

Get closer, Foote ordered. But the nearer the gunboats approached, the more punishment they took. Walke described the rebel fire striking the *Carondelet*:

> We heard the deafening crack of the bursting shells, the crash of the solid shot, and the whizzing of fragments of shell and wood as they sped through the vessel. Soon a 128-pounder struck our anchor, smashed it into flying bolts, and bounded over the vessel, taking away part of our smoke-stack.... Another ripped up the iron plating and glanced over; another went through the plating and lodged in the heavy casemate; another struck the pilot-house, knocked the plating to pieces, and sent fragments of iron and splinters into the pilots...and still they came, harder and faster, taking flag-staffs and smoke-stacks, and tearing off the side armor as lightning tears the bark from a tree.

And a crewman remembered:

> Two shots entered our bow-ports and killed four men and wounded others. They were borne past me, three with their heads off.... Our master's mate came soon after and ordered us to our quarters at the gun. I told him that our gun had burst, and that we had caught fire on the upper deck from the enemy's shell. He then said: "Never mind the fire; go to your quarters." Then I took a station at the starboard tackle of another gun and remained there until the close of the fight.

And so it was on the other ironclads, until Foote closed to within 350 yards of the Confederate batteries. The *Carondelet*'s Walke recalled:

> On looking out to bring our broadside guns to bear, we saw that the other gun-boats were rapidly falling back out of line. The *Pittsburgh* in her haste to turn struck the stern of the *Carondelet*, and broke our starboard rudder, so we were obliged to go ahead to clear the *Pittsburgh* and the point of rocks below. The pilot of the *St. Louis* was killed, and the pilot of the *Louisville* was wounded. Both vessels had their wheel-ropes shot away, and the men were prevented from steering the *Louisville* with the tiller-ropes at the stern by the shells from the rear boats bursting over them. The *St. Louis* and the *Louisville*, becoming unmanageable, were compelled to drop out of the battle, and the *Pittsburgh* followed; all had suffered severely from the enemy's fire.

That left the *Carondelet* to face the batteries on the bluff. Confederate gunners concentrated their fire on the lone gunboat, aiming low, hitting the *Carondelet* below her bow's waterline and shattering her plating, but still Walke fought back. "Before the decks were well sanded," he wrote later, "there was so much blood on them that our men could not work the guns without slipping." And Walke kept firing—"to keep the enemy from seeing us through the smoke." Then, finally, he withdrew.

General Grant, realizing that Fort Donelson would not go the way of Fort Henry, learning that Commodore Foote had been wounded by the rebel shell that killed the *St. Louis*'s pilot, aware that the gunboats were all but out of the campaign for the time being, began thinking in terms of a siege. Inside Confederate lines, however, thinking of a very different sort prevailed: Floyd and his other brigadier generals agreed that they would have to fight their way out of Donelson at sunrise.

Such a decision was ironic, for the rest of the men in Fort Donelson's garrison were jubilant. And so had been Floyd, until he talked the situation over with Gideon Pillow and the only professional soldier in the group, Simon Bolivar Buckner. To Pillow's troops went the honor of attacking the eastern segment of Grant's crescent-shaped line, where McClernand was in command, the objective being to open the road to Nashville. Buckner would support Pillow, then serve as rear guard.

Before dawn on Saturday, February 15, Grant read a message from Foote. The wounded commodore could not visit him, so would the general ride northward a few miles to the landing and come aboard the *St. Louis* for a conference before she moved downstream for repairs? Certainly, Grant decided. And before he left his headquarters house, near old C. F. Smith's division at the line's western end, he issued orders for his commanders to hold their present positions.

Pillow's brigades attacked McClernand—early and hard —and after a few hours the Yankees were falling back and the road to Nashville was open. Curiously, Floyd failed to take advantage of Pillow's gate opening. And while the victors were catching their breath, holding the ground they had gained, Grant returned from his trip to see Commodore Foote.

All was lost, Grant heard a panicked aide declare. Exactly what the general did next may have been less important than two things he said. Suspecting perhaps that there comes a time in any battle when both sides are exhausted, Grant remarked to his staff: "The one who attacks now will be victorious." And: "Gentlemen, the position on the right must be retaken."

McClernand was on the right, and Grant sent him forward to

regain the ground Pillow had taken, but Smith's division was fresh, and he also ordered him to advance. To Foote, Grant sent a request for any gunboats available to come up the Cumberland and merely fire a few diverting shots.

Smith's assault, led gallantly by the old soldier waving his saber with his hat on the tip, broke Floyd's depleted line and facilitated McClernand's counterattack. By nightfall Union artillery was on high ground the rebels had abandoned to Smith. And no longer was Grant thinking about a siege.

That night Floyd sat down again with Pillow and Buckner to decide what to do next. With them was Colonel Nathan Bedford Forrest, Tennesseean, commander of the cavalry. All the routes of escape were closed except for the river, on which there was a steamboat that had just landed 400 troops sent from upstream. Forrest said the men could get out if they waded a waist-deep creek, but a surgeon cited the bitterly cold night air as a reason not to try that. The generals decided to surrender.

Floyd—mindful, perhaps, that if captured he would be prosecuted for treason because of his actions as Buchanan's secretary of war—passed the command to Pillow, commandeered the only steamboat available and loaded his troops aboard it, and headed for Nashville. Pillow quickly followed Floyd's example, though he could save only himself. Forrest showed his contempt for Floyd and Pillow by taking all his cavalry out, using the route he had recommended for the entire garrison.

This left Simon Buckner with orders to surrender more than 12,000 troops to his friend in happier days, Grant. Buckner sent a message asking for terms. Soon came a reply he found surprisingly harsh: "No terms except an unconditional and immediate surrender can be accepted. I propose to move immediately upon your works."

Grant's threat, Buckner knew, was genuine: Smith had guns on high ground, and the federal force of more than 27,000 men was twice the size of the garrison Floyd, Pillow, and Forrest had left behind. Reluctantly, Buckner followed the orders he had inherited and went into captivity with his troops.

Newspapermen alert for coincidences quickly dubbed Fort Donelson's victor "Unconditional Surrender" Grant, using his first two initials as inspiration. Surely this little touch of fame was welcome to a man whose life earlier had been devoid of it. But from this point onward his challenge would be to keep his new reputation intact, and that would prove to be a burden.

Chapter 6

The Young Napoleon Falters

"T hus my husband entered his martyrdom," Varina Davis was to write long after February 22, 1862, the day on which he was inaugurated as the first elected president of the Confederacy. Dismal weather was an inauspicious omen, she had thought during her ride to Capitol Square; also unsettling were the carriage's slow pace and outside it, escorting it on either side, black men, white cotton gloves on their hands contrasting sharply with the black suits they wore, marching slowly, with solemn expressions on their faces.

Ordering the driver to halt, she demanded to be told the reason for the presence of "pall-bearers."

"This, madam," he explained, "is the way we always does in Richmond at funerals and sich-like."

And it certainly seemed at the time that Jefferson Davis had indeed "entered martydom." All the news was depressing: Fort Donelson was lost; so was Nashville. Sidney Johnston was trying to concentrate Confederate forces scattered throughout the west as he retreated. Roanoke Island on North Carolina's coast had been captured. Joe Johnston was uneasy over McClellan's buildup of troops within easy striking distance of Manassas.

Now that all of Kentucky was lost to the Yankees and much of Tennessee as well, critics were howling for scalps. Albert Sidney Johnston offered to take all the blame. "The test of merit in my profession," he wrote Davis, "is success. It is a hard rule, but I think it right."

Davis said in reply: "My confidence in you has never wavered, and I hope the public will soon give me credit for judgment rather than continue to arraign me for obstinacy."

Earlier, the other Johnston had come to Richmond to warn Davis and the cabinet that his little army at Manassas would have to retreat sooner or later. No decision was either asked for or made at that meeting. As Joe Johnston passed through the lobby of his hotel, however, he heard rumors that his line at Manassas was about to be abandoned. Dismayed, suspecting a Union spy was already relaying the gossip to George McClellan, he hurried northward to rejoin his troops.

That incident destroyed whatever confidence Joe Johnston may have had in his civilian superiors' abilities to understand wartime realities. Shattered as well was his willingness to tell them what he meant to do, provided McClellan gave him time enough in which to do anything. ■

Confederates might have breathed easier had they known about the war within a war raging in Washington—a struggle between the Army of the Potomac's commander and his president.

All along McClellan had given the public, newspapermen, Congress, and Abraham Lincoln the impression that he was either unwilling or afraid to attack Joe Johnston's lines. And he had seemed to confirm his critics' allegations of indecision and cowardice by refusing to tell anyone what better use he might have for his huge army, now numbering over 100,000 superbly trained and equipped men.

A general could claim military necessity in defense of his silence, but a president could neither ignore popular demand for action nor let it be known that whatever McClellan planned to do was a deep secret even to him. When Attorney General Edward Bates reminded Lincoln of his constitutional duty to "command the commanders," however, he heeded the advice. On January 27 he prepared and issued "President's General War Order No. 1," directing "that the 22d. day of February, 1862, be the day for a general movement of the Land and Naval forces of the United States against the insurgent forces." In it he refrained from specifying targets, but he put everyone in the chain of command on notice that they would be "held to their strict and full responsibilities" for full compliance.

Getting McClellan to act may have been the president's only goal. Halleck and Buell, out west, needed no prodding; the navy was about to put army troops ashore on Roanoke Island; and Secretary Welles's planners were massing ships and soldiers for a strike up the Mississippi to take New Orleans.

Four days later, on January 31, came "President's Special War Order No. 1." It narrowed his focus, calling for seizure of a railroad point "southwestward of" Manassas Junction on or before February 22. McClellan reacted by sending the secretary of war a long document in which he revealed his intention to move his troops in a huge fleet of ships down the Potomac and through Chesapeake Bay, then up the Rappahannock River to Urbanna, Virginia; from there he would advance roughly thirty miles westward and take Richmond.

The information Lincoln had finessed left him with serious misgivings. It seemed unthinkable that the Young Napoleon could fail to comprehend Washingtonians' deep and continuing concern for the capital's safety—or blithely ignore the presence of the 115,000 Confederates he claimed Joe Johnston had at Manassas—and take the Army of the Potomac more than 100 miles to the south, leaving the city and others north of it wide open to rebel invasion.

Radical Republicans in Congress, for reasons of their own, were disgusted with McClellan and applied heavy pressure on the president to get rid of him. Grant's success in the west showed what a real fighter could do with forces tiny compared to McClellan's. Why delay sacking "Little Mac?"

Secretary of War Stanton forgot his once-close friendship with McClellan and turned against him, as did Secretary of State Seward, who had been his ally during the campaign to force old General Scott into retirement. Even so, Lincoln reserved decision. His mind was elsewhere: Willie, his second son, was ill and not expected to live.

But the president really had no alternative to accepting McClellan's plan, which he did with great reluctance in mid-February. Then he persuaded his general-in-chief to send Major General Nathaniel Banks up the Shenandoah Valley to threaten Jackson's garrison at Winchester, a movement Lincoln believed Joe Johnston might consider serious enough to shift at least some of his troops westward from Washington.

McClellan went to Harpers Ferry to supervise the building of a pontoon bridge over the Potomac for Banks. But the boats the Young Napoleon meant to use as supports for the bridge were six inches too wide to get through the Chesapeake & Ohio Canal's locks, embarrassing the general and infuriating the president. Treasury Secretary Chase reduced Lincoln's anger somewhat by remarking: "The expedition died of lockjaw."

Not quite: Banks did cross, and before long he would move southward. Meanwhile, McClellan drew more presidential wrath by opposing Lincoln's suggestion that the Army of the Potomac's proliferating divisions be grouped into corps, a change the general ought to have sought himself, since it would enable him to deal with four key subordinates instead of a dozen or more. The Young Napoleon lost this fight, too, even having to accept the officers the president designated to be corps commanders.

And there was more humiliation in store for McClellan. Lincoln called the general to the Executive Mansion on March 8 and warned him, man to man, that others were calling him a traitor, a charge McClellan angrily denied. But the incident further eroded their relationship, and at a critical time.

So, though he knew nothing of any of this, Joe Johnston, at nearby Manassas, had no real cause to fear that his once-dear friend McClellan would force his withdrawal. Neither could the Confederate general have foreseen the events in Hampton Roads.

She had been the USS *Merrimack* until April 1861, when the federals burned her to her waterline before abandoning the navy yard at Norfolk to secession-bent Virginians. Confederate navy secretary Stephen Mallory ordered her salvaged and rebuilt as an ironclad. By Saturday, March 8, 1862—the day Lincoln was warning McClellan that others suspected him of treason—the frigate had been renamed the CSS *Virginia*, and she was steaming out into Hampton Roads on a trial run.

Burdened by heavy armor plate and guns, drawing twenty-two feet of water and sluggish in her response to hard rudder, the *Virginia* was nothing to throw a naval cap in the air about. But within a few hours she rammed and sank the USS *Cumberland*, blasted the USS *Congress* into surrender, and drove three more federal warships aground in waters too shallow for her to risk entering.

The *Virginia* was only slightly damaged despite repeated hits from the fire of a hundred Yankee guns; her twenty-one casualties were minor compared with heavy Union navy losses. And though she had been obliged to leave some enemy vessels to await certain destruction the next day, the *Virginia*'s cruise had in fact doomed all the wooden ships in the world's navies to obsolescence.

News of the disaster reached Washington early enough the next morning for Lincoln to gather his cabinet at the Executive Mansion for a sunrise meeting. Edwin Stanton, the ruthlessly efficient War Secretary, broke apart in panic. The *Virginia*, he declared, would dominate all the Union's seaboard cities: "Not unlikely, we shall have a shell or a cannonball from one of her guns in the White House before we leave this room."

Lincoln and Secretary of the Navy Gideon Welles tried to calm Stanton by telling him about the the USS *Monitor*, a gamble they had accepted months before when John Ericsson, a Swedish-born engineer, had come to Welles with the design for a warship unlike anything yet seen. The *Monitor*, they assured Stanton, was reported entering Hampton Roads; her two eleven-inch rifles, mounted in a revolving turret, might make a powerful difference, eliminating any cause for spreading alarm throughout the Union.

To the surprise of no one present except Stanton, the meeting ended without the *Virginia* appearing on the Potomac. She was fully occupied in Hampton Roads that day, fighting a duel with the *Monitor* that left both ships battered but still afloat. But there was something else visible from the White House: a plume of dark smoke rising ever higher in the western sky.

Though Joe Johnston certainly had not intended it as such, that mounting plume was his farewell salute. Rainy weather and wagon shortages had kept him from removing more than a fraction of his supplies before he sent his columns marching southward; the rest, including more than a million pounds of meat, had to be burned. Into the flames also went blankets, extra clothing, and other belongings Johnston's troops could neither carry with them nor replace. And not all the guns he had to leave behind were logs painted black.

But there were enough "Quaker" guns in Johnston's deserted lines to give Northern newspapermen rich material for stories — and the reporters got to Manassas almost as soon as the first federal patrols entered the area. At no time, observers inspecting the ruins concluded, could Johnston have had more than 60,000 men there. "Our enemies, like the Chinese," wrote a correspondent, "have frightened us by the sound of gongs and the wearing of devils' masks."

Atop McClellan's Manassas humiliation another was soon heaped: On March 11 he read in a newspaper that the president had relieved him as general-in-chief. Stunned and also stung, he assumed Lincoln's manner of informing him was intentionally insulting. Not so, McClellan soon learned from the emissary who had not reached him in advance. Since the general was departing to lead the Army of the Potomac into battle, this mutual friend explained, the president did not want him to feel burdened by other responsibilities.

There was truth in that and also in what was left unsaid: McClellan could not "do it all." Actually, no one seemed to know precisely what a general-in-chief's duties really were. Perhaps Lincoln meant to define them or to set an example; in any case, he did not appoint anyone to succeed McClellan, taking on the task of directing the Union's armies himself.

McClellan took some comfort from the possibility that he would be reinstated after he took Richmond. He also revised his plans, adjusting them for the fact that he could no longer hope to trap Johnston. Instead of landing at Urbanna, he would put his divisions ashore at Fort Monroe. Using it as his base and with the navy protecting his flanks on the James and York rivers, he would advance northwestward up the long peninsula and seize the rebel capital.

Now there was only one question not yet settled: Lincoln's insistence that McClellan leave enough troops behind to protect Washington. But Little Mac was concentrating on moving his army, a huge task involving the loading of 113 steamers, 188 schooners, and 88 barges. For days, from March 17 onward, columns of troops passed through Alexandria on their way to docks on the south shore of the Potomac; afterward came guns, horses, cattle, and wagons carrying provisions for 146,000 men.

Thick clouds of black steamboat smoke and the comings and goings of so many ships on the Potomac merely confirmed all the other reports the Confederates had of McClellan's departure. Joe Johnston was leading his troops southward, vexed because the single-track Orange & Alexandria Railroad had been unable to move more of his supplies, still not communicating with the authorities in Richmond. And in that city the minds of most people were not so much on Manassas as Hampton Roads; despite the *Monitor*'s appearance, the *Virginia* seemed to have won enough of a victory to justify celebration.

Johnston had a different reason for at least some elation. President Davis had shifted Judah Benjamin over to the post of secretary of state, and he had also called General Lee back from South Carolina to act as military adviser. Lee, Johnston hoped, was still respected enough to prevent the civilians from inflicting further damage on his little army's operations.

Smaller still—perhaps 4,600 men—was Major General Jackson's garrison at Winchester, well west of Manassas, over in the Shenandoah Valley. Colonel Turner Ashby's cavalry had been watching a force of 38,000 federal troops moving slowly southwestward from Harpers Ferry: Nathaniel Banks's corps. And Jackson's orders were to withdraw if and when Johnston's army abandoned Manassas.

Attacking was Jackson's preference. Writing Johnston to ask for reinforcements, he said this:

> If we cannot be successful in defeating the enemy should he advance, a kind Providence may enable us to inflict a terrible wound and effect a safe retreat in the event of having to fall back.

And to Confederate congressman Alex R. Boteler he wrote, "If this Valley is lost, Virginia is lost."

A curious man, Jackson: austere, deeply religious, very strict in imposing discipline on himself as well as his men, a mystery even to members of his carefully chosen staff officers. But though he seldom spoke, what he said on paper on those two occasions in early March gave as clear an indication as anyone could wish to have of how his mind was working.

The orders he gave reflected that. Even before Johnston's retreat began Jackson moved all his supplies southward. Then, on March 11, as Banks's Yankee regiments neared Winchester and his own men were withdrawing, he called his brigade commanders together to help him decide what to do. Jackson wanted to hit Banks with a night attack. No, he was told, the troops had already marched too far southward.

Reluctantly, angrily, Jackson accepted the fact. "That is the last council of war I will ever hold," he told his medical director, Dr. Hunter McGuire, soon afterward.

Southward up the Shenandoah Valley Turnpike the general rode, past Kernstown, a few miles south of Winchester, then Strasburg, finally halting his force at Mount Jackson. Now he was forty-two miles from Winchester. But Ashby's scouts were active well to the north of Jackson's camp. On March 21 the colonel reported that the Yankee division at Strasburg led by Brigadier General James Shields was moving north, back toward Winchester.

General Johnston had told Jackson he wanted all of the federal forces then in the Shenandoah Valley kept there to make it more difficult for McClellan to defend Washington while he was moving the Army of the Potomac away from the capital. To Jackson, that expression of intent was as valid as a direct order. "Press on!" he urged his men as they marched toward Strasburg, halfway to Winchester, on Saturday, March 22. And onward they pressed the next day, Sunday, almost to Kernstown.

There, four miles south of Winchester, at two o'clock that afternoon, Jackson paused. The Yankee troops in sight, Ashby said, were merely a rear guard. Jackson was tempted to attack. But the northward march's fast pace had left many stragglers exhausted along the Valley Turnpike; he had only about 3,000 men he could throw against however many Shields might have. And there was another risk he had to evaluate. Would the Lord condone his fighting a battle on the Sabbath?

A worse sin, the devout Jackson concluded, would be to allow the enemy to escape. Quickly he scanned the terrain, sent his regiments where he thought the Yankee line weakest, got his guns into position, and ordered his line forward.

And forward they charged, gallantly, into federal fire so heavy that Jackson's old Stonewall Brigade seemed to be pulling back. He rode northward·to learn why. Their ammunition was all gone, a soldier told him. "Then go back," snapped the general, "and give them the bayonet!"

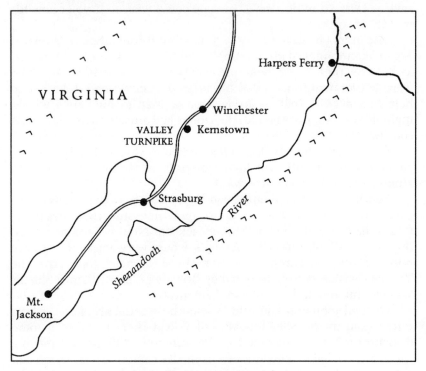

Shenandoah Valley; Kernstown

Confusion prevailed. The federals, more numerous than he had thought, came at Jackson from the woods on his left. He tried to rally his men; that failing, he ordered his reserve regiments forward, only to learn they were already in the line. Finally, he ordered his commanders to withdraw, taking with them each wounded man and every weapon.

Ashby's cavalry covered the retreat, which stopped near Newtown, about five miles to the south. Fighting not a rear guard but 9,000 Yankees had cost Jackson about 700 casualties. Shields lost almost 600 men. Later, Jackson would learn that by striking Shields at Kernstown, he had kept Nathaniel Banks's corps from leaving the Shenandoah Valley for Washington.

In fact, Jackson had accomplished even more, with some inadvertent help from George McClellan. Lincoln, uneasy over whether Little Mac had left enough troops behind to protect

Washington, discovered that instead of 40,000 there were fewer than 20,000 available, many of them untrained recruits. McClellan's explanation was both ingenuous and bewildering; by his reckoning, 73,456 men were defending the capital. Unconvinced, the president halted Irvin McDowell's corps, the only one still awaiting shipment to Fort Monroe, and kept it nearby under his control.

A little earlier, at the end of March, Lincoln had given Major General John C. Frémont the chance to try to "free" the Unionists in East Tennessee by advancing southwestward through the rugged Alleghenies west of the Shenandoah Valley. And to Frémont's force the president had added a division detached from McClellan's army. McClellan had protested at the time; now, with McDowell's corps also denied him, he considered himself the victim of a conspiracy.

But by April 5, McClellan was down on the peninsula with his leading units as they approached the Confederate defenses near Yorktown. Rains had turned the roads behind him into mud wallows. And from all reports, fire from the rebel line was heavy. Quickly the Young Napoleon's messages to Washington stopped predicting fighting and began reflecting his decision to halt the Army of the Potomac's advance and take Yorktown by employing time-consuming siege operations.

That decision was curious. On March 22, many days before he reached the peninsula, McClellan had ordered siege guns sent to Fort Monroe. Then, once on the scene, apparently he made no attempt to use the two divisions he had up front to feel out the Confederate defenses.

Had McClellan done so, he might have been shocked to find how weak Major General John B. Magruder's line really was. For fourteen miles it stretched, east to west; and though General Lee had increased "Prince John's" strength from 12,000 to double that, he was obliged to resort to the amateur theatricals (hence his nickname) for which he was admired in the Old Army. Magruder, outnumbered five to one, shifted his guns from one visible spot to the next. He even used the hoary "Indian trick," parading the same soldiers in view of McClellan's observers around and around a forest's segment that concealed their circumambulations.

Even before stage manager Magruder had his actors moving, however, Lincoln—general-in-chief now by default, perhaps remembering the Munson's Hill and Manassas humiliations—gave Mc-Clellan some advice: "I think you better break the enemy line from Yorktown to Warwick River at once." It was ignored.

Concentration, a principle preached to West Point cadets since 1830 by Professor Dennis Hart Mahan, was evident in the Young

Napoleon's massing of forces before he launched his peninsula
campaign. Conserving what he had achieved was one valid reason
McClellan had for protesting when the president chopped off first a
division and then McDowell's corps for the defense of Washington.
And General Halleck—Old Brains, now commander of all federal
forces in the west—was reflecting both Mahan and his own doctrine, as proclaimed in his *Elements of Military Art and Science,* by
ordering Grant to Pittsburg Landing on the Tennessee River and
directing Buell to shift his troops southwestward to join Grant there.

Confederate General Sidney Johnston, too, was pulling his units
together, some from as far away as Columbus, Kentucky, and his
president had ordered Major General Braxton Bragg to move northward from Florida's coast to replace Fort Donelson's losses. But
Johnston was employing another principle as well: deception. He
made enough southeastward motions to persuade his most dangerous adversary, Ulysses Grant, that he meant to concentrate his
army at Chattanooga; instead, by early April, Johnston had his
40,000 men far west of there at Corinth, a strategically important
railroad-junction town in northern Mississippi, within short striking distance of Grant's camp at Pittsburg Landing.

One task—concentration—behind him, Sidney Johnston faced
many more. His force, assembled from all over the South, with no
experience in working as a unit, was more of an armed rabble than
anything else. Given a few weeks, he might have trained them, but
time was not on his side. He had to attack Grant before Buell's forces
reached Pittsburg Landing. And to his rear pressure was mounting
on him to avenge not only his losses of Forts Henry and Donelson
but one out in Arkansas.

Months earlier, federal forces had driven Sterling Price's militiamen out of Missouri to the Boston Mountains in northwest
Arkansas. In the spring came Major General Earl Van Dorn with
fresh Confederate units and hopes of invading Missouri, and by
March 6 a Texas regiment in which comet watcher A. W. Sparks was
marching had chased the Union defenders from Bentonville northeastward to a plateau called Pea Ridge.

West Pointer Van Dorn decided to go north and then east to cut
Brigadier General Samuel R. Curtis's federals off from their escape
route, which produced a fight in which the Yankees faced northward. Actually, there were two engagements, one west of the main
Union position; in it some of Van Dorn's Indians—drawn from what
would later be called Oklahoma—may or may not have taken a few
scalps on March 7. But Earl Van Dorn, ill and trying to direct
operations from an ambulance wagon, was unable either to coordi-
nate his forces or keep them supplied with ammunition. Curtis

attacked northward on March 8, driving the Confederates eastward
from Pea Ridge into a retreat that completed their long, circular
march around the Yankees.

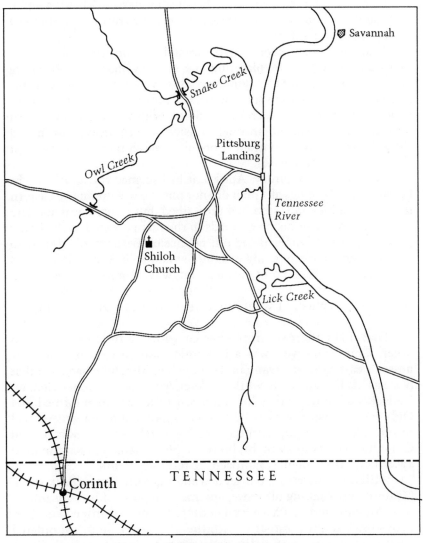

Shiloh Battle Area

Apart from roughly 1,500 casualties on each side (more for the
rebels, fewer for the Union) the three-day battle caused Van Dorn to
abandon his plan for invading Missouri. The deep depression his failure
produced throughout the Confederacy in the following weeks made it
all the more urgent that Sidney Johnston win a victory—and soon.

Johnston's intent was to advance northward from Corinth and destroy Grant's divisions at Pittsburg Landing before Don Carlos Buell's troops reinforced them. The main Confederate attack, then, would be along the west bank of the Tennessee River. And in keeping the federal forces separated, he meant to rely on another key principle of war: surprise.

Beauregard was second in command at Corinth, and on him Johnston had relied for planning the one-day march to Pittsburg Landing and the attack. Johnston discovered too late that his lieutenant's orders were too complex. Columns advancing on converging roads ran into each other. Some brigades wound up mixed with those belonging to another division. Worse, heavy rain mired the guns and wagons in mud. A one-day march took three, the last the most frustrating of all.

For a time on Saturday, April 5, it had seemed the attack might be launched. Beauregard's plan did not put the weight on the eastern flank that Sidney Johnston had prescribed, but again it was too late to remedy that. Confusion on roads in the rear persisted as the hours passed. Call the whole thing off, counseled Beauregard; return to Corinth and fortify. No, said Bishop/General Polk, Sidney Johnston's roommate at West Point, attack, anyway. Tomorrow morning, Johnston declared. Once more Beauregard protested. The army commander replied: "I would fight them if they were a million."

That night the two armies rested within a mile or so of each other. Grant, however, was a few miles downstream on the Tennessee's east bank at Savannah. For much of March he had used that place as his headquarters while he defended himself against General Halleck's allegations that he had failed to keep him informed and Old Brains's suspicions that the newly appointed major general had resumed his love affair with the whiskey bottle. All that was behind Grant on that Saturday night, however. He remained in Savannah to await news from Buell's approaching reinforcements.

William T. Sherman, befriended and supported by Halleck while "Cump" was shaking off newspapermen's reports of his "insanity," was in command at Pittsburg Landing. Grant had inspected Sherman's lines and was satisfied with them. True, Halleck had ordered entrenchment; but many officers at the time, including both Grant and Sherman, thought digging in eroded the offensive spirit in soldiers, and this was not done.

Up in Kentucky, Sherman had almost destroyed his usefulness by appearing too panicky. Now he was erring in the opposite direction, dismissing reports of rebel cavalry patrols, even telegraphing Grant: "I do not apprehend anything like an attack upon our position."

And a good one it was, on a plateau between two creeks that fed the Tennessee. Sherman's division was farthest from the river, westernmost, near a little Methodist church called Shiloh. With him he had 33,000 men.

Even on Sunday morning, April 6, Sherman refused to heed the warnings some of his troops brought him. Finally, he got on his horse for the ride through blossoming peach trees and past the tents where cooks were preparing breakfast to a clearing in which a soldier had said the rebels were "thicker than fleas on a dog's back!"

Sherman was scanning the field when shots rang out and the orderly near him fell dead. "My God," said the general, "we're attacked!" Back to the camps he galloped, ordering his men to grab their rifles and get into line.

Some did—enough to slow the Confederate advance as it swept toward them through the underbrush. Others ran for their lives. But Brigadier General Benjamin Prentiss's troops stood fast, and John McClernand rushed his division toward the sound of rifles blazing. Sherman rallied his regiments, getting shot in the hand and nicked in the shoulder as he did.

"Tell Grant if he has any men to spare I can use them," he said to an aide. "If not, I will do the best I can. We are holding them pretty well just now. Pretty well; but it's hot as hell."

It might have been hotter for the Yankees if Beauregard's plan of attack had conformed to Sidney Johnston's intent. As it turned out, troops in the second and third waves stumbled over the bodies of men cut down in the initial assault. Units became scrambled; officers led any troops they could get to follow them; soon Johnston's army was a 40,000-man mob.

Like Sherman, Sidney Johnston did his best—riding into the thick of the fight, shifting brigades and then leading them forward, sending an order back to Brigadier General John Breckinridge to attack on the eastern flank, along the river, where from the outset he had wanted to throw his heaviest weight.

By noon the Yankees had pulled back a mile or so away from Shiloh Church, their line moving first northeastward and then eastward like a door closing toward the riverbank, its hinge a stubborn bunch of Benjamin Prentiss's troops who were holding a sunken wagon trail men were beginning to call the Hornets' Nest. Grant had been there since ten but had found little to do except first to order Major General Lew Wallace southward from downriver to help Sherman and then to send a message to Buell's divisions on the Tennessee's other side to hurry to Pittsburg Landing. Mostly, Grant encouraged Prentiss to hold on and kept him supplied with ammunition.

For hours the fighting had been straight ahead, gallant charges by Confederates into equally gallant knots of federals resisting them, casualties piling up all over the battlefield, but especially south of Prentiss's Hornets' Nest. East of that obstacle was a Union force under Brigadier General Stephen A. Hurlbut, the friend Lincoln had sent to Charleston before Fort Sumter to sample the attitudes of South Carolinians. The best way to take the Hornets' Nest, Sidney Johnston decided, was to get around its flank, which meant driving Hurlbut northward.

Breckinridge's troops had tried to do that often enough to respect the guns Hurlbut had under the pink blossoms in the peach orchard up ahead. But Johnston wanted one more effort. Dragging a Yankee's tin cup along the tips of his soldiers' bayonets he said: "These must do the work. I will lead you!"

Their hearts quickened by the example of the handsome general, eyes flashing, the men followed him into the hail of minié balls stabbing out from Hurlbut's line. Cheers rang out as the federals fled.

Back from the charge rode Johnston, his uniform ripped in several places, a boot sole flapping. To Tennessee's governor Isham Harris, a volunteer aide, he quipped: "They didn't trip me up that time."

Soon Harris saw Johnston's body swaying, almost falling from his saddle. The general had sent the surgeon to treat Union wounded, and Harris did not know what to do. Within only a few minutes Albert Sidney Johnston, shot through an artery above his knee, bled to death.

It was Beauregard's battle now, and from Shiloh Church he ordered artillery fire concentrated on the Hornets' Nest. Late in the afternoon an assault took it—General Prentiss, too—but elsewhere along the line the Confederate advance lost its momentum. Or so Beauregard believed, apparently, when he sent messages to all his commanders directing them to break contact and withdraw. Most of them could hardly believe it. One more attack and the Confederates might (as Albert Sidney Johnston had predicted) water their horses in the Tennessee River.

Grant knew how near disaster was. Fugitives cowered below the bluff at the landing, and more were pouring in as sundown came. Genuine battle casualties had been heavy. Fire from two wooden gunboats, aimed high to clear the western riverbank, might do no more than scare the rebels, but it could discourage them from more attacks against Sherman's lines. And the rain a spring thunderstorm was bringing would create problems for the Confederates, dependent as they were on twenty miles of roads back to Corinth for resupplies of food and ammunition.

"Delay counts everything with us," said Grant to a staff officer. "Tomorrow we shall attack them with fresh troops and drive them, of course." This was a statement, not a boast, for Buell's men were arriving.

Beauregard, sheltered from the rain by Sherman's tent near Shiloh Church, had gone to sleep satisfied that he had won the battle. So he had reported to Richmond, along with the news of Sidney Johnston's death.

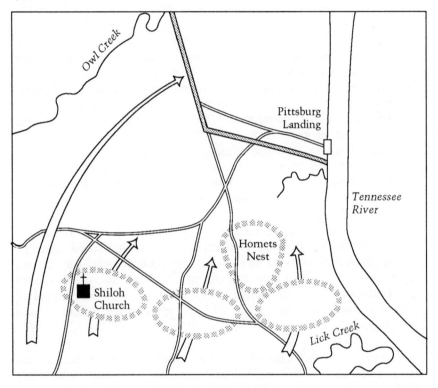

Shiloh, End of First Day

Outside in the storm, though, Nathan Forrest was searching for the commanding general. Forrest had climbed the bluff and he had seen Buell's men streaming ashore at Pittsburg Landing. But no one he asked could tell him where Beauregard might be.

Early the next morning, Monday, April 7, Grant sent his heavily reinforced line forward, using no military art beyond the simple order to advance. The only remarkable thing about the second day's fighting was that Beauregard held his forces together until midafternoon. But before the scattered showers on that day passed, the remnants of Sidney Johnston's army were back on the muddy roads to Corinth.

It had been Cump Sherman's battle earlier, and to him went the honor of leading a brigade in the pursuit. At first the going was easy, through rolling terrain on a muddy road lined by underbrush, but when he spotted Confederate cavalry ahead, he deployed his units.

"Charge!" Nathan Bedford Forrest yelled, waving his saber over his head, leading his troopers into the federals. Soon he alone was in their midst, slashing, turning his horse to slash again. Dodging the arc of Forrest's lethal blade, a federal soldier rammed the muzzle of his rifle into the cavalryman's side and fired. Forrest jumped upward from the saddle, but only for a moment. Angrily cutting his way forward, he jerked a blue-clad up by the neck to shield his own body from fire and held the man there as he rode southward. Once beyond the federals' range, Forrest threw the Yankee to the ground.

That was enough to persuade Sherman to call off the chase. He led his awed brigade back to Shiloh, where the grim task of collecting the wounded and counting the dead was beginning.

When it ended, there was cause for enormous grief on both sides. Grant's casualties were a little over 13,000 men; the Confederacy's, nearly 11,000. Roughly one man of every four in the fight had been killed, hit, or captured.

Neither the Confederates nor the federals had won a clear victory at Shiloh. Because the imperturbable Grant had held his ground, however, perhaps he had the stronger case. But he gained no glory, only criticism: Grant had not insisted that Sherman's troops dig entrenchments, the longest casualty lists yet seen appalled people throughout the Union, and the ghastly battle had settled nothing at all.

Jefferson Davis's Confederacy had much more to mourn during that April than Shiloh's dead and the loss of Sidney Johnston's leadership in the west. It was as though everything that might go wrong did, with results that brought the Union nearer to winning the year-old war than anyone in the North perceived.

Before the firing at Shiloh ceased on Monday, April 7, the South lost control of 100 miles of the upper Mississippi with the surrender of Island No. 10, together with the 7,000 troops and many irreplaceable guns defending that fortified sandbar. As on the Tennessee and Cumberland, gallant Captain Henry Walke had risked destruction of his little ironclad *Carondelet*, this time in the middle of the night and with a fierce spring thunderstorm raging. Once Walke had proved that the *Carondelet* could run past the dreaded Confederate batteries and survive, enough other Union steamboat skippers followed his example to enable Brigadier General John Pope's troops to isolate Island No. 10's garrison and compel its surrender.

Below Island No. 10 in the Mississippi, for at least as far downstream as Memphis, there was nothing much Union troops could do that Union gunboats could not. Soon General Halleck ordered Pope to load his 20,000 men on steamboats and move them to Pittsburg Landing to join the 80,000 either there or nearing that battle-swept plateau. Old Brains was concentrating his forces, planning to lead them himself southward to Corinth for the purpose of annihilating what was left of Beauregard's army.

Anyone with access to a map could see why else Halleck wanted Corinth: control over the railroad connecting Memphis to Chattanooga and the rest of the Confederacy. From Corinth as a base and with a huge army to command, he would be able to move westward, southward, eastward—and, possibly, win the war.

With Beauregard, digging in to defend Corinth, were troops Jefferson Davis had sent earlier from New Orleans to reinforce Sidney Johnston. Now those men were needed at home: Federal ships in the Gulf of Mexico were standing off the Mississippi's mouth, preparing to move up the river for an attempt to seize the Crescent City. But Beauregard could not afford to let the Louisianans go; even with reinforcements from Arkansas he had few more than 40,000 men to face Halleck's 100,000.

It was the same with the wooden Confederate gunboats on the Mississippi. There were only five of them, none a match for a Union ironclad, and though based in New Orleans they were above Memphis. The little flotilla's commander thought his ships' best use would be against the wooden fleet gathering off the river's entrance. No, declared the allocators of shortages in Richmond, reflecting the defend-everywhere thinking that was causing the Confederacy to lose everywhere.

Ironic, old General Scott may well have thought as Union forces began to carry out this part of his ridiculed Anaconda strategy: cutting the Confederacy in two by regaining control of the entire Mississippi River. Yet this was not happening so much by design as in response to openings the South's inherent weaknesses were providing. And few points along the rebels' threatened perimeter were as vulnerable as New Orleans.

Too many mouths and channels were available to invaders where the Mississippi's waters emptied into the Gulf, so the best place to stop any enemy fleet was in an almost mile wide stretch of the river about seventy-five miles south of New Orleans. On the south bank was Fort Jackson, pentagonal, brick-faced, the main deterrent; a little upstream on the north bank stood Fort St. Philip, smaller but still formidable. Together they could mass the fire from more than a hundred guns on any ship trying to run upstream past them, provided obstacles in the river slowed the target and gave the forts' gunners enough time.

Success in reducing the rebel forts and taking New Orleans was what Secretary of the Navy Gideon Welles required of Flag Officer David Glasgow Farragut, then sixty-one, a sailor since the age of nine when he became a midshipman, veteran of the War of 1812, still as vigorous as those serving under him on the USS *Hartford*. Farragut knew New Orleans; his mother was buried there. And he had a special reason for relishing his mission: Welles's associates had given it to him—thirty-seventh on the list of possibles—despite his age and their misgivings over his prewar Southern linkages.

With Farragut as the fleet entered the Mississippi in mid-April was David Dixon Porter, a year earlier Premier Seward's ally in diverting the *Powhatan* to Florida. Commander Porter had twenty barges, each bearing a thirteen-inch mortar. His role was to get these platforms within range of the forts and soften them up by dropping these explosives on the Confederate defenders.

This Porter did, lobbing almost 17,000 mortar rounds, but without seeming to do much damage to either target. Finally, recognizing that Porter's fire alone could not reduce the forts, Farragut said: "I guess we'll go up the river tonight."

First Farragut sent sloops up to break the log boom the Confederates had improvised to stop the Yankee ships. Then up came the *Hartford*, taking all the punishment the Confederates could inflict: concentrated gunfire, blazing fire rafts grappled to her hull, ramming.

"My God," someone heard Farragut say, "is it to end this way?" No, he decided. At the moment of greatest danger to his ship, he shouted to his men: "Don't flinch from that fire, boys. There's a hotter fire than that waiting for those who don't do their duty!"

By sunrise on the morning of April 24, Farragut's *Hartford* was anchored in the river above the forts, her crew washing down the blood and charred debris from her decks, most of the other vessels in his fleet with him. Porter, downstream, fired all his remaining mortar rounds into the still-defiant rebels inside the battered hulks of masonry on which the authorities in faraway Richmond had placed too much reliance.

In New Orleans, crowds gathered at the wharf in a dismal rain on Saturday morning, April 26, and watched the *Hartford* tie up. It took a day or two for the people of the city to absorb that shock. As they did, they began hiding everything they had of value from the 18,000 loot-bound troops Farragut had brought upriver with him under the command of Ben Butler—soon to be nicknamed "Spoons" by families whose homes his men plundered.

Chapter 7

General-in-Chief Lincoln Sets a Trap

In Richmond, General Robert E. Lee, now military adviser to President Davis, was facing enough discouragements to make an ordinary man question the wisdom of resisting any longer. Many Confederate soldiers' one-year enlistments were expiring, and men were heading homeward, some only on sixty-day furloughs before returning but others having to be drawn back to duty by a new conscription act. Richmond's arsenal had sent out its last rifle, and there was talk of manufacturing pikes, obsolete for a century or more. And wherever on Virginia's map Lee looked, federals threatened to overwhelm weak Confederate defenders.

In the Alleghenies a force under Pathfinder Frémont was moving toward the railroad connecting Staunton and Knoxville. Banks's troops occupied Winchester and the lower Shenandoah Valley. Near Alexandria, Lincoln was holding Irvin McDowell's corps. And southeast of Richmond, at Yorktown, McClellan was preparing to assault Prince John Magruder's thin line.

If all the Union commanders attacked at the same time, Lee could do nothing directly to prevent the utter crushing of the Confederate war effort in Virginia. He was merely the agent through whom President Davis's decisions were carried out; he could advise but not command. And since the president and Joe Johnston were not in communication, Lee was obliged to draw upon the trust both men had in him to avert catastrophe.

General Johnston was slow to recognize that McClellan's army was making the main federal effort. After a visit to Magruder's position, however, he advocated withdrawal almost to Richmond; there he would concentrate all Confederate forces in Virginia, the Carolinas, and Georgia and await attack. No, Davis decided, agreeing with Lee that McClellan should be kept as far from Richmond as possible for as long as possible. To do this, Johnston moved the divisions he had been holding west of Fredericksburg to Yorktown. But sooner or later, he still believed, the climactic fight would be just outside Richmond.

Johnston's authority was Virginia-wide. However, he left a small detachment at Fredericksburg, Brigadier General Richard Stoddert Ewell's division between there and the Blue Ridge Mountains, Jackson's little force in the upper Shenandoah Valley watching Banks's corps, and Brigadier General Edward Johnson's troops facing Frémont in the Alleghenies northwest of Staunton.

Messages from these units were routed to General Lee in Richmond, Johnston being fifty miles to the southeast and busy dealing with McClellan. Although administrative necessity was far short of command authority, Lee seized the opportunity to communicate with the four commanders—and in so doing, to introduce his ideas as to what they should do. Afterward, mindful of Johnston's touchiness in matters affecting his prerogatives, he reported his actions to the army commander, adding that they were subject, of course, to his concurrence.

Such were the circumstances on April 21 when Lee wrote a letter to Jackson in which he outlined several possibilities aimed at achieving the same goal: preventing reinforcements from being sent to McClellan. Action was what Lee proposed, not waiting for federal blows to fall but striking out at the invaders, and this fresh spirit prompted Jackson to respond with a daring though complex plan of his own.

On May 1, General Lee told Jackson to use his discretion. Quietly, Jackson slipped away from Banks's corps, moved his little force through Staunton and then up to join Edward Johnson's men in the Alleghenies, lashed out at Frémont's troops in a sharp fight on May 8, then sent Lee a one-sentence report on the ninth: "God blessed our arms with victory at McDowell yesterday."

Jackson meant McDowell, Virginia; Lee's mind had been on Union General McDowell, whose corps was now at Fredericksburg. From there McDowell might drive fifty miles southward along the Richmond, Fredericksburg & Potomac Railroad (RF&P) and provide the anvil on which McClellan could hammer Johnston's army to pieces.

April had been a glorious month for the Union but not for George McClellan. The navy could not move up the York or James rivers lest the CSS *Virginia* come out from Norfolk on another rampage. All his maps proved unreliable. Roads thought to be all-

weather turned into mud wallows each time rain fell, and a lot did.
Magruder's line's growing strength was ominous. And again Lincoln
was prodding. "The country will not fail to note —is now noting—
that the present hesitation to move upon an intrenched enemy is but
the story of Manassas repeated," he wrote, concluding earnestly and
emphatically: "*But you must act.*"

McClellan did. From "Camp Winfield Scott" he sent a long,
detailed description of his preparations for the siege of rebel lines his
troops had never tested by assault. Onward those preparations went.
April ended, May began. On the third, after midnight, he wrote
Mary Ellen Marcy McClellan:

> I need rest—my brain is taxed to the extreme—I feel that
> the fate of a nation depends upon me, & I feel that I have not
> one single friend at the seat of Govt—any day may bring an
> order relieving me from command—if such a thing should
> be done our cause is lost. If they will simply let me alone I
> feel sure of success—but, will they do it?

It was, exactly as Lincoln had warned him, the story of Manassas repeated. On the eve of the day set for his army's destruction,
Johnston had withdrawn his men from Magruder's old line and was
taking them up the peninsula toward Richmond.

"Yorktown is in our possession," McClellan telegraphed to
Secretary of War Edwin Stanton on May 4, neglecting even in a
subsequent message that day to mention his enemy. But Stanton had
left "the seat of Govt" for Fort Monroe, Abraham Lincoln and
Treasury Secretary Salmon Chase with him, to find out why so little
had been done by so many in such a long span of time.

Leaving General McClellan alone, though they were within a
few miles of Camp Winfield Scott, Stanton and his distinguished
associates asked seventy-eight-year-old General John Wool why the
Young Napoleon had done nothing toward recapturing the Norfolk
navy yard. Wool offered no excuses, but he did provide two tugboats
that the visitors promptly used to reconnoiter possible sites for troop
landings on Norfolk's side of Hampton Roads.

Quickened, perhaps, by the presidential presence, Wool sent a
force to take the only place of refuge the CSS *Virginia* had. Salmon
Chase went along; Stanton kept Lincoln back at the fort to await
developments. Lincoln, questioning officers Wool had left behind
and disgusted by their answers, threw his stovepipe hat on the floor.
Angrily he dictated an order for the advance to be given full support.

Valiant Chase met no enemy troops, only another politician —
Norfolk's mayor, who by going through a lengthy welcoming

ceremony gained time for Confederates to remove everything they could from the navy yard. That done, federal units moved in, and the *Virginia* moved out. She had not steamed far when her captain concluded she could not retreat up the James—her draft was too deep—and, sadly, set her afire and abandoned her. Echoes of her magazine exploding reached Fort Monroe, giving the amateur warriors a memory to cherish as, soon afterward, they returned to Washington.

However quixotic the Stanton-Lincoln-Chase exploit may have seemed to the very few people who knew about it, by May 15 the Union navy controlled the York River on the peninsula's northeastern side all the way up to West Point and the James to the unfinished positions for batteries on Drewry's Bluff, within a few miles of Richmond. On the York, McClellan had a new supply base within thirty miles of the rebels' capital. And below Drewry's Bluff, the USS *Monitor* and USS *Galena* were threatening to shoot their way to the city's wharves.

Fortifying Drewry's Bluff had been one of General Lee's projects, and on the morning of May 15 he was riding out to inspect the work when he heard heavy guns firing up ahead. Spurring his great gray warhorse Traveller into a gallop, he arrived on the north bank in time to watch the Confederate gunners—some of them the *Virginia*'s crewmen—pour enough fire on the federal gunboats to send them back downstream.

It had been a close call, one that added urgency to the concern Jefferson Davis and his cabinet had felt for Richmond's security ever since General Johnston had slipped away from the Yorktown lines. At a meeting to discuss the next place a stand could be made, Lee mentioned the Staunton River, far west of the city. "But," he said, emotion rising, tears in his eyes, "Richmond must not be given up; it shall not be given up!"

Abraham Lincoln could begin to relax a little. Out in the west General Halleck's 100,000-man army was moving southward at the pace of a snail on the road to Corinth, heeding admonitions to dig in at every pause along the way. McClellan had finally shown some dash by leading his 115,000 troops northwestward up the peninsula's muddy routes in pursuit of Joe Johnston's army. And in the Shenandoah Valley, Jackson had disappeared after his strike at Frémont.

All along General McClellan had been begging for more men — specifically for McDowell's corps, which he wanted shipped from Aquia Landing to Fort Monroe. In mid-May, Stanton advised McClellan that something might be done when Shields's division returned to Fredericksburg from the Valley. Then, on the seventeenth, Lincoln ordered McDowell to move southward along the RF&P's tracks so that troops might be called back if a Confederate threat to Washington developed. No, protested McClellan in a lengthy message, arguing that he should have full control over McDowell's corps and insisting they be sent to him by water.

While this squabble continued, another one began, this one on the Confederate side of the long line a few miles east of Richmond stretching from near Drewry's Bluff northward beyond the Chickahominy River. Joe Johnston had his 70,000 men where (a month earlier) he had told President Davis it ought to be, and, like McClellan, he wanted more troops. But Lee had urged Jackson and "Dick" Ewell to do whatever they could to prevent federal troops in the Valley from reinforcing McClellan. And when Ewell, from Swift Run Gap in the Blue Ridge, reported Shields's division heading east toward Fredericksburg and Banks's men going down the Valley northward to Strasburg, Lee saw his strategy failing. Worse, ignoring Lee, Johnston gave Jackson cause to fear he was about to lose Ewell's division. From near New Market on May 20, Jackson wired Lee:

> I am of opinion that an attempt should be made to defeat Banks, but under instructions just received from General Johnston I do not feel at liberty to make an attack. Please answer by telegraph at once.

Jackson had risked being sacked for insubordination by contacting Lee. Compounding audacity, Lee told Jackson to go ahead and attack.

Whether or not Abraham Lincoln merely wanted to get away from Washington for a little while, on May 22 he took Stanton and Commander John A. Dahlgren with him on a steamboat ride down the Potomac bound for Aquia Landing and later McDowell's headquarters at Falmouth, across the Rappahannock River from Fredericksburg. The president's mood was light, his temptation to tease the tense secretary of war strong.

"That's Mr. Stanton's navy," said Lincoln to Dahlgren as the ship passed shoved-aside, rock-filled barges, ordered there by the panicked cabinet officer back on March 9, when he feared the CSS *Virginia* was about to shell the Executive Mansion, "as useless as the paps of a man to a suckling child."

If that barb made Stanton wince, worse was in store the next morning when the presidential party got on a train for the twelve-mile ride to Falmouth. General McDowell met them at Potomac Creek Trestle, a span 400 feet long and about 100 feet above a deep

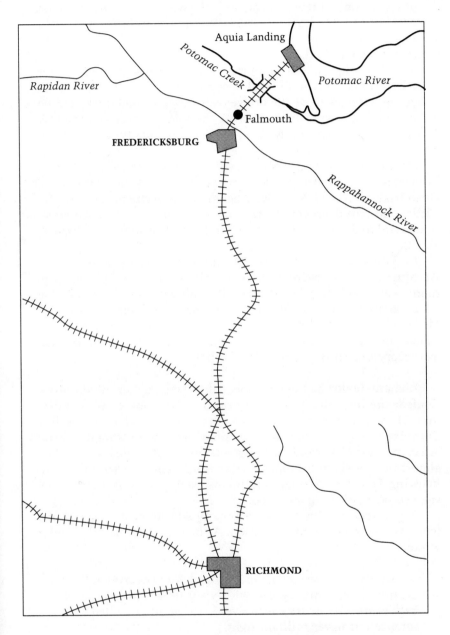

Aquia Landing–Richmond Corridor

ravine. McDowell, proud of engineer Herman Haupt's having built the bridge in only a few days (as Lincoln would later put it) out of nothing but "beanpoles and cornstalks," suggested that they walk across. Dahlgren, sensing Stanton's dizziness, helped him make it to the trestle's south end.

At Falmouth, Stanton saw more of what Haupt, a West Pointer he had recruited to rebuild rebel-ravaged railroads, had done. Haupt was ready to reconstruct the bridge over the Rappahannock, and he had materials stockpiled for repairing the RF&P's tracks all the way into Richmond, assuring McDowell of fast resupply when he advanced southward.

On that Friday, James Shields's division was at Falmouth, too, footsore and weary after the long march from the Valley. How soon, Lincoln asked, could McDowell begin the movement to join McClellan? In two days, replied the corps commander. No, the president said, "make a good ready" on Sunday and go south on Monday, May 26.

By Saturday afternoon, May 24, the three travelers were back in Washington. If they were pleased as well as refreshed by their trip, there was good reason. McDowell's advance might cause Joe Johnston to stretch his already thin lines northward enough for McClellan to break through them and take Richmond before May ended. But grim news awaited Lincoln and Stanton: Jackson had reappeared in the Shenandoah Valley.

Richard Taylor had never expected to be a soldier, much less a Confederate brigadier general, but on the afternoon of Wednesday, May 21, he was leading his troops northeastward along the Valley Turnpike to join a force being assembled by Major General Jackson at a camp near New Market. Taylor's Louisiana Brigade had marched almost twenty-six miles that day. But as his men drew near the goal, knowing Jackson's veteran Virginians were watching them, they stepped out with snap and vigor.

Taylor reported his arrival to a man perched on the top rail of a fence overlooking the road: Jackson. As he waited for a reply, Taylor wrote:

> I had time to see a pair of cavalry boots covering feet of gigantic size, a mangy cap with visor drawn low, a heavy, dark beard, and weary eyes—eyes I afterward saw filled with intense but never brilliant light.

Jackson told the newcomer he was impressed by the lack of stragglers in the Louisiana Brigade, adding that Taylor must teach the Valley army his secret. Suddenly, the creoles' band struck up a waltz, and the men began dancing. "Thoughtless fellows for serious work," remarked Jackson as he returned his attention to the lemon he had been sucking.

Late that night Jackson appeared at Taylor's campfire, sat down, said the march would begin at dawn, asked a few questions about march discipline, then lapsed into a silence that lasted for hours. Earlier, when Jackson had taken his force off into the rains that made the march to McDowell miserable, Taylor may have heard Dick Ewell declare that Jackson was crazy, for so his division commander had maintained, left as he was at Swift Run Gap in the Blue Ridge with scant instructions and no hint as to where Jackson was headed or why. Now Taylor, as though he sensed that Jackson was praying as he gazed into the fire, respected his visitor's prolonged silence.

The contrast between the two men could hardly have been greater. Jackson was from humble origins in western Virginia, Taylor a former president's son, educated at Harvard and Yale and in Europe, a planter and state senator in Louisiana before the war. What Jackson had attained, little though it was, he had earned. Taylor was open to suspicion that the president (years before, for a few months, his brother-in-law, until Sarah Taylor Davis died of a fever) had advanced his career.

Davis had done nothing of the sort. Taylor had brought his Louisiana regiments this far, along the way winning the respect even of Major Roberdeau Wheat's fierce Tigers—most of them well known to New Orleans's police, three companies of men too unruly for any officer but Taylor to allow within his command—and of Rob Wheat, who had fought in Mexico, Cuba, Nicaragua, and Italy before he led the Tigers at Manassas.

All "Dick" Taylor knew of the Shenandoah Valley's terrain he had seen from Swift Run Gap in the Blue Ridge and on the roads to New Market. Jackson had improved his own knowledge of the region by having Major Jedediah Hotchkiss prepare a map of the valley from Lexington northeastward to Harpers Ferry. And with Hotchkiss's help, the army commander had worked out a table of distances between key points.

As Jed Hotchkiss's map revealed, the Shenandoah Valley was a corridor roughly 25 miles wide and more than 120 miles long (as measured from Staunton northeastward to Harpers Ferry), yet there were few places in it that were flat. Between the Blue Ridge on the east and the Alleghenies west of it the Valley's main terrain features were a strange timbered rock mass known as the Massanutten and the Shenandoah River's forks on either side of it. Beginning near Harrisonburg, about twenty-five miles to the northeast of Staunton, the Massanutten jutted up as high as the Blue Ridge for forty miles or more, ending abruptly near two small towns, Strasburg on the west and Front Royal, nearly ten miles east of Strasburg. At Front Royal the forks of the Shenandoah joined; then the river's waters rushed northward to join those of the Potomac at Harpers Ferry.

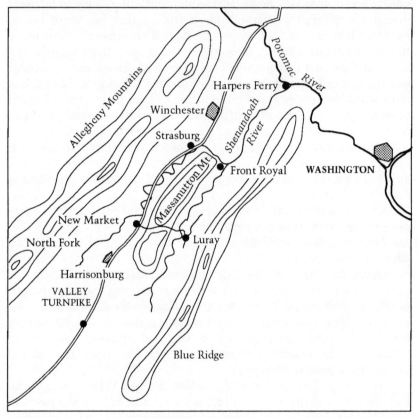

Shenandoah Valley

Roughly twenty miles northeast of Dick Taylor's campfire near New Market, Nathaniel Banks's 7,000 men were fortifying Strasburg on the theory Jackson would continue moving down the turnpike and attack them. Shields, now at Fredericksburg, had left a Maryland regiment behind at Front Royal. But all Jackson had said to Taylor that night was that they would move out at dawn.

Indeed, at first light on Thursday, May 22, Jackson put Taylor's brigade in the lead, sending it not toward Strasburg but up through a gap leading to the Luray Valley, the corridor between the Massanutten and the Blue Ridge east of it. Past the village of Luray, on the South Fork of the Shenandoah about ten miles south of Front Royal,

Jackson halted the column for the night.

There, Taylor noted, his men were almost at the beginning point for their marches around the Massanutten's southwestern tip past Harrisonburg to New Market. Having made that long circuit, he began to think, he wrote afterward, "that Jackson was an unconscious poet, and, as an ardent lover of nature, desired to give strangers an opportunity to admire the beauties of his Valley."

Dick Taylor would see more of it the next day, Friday, May 23, as he led his brigade northward down the Luray Valley. Jackson, silent as usual, rode with him. And behind, in the 16,000-man column, was the rest of Dick Ewell's division.

Meanwhile, Colonel Turner Ashby's cavalrymen were sweeping down from the Massanutten's steep northern slope midway between Strasburg and Front Royal to attack federal troops at a depot along the railroad connecting the towns. While some of Ashby's men cut the telegraph wires, the others fought a savage little battle that prevented Banks at Strasburg from learning about Jackson's movement toward Front Royal.

General Taylor and Lieutenant Henry Kyd Douglas, one of Jackson's staff officers, were riding down the northern slope of the last hill south of Front Royal when they saw a young woman running toward them. Nearly out of breath from dodging Yankee fire during her dash from the town, Belle Boyd told Douglas and Taylor that the town was filled with federals, their camp was west of the river, their guns covered the wagon bridge but not the railroad bridge north of it, and—in effect—no one expected Jackson to be anywhere near Front Royal. Then, after refusing Douglas's offer of protection and telling him to pretend he had not seen her if they met later, she went back toward the town.

Kyd Douglas and Belle Boyd had been friends for years. He knew she had been sending out reports of Yankee troop movements from her grandmother's hotel in Front Royal, General Shields's headquarters while his division had been there. Last Fourth of July, Belle had shot and killed a Yankee who invaded their home in Martinsburg, north of Winchester, demanding that her mother give him any Confederate banners hidden in the house. And now Belle's father was a private in one of Jackson's brigades.

Jackson rode up shortly after the girl had left. As he listened to Douglas's summary of what she had said, he showed no surprise; he merely ordered a Confederate Maryland regiment forward to join Taylor in the attack, remembering that Union Marylanders were said to be in Front Royal's garrison.

As Taylor's brigade swept down the hill and through the town, the federals fired and fell back, setting the bridge over the Shenandoah's North Fork ablaze as they fled. Rob Wheat's Tigers paused to loot the Yankee camp while other men in the Louisiana brigade stopped the flames from destroying the vital bridge. Taylor, singed as he rode across, started to pursue the federal survivors; then came Jackson, moaning because he had no artillery with him to blast the fugitives.

Suddenly from up the Shenandoah's North Fork came Colonel Thomas Flournoy's cavalry. They almost rode over Jackson as they chased the last of Front Royal's defenders northward along the road to Winchester, pausing finally near Cedarville.

Kyd Douglas had paused, too, in Front Royal as he rode by the hotel, but only long enough for Belle Boyd to pin a red rose on his uniform.

From the messages Abraham Lincoln read when he and Edwin Stanton returned to Washington on Saturday, May 24, it was hard to make out exactly what had happened at Front Royal. But before the fog of war got any thicker, Lincoln had Stanton send a warning to General McDowell at Fredericksburg that unforeseen events would probably necessitate a change in his orders.

That Jackson had suddenly descended upon Front Royal from out of "the mountains," as Banks had said, was a fact. Acting General-in-Chief Lincoln's opinion was that Banks could not long remain in Strasburg; indeed, that with only 7,000 men he might never reach the Potomac's Maryland side. No significant Union forces were along that river except for a small unit at Harpers Ferry that had no guns. What could be done?

Well, General Frémont had 15,000 troops in the Alleghenies bound southwestward for East Tennessee. And Irvin McDowell had 40,000 down at Falmouth preparing to march southward to help McClellan take Richmond.

"You must act," Lincoln had admonished McClellan not long before. Now he took his own advice, sending this message—signed by Stanton—to General Frémont:

> You are therefore ordered by the President to move against Jackson at Harrisonburg, and operate against the enemy in such a way to relieve Banks. This movement must be made immediately. You will acknowledge the receipt of this order and specify the hour it is received by you.

Harrisonburg, Frémont's new objective, was more than forty miles southwest of Front Royal, deep in Jackson's rear. And once there, Frémont's force might serve as an anvil, provided Lincoln could use McDowell's corps as a sledgehammer.

Only the day before, of course, Lincoln had been face-to-face with McDowell at Falmouth. Now he was obliged to reverse all the plans and agreements they had made and order McDowell to move his entire force to the Valley, to Front Royal.

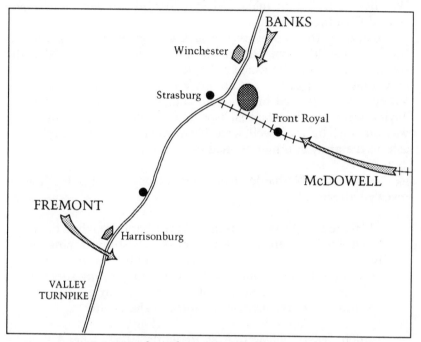

Lincoln's Plan to Trap Jackson

No telegram could convey Lincoln's reasons for this, much less the urgency and importance of the general's compliance, so he sent for Treasury Secretary Chase—McDowell's supporter before and after Bull Run—and asked him to go at once to Falmouth and explain to the general the president's seemingly abrupt decision. Chase left; then Lincoln read a terse reply from McDowell to the warning sent earlier. Very well, he said in effect, concluding: "This is a crushing blow to us."

Jackson had planned more crushing blows the night before as he sat, silent, staring at Taylor's campfire north of Front Royal. Striking Banks was Jackson's intent, but where?

It was, in a way, a problem in geometry. Jackson may have envisioned a triangle formed by Strasburg at the base's western point and Front Royal the eastern, with Winchester at the peak.

Banks, Jackson may have presumed, was studying the same

triangle, but for a different purpose: to decide whether to stay at Strasburg and fight or to escape. If the federal commander chose to flee, he might abandon the triangle, move westward into the Alleghenies, and join Frémont; or he could try to retreat northward to Winchester; or if he thought Jackson would block him at Winchester, he might make a dash eastward through Front Royal toward Washington.

Adding to the complexity of Jackson's geometry problem was the fact that his own command was scattered from Cedarville southward. Even as he gazed at Taylor's campfire on Friday night, only a few of his guns were up, his wagon trains still in the Luray Valley. This narrowed his possible courses of action considerably. Taylor, watching the silent Jackson as the hours passed, thought he was praying; he may well have been, for by the time Taylor fell asleep, the army commander had given no orders.

Neither had Nathaniel Banks, as Colonel George H. Gordon revealed afterward:

> I labored long to impress upon him what I thought a duty, to wit, his immediate retreat upon Winchester, carrying all his sick and all his supplies that he could transport, and destroying the remainder. Notwithstanding all my solicitations and entreaties, he persistently refused to move, ever repeating, "I must develop the force of the enemy."

Gordon, frustrated, left. A short while later, General Banks's chief of staff urged Gordon to make one more effort to persuade the former governor of Massachusetts to withdraw. The result:

> Moved with an unusual fire, General Banks, who had met all my arguments with the single reply, "I must develop the force of the enemy," rising excitedly from his seat, with much warmth and in loud tones exclaimed, "By God, sir, I will not retreat! We have more to fear, sir, from our friends than the bayonets of our enemies!" The thought so long the subject of his meditations was at last out. Banks was afraid of being thought afraid.

Colonel Gordon returned to his brigade, told his men to get ready to march, and sent his own wagons on down the Valley Turnpike northward to Winchester. Not until ten o'clock on Saturday morning did he receive orders for his troops to move to Middletown, six miles down the turnpike toward Winchester, and to take such action as Gordon might deem proper to oppose the rebels, reported to be on a road between Front Royal and Middletown.

Whoever wrote Gordon's orders must have learned, somehow, that Jackson had decided to move neither toward Strasburg nor Winchester but to send Colonel Turner Ashby's cavalry and Dick Taylor's infantry along a seldom-used road from Cedarville to Middletown. By so doing, Jackson's brigades still near Front Royal could prevent Banks's troops from trying to shoot their way eastward, and the Confederate commander would not have to risk defending a position near Winchester with too few troops supported by too few guns. To head westward for Middletown was a compromise, but at least it would get his men back on the Valley Turnpike, the road he had left at New Market on Thursday morning.

At around eleven A.M. on Saturday, Jackson's cavalry reported a Yankee wagon train (Gordon's) at Newtown, five miles north of Middletown: Banks was getting away. Jackson rode along the heavily wooded trail westward, reaching the high ground east of the turnpike in midafternoon. Below him for as far as he could see northward or southward the road was jammed with Banks's wagons. Shells from Jackson's guns halted the column; he watched as first Ashby's cavalry and then Taylor's men swept down and drove the mounted guards away.

While Wheat's Tigers were looting the wagons, Lieutenant Kyd Douglas placed a company of Taylor's Louisianans behind a stone wall just in time to stop a federal cavalry charge with volleys that littered the ground with blue-clad bodies. Many of the dead had been strapped into their saddles; some wore steel breastplates. Taylor deployed a regiment to block other units coming his way from Strasburg, then rode into Middletown to get information from the village's cheering citizens.

Banks's main force had passed through earlier, Taylor found out. Jackson ordered a pursuit and also sent word to Ewell, who was already leading a brigade northward on the empty Front Royal –Winchester road. For the Confederates on the turnpike, however, the going was slow. Taylor's men were worn out, and the wagons' contents were too tempting. Turner Ashby's ranks thinned as his cavalrymen who lived nearby led Yankee horses and mules homeward. But Jackson pressed on with any men he and Taylor could gather, pausing only to clear the road ahead when they came upon small Union delaying forces.

On through the night Jackson plodded, through one ambush after another, until after two o'clock on Sunday morning, when Colonel Samuel Fulkerson of the 37th Virginia came up. His men were exhausted, said Fulkerson, and must have some sleep.

"Colonel, I yield to no man in my sympathy for the gallant men under my command," replied Jackson, "but I am obliged to sweat them tonight, that I may save their blood tomorrow. The line of hills southwest of Winchester must not be occupied by the enemy artillery. My own must be there and in position by daylight. You shall, however, have two hours' rest."

Jackson alone stood guard over the sleeping members of his staff until near daylight. Ewell, he knew, was not far to the east and ready to attack. Once again Jackson would have to mar the Sabbath calm with battle, but there was no choice.

By dawn's first light Jackson saw Banks's army lining the hilltops just southwest of Winchester. First he sent his old Stonewall Brigade up to take a hill west of the turnpike; then he added his guns to the position. He led Taylor and his Louisianans past that hill and northwest of it, drawing the attention of Yankee gunners. "What the hell are you dodging for?" yelled Taylor to his men, forgetting the pious Jackson's presence. "If there's any more of it, you'll be halted under this fire for an hour!"

Jackson rode nearer and touched Taylor's shoulder. "I'm afraid," he said, "you are a wicked fellow."

Soon after Jackson left, Taylor had his brigade formed for the attack. He rode to the center of the line, drew his saber, watched a bluebird fly by with a worm in its mouth, then led his regiments in a charge up the hill directly into the muzzles of Banks's guns. The defenders fled, pouring into Winchester's streets, running northward.

Loud cheers rose from the rest of Jackson's brigades; then they, too, advanced. Within minutes they were rushing through Winchester, chasing the panicked Yankees, their pursuit slowed only by throngs of celebrating people greeting their heroes.

Jackson pressed on. "Never was there such a chance for cavalry!" he moaned. "Oh, that my cavalry was in place!"

He sent his guns down the Martinsburg road, but they could not catch up with the fugitives. Unhitch the horses, Jackson told the artillerymen, and charge like cavalry—which the gunners did, but in vain.

In the town the counting began. Since Friday at Front Royal the Valley army had deprived Banks of 3,500 men, 3,000 of them prisoners; more than 9,000 infantry weapons; quantities of supplies beyond reckoning; and, in Winchester, warehouses filled with of medical stores the South needed badly. In all, Jackson had lost 400 men, but he had also given the Confederacy its first significant victory since Manassas.

* ★ ★

In the War Department's telegraph room that Sunday, May 25, most of the news had come from Falmouth: Chase's assurances that General McDowell was cooperating fully, later a message saying that Valley veteran James Shields was returning with the treasury secretary to share his knowledge of the region with Lincoln and Stanton while his division marched westward again to Front Royal. Some of McDowell's other units were en route up the Potomac in case Jackson moved eastward or the president had to cope with panic in Washington merely because of the rebel army's reappearance.

Around noon, Lincoln prepared a message to McClellan in which he described the situation in the Valley and the fresh orders given to McDowell and Frémont, adding:

> Apprehensions of something like this, and no unwilling-
> ness to sustain you, have always been my reason for with-
> holding McDowell's corps from you. Please understand this,
> and do the best you can with the force you have.

News kept on clacking into the telegraph room, all of it bad, the worst a message from Banks sent from Martinsburg, about twenty-five miles north of Winchester and roughly fifteen miles south of a bridge over the Potomac into Maryland. After a terse description of the fight he had lost that morning, Banks said he expected he could cross the river "in safety."

Lincoln could draw some comfort from that, but not from anything else Banks reported. To McClellan he telegraphed at around two o'clock that Sunday afternoon: "I think the time is near when you must either attack Richmond or give up the job and come to the defense of Washington. Let me hear from you instantly."

General McClellan responded:

> Telegram received. Independently of it, the time is very
> near when I shall attack Richmond. The object of the
> movement is probably to prevent re-enforcements being sent
> to me. All information from balloons, deserters, prisoners,
> and contrabands agrees in the statement that the mass of
> rebel troops are still in the immediate vicinity of Richmond,
> ready to defend it.

That Sunday ended with McClellan behaving as he usually did and both Frémont and McDowell days away from where their forces could strike the Confederates. In the day's messages, however, inadvertently both McClellan and the president had declared Jackson's Valley campaign a success—Lincoln by conceding that protecting Washington might prove more important than McClellan's effort to take Richmond, the general by recognizing Robert E. Lee's strategic intent.

A few miles east of Richmond, as far as Joe Johnston knew, McClellan seemed to be stretching his line northward to make it easier for McDowell to come down from Fredericksburg and join him—as though "Beloved Mac" did not already have more than enough troops to take Richmond. And when McDowell arrived, the last hope of saving the capital would be gone—meaning that if anything were to be done, it would have to be done quickly.

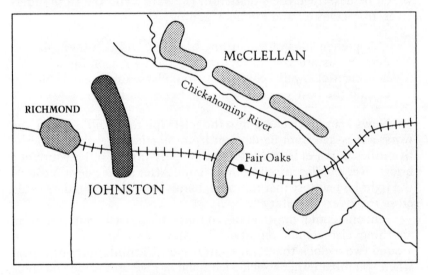

McClellan's Threat to Richmond

For both Johnston and McClellan the Chickahominy River was the key to whatever might be attempted. To the Union army the stream was an annoyance, forcing the Young Napoleon to place three of his corps north of the stream and build bridges along it to maintain communication with the two corps south of it. But if Johnston could mass his units up near the creeks forming the Chickahominy, he might strike McClellan's corps north of the stream and block McDowell's advance.

The risk involved was so enormous that Johnston kept his plan a secret from Jefferson Davis. Better to withstand presidential wrath, the army commander may have reasoned, than to have to endure his meddling. So matters stood on Monday, May 26, when General Lee rode out to visit Johnston. To Lee, Joe Johnston revealed his intention to attack north of the rain-swollen Chickahominy on Thursday. Lee, delighted, offered to send Johnston all the reinforcements he could scrape together.

Later in the day came news from Jackson: "God has blessed our arms with brilliant success," the dispatch from Winchester began. Lee responded by urging him to demonstrate along the Potomac as though he meant to invade Maryland.

Abraham Lincoln and his secretary of war had been massing Union strength to destroy Jackson since Saturday, May 24, and by Monday the twenty-sixth they were able to assess the effectiveness of their efforts. Northern governors were sending Stanton all the militiamen they had and could enlist, using the Stanton-controlled railroads to expedite troop movements. McDowell was carrying out his part of the plan to trap the rebel force: James Shields's division was moving toward Front Royal. And, presumably, Frémont would soon be in place at Harrisonburg.

Not until Tuesday night did Lincoln discover that Frémont was roughly forty miles northeast of Franklin, moving *away* from Harrisonburg. To the Pathfinder he wired: "I see that you are at Moorefield. You were expressly ordered to march to Harrisonburg. What does this mean?"

Frémont's reply on Wednesday cited the poor condition of his men and the shortage of food as reasons for his apparent disregard of the direct order the president had sent him on Saturday, then concluded:

> In executing any order received I take it for granted that I am to exercise discretion concerning its literal execution, according to circumstances. If I am to understand that literal obedience to orders is required, please say so. I have no desire to exercise any power which you do not think belongs of necessity to my position in the field.

Perhaps Lincoln took a second look at the acknowledgment Frémont had wired Stanton from Franklin Saturday night:

> Your telegram received at 5 o'clock this afternoon. Will move as ordered, and operate against the enemy in such [a] way [as] to afford prompt relief to General Banks.

No mention of hungry troops or discretion—and "Will move as ordered" implied Frémont was heading for Harrisonburg. But instead of making that thirty-mile march and despite the poor condition of his men, Frémont had subjected his division to a forty-mile hike and would have to press them at least another forty miles to reach Strasburg. Moreover, Frémont being Frémont, there was no assurance when or if he would get that far.

Such was the penalty Abraham Lincoln was having to pay for appeasing Frémont's supporters in Congress who had demanded that the president give the general a second chance. Surely Lincoln was tempted to relieve Frémont from command. But the amateur general-in-chief may have realized that part of the blame was his; in his Saturday order he had mentioned the need to help Banks, thus inadvertently giving Frémont a choice. Worse, there was some truth in what Frémont had said about discretion. Making war from a distance, from a map, had its limitations no matter how brilliant the strategic concept or how determined the will of the strategist might be.

Curiously, out in northern Mississippi Old Brains was employing no strategy at all in his cautious advance southward to Beauregard's defenses at Corinth. Not making a mistake was uppermost in Henry Halleck's thinking, or so it seemed to his men, who saw no reason for all the digging in he insisted upon.

Puzzled, too, were some of Halleck's officers—Ulysses S. Grant in particular, nominally second in command but left with nothing to do. Move John Pope's division out of the swamps and onto the ridge leading into Corinth, Grant had suggested to the general commanding, receiving only a frosty stare in return. All the glory Unconditional Surrender Grant had won at Fort Donelson had been replaced by blame for the heavy Union losses at Shiloh. Politicians wanted Grant's scalp and took their complaints all the way to the Executive Mansion, but Abraham Lincoln had replied: "I can't spare this man, he fights."

Only Cump Sherman's friendly persuasion kept Grant from resigning. He would wait a while, he conceded, but not long.

The nearer to Front Royal James Shields's division got, the more attention acting General-in-Chief Lincoln was giving to the new trap he was setting at Strasburg. Time, he seemed to realize, was of the essence now that federal troops would not be in Harrisonburg to await Jackson's retreat if the wily rebel got past Shields. To McDowell, Lincoln telegraphed: "I think the evidence now preponderates that Ewell and Jackson are still about Winchester. Assuming this, it is for you a question of legs."

Nathaniel Banks, now north of the Potomac, was of no concern to Jackson; after observing a delayed Sabbath on Monday the twenty-sixth, he signaled a return to strict discipline the next day by ordering his men to stop looting captured stockpiles of Yankee equipment. On Wednesday he sent nearly all of his brigades northeastward to threaten Harpers Ferry. By Thursday he was near there himself, under federal artillery fire, sending forces to take positions on the heights overlooking the little village where John Brown had earned a hangman's rope.

"Old Jack'"'s studied indifference to the perils inherent in such an advanced position caused his artillery commander, Colonel Stapleton Crutchfield, to remark to Kyd Douglas: *"Quem deus vult perdere, prius dementat."* Driven mad by war's gods before they destroyed him Jackson may well have seemed; yet, silent as ever, he had Quartermaster John Harman out borrowing all the wagons he could find, loading them with Yankee supplies captured in Martinsburg as well as in Winchester, and starting them on the hundred-mile trip southward up the Valley Turnpike, past Strasburg, and through Harrisonburg to Staunton.

On Friday morning, May 30, riders brought Jackson warnings that Shields's troops were approaching Front Royal and Banks was regrouping his forces at Williamsport for a drive southward. Dismissing the couriers, he calmly greeted a delegation of women from Charles Town, then made a brief check of the progress his units were making toward surrounding Harpers Ferry. Satisfied, and with rain starting, Jackson stretched out under the shelter of a tree and fell asleep.

When Jackson woke up, he saw Confederate congressman Alex Boteler sketching him. After a glance at the product and some remarks about how difficult West Point's drawing course had been for him, the army commander outlined the situation and asked Boteler to go to Richmond immediately and try to get reinforcements sent to him. Jackson's purpose: to "raise the siege of Richmond and transfer this campaign from the banks of the James to those of the Susquehanna"—in Pennsylvania.

Chapter 8

Old Jack Finds "Delightful Excitement?"

General Jackson might not have been quite so relaxed or so far ranging in his thinking on that Friday in May had he known what had been happening elsewhere in the Confederacy.

Out in Corinth, Mississippi, on Sunday, May 25, General Pierre Beauregard and his subordinate commanders agreed their situation was hopeless. The next day they kept up a show of force in the lines while trains began removing sick soldiers and all the supplies that could be crammed into rail cars. On Tuesday and Wednesday they continued deceptive tactics Prince John Magruder would have admired. Then, on Thursday night, with the last locomotive shuttling up and back over the same stretch of track, its whistle blasting and men cheering, Beauregard quietly removed all his units from the line and led them toward Tupelo, fifty miles to the south.

On Friday morning, Halleck, delighted, declared his bloodless victory "all I could possibly desire." Jefferson Davis's anger matched the elation of Old Brains. Only days earlier Beauregard had assured his president that he would hold Corinth "to the last extremity." Losing the vital railroad hub was galling enough; giving it up without a fight was totally unacceptable.

That Friday would have been a difficult one for Davis in any case, for he had waited in vain on Thursday for the sounds of Johnston's artillery signaling the opening of his attack north of the Chickahominy. Finally, the president and Lee had gone out to learn why nothing was happening. Young Jeb Stuart had arrived Wednesday night, Lee was told, with electrifying news: McDowell was moving his troops out of Fredericksburg but *not* toward McClellan.

Relying on the cavalryman's report, Johnston had decided to postpone his attack.

But Johnston had neglected to tell Davis about that, or about anything else, including the new plan he was preparing. Heavy rainstorms had swollen the Chickahominy River to its highest levels in twenty years, washing out some of McClellan's new bridges, making it seem doubtful that he could move units to the south bank if Johnston struck the two corps on that side. Taking advantage of Little Mac's plight, his forces split now by a flooded stream, was what Joe Johnston decided to do. He meant to do it on Saturday, May 31. But he did not reveal his intentions to anyone in Richmond.

On Friday, May 30, while Jefferson Davis fumed over the stubborn silence of an army commander only five miles from his desk, in Washington the other president was frustrated by a general out in the Alleghenies whose messages were plentiful but unsatisfactory.

The day before, Thursday the twenty-ninth, Abraham Lincoln had telegraphed Pathfinder Frémont:

> General McDowell's advance, if not checked by the enemy, should, and probably will, be at Front Royal by 12 (noon) to-morrow. His force, when up, will be about 20,000. Please have your force at Strasburg, or, if the route you are moving on does not lead to that point, as near Strasburg as the enemy may be by the same time.

And to McDowell:

> General Frémont's force should, and probably will, be at or near Strasburg by 12 (noon) to-morrow. Try to have your force or the advance of it at Front Royal as soon.

"To-morrow" meant Friday, May 30.
Then, on Thursday, came Frémont's reply:

> My command is not yet in marching order. It has been necessary to halt to-day to bring up parts of regiments and to receive stragglers, hundreds of whom from Blenker's division strewed the roads. You can conceive the condition of the command from the fact that the medical director this morning protested against its farther advance without allowing one day's rest, the regiments being much reduced, and

force diminished accordingly. I could not venture to proceed with it in disorder, and cannot with safety undertake to be at the point you mention earlier than by 5 o'clock on Saturday afternoon.

Both General Frémont and his medical director may have been fortunate in that they were roughly eighty miles west of the War Department's telegraph room. Another day's delay, added to the Harrisonburg fiasco, must have stretched Lincoln's patience to its limits. But he had to take what Frémont would allow, and to him he replied:

Yours, saying that you will reach at Strasburg or vicinity at 5 P.M. Saturday, has been received and sent to General McDowell, and he directed to act in view of it. You must be up to time you promised, if possible.

But on Friday came good news: Shields had reached Front Royal an hour earlier than directed, at eleven o'clock, and by so doing he had closed Jackson's Luray Valley escape route. The fight there had been brief. Almost all the supplies the rebels had captured in the town a week earlier had not yet been moved.

If only Frémont could have been at Strasburg as ordered the trap would be shut. But he was not, so Saturday now loomed as the day on which Jackson might—might—be destroyed.

After Jackson's nap and his conversation with Congressman Boteler on that Friday afternoon the Valley army's commander told the officers pressing Harpers Ferry to cease their effort and start moving their men and guns southward; then he boarded a train for Winchester. On the way he slept, even after he was awakened briefly to be given the news that Shields was in Front Royal. That night, in Winchester's hotel, he had a brief talk with the commander of Front Royal's Confederate garrison and then ordered the colonel placed under arrest because he had not fought. Later, visiting Boteler again, Jackson astonished his friend by sipping some whiskey the congressman had offered him.

"Do you know why I habitually abstain from intoxicating drinks?" the general asked.

"No," said Boteler.

"Why, sir, because I like the taste of them, and when I discovered that to be the case I made up my mind to do without them altogether."

Outside, in the heavy rainstorm sweeping from high in the

Alleghenies across Virginia through Winchester and eastward to the headwaters of the already-flooded Chickahominy, Major John Harman's wagons were already moving along the Valley Turnpike. Behind them, at three o'clock Saturday morning, Jackson sent his troops. He remained in Winchester until two-thirty that afternoon, starting southward only when all his infantry units except the Stonewall Brigade, his little army's rear guard, were marching toward Strasburg.

Jackson knew Frémont was headed that way, too. But he had no way of knowing that an anxious man over in Washington was expecting the Yankee force to close his only escape route in another two and a half hours.

General Joseph Eggleston Johnston's plan seemed simple—on the map. He meant to attack Union Major General Erasmus D. Keyes's corps, which was near the Fair Oaks station on the York River Railroad, about a mile northwest of a little village called Seven Pines. To reach Keyes's positions Johnston had three roads available, and he would use all of them. If his divisions converged on Keyes's position at about the same time Johnston might destroy his forces before Major General Samuel Heintzelman's corps could move westward. And Friday night's rainstorm would raise the Chickahominy's waters even higher, preventing McClellan from sending any support to Keyes.

On Saturday, May 31, however, nothing happened according to Johnston's plan. Confederate Major General James Longstreet decided to take his division eastward on the Williamsburg Road instead of the Nine Mile Road, and this threw other units' movements into hopeless confusion, creating snarls of troops and wagons and causing hours of delay. By early afternoon Major General D. Harvey Hill's division was the only one in Johnston's army in position to attack. Disregarding his lack of contact with any Confederate troops on his flanks, Hill led his men forward, driving Keyes's defenders back a mile or so, overrunning their camps, and taking their guns. But McClellan had ordered Major General Edwin V. Sumner to take his corps across the swollen, boiling Chickahominy and save Keyes. Confederates arriving late, then, had to keep Sumner from attacking their northern flank as they advanced toward Keyes.

Around noon on that Saturday, General Lee, too curious to remain in Richmond, rode out to Johnston's headquarters. There he learned little, primarily because the commanding general knew next to nothing about the progress of his battle and told Lee less. Finally, sounds of firing reached their ears—just before the president arrived. Ignoring him, Johnston mounted and galloped down the Nine Mile Road. Lee and Davis followed him.

Along the way the visitors came under Yankee fire. Davis, sensing an opportunity, paused amid the smoke and noise to send an order to Prince John Magruder to make a flanking march. On they rode until, so late in the day nothing much more could be done, they saw men carrying Joe Johnston's body on a litter.

Up front, General Johnston had been shot through his right shoulder and hit in the chest by a shell fragment. Conscious but in great pain, he asked someone to go back and bring his sword and pistols to him.

The president knelt beside the litter and took Johnston's hand in his. Set aside now were all their differences. Davis expressed his regret and his hope that the general's wounds would heal quickly so he could rise to fight again.

The stricken general was taken off to Richmond, leaving it to Major General G. W. Smith to carry on the battle. In fact, it was over for the day, for "Bull" Sumner's troops had stormed across the Chickahominy over McClellan's wavering bridges just in time to hit Johnston's northern flank and stop his attack.

Smith had been in Sumner's path, and when he reported to Davis and Lee, he seemed stunned—too much so to tell them where Johnston's forces were or what he intended to do with them in the morning. Hold in place, Davis advised Smith.

On their ride back toward the city the president turned to General Lee and said, "I am assigning you to the command of the army. When we get to Richmond, I shall send you the official order."

Not until late on that Saturday would Lincoln learn that a fight was in progress east of Richmond, and even then the only reports he got told him little, in part because McClellan was sick and had remained north of the Chickahominy. But there had been some news from the Shenandoah Valley, most of it mixed.

First came a message from General McDowell:

> Major-General Shields reports from Front Royal that the enemy is at Winchester, his force variously estimated at from 20,000 to 40,000.... The rain-storm, which continues violent, may delay us; but it will be worse for the enemy, who has no railroad, than it is for us. Our successful attack upon their rear cannot fail to make the enemy fall back from the Potomac both from General Banks and General Saxton. I beg to suggest that it would be well if these officers were to hang upon the enemy's rear and keep up a continued attack.

Since Monday, Banks had been above the Potomac; by now he should have his forces reorganized and resupplied. Late on Saturday afternoon, Banks replied from Martinsburg. For him to be only twenty miles north of Winchester was reassuring, but not the rest of his message:

> My command, I regret to say, is not in condition to move with promptitude to any great distance....My troops are yet much scattered, and want army blankets and cooking utensils, that are required for any movement.

Five o'clock—Frémont's promised time of arrival "at or near" Strasburg—passed with no word from him. Finally, as the first few scraps of news about the firing at Seven Pines began coming in, around eight that evening Frémont broke his silence. From Wardensville, fifteen miles west of Strasburg, the Pathfinder reported: "Roads heavy and weather terrible. Heavy storm most of yesterday and all last night." But his cavalry had sighted Confederates on the turnpike. "The army is pushing forward, and I intend to carry out operations proposed."

Now it was "a question of legs" for Jackson's army, especially for the Stonewall Brigade. Charles Winder's men had kept the Yankees at Harpers Ferry amused until the last moment, then started the long march southward. Winder knew Winchester might be abandoned before he got there. If so, he would have to find a way of bypassing the town.

After Jackson had left Winchester in the middle of that Saturday afternoon, he rode past his columns of infantry and wagons moving up the Valley Turnpike. Along the way he got word of a clash that had occurred between Strasburg and Front Royal: Shields might cut him off if Frémont had not already done so. Jackson pressed on.

From a point just north of Strasburg he could see no signs of Yankees anywhere ahead of him. Skirmishers he sent out drew no fire. Let the wagons go on up the turnpike, he ordered, and as infantry units reached him, he sent them to positions from which they could hold off both Shields and Frémont.

For Strasburg to have been empty was indeed a blessing. But Jackson would have to defend the town until the Stonewall Brigade arrived, however long it might take it to get there.

That evening, Jackson sat down at Dick Taylor's campfire. He was more communicative, Taylor wrote later, than before:

> He said Frémont, with a large force, was three miles west

of our present camp, and must be defeated in the morning. Shields was moving up Luray Valley, and might cross Massanutten to Newmarket, or continue south until he turned the mountain to fall on our [wagon] trains near Harrisonburg. The importance of preserving the immense trains, filled with captured stores, was great, and would engage much of his personal attention; while he relied on the army, under Ewell's direction, to deal promptly with Frémont. This he told in a low, gentle voice, and with many interruptions to afford time, as I thought and believe, for inward prayer.

And Taylor added: "The men said that his anxiety about the wagons was because of the lemons among the stores."

Jackson did leave Frémont to Ewell, who attacked westward —as ordered, at "early dawn" on Sunday morning, June 1—but Ewell could not provoke the Pathfinder's troops into much of a fight. Taylor offered to take his brigade around Frémont's northern flank— and did. His Louisianans rolled up the Yankee line until they came under Ewell's fire.

If Frémont had been timid, his gunners were not. Federal artillery fire was raking the woods behind Ewell's lines when Jackson came upon Tom Strother, Taylor's black servant, who was holding the general's horse. Strother had grown up with Taylor and had insisted on coming to the war with him.

To Jackson's suggestion that he move to a safe place, Strother, ignoring the shell bursts in the treetops overhead, replied: "If you please, sir, I'll just stay here, so's General Taylor can find me when he gets back—this artillery don't trouble me."

Several nights later, by another of Taylor's campfires, Jackson would rise and shake Tom Strother's hand, silently commending him for his devotion to duty.

While Ewell's division held Frémont west of Strasburg and Jackson's other troops guarded the approaches from Front Royal, at the head of the Stonewall Brigade Charles Winder heard guns firing. His men said nothing, but they may well have shared the thoughts of their commander: too late. But Winder did what he could to keep his troops plodding southward. That task was not easy; some of his regiments had marched thirty-six miles Saturday, the rest at least thirty. Old Jack always left the most dangerous jobs for them to do, veterans grumbled, lest he be accused of favoritism. But their snarls ceased as they saw Colonel Turner Ashby ride toward them from Strasburg. Jackson had waited for them; and, realizing he had, now they marched faster.

Abraham Lincoln had two battles to worry about on that Sunday, June's first day. No news came from the Shenandoah Valley. And from what General McClellan had reported it seemed that the rebels had caught him at Seven Pines with his pants down. "This morning the enemy attempted to renew the conflict," the Army of the Potomac's commander had said in a message, "but was everywhere repulsed." If so, neither side must have won. Another message was more specific: Federal casualties were about 5,000; the Confederates', around 6,100.

From the Shenandoah Valley some news came the next morning, Monday, June 2. General Frémont telegraphed:

> A reconnoitering force just in reports the enemy retreating, but in what direction is not yet known. Our cavalry will occupy Strasburg by midnight. Terrible storm of thunder and hail now passing over. Hailstones as large as hens' eggs.

Grateful as acting General-in-Chief Lincoln may have been for the former explorer's weather report, it must have been difficult for the president to keep from punching a hole in the telegraph room's wall. How could Frémont say Jackson was retreating and not know in which direction? It had to be south. Clearly, Jackson had escaped. And now for Lincoln's forces it was a question of legs all over again.

A question of weather, too. Heavy rain lingered long enough for Jackson to get south of a loop in the Shenandoah's North Fork and burn a bridge. Lest James Shields's division get up the Luray Valley so far he could cross the New Market gap in the Massanutten, block the turnpike, and attack his precious wagon trains, Jackson sent cavalry over to destroy bridges on the rampaging river's South Fork as well.

Harrisonburg was much on Old Jack's mind, though he said nothing except "Press on!" To get that far up the Valley before Shields, though, Jackson's army would have to live up to the nickname some newspaper reporters were giving it: foot cavalry.

Jefferson Davis had asked Mrs. Johnston to let the wounded general be brought to the presidential mansion and to stay there while he recovered, but she had made other arrangements. To the house she rented came a visitor who told Joe Johnston that his loss was a calamity to the South.

"No, sir," said General Johnston. "The shot that struck me down is the very best that has been fired for the Southern cause yet. For I possess in no degree the confidence of our government, and now they have in my place one who does possess it, and who can accomplish what I never could have done—the concentration of our armies for the defense of the capital of the Confederacy."

Robert E. Lee, he meant, the man in whom many Southerners had long since lost all faith. He had been called "Granny Lee" and "Retreating Lee," the "King of Spades." His troops, fatigued from digging the long stretches of entrenchments Lee had ordered, missed "Old Joe." So did the army's division commanders. To them Lee was only a "staff officer," a general totally inexperienced in leading units in battle.

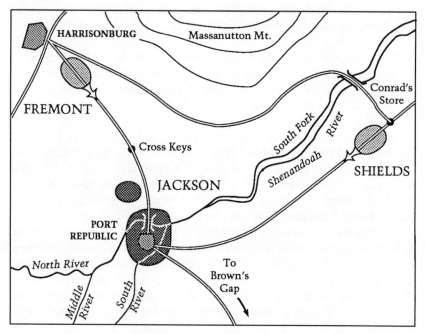

Cross Keys and Port Republic

McClellan, when he heard about the change in Confederate command, agreed. "I prefer Lee to Johnston," he said, adding that Lee "is too cautious and weak under grave responsibility. Personally brave and energetic to a fault, he is yet wanting in moral firmness when pressed by heavy responsibility, and is likely to be timid and irresolute in action."

Strange words these, coming as they did from the veteran of Rich Mountain and the abandoned positions at Munson's Hill, Manassas, and Yorktown. But George McClellan's opinion matched the rest—except Joe Johnston's, who was wrong only in one important detail. If General Lee concentrated the Confederate armies at Richmond, it would not be merely to *defend* the capital.

On the way up the Valley Turnpike from Strasburg, Jackson had decided to head for Port Republic, a little town south of the Massanutten's end where two rivers converged to form the Shenandoah's South Fork. He could hardly have selected a more dangerous place: Port Republic was on the road Shields's troops were taking up the Luray Valley, and if Frémont suddenly became aggressive, the Valley army could be trapped, after all. On the other hand, from the central position Port Republic afforded Jackson might strike blows at each federal force separately. And if worse came to worst, he could withdraw through Brown's Gap in the Blue Ridge.

At Harrisonburg on Thursday, June 5, Jackson turned off the macadamized Valley Turnpike and led his men southeastward. Now, for the first time in days, he had to contend with deep mud, and the columns were soon mired in it. Onward he pressed on Friday morning, leaving newly promoted Brigadier General Turner Ashby and some of his cavalry behind to guard against Frémont's approach. And by that night some of his other units were on the high ground north of Port Republic.

There sad news reached him. Frémont had sent cavalry southeast of Harrisonburg in Jackson's wake; Ashby met the federal charge with a countercharge and drove the Yankees back, but Union infantry appeared in the woods. Ashby, on foot because his horse had been killed, was leading some of Ewell's troops up to engage them when he ran into bluecoats. They shot him down as he was shouting, "Forward, my brave men!"

More news came: Shields's southernmost unit was about two miles north of Conrad's Store in the Luray Valley, which put him roughly twelve miles from Port Republic. Frémont was nearer. On Saturday, Jackson rode a few miles west, to Cross Keys, and tried to lure Frémont into a fight with Ewell's division. But the Pathfinder held back, disappointing Jackson and increasing the possibility that the Valley army might have to face both federal forces at the same time—that, or withdraw.

A bridge over the river at Port Republic's northern edge was the key to what Jackson could do. For as long as he held it, he would be able to handle Frémont. But if Shields came at him first, Jackson would have to bring Ewell eastward over the bridge, then burn it, giving up his last hope of destroying Frémont. Worse, leaving Frémont unopposed would allow the Union general to put his guns on the high ground overlooking the place where Jackson might be fighting Shields.

Early on Sunday, June 8, the general had just told a staff officer that there would be no military operations when up rode a cavalryman: Federals were in Port Republic's northern edge, he warned, and a moment later sounds of firing broke the morning calm.

"Go back and fight them!" said Jackson, starting out on foot toward the noise. A servant brought his horse; he mounted and rode at a gallop over the bridge to the high ground beyond it, narrowly escaping capture by Colonel S. S. Carroll's cavalry. Not so fortunate were several of Jackson's staff officers. Yankees soon discovered the unguarded wagon train. And Carroll had two guns positioned to blow away the bridge.

From the high ground overlooking Port Republic, Jackson sent infantry down to save the bridge and drive the invaders out of the village. Jackson, impatient, rode down to lead them across the bridge. Carroll's troops gave way, retreating down the Luray Valley, leaving behind their prisoners and two guns.

Scarcely had the Sabbath's calm been restored when gunfire broke out in the west, near Cross Keys: Frémont was attacking Ewell's division. Did Carroll's probe, followed by this, mean that Shields would soon be striking Port Republic in force from the northeast? No, said Jackson. "He cannot do it; I should tear him to pieces!" But he left Frémont for Ewell to handle and stayed at Port Republic, just in case.

Roughly seven miles west of there one of Ewell's brigades waited until Frémont's attackers were right in front of them, then fired a volley that stunned the federals. By the second volley the survivors were retreating.

Ewell, tempted to pursue, had to restrain himself as well as his men. Around noon Jackson appeared. Frémont showed no signs of wishing to renew the fight, and Jackson was content to leave it at that.

Shields's force in the Luray Valley was still on Jackson's mind, and before that Sunday ended, he had decided what to do about it: attack on Monday morning. Some of his orders caused his staff officers to think the general had gone mad. Ewell was to send his supply wagons eastward once his men had been fed, then all the trains would start up the road to Brown's Gap in the Blue Ridge. At early dawn Ewell would withdraw from Cross Keys, leaving only a token force to amuse and deceive Frémont, then join Jackson's forces in striking out at Shields northeast of Port Republic. That done, the Valley army would recross the bridge, return to Cross Keys, and smash Frémont.

Mad or not, at early dawn on Monday, June 9, Jackson led Charles Winder's Stonewall Brigade across the fords of the South Fork, not knowing the size of Shields's units or what others might be within supporting distance, not waiting for Ewell's troops to begin arriving from Cross Keys. For a mile or so Winder's men advanced through open country, spurs of the Blue Ridge east of them, high ground beyond the Shenandoah's South Fork to their west.

Then, soon after the Stonewall Brigade's skirmishers met those of Union Brigadier General E. B. Tyler, a fierce fight developed in the Lewis farm's wheat fields. Tyler's 3,000 men threw Winder's back while Union artillery on a high plateau off to the east poured fire on the stunned Confederates. Jackson did his best to rally them, sending troops and guns eastward to silence the federal batteries, dispatching messengers to Ewell to hurry forward.

Defeat was looming. The men trying to reach Tyler's guns were stopped by tangles of laurel and rhododendron. Winder's regiments were running out of ammunition, falling back under heavy fire from Union infantry to their front and artillery on the plateau east of them. Then, amid the shell bursts, up rode Richard Taylor.

"Delightful excitement," said Jackson; then he ordered the Louisiana Brigade's commander to capture Tyler's guns. This Taylor and his Tigers did, but only after hacking their way up the slope through the laurel and rhododendron and then getting thrown back from their objective twice, repulsed by Yankees firing from behind dead horses, swinging rammer staffs to ward off bayonets. Finally, on the third charge, the Louisianans drove away the last of the batteries' defenders.

To recover the guns Tyler's infantry surged up the slope. "There seemed," Taylor wrote afterward, "nothing left to do but set our backs to the mountain and die hard." But Dick Ewell made that unnecessary by leading two regiments into the Yankees' flank, supported by Winder's guns down below.

Ewell's brigades had arrived just in time to reinforce the Stonewall Brigade's fought-out men. Up to the plateau he ran, emerging as Taylor's men were aiming the captured artillery pieces at the fleeing federals; he dashed over and began serving one of the guns himself.

Jackson, elated, came up. First he shook Dick Taylor's hand, then awarded the guns to his brigade. Turning to Ewell, Jackson said, "General, he who does not see the hand of God in this is blind, sir, blind!"

Frémont, hearing the roar of battle in the east, advanced, responding to Shields's request that he come "thundering down" on Jackson's rear. His leading unit reached Port Republic's bridge, found it burned, and stopped.

The Pathfinder sent his artillery up to the high ground north of the demolished span. But when the guns got into position, their only targets were ambulance wagons moving slowly over an almost deserted battleground littered with dead and wounded soldiers.

Jackson's victorious army was following his wagons up the road leading southeastward to Brown's Gap in the Blue Ridge.

At about the same time on that Monday, June 9, Lincoln was replying to a message Frémont had sent from Harrisonburg, one in which the Pathfinder announced his arrival there on Friday. Lincoln, a day short of learning about the fight at Cross Keys, telegraphed:

> Halt at Harrisonburg, pursuing Jackson no farther. Get your force well in hand and stand on the defensive, guarding against a movement of the enemy either back toward Strasburg or toward Franklin, and await further orders, which will soon be sent you.

But Lincoln must have made that decision on Sunday, for on that day McDowell wired his chief of staff from Washington:

> Send to General Shields the following: That it being the intention of the President that the troops of the Rappahannock be employed elsewhere, General Shields will cease all further pursuit, and bring back all his division to Luray and get it ready for the march to Fredericksburg.

Meanwhile, on Sunday, Frémont had lost 684 men at Cross Keys; the next day, near Port Republic, Shields's ranks were thinned by 1,018 in defeats the telegraph might have prevented but did not. Both sides' dead would be in their graves before either Frémont or Shields would find out that the president had called off the chase two days before Jackson signaled the end of his Valley campaign himself, Monday afternoon, by vanishing from the Port Republic battlefield into the Blue Ridge.

Curiously, Jackson had already decided what his next move ought to be on Friday, June 6, when he reached Port Republic. He wrote to Richmond that if his forces were needed there, he could march them to the Virginia Central Railroad's Mechum River Station, adding: "I do not see that I can do much more [here] than rest my command and devote its time to drilling."

After fighting at Cross Keys and Port Republic, Jackson's little army did get some rest. When his scouts reported that Frémont had pulled back beyond Harrisonburg and Shields was on his way down the Luray Valley toward Front Royal, Jackson led his weary troops back to Port Republic and let them relax.

Jackson's men were weary indeed. Some had marched more than 400 miles in six weeks, Ewell's almost 200 miles in the past three weeks. Their commanding general, too, was worn out. On Saturday night, Jackson had not put adequate guards around the wagon train at Port Republic, to Yankee Colonel Carroll's short-lived delight on Sunday morning, and he had been rash in committing the Stonewall Brigade alone to the attack on Tyler's forces on Monday.

Even so, in exchanges of messages with General Lee there were no signs of fatigue on Jackson's part. Lee had given much thought to Jackson's proposal for an invasion of Pennsylvania, but the Army of Northern Virginia's commander recognized that the Confederacy could not provide enough men for that. Lee did send Jackson a few reinforcements and encouragement: "Should an opportunity occur for striking the enemy a successful blow," he wrote, "do not let it escape you." Preventing federal troops from reaching McClellan was still on Lee's mind. But Jackson, who had already offered to move his entire army to Richmond if it could be of more effective service there, replied:

> So far as I am concerned my opinion is that we should not attempt another march down the Valley to Winchester, until we are in a condition under the blessing of Providence to hold the country.

Hardly anyone—least of all Jackson, who had been both busy and late in learning of Joe Johnston's wounding—knew exactly what Robert Lee intended to do to George McClellan. Lee's ordering the digging of entrenchments east of Richmond seemed a defensive action. Parading troops bound for Jackson's army through the streets of Richmond made no sense at all.

But Jefferson Davis understood, for Lee had told him every detail of his plan. Public displays of Valley-bound brigades were for McClellan's benefit, the idea being to make him believe Lee had more forces than he needed to hold Richmond. And those trenches were for the very few men Lee meant to leave there, making demonstrations to hold the corps McClellan had south of the Chickahominy, while he massed the rest of his army north of the river and attacked eastward to achieve two goals: cut McClellan's supply line and force him to fight in the open—on ground Lee chose.

Having known all this from Lee's earliest days in command of the army and being a fighter himself, President Davis had no problem with the astonishing risk involved. He gave Lee his full support. But how could Jackson, out in the Valley, who hardly knew Lee except through messages, have possibly sensed as early as June 6 that the general commanding had a plan that required his "foot cavalry" to ensure devastating success?

Whether or not an intuitive link existed between the two generals, Jackson's "opinion" triggered a reply on June 16 in which Lee directed him to leave enough men behind to keep the Yankees fearful of another northward strike while the rest of the Valley army started toward Richmond in utmost secrecy.

Chapter 9

"Granny" Lee Begins to Learn

In the aftermath of his defeat in the Shenandoah Valley, Abraham Lincoln agreed to send McDowell's corps to McClellan. McCall's division was already on the way when on June 14 from "Camp Lincoln" the Young Napoleon complained:

> I received a telegram from [McDowell] requesting that McCall's division might be placed so as to join him immediately on his arrival. That request does not breathe the proper spirit.... If I cannot control all his troops, I want none of them, but would prefer to fight the battle with what I have, and let others be responsible for the results.

By June 20 General McClellan appeared to have calmed down enough to describe his situation:

> There is not the slightest reason to suppose that the enemy intends evacuating Richmond. He is daily increasing his defenses. I find him everywhere in force, and every reconnaissance costs many lives, yet I am obliged to feel my way foot by foot at whatever cost, so great are the difficulties of the country. By to-morrow night the defensive works covering our position on this side of the Chickahominy should be completed. I am forced to this by my inferiority in numbers, so that I may bring the greatest possible numbers into action and secure the army against the consequences of unforeseen disaster.

At the time, McClellan had 127,327 troops and Lee roughly half that number, but the Army of the Potomac's commander was estimating the Confederates' strength at 200,000;—hence, his forebodings of disaster. Yet his mind was not entirely on the difficulties he perceived, for in the same message to Lincoln he added:

> I would be glad to have permission to lay before Your Excellency, by letter or telegraph, my views as to the present state of military affairs throughout the whole country. In the mean time I would be pleased to learn the disposition as to numbers and position of the troops not under my command in Virginia and elsewhere.

Lincoln, replying, discouraged the use of the mails. "I would be very glad to talk with you, but you cannot leave your camp and I cannot well leave here."

So the president said on June 21. Not long afterward, however, he left Washington secretly on a special train bound for West Point. Lincoln did want a senior soldier's views "as to the present state of military affairs throughout the whole country"—not George McClellan's but old Winfield Scott's.

Nothing much would ever be known regarding precisely what the retired general-in-chief and the acting one discussed when they met on June 23. At a minimum, this was an opportunity for Lincoln to reveal to Scott his innermost thoughts and to ask the most searching questions, possibly even to concede his own inadequacies as a war manager, knowing that for once whatever either man said would be kept confidential.

And so it was. But from some of the actions Lincoln took shortly after his return to Washington, it was clear that the visit had not been merely to admire the gorgeous scenery of the Hudson Highlands.

On that Monday, June 23, while Lincoln and Scott were at West Point sorting out the problems besetting the Union's high command, roughly 400 miles to the south Robert E. Lee was waiting in a farmhouse east of Richmond for four of his army's generals to arrive for a conference. D. H. Hill saw when he rode up that one was already outside: a man leaning against a fence with his head bowed, his cap pulled down over his face. Then, astonished, Hill realized the stranger was Jackson. He had been told General Lee was busy, Tom Jackson explained to his brother-in-law, so he had taken the opportunity to catch some rest from what had been a long and very hard journey.

When the army commander called them inside, a glass of milk

was the only refreshment the hero of the Valley campaign would accept, though he had been riding for the past fourteen hours during the last segment of his six-day trip from Port Republic. Soon came Longstreet and Major General A. P. Hill, often referred to as Powell Hill to distinguish him from D. H. Hill, whose middle name was Harvey. Jackson sat down with the others to listen as Lee presented his analysis of the situation.

Richmond could not withstand a siege, Lee said, so the Army of Northern Virginia would have to prevent one. Given McClellan's superiority in troop strength and the power of his artillery, a frontal assault was out of the question. But the federal army was astride the Chickahominy and vulnerable to a turning movement, particularly one launched against the only corps north of the Chickahominy, Fitz-John Porter's, which held a thin line from the river to Mechanicsville.

That Porter's northern flank was "in the air" was the first thing Jeb Stuart, at twenty-nine a brigadier general commanding Lee's cavalry, had learned while leading 1,200 picked troopers on a ride all the way around McClellan's army between the twelfth and fifteenth of June. Stuart had started from north of Richmond, moved eastward around Porter, crossed the roads and the track of the York River rail line McClellan was using for moving supplies from his base at White House to his five corps, then cut southward deep in the Yankees' rear and returned. Along the way there had been some skirmishing, a few tight moments, but only one Confederate casualty.

So the plan was, General Lee continued, to drive Porter out of his lines near Mechanicsville, then threaten the Union army's supply line. McClellan would have to come out of his entrenchments and fight in the open or withdraw south of the Chickahominy and try to get supplies from some point on the James River's bank.

To do this, however, the Confederate army would have to be concentrated north of the Chickahominy. The few men left in Lee's fresh-dug trenches east of Richmond would have to hold off most of McClellan's divisions if he sensed their weakness and decided to attack westward through it.

Jackson's divisions would be arriving from the west, but they would not join the main body. Instead, he was to begin the attack by moving eastward from Ashland, about ten miles northwest of the Meadow Bridge, where the other divisions would be waiting, south of the Chickahominy. Jackson was to sweep north of Porter's line and get behind it. Powell Hill, hearing Jackson's guns, would cross the Meadow Bridge. Once Porter realized his peril and withdrew, Powell Hill's division would press him. As Porter retreated on down the Chickahominy, the Mechanicsville Pike Bridge would become available for Harvey Hill and Longstreet; their divisions would cross and join the pursuit.

At that point, according to General Lee's plan, the Army of Northern Virginia's forces would be in a line. Jeb Stuart's cavalry would be the northernmost unit, then Jackson, Harvey Hill, Powell Hill, and nearest the Chickahominy, Longstreet.

Lee left the room so that his generals could discuss what they had just been told. Obviously, much depended on Jackson; only his divisions were not within striking distance of George McClellan's army. How soon, Longstreet asked him, could his forces be at Ashland, ready to advance?

On the twenty-fifth, Wednesday, Jackson replied. Longstreet said he thought that might be too soon. Then the next day, Jackson suggested, Thursday, the twenty-sixth. That was the date reported to General Lee when he returned.

Around dark on that Monday, the twenty-third, Jackson mounted and rode westward to find his men and urge them to "Press on!"

So began what would later be ranked high among the war's truly critical weeks. Lee was risking Richmond's safety, and possibly the Confederacy's future, on his daring but complex plan. And in Washington, emboldened perhaps by General Scott's counsel, Abraham Lincoln was about to make major changes in the management of the Union's military effort.

First, on June 26, the president issued an order combining almost all the forces still in the Shenandoah Valley into what he called the Army of Virginia and appointed Major General John Pope as its commander. Lincoln had ordered Pope to Washington before he left for West Point; apparently Scott's blessing was bestowed on the creation of the new field army in their talks.

General Frémont, however, flatly refused to serve under an officer junior to him in rank. Lincoln quickly accepted his resignation and replaced him with Major General Franz Sigel.

By including Irvin McDowell's corps in the new army, the president was, in effect, telling General McClellan that he would have to get along with the reinforcements already sent him. And if the Young Napoleon complained, Lincoln could remind him— again—that federal forces in the Shenandoah Valley were keeping Jackson's 17,000 troops from joining Lee, which was as good as having that many more men in the Army of the Potomac.

Well, not quite. On Tuesday, June 24, McClellan learned from a rebel deserter that Jackson was on the way eastward and intended to attack Fitz-John Porter's northern flank. On the next day, he heard that Beauregard had arrived in Richmond with reinforcements for Lee's army, which would increase its size to at least 200,000 men. On Wednesday night McClellan telegraphed to Secretary Stanton:

> I shall have to contend against vastly superior odds if these reports be true; but this army will do all in the power of men to hold their position and repulse any attack. I regret my great inferiority in numbers, but feel I am in no way responsible for it, as I have not failed to represent repeatedly the necessity of reinforcements; that this was the decisive point, and that all the available means of the Government should be concentrated here. I will do all that a general can do with the splendid army I have the honor to command, and if it is destroyed by overwhelming numbers, can at least die with it and share its fate. But if the result of the action, which will probably occur tomorrow, or within a short time, is disaster, the responsibility cannot be thrown on my shoulders; it must rest where it belongs.

Ironically, helping McClellan was among the reasons the president had created Pope's army. "The Army of Virginia," he had ordered, "...shall in the speediest manner attack and overcome the rebel forces under Jackson and Ewell, threaten the enemy in the direction of Charlottesville, and render effective aid to relieve General McClellan and capture Richmond."

That was on June 26. John Pope would not be ready to move for weeks, but George McClellan was already providing excuses for a disaster that had not occurred.

Lincoln's other change in the Union's war management was to ask General Halleck, then at Corinth in Mississippi, to come to Washington for "consultation." In the fall of 1861, Winfield Scott had recommended Halleck to succeed him as general-in-chief; Lincoln had appointed McClellan instead, then tried to fill the position himself. Presumably, at West Point on June 23, Scott had reiterated his belief that Old Brains was the man the president needed.

Halleck's reply to Lincoln's invitation for a visit was, in effect, that he had rather not make the trip. After taking Corinth at the end of May, he had sent Sherman toward Memphis and Buell eastward, with Chattanooga as his goal; progress was slow because both forces were repairing the East-West railroad as they advanced. Clearing Tennessee of rebels, he believed, was "worth three Richmonds."

Lincoln did not press Old Brains. But he did send Rhode Island's governor William Sprague out to Corinth to nudge him.

When General Jackson reached his army on Tuesday morning,

the twenty-fourth, having been in the saddle for the second night in a row, he found that only a few of his units were up. Wagons and artillery lagged because of muddy roads. He was about twenty-six miles west of where his forces had to be on Wednesday night: roughly six miles east of Ashland, ready to begin executing the entire plan precisely at 3:00 A.M. Thursday. Even so, he waited all day on Tuesday for the rest of his troops and wagons.

On Wednesday morning, Jackson's sense of urgency—absent the day before—was evident. "Press on!" he told his troops, but delays were many and frequent. Bridges were out, streams high from the rains, roads muddy. Near Ashland he decided to go into camp. He reported by courier to General Lee that he had been delayed but would begin Thursday morning's advance half an hour earlier than ordered.

George McClellan spent most of that Wednesday, June 25, near Oak Grove watching a brisk skirmish between Heintzelman's corps and Confederates west of them. Little Mac wanted to advance this part of his line a mile or so to support the attack Sumner's and Major General William Franklin's corps would launch on Thursday to seize Old Tavern on the Nine Mile Road.

McClellan's campaign was approaching the climax he had envisioned back in the winter: Richmond's siege. That required guns too heavy to move except by water and rail, which is why he had made White House on the Pamunkey River his base. From there the York River Railroad could move the ponderous weapons almost to within range of Richmond, minimizing dependence on roads with frail bridges.

Could McClellan, instead, have used a landing on the James River, south of the peninsula, nearer Richmond, as his base? No, there was no railroad on that side, only a network of roads and creeks and swamps. Hence, his deployment: To protect White House and the York River Railroad, McClellan kept Major General Fitz-John Porter's corps north of the Chickahominy River and reinforced it with McCall's division even after he no longer expected McDowell's corps to join him. All Porter's 35,000 men had to do was defend; the purpose of the 74,300 troops in the four corps south of the Chickahominy—nearest it Franklin's, then Bull Sumner's and Heintzelman's, southernmost Keyes's—was to get near enough to Richmond for the siege guns to blast the Confederacy's capital to rubble. McClellan's headquarters, too, were south of the river now, making it more convenient for him to supervise his short stabs westward, such as Oak Grove and the one planned for Thursday to take Old Tavern.

Robert E. Lee, too, had watched the fighting at Oak Grove that day, wondering, as it raged, whether his plan could still be carried out. All along he had assumed that McClellan was not bold enough to use his 74,300 troops south of the Chickahominy in a frontal attack, yet the Confederate general was viewing the kind of skirmishing normally preceding one. Did McClellan know that Lee was shifting all but Magruder's division and Major General Benjamin Huger's northward or that Jackson was coming? Should he cancel his orders?

This was, after all, the first campaign General Lee had ever had the opportunity to plan and lead. It might be his last chance to redeem his earlier failures. And now, before his eyes, the one thing he had feared most might be beginning.

Lee had remembered Prince John Magruder's theatricals down the long peninsula back in April, when he had halted McClellan's advance short of Yorktown. Now he was counting on Magruder and his 12,000 men not only to repeat that fine performance but to enhance it. Huger's 9,000 troops would be in this thin line, too, south of Magruder, but Lee knew that neither commander had a chance of stopping McClellan if this fight at Oak Grove was in fact the foreshadowing of a sustained federal drive.

Lee ordered General Huger to hold his position at any cost the next day and, if possible, to advance. There would be no change in his decision to get at "those people"—the way in which he habitually referred to the invaders of his beloved Virginia and the new nation of which she was, at the moment, the most critical part.

"If I had another good Division," telegraphed McClellan to Stanton on Wednesday night, "I could laugh at Jackson."

As matters stood, he canceled the orders for Thursday's attempt to seize Old Tavern, urged Fitz-John Porter to be alert for Jackson's approach, and—perhaps remembering Jeb Stuart's ride around the Army of the Potomac two weeks earlier—warned the White House base's guards they might be raided. Also, lest he overlook any detail, McClellan directed the ordnance officer at White House to send a supply of ammunition by ships around to the James River.

In Washington, Abraham Lincoln was preparing a reply to the telegram McClellan had sent Stanton earlier on that Wednesday evening, when the deserter and the runaway slave had reported Jackson's movement and the supposed arrival of Beauregard's troops (which were still in Mississippi). Lincoln wrote:

The [wire] of 6.15 p.m., suggesting the probability of your being overwhelmed by 200,000, and talking of where the responsibility will belong, pains me very much. I give you all I can, and act on the presumption that you will do the best you can with what you have, while you continue, ungenerously I think, to assume that I could give you more if I would. I have omitted and shall omit no opportunity to send you re-inforcements whenever I possibly can.

And the president added:

P.S.—General Pope thinks if you fall back it would be much better toward the York River than toward the James.

Sunrise on Thursday, June 26, found three of Fitz-John Porter's federal divisions entrenched along the eastern bank of Beaver Dam Creek, a stream flowing southward in an arc from north of Mechanicsville (and east of it by maybe a mile) to the Chickahominy. Looking westward across some open fields, Union artillerymen could see the village: nothing much, a cluster of houses and outbuildings where roads crossed. Beyond the tiny settlement, farmlands extended to the Chickahominy's tree-lined course. On the river's far side were bluffs, perhaps three miles west of where Porter's artillery pieces were in position. But if the gunners shifted their gaze northwestward, seeking signs of Jackson's approach, as surely they had been alerted to do, higher ground blocked their view.

Major General Porter had not neglected his open flank. Cavalry patrols were operating north and west of it. And in the countryside that his artillerymen were watching, detachments of infantry were posted to act as skirmishers.

General Lee could see little of this through his field glasses on that Thursday morning from the bluff above the Chickahominy's mile-wide thickets. Earlier, three divisions had moved northward from near Prince John Magruder's line; two, Longstreet's and Harvey Hill's, were resting not far away from the army commander's vantage point. Off a mile or more to the west Powell Hill's men were waiting to cross the Chickahominy at the Meadow Bridge above a fork in the river.

President Davis, accompanied by other curious government officials, arrived. Where was General Jackson? All the Army of Northern Virginia's commander could tell them was that Jackson had been delayed.

Set aside in Lee's earlier thinking had been the axiom that nothing in war is more difficult than combining forces on a battlefield in the face of the enemy. This enormous risk might have been on the mind of young staff officer Porter Alexander, as well, but he may have remembered something else, Colonel Joseph Ives's comment two weeks earlier: "Alexander, if there is one man in the army, Confederate or Federal, head and shoulders above any other in *audacity*, it is General Lee! His name might be Audacity. He will take more desperate chances and take them quicker than any other general in this country, North or South; and you will live to see it, too."

But as noon passed with no word from Jackson, Alexander and the rest of the men watching the solitary figure standing on the bluff may have wondered if Lee's inexperience had led him—and them— into a fiasco. He had sent no riders out to search for the tardy Jackson. Was Lee's calm genuine? Was he really that composed, or was he merely setting an example?

George McClellan, too, had been up since first light on that Thursday morning. He inspected his lines south of the river dividing his army, then sent a message to Washington: "All things very quiet on this bank of the Chickahominy. I would prefer more noise."

There had been some noise earlier, most of it made by the heavy guns McClellan had placed on Dr. Gaines's farm on the river's north side. Magruder's artillery had replied, then pulled back, but Prince John's infantry seemed active, so much so that the Union corps commanders watching them were becoming increasingly apprehensive.

Around noon McClellan got off another report to Stanton:

> I have just heard that our advanced cavalry pickets on the left bank of the Chickahominy are being driven in. It is probably Jackson's advance guard. If this be true, you may not hear from me for some days, as my communications will probably be cut off. The case is perhaps a difficult one, but I shall resort to desperate measures, and will do my best to outmaneuver, outwit, and outfight the enemy. Do not believe reports of disaster, and do not be discouraged if you learn that my communications are cut off, and even York- town in possession of the enemy. Hope for the best, and I will not deceive the hopes you formerly placed in me.

General McClellan also took the time to send a wire to Flag Officer Louis M. Goldsborough, who had been offended by the tone of quartermaster Brigadier General Stewart Van Vliet's request that the navy send provision ships to the James River. Comply, he urged: "It is a matter of vital importance & may involve the existence of this army."

Such, apparently, was Jackson's power over McClellan's mind, though no man in the Valley army had yet fired a round.

General Magruder's latest theatrical production seemed to be a success, but staging it hour after passing hour was making him jittery. All morning he had listened in vain for sounds of battle to the north of his thin line. Not a word had Lee sent him. By early afternoon Prince John could bear the strain no longer. Unwilling to let Lee perceive his distress by risking a written inquiry, he sent Major Joseph L. Brent, his ordnance officer, to Lee merely to report that the Yankees were inert; Brent's appearance, Magruder was certain, would prompt Lee to end the agonizing suspense.

As Brent rode northward past houses in Richmond's eastern fringe, he saw children playing in the yards as though this day were no different from any other. And it might not be, Brent may have concluded when he passed the troops resting along the Mechanicsville Turnpike, for it was then three o'clock and the hours of daylight remaining were few and dwindling.

Major Brent found Lee standing on the bluff, silent, calm. The general guessed Brent's purpose immediately. "We have been waiting for General Jackson," Lee told him, "from whom we have not heard. I wish you to remain here until I am ready to send a message to General Magruder."

Very shortly afterward came the sound of rifle fire, from the Meadow Bridge where Powell Hill's division had waited all day for signs of Jackson's approach. Now things happened very quickly. Lee ordered Longstreet and Harvey Hill to move down the Mechanicsville Turnpike. President Davis and his entourage came to the bluff to watch Powell Hill's troops sweep eastward, driving Fitz-John Porter's skirmishers beyond the village.

More delay: Bridges had to be repaired before guns could cross the Chickahominy. Davis, losing patience, led his party across the stream; General Lee followed.

A. P. Hill's men came under the fire of Porter's artillery as they neared Mechanicsville. There was only one thing to do: keep advancing. That they did, toward Beaver Dam Creek.

When General Lee reached Mechanicsville, he learned that Powell Hill had moved out because his anxiety, like Magruder's, had driven him to do something. Heavy firing along Beaver Dam Creek made it clear that Jackson had not gotten around Porter's flank. A frontal assault, the very thing Lee wanted Jackson's sweep to prevent, was inevitable. And even now, with the fight too hot to break off, no one knew where Jackson was.

Through federal shell bursts, killing and maiming attackers and

disabling the few guns Harvey Hill's men had gotten across the
river, Lee saw Davis and the politicians riding with him. "Mr.
President," said the general after saluting, "who is all this army and
what is it doing here?"

"It is not my army, General."

"It certainly is not my army, Mr. President, and this is no place
for it."

"Well," said Jefferson Davis, stunned, "if I withdraw, perhaps
they will follow me."

Davis lifted his hat briefly, then led the group down to some
woods. Lee fed some of Harvey Hill's arriving brigades into the fight
centering on Ellerson's Mill, where there was a bridge over Beaver
Dam Creek. Davis, too, sent men forward.

Nothing could have pleased Fitz-John Porter more. From their
triple-tiered trenches on the ravine's eastern slope his riflemen all
but destroyed each Confederate unit that tried to wade the stream.
Those who crossed died quickly, their bodies —as a federal soldier
said afterward—"as thick as flies in a bowl of sugar."

Finally, with the sun almost down in the west, Lee faced not
only defeat in his first battle as a commander but ruin if he made the
wrong decision now. McClellan had to know what Lee had intended
to do, and Lee had to expect his adversary to take full advantage of
the situation: to send his four corps south of the Chickahominy
attacking straight ahead, crushing Magruder and Huger, driving all
the way into Richmond. Short of that, McClellan could easily
reinforce Porter. Either way, Lee's campaign was stopped, wrecked
possibly beyond salvaging.

After sundown the fighting eased off. General Lee told his
division commanders to hold the ground they had, which was all he
could do, at least until he found out where Jackson was. Curiously,
Lee sent no riders in search of him.

In midafternoon on that Thursday, as Powell Hill grew too
impatient to wait any longer for Jackson to appear, McClellan wired
Fitz-John Porter from Camp Lincoln: "I will hold everything in
readiness here to move all available troops to your support when
needed. We must save all baggage & guns."

There was more, mostly requests to keep him informed. An hour
or so later, as the fight was intensifying along Beaver Dam Creek,
McClellan finished the text of a telegram he wanted the War
Department to relay to his wife, in New Jersey:

Dear Nell. I may not be able to telegraph or write to you
for some days. There will be great stampedes but do not be

alarmed. I think the enemy are making a great mistake, if so they will be terribly punished. There will be severe fighting in a day or two but you may be sure that your husband will not disgrace you and I am confident that God will smile upon my efforts & give our arms success. You will hear that we are cut off, annihilated etc. Do not believe it but trust that success will crown our efforts. I tell you this darling only to guard you against the agony you would feel if you trusted the newspaper reports. I give you my word that I believe we will surely win & that the enemy is falling into a trap. I shall allow the enemy to cut off our communications in order to ensure success.

Having reassured Mary Ellen, the general ordered Franklin to have a division ready to assist Porter if needed. Next he asked the other idle corps commanders how many troops they could spare: None, replied Keyes; a third of his, Heintzelman said; Sumner, half—in all, 50,000 men.

McClellan went over to the Chickahominy's north side, saw Porter's repulse of the rebels, and wired Stanton: "Victory of to-day complete and against great odds. I almost begin to think we are invincible."

Porter's 35,000 had held off only 14,000 of the 56,000 Confederates Lee had north of the Chickahominy—roughly 1,400 fewer now that the firing was dying out. And, ironically, Porter learned where Jackson was well before Lee did: Jackson was in fact on Porter's flank, going into camp near Hundley's Corner, and he had been there within the sounds of the firing along Beaver Dam Creek since about five o'clock that afternoon.

That was all McClellan needed to know, apparently, for—as though he had forgotten the 50,000 reinforcements available south of the Chickahominy—he ordered Porter to withdraw to a position several miles to the east, near Gaines's Mill, before sunrise. Earlier he had directed officials at White House to load all supplies on freight cars and wagons and send them to him, then to prepare to abandon that base and establish a new one on the banks of the James River.

It did not seem to occur to George McClellan that these were strange actions to take if the day's victory had indeed been "complete."

Jackson's Valley army did not begin its march to get north of and behind Fitz-John Porter's flank at two-thirty or even three A.M. on that Thursday, June 26. At daylight, some of the men were filling their canteens in anticipation of the fourteen-mile march still ahead of them. Not until nine o'clock did they pass the place General Lee had directed Jackson to stop the night before. They were already six hours late, the day was hot, Yankee cavalry active east and south of their route.

Delays continued all morning. At noon, Jackson halted to give his men an hour's rest. At one, the march resumed. Up rode Jeb Stuart; he conferred briefly with Jackson, then went eastward again. As men stopped at farmhouses to refill their canteens, officers let them take their time. Each pause made the entire column wait. A bridge the federal troopers had tried to burn had to be repaired. And at each fork in the road more time was lost as Jackson queried the guides.

By midafternoon Jackson had skirmishers out, slowing the advance even more. From the south came the sounds of firing. This was not in accordance with General Lee's plan, but Jackson sent no riders to find out what that noise meant, nor did any messengers come to him.

On Jackson pressed until, at around five, he passed Pole Green Church. Hundley's Corner was just ahead. This was his objective, the one designated in his orders. He ordered his unit commanders to go into camp and waited for the brigades and wagons filling the road behind him to catch up.

Now, with evening coming on, that firing off to the south grew heavier, but it seemed miles away. Nothing matched Lee's plan. Harvey Hill's division should be on his right, but there was no sign of him—or of the enemy.

Stopping, apparently, was the only thing Jackson could think of to do. He had complied with his orders. No new ones had reached him, nor did he send anyone to report his arrival to General Lee. To act on his own, worn out as he was and with men tired from the day's march, in unfamiliar country, not knowing anything about the situation south of him, might be contrary to the army commander's wishes. So he would wait.

Concurrently, General Lee was waiting to hear from Jackson, and in the hope it might help him make sense of the day's events, that Thursday evening he called his division commanders to a meeting at a farmhouse near Mechanicsville. Lee asked questions, mostly, and listened. Yes, mistakes had been made. But he assigned no blame, nor did he give any new orders; the battle would have to be resumed in the morning. Could anything more be done? No, not until Lee found out where Jackson was.

Chapter 10

Gaines's Mill:
McClellan Self-Destructs

Fitz-John Porter's position along Beaver Dam Creek had proved ideal for the kind of battle Thursday's had been. His casualties had been light, less than 400, and the morale of his men was soaring. But with Jackson on his northern flank, Porter could not argue when McClellan said he should withdraw.

Brigadier General John Barnard, the Army of the Potomac's senior engineer, had been scouting while the fighting was going on. Move Porter's divisions several miles to the east, Barnard advised McClellan and the corps commander after midnight, past a creek called Boatswain's Swamp, and prepare to defend the plateau on which a family named Watt lived. From that plateau a road led southward to Grapevine Bridge over the Chickahominy, assuring communication between Porter and the bulk of the army and providing an escape route if one might be needed.

Quickly, McClellan approved Barnard's suggestion, though he delayed giving Porter the formal order to commence his movement until three o'clock on that Friday morning, June 27. White House, apparently, was also on the army commander's mind; if Porter could not hold the Watt farm's plateau, the supply base would certainly have to be abandoned. And, as though he assumed the worst would happen, McClellan alerted his headquarters—well south of the Chickahominy—to be ready to move.

When Robert Lee had gone to bed, he had every reason to consider himself defeated, Richmond in greater peril than ever, his plan a ghastly mistake, his ability to control his forces in battle tragically deficient, the prospects for Friday as dreadful as the disaster at Beaver Dam Creek had been. But using the forces he already had in place as best he could was on General Lee's mind at dawn, apparently, for he told Powell Hill to renew his attack along Beaver Dam Creek while Harvey Hill moved northeastward in search of contact with Jackson.

Soon Powell Hill's men drove away the few defenders and took the east bank of Beaver Dam Creek. Almost as quickly General Lee ordered Hill to pursue Porter's rear guard eastward on the road the fugitives had taken. He sent Longstreet along a parallel route near the Chickahominy. Harvey Hill's division had already gone north of Beaver Dam Creek's headwaters, using a third road eastward, one that also passed the branches that created Powhite Creek—the next good defense position shown on Lee's map, the line he assumed Porter now meant to hold.

Sounds of firing along Beaver Dam Creek had prompted Jackson to move, but he had done it cautiously, knowing nothing about the terrain ahead or what Yankee forces might be in the woods on his flanks. It had taken him fourteen hours to cover fourteen miles the day before, in part for the same reasons; now, on Friday morning, acting without orders, Jackson's pace was even slower. By around eleven o'clock, however, he was at Walnut Grove Church. And there he found Powell Hill.

After Jackson and Hill had been talking for a little while, General Lee rode up. Hill left to rejoin his division, passing eastward-bound on the road to Old Cold Harbor. Lee and Jackson moved away from the troops staring at them—Valley veterans who had never seen the army commander, staff officers who wanted a look at the famous "Stonewall."

No one would ever know what the immaculate, much older man, sitting on a tree stump, and the one holding a dusty cadet cap said to each other. Some of those who watched them later reported that neither general showed any emotion: no sign of understandable anger on Lee's part, no visible indication that Jackson felt rebuked. Only from that Friday's subsequent events could anyone even guess what they had discussed.

After General Lee mounted Traveller and led his staff off to the east, Jackson got his men moving in the same direction, but on a different road. Whether or not Lee had made it clear to him, Jackson's mission was the same as it had been the day before: to turn Porter out of his defensive position, but this time above Powhite Creek.

Engineer Barnard had looked at Powhite Creek and found that twin of Beaver Dam Creek equally vulnerable to a rebel turning movement, which is why he had recommended building a line eastward on the far side of Boatswain's Swamp. And when Fitz-John Porter reached the Watt farm's plateau he may well have been glad George McClellan had listened to Barnard.

It was as though nature had prepared the position exactly for the purpose it was about to serve. From its headwaters south of Old Cold Harbor, Boatswain's Swamp ran westward for about a mile, south-westward for nearly two more, then mostly to the southeast for another mile or so before emptying into the Chickahominy. Below its origins the creek's waters had carved ravines along its course; trees and dense underbrush lined it, and only two farm roads crossed it.

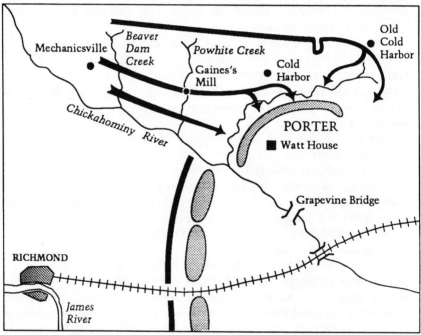

Gaines's Mill

Porter deployed his divisions along the moat's long arc, knowing he could shift them and his artillery easily if he had to. At the plateau's eastern edge was a road from Old Cold Harbor southward to Grapevine Bridge and—south of it—the rest of the army. General McClellan would have no problem in reinforcing him and keeping his guns and troops well stocked with ammunition.

Off to the west there were sounds of skirmishing—the rear guard delaying the rebels east of Gaines's Mill. This meant Porter's unit commanders would have more time in which to place their men and have them dig in. By early afternoon they would have at least two lines of fortifications ready, in some places three. And the longer Lee's forces took to get there, the deadlier their reception would be.

Afterward the battle would be called Gaines's Mill, though the only fighting near it took place around noon on that Friday when Brigadier General Maxcy Gregg's South Carolinians easily drove Porter's skirmishers eastward and crossed Powhite Creek in pursuit. Gregg advanced on through New Cold Harbor; there he was on ground high enough to look southeastward over the tree-lined moat to the plateau beyond, and what he saw was a mass of troops in blue protected by an obstacle nigh impossible to get through and all too simple for the Yankees to defend.

Powell Hill came up to join Gregg, then General Lee. On Lee's map there was no creek where the arc of Boatswain's Swamp ought to have been drawn, but that no longer mattered. Getting at Porter did. And that obliged him to improvise a plan.

The roads, at least, were advantages Lee could use—or continue to use—for he had already sent Harvey Hill eastward to Old Cold Harbor and Jackson would be there, too, directing Hill temporarily. At Old Cold Harbor they would control the only road north of the Chickahominy Porter could take if his intent was to protect McClellan's supply base at White House. As Porter retreated, Jackson's guns and Harvey Hill's could shell the columns trying to move eastward.

But what if Porter was determined to hold his fortress? Again, Jackson was on Porter's northeastern flank. Behind Lee, on another road, Longstreet was coming up; he could press the federal line south of Powell Hill.

Remembering, perhaps, the chaos at Mechanicsville, Lee meant to avoid piecemeal commitment of his troops. He wanted to hit Porter with his whole army. But it would take time to get all his divisions ready to make the assault, it was then afternoon, and he was by no means certain that Jackson and Harvey Hill were actually at Old Cold Harbor.

While General Lee sent riders off bearing orders, Powell Hill decided to feel out Porter's lines. He sent Maxcy Gregg's men in first, charging across an open field through the flame and steel and concussion from federal artillery bursts and then plunging through vines and underbrush until they were stunned by murderous volleys from the Yankees entrenched above them. Still Gregg's men fought, some using their rifles as clubs; finally, they had to fall back toward the creek.

All Powell Hill knew was that a fight had started, and being a fighter, he threw more brigades into the creek line's green hell west of Gregg. Soon almost his entire division was deep in the ravine, lost from view below dense battle smoke, too hotly engaged to turn away, too weak to break through.

By midafternoon on that scorching day Jackson was where General Lee had hoped, near Old Cold Harbor, and so was Harvey Hill. Pouring artillery fire on retreating Yankees appeared to be more on Old Jack's mind than anything else, for he had told Hill to break off an attack against Porter's division guarding the corps' eastern flank and the road to Grapevine Bridge—an unfortunate order, for a little more pressure there might have caused Porter to shift some units away from where Powell Hill's men were hammering in vain and at a terrible cost. And as time passed, no federal fugitives came within range of the waiting Confederates' guns.

If that vexed Jackson, much else on that Friday also had. Early in the morning his shelling of the woods had hit some of Maxcy Gregg's men. After he had conferred briefly with General Lee, his march eastward had been slow, delayed by taking the wrong turn and having to double back. And now Jackson was not sure where all of his units were, what they were doing, or what he ought to have them do if he could find them.

Or so it seemed, for the easternmost wing of Lee's still-scattered army was present but not really in the battle. And time was getting away, as only a glance toward the western sky could verify.

Such wind as there was on that Friday had kept most of the noise of fighting away from Camp Lincoln. From there, around one o'clock in the afternoon—before Powell Hill's attack—General McClellan sent a report to Secretary Stanton:

> We are contending at several points against superior numbers. The enemy evince much desperation but as we have no choice but to win you may be sure that we will do all that can be expected.... As this may be the last dispatch I send you for some time I will beg that you put some one General in command of the Shenandoah & of all the troops in front of Washington. For the sake of the country secure unity of action & bring the best men forward. Good bye & present my respects to the President.

Word from Porter regarding the attack Powell Hill had launched spurred McClellan into suggesting to Franklin that he send a force northward across the Duane Bridge and strike Lee's flank. No, replied Franklin, he could not; he had burned the bridge, lest the rebels use it. Later, McClellan wired Porter he had ordered Slocum's division to leave Franklin's line, where Prince John Magruder was active, and to move to Porter's support. Then, at four-thirty P.M., he telegraphed to Porter:

> Send word to all your troops that their general thanks them for their heroism, and says to them that he is now sure that nothing can resist them. Their conduct and your own has been magnificent, and another name is added to their banners. Give my regulars a good chance. I look upon to-day as decisive in the war. Try to drive the rascals and take some prisoners and guns. What more assistance do you require?

James Longstreet, whose division was between Powell Hill's and the Chickahominy, had learned right away that Porter's guns would catch his troops in a deadly crossfire if he advanced. This disappointed General Lee, who had hoped Longstreet could make enough of a demonstration to lure Porter's defenders away from Powell Hill, but Lee agreed that Longstreet should wait until he knew Jackson was ready to join in a general assault.

So matters stood when, with A. P. Hill's men fought out for the second straight day, Dick Ewell appeared on the road linking the two Cold Harbors. Lee sent Ewell's division into the ravines east of Hill, but no more than Hill's remnants could they advance.

Isaac Seymour, commanding the Louisiana Brigade in place of ill Dick Taylor, was killed early in the attack. Down, too, went Roberdeau Wheat; he had told another officer he expected to die that day, and when his premonition became a fact, his Tigers fell back, too stunned to fight on.

Suddenly, from out of the east on the Old Cold Harbor road, up rode Jackson. "Ah, General," said Lee, "I am very glad to see you. I had hoped to be with you before."

Battle noise smothered Jackson's response.

"That fire is very heavy," Lee continued. "Do you think your men can stand it?"

"They can stand almost anything. They can stand that!"

Jackson listened to the army commander's instructions, then, sucking on a lemon, he rode eastward. As the first of his brigades appeared, Lee sent them to plug gaps in his line. Farthest to the east, Harvey Hill was ready to attack the federal regulars commanded by his roommate at West Point, George Sykes. Now only two brigades remained to be committed: Evander Law's and John Hood's.

Lee explained to Hood the need to dislodge Porter. "This must be done," he added. "Can you break his line?"

"I will try," said Hood.

Lee raised his hat. "May God be with you."

It took Hood and Law about half an hour to get their men into position, a half hour in which the sun went down behind the trees and darkness deepened in Boatswain Swamp's hollows. Wade Hampton's Legion would be on Hood's left, Law's brigade on his right, three Texas regiments in the center, his Fourth Texas in reserve.

Once John Hood had reviewed his battle line, ignoring the Yankee artillery bursts, he ordered the troops forward, setting a steady, unhurried pace. To the right of Law's Georgians, Hood noticed, was an open field. Beyond the little stream he could see Fitz-John Porter's fortified lines and guns nearly hub to hub. And from south of the Chickahominy, he knew, McClellan's long-range artillery could sweep the clearing with enfilade fire.

Yet the thing must be done. Hood rode back to the 4th Texas, the regiment he had brought to the war, and gave orders for it to march by the right flank into the open field. Then, when the Texans reached it, Hood gave them their final orders.

No man was to fire until he said so. They would stay in formation, keeping the line intact.

Hood, dismounted now, saber drawn, led the Texans as if they were on parade. Federal rounds—many, the dreaded canister—cut into his neat lines, thinning them, but Hood marched on toward the creek. To his left he could see Hampton's Legion moving steadily but slowly through the smoky thickets. Over on the right, in Evander Law's front, some of Powell Hill's weary men were breaking for the rear, no longer able to take the heavy pounding from the Yankee artillery.

Now, just short of the creek line, Hood and his men had to step over the bodies of men who had fallen hours before in futile attempts to reach Porter's trenches on the bluff beyond. Rifle fire plunged into Hood's line, tearing huge gaps in it, but his men came on, tempted to halt and shoot back but remembering his order to hold their fire.

Once across the stream, with nothing but the deadly slope left in front, Hood paused. Fix bayonets, Hood told his men, and waved his saber forward.

With fierce yells the Texans scrambled up the bluff behind Hood, many of them falling as Yankee rifle fire stabbed out at them, others returning it as quickly as they could reload and aim. Hood, saber flashing, ordered a volley, then dashed toward the first trench. Blue-clad defenders turned and ran for the one above it, but the panic was spreading. Hood's Texans paused only to fire. He raced ahead, crossing the abandoned lines, until he reached the plateau. Behind him came Law's troops and Hampton's Legion. Soon yelling Confederates were emerging all along the rim of the plateau.

Now, in the gathering darkness, confusion proliferated. Officers on both sides lost control of their men. While two federal regiments surrendered immediately and other troops ran southward, littering the ground with thrown-away weapons and knapsacks, some units formed knots of resistance. Brigades that McClellan had sent Porter arrived too late to stem the gray tide, and when Brigadier General Philip St. George Cooke's cavalry charged the Confederates, chaos was complete.

Cooke was Jeb Stuart's father-in-law, still humiliated perhaps by his inability to catch Stuart during the ride around the Army of the Potomac in mid-June. Toward the rebels Cooke sent the 2d U.S. Cavalry, Lee's old outfit and Hood's, and the 5th. But in charging, the riders got in the way of artillerymen who were about to fire. Hood's men stood firm, emptying Union saddles, stopping Cooke's horsemen and then capturing the guns.

Only on the eastern end of Porter's line was the retreat orderly. George Sykes's regulars held back Harvey Hill's men for long enough to form a rear guard, giving Porter time in which to start his withdrawal over the Grapevine Bridge.

John Hood's breakthrough had cost his brigade a thousand troops. In all, Confederate casualties that day exceeded 8,300 — almost a division. Porter lost more than 6,800 men.

It would take Lee's quartermasters three days to gather all the rifles and equipment scattered on the Watt farm's plateau, but the twenty-two guns Porter had abandoned would be turned against the Army of the Potomac the next morning.

Inadvertently, George McClellan paid a high compliment to Prince John Magruder's skill in the dramatic arts when he said in a wire to Secretary Stanton on that Friday evening:

> Have had a terrible contest—attacked by greatly superior numbers in all directions. On this [the Chickahominy's south] side we still hold our own, though a heavy fire is still kept up.
> On the left bank of the Chickahominy the odds have been immense. We hold our own very nearly. I may be forced to give up my position during the night, but will not if it is possible to avoid it. Had I (20,000) twenty thousand fresh & good troops we would be sure of a splendid victory tomorrow. My men have fought magnificently.

McClellan's last sentence was true; later, in the reports they wrote, Confederate commanders who had fought Porter's men on that grim Friday would praise their valor and the skill of their corps commander. But the Young Napoleon had to be vague in what he told Washington: McClellan had remained at Camp Lincoln all day.

Within the next two hours news of what had happened on the Watt farm's plateau must have reached the Army of the Potomac's commander, or so a wire he sent at ten-thirty P.M. to Flag Officer Louis Goldsborough indicated:

> I am obliged to fall back between the Chickahominy and the James River. I look to you to give me all the support you can, in covering my flanks as well as giving protection to my supplies afloat in the James River.

Those supplies afloat were critical now, for earlier Quartermaster Colonel Rufus Ingalls had telegraphed the officer in charge of the base at White House:

> Run the cars to the last moment, and load them with provisions and ammunition. Load every wagon you have with subsistence, and send them to Savage's Station by way of Bottom's Bridge...burn everything that you cannot get off. You must throw all our supplies up the James River as soon as is possible and accompany them yourself with all your force. It will be of vast importance to establish our depots on James River without delay....I will keep you advised of every movement so long as the wires work; after that you must exercise your own judgment.

Now, with Lee's forces north of the Chickahominy within fifteen miles of White House and no federal units to speak of in their way, Ingalls's instructions would have to be carried out. All Mc-Clellan could do was hold his ground for long enough to get his wagon trains moving on southward. That, more or less, was what he told his corps commanders before midnight that Friday—adding that Keyes's and Porter's corps would be the first to begin making what the army commander insisted was merely a change of base.

Next, McClellan prepared a telegram to Secretary Stanton:

> I now know the full history of the day. On this side of the river (the right bank) we repulsed several strong attacks. On the left bank our men did all that men could do, all that soldiers could accomplish, but they were overwhelmed by

vastly superior numbers, even after I brought my last reserves into action. The loss on both sides is terrible. I believe it will prove to be the most desperate battle of the war.

The sad remnants of my men behave as men. Those battalions who fought most bravely and suffered most are still in the best order. My regulars were superb, and I count on what are left to turn another battle, in company with their gallant comrades of the volunteers. Had I 20,000 or even 10,000 fresh troops to use to-morrow I would take Richmond, but I have not a man in reserve, and shall be glad to cover my retreat and save the material and personnel of the army.

If we have lost the day we have yet preserved our honor, and no one need blush for the Army of the Potomac. I have lost this battle because my own force was too small. I again repeat that I am not responsible for this, and I say it with the earnestness of a general who feels in his heart the loss of every brave man who has been needlessly sacrificed to-day.

I still hope to retrieve our fortunes, but to do this the Government must view the matter in the same earnest light that I do. You must send me very large reenforcements, and send them at once. I shall draw back to this side of Chick-ahominy, and I think I can withdraw all of our material. Please understand that in this battle we have lost nothing but men, and those the best we have.

In addition to what I have already said, I only wish to say to the President that I think he is wrong in regarding me as ungenerous when I said that my force was too weak. I merely intimated a truth which to-day has been too plainly proved. If, at this instant, I could dispose of 10,000 fresh men, I could gain a victory tommorrow. I know that a few thousand more men would have changed this battle from a defeat to a victory. As it is, the Government must not and cannot hold me responsible for the result.

I feel too earnestly to-night. I have seen too many dead and wounded comrades to feel otherwise than that the Government has not sustained this army. If you do not do so now the game is lost.

If I save this army now, I tell you plainly that I owe no thanks to you or to any other persons in Washington.

You have done your best to sacrifice this army.

On Saturday, June 28, when General McClellan's message

reached the War Department, an alert duty officer took it to his supervisor, Edward S. Sanford, earlier president of the American Telegraph Company. On his own responsibility, suspecting treason in McClellan's last two sentences—"If I save this army now, I tell you plainly that I owe no thanks to you or to any other persons in Washington" and "You have done your best to sacrifice this army"— Sanford deleted them.

Chapter 11

The Beginning's Deplorable Ending

For most of Lee's army Saturday was a time for collecting the last of the wounded, burying the dead, regrouping, and resting. Lee sent Jeb Stuart's cavalry eastward to White House; Ewell's division moved along the Chickahominy's north bank in support. Pursuing Porter was impossible: Yankees had burned Grapevine Bridge, and federal gunfire kept Lee's engineers from rebuilding it. And east of Richmond, according to reports from Magruder and Huger, McClellan's forces were making no threats.

By late Saturday afternoon General Lee had indications, at least, that the next fight would be south of the Chickahominy. Ewell and Stuart had encountered no significant opposition. And across the river from the Watt farm's plateau a plume of smoke was rising. Intermittent explosions added to Lee's supposition that McClellan was burning the stockpiles of supplies he could not carry off. But it was too late in the day to start units southward over New Bridge, so Magruder and Huger would have to spend another night—their third—intimidating McClellan.

Before dawn on Sunday morning two of Lee's engineers crossed the Chickahominy on a raft, reconnoitered the federal shore and probed southward, then reported that the Yankees were gone. That clinched it: Lee, leaving Stuart and Ewell where they were and Jackson to rebuild the Grapevine Bridge, told Magruder to pursue McClellan's rear guard; he sent Huger on a road farther to the south to press "those people" as they made their way through White Oak Swamp. Powell Hill and Longstreet faced a longer march, one intended to trap McClellan.

Since Thursday afternoon at Mechanicsville General Lee had been improvising plans, all of which were sound in concept but few—as it had turned out—within the capabilities of his subordinates to execute. And so it was again on that Sunday.

Magruder, exhausted from his days and nights of stage-managing Richmond's defense, finally drove the Yankees back to Savage Station on the York River Railroad. There elements of three Union corps made a stand while more supplies were moved and the rest burned. Heavy rain began to fall as the sharp fight ended. Huger, having achieved nothing, went into camp.

For George McClellan's Army of the Potomac that Sunday night was similar to Hernán Cortés's *noche triste*, in Mexico in 1520, when the *conquistador* had been compelled to retreat in the rainy darkness along a narrow causeway from Tenochtitlán, pursued by Aztecs. Behind him at Savage Station the Union commander had left about 2,500 of his wounded men in a field hospital: Cortés had pressed on, powerless to save 700 of his 1,300 troops. And like Cortés, McClellan knew nothing about what would happen next, for although the Army of the Potomac had been in the area for many weeks, the Young Napoleon had not sent scouts out to reconnoiter routes to the James's banks.

McClellan's immediate problem on his army's *noche triste* was to get through White Oak Swamp, a boggy northward-flowing tributary of the Chickahominy crossed by two roads, though he was aware of only one. Over its bridge he had to cram a herd of 2,500 slow-moving beef cattle, perhaps 3,600 wagons and 700 ambulances, and most of his 100,000 troops and their artillery.

"A commander should not abandon his line of operations," wrote the real Napoleon in his *Maxims*, "but one of the most skillful maneuvers in war is to know how to change it when circumstances demand it." For days, notably in his wires to Flag Officer Goldsborough, McClellan had been implying a change of base might be necessary. Now that the need was upon him, however, Little Mac had only the skill of his subordinates on which to rely—unless Robert E. Lee made a mistake.

On Monday morning, June 30, once again General Lee was improvising. Once again his plan called for Powell Hill and James Longstreet to get south of McClellan's supposed position while Huger and Magruder struck the federal army's flanks from the west and Jackson pressed southward through White Oak Swamp from the north, driving Yankees before him so that the Confederate divisions below might destroy them.

No long marches were involved, only obedience and closer communication. Lee received neither on that Monday.

Jackson, always reluctant to mar the Sabbath, had done next to nothing on Sunday toward repairing Grapevine Bridge, disappointing Magruder, who could have used his presence in the fight at Savage Station. Early on Monday morning he appeared briefly at Magruder's headquarters, had another conversation with General Lee, then vanished eastward. No one would see or hear much more of Jackson on that Monday except for members of his staff. He had not seemed his usual self for days. True, at moments his familiar spark glowed—late on Friday, as Hood was making his charge, Jackson had told all his commanders: "Sweep the field with the bayonet!"—but the men sitting at the supper table with him on that Monday evening grew alarmed anew when Old Jack seemed to fall asleep right after he had put the edge of a biscuit into his mouth.

General Lee's other forces would accomplish little that day, though some stabbed hard into McClellan's flank late in the afternoon near Frayser's Farm or Glendale or Riddell's Shop—in any case a crossroads where the federals held off repeated Confederate thrusts. The fighting was as intense as any back at the Watt farm's plateau on Friday, except that this time there had been no breakthrough. And Jackson had disappointed everyone by not coming down through White Oak Swamp from the north.

Something most unusual was happening, though no one would realize it until much later. General Lee was overdrawing his fund of energy to get his divisions within striking range of McClellan's army but failing consistently. Concurrently, the federal forces were eluding Lee's successive traps mainly through the efforts of leaders who worked things out for themselves, as though certain they would get no direction from McClellan.

On Sunday, for example, as the fight at Savage Station was nearing a critical point, a Union corps commander had to send an aide southward to find the army commander, get instructions, and bring them back. The order was to withdraw. In carrying it out, some of the units used a hidden road discovered only through the initiative of another corps commander.

On Monday morning, General McClellan did spend some time with his subordinates at Glendale. Before Lee's forces threatened the Union lines, though, he rode away—and did not return. After inspecting Malvern Hill, down on the James near the area where the wagons were being parked as they arrived from the north, McClellan boarded the gunboat *Galena* for a ride upriver to shell a column of Confederate troops moving eastward.

The *Galena*'s target that evening was a division General Lee had ordered Brigadier General Theophilus H. Holmes to bring over from the James's south bank to help in the effort to trap McClellan. At one point Lee had been with the newcomers, for his cavalrymen had reported that Porter and Keyes were busy fortifying Malvern Hill. Lee had been to all his other divisions except Jackson's that Monday afternoon as well, urging them forward, correcting mistakes, doing his best to keep any more of "those people" from reaching Malvern Hill. And among many other things, again Lee had been obliged to tell President Davis he should not be in such a dangerous place; Powell Hill ordered both Lee and Davis away.

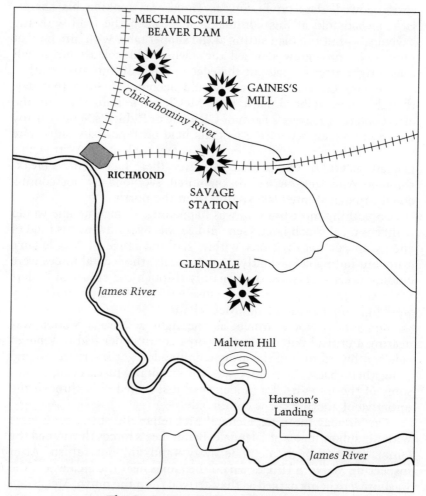

The Seven Days End at Malvern Hill

Lee's blows were not as hard as he wished, and he threw them late, but they gave the three federal corps commanders at Glendale—operating independently, for McClellan had not left anyone in charge—a fight they almost lost. Valor, mostly, saved the absent McClellan from utter defeat. Yet Frayser's Farm, as the Confederates would later call the battle, was in Lee's mind the bitterest of disappointments; so close had he come to a stunning victory, only to see the sun set on another failure.

By dawn on Tuesday morning, July 1, both armies had just about run out of maneuvering space. McClellan had reached the James. Engineer Barnard and Fitz-John Porter were fortifying Malvern Hill. And Lee could not strike southeastward for as long as federal troops controlled such a dominant position, apart from the fact that his forces were still too scattered near Glendale for him to get them back in hand quickly.

"Save your Army at all events," President Lincoln had told General McClellan in a much-relayed message. That was what Little Mac had been doing, mostly, since Wednesday evening, when news of Jackson's approach reached him. All his orders from that moment onward suggested that he no longer meant to seize Richmond. He was, instead, changing his base; yet only on Monday afternoon, when the *Galena*'s commander had shown him Harrison's Landing, seven miles or so downstream from Malvern Hill, had he known where the new one would be.

Now, on Tuesday, McClellan's wagon trains were moving south-eastward to his army's destination. So was he, back on the *Galena* by midmorning. Barnard and Porter, he knew from a brief inspection ride, were busy completing the task they had started the day before—creating a fortress along Malvern Hill's crest, their backs to the James River about a mile to the south, their effort strengthened now by the three corps that had withdrawn from the Glendale fight after no orders to the contrary had come from the Army of the Potomac's commander.

At Harrison's Landing General McClellan went ashore, rode over the plantation, found it to his liking, then reboarded the *Galena*. "I pray that the enemy may not be in condition to disturb us today," he had wired earlier to Fort Monroe. As the gunboat neared Malvern Hill in midafternoon, though, McClellan was about to learn that his prayer would not be answered.

Actually, neither the Army of Northern Virginia nor its commanding general were in condition to fight that Tuesday. For nearly a week Lee had been under enormous strain. On the previous Wednesday the skirmish at Oak Grove had threatened to wreck his plan; everything had gone wrong on Thursday at Mechanicsville; Friday's attacks along Boatswain's Swamp had succeeded only at the last possible moment, and Saturday's respite was all too brief; then, on Sunday and Monday, the pursuit had failed despite the sharp fights at Savage Station and Frayser's Farm.

That Lee's calm had its limits became apparent on Tuesday morning, near Glendale, when Brigadier General Jubal A. Early said something about McClellan's escape. "Yes," snapped Lee, "he will get away because I cannot get my orders carried out!"

Lee asked Longstreet to stay with him. At Willis Church they found Harvey Hill, who repeated a description of Malvern Hill a native of the area had given him. "If General McClellan is there in strength," he added, "we had better let him alone."

"Don't get scared," said Longstreet, "now that we have got him whipped."

Leaving McClellan alone was beyond Lee. Malvern Hill was less than three miles to the south. He sent Jackson and Magruder toward it; the rest of the army would follow once the road was clear. Lee and Longstreet rode behind Jackson.

In some ways, they discovered, Malvern Hill resembled the Watt farm's plateau. Again there was a creek line that would have to be crossed, and again the federals had positioned their troops to take full advantage of the terrain. This time, though, the Union commanders had massed all their artillery on the hill.

General Lee could see that Jackson was placing his units astride the road north of the creek, but he was unaware that Magruder had gone astray. All Lee could do at the moment was hunt for some way of getting around Malvern Hill. He sent Longstreet to scout the possibilities west of Willis Church Road; Lee rode eastward, but not very far.

Longstreet returned with an idea. He had found a place west of Jackson's line, where Lee meant for Magruder to go in, that was ideal for artillery. Jackson had another good site in his sector. Fire from both positions could converge on the Yankees' fortress, destroying their guns and opening the way for infantry to assault the survivors.

Let bombardment be tried, Lee ordered. Longstreet left to direct the preparations at the site he had located; Jackson moved guns eastward. Lee, thinking ahead, told his adjutant to prepare a message and send it by couriers to troop commanders. Colonel Robert Chilton wrote:

Batteries have been established to rake the enemy's lines. If it is broken, as is probable, Armistead, who can witness the effect of the fire, has been ordered to charge with a yell. Do the same.

Brigadier General Lewis Armistead, whose men were to do the first yelling, was westernmost in Lee's line. He had drawn federal gunfire in approaching from the northwest; soon his men were skirmishing with Yankees.

Colonel Henry J. Hunt, commanding the Army of the Potomac's massed artillery, had watched the Confederates building their line during the morning. At times, he had ordered his gunners to shell the area. By early afternoon he saw rebel guns being put into positions in two clearings. Hunt quickly shifted his fire, and almost as quickly the distant batteries disappeared.

Never before had so much federal firepower been employed. Some of it, ready to fire canister at assaulting infantrymen, was well down the open slope. Along the crest Hunt had about eighty guns nearly hub to hub. Behind Malvern Hill's crest were fourteen siege guns. And on the James the navy's gunboats were standing by, prepared to cover the army's flanks if Lee tried to get around either one or both.

Fitz-John Porter's infantry line began at Malvern Hill's western edge, a bluff. East of Porter were Sumner's corps and Heintzelman's, and Franklin's divisions were east of them.

General McClellan made no changes in the deployment when he returned in midafternoon from Harrison's Landing. After leaving Porter in charge of the hill's western defenses, the army commander rode about two miles eastward to a position from which he could hear Henry Hunt's guns.

"I cannot get my orders carried out!" General Lee had said to Jubal Early. Now, ironically, one commander after another executed the instructions he had told Chilton to send them. It was as though everyone—even Lee—had forgotten that the yelling and the charging were to take place only after Lewis Armistead saw that the bombardment had succeeded. It had never even gotten started, but Armistead's brigade was yelling and fighting anyway, and by late afternoon his men and some from other units were near enough to Porter's lines to force Colonel Hunt to move a few guns.

Magruder sent troops up toward Armistead, as did Harvey Hill and later Ewell, committing them piecemeal, only to see them blasted by the murderous federal artillery fire. Calls for reinforcements brought few responses; some units trying to advance were blocked by stragglers and streams of wounded men or delayed by the underbrush and vines in the creek bed.

Still Armistead's men and the brigades with him fought on, making assault after assault, sometimes getting within revolver range of Hunt's gunners, until it was too dark to do more than hold their ground—which they did. Behind them, troops that had tried to reach them could no longer see Yankees to shoot.

Confusion had prevailed all day, and it would continue as the Confederate commanders tried to reassemble their shattered units. Cries of wounded men filled the evening air now that the Union guns were silent. Tuesday's fight was over.

Fitz-John Porter sent a message to General McClellan in which he reported his victory, adding that if resupplied with ammunition and reinforced, "we will hold our ground and advance if you wish." Porter was too late. McClellan had already ordered the withdrawal of the army to Harrison's Landing.

Brigadier General Philip Kearny could not believe it. Kearny had lost an arm at Mexico City and fought again on the French side in Italy afterward, and on this Tuesday his men had held off Harvey Hill's charges.

"I, Philip Kearny, an old soldier," he told his staff, "enter my solemn protest against this order for retreat. We ought instead of retreating to follow up the enemy and take Richmond. And in full view of the responsibility for such a declaration, I say to you all, such an order can only be prompted by cowardice or treason."

At Malvern Hill, General Lee had lost another 6,000 men, the federals, perhaps 2,000. During the series of battles that would become known as the Seven Days, more than 36,000 young Americans had been killed, wounded, or captured—a total far surpassing any previous clashing of the armies.

For General Lee the outcome was a deep disappointment. He had lost all the Seven Days' engagements but one, taking very heavy losses in the process; silently he had endured disappointments as Jackson failed time and again to perform as ordered; now he would have to remove leaders who had proved unreliable in open warfare, among them Prince John Magruder, to whom he owed much; and— most crushing of all his regrets—he had failed to destroy McClellan's army.

True, yet Lee had driven a far superior force more than twenty miles southeast of Richmond and confined it to the limits of Harrison's Landing's defenses. Along the way quartermasters had picked up vast quantities of rifles, ammunition, equipment, even batteries of badly needed artillery. And in the midst of his remorse he may have overlooked something perhaps of more importance than anything else: though in command for less than a month, despite his age and inexperience and failures earlier, he had demonstrated that he could lead men in battle.

That Robert E. Lee would have more battles to fight was one 'ironic result of his success. During the Seven Days' Battle, and stimulated in part by McClellan's oft-repeated warnings of disaster, Abraham Lincoln had set in motion an effort to get fresh troops. This was not easy; months earlier, in a moment of overconfidence, Secretary Stanton had closed recruiting offices, only to find results discouraging when Jackson's Valley campaign forced him to reopen them; and, understandably, governors would find it awkward to call more men to the colors at a time when McClellan was being driven away from Richmond and casualty lists were growing longer.

The Union's president sent Secretary of State Seward to New York, armed with a letter to the governors meeting there. In it Lincoln set forth the military situation and asked for 100,000 additional troops, adding in conclusion:

> I expect to maintain this contest until successful, or till I die, or am conquered, or my term expires, or Congress or the country forsake me; and I would publicly appeal to the country for this new force, were it not that I fear a general panic and stampede would follow—so hard it is to have a thing understood as it really is.

Drawing upon the president's candor, Seward persuaded the governors to sign an appeal he put before them, one in which *they* urged Lincoln to call upon the states to provide as many volunteers as final victory might require. Thereupon Lincoln, on Wednesday, July 2, responded. He asked for 300,000 troops.

"So hard it is to have a thing understood as it really is," Lincoln had said, and his words summed up the challenge George McClellan faced on that rainy Wednesday when he sat down at Harrison's Landing to write a message to the president. "I have not yielded an inch of ground unnecessarily," he said near the close, "but have retired to prevent the superior force of the enemy from cutting me off and to take a different base of operations."

So General McClellan believed, though the true magnitude of his defeat would soon become apparent. Yet, for the rest of his life, he would go on trying to make others believe that during the Seven Days he had merely changed his base.

PART TWO

Audacity's Noontime

Chapter 12

Moves on a Huge Chessboard

Ⅰt took a while for the impact of the Seven Days to be felt in the North, partly because General McClellan had sent newspaper reporters away from the Army of the Potomac before the fighting began. Gradually, however, the grim truth emerged. When it did, people throughout the Union were first stunned and then enraged.

Richmond's fate was supposed to have been something like Corinth's, where Union Major General Halleck had massed more than 100,000 troops and merely kept pressing southward until Beauregard recognized the futility of defending any longer and skedaddled. Now, suddenly, unbelievably, the powerful Army of the Potomac was penned up on the bank of the James River more than twenty miles southeast of Richmond. McClellan maintained that he had not been beaten, only that he had failed to win, yet long casualty lists raised a disturbing question: If he had merely been changing his base, why had nearly 16,000 Union soldiers been killed, wounded, or captured?

Even Lincoln, as prepared as anyone in the North for the answer, was shocked and saddened anew on July 3 when Brigadier General Randolph Marcy, McClellan's chief of staff and father-in-law, told him the full story. Marcy, there to plead for 50,000 reinforcements, added that he would not be astonished if the army were obliged to capitulate. "That," snapped Lincoln, "is a word not to be used in connection with our army."

Treason was the cause of the disaster, Radical Republican congressmen were alleging. They and others cried out for the South to be punished in every conceivable manner. Pressure intensified to make abolition of slavery a war aim.

All of this and more reflected frustration—and ignorance, for everyone seemed to agree with McClellan that Lee must have had 200,000 men. How else could Lee have driven the Army of the Potomac so far away from Richmond and given it such a heavy mauling?

Fear, too, was embedded in the Union's reaction. If Lee had 200,000 troops, what could stop him from taking Washington? John Pope's new Army of Virginia? Perhaps; but Pope had only 43,000 men, and they were not yet in positions from which they could block a Confederate advance northward.

Clearly something had to be done—by McClellan, or about him or to him. It was up to Lincoln either to get the Army of the Potomac moving again or sack its commander. But he could do nothing without finding out for himself what the situation really was; so, shortly after the Fourth of July observances, he boarded the steamer *Ariel* and headed for Harrison's Landing.

But nothing much was wrong with the Army of the Potomac, the Union's president discovered soon after he arrived. If anything, he was surprised to find survivors of the Seven Days resting and refitting in such a pleasant haven. Some of the questions he had brought down on the *Ariel* evoked less than reassuring answers: On whether the Army of the Potomac ought to stay and renew the fight, Lincoln's main concern, McClellan's corps commanders were divided. McClellan said he thought withdrawing his forces would be a delicate and very difficult maneuver; he was silent regarding any plans.

As the president was about to depart, however, McClellan handed him a letter in which he set forth his views on policies the Union ought to follow in the conduct of the war. Among other things, Lincoln read: "Neither confiscation of property, political executions of persons, territorial organization of states or forcible abolition of slavery should be contemplated for a moment."

Much of which, the visiting president knew, Congress was not only contemplating but seemed hell-bent on incorporating in new laws. Lincoln thanked the general, folded the letter and put it in his pocket, and never said another word about it.

Although the president accomplished very little by going to Harrison's Landing—ironically, military matters had been uppermost in the politician's mind, while politics preoccupied the general—the trip may have convinced Lincoln that it was time he disentangled himself from the vexing problems McClellan created. In any event, on July 11 he appointed Henry Halleck general-in-chief of the Union armies.

General Halleck had deep misgivings about leaving the war in the west, exchanging what he thought he understood for "the quarrels of Stanton and McClellan"—or so he told friends. For all their many differences, Ulysses Grant was sorry to see Halleck go. "He is a man of gigantic intellect and well studied in the profession of arms," he wrote Congressman Elihu Washburne. And Sherman protested in a letter to Halleck, who had restored him to usefulness after the insanity accusations:

> The man who at the end of this war holds the military control of the Valley of the Mississippi will be the man....Instead of that calm, sure, steady progress which has dismayed the enemy, I now fear alarms, hesitations and doubt. You cannot be replaced here and it is too great a risk to trust a new man from the East.

Halleck's critics, however, had already been dismayed by his failure to do anything much with his huge army after he had intimidated Beauregard into abandoning Corinth. Old Brains had in fact scattered it, sending Sherman westward to Memphis and Buell east to take Chattanooga; such uses for his troops seemed preferable to wearing out a concentrated force either pursuing Beauregard or moving toward Vicksburg during Mississippi's hot and humid summer. But if the rebels surprised him by starting an active campaign, Halleck had told Stanton, he would change his dispositions accordingly.

Now it would be up to Grant to watch the Confederates. But his new command did not include East Tennessee, Don Carlos Buell's objective, which may have been Halleck's first mistake as general-in-chief.

Jefferson Davis took advantage of the lull after the Seven Days' battles by trying to make something happen in the west. General Beauregard, citing illness, turned command of his forces at Tupelo over to Braxton Bragg, saving Davis the embarrassment of having to relieve Sumter's hero. But Bragg needed more men. None were available. Could audacity make up for them?

Perhaps, but as Jackson had proved, audacity was not something anyone could rely upon. Worse, there was nothing in Braxton Bragg's style of leadership to suggest that he would do anything bold. Like McClellan, Bragg was good at whipping raw troops into soldiers and restoring their morale after a defeat. But he seemed as content to remain at Tupelo as Little Mac was to relax in his captivity at Harrison's Landing. Bragg offered Davis no plans, only requests for more men and wagons.

Fortunately for the Confederate president, however, there was another small force in East Tennessee under the command of Major General Edmund Kirby Smith. At Manassas a year before he had helped win that battle by leading his just-arrived brigade into the thick of the fighting at precisely the right moment. And having tasted glory once, Kirby Smith wanted more.

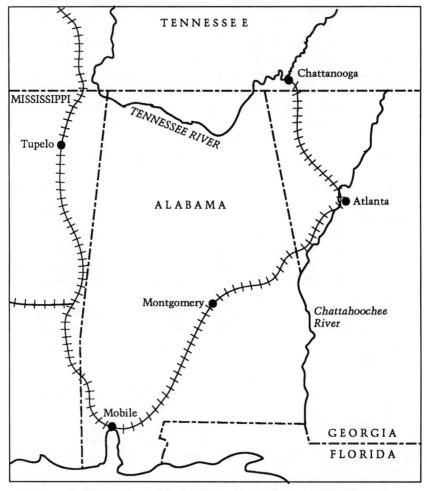

Western Battle Area

Eastern Kentucky was on his mind, and on Colonel John Hunt Morgan's as well. Early in July, Morgan took his cavalry northwestward from Knoxville into his home state, striking federal supply points and destroying railroad tracks and bridges. (One day Morgan captured a telegraph office and had his own operator send messages to confuse the Union forces pursuing him, making them think his

900 troopers were 5,000 and causing General Buell to halt his advance toward Chattanooga.) By mid-July, Morgan had gone as far north as Frankfort and Lexington. And though his sweep had been only a series of sharp hit-and-run raids, Morgan had proved that federal units in eastern Kentucky were more vulnerable than anyone had believed.

Concurrently, Colonel Nathan Bedford Forrest was rampaging in central Tennessee. With about 1,200 men he rode westward from Chattanooga on July 9; on the thirteenth he captured the federal garrison at Murfreesboro, then moved northward to threaten Nashville. Time and again Forrest led charges into Yankee positions, gathered weapons and supplies and sent them eastward in wagons driven by prisoners, then eluded federal pursuers by taking little-used roads—once a dry creek bed.

These displays of audacity impressed General Bragg enough to show some of his own. Earlier he had sent a brigade up to reinforce Kirby Smith's men in Chattanooga, and he had done it by rail from Tupelo southward to Mobile, then via Montgomery and Atlanta. Now he would send most of his troops over the same 776-mile route, using six rail lines, leaving behind two detachments to watch Vicksburg and northern Mississippi while he and Kirby Smith first destroyed Buell's divisions and then rescued East Tennessee and Kentucky from Yankee occupation.

Morgan and Forrest had captured Halleck's attention, too, but figuring out what to do with McClellan's army had a higher priority. Soon after the new general-in-chief arrived in Washington he found himself on a steamer bound for Harrison's Landing. And behind him he had left a situation that might prove as vexing as the one involving McClellan.

John Pope was the cause. On assuming command of the Army of Virginia, the general had issued a proclamation intended to inspire his troops:

> I have come to you from the West, where we have always seen the backs of our enemies; from an army whose business it has been to seek the adversary and to beat him when he was found; whose policy has been attack and not defense....I desire you to dismiss from your minds certain phrases, which I am sorry to find so much in vogue amongst you. I hear constantly of "taking strong positions and holding them," of "lines of retreat," and of "bases of supplies."...Let us look before us, and not behind. Success and glory are in the advance, disaster and shame lurk in the rear.

All Pope's bombast inspired, though, was ridicule. Fitz-John Porter wrote a friend that he regretted that the general "has not improved since his youth and has now written himself down what the military world has long known, an ass." Pope's troops resented the newcomer's slurs toward easterners. His implied criticisms of McClellan evoked sympathy for Little Mac even from those who had recently been denouncing him.

There was much irony in all this. Stanton, not Pope, had supplied the counterproductive language. But Pope would have to live with it, and more. "Headquarters in the Saddle," his messages began, prompting Confederates to quip that he had his headquarters where his hindquarters ought to be.

And as if to underscore the difference between his style of warfare and McClellan's, on July 18—four days after the harangue to his troops—Pope (again assisted by Stanton) issued a series of orders calling for his soldiers to live off the land they invaded, to force Virginians within a five-mile radius of any guerrilla-type damages to railroads or telegraphs to repair them, and to subject civilians to an unprecedented degree of military coercion, with death by shooting among the penalties for disobedience.

Southerners found those orders proof of Yankee depravity. Lee termed Pope a "miscreant" who had to be "suppressed."

If General Halleck assumed that McClellan viewed Pope in much the same way, he was correct. His host at Harrison's Landing was in a nasty mood in any case. "A slap in the face," McClellan had called Halleck's appointment when he read about it in a newspaper. To a friend in New York he had written, on July 15:

> I do not care if they do remove [me] from this Army— except on account of the Army itself. I have lost all regard & respect for the majority of the Administration, & doubt the propriety of my brave men's blood being spilled to further the designs of such a set of heartless villains.

To Halleck, however, McClellan said merely that he would cross the James River, seize Petersburg, cut the railroads on which Richmond was depending, and take the capital—provided he got massive reinforcements, meaning Pope's troops. No, the general-in-chief told him, only 20,000 could be sent. That would do, McClellan replied.

Halleck returned to Washington with deep misgivings. And soon a message from McClellan arrived: Twenty thousand reinforcements would not be enough. Sending troops to him, Lincoln had said, was like trying to shovel fleas across a barn lot. And to

Attorney General Bates the president remarked that if he gave McClellan 200,000 men, the general would wire the next day that he could not possibly advance because Lee had 400,000.

Now a decision had to be made. Whatever their size, Lee's forces were between Pope and McClellan. Pope's new army, even with reinforcements being added, would still be too small to assure Washington's safety. Concentration, then, was the only remedy: McClellan would have to abandon the Peninsular campaign and return to northern Virginia.

So General-in-Chief Halleck ordered, on August 3.

And on August 8, McClellan wrote his wife:

> Their game is to force me to resign—mine will be to force them to place me on leave of absence, so that when they reap the whirlwind they have sown I may still be in position to do something to save my country.

That whirlwind was in the making, both in Washington and in Richmond, and soon its funnels would combine. But its origins were different in ways other than in location.

Slavery, the sin of long-dead fathers, a proximate cause of the war, put spin on the Northern twister after the Seven Days' Battles. Congress, in its frustration, had tried to achieve through legislation what the president had said he was not ready to do: abolish the "peculiar institution."

During the four months he had been acting as the Union armies' general-in-chief, Lincoln had learned that restoring the Union to what it had been earlier, his and the Congress's only stated goal, might not be attainable unless he could find some new way to retain and enhance both public and military support. Moreover, astute politician that he was, Lincoln recognized the need for action on his part to protect his presidency from Radical congressional usurpation.

The idea of offering money to rid border states of slavery having been ignored and after Northern black leaders gave his resettlement plan a cool reception, Lincoln began considering emancipation by presidential decree as a viable alternative to doing nothing. While in a carriage on the way to the funeral of the Stantons' infant child, he told Secretary of State Seward and Navy Secretary Gideon Welles that he had "about come to the conclusion" that he would either have to free the slaves or lose the war. Did Seward and Welles, Lincoln asked, agree?

Emancipation was too momentous a step to take without more thought, replied Seward. Welles concurred. Then, for days afterward, the president used Major Eckert's desk in the War Department's telegraph office on which to draft a proclamation. This was in the middle of July, at about the same time General Pope was issuing draconian orders to punish Southern civilians, and it may be the reason Lincoln let them stand. "I shall not surrender this game leaving any available card unplayed," he wrote a friend on July 22, the day on which he also finished getting his decision regarding emancipation on paper.

And later on that day the president read the product to his cabinet, asking only for their comments. Seward's was the only one that mattered: "I suggest, sir, that you postpone its issue until you can give it to the country supported by military success, instead of issuing it, as would be the case now, upon the greatest disasters of the war."

Lincoln agreed. But when would military success come?

That depended on how soon the Northern whirlwind met the one gathering momentum around Richmond and on what happened when they did. General Lee and his president agreed that the calm following the Seven Days was temporary. Less clear to them, however, was whether to use such combat power as Lee had against the "miscreant" Pope or the curiously inert McClellan.

At first, Lee used the lull to give his troops some rest and to simplify the army's command structure. Now he would rely mainly on Longstreet and Jackson, in effect making them corps commanders, and on Stuart. And since he would have to strip Richmond of defenders if he launched another offensive, Lee ordered the city's fortifications strengthened.

Jackson, cured now of the acute fatigue that had plagued him since he left the Shenandoah Valley, was eager to attack the forces Pope was sending southward. Lee reserved judgment. Discussing this one day with Congressman Alex Boteler, Jackson made it clear that he was not complaining about Lee's silence. "With the vast responsibilities now resting upon him, he is perfectly right in withholding a hasty expression of his opinions and purposes," he said, then added: "So great is my confidence in General Lee that I am willing to follow him blindfolded."

McClellan's presence at Harrison's Landing was one reason for Lee's hesitancy. But on July 12 the army commander learned that Pope was occupying Culpeper, only twenty-seven miles from the vital Virginia Central Railroad at Gordonsville. The next day, Lee sent Jackson's two divisions northward—by rail.

For the next week or so General Lee weighed all the facts he had regarding Pope's activities north of Richmond and those of Mc-

Clellan to the southeast. But there was a third force, Ambrose Burnside's, more difficult to watch because it was on ships awaiting orders. Then Lee learned that those troops would not be sent to McClellan, and he began to think in terms of "suppressing" Pope before anyone could reinforce him. So matters stood on the morning of August 7 when he gave Jackson discretion as to whether he should attack Pope's forces with such troops as he had.

Jackson, meanwhile, had learned that Pope's leading units were moving toward him. He began marching northward before Lee's message arrived, and by noon on August 9 his men were near Cedar Mountain—also known as Slaughter Mountain—a hill roughly halfway between Culpeper and Gordonsville.

"I am not making much progress," Jackson admitted in a wire to Lee. The heat that Saturday was scorching, the roads dusty, the ground ahead unfamiliar. Jubal Early's brigade got past Cedar Mountain's northwestern shoulder, then halted: Union cavalrymen, the Confederates saw, were waiting in a line across wheat and corn fields, artillery pieces spotted nearby, with infantrymen coming up rapidly.

Now it was as though the commanders on both sides were more mindful of the recent past than they were of the present. Jackson, lethargic during the Seven Days, rashly ordered his troops to attack before he had much of a grasp of the situation, and Nathaniel Banks, perhaps recalling Pope's admonition that "success and glory are in the advance" and knowing he was facing the man who had humiliated him in the Shenandoah Valley, threw his 8,000 men at Jackson's 24,000.

Success was Jackson's first, then Banks smashed part of the Confederate line. For the first time in the war Old Jack drew his saber, rallying his troops, shouting, "Follow me!" Yet, by sundown, both generals' forces were about where they had been before the shooting had started.

Cedar Mountain settled nothing at considerable cost—roughly 2,500 federal casualties, 1,400 Confederate—but, like Kernstown back in March, the battle foreshadowed violence to come. Pope had meant for Banks merely to hold his position while he got the rest of the Army of Virginia concentrated. To this extent, Banks succeeded. Jackson could claim victory only in that he occupied the devastated corn and wheat fields for two more days, long enough to bury the dead. But he had also given General Lee a little more time in which to decide what to do with the remainder of the Army of Northern Virginia.

Lee started Longstreet's divisions toward Gordonsville on August 13. The next day, he learned that the withdrawal of McClellan's

Army of the Potomac from Harrison's Landing was beginning, and this spurred Lee into a race of sorts: Pope *could* be suppressed—if Lee could force the "miscreant" to give battle before any of those reinforcements reached him.

Now it seemed as though all the pieces on the war's vast chessboard were moving at the same time. Clearly the shifting around meant that a new phase of the struggle was beginning.

This was not at all the way things were supposed to have worked out. Northern war weariness was reflected in the sullen response to Lincoln's call for 300,000 more volunteers and in resistance to moves toward conscription. Was restoring the Union really worth still more sacrifice?

Southerners, too, felt the strain. Protecting Texas had been A. W. Sparks's motivation in 1861 when he enlisted in the Titus County "Grays." But the fighting he had been in was in northwestern Arkansas, at Pea Ridge, and by the summer of 1862 he was in Vicksburg, Mississippi. So it surely was with other men whose loyalties to their states far surpassed any notions of serving the vague and amorphous blob called the Confederacy. The farther away from their own homes Southerners could kill Yankees, men such as Sparks may have reasoned, the better. But this was soldier logic, understandably unconvincing to families of those now buried at distant places unheard of earlier and hard to find on any map: Manassas, Shiloh, Gaines's Mill.

Some Southern governors sent protests to President Davis in which they alleged infringements of states' rights. Others asked for kinds of support the central government could not provide. Inflation crippled everyone. Granted, independence seemed attainable. But was it truly worth the cost?

In mid-1862 the only thing that seemed likely to upset the balance of military power was foreign intervention. All along the British and French had been scanning news of the war raging in America, but after the Seven Days' Battles their interest intensified.

At the outset, most foreign observers expected the war to be won by the Union within a few months, certainly before the huge stocks of cotton in European warehouses could be depleted. Thereafter, defeated Southerners would be eager to sell their white gold for any price they could get. Government policies toward the Confederacy seemed based on this theory—hence the failures of Jefferson Davis's emissaries in London and Paris to accomplish anything toward their goal, diplomatic recognition.

By August 1862, however, conditions on both sides of the North Atlantic had changed remarkably. Confederate farmers near enough to deal with Yankee buyers were getting top prices for the cotton they sold, burning the rest. And in the British midlands closings of textile mills were forcing 150,000 laid-off workers to press Her Majesty's government to do *something*.

Tracking the various armies' movements would be almost as difficult for Americans as for policymakers an ocean away, in part because so many events would be happening concurrently in Virginia and Tennessee. In the east, Lee was stirring. John Pope was about to demonstrate whether his generalship exceeded his (and Stanton's) bombast. And how quickly could McClellan's army reinforce Pope's?

West of Virginia's Shenandoah Valley distances were vast, both sides' forces widely dispersed. No commander out there had the glamour of a Lee or a Little Mac. Nothing decisive seemed likely to occur, given the Union armies' possession of rivers and rail lines stretching southward from the Ohio River through Kentucky into western and central Tennessee.

Lincoln considered it imperative for Don Carlos Buell to take Chattanooga, move northeastward to Knoxville, and free East Tennessee's Unionists from Confederate oppression. But Forrest's and Morgan's raids in July had made General Buell more cautious than ever, reminding him of his dependence on 285 miles of railroad track for supplies now that the hot and very dry summer had left both the Tennessee and Cumberland rivers too shallow for steamboats to reach him.

Haunting Buell, surely, was the memory of how Morgan had shut down the Louisville & Nashville Railroad. Confederate cavalrymen had shoved flaming boxcars into a tunnel to burn away the supporting timbers; the tunnel collapsed, and so, too, for a time, did Buell's advance. Only by posting small detachments at the rail line's hundreds of vulnerable places could the federal general counter such threats. But for how long, unless Halleck sent him reinforcements, could Buell both guard his troops' long lifeline and still remain strong enough to take Chattanooga, assuming he could ever get there?

Preventing Buell from reaching his first goal was up to the rather jittery Edmund Kirby Smith, commanding general for the Confederate Department of East Tennessee, headquartered in Knoxville, who had only 9,000 men—including troops Bragg had sent him—in Chattanooga's defense lines. Not knowing that Bragg was already in the process of moving the major portion of his forces there, Smith had written him on July 24 to suggest precisely the action Bragg was taking and also to propose the merging of their forces to drive the Yankees out of central Tennessee and possibly even Kentucky. Smith, technically not subject to Bragg's orders though junior by far to him in rank, underscored this by offering to serve as his subordinate in such a campaign.

Buell was stalled roughly twenty miles west of Chattanooga at the end of July when Bragg's infantrymen reached there after their 776-mile train ride from Tupelo, via Mobile and Atlanta. General Bragg was with them. Kirby Smith hurried down from Knoxville to confer with him.

On August 1 Bragg reported to Richmond the conclusions he and Smith had reached during their talks. In essence, they agreed that Smith would move northeastward from Knoxville and try to remove the federal force at Cumberland Gap while Bragg waited in Chattanooga for his horse-drawn artillery and wagon trains to arrive from Tupelo. Thereafter, Bragg's and Smith's combined forces would destroy Buell's army in central Tennessee while the units Bragg had left behind in Mississippi attacked Grant in western Tennessee. With the fragments of the federal army Halleck had brought to Corinth eliminated, the way into Kentucky would be open.

All of this was appealing, even exciting. But Richmond could do little or nothing to help, and the command situation in the west was muddled. Though Earl Van Dorn and Sterling Price were Bragg's subordinates, they were inclined to take advantage of the discretion he had given them. And Van Dorn wanted to protect his base, Vicksburg, by driving away the Union forces threatening it from the south.

At about the time Bragg's train riders began arriving at Chattanooga, Van Dorn sent Breckinridge and roughly 4,000 troops down the Mississippi's east bank to take Baton Rouge. Joining Breckinridge in the attack on Louisiana's capital would be the newly built Confederate ironclad *Arkansas*. And if Baton Rouge could be recovered, so might New Orleans.

Earlier, the *Arkansas* had helped prevent federal Flag Officer David Farragut's fleet from seizing Vicksburg and with it full control of the Mississippi from Minnesota down to the Gulf of Mexico. But those sharp fights on the river left the little ironclad in need of repairs, and as she approached Baton Rouge on August 5, one of her engines quit.

Breckinridge, his force reduced to about 2,600 by disease, launched his attack that morning before he knew the *Arkansas* would not arrive. Sickness had cut Baton Rouge's federal garrison down to equal size, but fire from Union gunboats assisted its commander in holding off Breckinridge's assaults. Four miles up the

Mississippi, the *Arkansas*'s gunners kept other Yankee ships at a respectful distance while her crew worked to fix the trouble. Breckinridge withdrew to give the crippled ironclad protection overnight, but another breakdown the next morning left the *Arkansas* aground and unable to fire more than one gun at the advancing USS *Essex*. The *Arkansas*'s captain had no choice but to destroy her, and down with her went Breckinridge's hopes of seizing Baton Rouge. But there was some gain: Breckinridge fortified a high bluff at Port Hudson, south of where the Red River flowed into the Mississippi, and for a time the Confederacy would control more than 100 miles of the Big Muddy.

Fine, Braxton Bragg may have thought, but he had wanted Van Dorn to move north instead of south, or at least to get ready to. And Kirby Smith was edging away from the plan he and Bragg had worked out in Chattanooga. Smith, emboldened by John Morgan's report that Kentuckians were eager to join Confederate ranks as soon as an army came northward to free them, now wrote of bypassing the Union force holding Cumberland Gap and taking his 21,000 men directly into the Bluegrass State. If he did, Bragg would have only about 31,000 troops to throw against Don Carlos Buell's federal army in central Tennessee. But Bragg told Kirby Smith to go ahead: "Van Dorn and Price will advance simultaneously with us from Mississippi on West Tennessee, and I trust we may all unite in Ohio."

And so it was that four Confederate generals, each with streaks of independence and rather hazy intermediate goals, undertook the recovery of two large states—nearly 81,000 square miles—on August 14 when Kirby Smith led his forces northward from Knoxville.

"Be as patient as possible with the generals," Assistant Secretary of War Peter Watson would later tell Herman Haupt, the Union's railroad genius. "Some of them will trouble you more than the enemy."

Watson's sound advice might better have been directed to Lincoln's new general-in-chief, however, for the war in the west would place heavy demands on Henry Halleck at the same time he was trying to concentrate his forces in the eastern sector. And again the telegraph would prove seductive: Halleck could get information quickly and issue orders based on it, but as Lincoln before him had learned, most of the generals on whom he was relying had reaction speeds slower than those of wagon-pulling mules.

George McClellan promised much but did little. To Mary Ellen he wrote on August 10:

> I have a strong idea that Pope will be thrashed during the

coming week—& very badly whipped he will be & ought to be—such a villain as he is ought to bring defeat upon any cause that employs him....

The absurdity of Halleck's ordering the army away from here is that it cannot possibly reach Washn in time to do any good, but will necessarily be too late....

I am satisfied that the dolts in Washn are bent on my destruction if they can accomplish it—but I believe that Providence is just enough to bring their own sins upon their heads & that they will before they get through taste the dregs of the cup of bitterness. The more I hear of their wickedness the more am I surprised that such a wretched set are permitted to live much less to occupy the positions they do....

The next few days will probably prove decisive. If I succeed in my coup [a planned thrust toward Richmond] everything will be changed in this country so far as we are concerned & my enemies will be at my feet. It may go hard with some of them in that event, for I look upon them as enemies of the country & of the human race.

"You will send up your troops as rapidly as possible," Halleck wired McClellan. Washington's danger was uppermost in General Halleck's mind. Lee was moving toward Pope, and Pope knew it. "Make McClellan do something," he wired Halleck, "to prevent [Confederate] re-enforcements being sent here."

Ambrose Burnside was among McClellan's closest friends, and on August 14 Halleck sent him to Harrisons Landing to try friendly persuasion. "Count on my full cooperation," the Young Napoleon assured the general-in-chief. And apparently he meant it: By sundown on August 16 only blue uniforms stuffed with straw remained to guard Harrisons Landing's defenses.

All summer Abraham Lincoln had been under heavy pressure to do something. He must, a friend urged him, take decisive action; trying to please everybody would satisfy nobody.

On August 20, *New York Tribune* editor Horace Greeley added his advice in an editorial entitled "Prayer of Twenty Millions." Lincoln's attempts to quell the rebellion while leaving slavery intact, wrote Greeley in effect, were preposterous and futile.

Nearly a month earlier Lincoln had drafted a preliminary Emancipation Proclamation; it rested in a drawer, awaiting a Union victory. In response to Greeley on August 22, however, he merely stated the case as he saw it:

I would save the Union. I would save it the shortest way under the Constitution. The sooner the national authority can be restored; the nearer the Union will be "the Union as it was." If there be those who would not save the Union, unless they could at the same time *save* slavery, I do not agree with them. If there be those who would not save the Union unless they could at the same time *destroy* slavery, I do not agree with them. My paramount object in this struggle *is* to save the Union, and it is *not* either to save or to destroy slavery. If I could save the Union without freeing *any* slave I would do it, and if I could save it by freeing *all* the slaves I would do it; and if I could do it by freeing some and leaving others alone I would also do that. What I do about slavery, and the colored race, I do because I believe it helps to save the Union; and what I forbear, I forbear because I do *not* believe it would help to save the Union. I shall do *less* whenever I shall believe what I am doing hurts the cause, and I shall do *more* whenever I shall believe doing more will help the cause. I shall try to correct errors when shown to be errors; and I shall adopt new views so fast as they shall appear to be true views.

I have here stated my purpose according to my *official* duty; and I intend no modification of my oft-expressed *personal* wish that all men every where could be free.

So Abraham Lincoln wrote. But despite the power of his deceptively simple words and balanced phrases, he had changed few minds; the position he had taken was too far short of what abolitionists demanded, and for that he would reap only more harsh criticism.

But saving the Union was something Lincoln's generals and their troops would have to do, and in mid-August there was no assurance that McClellan's forces could reach John Pope's soon enough to keep Lee from taking Washington.

After Jackson withdrew southward from Cedar Mountain and recrossed the Rapidan, Pope concentrated his corps north of that river. Lee sent Jackson's divisions upstream and placed Longstreet's east of them, hoping to trap Pope's forces between the Rapidan and the Rappahannock and cut both of Pope's supply lines—the Orange & Alexandria's tracks and roads connecting the federal army and Fredericksburg—thus destroying the "miscreant" before Burnside's men or McClellan's could arrive.

Such a move also seemed General Lee's only hope. Having drawn northward almost all of Richmond's defenders, he knew his

55,000 men would soon be vastly outnumbered. Lee meant to open his drive around Pope's eastern flank on August 18, but his army was not ready; and that proved to have been a blessing because of something that had happened early that morning.

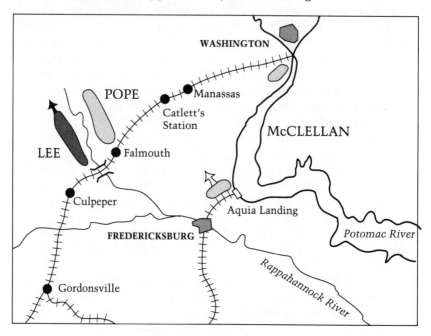

Lee vs. Pope—Early August

Jeb Stuart, confident that no Yankee cavalry patrols were in the vicinity, spent the night on the front porch of a house near Verdiersville. Early on the morning of the eighteenth, however, he barely got away—leaving behind his cloak and his plumed hat—when federal troopers appeared suddenly, scattering his staff, capturing a major who had a copy of Lee's attack order.

On the next day General Lee revised his plan, intending to strike Pope from the east on the twentieth, then he and Longstreet went to the top of Clark Mountain to observe what was happening north of the Rapidan. Union army wagons were moving northward. Following them were dust clouds raised by soldiers' feet.

"General," said Lee to Longstreet, "we little thought that the enemy would turn his back on us so early in the campaign."

By then, late afternoon on August 19, not enough time was left for a pursuit. Again Lee modified his orders. At four A.M. on August 20 the army would cross the Rapidan and march up to the southern banks of the Rappahannock.

Once there, Lee found the geography favoring the federals. The Rappahannock's course was almost north to south. Union guns on the bluffs dominated approaches to the fords. Any attempt to force a crossing downstream, to get east of Pope's positions, might prove too costly. And moving upstream would take the army northward, too far away from Richmond to return if McClellan stopped withdrawing, turned around, and attacked.

Yet Lee could not stand still. "Those people," he knew, would use whatever time he gave them to rush reinforcements to Pope. Accordingly, on August 21 he ordered Jackson to begin moving up the Rappahannock's western bank, to keep advancing northward until someone found a place where the federal flank had not yet been stretched. Longstreet's men were to follow, and closely, lest a sudden Yankee thrust across the river cut the Confederate army in two.

Lee had lost no time, but geography had deprived him of surprise. All along the line, from Jackson's scouts southward to Longstreet's rear guard, federal eyes watched the advancing columns, and Union guns fired. And whenever Jackson sent probes across the river, Yankees were there to drive them back.

"Fight hard," General Halleck had wired John Pope on August 18, when Pope began moving toward the Rappahannock, "and aid will soon come." From McClellan, Halleck meant. But Pope neither liked nor trusted George McClellan, and it would take days for any of his troops to arrive. And even after Pope had his little army on the high ground north and east of the Rappahannock, he was still uneasy. That river, he told Halleck in a message, got less impressive for defensive purposes the farther north anyone scouted it. But on August 21 the general-in-chief wired him: "Dispute every inch of ground, and fight like the devil till we can re-enforce you. Forty-eight hours more and we can make you strong enough."

"Dispute," said Halleck, not hold. So as the Confederates slipped northward, so did Pope—but with some reluctance, for he had not one line of communications to worry about but two. And the O & A was a mess. Herman Haupt had been cleaning it up, but slowly, primarily because General Pope's quartermasters were hoarding boxcars to use as warehouses at the line's southern end. Haupt wanted those cars returned to Alexandria to use when McClellan's men arrived as well as for moving more supplies to Pope.

That is one reason why Haupt was at Pope's headquarters (under a tree, not in the saddle) on August 22. After West Point graduate Haupt had listened to aides' reports for two hours or so, he asked the general commanding: "What is to prevent the enemy from going even as far north as Thoroughfare Gap and getting behind you?"

"There is no danger," Pope replied.

Haupt, assuming the general's information must be far more complete than his own, left it at that and climbed aboard the next northbound train.

Railroad bridges were on Jeb Stuart's mind that afternoon, now that General Lee had told him to go ahead and do something, somewhere, to break the irritating pattern of Pope's matching Jackson's northward pace along the Rappahannock. A map showed Cedar Run passing under an O & A bridge at Catlett's Station, so Stuart selected 1,500 of his boldest cavalrymen and led them about twenty miles upstream and another ten eastward to Warrenton, then five more to Auburn Mills, roughly that distance from Catlett's.

By the time Stuart reached Auburn Mills, though, darkness and rain combined against him. So heavy was the downpour, he assumed his horse-drawn artillery would never catch up. And behind Stuart the creeks would soon fill the Rappahannock, flooding the fords he had used earlier that day.

Suddenly, luck intervened. Up came a black man who had seen Stuart elsewhere nearly a year earlier, a "contraband" who had been forced to be a Union officer's servant but whose heart (he declared) was still with his "own folks." He offered to guide the Confederates directly to General Pope's tent.

Trust was what this black was expressing, or so Jeb Stuart must have recognized, for he decided to stake everything—his life, the lives of his men, the success of his mission—on the trust he placed in this man.

Stuart was not disappointed. In the unrelenting rain and utter darkness and after a short fight marked mostly by the confusion the raid's abruptness caused, amid lightning flashes the Confederates plundered the absent Pope's tent and those of his staff officers. But the railroad bridge was too wet to burn and too stout for axes to damage, and without artillery there was no way to destroy it.

Stuart led his men westward, then southward, taking along more than 300 prisoners, many of them officers; General Pope's dispatch book and letters; and, among other trophies, a uniform frock coat adorned by the shoulder straps of a major general. The O & A bridge at Catlett's Station was intact, but now Stuart would no longer have reason to mourn the loss of his cloak and plumed hat five nights earlier. And General Lee would soon have both a talkative Yankee quartermaster major to question and Pope's personal files to read.

But Lee would not get to that right away, for something else had happened in Stuart's absence. Jackson had sent two of Dick Ewell's brigades across the Rappahannock on the afternoon of the twenty-second, and the same thunderstorm Stuart had endured up at Catlett's Station isolated Jubal Early's regiments on the east side of the flooded Rappahannock.

For a time, a long one to "Old Jube's" troops, who had no rations with them and no hope of getting any, it seemed that the Confederates' presence east of the river was attracting Pope's entire army. Worse, on the western bank Isaac Trimble —his brigade left behind as rear guard until Longstreet's men arrived from the south to relieve him—learned that Yankees were stealing mules and ambulances from Jackson's wagon train. Trimble's men recovered them, but then a spy said bluecoats in great numbers were behind the repelled marauders.

Trimble, like Early across the river, could neither attack nor retreat. All he could do was wait for Longstreet's troops to appear. When they did, John Hood's Texans were leading the column. His brigade supported Trimble's in thinning the ranks of the Yankees scrambling back across the Rappahannock.

Jubal Early's plight would be more prolonged. Fearing his men might run out of ammunition too soon, he told them to hold their fire when federal skirmishers probed. Not until predawn hours on the twenty-fourth could Early and his men be withdrawn, and then only because the Rappahannock was back at a level they could wade. Nearly two days without food, glad to be alive, they surged across.

So, on August 24 Jackson had still not found the northern end of the Army of Virginia's flank. And as General Lee read through the papers Jeb Stuart's men had captured at Catlett's Station, he recognized that his campaign was about to end in failure. No longer was there any doubt regarding the Army of the Potomac's destination. Within a few more days, a week at most, McClellan's forces then at Aquia Landing and nearing it would increase Pope's strength from only a little more than 40,000 to 130,000. If that happened, Lee saw, he would have to retreat.

But could Pope be defeated in the meantime? No opening had he given Lee while this sparring had been going on. Even so, was it possible to lure Pope northward, to draw his army away from the reinforcements moving toward him?

Principles of war are not mocked with impunity, Lee may have remembered from the Seven Days. He had violated two of them, splitting his army and attempting to combine his forces on the battlefield, and the price had been humiliatingly high: failure to destroy McClellan. And this time retribution might well cost the

Confederacy even its hopes for survival.

Yet, General Lee decided, the risks could not be avoided. He rode to Jackson's headquarters, talked with him briefly, listened intently, watched the excited Jackson make some marks on the sandy ground with his boot, nodded, then left.

Chapter 13

Second Manassas: John Pope's Time of Trial

If Lee and Jackson had hoped the movement could be kept secret, they were to be disappointed. Alert federal observers on John Pope's high ground began sending him detailed reports early on Monday morning, August 25. From Warrenton he wired Washington that an estimated 20,000 Confederates were moving northwestward—bound, he guessed, for the Shenandoah Valley.

Other matters were on Pope's mind, of course, including some trouble involving Brigadier General Samuel Sturgis, whose troops were assigned to Pope but were still up near Alexandria awaiting transportation. In a fit of frustration, compounded by ignorance and possibly a little too much whiskey, Sturgis told railroad operator Herman Haupt he was taking charge of the O & A and placing him under arrest.

> I replied [wrote Haupt, much later] that I was acting under the orders of General Halleck; that so far as my personal comfort was concerned, the arrest would be quite a relief...and a few hours of rest would be quite refreshing, but he must understand that he was assuming a very grave responsibility; the trains were loaded with wounded; the surgeons, with ambulances, were waiting for them at the depot; the engines would soon be out of wood and water, and serious delays would be caused in the forwarding of troops to General Pope.

"I don't care for John Pope a pinch of owl dung!" Sturgis retorted. And there the case remained until the arrival of an order to Haupt from the general-in-chief: "No military officer has any

197

authority to interfere with your control over railroads. Show this to General Sturgis, and if he attempts to interfere, I will arrest him."

Haupt, once liberated, lost more sleep trying to untangle the confusion Sturgis's brief seizure of the O & A had caused. He was still at the task on Monday morning when Pope's observers reported that Confederate troops were marching northwestward.

All of this was puzzling to Pope. How could he expect to get McClellan's men, who might be disembarked at Alexandria, when he could not get his own delivered to him?

Just at that point the federal cavalry wore out, leaving Pope blind, devoid of information mounted scouts normally provide. So he remained for most of Tuesday, August 26. But some of George McClellan's men were not far away: Heintzelman's corps was at Warrenton Junction, and Fitz-John Porter's leading division was ten miles or so south of there.

Then, at eight o'clock on that Tuesday night, Manassas's O & A telegraph operator could not complete a message because rebel cavalry had cut the wires. And now many things General Pope had not known began to make a profound difference.

Overnight on August 24–25 cooks were preparing three days' rations for Jackson's troops; only a small herd of cattle would follow them, mixed in the column with the artillery and wagons loaded with ammunition and nothing more. At early dawn, Old Jack's favorite starting time, 23,000 Confederate soldiers followed him northward, colors flying in the morning breeze. None of them knew where they were going, but that was nothing new: Jackson never told even his division commanders anything until he had to. "Close up, close up!" was about all anyone heard him say on Monday, August 25.

Near Salem, after a march that day of twenty-five miles, Jackson decided to halt for the night. He moved off to the side of the road to watch his weary men pass, and when they saw him they cheered. Jackson, thinking Yankee cavalry scouts might hear it, waved that down, and as the rest of his soldiers came by, they silently raised their caps or smiled and waved a hand.

"Who," said Jackson to a staff officer, "could not conquer with such troops as these?"

From Tuesday's dawn onward the route was uphill, toward Thoroughfare Gap. Stuart's cavalrymen screened the advance of Jackson's divisions through it and southeastward from it. Now Bristoe Station on the O & A was directly ahead. General Lee wanted the railroad cut: Jackson ordered that it be cut.

And so it was, but not by burning bridges. Once the small federal garrison had been disposed of, Jackson's men tried to damage the track enough to derail a northbound train. It got by, puffing rapidly on toward nearby Manassas, where surely the train's crew would pause long enough to wire Washington that there was trouble at Bristoe.

Some of the departed Dick Taylor's unruly Louisiana Tigers heard another northbound train's whistle; this time an alert soldier opened a switch. The engine's momentum made it tumble off an embankment, taking into the wreck half the cars it had been pulling. Soon from the south came another train, moving too fast to avoid plunging into the cars ahead of it. To the loot-hunting Tigers' dismay, though, the cars were empty. The train behind it stopped short of the smashup, then backed southward. Now the Yankees at Warrenton would know the line was blocked—and why.

There was, however, one cause for Confederate laughter. President was the name of the derailed engine, and on its side, through a painted likeness of Lincoln, was a bullet hole.

After Jackson departed on Monday, Longstreet's men had sparred with Pope's as usual. On Tuesday, General Lee detected a subtle diminishing in the Yankees' aggressiveness. Before sundown he had Longstreet's troops moving northward. They marched eleven miles before halting for the night near Orleans.

Longstreet had about 32,000 under his command, but 5,000 had been left behind to "amuse" Pope, whose forces numbered roughly 75,000 now that McClellan's units were arriving. But if Lee was aware of how close he was to losing his gamble, he showed no sign of it. At a lavish dinner with the Marshall family near Orleans on that Tuesday evening, the twentieth-sixth, he was (a staff officer recalled) "a genial cavalier."

While Lee relaxed, east of him Jackson was still pressing on. When citizens of Bristoe had described the federal supply depot seven miles up the O & A at Manassas Junction, Old Jack sent Trimble's brigade northeastward along the tracks, then Stuart's cavalrymen. By early Wednesday morning the Confederates were in possession of the largest and richest stocks of food and sutlers' luxuries any of them had ever seen.

For a time officers tried to keep their hungry men from looting—unsuccessfully, until help in restraining them came from an unexpected source: federal artillery. Jackson rode out, spotted the glint of Union soldiers' bayonets off to the northeast, and sent Powell Hill's troops to block the threat.

Herman Haupt was responsible for that response to Jackson's

audacity. On the evening before, from his office at the Alexandria terminal, he wired General-in-Chief Halleck:

> I am just informed that the four trains following the engine Secretary are captured, and that the rebels are approaching Manassas with artillery. These may be exaggerations, but the operator and agent are leaving, and prompt action is required.

Then, soon afterward:

> The wire is cut between Manassas and Warrenton. We have transportation for 1,200 men; this number might be sent to Manassas to protect the road while we repair it. I suppose the bridge at Bristoe will be destroyed.

Within a few minutes, Haupt had Halleck's reply:

> General Smith, General Slocum, General Sturgis, or any other General Officer you can find, will immediately send all the men you can transport to Bristoe Bridge or Manassas Junction. Show this order.

That was at 9:25 P.M. It took Haupt until midnight to find a general officer. "The attractions of Washington," he wrote later, "kept most of the General Officers in that city." But the one he found, Brigadier General Winfield Scott Hancock, promptly ordered Brigadier General George W. Taylor to load his two regiments on Haupt's cars and protect the repair crews.

By early Wednesday morning, the twenty-seventh, Taylor's men were off the train and, contrary to Hancock's orders, advancing, bayonets fixed, toward Manassas. Their attack was gallant but doomed; in it, Taylor was killed; and after his successor in command finally stopped the panicked troops' flight, all he could do was lead the survivors' march back to Alexandria.

That federal threat beaten off, now Powell Hill's soldiers could and did join in the plundering. Jackson permitted it, having ordered the whiskey surgeons could not carry away dumped and knowing he had too few wagons to take anything but captured ammunition along. So, for men who had marched fifty-four miles in two days on light rations, Wednesday was a day of feasting:

> It was hard to decide what to take [one veteran wrote].

Some filled their haversacks with cakes, some with candy, others oranges, lemons, canned goods, etc. I know one who took nothing but French mustard, filled his haversack and was so greedy that he put one more bottle in his pocket. This was his four days' rations, and it turned out to be the best thing taken, because he traded it for meat and bread, and it lasted him until we reached [Maryland].

Sutlers' wares also disappeared quickly, as one of Maxcy Gregg's men recalled:

Fine whiskey and segars circulated freely, elegant lawn and linen handkerchiefs were applied to noses hitherto blown by the thumb and forefinger, and sumptuous under-clothing was fitted over limbs sunburnt, sore and vermin-splotched. Many a foot more worn and more weary than those of the olden time pilgrims here received its grateful protection from the rocky soil. At the Junction there was a general jubilee. Hard-tack and bacon, coffee and sugar, soap even, was distributed to us, and we were invited to help ourselves to anything in the storehouses, from a dose of calomel to a McClellan saddle.

Presumably, the saddle Captain George McClellan designed and the army adopted as standard cavalry issue in 1857 drew as few takers as the calomel. A discerning officer took "a tooth brush, a box of candles, a quantity of lobster salad, a barrel of coffee and other things which I forget."

General Ewell's men had missed the fun, spending the day at Bristoe Station to block a federal advance from the south. One developed, and by the middle of that Wednesday afternoon Ewell thought it best to use the discretion Jackson had given him. Jubal Early's troops covered the beginning of the seven-mile withdrawal to Manassas, rejoining the main body near dark, in time to plunder some before Old Jack ordered everything that could not be eaten, stowed, or otherwise carried off burned.

General Pope knew nothing about the gastronomic orgy his 23,000 uninvited guests were enjoying up at Manassas Junction, but the cutting of the telegraph wires Tuesday evening had told him he had better get between there and Washington quickly. On Wednesday morning Pope wired Halleck:

Under all the circumstances I have thought it best to

interpose in front of Manassas Junction, where your orders will reach me. Neither Sturgis' nor Cox's commands have come up. Heintzelman's has no artillery. I am pushing a strong column to Manassas Junction to open the road.

And Irvin McDowell had made an interesting suggestion: If Lee had split his army, as was becoming increasingly evident, why not attack each portion of it separately?

So far in August 1862 neither Abraham Lincoln nor his secretary of war had taken any part in the management of the Union's military operations. That the president was monitoring the messages reaching the War Department's telegraph room was evident, however, for occasionally he sent a tersely worded question to one general or another. This being so, to this point Lincoln must have felt comfortable about his choice of John Pope. Liar, braggart, ass, even miscreant, others might consider him; but for a week Pope had held the dreaded Lee in check, and now Pope seemed poised to destroy him.

Longstreet's force was still miles to the west of Pope on Wednesday morning, the twenty-seventh. The day was hot, the road dusty, watering places scarce. A messenger from Jackson brought good news and no hints of danger. General Lee saw no need to press Longstreet's men, and he was content to halt at White Plains so that the stragglers could catch up overnight.

While Longstreet's troops rested, Jackson's were moving. Old Jack had cut the O & A Railroad, burned enough bridges to ruin it for days, and for the time being that was enough. Now he would have to wait for as long as it took General Lee and Longstreet to arrive; to move toward them would be retreating and therefore unthinkable; yet he had to be near enough for them to reach him and on ground he could defend in the meantime. Where was it?

Memory served Jackson well that Wednesday night. About seven or eight miles north of the flames at Manassas Junction was Stony Ridge, near the base of which ran the embankment of an unfinished railroad. If he could place his troops on that embankment, they would be looking southeastward at the nearby turnpike connecting Warrenton and Washington. Once General Lee and Longstreet descended from Thoroughfare Gap to Gainesville, they could take the turnpike to reach him; while he waited, his men would be concealed from Yankee eyes.

Jackson got one division headed toward the new position, which local folks called Groveton. But apparently Old Jack told his other commanders too little, or his instructions were confusing, or guides tried short cuts. In any case, for hours Powell Hill's troops wandered over the old Manassas battlefield in the dark, and so did most of Ewell's. It was not until early on Thursday that Jackson had his half of Lee's army where he wanted it. Ironically, that was about a mile west of Henry House Hill, where General Bee, a little over a year before, had said something about a man standing like a stone wall.

With no direct telegraph link to Pope, less than forty miles from his office in the War Department building, General-in-Chief Halleck had to rely on scraps of information railroader Haupt sent him in order even to guess what was happening so near to Washington. But his mind was also on that other war, the one 600 or 700 miles out west, and both situations were vexing.

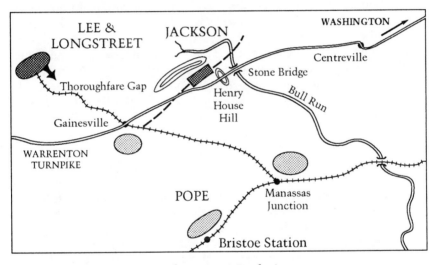

Second Manassas Battle Area

Halleck had erred by believing Don Carlos Buell could take Chattanooga. As early as August 16 Buell had made it clear that he was all but abandoning that effort when he reported that Kirby Smith's Confederate forces were invading Kentucky and that he expected the rebels to try to recover Tennessee as well. For Buell, getting reinforcements from Halleck and Grant to cope with the drives led by Kirby Smith and Braxton Bragg was what could be called Problem 1. Problem 2 came in the form of a wire from the general-in-chief on August 18:

> So great is the dissatisfaction here at the apparent want of energy and activity in your district, that I was this morning

notified to have you removed. I got the matter delayed till we could hear further of your movements.

At once came Buell's reply:

> My movements have been such as the circumstances seemed to me to require. I beg that you not interpose in my behalf; on the contrary, if the dissatisfaction cannot cease on grounds which I think might be supposed if not apparent I respectfully request that I may be relieved.

Ulysses Grant owed Don Carlos Buell much—Buell's men had saved Grant's army at Shiloh by arriving in time to power the second day's counterattack—and he had sent northeastward from northern Mississippi all the troops he could spare. Old Brains, too, had tried to respond to Buell's plea for cavalry "to keep open the 400 miles of railroad on which this army is dependent for subsistence" and along which Confederate troopers were "swarming." Yet Buell's Problem 1 was becoming more and more serious on August 25 when Halleck tried to solve Problem 2 by sending a challenge of sorts to Major General Horatio G. Wright, newly placed in charge of operations in Kentucky:

> There must be more energy and activity in Kentucky and Tennessee, and the one [Buell or Wright] who first does something brilliant will get the whole command. I therefore hope to hear very soon of some success in your department. I can hardly describe to you the feeling of disappointment here in the want of activity in General Buell's large army.
>
> The Government seems determined to apply the guillotine to all unsuccessful generals. It seems rather hard to do this where the general is not at fault, but perhaps with us now, as in the French Revolution, some harsh measures are required.

If Henry Halleck had made a mistake by expecting too much of Buell, he was on the brink of another error regarding the amount and sincerity of support he thought George McClellan and some of his corps commanders would provide to John Pope. A key point Halleck missed was the unique relationship between the officers and men of the Army of the Potomac and their commander. An example: Halleck placed Fitz-John Porter's corps under John Pope's control, but this did not sever the link with McClellan. On August 27 Porter wrote Burnside, referring to Pope's Army of Virginia: "I wish myself away from it, with all our old

Army of the Potomac, and so do our companions."

Nostalgia? No, loyalty—of a sort. And misdirected or even undeserved though it may have been, it was a force unknown to anyone except McClellan and his men.

On the morning of August 28, however, all the general-in-chief knew was that Pope meant to place his forces between the wings of Lee's army, keep them separated, and attack the nearer one: Jackson's. This news reached Halleck via Fredericksburg, and it was reassuring: Pope appeared to be taking advantage of his central position to defeat fragments of his enemy's army before they could be combined against his own.

Such were the potentials and hopes for that Thursday's actions, but the reality proved otherwise: Jackson's marauders had disappeared. Pope, following up on reports of Confederates having been seen the night before around Centreville and other places north of the old Manassas battleground, sent forces all over it in search of the foe. But in so doing, apparently Pope neglected to worry enough about that other wing of Lee's army.

General Jackson's divisions had marched to Bristoe Station in two days; now Longstreet's men had been on the same road for that long and more, but Thoroughfare Gap was still east of them by midafternoon of the twenty-eighth. Longstreet's pace was that of the army's wagon trains. And though Jackson's couriers assured General Lee the road to Groveton was open, the army commander thought it prudent to send Brigadier General D. R. Jones's division forward to occupy the heights overlooking the pass.

Suddenly, firing broke out at the place General Lee had feared it might. He rode over to a hilltop. For a while he studied the terrain through his field glasses; then, showing no sign of concern, he ordered John Hood to get around the federals' northern flank. Three miles north of Thoroughfare Gap was Hopewell Gap. Take three brigades there and hold it as an alternative, Lee told Brigadier General Cadmus Marcellus Wilcox.

These efforts launched, General Lee accepted an invitation to an early dinner at a nearby home. Again his mood was genial, though (as an aide wrote afterward) "victory or defeat hung trembling in the balance."

Not quite—at least not then. General Lee knew from the messages couriers had brought during the day that Jackson was in a strong position. Union forces blocking Thoroughfare Gap were small. Delay mattered little; he wanted Longstreet's men to be well rested the next day when they joined Jackson's.

After dinner, though, General Lee and all the others at Thoroughfare Gap heard the distant rumble of artillery fire. Everyone knew what it meant, and now no one could rest easy.

Resting was how most of Jackson's men had spent the better part of that Thursday, once all the units that had gone astray the night before were in concealed positions a little to the west of the old Manassas battlefield. But before noon Old Jack had read some captured federal messages and questioned at least one prisoner, and though some of the information confused him, it indicated that John Pope, too, was confused.

Even so, a few facts emerged. Pope seemed to be drawing his forces together at the smoking ruins of Manassas Junction for the purpose of attacking Jackson, but the Yankees did not know where he was hiding. Some of McClellan's troops and also Burnside's were in the vicinity. And Jeb Stuart's cavalrymen reported a federal column marching along the Warrenton Turnpike toward Sudley's Ford, across Jackson's front.

Jackson prepared to strike the Yankee column, then saw it turn southeastward, away from him. Later that afternoon he learned another contingent was coming his way and had not made the turnoff. This he wanted to check personally. He rode out alone to within rifle range of the bluecoats. They paid him no attention, for of all Confederate soldiers Jackson may well have been the shabbiest looking.

Finally, his curiosity satisfied, Old Jack returned to the officers who had been watching him inspect the Yankee column. "Bring up your men, gentlemen" was all he told them.

They did more. Brigadier General William B. Taliaferro led Jackson's old division out of the woods, the men cheering as they advanced, and after them came two of Dick Ewell's brigades. Isaac Trimble yelled in his finest battle voice: "Forward, guide center, march!" From behind three batteries of Jackson's artillery opened fire.

Had Jackson miscalculated? There were only six federal regiments out there on the turnpike, but they fought as though their numbers equaled the Confederates'. Among their leaders were Fort Sumter veteran Abner Doubleday, a brigadier general now, as was John Gibbon, whose midwesterners wore distinctive black hats and that day won a new nickname: the Iron Brigade.

Neither side, though, won the bitter, stubborn, stand-up, close-in fight, which lasted more than two hours and settled nothing at all at an appalling cost. Jackson's Stonewall Brigade, 635 troops strong earlier, lost one man out of three. Both of the Confederate division commanders were wounded; Taliaferro was able to see the scrap through, but Dick Ewell's knee was shattered by a minié ball, and he had to be rushed to the rear, where a surgeon amputated his leg. And of the 2,800 federals, nearly 1,100 were killed or wounded.

Such were the causes of the faint booming General Lee and the rest of the Army of Northern Virginia, in Thoroughfare Gap nineteen miles to the west, heard until about nine o'clock that evening. But why had General Jackson been so impulsive?

Attracting Pope's army as far northwestward as possible had been and still was Jackson's mission. Holding Pope at Groveton, then, had been of paramount importance—as keeping 40,000 Union troops in the Shenandoah Valley and away from McClellan had been three months earlier. But if General Lee could not bring Longstreet's divisions down from Thoroughfare Gap early the next morning, victory or defeat might well hang trembling in the balance.

On that Thursday, General Pope lost control of his forces. They moved in fragments, as had the brigades under Gibbon and Double-day or the division Brigadier General James B. Ricketts took up to Thoroughfare Gap, as though the Army of Virginia's commander no longer knew what to do.

General Halleck avoided badgering Pope, concentrating instead on rushing men and supplies to him. Halleck was busy both prodding and helping Don Carlos Buell as well, and he was finding General McClellan's presence across the Potomac in Alexandria more of a hindrance than anything else.

Halleck had wired McClellan on Wednesday the twenty-seventh that "Franklin's troops should move out by forced marches, carrying three or four days' provisions." McClellan's reply, bordering on incoherent nonsense, must have stunned the general-in-chief:

> Franklin's Artillery have no horses except for (4) four guns without caissons. I can pick up no cavalry. In view of these facts will it not be well to push Sumner's Corps here by water as rapidly as possible. To make immediate arrangements for placing the works in front of Washington in an efficient condition of defense. I have no means of knowing the enemy's force between Pope & ourselves. Can Franklin without his Artillery or Cavalry effect any useful purpose in front? Should not Burnside at once take steps to evacuate Falmouth & Acquia [Landing] at the same time covering the retreat of any of Pope's troops who may fall back in that direction? I do not see that we have force enough in hand to form a connection with Pope whose exact position we do not know. Are we safe in the direction of the valley?

That Pope would be defeated the seemingly addled McClellan appeared to take for granted; and if saving Washington was only alluded to in that wire, he made his thinking on this point clear at the end of the next one:

> I still think that we should first provide for the immediate defence [sic] of Washington on both sides of the Potomac. I am not responsible for the past and cannot be for the future, unless I receive authority to dispose of the available troops according to my judgment. Please inform me at once what my position is. I do not wish to act in the dark.

On the night of August 27–28 McClellan spent several hours in Washington conferring with Halleck, but in their exchanges of messages the following afternoon—Thursday—Halleck was still spurring him to push "as large a force as possible toward Manassas, so as to communicate with Pope before the enemy is re-enforced." And to McClellan's "it would be sacrifice to send them out now" response, Old Brains shot back:

> They must go to-morrow morning ready or not ready. If we delay too long to get ready there will be no necessity to go at all, for Pope will either be defeated or be victorious without our aid.

And, at ten P.M., from McClellan:

> Franklin's Corps has been ordered to march at 6 o'clock tomorrow morning.... Reports numerous from various sources, that Lee & Stuart with large forces are at Manassas. That the enemy with 120,000 men intend advancing on the forts near Arlington and Chain Bridge, with a view of attacking Washington & Baltimore.

Presumably, General Halleck did not try to relay to John Pope either the news that 120,000 Confederates were upon him or that he could expect Franklin's corps. However, nearly two full days after the general-in-chief had so directed, Franklin did march on Friday morning, August 29. He moved five miles, then halted: by order of Major General McClellan.

For Pope that Friday was off to a bad start in any case. His orders for Jackson's destruction, issued the night before, could not be carried out because Pope's forces were not where he had thought they were. Getting his troops back in hand was the purpose of the plan Pope made early on the twenty-ninth. "It may be necessary to fall behind Bull Run at Centreville to-night," he wrote his corps commanders. "I presume it will be so, on account of our supplies."

It was curious that Pope's plans for Friday included nothing about attacking anyone. He appeared to believe Jackson had been withdrawing late on Thursday. Pope's ability to cope was further impaired later that morning when McDowell failed to forward to him a message Brigadier General John Buford had sent by a courier: Some of Longstreet's forces had passed through nearby Gainesville at 8:45. Was the ill fate following Irvin McDowell since he lost a battle on that same ground in mid-July 1861 now overspreading John Pope?

After the fight with Gibbon's Black Hats and Doubleday's men late on Thursday, General Jackson took his forty guns and the 18,000 infantrymen he had remaining and deployed them along a front of about 3,000 yards on the embankment of the unfinished railroad. There they were, waiting, on Friday morning. Powell Hill's division was northeasternmost lest some of McClellan's corps come rushing down the Warrenton Turnpike from Alexandria. Stretching southwestward from Hill were brigades hardly larger now than regiments were supposed to be.

Jackson had expected the federals would try to get between him and the road leading down from Thoroughfare Gap, so he was not surprised when Yankees began probing the southwest end of his line. He gave less attention to those demonstrations than to red dust clouds he saw when he looked toward Gainesville. Were the troops moving into positions south of him federals?

"It's Longstreet!" a returning courier shouted, and cheers rippled northeastward along the embankment as the word spread. John Hood's Texans had led the way down from Thoroughfare Gap, and soon the Army of Northern Virginia would be reunited—and in *northern* Virginia, which may have been General Lee's point back on June 1 when he had given his new command its name.

But on this Friday, August 29, the work would be Jackson's to do. His gunners' replies to the federal shelling earlier gave Yankee commanders an idea of where Jackson's line was. Probes confirmed it. And by early afternoon Powell Hill was hard-pressed.

The Confederates' presence had drawn some of the Union's best-led divisions toward them: one-armed Phil Kearny's, Major General Joseph Hooker's. All Friday afternoon waves advanced, each making an assault almost strong enough to break through.

Maxcy Gregg's men seemed to be in the way of the heaviest surges. During one a worried Powell Hill asked Gregg if he could hold out. His ammunition was about gone, the former astronomer replied, but he still had the bayonet.

Jackson rode up, heard Hill's description of the nigh-hopeless situation, and said: "General, your men have done nobly; if you are attacked again, you will beat them back."

Doing that once more was mostly up to Maxcy Gregg and his South Carolinians. Overpowered, Gregg pulled them back as far as he dared, then shouted: "Let us die here, my men; let us die here!"

Gregg's men held. Powell Hill sent a message to Jackson reporting that the Yankee assaults had been beaten back.

"Tell him," said Jackson, "I knew he would do it."

But it had taken a long time, so long that some Confederates wondered if the sun was standing still. When it finally set, Maxcy Gregg had lost 600 men, among them 40 officers. Valiant Isaac Trimble had been hit by an explosive bullet. Federal dead and wounded heaped below the embankment could be replaced, and would be, but not Jackson's casualties.

Surgeon Hunter McGuire found Old Jack and said he thought the day had been won by "nothing but stark and stern fighting."

"No," said General Jackson, "it has been won by nothing but the blessing and protection of Providence."

So Old Jack doubtless believed; certainly, Longstreet had provided no help. From a hilltop south of the embattled railroad embankment General Lee had watched the federals attacking Jackson. And he had asked Longstreet several times if he thought they should strike those people. Not yet, said Longstreet, not before he rode out and studied this new terrain and found where the rest of Pope's forces were.

Lee, trusting Jackson and accepting Longstreet's advice for the time being, waited. Jeb Stuart sent the army commander a report of blue-clad troops approaching Longstreet's flank from Manassas Junction. That, together with what Longstreet had learned from his reconnaissance, seemed to persuade General Lee that he should allow the commanders of his army's now-united wings to proceed as each thought best.

Longstreet used his discretion by sending John Hood and his men out to probe. But that was late in the day, and about all Hood learned was that Stuart had been right: Jackson had not drawn northward all the federal units that were out there.

Among Pope's uncommitted forces was Fitz-John Porter's corps, the one best positioned that Friday afternoon to get behind the southern end of Longstreet's line. Do this, in effect, Pope ordered Porter at about four-thirty P.M. Porter did not obey. Some of his troops had skirmished with Longstreet's, and his awareness of Confederate positions and strength had to be sharper than that of his distant army commander. But had there been a deeper reason for Porter's disobedience? Perhaps: that morning, in another message to Ambrose Burnside, he had said: "I hope Mac is at work, and we will soon get us out of this."

Indeed, McClellan was at work. That Friday afternoon, in reply to a wire in which Abraham Lincoln had asked, "What news from Manassas Junction? What generally?" he wrote:

> The last news I received from the direction of Manassas was from stragglers to the effect that the enemy were evacuating Centreville & retiring towards Thoroughfare Gap. This is by no means reliable. I am clear that one of two courses should be adopted—1st To concentrate all our available forces to open communications with Pope—2nd To leave Pope to get out of his scrape & at once use all our means to make the Capital perfectly safe. No middle course will now answer. Tell me what you wish me to do & I will do all in my power to accomplish it. I wish to know what my orders & authority are—I ask for nothing, but will obey any orders you give.

Leave Pope to get out of his scrape?

Could any Union soldier even contemplate, much less admit—and in a message to the president of the United States, his commander-in-chief—that he would abandon another, especially one commanding a large field army at that moment engaged in a battle that could be decisive?

Information was all Lincoln had asked for, but what he got was sheer nonsense followed by gratuitous, self-serving advice bordering on treason, with a crass attempt to go over Halleck's head to gain power tacked on. This was stunning, appalling, and also tragic.

Having responded to the president, McClellan then wrote a letter to Mary Ellen:

> I have a terrible task on my hands now—perfect imbecility to correct. No means to act with, no authority—yet determined if possible to save the country & the Capital. I find the soldiers all clinging to me—yet I am not permitted to go to the post of danger! Two of my Corps will either save that fool Pope or be sacrificed for the country. I do not know whether I will be permitted to save the Capital or not—I

have just telegraphed very plainly to the Presdt & Halleck what I think ought to be done—I expect merely a contemptuous silence.

Regarding McClellan's second suggestion—"leave Pope to get out of his scrape"—Lincoln did remain silent, probably with cold contempt. But he agreed that concentrating forces to open communications with Pope was the right thing to do, and as if to remind McClellan that there existed a chain of command, the president added: "I do not wish to control. That I now leave to Genl Halleck aided by your counsels."

"I am tired of guesses," Henry Halleck had declared in a message to McClellan earlier on that Friday, and he was tired of a great deal more—McClellan's transparent attempts to hold back Franklin's and Sumner's corps, the hectoring tone of McClellan's messages, and in the west, the failure of anything much to come of his efforts to aid and also to spur Buell. And as Halleck had feared back in July, before he came east, now he was caught up in "the quarrels of Stanton and McClellan."

By Thursday afternoon Edwin Stanton's long restraint had apparently reached its limit, for on the twenty-eighth he asked the already overburdened general-in-chief to provide him with the answers to three questions pertaining to General McClellan's conduct of the Peninsular campaign and also the current one. Lawyer Halleck must have sensed lawyer Stanton's purpose: to convince lawyer Lincoln that McClellan must be removed.

Such was the disarray prevailing not far behind John Pope at the very time he most needed support. And compounding the Union's peril was his belief, on Saturday morning, that Jackson had withdrawn toward Thoroughfare Gap or that he meant to.

There was some shifting going on. Jackson knew that men who had beaten back 30,000 federals the day before, thinning the blue-clad ranks by 8,000, needed rest; they could get some by moving to the low ground between the embankment and Stony Ridge west of it; and so he told most of them to relax while a small force stood guard along Friday's line.

"It looks as if there will be no fight today," said Old Jack to the Stonewall Brigade's commander, "but keep your men in line and ready for action."

That Saturday, August 30, was hot and sultry. Confederates watched a few Yankee columns moving northward in the distance. Only an occasional cannon boom broke the calm. With little else to do, Jackson rode southward to the hilltop where General Lee had been the day before; there had been no other opportunity to talk with him for nearly a week.

Along the way the former VMI professor of artillery must have passed the eighteen guns Fort Sumter veteran Colonel Stephen D. Lee had put into position on high ground. From up there Lee's gunners could hit anything that moved in front of either Jackson's or Longstreet's lines within 2,000 yards. Such wide coverage was possible because Longstreet had placed his five divisions at a slight angle to Jackson's three.

Old Jack found General Lee and Longstreet together, and soon Jeb Stuart joined them. Longstreet seemed eager for Pope to attack; the army commander feared the "miscreant" would not, however, and he had already started planning a move northward to get west of the federal army's flank. But Stuart confirmed an earlier report (one sent by a man perched high in a walnut tree) that Pope was massing his corps near the northern end of Jackson's line.

Pope could do Lee no greater favor than to attack, soon, before arriving units made the federal force too powerful to be resisted. Orders to get ready spread through the Army of Northern Virginia: roughly 17,000 men in Jackson's depleted wing, about 30,000 in Longstreet's, 2,500 riders with Stuart. Then, for a time, it seemed the watcher in the walnut tree and General Stuart had been wrong. Noon passed, the heat and humidity grew oppressive. Confederates, weary from long hours of waiting, dozed.

As early as five A.M. on that Saturday, General Pope had gotten off a wire to the general-in-chief. In it he reported Friday's action and forecast his intentions: "Our forces are too much exhausted yet to push matters, but I shall do so as soon as Fitz-John Porter's corps comes up from Manassas."

But John Pope also seemed aware that McClellan's other units were not rushing to join him. To his dispatch he added:

> I received a note this morning from General Franklin, written by order of General McClellan, saying that wagons and cars would be loaded and sent to Fairfax Station as soon as I would send a cavalry escort to Alexandria to bring them out. Such a request, when Alexandria is full of troops and we are fighting the enemy, needs no comment.

Indeed, it most certainly did not: Halleck had been trying from Wednesday onward to get Franklin's corps moving to join Pope, and now it was Saturday. Also, Halleck's map would show Fairfax Junction roughly fifteen miles short of the battle area. General

McClellan, too, got off to an early start. From Alexandria, fifteen miles or so east of Fairfax, he wired Halleck that he had heard artillery firing "this side of Fairfax" and suggested that "the garrisons in the works on the north side of the Potomac are altogether too small," implying that Sumner's corps, too, should be held back from Pope—for the purpose of defending the city of Washington, the capital itself.

Halleck replied: "Franklin's and all of Sumner's corps should be pushed forward with all possible dispatch. They must use their legs and make forced marches. Time now is everything."

Pushed forward to Pope, General Halleck meant, dismissing as fantasy McClellan's embedded implication that the rebels were about to cross the Potomac. Then, gambling that McClellan would obey his order, at two P.M. Halleck wired Pope:

> Thirty thousand men are marching to your aid. Franklin should be with you now and Sumner to-morrow morning. All will be right soon, even if you are forced to fall back. Let your army know that heavy re-enforcements are coming.

That afternoon had been so somnolent that the Confederates' horses were no longer swishing their tails, but the sudden clatter of rifle fire on the embankment's southern end made adrenaline surge through man and beast alike. Yankees too numerous to count were coming not only toward what was left of the Stonewall Brigade but in the center and against Powell Hill's men at the thin line's northern end. Yesterday's assaults had been fierce, but these were heavier, and behind blue masses Jackson's troops could shoot at without missing, two more waves were advancing.

Only the ammunition the Confederates had scavenged from the bodies of Friday's dead Union soldiers kept this new thrust from breaking through. For some of Jackson's hardest-pressed outfits soon there was nothing left to do but claw rocks out of the railroad embankment and throw them at Yankees not ten yards away—or swing rifle stocks at attackers' heads—or charge blue-bellies with fixed bayonets.

Jackson, knowing valor alone was not enough, asked General Lee for one of Longstreet's five fresh divisions. Rush it, Lee ordered Longstreet. "Certainly," he replied when the message reached him; then he told Stephen Lee's gunners to open fire on the federal masses about to destroy Jackson.

Longstreet figured artillery delivered instantly would do Jackson more good than any number of troops no matter how fast they marched. "Old Pete" had seen it all developing, knew how eager the gunners were, and hoped Pope would soon throw in his last reserves. Now Pope had. The entire federal army was out there on the plain, within easy reach of Stephen Lee's eighteen guns and all the others along his and Jackson's lines. Blasted from their flank, the Yankee masses reeled in surprise, broke their neat ranks, and scrambled wildly in search of cover. They died by the dozens as Confederate shells shredded them, plunging into blue clumps all over Jackson's front, absorbing at least some of the punishment Lee's army had taken at Malvern Hill.

General Lee sent word to Longstreet to attack, but John Hood's Texans were already yelling northeastward in pursuit of the bombardment's panicked survivors; the rest of Old Pete's men were not far behind. Bull Run was their objective, the old Stone Bridge's bottleneck the place where the "miscreant" John Pope's suppression might be made complete, his army destroyed.

Jackson's forces off to the west of the killing ground could do little more than shriek their yells, having run out of nearly everything but rocks, but some of them joined the chase. And at times their fire, such as it was, proved enough to drive even the most gallant knots of Yankee defenders away from their positions along Longstreet's western flank.

Clearly a victory it was, but darkness came early because rain clouds were arriving. And the farther north Hood pursued, the stiffer federal resistance got. Just south of Henry House Hill the Confederates had to halt. North of it, over the Stone Bridge, John Pope's men streamed toward Centreville.

Jackson rode back to the embankment. Reaching it, he saw a wounded boy struggling, trying to rise, asking him, "Have we whipped them?"

Old Jack, dismounted now, said it was so. What was the boy's regiment? "I belong," said the very young soldier, "to the Fourth Virginia, your old brigade, General. I have been wounded four times but never as bad as this. I hope I will soon be able to follow you again."

Chapter 14

Confederates Invade Kentucky and Maryland

Jefferson Davis's hands must have trembled when he read the message General Lee sent him from the rain-swept battleground at ten o'clock on Saturday night, August 30: "This Army today achieved on the plains of Manassas a signal victory over combined forces of Generals McClellan and Pope."

It was typical of Robert Lee to leave it to the president and posterity to judge his role. In three short months this modest man's audacity had moved the war a hundred miles, from Richmond's edge to Washington's—a fact the governments of cotton-short Great Britain and France were bound to note with astonishment and, possibly, recognition of the Confederacy.

Moreover, the news Jefferson Davis was getting from the west was reassuring. On the very same day General Lee's army was sweeping across the plains of Manassas, Kirby Smith had won a victory at Richmond, Kentucky, that was as near to a battle of annihilation as any had been so far in this war.

There was irony in that fight's having been at a place also named Richmond, more in how it came about. Unlike Abraham Lincoln, the Confederate president had not yet learned that he could not run a government and manage his nation's war effort at the same time without neglecting, too much, one duty or the other. And so it was that Jefferson Davis made the mistake that enabled Kirby Smith to reach that other Richmond.

Jefferson Davis had been a soldier, planter, politician, and senator. But left over from his years as secretary of war was his tendency to think and perform like a bureaucrat. So it seemed in the summer of 1862. Having separated the west into several departmental com-

216

partments and placed generals he considered competent in charge of them, he overlooked the need to adapt his arrangements when Bragg moved most of his army from Tupelo to Chattanooga—from his own department into Kirby Smith's.

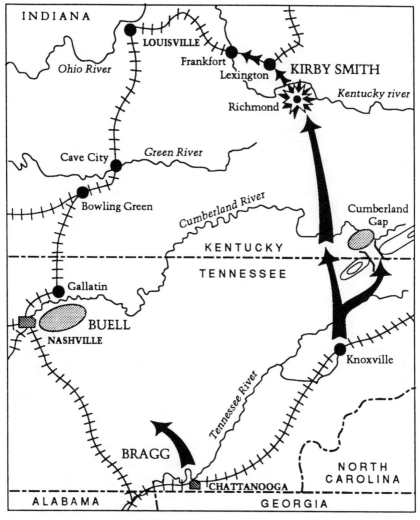

Confederates' Western Advances

Lacking an order from Davis for Bragg to assume command of all the forces in the west, in early August the two generals had agreed to cooperate. This was reassuring but also contrary to 2,000 years of military experience: contrary, as well, to all that Davis, Bragg, and Smith had been taught at West Point.

Yet Kirby Smith had Bragg's approval on August 14 when he moved northward from Knoxville. And with Kirby Smith were two fine brigades Bragg had sent him, Brigadier General Patrick R. Cleburne's and Colonel Preston Smith's, loaned for the purpose of driving the Union force out of Cumberland Gap. But Kirby Smith bypassed the federal division there and kept advancing. By the morning of August 18, his troops were in Barboursville, Kentucky, and he was in trouble; his supply wagons were far behind him and he was in the midst of Unionists determined to make the Confederates scavenge even for green corn.

Fortunately for Kirby Smith, leaving 9,000 men behind near Cumberland Gap to watch Union Brigadier General George Morgan's division meant that he now had only 12,000 Confederate mouths to try to feed. And everything would be better once he crossed the "barrens" and reached the bountiful bluegrass region.

While waiting at Barboursville for his wagons to catch up, Kirby Smith wrote a letter to Bragg in which he described his plight and all but canceled his pledge to help Bragg destroy Don Carlos Buell's army. He also wrote his wife:

> My expedition is something like Cortez. I have burnt my ships behind me and thrown myself boldly into the enemies country—the results may be brilliant and if successful will be considered a stroke of inspiration and genius.

Whether or not young Cassie Smith in Lynchburg, Virginia, expecting their first child, understood her husband's allusion to Hernán Cortés's conquest of Mexico, Braxton Bragg knew from the letter Kirby Smith had sent him that "cordial cooperation" had ended—if, in fact, it had ever been intended. Now Bragg would have to deal with Buell's Yankee army without Smith's forces. Powerless to command the ship burner, he acquiesced.

Kirby Smith started northward from Barboursville on August 27, the day Jackson's foot cavalry looted Manassas Junction. By Friday the twenty-ninth, Smith's troops were beyond the barrens, atop Big Hill, gazing northward in the late-afternoon sunlight at the lush bluegrass country as though it were the Promised Land. And cavalry reports were encouraging. Federal forces were deployed south of Richmond, within easy striking distance, and not (as Kirby Smith had feared) along the bluffs of the Kentucky River north of the town.

That Friday evening, Smith gave Pat Cleburne the honor of leading his and Preston Smith's brigades in the attack first thing Saturday morning. At sunrise the Irish-born Cleburne had his force advancing, and by sunset his men had killed 206 Yankees, wounded 844, and captured 4,303. Only about 1,200 of the original 6,500 or so federals managed to flee the scene.

Only later would Pat Cleburne find out what had happened on August 30. A Yankee bullet had hit his cheek, removed some of his teeth, and exited via his open mouth. Preston Smith had taken over and finished the battle—capturing, in the process, nine Union guns, 10,000 rifles and pistols, and a supply-laden wagon train at a cost of less than 500 Confederate casualties.

Few of the Yankees, recruits rushed across the Ohio River from Indiana and Ohio with scant training, had rallied when Major General William Nelson, setting a gallant example by baring his 300-pound, six-foot-five body to heavy Confederate fire, had cried, "If they can't hit me they can't hit anything!" *They* nicked the giant Yankee general's body twice but did not stop him. Neither could Nelson stop his green troops from surrendering in droves.

No federals remained between Kirby Smith and Lexington. His men got there the next day, and to Frankfort, Kentucky's capital, two days later, replacing the statehouse's Union flag with the colors of the 1st Louisiana Cavalry. Now Kirby Smith was where he had wanted all along to be, and Braxton Bragg was a day or so north of Chattanooga, and it was as though there had never been any agreement to cooperate at all.

Second Manassas (in the North, Second Bull Run) was fought on roughly the same ground, and again the Confederates won, but there the resemblance to First Manassas ended. As the heavy rain fell that Saturday evening, Major General John Pope's troops withdrew, but they did it in an orderly manner, destroying the Stone Bridge when the last bluecoat had crossed Bull Run and halting at Centreville to regroup. There was no panic, no rush toward Washington.

At 9:45 P.M., August 30, Pope sent a reassuring message to General-in-Chief Halleck:

> The battle was most furious for hours without cessation, and the losses on both sides very heavy. The enemy is badly crippled, and we shall do well enough. Do not be uneasy. We will hold our own here.

Henry Halleck must have been overwhelmed by thoughts of what might have been. "If re-enforcements reach [Pope] in time," he had said in a telegram to General McClellan three hours earlier, "we shall have a glorious victory." McClellan's two corps, 30,000 troops, had been so near, yet not a man in either one had gotten close enough to pull a trigger.

Then came a wire from Alexandria, from McClellan:

> I cannot express to you the pain & mortification I experienced today in listening to the distant sound of the firing of my men. As I can be of no further use here I respectfully ask that if there is a probability of the conflict being renewed tomorrow I may be permitted to go to the scene of the battle with my staff— merely to be with my own men if nothing more—they will fight none the worse for my being with them.
>
> If it is not deemed best to entrust me with the command even of my own Army I simply ask to be permitted to share their fate on the field of battle. Please reply to this tonight.
>
> I have been engaged for the last few hours in doing what I can to make arrangements for the wounded.

Compassion had set Secretary of War Stanton in motion as well. Hearing the distance-muffled booming and sniffing the acrid traces of gunpowder winds were bringing into Washington from the southwest that Saturday afternoon, Stanton seized all the carriages and buggies he could to move convalescent men to the railroad station and ordered trains to take them northward to Philadelphia, even New York. Having cleared Washington's cots, Stanton sent out circulars to recruit government employees and indeed anyone to go to Fairfax and serve as nurses, with rail transportation to be provided.

Colonel Herman Haupt would have to do the providing, of course, and when he learned of Stanton's action, he protested. Military supplies, not a "promiscuous rabble," should have top priority. But he was told that the invitations had gone out and that the secretary could not rescind his orders to Haupt "even though it [the whole thing] might have been a mistake."

Long afterward, Haupt described the result:

> I sent on a train, and when it reached Alexandria [from Washington] it was packed full, inside and on top. Some women even had forced themselves into the cars, which were ordinary freight cars without seats. It was night. Superintendent [J. H.] Devereux came to me, after inspecting the train, and begged me to have it sidetracked; that it would not do to send it forward; that half the men were drunk and nearly every one had a couple of bottles of whisky.

Stanton's orders were peremptory, Haupt told Devereux. But Haupt delayed as long as he could and also wired an officer at Fairfax to arrest the drunks when the train got there. Haupt recalled the aftermath:

> Those who were sober enough straggled off as soon as it was light enough [on Sunday morning] to see and wandered around until whisky and provisions became exhausted, when they returned to the station to get transportation back. In this, most of them were disappointed. The orders had been to take them out, but none to bring them back, and although it seemed cruel to compel them to walk, cold, hungry and wet with rain, it would have been far more cruel to let the wounded lie on the ground to perish.

And, reminiscing, Haupt added, perhaps with a chuckle: "Telegrams came in from officers, 'don't send out any more civilians.'"

Sunday morning's rain pelted the hangover-plagued "nurses" and General Lee's troops alike, obliging the fifty-five-year-old man who commanded the Army of Northern Virginia to put on rubber overalls and a poncho when he got to work early on August 31. Cavalrymen arrived, reporting all roads except the Warrenton Turnpike muddy, Bull Run nigh impassable, and federals beyond counting present in the defensive positions Joe Johnston's men had dug near Centreville after First Manassas.

Make the most of the scraps of time had long been one of Robert Edward Lee's personal maxims, and he had followed it on Saturday morning—while John Pope did not appear to be doing anything much—by planning his next move. So he was prepared on that rainy Sunday to order General Jackson to make another flank march, northward again, the purpose being to force Pope to abandon Centreville.

"Good," said Jackson.

Then, not long after this man of few but significant words departed, someone yelled: "Yankee cavalry!"

Traveller, Lee's magnificent war horse, stirred. General Lee tried to reach Traveller's reins, but he slipped in the mud and fell, breaking a small bone in one hand and spraining the other. No federals appeared. But for days to come, with both his hands bandaged, General Lee would have to command his army from an ambulance wagon.

General McClellan had given the rain-swept new day a depressing start by sending the general-in-chief a message from Alexandria at 3:30 A.M.:

My aide just in. He reports our army as badly beaten. Our losses very heavy. Troops arriving at Centreville. Have probably lost several batteries. Some of the Corps entirely broken up into stragglers.

Halleck got a very different impression from the report General Pope sent him from Centreville at 10:45 A.M.:

Our troops are all here in position, though much used-up and worn out. I think perhaps it would have been greatly better if Sumner and Franklin had been here three or four days ago; but you may rely on our giving them [Lee's army] as desperate a fight as I can force our men to stand up to.

I should like to know whether you feel secure about Washington should this army be destroyed. I shall fight it as long as a man will stand up to the work. You must judge what is to be done, having in view the safety of the capital.

"My dear General," began Halleck in the reply he wired to Pope at once. He continued:

You have done nobly. Don't yield another inch if you can avoid it. All reserves are being sent forward....Can't you renew the attack?...I am doing all in my power for you and your noble army. God bless you and it.

Then came the news from Kentucky, and it was discouraging enough to make a stone crack. Kirby Smith's rebels had smashed Nelson's green troops and were about to seize Lexington. No federal force remained to keep the Confederates from rushing northward to the Ohio River and crossing it, bringing the war into Indiana and Ohio. "We must have help of drilled troops," telegraphed Brigadier General J. T. Boyle from Louisville, "unless you intend to turn us over to the devil and his imps."

General Halleck intended no such thing, and for days and nights he and his pitifully small staff had been working beyond the limits of human endurance to support Union operations in Tennessee and Kentucky as well as Virginia. But now the devils seemed to be winning everywhere, at the same time, and for disasters such as these there would have to be a scapegoat.

It was perhaps as Halleck had feared, back in July, when he had all but refused to come to Washington. But he worked on through Sunday and into Sunday night, dividing his attention among the three widely separated points of Union vulnerability, peppered by

McClellan's misleading and insolent messages, until at 10:07 on the night of August 31 Halleck wired him:

> You will retain command of everything in this vicinity not temporarily belonging to Pope's army in the field. I beg of you to assist me in this crisis with your ability and experience. I am utterly tired out.

It was a surrender of a sort; so it would be interpreted later; but McClellan took it as such immediately. "I am ready to afford you every assistance in my power," he replied only eighteen minutes later, "but you will readily perceive how difficult an undefined position such as I now hold must be."

Then, at 11:30 P.M., McClellan added:

> To speak frankly—and the occasion requires it—there appears to be a total absence of brains, and I fear the total destruction of the army....It is my deliberate opinion that the interests of the nation demand that Pope should fall back to-night if possible, and not one moment is to be lost....I shall be up all night and ready to obey any orders you may give me.

General McClellan, Halleck may have sensed, would not be the scapegoat, though, at the beginning of his effusion, he had let it slip that his information came from a sergeant whose cavalry unit had tangled with the rebels more than nine hours earlier. All McClellan's judgments and urgings were apparently based upon this sole source, which was appallingly shallow, and even dangerous. If Pope were destroyed, however, McClellan could stand before the Congressional Committee on the Conduct of the War and solemnly swear, "I warned the General-in-Chief."

Again Halleck would be up all night. Around one-thirty on the morning of Monday, September 1, he wired McClellan:

> My news from Pope was up to 4 p.m. and he was then all right. I must wait for more definite information before I can order a retreat....I am fully aware of the gravity of the crisis and have been for weeks.

Heavy rain, scant rations, low ammunition stocks, fatigue—all these made General Jackson's attempt to get north and west of the federal army's flank difficult. On Sunday, the thirty-first, his men crossed Bull Run at Sudley's Ford and slogged along muddy back roads to the Little River Turnpike, turned southeastward, and camped for the night near Pleasant Valley. In all they had marched ten miles.

Centreville was about five miles south, but that no longer mattered, for on Monday morning Stuart's cavalrymen reported that Pope's forces had moved eastward to Fairfax Court House. There the Little River Turnpike met the Warrenton-Washington Turnpike. But by afternoon Jackson's three hungry and weary divisions had covered only three miles, storm clouds loomed overhead, and it was apparent that his troops would not get much beyond the once-gracious Chantilly mansion.

Late on that Monday, September 1, Stuart's cavalry patrols collided with Union infantry near Ox Hill. Jackson deployed his units while Stuart tried to determine whether the Yankees were advancing or retreating. Heavy rain was falling now, and heavy as well was the fire the Confederates encountered; as often as they tried to advance, they were repulsed. Darkness and the miserable weather ended the fight, one in which Union losses were around 1,000 and Jackson's about 500.

Chantilly had been a meeting engagement, nothing more, and it was memorable mainly because it cost the Union the services of two generals of great promise.

One was Brigadier General Isaac Ingalls Stevens, first man in West Point's class of 1839 (Henry Wager Halleck was third), wounded outside Mexico City at Churubusco in the same battle in which Phil Kearny lost an arm. On this dreary Monday afternoon, Stevens had just taken a regiment's colors from the hands of a dying man and was leading his troops forward when he was shot through the head and died instantly. At about that moment, so Porter Alexander wrote, "the authorities in Washington were about to supersede Pope, and place Stevens in command of the now united armies of Pope and McClellan."

Chantilly was gallant Phil Kearny's final fight as well, and his death saddened men on both sides. Kearny, a veteran of fighting in Algeria, Mexico, Italy, and McClellan's Peninsula campaign, was killed while trying to shoot his way through a ring of Confederate skirmishers. Remembering Churubusco, perhaps, General Lee returned his old friend's body to the federal lines under a flag of truce.

So ended the Second Manassas campaign, in which the South lost roughly 9,100 men that nation could not replace. Union casualties totaled nearly 14,500. Along the way from Cedar Mountain, Lee's troops took thirty guns and picked up more than 20,000 abandoned small arms, apart from luxuries such as shoes, toothbrushes, canned delicacies, and fine wines Jackson's men had looted from Pope's treasure houses at Manassas Junction.

On September 1, 1862, both eastern armies were nearly where they had been in late July 1861. This was curious, but such a situation could not last. John Pope had not quit fighting, as Jackson had learned at Chantilly. Lee had to move out of northern Virginia's ravished counties or watch his army starve. And the only direction in which Lee could move was northward, into Union-held Maryland.

John Hay, one of Abraham Lincoln's secretaries, had seen the president's mood swing like a weathervane in erratic winds during the last days of August until, on the morning of the thirty-first, Lincoln looked up from a message and said, "Well, John, we are whipped again, I am afraid."

It was not so much a cry of despair as the facing, once more, of a fact and an acceptance of its consequences. These, Lincoln knew from experience, he would begin to feel as soon as more wounded Union soldiers were brought into Washington and newspaper reporters heard their stories.

This time, however, the Northern public's reaction went beyond shock and sadness and anger to vindictiveness. People agreed with the judgment of a *New York Tribune* reporter who wrote: "We have been whipped by an inferior force of inferior men, better handled than ours."

This was galling, the more so because there was truth in the charge that inferior generalship was the main cause of the Union's humiliation. Later reports would be more specific, accusing George McClellan and Fitz-John Porter and other slow-moving officers from the Army of the Potomac of contributing to John Pope's defeat. Pope was considered merely incompetent. Senior officers' jealousy, treachery, misdirected loyalties—these, Northerners were led to believe, suggested that something in the national character was rotten.

Was this new punishment falling upon bewildered children because of the long-ago sins of the fathers? Or because of laxity on the part of the current president? Whatever the fault, Lincoln knew he would have to correct it. Doing so would not be easy. Pressure on him was increasing, time was short, and his possible courses of action were few in number. But what was the least wrong thing to do?

The Union's commander-in-chief had spent enough hours in the War Department's telegraph office to know that Halleck had done all he could to support and encourage John Pope. Sacking goggle-eyed, elbow-scratching Old Brains, then, was neither deserved nor likely to stop the howling of those who, in Secretary of War Stanton's words, "sell news."

McClellan's head was the one many in the mob demanded, the president's not being available. Stanton started the process of decapitating McClellan. Relying on answers to the questions he had put to Halleck regarding the general's conduct, Stanton prepared a memorandum to the president—a "remonstrance"—that he expected most other cabinet members would sign.

In the text Stanton accused McClellan of incompetence and imperiling Pope's army through inactivity and disobedience of orders. He asserted that the signers feared "destruction of our armies," the war's protraction and the waste of national resources, even overthrow of the government—"the inevitable consequence of George B. McClellan being continued in command."

Treasury Secretary Salmon Chase agreed to sign, saying "McClellan ought to be shot!" Gideon Welles thought so, too, but he considered the "remonstrance" procedure a discourtesy to the president. Attorney General Bates signed a revised text.

But it was all for naught. At a cabinet meeting on September 2, Lincoln astonished its members—and infuriated Stanton and Chase—by announcing that he had given McClellan command of both Union armies in the Washington area.

Lincoln took full responsibility, admitting that the general had the "slows" but explaining that McClellan was good at organizing and training and that these skills were what the immediate situation required. General-in-Chief Halleck, the president added, agreed.

Curiously, neither Lincoln nor Stanton put their names on the order appointing McClellan. This they left for Halleck to do—and to relieve John Pope and reassign him to faraway St. Paul, Minnesota, where quelling Indian uprisings would be his primary duty. From there Pope would ask repeatedly and with considerable justification for a court of inquiry to clear his reputation; repeatedly, his requests were denied, the blows softened only by Halleck's expressions of his personal regrets and assurances of his respect.

John Pope deserved respect, for in almost his last message as a combat commander he showed he still wanted to fight. At about the same time, George McClellan was having forces prepare to burn the houses in Arlington, directly across the Potomac from Washington, when the enemy came near. Earlier, someone—the president, presumably—had countermanded McClellan's order to demolish the Chain Bridge.

Persons nearest Abraham Lincoln and certainly his critics were convinced he had selected the worst possible man to merge the federal armies and reorganize them, but the weary men in the camps near Fairfax Court House felt otherwise. They cheered and threw their caps and knapsacks high in the air as they saw the familiar figure astride Dan Webster riding toward them, and the yelling intensified and spread ahead of him. It reached John Pope before McClellan did. It was surely the bitterest of the memories he would be taking out to Minnesota.

Why had General Lee not ordered Jackson to press on from Chantilly and pursue the "miscreant" Pope into Washington's lines? "My men had nothing to eat."

There were, of course, other reasons for moving northward. The farther from Richmond Lee advanced, the more federal forces his army attracted and the more secure would be the Confederate capital. Maryland was to Southerners a sister state in need of rescue from Yankee forces. Foreign military observers might recommend diplomatic recognition and aid. And the longer Lee's army remained north of the Potomac, keeping Union troops out of Virginia, the more time farmers throughout the Shenandoah Valley would have for harvesting their crops.

So it was that on Thursday afternoon, September 4, 1862, less than a month after they had left the old battlegrounds east of Richmond, more than a hundred miles south of them, the first of General Jackson's troops waded the Potomac, cheering as they reached the northern shoreline, some singing as they heard the band playing "Maryland, My Maryland."

Decades later, Douglas Southall Freeman reconstructed the scene as effectively as any historian ever may:

> The country people seemed glad to see them, but they must have wondered how such an army could have won the victories emblazoned on its faded flags. Lank and lagging horses bore tattered riders ahead of the ragged columns of dirty, unshaven, and cadaverous infantrymen, neat in nothing but the well-tended rifles they carried. Scarcely a shining button or a trim uniform was to be seen, even in brigades the very names of whose officers had the ring of iron discipline. Hats hung in battered brims; shocks of hair stuck through the holes; caps had lost their color. Toes gaped from flapping shoes and naked feet limped in protest at the hardness of Maryland's stony roads. Smoke-covered caissons rattled; dilapidated wagons groaned; the worn wheels that carried the lean guns of the artillery complained.

Justified though General Lee may have considered the move

northward, he soon discovered that his thinking was not shared by a surprising number of his men. Many of them were serving in the army merely to drive the Yankees off Southern soil and punish them for having invaded it. Some were stretching their principles to defend states other than their own. To expect them to cross the Potomac, to commit the sin the Northerners had, was simply too much; they could not do it.

Estimates of how many soldiers abandoned Lee's army during the first week of September ranged between 10,000 and 20,000. In any case, the number well exceeded his losses in combat since the early part of August. Fortunately for him, President Davis had sent up virtually all Richmond's defenders. Even so, if Lee had 53,000 men on September 5, they would be roughly 18,000 fewer by the middle of that month.

But what worried the Army of Northern Virginia's commander most was running out of ammunition, or so he wrote Davis. He was indeed dangerously far extended, forced to rely on wagon trains to make the slow 100-mile trip northward from Culpeper at a time when his thoughts were centered on how to advance another seventy miles to Harrisburg, Pennsylvania's capital. Yet he pressed on from the Potomac to Frederick, Maryland, reaching there on September 7 and ordering his men to remain in their camps near the town.

Marylanders' receptions varied from guarded welcomes to curiosity. Well aware that the federals might return once his army had passed on, Lee did not allow himself or his troops to become too friendly with any citizens, even those who showed no fear of Yankee reprisals. This was the western, heavily pro-Union part of the state; most Confederate sympathizers lived in distant counties, along the eastern shores of Chesapeake Bay.

But there was the chance something might be gained by a proclamation to all the people of Maryland, and from Frederick on September 8, General Lee issued one. In part it said:

> Marylanders shall once more enjoy their ancient freedom of thought and speech. We know no enemies among you, and will protect all, of every opinion. It is for you to decide your destiny freely and without constraint. This army will respect your choice, whatever it may be; and while the Southern people will rejoice to welcome you to your natural position among them, they will only welcome you when you come of your own free will.

It was perhaps as near an expression of Robert Lee's own political philosophy as anything he ever wrote. And while his mind was on such matters, the general prepared a letter to the president in which he said he thought the military situation enabled the Confederacy to make a peace proposal, one designed to obtain its independence. Near the close, Lee said:

> The rejection of this offer would prove to the country that the responsibility of the continuance of the war does not rest upon us, but that the party in power in the United States elect to prosecute it for purposes of their own. The proposal of peace would enable the people of the United States to determine at the coming elections whether they will support those who favor a prolongation of the war, or those who wish to bring it to a termination, which can but be productive of good to both parties without affecting the honor of either.

Lee then reverted from statesman to soldier, recognizing that all his words would prove hollow unless he found ways of sustaining his army's presence in Maryland for long enough to convince Northerners that this was no mere raid. Confederate dollars had bought about all the food and fodder available in Frederick's vicinity. Soon he would have to move on. But Lee could not head for Pennsylvania until he removed the federal threats to his supply lines in Virginia's Shenandoah Valley.

Strong federal garrisons at Harpers Ferry and Martinsburg had to be removed before Lee's new 150-mile lifeline down the Valley from Staunton could do him much good. But should he split his army to achieve this?

As it turned out, General Lee not only divided his little army but broke it into *four* fragments.

"Again I have been called upon to save the country," wrote General McClellan to his wife on September 5, adding:

> It makes my heart bleed to see the poor shattered remnants of my noble Army of the Potomac, poor fellows! and to see how they love me even now. I hear them calling out to me as I ride among them—"George—don't leave us again!" "They *shan't* take you away from us again" etc etc. I can hardly restrain myself when I see how fearfully they are reduced in numbers & realize how many of them lie unburied on the field of battle where their lives were uselessly sacrificed. It is the most terrible trial I ever experienced—Truly God is trying me in the fire.

No, not quite. But the wisdom of returning McClellan to command of the Army of the Potomac *was* being questioned. Lee had bypassed Washington, so Little Mac's defensive skills were not needed. And Lincoln was not so sure he was willing to trust a general afflicted with the "slows" with the task of turning back a Confederate invasion of the North.

Once before, thinking of getting rid of McClellan, the president had offered command of the army to Burnside; again he did, and again Burnside told him he did not consider himself capable of leading so large a force. And Fitz-John Porter's name had to be erased from the already short alternatives list: his recent conduct at Manassas was widely thought to be a proximate cause of Pope's defeat. So Lincoln was stuck with McClellan, a general who was at least good at building armies.

Fortunately for the Union, the Army of the Potomac needed little refitting—ironically, because McClellan had kept so much of it east of Manassas. At his headquarters in his house in Washington the general quickly made changes in his command structure. Although McClellan's authority to take the army beyond the defenses of Washington was not entirely clear, by Sunday, September 7, he could write to Mary Ellen:

> I leave in a couple of hours to take command of the army in the field. I shall go to Rockville [Maryland] tonight & start out after the rebels tomorrow. I shall have nearly 100,000 men, old & new, & hope with God's blessing to gain a decisive victory. I think we shall win for the men are now in good spirits—confident in their General & all united in sentiment. Pope & McDowell have morally killed themselves—& are relieved from command—a signal instance of retributive justice. I have done nothing towards this—it has done itself. I have now the entire confidence of the Govt & the love of the army—my enemies are crushed, silent & disarmed—if I defeat the rebels I shall be master of the situation.

But at Rockville, twelve miles northwest of Washington and roughly twenty-five miles from Frederick, the army commander lingered. At one point he thought Lee was moving toward Baltimore. His estimates of the Confederate army's strength varied from wire to wire, ranging wildly until on September 11, when he telegraphed the general-in-chief that it was "not less than 120,000 men." Halleck released Fitz-John Porter's 21,000 men from the defense of Washington and sent them, and more, up to McClellan.

Hagerstown, twenty-odd miles northwest of Frederick, was where General Lee wanted to be. From Hagerstown he could move into Pennsylvania, burn the railroad bridge over the Susquehanna at Harrisburg, and force the federals to resort to a roundabout route near the Great Lakes for East-West rail shipments. This would vex "those people" severely and also cause them to worry about the safety of Baltimore and even Philadelphia. Presence of a Confederate army in Pennsylvania would not go unnoticed in London and Paris; and the commonwealth north of Maryland could provide food for his men and fodder for the army's animals.

First, though, the Army of Northern Virginia's commander had to have a secure supply route (for ammunition, if nothing more) from Staunton northeastward through Hagerstown and Chambersburg to wherever his forces might be. On Tuesday, September 9, General Lee issued Special Order No. 191, a detailed set of instructions calling for Jackson to eliminate the Union detachment at Martinsburg, then the one at Harpers Ferry, destroying segments of the Baltimore & Ohio Railroad along the way. Two other Confederate forces were to move by different routes to seize the heights north and east of Harpers Ferry, prevent its Yankee garrison from escaping, and assist Jackson in capturing it. The fourth force, Longstreet's, would move directly toward Boonsboro and Hagerstown. Jeb Stuart was to assign cavalry to accompany each of the army's fragments. The army would reassemble at Hagerstown. And with McClellan back in command of the federal army, Lee was confident he would have enough time in which to execute his plan.

All of Lee's troops left Frederick early the next morning, Wednesday, the tenth. By Thursday night he and Longstreet were in Hagerstown. On Friday, the twelfth, all he learned was that McClellan was nearing Frederick, which was a surprise. Word came on the thirteenth, Saturday, that Jackson had only then reached Martinsburg and was driving about 3,000 federals toward Harpers Ferry. Other reports said the Yankees were past Frederick and approaching South Mountain, northeast of Harpers Ferry.

Now, with Jackson late and McClellan astonishingly early, Lee improvised, ordering Harvey Hill to move southeastward from Boonsboro to Turner's Gap on South Mountain (as the Blue Ridge is called where it crosses Maryland) and hold it. Longstreet's divisions would follow first thing in the morning.

But to Lee at around ten o'clock that Saturday night came a message from Jeb Stuart. A Southern sympathizer, reported the cavalryman, had found him near Turner's Gap just after dark and told him he had been at McClellan's headquarters late that morning and had seen the general get very excited about a piece of paper someone had brought him. This suggested that the Union army might be about to launch an offensive.

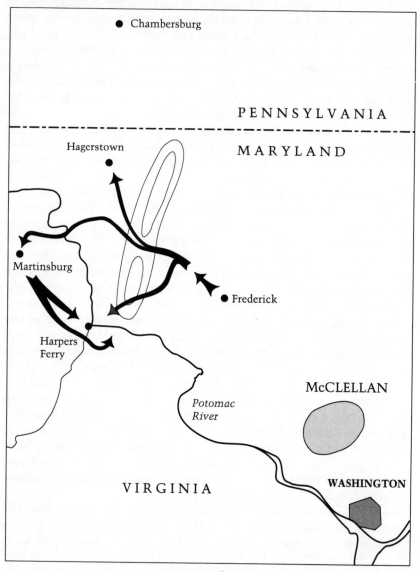

Lee's Scattered Army

Longstreet had never been comfortable about splitting the army into four fragments—now five, with Harvey Hill moving to Turner's Gap. Old Pete told General Lee he thought it would be better to let the federals have the passes on South Mountain and to concentrate his whole army at Sharpsburg. No, Lee decided, the orders he had given would stand: Turner's Gap and Crampton's south of it must be defended—to give Jackson enough time to capture Harpers Ferry and its Yankee garrison.

General McClellan wanted the men defending Harpers Ferry added to his own force. No, said the general-in-chief; the B & O railroad bridge over the Potomac had to be protected, meaning that Colonel Dixon S. Miles would have to hold at all costs.

So matters stood earlier in the week when McClellan began advancing from Rockville toward Frederick. Six miles per day was about all the marching McClellan could get from the Army of the Potomac, in part because Marylanders along the route welcomed the troops with pastries, apples, tubs of water, and in at least one instance, whiskey.

Early on Saturday morning, the thirteenth, McClellan rode into Frederick. Cheering citizens pelted him with flowers and handed babies up for their hero to kiss. That interlude past, at his new headquarters the Army of the Potomac's commander began a conference with a small group of civilians regarding the troops' presence near Frederick. He would send Burnside's corps, under the temporary command of Major General Jesse Reno, westward toward South Mountain lest Frederick's people have too many guests too close by. Most of his other corps would settle in east of the town.

The 27th Indiana had already moved into a campsite the Confederates had used during their stay. Corporal Barton W. Mitchell noticed a bulky white envelope on the ground, picked it up, and found three cigars inside wrapped in a piece of paper. Mitchell knew what to do with the cigars, but there was something unusual about their wrapper. Thinking it might be a Confederate order of some sort, the corporal passed it up the chain of command; quickly it reached army headquarters.

McClellan was still talking with his visitors when an officer drew him away from the group and handed him the piece of paper Corporal Mitchell had found. For a moment the general studied it. Then, as one of the civilians told Jeb Stuart some hours later, McClellan grew very excited and said: "Now I know what to do!"

Though the observer had been unaware of it, the document McClellan had read was a copy of Lee's Special Order No. 191, dated September 9, 1862. From it the Young Napoleon learned not only that Lee had split his army but also where he had sent each of the four fragments and what their missions were.

"I think Lee has made a gross mistake," the jubilant general wired President Lincoln at noon, "and that he will be severely punished for it." McClellan continued:

> I hope for a great success if the plans of the rebels remain unchanged....I have all the plans of the rebels, and will catch them in their own trap if my men are equal to the emergency. I now feel that I can count on them as of old. All forces of Pennsylvania should be placed to co-operate at Chambersburg. My respects to Mrs. Lincoln. Received most cordially by the ladies. Will send you trophies. All well, and with God's blessing will accomplish it.

On Monday the eighth McClellan had wired General-in-Chief Halleck: "As soon as I find out where to strike, I will be after them without an hour's delay." But almost seven hours passed between his sending of regards to Mrs. Lincoln and the issuing of orders to get "after them." And neither directive called for movement until the next morning.

William Franklin was to move his corps, then within easy marching distance of Crampton's Gap on South Mountain, and attack the rebel force holding Colonel Miles's garrison captive at Harpers Ferry. Worse, McClellan was allowing the divisions west of Frederick to spend that night in the valley east of South Mountain, a few miles below lightly defended Turner's Gap.

General Jackson, two years earlier professor of artillery at the Virginia Military Institute, spent most of Sunday, the fourteenth, trying to arrange for all the guns ringing Harpers Ferry to pour their fire on the 13,000-man federal garrison *concurrently*. Old Jack knew the rugged terrain well; a frontal assault would be costly; the Yankees' surrender was what he wanted; stunning was the way to obtain it; hence, the importance of artillery.

But Jackson knew, also, that for him time was running out. Marching sixty-two miles since leaving Frederick on Wednesday morning had made him reach his goal later than the date General Lee had designated in Special Order No. 191. Word had reached Old Jack that McClellan's advance had been uncharacteristically rapid. Harvey Hill, even with help from Longstreet's divisions, could not hold South Mountain's gaps for very long. Unless Jackson finished his work at Harpers Ferry immediately, the Maryland-Pennsylvania campaign would have to be aborted.

At 8:15 P.M. on that Sunday, the fourteenth, Jackson sent such assurance as he could to General Lee: "Through God's blessing, the advance, which commenced this evening, has been successful thus far, and I look to Him for complete success tomorrow."

Chapter 15

Time Runs Out Along Antietam Creek

George McClellan was counting on God's blessing, and Thomas J. Jackson was grateful for it and hoping for more. Abraham Lincoln also had been meditating upon divine will. Early in September he had written down some of his thoughts:

> The will of God prevails. In great contests each party claims to act in accordance with the will of God. Both *may* be, and one *must* be wrong. God can not be for, and *against*, the same thing at the same time. In the present civil war it is quite possible that God's purpose is something different from the purpose of either party—and yet the human instrumentalities, working just as they do, are of the best adaptation to effect His purpose. I am almost ready to say this is probably true—that God wills this contest, and wills that it shall not end yet. By his mere quiet power, on the minds of the now contestants, He could have either *saved* or *destroyed* the Union without a human contest. Yet the contest began. And having begun He could give the final victory to either side any day. Yet the contest proceeds.

Had Lincoln witnessed the fighting on South Mountain on Sunday the fourteenth, he might have been as perplexed as ever. As the day began, only a small Confederate force held Turner's Gap. At nightfall, two Union corps had failed to get through it.

The contest was another classic meeting engagement, one in which both sides began with modest numbers of troops engaged where no one had expected much more than a holding action's skirmishing. But as both sides fed more and more men in, a battle

235

developed that would last all day and increase in ferocity hour by hour.

Harvey Hill, defending Turner's Gap, never had enough men to do anything beyond trading blood for time while he waited for Longstreet's divisions to arrive from Hagerstown. Hill's main problem was that the Yankees had found trails right and left of the National Road, trails that led upward through the woods to his brigades' flanks on the ridgeline.

True, Hill was in a central position. But he was having to hold back federals south and north of him and worry about being hit from the east, on the National Road, as well. In mountainous terrain artillery was ineffective, except briefly. The battle was mostly a series of sharp firefights in which one side gained ground, then lost it, with second efforts by the Yankees—growing rapidly both in numbers and killing power—hammering both of Hill's flanks on the ridgeline, squeezing the Confederates back into the pass.

Longstreet's arrival late on that Sunday afternoon made little difference. His men were tired, and by then the only question was whether Burnside's corps would take the pass from the south or Joseph Hooker's from the north. It took sundown to stop the firing, but Harvey Hill still held Turner's Gap.

All of which, had he seen it, would have revealed far more about the valor of American soldiers to Abraham Lincoln than it might have helped him discern signs of divine will.

At Crampton's Gap, roughly eight miles to the south along South Mountain's spine, Confederate Major General Lafayette McLaws's weak forces proved unable to hold back Franklin's federal corps and retreated. In Pleasant Valley, not far north of Harpers Ferry, McLaws built the best line he could. But near sundown Franklin decided to wait until Monday morning to smash through McLaws's defenses.

That proved to be a mistake. Early on Monday morning, the fifteenth, echoes of Jackson's concentrated bombardment of Harpers Ferry bounced from mountain to mountain, but before the lethargic Franklin could get his men moving, the firing ceased. Correctly, he took that to mean Colonel Miles had surrendered; he called off his attack and waited for McClellan's orders.

After Sunday's fights on South Mountain, and reluctantly, General Lee had ordered the commanders of his army's fragments to bring their forces to Sharpsburg. Now, on Monday morning, September 15, he had with him at the little village not far from the Potomac only Longstreet's men, about 18,000. Still some miles off to the southeast were the rest.

Near noon a message came from General Jackson:

> Through God's blessing, Harper's Ferry and its garrison are to be surrendered. As [Powell] Hill's troops have borne the heaviest part in the engagement, he will be left in command until the prisoners and public property shall be disposed of, unless you direct otherwise. The other forces can move off this evening so soon as they get their rations.

"That is indeed good news," the general remarked, "let it be announced to the troops." More news arrived: Jackson had captured more than 11,000 Yankees—all but a cavalry force that had fled earlier—and roughly 13,000 rifles and pistols, 73 artillery pieces, over 200 wagons, and various kinds of supplies. No mention was there of McLaws, but the roads were open for all the divisions to use in marching to Sharpsburg.

Along the way Jackson had cleared Martinsburg, which meant the Valley Turnpike supply route from Staunton was also open. All Lee had intended when he issued Special Order No. 191 had been achieved except that the reassembly point was not Hagerstown. Sharpsburg would have to do. "We will make our stand," General Lee had decided before the encouraging news had reached him. But now he would have to make good that commitment, for on the eastern side of Antietam Creek "those people" were moving in.

Out in the west a different kind of war was going on, yet there were some similarities to the eastern one. Confederate forces had streaked from Chattanooga and Knoxville into central Kentucky, marching about as far as Lee's army had moved from Richmond. The Union's ranking general, Don Carlos Buell, had been obliged to react to Southern initiatives (as John Pope had been in late August), and Buell, like McClellan, was not the man the federal high command wanted. And, as in the east, much depended on the outcome—internationally as well in terms of public attitudes toward continuation of the war.

Kirby Smith's victory at Richmond, Kentucky, on August 30 was minor in comparison with the concurrent Battle of Second Manassas, but it opened the eastern half of the Bluegrass State and set Northern civilians in Cincinnati to digging trenches, ten miles of them, south of the Ohio River. Braxton Bragg's achievements were more modest; he did not leave Chattanooga until August 28 and then had to keep an eye on Buell's federal divisions. But by the time Lee was invading Maryland, Bragg was at Sparta—east of Nashville—deciding which route to take northward after his 28,000 men entered Kentucky.

Bragg's problem was much the same as Lee's had been: food. There would not be much of it available until he got well into Kentucky, which meant his troops would be on short rations on their ninety-mile march to Glasgow. But for the moment he could press northward without worrying greatly about Buell. Nathan Bedford Forrest's cavalrymen had been harassing the Yankees around Nashville; and like McClellan, Buell was afflicted by what Abraham Lincoln called "the slows."

That was not entirely Don Carlos Buell's fault, for he had been forced to scatter his forces along his railroad lifeline, and he had a nervous Unionist governor in Nashville to placate—Andrew Johnson, an East Tennesseean who wanted Buell to forget about Kentucky and keep the bulk of his army nearby. Ulysses Grant had sent about 10,000 troops northeastward from Mississippi to replace Buell's. Even so, to appease Johnson, Buell had to leave Major General George H. Thomas's corps behind at Nashville on September 7 when he took five divisions up the Louisville & Nashville Railroad (L & N) to try to reach Louisville before Bragg did.

Bowling Green was Buell's first objective. It took him a week to get there. And when he did, he learned that Bragg was nearly forty miles northeast of him, threatening Munfordville—a key point on the L & N, one Buell could not afford to lose.

It had been a race throughout early September, reminiscent of Lee's in August to beat McClellan's forces to Manassas, but now the differences between the eastern and western campaigns began to appear. Weeks earlier, Braxton Bragg had wanted to destroy Buell's army first, then invade Kentucky. But Kirby Smith had gone his own way, so slipping past Buell's army had been Bragg's only option. And now, no matter how much Bragg may have wished he could concentrate all of the Confederate forces in Kentucky to smite Buell, he lacked the authority to order Kirby Smith to do anything. Another difference: Unlike Lee, Bragg seemed uncertain as to what he really meant to do.

"We come to guarantee to all the sanctity of [Kentuckians'] homes and altars, to punish with a rod of iron the despoilers of your peace, and to avenge the cowardly insults to your women," Bragg had proclaimed on September 14. This was a lot for a general with such a small force to promise. And for his rhetoric to attract recruits and broad support, he would have to convince Kentuckians he could protect them, statewide, indefinitely. But Bragg made clear in his final paragraph that his army's presence was highly tentative: "If you prefer Federal rule, show it by your frowns and we shall return whence we came."

From proclaiming Bragg returned to planning. Food stocks were low; Buell's 35,000 Yankees were getting closer; joining Kirby Smith for a drive toward Cincinnati seemed too ambitious. He would move northeastward into the fertile bluegrass country, Bragg decided, link up with Smith, then seize Louisville.

Bragg did what he could to slow Buell's advance, sending some forces to the L & N Railroad to wreck it and others probing northward. From Cave City, Brigadier General James R. Chalmers moved ten miles or so up to attack a federal outpost south of the Green River and Munfordville—and got repulsed. Chalmers backed off and demanded the 4,000-man garrison's surrender. Union Colonel J. T. Wilder replied: "If you wish to avoid further bloodshed keep out of the range of my guns."

News of this abrupt challenge upset Bragg's plans; quickly he sent his divisions to surround the federals at Munfordville. Bragg reiterated Chalmers's two-day-old surrender demand and got a prompt refusal. But the federal commander had been a soldier for only a little over a year, and he knew Kentuckian Simon Buckner was in Bragg's force, so he came out of his fort under a truce flag to talk to the man he trusted. Buckner abstained from persuasion, merely taking his unexpected guest on a tour of the lines and letting Wilder count the guns and guess at the number of the troops he saw. "I believe," said Colonel Wilder to Buckner early on September 17, "I'll surrender."

And so it was that about the same time Lee and McClellan were moving their forces into confrontation on opposite sides of Antietam Creek in Maryland hundreds of miles eastward, Bragg won a victory at Munfordville that almost matched Kirby Smith's earlier one. At a cost of less than 300 men, Chalmers's loss in his first assault, Bragg had captured more than 4,000 Yankees, 10 guns, about 5,000 rifles, horses and mules the Confederates needed badly, and all sorts of supplies. But this had been a tactical diversion, not much more, and after the savoring of it there remained the question of whether this time Kirby Smith would agree to join forces with Bragg—and beyond that, what to do next, now that he was within fifty miles of Louisville, the Ohio River frontier, and Indiana north of it.

Neither side's anxious war managers knew much about what was happening either in Kentucky or Maryland on September 16, 1862, because most communication was at the speed of the horse or delayed by telegraph operators' time-consuming relays. This mattered little in Kentucky, where commanders relied mainly on mounted couriers, or to General Lee. But McClellan had gotten Abraham Lincoln's interest aroused by the message he had sent from Frederick on the thirteenth ("Will send you trophies"), and the Union's president had something else on his mind as well.

It was the Emancipation Proclamation, finished nearly two months earlier but ready to be issued the moment there was a Union victory. A month had passed since Lincoln had replied to Horace Greeley's "Prayer of Twenty Millions." Since then, John Pope had been whipped at Manassas, and Lee had invaded Maryland.

Then, on September 13—the day McClellan was given "all the plans of the rebels"—there came to the Executive Mansion a delegation of clergymen from a multidenominational meeting of Christians held in Chicago the previous Sunday. Proclaiming the national emancipation of slaves, his visitors told Lincoln, was the only means of preserving the Union.

"What possible good," he asked—playing devil's advocate— "would follow from the issuing of such a proclamation as you desire?" Europeans would be impressed favorably, the ministers suggested, and it might appeal "to the God of the oppressed and down-trodden for His blessing."

Those clergymen differed from many others only in that they had talked with Lincoln. The Reverend O. B. Frothingham had not, and on the next day—Sunday—he declared from his pulpit in New York:

> In spite of all that is said to the contrary, the belief deepens that the significance of slavery in this conflict is seen with more and more distinctness—that the character of slavery is viewed with more and more detestation—that the resolution to have done with slavery knocks louder and louder at the gates of Washington—that the answer to that resolution will soon come from the occupant of the White House.

Many Northerners' views were far more moderate than the abolitionists', but most of them were disappointed, bewildered, impatient for victory. They were turning to their ministers, to newspaper editors, to anyone who might have some sort of answer. Now molders of opinion were pressing the president, who surely would have pressed General McClellan if he could have reached him. And the measure of McClellan, the man at the apex of this pyramid of dependence, was about to be taken by the Confederate Army of Northern Virginia.

"We will make our stand here," General Lee had said Monday

when he got to the plateau west of Antietam Creek, overlooking it and the gently rolling terrain beyond—wooded, part of it, with corn fields and other clearings checkerboarding the ground eastward for as far as he could see. Antietam Creek would not be much of an obstacle to "those people." Certainly it could be forded north of the stone bridge to his front, as he viewed it from just east of Sharpsburg—and there were other bridges upstream, for the village was well connected by roads leading to Hagerstown, Boonsboro, and to Harpers Ferry.

Had a balloonist gone up from General Lee's vantage point he might have reported that the Confederate troops were moving in along the north-to-south peninsula formed by the Potomac to Lee's rear, two or three miles west and south of Sharpsburg, and Antietam Creek before it flowed southward into the Potomac. But Lee was well aware not only of how near he was to the Potomac but of what being driven into its waters would mean to his nation's hopes for survival and foreign recognition. Wrote an observer afterward, "If he had had a well-equipped army of 100,000 veterans at his back he could not have appeared more composed and confident."

More so, Lee may have been at noon on that Tuesday, September 16, when Jackson arrived and said his troops were not far behind him. Now Lee could at least hold the plateau he was on until his other three divisions came up.

And there was something else: Never had George McClellan dared attack the entire Army of Northern Virginia.

Mist covered the ground along the Antietam early on the morning of Tuesday, the sixteenth, delaying the reconnaissance the Union army's commander had intended to make. But from what McClellan had seen on Monday afternoon, he knew that there was no possibility for maneuvering except within the area about a mile wide facing a Confederate battle line four miles long. And fog of a different kind affected McClellan's thinking. He still believed Lee had upwards of 120,000 troops—at the time the actual figure was closer to 35,000—and McClellan was not sure he had his 71,500-man army well in hand.

While reorganizing his forces back in Washington, he had grouped his corps into three "wings," to be led by his close friend Burnside, old Bull Sumner, and Franklin. But once the sun burned away the mist on this Tuesday, McClellan planned mainly in terms of corps as he and his staff rode over the ground east of the Antietam. Curiously, he made no great use of his cavalry or patrols to probe Lee's line or even to get more information about the terrain over which his forces would be advancing—tomorrow, maybe.

Based mostly on what he had seen from the saddle, McClellan

decided to put Joseph Hooker's corps at the northern end of his battle line. Supporting Fighting Joe would be another corps commanded by newly arrived Major General Joseph K. F. Mansfield (who had seen no fighting since the Mexican War). And if more strength were needed to crush Lee, he would call upon Sumner—or Franklin's corps, if it arrived in time on Wednesday. Then, having placed the main weight of his army's attacking power on the northern end of his line, McClellan designated Burnside's corps as the one to assault Lee's defenses at the southern end, nearest the Potomac.

So McClellan would be striking across the Antietam first from the north, then maybe from the south, and when either or both of these blows crumpled Lee's line, he would attack with the forces in his center. These would consist of Brigadier General Alfred Pleasonton's 4,300 cavalrymen, Franklin's unused divisions, Fitz-John Porter's corps (in army reserve), plus—if needed —a division that might be ordered westward from Frederick, one led by Brigadier General Andrew A. Humphreys.

These decisions made, General McClellan told each of his corps commanders what he wanted them to do. He added no facts regarding the rebels' defenses, issued no general order, held no conferences, and left it to Hooker to open the battle whenever he felt he had light enough to do so on Wednesday morning. Few flaws would anyone reviewing his plan later find. Yet there was a strange subtlety in McClellan's troop dispositions: A large portion of the soldiers in the assault forces would be men he had inherited from John Pope's Army of Virginia.

On Monday and Tuesday General Lee had made the most of the scraps of time, riding Traveller along the north-south highway roughly paralleling the Antietam, learning that ravines west of the creek cut the plateau into three segments.

Lee put Jackson's three divisions in the northernmost, where John Hood's Texans had been since Monday. The center segment and most of the southern one would be Longstreet's. With Hood remaining near Jackson, Longstreet put Harvey Hill's division in the center and told Brigadier General John Walker to stretch his men southward beyond the stone bridge over the Antietam nearest the Potomac. Most of Stuart's cavalry would be guarding Jackson's northern flank, but some of his troopers were with Powell Hill at Harpers Ferry or operating between there and Sharpsburg to cover Lee's southern flank.

Late on Tuesday afternoon George McClellan gave Lee one more gift by moving Hooker's corps west of the Antietam to a position

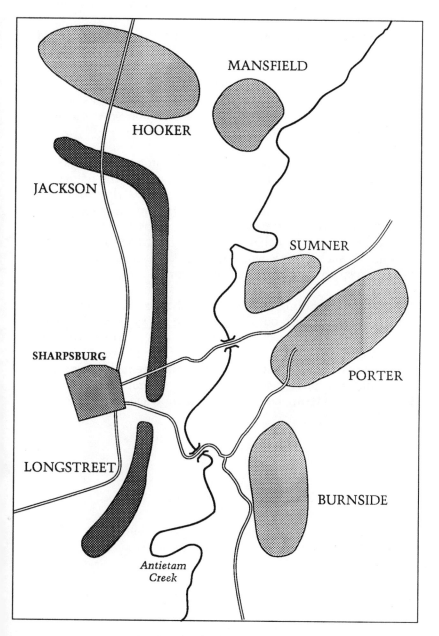

Pre-Battle Positions

opposite Jackson's troops. Now the Confederates knew there would be no surprises.

Still absent at sundown on Tuesday were McLaws's division and Major General Richard H. Anderson's, but they were moving. Lee sent a terse order to Powell Hill at Harpers Ferry: Hurry!

Porter Alexander had not remained in Sharpsburg on that Tuesday for very long, but he knew enough about the situation to be able to imagine what General McClellan's common sense ought to be *shouting* to him:

> Your adversary is backed against [the Potomac], with no bridge & only one ford, & that the worst one on the whole river. If you whip him now, you destroy him utterly, root & branch & bag & baggage. Not twice in a lifetime does such a chance come to any general. Lee for once has made a mistake, & given you a chance to ruin him if you can break his lines, & such game is worth great risks. Every man must fight & keep on fighting for all he is worth.

A light rain was falling, making the night more miserable, sleep fitful, fears harder to push out of mind. Some of the troops on both sides had been looking at each other for the better part of two days, shooting at each other now and then, all of them aware that this fight was going to be different. Here everything seemed so confined, death or painful wounding so certain. Even veteran soldiers could not keep from wondering how much luck they had left.

Chapter 16

Sharpsburg:
Fourteen Hours of Slaughter

At first light on Wednesday, September 17, Joseph Hooker sent three divisions—Abner Doubleday's on the right, James Ricketts's on the left, George Meade's behind them—due southward on the road leading to Sharpsburg. Hooker knew that John Mansfield's corps was off to the east of him, but he had received no fresh orders from General McClellan and assumed this part of the battle would be up to him and the 8,600 men under his command.

A mile south of Hooker's starting point was a plateau on which he could see a whitewashed building resembling a country schoolhouse; actually it was a church, one owned by the German Baptist Brethren sect known locally as the Dunkers. Nearer Hooker, also on the western side of the highway, were woods. In a thirty-acre field east of the road, ripening corn stood head high, with woods east of it and also to the north. Split-rail fences zigzagged along the edges of the fields and bordering farm roads—most of them east of the highway.

West of it, though, was Nicodemus Hill, a place no federal cavalry had gone to inspect. From this high ground, directly on the flank of Joe Hooker's advancing divisions, came Confederate artillery fire; suddenly more of it, fired from near the Dunker church, began thinning the federal ranks.

It had been misty earlier. Now smoke further obscured the scene as Abner Doubleday's guns got into action and the long-range Parrotts from east of the Antietam sent shells bursting into the woods ahead. And there was a different kind of noise shattering the morning calm now, rifle fire, mostly from the East Woods, so much of it that one of George Meade's brigades was soon out of ammunition.

The killing had started. It would go on all day long.

Jackson had brigades facing northward on both sides of the Hagerstown-Sharpsburg highway, but their depleted ranks were no match for the powerful waves of Yankees bearing down on them. Within minutes his line was shattered. Back from both the West Woods and the corn field came stories of desperate fighting and fearful slaughter. A company commander was the only man left in his outfit, and he was wounded. Jackson's old division had been swept aside; Georgians led by Brigadier General Alexander Lawton, wrecked.

Never in this war had there been any fighting as fierce and relentless as this. Near Manassas the unfinished railroad embankment had given Jackson's defenders at least a little cover and concealment; here there was none to be had, not in this lush farmland where shell bursts were making cordwood out of the timber stands east and west of the road and volleys of rifle fire slashed cornstalks and the bodies of men as though some gigantic scythe was sweeping across them time and again.

John Hood's men were in the rear, cooking their first meal in days, when their commander heard the firing. Quickly he got them up from their campfires and moving east of the road. At the edge of the corn field Hood saw Lawton's wounded body being carried out, and he met Harry Hays, the brigadier general who now commanded the Louisianans Dick Taylor had led in Jackson's Valley campaign. Half those veterans had just been shot down, and the rest had no ammunition; Hood told Hays to take the forty or so men with him to the rear and get ready to fight again.

Then Hood took his division into the corn field. In his words:

> Not far distant in our front were drawn up, in close array, heavy columns of Federal infantry; not less than two corps were in sight to oppose my small command numbering, approximately, two thousand effectives. However, with the trusty [Evander] Law on my right, in the edge of the wood, and Colonel [William T.] Wofford in command of the Texas brigade on the left, near the pike, we moved forward into the assault. Notwithstanding the overwhelming odds of over ten to one against us, we drove the enemy from the wood and corn field back upon his reserves, and forced him to abandon his guns on our left.

Jackson, hearing the yelling and furious, incessant firing as Hood's men advanced, sent Captain Alexander Pendleton over to find out what was happening east of the highway. "Tell General Jackson unless I get reinforcements," said Hood, "I must be forced back, but I am going on while I can."

And Hood's line surged on through the corn field and the East Woods. "Fear gave us wings," wrote a Yankee soldier whose outfit could no longer withstand the assault. The Confederates charged onward, shooting and being shot at, until they got to the edge of the North Woods and a rail fence on which Union troops were resting their rifles to steady their aim, watching through dense battle smoke for gray-clad legs.

Hood described the result:

> This most deadly combat raged till our last round of ammunition was expended. The First Texas Regiment had lost, in the corn field, fully two-thirds of its number; and whole ranks of brave men, whose deeds were unrecorded save in the hearts of loved ones at home, were mowed down in heaps to the right and left. Never before was I so continuously troubled with fear that my horse would further injure some wounded fellow soldier, lying helpless on the ground.

So, after his men had fired their last shot, John Hood withdrew. As he neared the Dunker church, someone asked him where his division was. Hood replied: "Dead on the field."

Joe Hooker was back where he had started, or near there, and his corps—Irvin McDowell's, earlier—was fought out, a third of it killed or wounded or borne away by the wings of fear. Ricketts could rally only 300 of the 3,150 men he had taken into the corn field and the East Woods. And survivors, along with Fighting Joe, were left to wonder why General McClellan had let them go in, and stay there for nearly two hours smelling hell and getting beaten, while Mansfield's corps and Bull Sumner's had been within supporting distance of them but hardly a man in either one had moved.

South of there, near the Dunker church, Jackson undertook the grim task of counting survivors. He had started Wednesday with roughly 7,700 troops; now he knew only an alarmingly low fraction of them remained to face the next fierce onslaught—which might well come in the gap between his south flank and Harvey Hill's lonely position in the Confederate center.

General Lee was nearby and well aware of the disaster looming. While Hood's brigades in the corn field were buying time for him, Lee was using every scrap of it to borrow troops from Longstreet. But the distance those men had to cover was great—Walker's had to march from the south end of the line, near the Potomac—so the army commander put the travel-bushed divisions of Lafayette McLaws and Richard Anderson in motion from Sharpsburg toward Jackson and Harvey Hill.

Hooker's corps was out of the action, but he was still in charge of the battle, or so Joseph Mansfield must have supposed, absent any word from Army of the Potomac headquarters east of the Antietam. Take over the sector east of the Sharpsburg highway, Hooker told Mansfield when he asked for orders, and attack southward through the corn field and the East Woods. Presumably, Hooker's men would hold the west side of the road and await developments.

General Mansfield's corps was Nathaniel Banks's old one, whipped back in May by Jackson in the Shenandoah Valley, so distrusted by John Pope it had drawn only guard duty during Second Manassas and now led by an officer so new to combat he insisted that troops remain in tight columns even under rebel artillery fire. But old Joseph Mansfield was a lifetime soldier more brave than stodgy, and he proved this by leading a few brigades near enough to the rail fence north of the corn field in time to encourage George Meade's Pennsylvanians to hold fast and shred the ranks of John Hood's 1st Texas. He could not do much more than that, for many of the troops he then fed into the fight were recruits who had not yet mastered the drill of loading and firing their rifles.

General Mansfield was as new as his men to this ghastly and deafening inferno of blasting and acrid gunsmoke and cries of the wounded. He was a West Pointer, too, taught never to commit forces to battle piecemeal, realizing possibly that in obeying Hooker he was compounding General McClellan's tragic error. It was all very confusing—so much so that Mansfield saw his men firing into what he mistook for his own units, ordered them to cease it, and got shot through the chest. As though nothing had happened, the general dismounted, led his horse to the rear a little way, then collapsed.

Brigadier General Alpheus Williams took over, conferred with Fighting Joe briefly, then tried to do what Hooker had told Mansfield earlier to do—drive south of the corn field and the East Woods. But at around nine o'clock on that bloody Wednesday, Williams had to tell his signalmen to wigwag some bad news to Army of the Potomac headquarters, a mile and a half or more away across the Antietam:

Genl Mansfield is dangerously wounded. Genl Hooker wounded severely in foot. Genl Sumner I hear is advancing. We hold the field at present. Please give us all the aid you can.

Bull Sumner was indeed advancing, his large corps off to a late start, though its commander had been ready to lead it into the fight since dawn. Patience was not high on Edwin V. Sumner's list of virtues; General McClellan had ignored the sixty-five-year-old soldier's presence at headquarters all morning; this was all the more galling because Sumner had thought he was a wing commander; and when orders to attack finally reached him, anger clouded his judgment.

Yet Sumner's first move was a good one. Rather than waste more time using a bridge upstream, he sent Major General John Sedgwick's division across the Antietam at a ford. Sedgwick's march took him south of where the remnants of first Hooker's and then Williams' corps had spent their strength, nearly due westward, his orders from Sumner being to cross the highway and then turn left and drive Jackson's defenders southward from the West Woods and the plateau on which the Dunker church stood.

Behind Sedgwick's division, south of it, would come two more divisions: Brigadier General William H. French's and, after it, Major General Israel B. Richardson's. Sumner's goal was to roll up the Confederate line east and west of the road to Sharpsburg and force Lee's army to flee toward the Potomac while McClellan's other corps struck its eastern flank.

But on this Wednesday nothing seemed to go as planned, and Sumner's scheme fell apart soon after he launched it. He had gone with Sedgwick's 5,400-man division, allowing French and later Richardson to drift southwestward, thus repeating the error—piecemeal commitment—that had plagued the federal effort from dawn onward. Worse, Sumner ordered Sedgwick to advance in three waves, a brigade in each, though he had no idea of what sort of opposition Sedgwick would encounter.

That proved to be Confederate artillery fire, from the flank of the three brigades' neat ranks, and it was murderous. But Sumner and Sedgwick pressed on through it until their men were in the West Woods—targets now for rebel riflemen, a small force composed of every man Jackson could put into it plus reinforcements General Lee had rushed northward. Caught in rebel crossfire, being shelled unmercifully, with some raw units riding the wings of fear across to the body-littered corn field, Sumner shouted: "By God, we must get out of this!"

Getting out was harder to do than getting in had been, for now the Confederates were leapfrogging artillery batteries to keep pounding Sedgwick's men as they retreated toward the North Woods. Behind the Union troops came rebels filling the smoky air with their demonic yelling and volleys from their rifles.

Now fragments of three federal corps mingled in the North Woods, another 2,300 casualties remained on the ground neither side could take and hold, and Bull Sumner had lost control of the rest of his corps. None of this, however, could the Army of the Potomac's commander see from the lawn of the Pry house, nearly two miles from the places where battle more savage than any yet seen in this war had been raging since sunrise.

Couriers had come and gone, and McClellan had read the messages wigwagged by signalmen, but so far he seemed content to leave it to the corps commanders engaged to do what they thought best. An exception was an admonition to Bull Sumner, dispatched too late to reach him: "General McClellan desires you to be very careful how you advance, as he fears our right is suffering."

It was, in fact, wrecked. By then, though, midmorning, the Union's commanding general was thinking about his left, Ambrose Burnside's wing. Attack, McClellan ordered the hapless officer who could only relay the message to Jacob Cox, leader of the sole corps. That done, Little Mac turned his attention to the one sector of the battlefield he could see through his telescope: the center of Lee's line.

All morning Harvey Hill's men had been under pressure. Of his division's five brigades, only those led by Brigadier Generals Robert E. Rodes and George T. Anderson were little damaged—because their position was in a trench of sorts, one created by generations of wagon ruts and erosion along a 500-yard stretch of farm road stretching east and then southeast from the highway. Soon, with a federal division approaching from the east, this depression would become Bloody Lane.

The Yankees were William French's men, strayed from the line of Bull Sumner's advance, and they died by the dozens as volleys stabbed out at them from the sunken road. General Lee had been there a few minutes earlier, but he missed the sight because he had gone northward to supervise the movement of the artillery pieces slaughtering Sedgwick's fugitives. Rodes's Alabamians and Anderson's North Carolinians in the trench kept firing their lethal volleys as French's men—bayonets fixed —came charging toward them, piecemeal, only to be scythed down, adding theirs to the hundreds of blue-clad bodies already covering the ground.

Next came Union general Richardson's 4,000-man division, which had been detained by McClellan to guard a ford over the Antietam until relieved by a reserve outfit. It, too, took heavy losses, but suddenly there was some mix-up in what the Confederates in the sunken road took to be orders. Part of the confusion came from officers being hit: Colonel John B. Gordon, for example, who had taken his fifth wound of the day. Whatever the cause, both of Harvey Hill's brigades abandoned the strongest defensive point along the entire Confederate line, and there was nothing Rodes or the wounded George Anderson or anyone else could do to stop the skedaddling westward.

At that moment, wrote Porter Alexander afterward, "Lee's army was ruined and the end of the Confederacy was in sight." But General Longstreet, wearing carpet slippers because of a bruised heel, found enough artillery pieces to stagger the Yankees' advance with canister. And young Colonel John R. Cooke, Jeb Stuart's wife's brother, got Captain John William Reedy's 3d Arkansas regiment to join with his own 27th North Carolina, and this improvised force—led by Cooke—moved straight toward the Yankees' flank, with his color-bearer racing because (as he told the colonel when warned to slow down) "I can't let that Arkansas fellow get ahead of me!"

Cooke's charge stopped Richardson's bluecoats, driving them to cover behind a rail fence, but the colonel knew his force was too weak to continue the attack. Reluctantly, he told his men to withdraw. As they did, they had to shoot their way through Yankees, some hiding behind haystacks, they had bypassed earlier.

When Cooke returned, he placed his force in a gap in Harvey Hill's line. Longstreet sent congratulations to him and an order to hold the ground he was on. "We will stay here," said Cooke to the courier, "if we must all go to hell together." He added: "Tell General Longstreet to send me some ammunition. I have not a cartridge in my command, but will hold my position at the point of the bayonet."

That, Cooke and his men did. The federals, caught in the fierce artillery fire coming from west of Bloody Lane, turned aside and then pulled back. And soon afterward—by now it was the middle of the day—the guns were quiet all along what was left of Lee's line.

"It is the most beautiful field I ever saw," General McClellan had remarked to a staff officer when it seemed his forces in the western distance had broken through, "and the grandest battle. If we whip them today it will wipe out Bull Run forever."

An attack by one of the divisions Franklin had brought up might have won a victory. But Richardson's drive stalled, and he was seriously wounded by an artillery burst: McClellan let the opportunity fade. The lull in the fighting was continuing at 1:25 P.M. when he wired General-in-Chief Halleck:

We are in the midst of the most terrible battle of the war,

perhaps of history—thus far it looks well but I have great
odds against me. Our loss has been terrific, but we have
gained much ground. I have thrown the mass of the Army on
their left flank. Burnside is now attacking their right & I
hold my small reserve consisting of Porter's (5th Corps)
ready to attack the center as soon as the flank movements
are developed. I hope that God will give us a glorious
victory.

Such was the text McClellan sent, after some editing. At first his
closing words had been: "It will be either a great defeat or a most
glorious victory. I think & hope God will give us the latter." The
change was prudent, yet it masked his uncertainty. How could Lee
be holding unless he had thousands of troops hidden from view west
of Sharpsburg?

True, Burnside was attacking. But he had not yet crossed the
Antietam several hours after he had been ordered to, and the army
commander had sent his inspector general to demand an explanation
and to give orders to advance at whatever cost.

"McClellan appears to think I am not trying my best to carry
this bridge," replied Burnside. "You are the third or fourth one who
has been to me this morning with similar orders." Jacob Cox could
explain the delay. West of the Antietam and the 125-foot stone
bridge spanning it, the terrain gave the rebels an enormous advantage, and they had been using it, and their infantry and artillery, to
prevent two of his divisions from getting anywhere near the creek. A
third division, sent down the Antietam a mile or more in search of a
ford, had not yet found one not covered by Confederates.

There was more to it than that. Neither Cox nor any of his
subordinates had done any reconnoitering to speak of, and Burnside
had not pressed them to. It was as though initiative had vanished
with the morning mist.

Vanished, too, was the division Cox had sent downstream. Cox's
idea had been that Brigadier General Isaac Rodman's men would
cross about a mile south of the stone bridge, then move northward
as Cox's other forces took the bridge; once combined, the corps
would sweep the rebels from Sharpsburg's heights. But the ford
McClellan's engineers had found the day before proved unsuitable,
so Rodman kept moving southward. Cavalry might have done that
for him had the Young Napoleon not kept all of it near his
headquarters miles to the north.

So matters stood in midafternoon when another officer from Pry
house reached Burnside. General McClellan had given him discretion to relieve Burnside if the wing commander did not seem likely

to do something aggressive. But by then two regiments had rushed across the stone bridge, securing it, and Cox's divisions were streaming over it, guns moving with the troops, massing on the far side of the Antietam for a drive up the slopes to Sharpsburg itself.

At about the same time Harvey Hill's men repelled the final federal assault against his line's center, Lee was asking Jackson to see what could be done to get around McClellan's northern flank and attack him. Not much, Old Jack would have been justified in replying. The morning's fighting had reduced his divisions and those Lee had brought northward from near the stone bridge almost to weak brigades; Yankees a-plenty remained in the North Woods, and more were in sight to the east.

But Jackson found Jeb Stuart, and between them they got a small force together. It was cavalry, mostly, but it included a battery in which young Robert Lee was serving.

"General," said the begrimed artilleryman to his father, "are you going to send us in again?"

"Yes, my son. You all must do what you can to drive those people back."

Whether Stuart's attempt might have succeeded would never be known, however, for when he approached the North Woods, he recognized the futility of pressing on.

All the fight had gone out of Bull Sumner, who was by default commanding the fragments of the three corps that had failed to destroy Jackson. Franklin had discovered Sumner's depression when he came to him with a proposal to combine their forces and smash the Confederates. No, said the old soldier, Franklin's newcomers were the only troops with any life left in them. Then came Lieutenant James Wilson bearing orders from McClellan to hold his position at all hazards. No, replied Sumner, his men were all cut up: "Tell him General Franklin has the only organized command on this part of the field!"

Finally, McClellan himself came, and he agreed, but he did not relieve Sumner, nor did he allow Franklin to attack, as he had Hooker, Mansfield, and Sumner: unsupported, piecemeal.

And so it was that though Jackson and Stuart had not given General Lee the flank march he had hoped for, George McClellan had feared it or some sort of audacious counterattack enough to immobilize all his forces except Ambrose Burnside's "wing." Back at his headquarters, through his telescope, Little Mac could see Cox's blue-clad troops moving up the ravines toward Sharpsburg, but he did nothing to support them, either.

Colonel Henry L. Benning's Georgians had held the ground opposite the stone bridge all morning, repulsing the Yankees each time they appeared on the Antietam's eastern bank, but by noon the Confederate brigade's ammunition was almost gone. A little later, federals began wading the creek upstream; then to division commander Brigadier General David R. Jones came the news that a Union division had crossed well south of the bridge and was headed toward Sharpsburg. Jones had no choice but to tell Benning to bring his men up to the line Brigadier General Robert Toombs had formed.

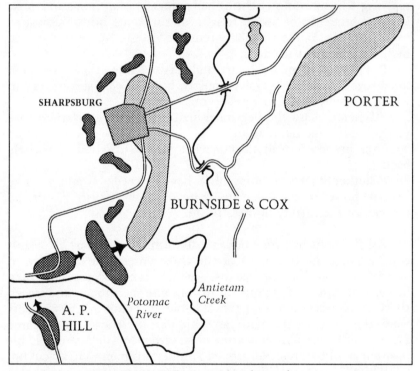

A.P. Hill's Arrival and Attack

That morning, General Lee had moved three divisions from this segment to help hold his northern and center ones. Now it appeared that Jones's brigades, overlooking swarms of Yankees crossing the bridge and forming assault waves on the creek's west bank, could do no more than delay the federals.

Only one hope remained: that Powell Hill could arrive from Harpers Ferry within a very short time. But Harpers Ferry was seventeen miles away, and the Yankees south of Sharpsburg might stop him; certainly the day's heat and the road's dust would slow his division's march. And with each passing minute the chances for

Powell Hill's coming to the rescue in time dwindled.

General Lee could move no men from elsewhere in his line — only such guns as he could find and bring southward—yet he seemed confident that David Jones could hold back "those people." He watched from a knoll west of Sharpsburg as Cox's blueclads hammered Jones's brigades into regiments and pushed them ever closer to the village, then into it. Only Toombs's Georgians seemed to be holding, and they could not stay where they were much longer. Behind them buildings in Sharpsburg were on fire, and around them Union colors kept advancing.

Then, just as it appeared the federals had cut Lee's only escape route and McClellan could now throw all his forces into the battle and destroy the Army of Northern Virginia, up from the south came one of Powell Hill's batteries. News of this spread quickly. General Lee heard it and scanned the southern horizon, unable to use a telescope because his hands were still bandaged. A lieutenant near him looked through it, saw first a United States flag, then, at Lee's suggestion, shifted his gaze to the right: Virginia and Confederate banners.

"It is A. P. Hill from Harpers Ferry," Lee said simply, then he told the lieutenant to shift his battery's aim to the federal forces he had first seen. That would attract their guns' fire, the officer warned the army commander.

"Never mind me," Lee assured him.

But he could not content himself with directing artillery or resist riding out to meet Powell Hill—easy to spot, for he was wearing his red hunting shirt, the one he always put on for battle. Within moments Hill had Maxcy Gregg's troops stabbing the Yankees' flank with murderous volleys and his other four brigades forming to join in driving the astonished bluecoats northeastward across the Antietam.

It had been as though Jacob Cox's southernmost troops, raw recruits many of them, never knew what hit them. At one moment they were surging up the slope toward Sharpsburg, almost within dashing distance of it, and in the next their ranks were being shredded from a totally unexpected direction.

Equally surprised were Ambrose Burnside and Cox. General McClellan saw their blue waves receding through his telescope, then turned and looked at Fitz-John Porter. As if in answer to McClellan's unspoken question, Porter shook his head.

Earlier, rebel gunfire—Jeb Stuart's—out west of the North Woods had been unsettling. Even more so was this visible calamity. Quickly McClellan and Porter rode southward until a courier from

Burnside stopped them. Guns and reinforcements were needed, McClellan was told, and Burnside could not hold his position half an hour without them.

"Tell General Burnside," said the Army of the Potomac's commander, "this is the battle of the war. He must hold his ground till dark at any cost. I will send him [Captain M. B.] Miller's battery. I can do no more. I have no infantry."

As the courier turned to go, McClellan added: "Tell him if he *cannot* hold his ground, then the bridge, to the last man!—always the bridge! If the bridge is lost, all is lost!"

Burnside held the bridge.

Nightfall ended the battle. As firing sputtered, then died out, the cries of wounded men could be heard all along the four miles of fought-over ground, from below Burnside's stone bridge northward past Bloody Lane and the corn field and in the shell-torn timber stands east and west of the highway to the North Woods. Men from both sides, some bearing lanterns, stumbled over bodies as they searched for friends and removed as many of the stricken living as they could.

To General Lee's headquarters, a campfire west of ruined Sharpsburg, came some of his generals. But one had stopped to help some women put out a fire. As the man rode up, Lee said: "Ah, here is Longstreet; here is my old war horse."

At one time or another almost every man in the Army of Northern Virginia, roughly 36,000 in all, had been in the fight; now 10,000 were gone, perhaps more. Nine generals had been killed or wounded mortally; fortunate was any officer who had not been hit at least once. Federal losses exceeded 12,000—even though at least 24,000 of McClellan's 80,000 or more troops had not been engaged at all or had taken next to no part in the battle.

Now the question uppermost in the minds of General Lee and his lieutenants was, what to do next? Withdrawal during the night would have been honorable; certainly, having fought so gallantly for so long, no one could blame Lee for saving what remained of the army upon which the survival of the Confederacy depended. Moreover, remaining seemed utterly pointless, even suicidal.

Such might have been the advice General Lee would have received had he asked for it. But that was not his practice, nor did he make any dramatic declaration. Instead, quietly, he gave orders for the men to be fed, the wounded gathered and cared for, and stragglers collected and returned to their units.

Robert E. Lee's intent was clear enough. He would stand his ground the next morning and again defy George McClellan to take it.

Chapter 17

Emancipation—and High Tide in Kentucky

For a time on the evening of September 17, 1862, officers at General McClellan's headquarters had every reason to expect Little Mac to give orders to renew the attack first thing on Thursday morning. True, Wednesday's losses had been severe, but William Franklin's corps was virtually intact, Fitz-John Porter's was hardly nicked, and two divisions were on their way to rejoin the Army of the Potomac. As soon as the corps Hooker, Mansfield, and Sumner had led could be sorted out, half or more of their initial strength ought to be available. And Burnside was still west of Antietam Creek, holding an excellent position from which he and Jacob Cox could sweep around the Confederate army's southern flank and destroy Lee before he could reach the Potomac's few fords.

But McClellan dashed those high hopes. His men, he told a staff officer, were to "hold the ground they occupy, but are not to attack without further orders." And on that Wednesday evening no orders were prepared. Nor were any issued early the next morning; instead, at eight o'clock, the army commander wired General-in-Chief Halleck:

> The battle of yesterday continued for fourteen hours, and until after dark. We held all we gained except a portion of the extreme left that was obliged to abandon a part of what it had gained [*sic*]. Our losses very heavy, especially in General officers. The battle will probably be renewed today. Send all the troops you can by the most expeditious route.

That duty done, McClellan promptly wrote his wife:

We fought yesterday a terrible battle against the entire rebel army. The battle continued *fourteen* hours & was terrific—the fighting on both sides was superb. The general result was in our favor, that is to say we gained a great deal of ground & held it. It was a success, but whether a decided victory depends upon what occurs today. I hope that God has given us a great success. It is all in his hands, where I am content to leave it. The spectacle yesterday was the grandest I could conceive of—nothing could have been more sublime. Those in whose judgment I rely tell me that I fought the battle splendidly & that it was a masterpiece of art. I am well nigh tired out by anxiety & want of sleep....

William Franklin rode westward with the army commander to consider seizing Nicodemus Hill, from which rebel artillery had shattered Hooker's assault the morning before. Bull Sumner advised against it; there the idea died. And along the way, apparently, McClellan got enough stomach-turning glimpses of dead soldiers— their bodies in the grotesque positions death had come to them, discolored, swollen—to seek no more battle that day. Instead, he agreed to a truce for removal of the wounded and burial of those who had fought their last fight.

That was the humanitarian thing to do, a decision a woman not far from Nicodemus Hill that Thursday morning might have shouted "Hoo-ray!" for if she had known of it and had enough energy left to shout at all. She was Clara Barton, earlier a teacher and then an employee of the Patent Office in Washington but from Fort Sumter onward too concerned over the plight of the Union's wounded to leave anything for anyone else to do.

Later, Clara Barton would be remembered as the founder of the American Red Cross. But she won fame of a different sort when, at almost the fiercest point in Wednesday's fighting, she halted her mule-drawn wagon filled with medical supplies and got to work. She was busy nursing a wounded man when a bullet passed through the sleeve of her dress and killed him. And on that Thursday she went on dealing with the war's reality and coping with it as best she could.

Leaving Lee alone was perfectly all right as far as the men in McClellan's army were concerned. There were enough dead and wounded on the field, more than in any other single day's fighting. But why? What made Antietam (or Sharpsburg, as the Confederates would call it) so costly to both sides?

It had been a long battle, lasting from dawn until after dark, in contrast to the fights during the Seven Days' Battles in which most of the shooting was done in the hours just before sundown. Here regiments had advanced to within very close range of the enemy's lines and remained there, exchanging volleys, firing and reloading, the defenders weakening but not breaking, until ammunition ran out. And there was the artillery. McClellan had more of it, but Lee used his batteries more effectively, placing them where they could blast the flanks of advancing Federal masses, at times putting guns so near them that the ranges were those of his infantrymen, using canister to drive "those people" back or at least slow them down.

But Wednesday's battle—McClellan's "masterpiece of art" — was in fact a two-level affair. Most of his men fought with uncommon valor and tenacity. And so might have the 24,000 or more troops he held out of the fight, veterans of the Peninsula campaign and the Seven Days' Battles. Gallantry alone, however, could not offset the failures at the highest level of the Army of the Potomac's command. It was as though McClellan never knew whether he was fighting an offensive or defensive battle. Worse, a telescope was no substitute for mounting Dan Webster and riding out to see what his corps and division commanders were too busy to report; sadly for the North, he may never have known how close his men had been to destroying Lee's Army of Northern Virginia.

Robert Edward Lee remembered those moments—so many of them!—when only one more federal effort, one final packs-off charge, would have broken his line and obliged him to watch the ruin of his forces and all his nation's hopes. But his army had survived the night, and on Thursday morning he wondered if he and his men might do more than wait for McClellan to resume his attacks. Lee rode to Jackson's segment of the line. Once there, he proposed another attempt to get around McClellan's northern flank. No, Jackson advised, the Union's artillery commander had belatedly shifted too many guns that way.

Professor Jackson's opinion carried great weight; enough, anyway, to persuade Lee to begin thinking about withdrawing to the Virginia side of the Potomac. From there, once stragglers were gathered and ammunition stocks replenished, perhaps he could take his army northward again.

Longstreet began crossing the Potomac after midnight. Lee remained at the ford until Friday morning, when he was assured all his men and guns were on Virginia soil. On Saturday, September 20, there was a flurry of activity when federal troops probed. Jackson took care of it, sending Powell Hill's division to give Fitz-John Porter's pursuit force a thrashing severe enough to preclude any more breaches of what General Lee hoped would be only a temporary lull.

"I wish it were a better time," said Abraham Lincoln to his cabinet's members on September 22, 1862. "The action of the army against the rebels has not been quite what I should have best liked."

The president meant General McClellan's failure to pursue and destroy Lee's Confederate army. That ghastly battle had been fought on the seventeenth. On the twentieth, General-in-Chief Halleck had wired McClellan:

> We are still entirely in the dark in regard to your own movements and those of the enemy. This should not be so. You should keep me advised of both, so far as you know them.

That evening, the general sent Halleck a terse and rather vague situation report, then added:

> I regret that you find it necessary to couch every dispatch I have the honor to receive from you, in a spirit of fault finding, and that you have not yet found leisure to say one word in commendation of the recent achievements of this Army, or even to allude to them.

And as usual, McClellan was much more candid in what he wrote Mary Ellen an hour later on the twentieth:

> I hope that my future will be determined this week. Thro' certain friends of mine I have taken the stand that Stanton must leave & that Halleck must restore my old place to me. Unless these two conditions are fulfilled I will leave the service. I feel that I have done all that can be asked in twice saving the country. If I continue in its service I have at least the right to demand a guarantee that I shall not be interfered with—I know I cannot have that assurance so long as Stanton continues in the position of Secy of War & Halleck as Genl in Chief. You will understand that it is a matter of indifference to me whether they come to terms or not.

Had Lincoln known of General McClellan's claim that he had twice saved the country, he might well have asked, "When?" As it was, the Union's president was baffled as well as pressured and mindful also of a promise he had made to God that if Lee's army could be driven out of Maryland, he would issue his Emancipation Proclamation. Absent real news from McClellan, Lincoln said to his cabinet: "I think the time has come."

He had told them more earlier, admitting that if anyone else could command a greater share of public confidence and if there was a lawful way for that person to be put in his place, "he should have it." And he added: "I must do the best I can, and bear the responsibility of taking the course which I feel I ought to take."

Thereupon he issued his Emancipation Proclamation, a document, wrote historian J. G. Randall, "more often admired than read." But those who did read it found some surprises.

Lincoln began by reaffirming his understanding of the war's purpose: restoration of the Union. He did not cite the abolition of slavery as a new war aim. The rest was mainly a promissory note, a declaration of what he meant to propose to Congress when it met early in December. Two of Lincoln's old ideas were embodied in the text: compensation to slave owners not in rebellion and in states whose laws were moving toward abolition, and continuation of efforts to gain consent of persons "of African descent" to be resettled elsewhere.

Emancipation applied, in fact, only to slaves in the states in rebellion, none of which were completely under Union control on September 22, 1862. However, by declaring slaves in those states "forever free," in effect Lincoln went beyond the goal of restoring the Union and implied a new one: delivering to the South's slaves the freedom he was then proclaiming—deliverance abolitionists could only hope Lincoln and his generals would achieve eventually through relentless use of superior federal military force.

Northern reactions to the Emancipation Proclamation were mostly favorable, ranging from praise by abolitionists and Radical Republicans to guarded acceptance in midwestern states where some feared an influx of job-seeking "freedmen." Not only had Lincoln taken the moral high ground; politically he was stronger now, having placed opponents in the position of seeming to be pro-slavery if they criticized his action.

There was, however, some question as to whether soldiers, particularly those in McClellan's Army of the Potomac, would support this change in Union war goals. No, suggested Fitz-John Porter to the editor of the antiadministration *New York World*:

> The Proclamation was ridiculed in the army—causing disgust, discontent, and expressions of disloyalty to the views of the administration, amounting I have heard, to insubordination, and for this reason—All such bulletins tend only to prolong the war by rousing the bitter feelings of the South—and causing unity of action among them—while the reverse with us. Those who fight the battles of the country are tired of the war and wish to see it ended soon

and honorably—by a restoration of the union—not merely a suppression of the rebellion.

While General Porter may have been reflecting the opinion held by his close friend and army commander, McClellan was less bold: Little Mac wrote businessman William H. Aspinwall, long a supporter and a leader in the Democratic party, for advice:

> I am very anxious to learn how you and the men like you regard the recent Proclamations of the Presdt inaugurating servile war, emancipating the slaves, & and at one stroke of the pen changing our free institutions into a despotism—for such I regard as the natural effect of the last Proclamation suspending the Habeas Corpus throughout the land.
>
> I shall probably be in this vicinity [Antietam] for some days &, if you regard the matter as gravely as I do, would be glad to communicate with you.

This letter was written on September 26, and attacks of apoplexy might have been the probable result had Halleck and Stanton and the president known of it—at a minimum, of the assurance McClellan gave Aspinwall that he would not move "for some days" in pursuit of Lee's battered army. Yet for George McClellan to have turned to Aspinwall for counsel may not have been out of a pattern: one that, if it really existed, might explain the Young Napoleon's curious conduct all along.

British journalist Frederick Milnes Edge, in *Major-General McClellan and The Campaign on the Yorktown Peninsula*, a book published in London in 1865, reported that in June 1861 (not more than a month after Fort Sumter) certain Southern Democrats twice met secretly in Baltimore with their Northern brethren to discuss ways of restoring their party to control of the Union government on a pro-slavery basis once the fighting ended. At their first meeting it was agreed that an army officer should be the eventual "Democratic chieftain." But which officer could supply all of the qualities each of the delegates specified? Only a week later the second meeting's Southern and Northern attendees were unanimous in their decision: George Brinton McClellan.

Never documented clearly enough to satisfy generations of historians were any instances indicating that McClellan was a knowing participant in any such scheme. British reporter Edge did not reach the United States until mid-July 1861, and his information may have been stale, at best, even had it not been planted by clever Confederates.

Yet anyone in later years puzzled by McClellan's behavior might well wonder if there had been some linkage between those ambitious Democrats and the man who may (or may not) have been their chosen instrument. If not this theory, what other one could explain so many departures from the kind of performance citizens of the Union had every right to expect from the senior major general?

Jefferson Davis was deeply disappointed when he learned that Lee had withdrawn to Virginia's Shenandoah Valley. But he gave no hint of this in a message of support, one ending: "In the name of the Confederacy I thank you and the brave men of your Army for the deeds which covered our flag with imperishable fame."
And the general replied:

I wish I felt that I deserve the confidence you express in me. I am only conscious of an earnest desire to advance the interests of the country and my inability to accomplish my wishes.

Earlier Davis's hopes had been soaring: Lee was in Maryland, and Bragg and Kirby Smith were well inside Kentucky, bound for the Ohio River. And Davis might have been even more optimistic had he known what was happening in London at about the time the guns were blazing along the western slopes of the Antietam's creek bed.
On September 14 Prime Minister Lord Palmerston, on learning of the federals' "very complete smashing" at Manassas, wrote Foreign Secretary Lord Russell: "It seems not unlikely that...even Washington and Baltimore may fall into the hands of the Confederates." In such an event, asked the prime minister, did Russell think Britain and France might "recommend an arrangement upon the basis of separation." The Foreign Secretary responded on September 17:

Whether the Federal army is destroyed or not, it is clear that it is driven back to Washington, and has made no progress in subduing the insurgent States....I agree with you that the time is come for offering mediation to the United States Government, with a view to the recognition of the independence of the Confederates.

Presumably, news that Lee was once more in Virginia caused the British statesmen to await further developments—one of which happened to be Lincoln's Emancipation Proclamation. Foreign Secretary Russell wrote:

There is surely a total want of consistency in this measure....If it were a measure of Emancipation it should be
extended to all the States of the Union. Emancipation is not
granted to the claims of humanity but inflicted as a
punishment.

And the *London Times* predicted that the proclamation would
inspire slave uprisings in the South, leading to "arson, the slaughter
of innocents, and a host of unmentionable horrors."

Perhaps, but with nothing happening along the Potomac, inter-
national attention shifted to the war in the west. Out in Kentucky
Kirby Smith remained in the bluegrass region, sending only one
probe toward Cincinnati, trying to recruit Kentuckians but acquiring few, rejecting Bragg's proposals that they join forces for a drive to
seize Louisville. No Kentuckians were coming forward to take any
of the 15,000 rifles Bragg had in his wagons. True, Bragg had gotten
north of Buell; but he had done nothing to convince anyone that the
Confederate campaigns were anything but glorified raids. And,
worse, the commanders Bragg had left behind in Mississippi were
not performing as he had ordered—that is, threatening Nashville,
thereby forcing Buell to leave George Thomas's divisions there.

In part, unintentionally, President Davis had contributed to
Braxton Bragg's plight. Back in August Davis had not sensed the
folly of "cooperation" and appointed one general to command the
entire western theater. Later, with communications with Bragg
almost nonexistent, Davis had responded to messages from Earl Van
Dorn in Mississippi by giving him discretion subject to any orders
from Bragg limiting Van Dorn's planned actions.

General Van Dorn, however, lacked authority to control the
small force led by Sterling Price except when their divisions were
combined: an echo of the Bragg–Kirby Smith difficulty up in
Kentucky. Van Dorn wanted Price to join him in recovering Corinth
from the Yankees; Price, thinking Bragg wanted him to advance
toward Nashville, ignored Van Dorn and seized Iuka, a village on the
railroad east of Corinth, in mid-September.

Neither of the Confederacy's generals in Mississippi had paid
enough attention to the locations of the federal forces Halleck had
left under Ulysses Grant's command. From Corinth, Grant sent
troops led by Major General William S. Rosecrans, the man who had
won the little fight at Rich Mountain back in July 1861 that had
drawn Lincoln's attention to the Young Napoleon. Rosecrans placed
his troops around Price's men in Iuka like the jaws of a shark. On
September 19, Sterling Price fought his way through one federal jaw

and escaped while the other, through some acoustical freak, failed to hear the firing and remained idle.

Near disaster at Iuka made General Price more receptive to cooperation with Van Dorn. But their objective would be the one Van Dorn had been coveting, Corinth, and for as long as it might require for them to take it, General Bragg would be denied their divisions' presence anywhere in Tennessee.

But in late September Bragg believed his little army might be caught between Buell to the south and vast hordes supposedly gathering at and north of Louisville. With Kirby Smith too far to the east to come to his rescue, he gave the L & N Railroad back to Buell and headed for Frankfort.

Kentucky's capital was Bragg's choice of destinations for political reasons, mainly. If Kentucky's young men would not volunteer, perhaps they could be drafted; but before Bragg had the power to use his nation's conscription laws, there must be a pro-Confederate state government. A governor was waiting to be inaugurated at Frankfort, which Kirby Smith's men held. Once the ceremony took place and the draft law took effect, the hoped-for recruits might deplete Bragg's wagons of those 15,000 otherwise useless rifles.

Sometimes nothing is a very good thing to do, someone has said, and General Buell proved that by waiting north of Bowling Green until first George Thomas arrived from Nashville with his divisions and then Braxton Bragg abandoned Munfordville. That wait had been possible because the cautious Buell had kept his supply wagons moving, thus offsetting Bragg's having blocked the L & N Railroad. Now, with Bragg headed eastward, Buell moved with uncharacteristic speed; by September 26 he had most of his army in Louisville.

The tortoise had won the race and seized the initiative from the hare, but Abraham Lincoln had long been displeased by General Buell's performance, and he wanted him replaced. Even before the Confederates got out of Buell's way a courier was bound for Kentucky bearing three orders: one to Buell telling him he was relieved, another appointing George Thomas as the army's new commander, and a letter from the general-in-chief to Thomas directing him to conduct "energetic operations."

For Don Carlos Buell September 29 would have been a bad day in any event. Shortly after breakfast came the first shock: William Nelson, one of his corps commanders, was dead. During a heated argument in a Louisville hotel an officer named (ironically) Jefferson C. Davis had shot Nelson, the hard-fighting, hard-drinking giant who had watched his raw troops flee from Pat Cleburne's Confederates at

Richmond back on August 30. Then the courier arrived from Washington and delivered Halleck's order removing Buell from command.

Buell wired the general-in-chief that he would comply, but General Thomas took a different view in his telegram:

> General Buell's preparations have been completed to move against the enemy, and I respectfully ask that he be retained in command. My position is very embarrassing, not being as well informed as I should be as the commander of this army and on the assumption of such responsibility.

Military necessity, not timidity or even loyalty to Buell, motivated Thomas—West Pointer, by birth a Virginian but by choice a defender of the Union, a good soldier in the Old Army and now relying once again on his sense of what was correct in the circumstances. Halleck, lacking faith in any other general officer on the scene, replied to Thomas: "You may consider the order suspended until I can lay your dispatch before the Government and get instructions."

There the matter would have to rest, for on October 1 the president arrived at General McClellan's vast camp east of the Antietam for a three-day visit. He reviewed the troops, rode over the battleground, and had several private talks with the Army of the Potomac's commander.

"I went up to the field," said Lincoln afterward, "to try to get [McClellan] to move." Two weeks had passed since the fight, but the general had given no indication that he had any plans to do anything but rest and refit. And in that interval Lincoln had issued his Emancipation Proclamation, so he may have wanted to learn firsthand how the army's officers and men were reacting to it. By the fourth, however, Lincoln was back in Washington, having left behind only one memorable remark, made to a friend as they gazed over the sea of tents: That army, he said, was "General McClellan's bodyguard."

On October 6, General Halleck reflected the true conclusion Lincoln had drawn from his inspection trip. It took the form of a peremptory order to McClellan: "The President directs that you cross the Potomac and give battle to the enemy or drive him south. Your army must move now while the roads are good." And, as if to underscore: "I am directed to add that the Secretary of War and the General-in-Chief concur with the President in these instructions."

First Braxton Bragg had lost sight of his campaign's main

requirement, which was to dominate the military situation in Kentucky; now, in early October, he seemed to lose control of his army even while he sought to augment its strength.

Bragg had never really controlled impetuous subordinate Earl Van Dorn, so he could hardly have been surprised when he learned what Van Dorn had done at Corinth on October 3 and 4. That was to attack the federal garrison commanded by William Rosecrans on the scene and by Ulysses Grant from a distance.

Van Dorn's men had to march a long way from the west and Sterling Price's an even longer stretch from below Iuka for their forces to combine southwest of Corinth and then continue northward to their goal. Apparently, Van Dorn's idea was to strike Corinth from the northwest before Grant could rush reinforcements from that direction to Rosecrans.

But Rosecrans had all the advantages over his West Point classmate, and he used them to thin Van Dorn's assault ranks on October 3. It was Price's turn the next day, supported by Van Dorn's men. But the heat as well as Rosecrans's federals took a heavy toll. And when Earl Van Dorn finally withdrew, he still had to fight his way through Union troops Grant had sent from the northwest. He did, but his venture had cost him roughly 5,000 men and the Federals about 3,000—an appalling cost for a fight that helped Bragg not at all but enabled Grant to tell Halleck that now he saw his way clear to move toward Vicksburg.

Up in Kentucky, General Bragg was watching the inauguration of a Confederate governor at Frankfort—an occasion curtailed by the sound of artillery firing not far from the city. Though he and Kirby Smith were at long last attempting to combine their commands to smite Buell, the federal commander had sent three columns southeastward from Louisville to destroy Bragg's widely scattered forces.

Drought had plagued the part of central Kentucky in which the fragments of Buell's and Bragg's forces were groping toward each other, so water sources were the real march goals for the troops on both sides. Doctor's Creek, near Perryville, drew them together on the evening of October 7. Confederates held the few pools along the otherwise dry streambed, and they would not let the Yankees near them.

One Union soldier refused to leave it at that: Brigadier General Philip H. Sheridan, a hater of Southerners who had been set back a year from graduation at West Point for aiming a bayonet at a Virginia-born cadet. Sheridan's early-morning attack on October 8 took the precious pools and some high ground as well.

That afternoon, Bragg massed his available divisions on the northern end of Buell's six-mile line and struck hard, renewing a

confused battle in which his 16,000 men drove 55,000 Union troops
back far enough for Bragg to think he had won. Sunset ended the
fight, which had added another 7,600 Americans to the war's
casualty lists—with about 1,000 fewer Confederate losses than
federal. But Bragg had only stunned Buell, whose forces vastly
outnumbered his own and would even after Kirby Smith's men
joined him, so he let the Yankees have such water as they might find
around Perryville. He used the moonlit hours of the next morning,
October 9, to move his army eastward to Harrodsburg. There, on the
tenth, Kirby Smith's troops joined his—finally. And from near there,
in another day or two, Bragg would begin the long march back
toward East Tennessee.

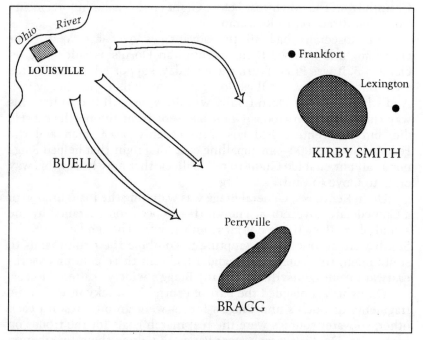

Moves Toward Perryville

As far back as September 25, General Bragg had warned the
authorities in Richmond that his campaign might end that way,
mainly because of his disappointment "at the want of action by our
friends in Kentucky." And he added:

> Unless a change occurs soon we must abandon the garden
> spot of Kentucky to its cupidity. The love of ease and fear of
> pecuniary loss are the fruitful sources of this evil.

But a greater evil had been Jefferson Davis's faith in the notion that four generals in three widely separated regions would "cooperate." As a West Point graduate, a Mexican War veteran, and a former secretary of war, he ought to have known better. True, Bragg and Kirby Smith—and Van Dorn and Price as well—had made their share of blunders. And it could be argued that the Confederates in the west had tried to achieve too much with too few men. But the fundamental flaw had been the president's failure to give Bragg command authority equal to General Lee's, and for that there was no excuse.

Davis's immediate problem was to defend Bragg against a host of critics, including Kirby Smith and many of the generals who had served under Bragg. To them the president conceded: "That another Genl. might excite more enthusiasm is probable, but as all have their defects I have not seen how to make a change with advantage to the public service."

Put another way, the Confederacy now faced a new shortage: general officers capable of commanding field armies.

Abraham Lincoln's long-held desire had been for Union forces to occupy East Tennessee and give its Unionists the freedom and protection Bragg had proved unable to provide to Kentuckians. Accordingly, after Perryville the general-in-chief set seizing Knoxville as Buell's goal and suggested two routes for reaching it.

General Buell tried the least feasible one and abandoned it, ignored the other more attractive route, and headed his army for Nashville—a destination in no danger—at a time when Bragg and Kirby Smith were retreating toward Knoxville in haste. To Lincoln this seemed direct disobedience of orders. On October 24, two weeks after Perryville and with the rebels hardly molested, down sped the angled blade: Buell was relieved of command and replaced by William Rosecrans.

Was this action a signal to the Young Napoleon that his days were numbered? Perhaps, but if so, he gave it no heed. Neither did George McClellan pay much attention to a letter the president wrote him on October 13, a week after Halleck's peremptory order to cross the Potomac and give battle to Lee's forces or drive them southward. Echoing conversations during Lincoln's visit nearly three weeks before, he wrote McClellan:

> You remember my speaking to you of what I called your over-cautiousness. Are you not over-cautious when you assume that you cannot do what the enemy is constantly doing? Should you not claim to be at least his equal in prowess, and act upon the claim?

As I understand, you telegraph General Halleck that you can not subsist your army at Winchester unless the Railroad from Harper's Ferry to that point be put in working order. But the enemy does now subsist his army at Winchester at a distance nearly twice as great from railroad transportation as you would have to do without the railroad last named. He now wagons from Culpepper C. H. which is just about twice as far as you would have to do from Harper's Ferry. He is certainly not more than half as well provided with wagons as you are. I certainly should be pleased for you to have the advantage of the Railroad from Harper's Ferry to Winchester, but it wastes all the remainder of the autumn to give it to you; and, in fact ignores the question of *time*, which can not, and must not be ignored.

Lincoln might have stopped there. That he did not may have reflected his concern over another ride Jeb Stuart's Confederate cavalrymen had made all the way around McClellan's army—one that began on October 9. Stuart's men failed to destroy a railroad bridge near Chambersburg, Pennsylvania, but in the course of their eighty-mile clockwise sweep they captured 1,200 horses and evaded the federal cavalry's frantic pursuit before returning to Lee's lines on October 12, the day before the president wrote McClellan.

Again, [continued Lincoln] one of the standard maxims of war, as you know, is "to operate upon the enemy's communications as much as possible without exposing your own." You seem to act as if this applies *against* you, but can not apply it in your *favor*. Change positions with the enemy, and think you not he would break your communications with Richmond within the next twentyfour hours? You dread his going into Pennsylvania. But if he does so in full force, he gives up his communications to you absolutely; and you have nothing to do but to follow, and ruin him; if he does so with less than full force, fall upon, and beat what is left behind all the easier.

This was remarkable. Had Halleck coached the president? Perhaps, although the wording and the tone were Lincoln's. And more he wrote:

Exclusive of the water line, you are now nearer Richmond than the enemy is by the route that you *can,* and he *must* take. Why can you not reach there before him, unless you admit that he is more than your equal on a march. His route is the arc of a circle, while yours is the chord. The roads are as good on yours as on his.

You know I desired, but did not order, you to cross the Potomac below, instead of above the Shenandoah and Blue Ridge. My idea was that this would at once menace the enemies' communications, which I would seize if he would permit. If he should move Northward I would follow him closely, holding his communications. If he should prevent our seizing his communications, and move towards Richmond, I would press closely to him, fight him if a favorable opportunity should present, and, at least, try to beat him to Richmond on the inside track. I say "try"; if we never try, we shall never succeed.... As we must beat him somewhere, or fail finally, we can do it, if at all, easier near to us, than far away. If we can not beat the enemy where he now is, we never can, he again being within the entrenchments of Richmond.... It is all easy if our troops march as well as the enemy; and it is unmanly to say they can not do it.

Then the Union's commander-in-chief added: "This letter is in no sense an order."

McClellan must have put more weight on that last sentence than anything else his president had said at Antietam early in October or—now—written. That Little Mac's mind was not on advancing was indicated by a message he sent regarding the availability of hospital tents: "If there are none, how long would it take to have them manufactured and delivered here in considerable amount, say three or four thousand?" And from his camps east of the Antietam he continued to ask Washington for weapons, uniforms, horses, and all sorts of equipment and supplies, though the railroads were so clogged by boxcars Army of the Potomac quartermasters had not unloaded that it took the presence of Herman Haupt to untangle the snarls.

Lincoln's patience was all the more amazing in view of the remark he learned that Major John J. Key, one of McClellan's staff officers, had made: Lee's army had not been pursued after Antietam because that "was not the game." What Key had meant, or so the president was told, was that both sides were to fight it out until both were exhausted and terms preserving slavery were worked out; only in this way could the Union be restored. Lincoln had Key dismissed from the army, but he gave him a letter in which he showed compassion for the staff officer's plight but said he felt compelled to make an example of him.

Whether George McClellan was following some game plan or not, his seemingly studied inactivity east of the Antietam gave General Lee a month and more in which to rebuild the Army of Northern Virginia. His men had enjoyed no such respite from marching and fighting since Lee assumed command in early June.

Now Lee became something of a quartermaster, directing the search throughout Virginia's lower (northern) Shenandoah Valley for better food and more of it for his men; fresh horses for the artillery and wagon trains; and, with winter coming, shoes and clothing. From Richmond came approval to establish corps—one composed of Longstreet's divisions, the second Jackson's—with those officers commanding and promoted to lieutenant generals. And, as the weeks passed, recruits arrived, and many stragglers returned voluntarily or were rounded up. By the end of October, Lee had more than 68,000 men present for duty, twice as many as had been with him at Sharpsburg on September 17 when someone remarked, "Only the heroes are left."

General Lee had learned from Stuart's ride around the Army of the Potomac that McClellan's army was not scattered. As had Lincoln, Lee defined the two routes "those people" were most likely to consider when they did move southward: up the Shenandoah Valley or east of the Blue Ridge using the Orange & Alexandria as a supply line. It had been a mistake, a welcome one, for McClellan to allow October's good fighting weather to slip by unused. But Lee could not assume his opponent would remain idle much longer. Rather than try to outguess him, Lee placed some of his forces—including Stuart's cavalrymen—in a ninety-six-mile screen stretching from Martinsburg eastward to Fredericksburg and waited.

As always, Lee used the scraps of time. He wrote a note of regret over the death of Union general Mansfield, thirty years earlier his commanding officer. And, answering the request of Phil Kearny's widow for her husband's horse and its gear, Lee had an appraisal made, paid the amount involved, and sent her the animal complete with the general's saddle and all the rest.

George McClellan also took time for amenities. Visitors came, among them William Aspinwall, the New York businessman and prominent Democrat to whom he had written regarding the president's Emancipation Proclamation. And Mary Ellen arrived, bringing with her their year-old daughter, for a stay of almost two weeks at a farmhouse east of the camps along the Antietam.

In reply to Lincoln's long letter the general said he was thinking of moving into the Shenandoah Valley but that his army was not yet in condition to go anywhere. Among many other items he wanted fresh mounts for his "fatigued" cavalry, thus provoking the president to respond: "Will you please pardon me for asking what the horses of your army have done since the battle of Antietam that fatigue anything?"

But by October 26, after many proddings from the general-in-chief, the Army of the Potomac was crossing its namesake river—not to invade the Shenandoah Valley, where McClellan believed General Lee had 130,000 troops, but to follow the O & A Railroad southward. It would take McClellan the better part of nine days to get his army over much the same stretch of the Potomac Lee's much smaller force had crossed in two days early in September. As this operation was being carried out, he kept on bombarding Washington with requests for weapons, supplies, and horses. And on October 27, in a message to Lincoln, he raised a question that could be interpreted as groundwork for more delay: Before going into action again, could an order be issued for drafted troops to fill the ranks of regiments whose losses had been heavy? Yes, Lincoln assured him, but he added:

> And now I ask a distinct answer to the question, Is it your purpose not to go into action again until the men now being drafted in the States are incorporated into the old regiments?

No, replied McClellan, he had no intention of postponing his advance for that reason. Lincoln might have gotten the wrong idea, explained the general, because a staff officer had added "before taking them again into action" to his text. But the damage was done: Lincoln had been using the word action, and McClellan spoke of advancing, which may have made the president wonder if the army commander knew the difference.

One thing, however, George McClellan did know, and he made it clear in a letter to Mary Ellen near October's end:

> It will not do for me to visit Washington now—the tone of the telegrams I receive from the authorities is such as to show that they will take advantage of anything possible to do me all the harm they can & if I went down I should at once be accused by the Presdt of purposely delaying the movement....If you could know the mean & dirty character of the dispatches I receive you would boil over with anger—when it is possible to misunderstand, & when it is not possible, whenever there is a chance of a wretched innuendo—there it comes. But the good of the country requires me to submit to all this from men whom I know to be

greatly my inferiors socially, intellectually & morally! There never was a truer epithet applied to a certain individual [Lincoln] than that of the "Gorilla."

Chapter 18

Exit McClellan, Enter Burnside

Congressional elections throughout the Union, held in some states in October and in the rest in early November, told the President that a great many voters were not as patient with his management of the war as he had been with his generals—with George McClellan, in particular. The people apparently knew the Young Napoleon could have destroyed Lee's army and did not, might have pursued Lee into Virginia but failed to do so, and had waited for the better part of two whole months before crossing the Potomac. And now, with the fall's good fighting weather wasted, McClellan gave the administration no reasons to expect any improvement in his performance.

Relieving General McClellan, however, entailed the risk of losing some Democrats' support for the war effort. And there was that lingering fear that the Army of the Potomac might in fact be, as the president had rather whimsically remarked near the Antietam back in early October, "McClellan's bodyguard."

On that point John Pope had been more specific, blaming his defeat in the battle Northerners called Second Bull Run in part on Fitz-John Porter's misplaced loyalty to a man rather than to the Union. For months to come, Porter would be obliged to try to convince a board of officers that Pope was wrong—as to him, at least—and he would fail, be cashiered from the army, appeal, and not succeed in clearing his reputation even legally for another thirty-four years.

But if Northerners were ever to have the victory they so clearly demanded, every risk had to be assumed. Now that all of the army was south of the Potomac, the President made the critical decision: McClellan must be removed from command.

Stanton and Halleck recognized that the amputation of George McClellan's head from a body made up of maybe 150,000 armed men from all over the North was not something to be left to an administrative guillotine. Surgery of the most sensitive sort had to be employed, cutting more delicate than had been needed nearly two weeks earlier in Don Carlos Buell's slicing.

Brigadier General Catharinus Putnam Buckingham, who had graduated four files behind Robert E. Lee in West Point's class of 1829 but left the army in 1831, was the War Department staff officer selected to carry out the mission. Railroader Herman Haupt, perhaps the only other person to know the nature of the elderly general's trip, provided him with a special train to Warrenton. From there, on November 7, and in the midst of a heavy snowstorm, General Buckingham rode westward to Waterloo in search of Major General Ambrose Burnside's headquarters.

Persuading Burnside to accept command of the Army of the Potomac was General Buckingham's first objective. If Burnside refused, Buckingham had been told, he should leave it at that and return to Washington. And for a time it seemed as though Burnside's reluctance to supersede his longtime friend would prevail; but finally he agreed, and he rode on with Buckingham through the storm to McClellan's headquarters near Rectortown.

By then in was late in the evening, around eleven o'clock. They found McClellan in his tent, writing a letter to his wife, one containing details of the military situation General-in-Chief Halleck might have wished he had. After his visitors left, McClellan returned to the unfinished letter:

> 11 1/2 pm. Another interruption—this time more important. It was in the shape of dear good old Burnside accompanied by Genl Buckingham, the Secy's Adjt Genl—they brought with them the order relieving me of the Army of the Potomac, & assigning Burnside to the command. No cause is given. I am ordered to turn over the command immediately & repair to Trenton, N. J. & on my arrival there to report by telegraph for future orders!!...
>
> Poor Burn feels dreadfully, almost crazy—I am sorry for him, & he never showed himself a better man or truer friend than now. Of course, I was much surprised—but as I read the order in the presence of Genl Buckingham, I am sure that not a muscle quivered nor was the slightest expression of feeling visible on my face, which he watched closely. They shall not have that triumph. They have made a great mistake—alas for my poor country—I know in my inner-

most heart she never had a truer servant....

Do not be at all worried—I am not. I have done the best I could for my country—to the last I have done my duty as I understand it. That I must have made many mistakes I cannot deny—I do not see any great blunders—but no man can judge of himself. Our consolation must be that we have tried to do what was right—if we have failed it was not our fault....

While General McClellan had been crossing the Potomac late in October, General Lee decided once again to split his army. He left Jackson's corps in the Shenandoah Valley; Longstreet's he took to Culpeper, east of the Blue Ridge. No matter which route southward McClellan took, he would risk having one of Lee's corps strike his rear and destroy his communications with his supply bases or face a reunited Confederate army.

Lee was still not certain what McClellan meant to do when the federal advance halted near Warrenton. Then, on November 10, Lee learned the reason: McClellan was no longer in command of the Union force. "We always understood each other so well," said Lee to Longstreet. "I fear they may continue to make these changes till they find someone I don't understand."

And for a while the Army of Northern Virginia's commander was uncertain as to what Burnside would do. A good guess was that he would approach Richmond via Fredericksburg; he had remained in that area during the recent fighting at Manassas and might prefer operating over terrain he knew. On the twelfth, General Lee alerted Jackson to be ready to move his corps eastward from the Shenandoah Valley. But he could do no more until Jeb Stuart's cavalry brought him fresh reports.

Ambrose Burnside's balding head, deep-set and rather sad eyes, and unique beard made him seem older than his thirty-eight years. So far he had been only on the fringes of glory—graduated from West Point in 1847 too late to see much of the Mexican War, in civilian life the inventor of a breech-loading carbine too far ahead of its time (the company he formed to manufacture it went into bankruptcy), holder of a railroad job only through George McClellan's compassion for him, and distinguished in this war only for the little-noticed campaign he had conducted on the coast of North Carolina. Fate frowned upon Burnside at Antietam as well: McClellan certainly had.

Abraham Lincoln must have known all of this when he gave Burnside command of the Army of the Potomac, and known, too, that this good soldier considered himself unworthy to lead so large a force. But Burnside was loyal, he had seen combat close up, and he might prove more effective than the general who had assured the president twelve months earlier, "I can do it all!"

To a message from Halleck, Burnside responded promptly that Fredericksburg would be his first objective, with Richmond the ultimate one; even better, he implied that defeating Lee's army was more important to him than cities on the map. And perhaps best of all, he seemed eager to have Halleck's counsel and War Department approval for whatever his next actions might be.

The general-in-chief went to Burnside's headquarters at Warren-

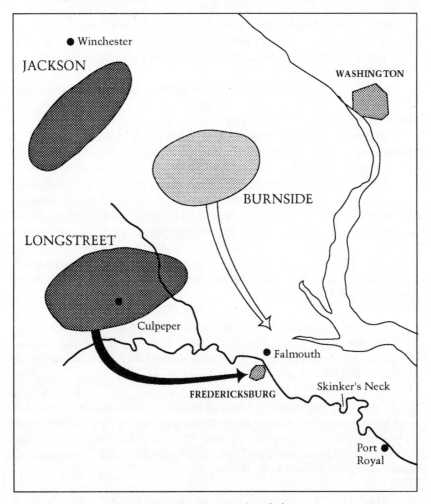

Both Sides' Moves to Fredericksburg

ton on November 12 for a conference regarding the planned advance to Fredericksburg. But lawyer Halleck had to refer the proposal to his client in *United States v. the Confederacy,* and not until near noon on November 14 did Burnside get the message he had been expecting: "The President has just assented to your plan. He thinks that it will succeed if you move rapidly; otherwise not."

General Lee had waited at Culpeper, getting few reports, considering all the moves Burnside could make. But on November 17, at about the time Burnside's most advanced unit was nearing Falmouth (across the Rappahannock and just north of Fredericksburg), Lee ordered Longstreet to send a division that way and to get the rest of his corps ready to follow it.

Lee deeply regretted the possibility that he might have to fight Burnside at Fredericksburg. There George Washington's mother had lived and died, and John Paul Jones had grown up, and Lee in his young manhood had courted Mary Custis on the lawns at Chatham, the Fitzhugh family's imposing mansion on Stafford Heights east of the Rappahannock. But it was not sentiment alone that made Lee shudder. Even if his forces could stop "those people" from advancing, the area's terrain would make it impossible for him to exploit a victory.

Setting regrets aside, by November 20, General Lee had all of Longstreet's corps on the hills west of Fredericksburg known as Marye's Heights. Through a heavy rain he could see Burnside's camps over on Stafford Heights and the low ground nearer the river. He had not thought he had been in a race with Burnside; even so, surely he was glad George McClellan's successor had not moved rapidly enough to seize Fredericksburg.

Bull Sumner seemed to be the Union general in charge on the Rappahannock's far side, or so General Lee learned the next day, November 21, when a letter from Sumner reached him. In it Sumner demanded the surrender of the town by five o'clock that afternoon; otherwise, federal guns on Stafford Heights would begin bombarding Fredericksburg at nine the next morning.

The army commander gave his assurance to the town's worried mayor that he would not expose Fredericksburg to damage by placing his forces in it—all Lee could promise. The mayor reported this in a reply to Sumner, adding that it would not be possible to remove innocent civilians within the time allotted. Sumner rescinded his threat. But Lee advised the mayor to get as many of the townspeople as he could out of harm's way as soon as he could, and the general watched the next day, with cold rain still falling, as families loaded their most precious possessions into wagons or carriages or onto the backs of mules and streamed westward or southward. Later, Lee wrote:

> History presents no instance of a people exhibiting a purer and more unselfish patriotism or a higher sense of fortitude and courage than was evinced by the citizens of Fredericksburg. They cheerfully incurred great hardships and privations, and surrendered their homes and property to destruction rather than yield them into the hands of the enemies of their country.

Compassion was not the only reason Fredericksburg was not reduced to rubble on November 22. The rains that had greeted General Lee on the twentieth persisted long enough to make all the Rappahannock's upstream fords impassable and the timely arrival of pontoon bridges General Halleck had ordered southward more uncertain and more important.

By November 25 some pontoons had arrived, but not enough, and on the next day Burnside was called to Aquia Landing for a visit from Abraham Lincoln. Halleck showed his confidence in Burnside by sending him another 15,000 troops, although the Army of the Potomac already had about 119,000 men near Falmouth and two corps remained to be ordered southward if needed.

But in December's early days General Burnside's mind was mostly on the Rappahannock and where he ought to cross it. By then Jackson's corps had arrived from the Shenandoah Valley, and the Confederates' shifting made each federal plan obsolete soon after it had been declared feasible.

Fifty miles or so northward, in Washington, Henry Halleck may well have considered Burnside's problem minor in comparison to others he faced. In the west General Rosecrans remained at Nashville, saying he must accumulate supplies before moving. Grant was preparing to open a campaign to seize Vicksburg, gain control of the Mississippi, and cut the Confederacy in two. Something might be done in North Carolina. Even in Texas.

All through the fall the general-in-chief had been moving forces from training camps to the armies and from one army to another, balancing military necessity with the president's priorities. Halleck remarked: "His fingers itch to be into everything going on."

As before, Lincoln wanted East Tennessee: That was Rosecrans's task, but first he would have to fight Bragg's army, which Rosecrans was willing enough to do. But Confederate cavalrymen kept tearing up the Louisville & Nashville's tracks, and only when Rosecrans' supply stockpiles made dependence on the rail line no longer critical could he attack. Halleck understood logistics better than the president; but as December opened, even the general-in-chief's patience was thinning.

General Grant's Vicksburg campaign as well was off to a slow start for the same reason: the need to gather supplies. But Lincoln added a complication by accepting an offer from Grant's subordinate John A. McClernand, an Illinois Democrat, to furnish a special force of midwestern troops and lead it in the drive to clear the Mississippi of Confederates. The general had gone first to Halleck with his plan, and Halleck—who considered McClernand incompetent—had turned him down; now the general-in-chief learned from a newspaper article that the president had reversed that decision.

All along Halleck had meant for Grant to be in complete charge of the Vicksburg operation, with able William Tecumseh Sherman as his primary subordinate troop leader. At a minimum, McClernand might eclipse Cump. And all Halleck could do was hope that Grant could complete the campaign before political influence wrecked it.

Less damaging, militarily, was the president's appeasement of New Englanders' demands that he invade Texas and seize rebel cotton for the North's mills. Lincoln met the challenge by giving command of the expedition to Major General Nathaniel Banks, former governor of Massachusetts, whipped by Jackson in the Shenandoah Valley and so distrusted by John Pope that he had been left to guard supplies at Second Manassas. "Oh, the curse of political expedience!" Halleck might cry (and did)—but Texas could wait.

Blasted now, though, were the general-in-chief's hopes that the armies' movements along the Mississippi and toward East Tennessee could be coordinated so as to smite the enemy's forces in the west at about the same time Burnside destroyed Lee on the Rappahannock. Halleck wrote to Major General John Schofield:

> I am sick and tired of this political military life. The number of enemies I have made because I would not yield my own convictions of right is already legion. If they would only follow the example of their ancestors, enter a herd of swine, run down some steep bank and drown themselves in the sea, there would be some hope of saving the country.

Henry Halleck might have been even more discouraged if he had given thought to the improvements Jefferson Davis had made in the Confederacy's war-management system during the fall of 1862. But Davis had made the changes gradually, some only under pressure;

few of them attracted much attention, and it would take time for many of them to make any difference.

With Grant's federals more active in Mississippi, Davis promoted John C. Pemberton to lieutenant general and made him responsible for Vicksburg. At a minimum, Pemberton's higher rank would relieve Earl Van Dorn and Sterling Price from having to "cooperate"—something they had not done effectively earlier. But how could Davis get Bragg and Pemberton to work together?

General Joseph Eggleston Johnston provided an answer in mid-November by turning up in Richmond to seek a command, now that he had recovered from the wounds he had suffered at Seven Pines back on the last day of May. The Davis-Johnston relationship had always been fragile, and so it might be again, but it would be hard for the president to explain why such a senior full general was idle when a supreme commander was needed in the west. Accordingly, Davis sent Joe Johnston to Chattanooga.

At least in theory, the Confederate commander-in-chief now had only three generals looking to him for guidance: Robert E. Lee in Virginia, Johnston in the west, and Pierre Beauregard in Charleston. Lee needed no control. Beauregard was parked out of action in South Carolina, where he was revered as the hero of Fort Sumter. But Davis had his doubts about Johnston.

Jefferson Davis's health was almost broken by the burdens of being both political and military leader of an embattled nation. Even so, in early December he took two aides with him on a secret trip to see for himself what conditions in the west really were. At Chattanooga he found that the newly arrived Johnston was still too bothered by his wounds to accompany the president to Murfreesboro, where Bragg's army was gathered. Davis went on, found Bragg's troops in excellent shape and eager to fight Rosecrans, and headed for Vicksburg.

Curiously, Davis left Richmond on his long western journey just at the time General Lee was waiting for Burnside to send his powerful army across the Rappahannock at Fredericksburg.

Among General Burnside's first actions after he took over the Union Army of the Potomac was grouping six of his seven corps into what he called grand divisions, three of them, led by Sumner, Franklin, and Hooker; he kept Franz Sigel's corps as a reserve. George McClellan had moved toward something of this sort before Antietam, only to drop it prior to that battle. But Burnside stuck with his new organizational arrangement, and on December 9 he made another departure from his predecessor's practice by summoning his senior commanders to a conference so that each would know not only what he was to do but how all of them were expected to operate within the plan for crossing the Rappahannock and destroying Lee.

First there would be a feint made at Skinker's Neck, fourteen miles downriver, to hold Jackson's divisions in that vicinity. William Franklin's two corps were to cross pontoon bridges a mile or so south of Fredericksburg, advance westward, and cut Lee's army in two. Sumner's two corps would cross over bridges built east of Fredericksburg and destroy Longstreet's forces on Marye's Heights west of the town. Hooker's grand division would be in reserve, prepared to exploit the victory as soon as the army commander so ordered.

Franklin's and Sumner's grand divisions would have their artillery with them when they crossed the Rappahannock, and on Stafford Heights Brigadier General Henry J. Hunt's longer-range guns were available for support. Anyone who remembered Hunt's masterful use of massed artillery at Malvern Hill back on July 1 could only be reassured by his presence.

Some of Burnside's generals, though, may have wondered if he had erred by expecting young Lieutenant Cyrus B. Comstock, only seven years out of West Point, to drive his engineers hard enough to throw five pontoon bridges at three designated sites across an ice-choked river at the times called for in the plan—regardless of enemy opposition. Everything depended upon those bridges. Never before had the Army of the Potomac made a river crossing under enemy fire, nor had its chief of engineers been a mere lieutenant.

It was almost midnight on Tuesday, December 9, when the conference ended at Burnside's headquarters in the Phillips house. Now, to the general-in-chief he could send a report:

> All the orders have been issued to the several commanders of grand divisions and heads of departments for an attempt to cross the river on Thursday morning [the eleventh]....I think now that the enemy will be more surprised by a crossing immediately in our front than in any other part of the river. The commanders of grand divisions coincide with me in the opinion, and I have accordingly ordered the movement....
>
> If the General-in-Chief desires it, I will send a minute statement in cipher to-morrow morning. The movement is so important that I feel anxious to be fortified by his approval. Please answer.

Halleck did: "I beg of you not to telegraph details of your plans,

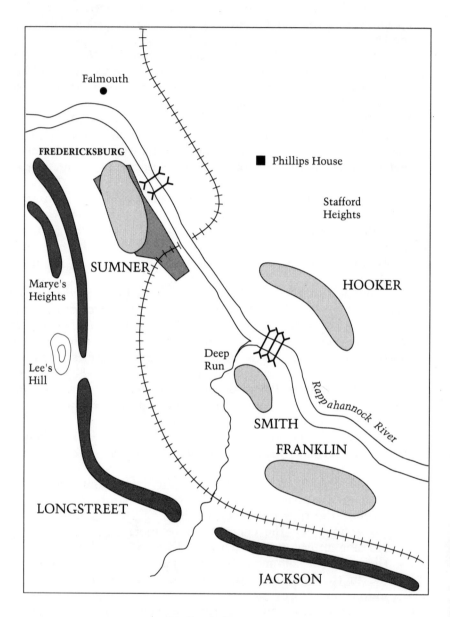

Pre-Battle Positions

nor the time of your intended movements. No secret can be kept which passes through so many hands."

True, but at the time, General Lee had no idea of where or when "those people" really meant to cross the Rappahannock. To guard against a sweep around his southern flank he had placed one of Jackson's divisions, Harvey Hill's, opposite Port Royal; about ten miles upstream, Jubal Early's division was watching the Yankees at Skinker's Neck. West of the Rappahannock, near the Richmond, Fredericksburg & Potomac's tracks, Jackson had two more divisions—his old one, led now by Brigadier General William B. Taliaferro, and Powell Hill's—either or both of which he could send to any threatened point along the river. Longstreet's divisions were scattered over seven miles or so of ridgeline stretching from the Rappahannock opposite Falmouth and along Marye's Heights southward to Deep Run.

Not during the day on Wednesday, December 10, would Lee know any more than he had earlier. And even that night all he had to go on was a rumor: A woman, some riverfront pickets reported, had shouted from the east bank that Burnside's troops had been given a large issue of rations and told to cook them. Was it possible that Burnside would attack Fredericksburg when he could so easily cross downstream and plant his huge Army of the Potomac between the Confederate forces and Richmond?

Yes, thought Lafayette McLaws, commander of the division on Marye's Heights most likely to be struck first by a federal assault. To Brigadier General William Barksdale, whose men were deployed along Fredericksburg's river frontage, McLaws sent word for the sharpshooters to be alert. And to General Lee he rushed a message: If he heard a signal gun fire twice, it would mean that the Yankees were indeed crossing.

Nothing could be worse, Lieutenant Comstock's engineers may have thought in the predawn hours of Thursday, December 11, than to be shot while they were unarmed and trying to put pontoons in place, then fall through the river's half-inch ice crust and drown in the frigid water beneath it. But from three A.M. onward, with the temperature at twenty-four degrees above zero, detachments worked at three bridge sites along the dreaded Rappahannock—directly opposite Fredericksburg, well above the ruins of the railroad bridge; a little below it; and a mile or so downstream across from Deep Run.

It was not just a matter of getting the pontoons out one beyond the other. They had to be lashed together, the planks brought out and secured. All of this took time, for cold fingers could not move with precision and there was always the fear that the nearer to the Confederate bank the bridging advanced, the easier it would be for a rebel marksman to aim and shoot to kill.

Most fortunate were the engineers putting the southernmost spans across the Rappahannock, for no rebels opposed them, and the single one below the old railroad bridge was completed even earlier that morning. Young Comstock's main problem was with the two bridges directly opposite Fredericksburg. There, at dawn and at a range of perhaps eighty yards, Confederate volleys stabbed out to make real the horrible death the engineers had dreaded, and this brought Comstock's work to a halt.

At four forty-five that foggy morning General Lee heard the two shots fired by Lafayette McLaws's signal gun. He rode to a hill south of Marye's Heights, but even after daylight he could not see very much because of dense fog.

Midmorning brought a lifting of the mist and with it the opening of a fierce federal bombardment of Fredericksburg: Burnside, furious at the delay Barksdale's sharpshooters had caused, told Henry Hunt to have every gun within range of the town fire fifty rounds into it.

Lee, mindful that some women and children might still be huddled in the cellars of their homes as shells exploded above them, was appalled as he watched Fredericksburg's houses and churches disappear under rubble-raised dust and smoke. He said, "These people delight to destroy the weak and those who can make no defense," he said, "it just suits them!"

And it was all in vain, for Barksdale's riflemen were back in action even as the final federal shells were landing. Again and again the Yankee engineers ventured out to resume work on the twin bridges; each time, fresh Confederate volleys sent them running to seek cover on the east bank.

Beyond the pillars of dark smoke rising into the still air over Fredericksburg General Lee could see masses of blue-clad troops and long lines of wagons and artillery batteries waiting for Comstock to finish his bridges. More blue blocks of men and strings of horse-drawn vehicles and gun carriages and caissons were off to the south, down near Deep Run, where two pontoon-borne spans had been in place and ready for use since eleven o'clock that morning.

John Hood's division of Longstreet's corps was all Lee had to oppose those blue blocks south of him if they began crossing the completed bridges, and Hood's troops were well back from the river on the ridgelines. The army commander had sent word to Jackson to hurry northward unless "those people" were making a crossing at

Skinker's Neck or Port Royal. But what if the huge federal force near Deep Run crossed and forced Hood back toward Marye's Heights before Jackson's divisions arrived?

Ambrose Burnside had told General-in-Chief Halleck he meant to launch his attack on this day, Thursday, December 11. He had tried to, but nothing much had gone as he had desired.

True, Sumner and Franklin had moved their grand divisions to the proper crossing places at the times designated. And Lieutenant Comstock had done nearly everything expected of him. But Burnside's timetable was in tatters, useless, because of those Confederates dug in along the Rappahannock's western bank. Artillery had not dislodged them. Something must.

Burnside may as well have been a West Point cadet again, standing at a blackboard working a mathematics problem, but not the one his instructor had assigned him. As early as eleven o'clock that morning he might have started Franklin's grand division over the southernmost bridges with orders to sweep westward and cut Lee's army in half. But his attention was instead riveted to the Fredericksburg crossing site, and now this short December day was getting away from him.

It may have been artilleryman Henry Hunt whose idea it was to fill some of the surplus pontoons with infantrymen and send them across. Once on the western bank, the troops could drive away the Confederate sharpshooters and hold a bridgehead, thus enabling Comstock's engineers to complete the twin spans over which Sumner's grand division could cross.

Soon after the suggestion was made, it was carried out. Infantrymen rowed through the broken ice. Though some were hit, enough got ashore. By dark Comstock's last bridges would be in place, and Sumner's troops could seize Fredericksburg.

This was apparent at four o'clock, when the army commander finally ordered Franklin to send his entire force across the spans threatening Lee's southern flank. Then, with William F. Smith's corps over on the western side, Burnside told Franklin to leave only one brigade over there to guard the bridgehead overnight. This meant that Smith's divisions had to recross the bridges, which they did.

And though all of Sumner's grand division might well have entered Fredericksburg before midnight on the eleventh, only enough troops did to drive Barksdale's brigade out of the town house by house, street by street. With this much done, however, the Army of the Potomac's commander seemed content. Fredericksburg and the Rappahannock's crossings were under his control.

But Burnside's problem that day had been Lee's army, and as night fell, the half of it he might have isolated remained unmolested on the high ground west of the town. Soon he would learn that in war, as in West Point's section rooms, there can be no credit given for solving the wrong problem.

In a way, though, the Yankees' general commanding may have been as much sinned against as sinner. All day long Brigadier General William Barksdale's Mississippians had fought as though they were determined to give General Lee the most precious gift of all in battle: time.

Barksdale had made sure in advance of the frustrated foe's bombardment that his men knew where to find shelter. During it a gallant woman came to tell him her cow had just been killed by a federal shell and that she did not want the Yankees to get the meat; his men were welcome to it, she told him, and after thanking her, he had a staff officer guide her to a safe place. And as the Union artillery fire died out, Barksdale instructed a courier: "Tell General Lee that if he wants a bridge of dead Yankees, I can furnish him with one!"

W. J. Cash later termed Southern effusions such as Barksdale's "extravagant profession," but the spirit was there, and it was shared by his Mississippians that day. Not until four-thirty that afternoon did he call his men back to Fredericksburg's Caroline Street, and not until seven did Barksdale obey the orders sent him by Lafayette McLaws earlier to withdraw to Marye's Heights.

To get there the Mississippians had to march over an open plain from the edge of town westward for several hundred yards. Halfway to the base of the hill they paused to form columns to cross one of the narrow bridges spanning an old canal—now more of a ditch about thirty feet wide and six feet deep—that ran from northeast to southwest, roughly parallel to Longstreet's lines. Finally, after another few hundred yards of flat ground, they crawled over a stone embankment and dropped onto the sunken 800-yard stretch of Telegraph Road.

As Barksdale deployed his regiments along the road, they could look up at Marye's Heights and the ranks of men and guns along its slope. Turning toward the river, they saw they were in a natural trench from which they could kill anything within range out there on the plain between them and Fredericksburg.

But not the next morning, Friday the twelfth, for fog covered the Rappahannock's valley. Only through momentary breaks in the haze could Generals Lee and Longstreet get quick glimpses of the masses of federal troops and guns streaming across the pontoon bridges into Fredericksburg. Was this happening south of there, near Deep Run, as well?

Definitely, Lee learned around noon when he and Jackson dismounted near an observation point one of Jeb Stuart's staff officers, Major Heros von Borke, had found. It was on flat ground, downstream from the southernmost bridges, within rifle range of the Yankees they were watching. von Borke breathed easier when his two irreplaceable guests walked back to their horses; but he had done them a great service, for even through the fog they had seen enough to know what to expect.

By early afternoon Jackson's first two divisions—Powell Hill's and Taliaferro's—were moving onto the ridgeline John Hood had occupied, and Hood took his brigades northward along it, nearer the rest of Longstreet's corps and Marye's Heights. This left Jackson with nearly two miles of hills to defend, all the way southward to a few houses on the railroad known locally as Hamilton's Crossing; from there Stuart's cavalry would guard the Army of Northern Virginia's southern flank eastward for a mile or so to the Rappahannock.

But Jackson needed his entire corps to hold those hills. He sent orders to Jubal Early and Harvey Hill, still eighteen to twenty-two miles down river southeast of him, to march all night and be certain they were with him at daybreak. This done, he rode along the base of his high ground, following the R F & P's tracks and scanning the Yankees' routes of approach over the plain. Then he rode up to the ridgeline and inspected it.

"I am opposed to fighting here," Jackson had told Harvey Hill some days earlier. "We will whip the enemy but gain no fruits of the victory."

So General Lee had felt all along; now all he said was: "I shall try to do them all the damage in our power when they move forward."

General Burnside went southward to see what he could of Jackson's hills. But it was late in the day, he was far from his headquarters at the Phillips house and perhaps eager to return to it, and he may not have given as much of his attention as he might have to William Franklin's proposal.

Franklin had placed Major General John Reynolds's corps in a position from which it might either sweep south of Jackson's flank or attack him directly. "Baldy" Smith's corps was north of Reynolds, guarding the bridges. Send other troops for that duty, Franklin urged Burnside, so that Smith could send his corps at Jackson while Reynolds got around the Confederates and behind them, thus forcing Lee to abandon Marye's Heights.

Burnside liked the idea, but he refused to approve it then and there. Orders would come later, he promised, then left.

Washington may have been more on the army commander's mind than Franklin's grand division. That morning, Herman Haupt had come to the Phillips house, disgusted because nothing was being done to repair the railroad bridge over the Rappahannock; he could not keep either civilians or soldiers from deserting the task. Presumably, Burnside explained what he was about to do. Then, suddenly, Haupt had rushed back to Washington.

He reached there around nine that evening, soon found John Covode—a friend who was a congressman from Pennsylvania—and described the situation at Fredericksburg to him. Covode took Haupt on to the Executive Mansion. Lincoln, starved for news and disturbed by what Haupt had told him, asked Covode and Haupt to walk with him to General Halleck's house. There, for the third time, Haupt gave a report of what he had seen and heard.

Long afterward Haupt wrote:

On its conclusion, the President asked General Halleck to telegraph orders to General Burnside to withdraw his army to the north side of the river. General Halleck rose and paced the room for some time, and then stopped, facing the President, and said decidedly: "I will do no such thing. If we were personally present and knew the exact situation, we might assume such responsibility. If such orders are issued, you must issue them yourself. I hold that a General in command of an army in the field is the best judge of existing conditions."

Lincoln listened to more information Haupt gave about the terrain facing Burnside. "When I finished," recalled Haupt, "the president sighed and said: 'What you say gives me a great many grains of comfort.'"

Whether Lincoln agreed with Halleck or suspected that the brilliant railroad manager might be backing down merely to ease the tension, that night the president sent Burnside no order.

And down on the frigid plain south of Fredericksburg, in William Franklin's tent, three generals waited in vain for the order the army commander had promised he would send.

Chapter 19

Fredericksburg:
A Worse Place Than Hell

Fog again covered the Rappahannock's valley at dawn on December 13, blanketing the movements of the armies drawn up so near each other the Confederates could hear the rumbling of federal artillery being moved over the frozen ground. Now, on Saturday, Burnside's forces were where he had meant them to be on Thursday. And in the interval Lee had brought all of his army together on the hills a mile or so west of the river.

Fredericksburg, looted by Union troops the day before, was in ruins, significant only as the place where Bull Sumner's grand division waited for the haze to lift and for a definite order to advance. William Franklin's situation was much the same several miles downriver. Not until almost eight o'clock that morning did he receive word from the army commander, and with Baldy Smith's corps still out of position, Franklin would have only John Reynolds's corps to send against Jackson's hills.

As the federal forces moved into their formations, General Longstreet rode his lines in the Confederate army's northern sector. Reaching Lieutenant Colonel Porter Alexander's guns, the corps commander spotted an idle one and asked if it might be used to kill Yankees when they approached Marye's Heights. "General," said Alexander, "we cover that ground so well that we comb it as with a fine-tooth comb. A chicken could not live on that field when we open on it!"

Jackson surprised his men early that morning by appearing in a uniform Jeb Stuart had given him back in October, one resplendent with gold braid and a hat instead of his familiar cap. "Come here, boys!" shouted an old campaigner, "Stonewall has drawed his bounty and has bought himself some new clothes!" Another, not so sure this was a good omen, shook his head and said: "Old Jack will be afraid of his clothes and will not get down to work."

Not quite. When Jackson joined General Lee, he wanted to strike the Yankees facing him before the fog lifted and federal gunners across on Stafford Heights could see to fire. This was typical of Jackson, but there may have been more to it. On the way to Lee's observation point he had noticed a gap between two of Powell Hill's brigades. "The enemy," he had remarked, "will attack here."

But Lee thought it best to restrain Jackson's desire to hit first. At around ten o'clock, when the fog dissipated and the generals could see all of Burnside's 105,000 combat troops and their artillery deployed for battle on the plains below them, it became obvious that the Confederate army commander's decision had been the correct one.

"Are you not scared," Longstreet teased Jackson, "by that file of Yankees you have before you down there?"

"Wait until they come a little nearer," Old Jack replied, "and they shall either scare me or I'll scare them!"

Jackson mounted. Longstreet asked, "What are you going to do with all those people over there?"

"Sir, we will give them the bayonet."

William Franklin had sixty thousand men in his Left Grand Division, but he could commit to the fight only John Reynolds's fraction, thanks to Ambrose Burnside's failure to make a firm decision based on what he had seen and heard the evening before. As if to make up for the nonavailability of Smith's corps, however, Burnside sent two of Joseph Hooker's reserve divisions to support Franklin's attack if he needed them.

Reynolds awarded the honor of leading the assault on Jackson's hills to George Meade's division, with assurances that divisions commanded by John Gibbon and Abner Doubleday would support him. But late in the morning, as Meade's brigades were moving westward, from their southern flank came artillery fire. Surprised, Meade had to halt his troops while his batteries and some of Doubleday's got rid of this threat.

It was not nearly as formidable a show of force as the Union commanders thought: Jeb Stuart's Major John Pelham had only two guns in action, but he was heating their barrels with the ferocity of his firing. For the federal gunners it was like trying to smash a fly with sledgehammers. After an hour, during which Pelham often changed positions, he ceased firing. With one gun disabled and his ammunition almost gone, he finally obeyed repeated orders to withdraw.

Now another hour passed as Union artillery blasted the hills Jackson's men held. Then, as Meade's brigades belatedly advanced over the flat ground and neared the R F & P's tracks, forty-seven Confederate guns opened fire on them.

Meade's men ran straight ahead toward the shelter of a salient of woods, and once there they kept moving westward up a ravine. Now it was the infantry's fight all the way uphill—a concentrated stab in which the determined federals shot their way past rebel brigades on both flanks until they were on the ridgeline.

All morning on that Saturday Confederate Brigadier General Maxcy Gregg, the scholarly South Carolinian who had fought so valiantly at Gaines's Mill and Second Manassas, had thought his troops were in reserve. Their arms were stacked. Resting, the first instinct of seasoned soldiers, was what they were doing as the Yankees came charging up the ravine toward them.

Confusion predominated. These had to be Confederate forces, or so Maxcy Gregg must have thought as he restrained his men from firing into them, only to be shot from his horse. Now some of his troops knew better. They held the Yankees back until Jubal Early arrived and launched a counterattack that sent the federals running back down the ravine, prodded by volleys from the brigades they had shoved aside earlier.

Now the confusion was federal, and it proliferated as the fugitives ran into blue-clad troops supporting them. But Early could not pursue them far; and although General Jackson hoped to exploit this repulse with a corps-wide advance that would push the Yankees into the icy Rappahannock, his awareness of Union artillery firepower on Stafford Heights made him leave his part of the battle where it stood.

And its worst moment had taken place exactly where, hours earlier, Jackson had predicted the Yankees would attack.

No one, least of all Ambrose Burnside, knew it, but the first part of his battle had ended as the remnants of George Meade's division streamed eastward back onto the plain. Burnside's headquarters at the Phillips house, however, was too far from Franklin's fight, and the messages the army commander got were too terse for him to have learned much. Moreover, he meant to press Lee everywhere until he broke him somewhere.

This may explain why Burnside—at around eleven o'clock, while Franklin's advance was getting off to a slow start—sent Sumner's grand division forward from Fredericksburg with Marye's Heights as his objective.

First to advance over the plain Barksdale's Mississippians had crossed Thursday night, ditch and all, were the brigades of Brigadier General William French's division. Behind them came Major General Winfield Scott Hancock's and Oliver Howard's.

Steadily, in ranks whose alignment the real Napoleon might have admired, French's troops marched toward the sunken road. As soon as rebel artillery rounds blasted holes in the federal waves, they were filled. Onward the bluecoats came, stalwart, determined, closing to within 400 yards of the embankment at the base of Marye's Heights, 300 yards, 200; then, suddenly, volleys fired from behind the stone wall shredded them.

Over the bodies of the fallen came another wave, another, and another, all to be cut down by the same incessant and nigh-inescapable fire from riflemen in the sunken road. Up through rebel artillery's canister and grapeshot came Hancock's brigades. No soldier wants to step on another, whether dead or wounded or only hugging the ground in fear, but after twenty minutes there was a blue carpet—thickened now as Hancock's men fell, riddled by Confederate infantrymen—and no one, however brave, could get beyond the westernmost Union soldier's body.

Next came Major General Howard's division. Howard had meant to incline to the north, to probe for a weaker place in the rebel line, but Hancock had called for support, and the man who had already lost his left arm at Seven Pines back in June promptly responded, only to see his brigades torn apart by the same withering combination of artillery and rifle fire.

Now, by midafternoon that Saturday, December 13, Major General Darius Couch's entire corps was wrecked—a mass of prone bodies, some of the living firing at the rebels from behind the dead and wounded but none advancing. None could: Burnside had sent Bull Sumner's Right Grand Division straight toward the five-mile Confederate line's strongest single point.

Nothing had been required of General Robert E. Lee on that grim Saturday, in stark contrast to all the improvising he had been obliged to do at Sharpsburg three months earlier with fewer than half the 78,000 men now with him. From the vantage point future mapmakers would call Lee's Hill he had watched as those people had charged over the plain toward the sunken road repeatedly, gallantly, only to be slaughtered a hundred yards and more short of it. Then Lee's attention had shifted to the south, where George Meade's brigades were disappearing into the spur of woods east of Jackson's lines.

Sounds were about the only means by which General Lee or

anyone near him could discern Meade's progress. At the worst moments, when it seemed those people had broken through and were on Jackson's ridgeline, the big thirty-pounder Parrott gun that had been firing only a few feet away from Lee exploded, scattering fragments that narrowly missed him. Then, as the dust settled, from the south came the cracks of savage rifle firing and, unmistakably, shrill rebel yelling.

Soon Lee saw bluecoats emerging from the woods, fleeing onto the plain, Confederates pursuing. Turning to Longstreet, he said: "It is well that war is so terrible—we should grow too fond of it!"

Below, in the sunken road, Lafayette McLaws's troops were in six ranks, some loading and passing rifles forward to men doing the firing. As artillery batteries' ammunition ran out, other units moved their guns in to replace them. Confederate wounded were taken to Mrs. Stevens's house, facing the road, where she not only remained to help but tore her petticoats to make bandages.

And the federal waves pressed on toward the sunken road, some mistaking the Confederate batteries' changeovers for the first sign of a retreat, only to discover to their horror that this was not so. No longer could the riflemen along the sunken road count the charges they had repelled. As dark fell, gunners were aiming their artillery pieces at flashes coming from the plain, drenched now with the blood of uncounted thousands, a vast and undulating blue rug.

Total darkness, made even more unsettling by the cries of the wounded east of the sunken road, was broken by streaks in the sky: the aurora borealis, a sight many Southern soldiers had never even heard about. The northern lights, some said it was. But many took the strange and ephemeral celestial fireworks to be an omen—and, like the Comet of Charles V back in 1860, one portending nothing good for the South.

At sundown Ambrose Burnside seemed determined to renew the battle the next day—repeating it, rather. This his three grand division commanders unanimously and vehemently opposed. But as late, or as early, as four o'clock on Sunday morning, December 14, Burnside wired Halleck and Lincoln: "We hope to carry the crest to-day. Our loss is heavy—say, 5,000."

It was nearer to 13,000, but even Burnside's rough estimate was appalling enough for his subordinates to persist in their appeals to him to call off the slaughter. This, reluctantly, he did, but only after declaring that he wanted to lead his old corps himself in an assault on Marye's Heights.

And so it was that Ambrose Burnside proved how correct he had been earlier when he had told the president and Buckingham that he was not qualified to command so large a force as the Army of the Potomac. Yet he had fought, certainly as hard or even harder than George McClellan ever had, harder than any of his subordinates thought prudent, and in the end he did not see himself defeated so much as let down by the unwillingness of his grand division commanders to keep on fighting.

Ironically, the Confederates were showing great respect for Burnside. Lee and the men with him were expecting the Yankees to come at them again and were preparing for it. An ammunition train from Richmond enabled the Confederates to replenish their dwindled stocks, and overnight the troops deepened the trenches they hoped would protect them from the federal artillery blasts presaging more assaults everywhere along the line.

But gallant Maxcy Gregg, who had still waved his hat to encourage his men to throw back George Meade's charging Yankees after one of them had put a bullet in his spine, knew he would not see even another morning fog. He dictated a farewell message to his state's governor, one ending: "If I am to die now, I give my life cheerfully for the independence of South Carolina, and I trust you will live to see our cause triumph completely."

General Jackson came to Gregg's bedside in the Yerby house and sat by him, holding his hand and listening to the dying man's explanation of an incident that had displeased Jackson earlier. "I fear," Gregg added, "I was discourteous."

"Let me ask you," said the corps commander, "to dismiss the matter from your mind and turn your thoughts to God and to the world to which you go."

"I thank you, I thank you very much."

The calm on Sunday, December 14, was broken only by sniper fire, behind which the federals collected such wounded men as they could reach and began burying the frozen bodies of the dead. If the Union position could be called a line, it was along the old canal, several hundred yards east of the sunken road.

In that intervening space General Lee could see that many of the corpses were naked, stripped during the night by some of his men, who argued that the Yankees going "below" had no need for warm clothing. That Confederates engaged in scavenging was understandable to Union Colonel Francis Winthrop Palfrey, who later wrote:

> [The Southerners'] stomachs were not seldom empty, their backs and feet ill-clothed and ill-shod, while the Northern soldiers were provided with everything. "I can whip any army that is followed by a herd of cattle," said

Jackson, and it was a pregnant saying....

A field won meant to [Confederates] not only a field won, but clothing for body and feet, food, money, watches, and arms and equipments as well. To the Northerners a field won was simply a field won.

This one, once looted, remained under a flag of truce for most of the next day, Monday, December 15, while the grim burials went on. Freezing weather had preserved many of the bodies in the grotesque positions death's agonies caused. Seldom, surely, on any battlefield had the inevitable task been so demanding on the emotions of those ordered to perform it.

Then, with a light rain falling on the morning of December 16, the Confederates discovered that Burnside had withdrawn all of his forces to the far side of the Rappahannock. Darkness and a wind from the west had masked the retreat from the eyes and ears of Southerners. And, giving mute assurance that for a time at least Burnside meant to fight no more, pulled against the Rappahannock's eastern shores were all the pontoon bridges.

For General Lee it had been a victory, but—as he and Jackson had predicted—a barren one. He could take no comfort when he learned that his 5,000 casualties were less than half Burnside's. Afterward he would write: "We had really accomplished nothing; we had not gained a foot of ground, and I knew the enemy could easily replace the men he had lost."

Reactions to Fredericksburg were predictable: in the South, rejoicing; gloom and anger throughout the Union. But Northerners placed the blame for Burnside's defeat much less on him than upon the man in the Executive Mansion. Among the most irate of Lincoln's critics was *Chicago Tribune* publisher Joseph Medill, who called the administration the "Central Imbecility." The *New York World* demanded that the president get rid of Edwin Stanton, Treasury Secretary Salmon Chase, and General-in-Chief Henry Halleck immediately.

In Congress the wrath of Radical Republicans centered on Secretary of State William Seward, charging that the "premier" had too much influence over Lincoln. At a caucus held three days after the Fredericksburg disaster, those Senators agreed that they had a duty to persuade the president to remove Seward and to send a delegation to Lincoln for that purpose.

Senator Preston King of New York warned Seward of what was happening, whereupon the secretary of state promptly sent his resignation to the president. It could hardly have reached Lincoln at a moment of greater depression. He had received little word from Burnside, and the general's optimistic tone had proved misleading; most of what he knew about the disaster he had read in a dispatch filed by newspaper reporter Henry Villard on the fourteenth, and the next day, the saddened president had remarked, "If there is a worse place than Hell, I am in it."

Now, on December 16, Lincoln realized that he had been given not only a fresh problem but a challenge to a key constitutional provision: the equality of the executive branch of the federal government with the congressional. Correctly, he saw the Radical Republicans' pressure on Seward as a naked attempt to wrest powers first the Founders and more recently the presidential Electoral College had entrusted to him, and no erosion or usurpation of those powers would he allow.

The Radicals, Lincoln told his friend Orville Browning, "wish to get rid of me, and I am sometimes half disposed to gratify them." No, advised Browning, stand fast. But to the president it seemed the country was on the brink of utter ruin. "It appears to me the Almighty is against us," he said, "and I can hardly see a ray of hope." And he added something to this effect: "I wonder why sane men can believe such an absurd lie as the charge of Seward's malign influence over me?"

If there was a lie, there had to be a liar; and on Thursday evening, the eighteenth, as Lincoln listened to the senators when the delegation paid its call on him, he tried to figure out who the liar may have been. A clue was embedded in the thrust of the visitors' complaints: The president did not make proper use of his cabinet. Possibly, but which member of it might have gone to the Radical with such a notion? Certainly not, in the circumstances, the once overly ambitious "premier." Could it have been Seward's bitter rival, Salmon Chase? Possibly. Chase was something of a hero to the Radical Republicans, and they might well want to see him become the dominant member of the cabinet once the mild Seward had been forced out of it.

Having heard the senators' allegations and demands, Lincoln sent them away with a promise to consider them. The next day, Friday, the nineteenth, he called his cabinet together, except for Seward, and told those present what had transpired. Since the problem appeared to be his relationship with the cabinet, he added, why not hold a joint meeting with the senators that evening? Who could object to that?

Well, Salmon Chase. But the other members' enthusiasm left the treasury secretary with no alternative, and he agreed.

When the senators arrived that night, Lincoln met with them

first and asked their permission for the cabinet members (other than Seward) to join them. There was no objection. In came the cabinet, and soon a session that lasted four hours began. Yes, the president conceded, he often acted without obtaining cabinet approval; but once he set policy, all its members supported it. Turning to them and looking directly at Chase, Lincoln asked: "Did they not?"

Nothing could Chase have said without condemning himself in the judgment of either the senators or the cabinet. Worse, he protested that he would not have attended the meeting if he had known he was to be arraigned.

Afterward, Senator Lyman Trumbull of Illinois said to the president: "Lincoln, somebody has lied like hell!" Deft, indeed, was the reply: "Not tonight."

But the problem was not solved by Salmon Chase's exposure. On the next day, Lincoln sent Navy Secretary Welles to Seward to find out if the "premier" was adamant about resigning. No, Welles was told; then he rushed back to the Executive Mansion. There he found Chase and Stanton waiting. Soon in came Lincoln.

"Did you see the man?" the president asked Welles, meaning Seward. Yes, Welles indicated. Then Lincoln turned to Chase, said he was deeply troubled by the situation, and when Chase offered him his letter of resignation, the president grabbed it, exclaiming: "This cuts the Gordian knot."

Later, Lincoln put this in another but no less cryptic way: "Now I can ride. I have got a pumpkin in each end of my [saddle] bag." What he meant was, he had all the complex forces neutralized. If the Radicals still wanted Seward out of the cabinet, Chase would go, too. This ought to block further congressional threats to presidential powers. And by pocketing both resignations for the time being, he could maintain the balance of tension as well as the capabilities he wanted within his cabinet.

Lincoln's performance in this instance was among the most adroit in American political history. And, in a sense, it was as important for him to have won this battle as holding Marye's Heights had been for Robert E. Lee.

But Second Fredericksburg, if a president's fighting off a raw congressional power grab might be called that, ended with Lincoln in a chastened mood. Lincoln never thought of himself other than as a man doing his best, leaving it to posterity to judge him. But the assaults had toughened the Union president, made him mindful of his own weaknesses and of those around him; and these he was determined to correct.

All of this Jefferson Davis, on his western journey at the time, missed though he might have learned little of his Northern counterpart's struggle had he remained in Richmond. The Confederate president had never doubted General Lee's ability to stop Burnside's army at Fredericksburg. And while Davis made his way westward, before and after the slaughter on the plains east of Marye's Heights, he had good cause to believe he was in the right region at the right time.

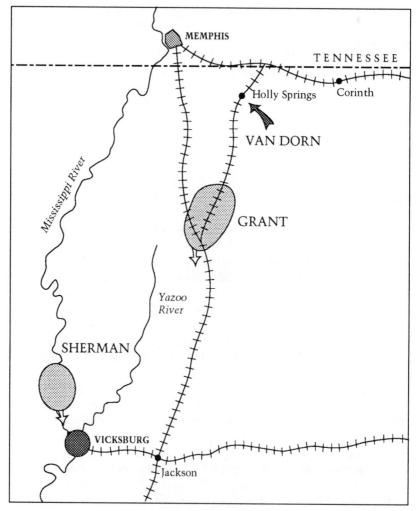

Grant's Vicksburg Plan

Davis could not possibly have known of it, but around December 8, Ulysses Grant ordered Cump Sherman to take a riverborne force from Memphis southward and seize the ground north of Vicksburg where the Yazoo River met the Mississippi. This thrust, Grant reasoned, would force Confederate General Pemberton to withdraw to Vicksburg the forces blocking his own inland drive down the railroad.

There was nothing much any Southerners could do to slow Sherman's preparations at Memphis. But Grant's long railroad supply line, stretching southward from Columbus up in Kentucky to his advance headquarters at Oxford in northwestern Mississippi, was vulnerable. As the Confederacy's president was touring, so was Brigadier General Nathan Bedford Forrest's cavalry. Striking rapidly and repeatedly in western Tennessee, Forrest's raiders tore up Grant's railroad so thoroughly it would not be repaired for years.

Then, on December 20, Earl Van Dorn's cavalry demolished the federal forward supply base at Holly Springs, Mississippi, Grant had been counting on. Grant, surprised and dismayed, had to abandon his portion of the proposed campaign and depend on Sherman to keep it alive. And with Grant no longer a threat, Pemberton could and did move southward to greet Sherman.

A week before Van Dorn's slash at Holly Springs, though, Davis was leaving Murfreesboro, south of Nashville, as the wedding of Brigadier General John Hunt Morgan and Martha Ready was about to begin. But Davis knew the story, and he must have relished it despite his regrets over missing the festivities.

"Mattie" Ready, twenty-one, had not met Morgan when she heard two Yankee officers condemning him. Not so, she declared; and when asked for her name, she gave it and added: "But by the grace of God one day I hope to be the wife of John Morgan." And so she became, on December 14, in a ceremony presided over by Bishop Leonidas Polk, his clerical robes draped atop his major general's uniform and with Braxton Bragg and his senior officers looking on.

A week afterward, however, Mattie's husband was off on another raid, one following much the same route up toward Louisville as had Bragg's forces back in September. Morgan's sweep was particularly important to Bragg; in Nashville Union Major General William Rosecrans seemed unlikely to remain where he was much longer, and another breaking of the Union supply line might delay him. But the bridegroom had tarried too long: on December 26, the federals began a march toward Braxton Bragg's army at Murfreesboro with the intent to destroy it.

There was another notable soldier's wedding that December, in Illinois, where John A. McClernand, fifty-one, married a lady who (some said) was his sister-in-law. Earlier, General McClernand had been recruiting in states along the upper Mississippi, carrying out the first part of the plan he had persuaded Lincoln to accept. Unlike Morgan, though, the Union general took his bride along when he boarded a steamboat at Cairo for Memphis. There McClernand expected to take command of his troops, take them down the Mississippi, and lead them in capturing Vicksburg. But they had left nearly a week before, while the general's mind was on his wedding.

Had Cump Sherman, as the outraged McClernand was quick to allege, stolen the forces? Was this some conspiracy by the West Point clique to prevent a citizen-soldier from showing the nation how incompetent the professionals actually were?

Well, no. Everything had been done according to orders, those the general-in-chief sent Grant and which Grant had attempted to forward to McClernand. True, lawyer Halleck may have used a touch of cunning in the process. But the Vicksburg venture was risky enough as matters stood, and time was of the essence— secrecy, as well—and it was unlikely, in the circumstances, that the general-in-chief or Generals Grant or Sherman knew that McClernand's plans were more matrimonial than military.

In any case, Sherman was armed with the authority to depart as soon as he could; correctly, he used it. He allowed no newspapermen on the expedition, remembering, perhaps, how they had not only declared him insane back in 1861 but had driven him almost into catatonia. The need to preserve secrecy, though, was ample justification for excluding all outsiders.

But for a flotilla of transports carrying more than 30,000 men and the gunboats escorting them to steam southward without being noticed was, of course, impossible. Confederates were in position, waiting, on December 29, when General Sherman sent his forces ashore with orders to attack Chickasaw Bluff, not far north of Vicksburg. But nothing he tried that day worked. He took a licking he had brought a lot of men a long way to get.

This fight had been no Fredericksburg. Cump had backed off, cutting his loss to fewer than 1,800 casualties, when he saw how recent rains were causing river levels to rise toward high-water marks on trees.

Not long afterward, McClernand caught up with Sherman, and McClernand had the satisfaction, of sorts, of telling him that Grant's advance had been halted. McClernand had more salt to rub into that wound: Sherman was now officially subordinate to him, ranking little higher than a division commander Sherman had thought about relieving for failure to lead his troops up Chickasaw Bluffs.

Chapter 20

Stones River: *Tragedy Opens 1863*

Nothing in the record since July indicated that bringing General Halleck to Washington had improved the Union's military situation one iota. Indeed, Old Brains's, performance had been deeply disappointing: Get rid of Henry Halleck, critics of the "Central Imbecility"—newspaper editorial writers, members of Lincoln's cabinet, congressmen, and more—were advising the president. And now maybe Lincoln would.

In this there was much irony. Halleck had resisted the order to come to Washington almost to the point of disobeying it; yet, once there, he had improved the army's administration enormously. But Halleck seems to have been easy to dislike. In appearance he was the opposite of the dashing McClellan: pudgy, balding, goggle-eyed, "an oleaginous Methodist parson in regimentals," a reporter wrote. His manner was abrupt, gruff, and he had the habit of pacing the floor, hands in his pockets or behind his back, and scratching his elbows.

"The fact is," said Lincoln of Halleck, "the man has no friends." Not quite; but the number was small and confined to men, such as Herman Haupt, whose intellects he respected, men who were as disinclined as he was to cultivate politicians' support, depending instead on devotion to duty to vindicate them in the eyes of posterity. Lincoln might have been more accurate had he said that Halleck had no defenders; and there would be none subsequently, for if historians have agreed on anything, it is that he was a disaster.

Perhaps. But at the end of December 1862 there was still no agreement as to what a general-in-chief's duties actually were. Having arrived in Washington just as the Confederates were seizing the initiative and pressing it in both the eastern and western theaters, Halleck was forced to improvise as he tried to manage two or three federal defensive efforts at once. Not until mid-November was he able to think much about taking the offensive in Virginia, Tennessee, and Mississippi. And in late December, despite Fredericksburg, it was still too soon to declare his three concurrent campaigns failures.

Rosecrans's army had finally left Nashville on the twenty-sixth, but Confederate cavalrymen were harassing the Union supply trains as they moved slowly toward Murfreesboro. Grant's inland drive southward in Mississippi was in trouble, and news from Sherman's riverborne force was slow in coming. And before Burnside could strike Lee's army again, something had to be done about reports of insubordination on the part of certain of his generals.

After the battle at Fredericksburg there was a brief lull, one in which a stunned Ambrose Burnside was said to have paced the floor in his tent at Falmouth, saying, "Oh, those men!"—meaning the dead east of Marye's Heights. "Those men over there! I am thinking of them all the time!" Soon, though, the Army of the Potomac's commander began thinking of moving down the Rappahannock, crossing again, and getting between Lee and Richmond. "In regard to movement we cannot judge here," Old Brains had wired Burnside, "you are the best judge."

But before General Burnside could get his troops in motion, the president intervened. On December 29 he telegraphed: "I have good reason for saying that you must not make a general movement without first letting me know of it."

What did Lincoln know that Burnside did not? The general rushed to Washington to find out. And what he learned on the morning of January 1, 1863, was dismaying. Two of his generals, names not given him, had come to the capital on the twenty-ninth to see a Massachusetts senator, only to learn he was out of town; they had gone to Secretary of State Seward; Seward had taken them to Lincoln. The army, the president was told, was too demoralized to carry out Burnside's proposed attack and might be thrown back to the Potomac.

After Burnside left on that New Year's Day, Lincoln sent a note to Secretary of War Stanton, addressed to Halleck, with instructions to pass it along to the general-in-chief:

> General Burnside wishes to cross the Rappahannock with his army, but his grand division commanders all oppose the movement. If in such a difficulty as this you do not help, you fail me precisely in the point for which I sought your assistance. It is my wish that you go with General Burnside to the ground, examine it as far as practicable, confer with

the officers, getting their judgment and ascertaining their temper; in a word, gather all the elements for forming a judgment of your own, and then tell General Burnside that you do approve or that you do not approve his plan. Your military skill is useless to me if you will not do this.

This task behind him, the president hurried down to his New Year's Day reception for foreign diplomats and other very important persons. For General Halleck it had already been a bad day: Rosecrans appeared to be losing a major battle near Murfreesboro, and both Grant and Sherman were contributing to his woes. Busy as Halleck surely was, however, apparently he paid a courtesy call at Stanton's residence, or so it seems from what he wrote to the secretary:

From the President's letter of this morning, which you delivered to me at your reception, I am led to believe that there is a very important difference of opinion in regard to my relations toward generals commanding armies in the field, and that I cannot perform the duties of my present office satisfactorily at the same time to the President and to myself. I therefore respectfully request that I may be relieved from further duties as General-in-Chief.

Having disposed of his career, presumably Halleck returned to his desk to help Rosecrans dispose of Bragg's army: Relief had not yet come, and duty remained. Like the slaves in enemy-held territory, whose emancipation became effective on that New Year's Day, he, too, might look forward to freedom.

Stanton's role was confined to that of a messenger. Lincoln had both authority and cause to order Halleck to go to Falmouth. And Halleck was correct in requesting relief rather than to (in effect) assume command of the Army of the Potomac, especially at a time when events critical to the success of his initiatives in Tennessee and near Vicksburg needed all the attention and support he could give them.

In the end, the president withdrew his letter, and Halleck took back his reply. But perhaps the kindest thing Lincoln ever said about his general-in-chief afterward was that he was "a first-rate clerk."

"The War Child rides tonight," Confederate Joseph Wheeler declared to his cavalrymen before leading them on a raid, and so he probably told them on December 29 as they rode northward from Braxton Bragg's lines near Murfreesboro. At twenty-six, only three years out of West Point, the "War Child" was a brigadier general senior to Nathan Bedford Forrest, forty-one, and John Morgan, thirty-seven, both off on raids of their own—Forrest wrecking Grant's railroad supply line in West Tennessee, Morgan striking the Louisville & Nashville in Kentucky.

Perhaps emulating Jeb Stuart, who had twice ridden around George McClellan's army and was even then raiding in northern Virginia almost to within sight of Washington, Joe Wheeler's goal was to lead his 2,500 troopers counterclockwise back to Bragg's army via the rear of the Yankee columns and wagon trains moving southeastward along the Nashville-Murfreesboro turnpike. By noon on Tuesday, December 30, Wheeler's men had already mauled a federal brigade and part of a wagon train when they reached La Vergne. There, halfway up the pike toward Nashville, they found a train of 300 wagons and burned it; that afternoon, they struck two more trains on the roads northwest of Murfreesboro. And along the way the War Child's raiders had captured enough horses to replace their worn-out mounts and could arm a brigade with Union-made carbines and rifles.

Wheeler's cavalrymen were back with Bragg's army by two A.M. on New Year's Eve. In their absence, Rosecrans's federals had gone into a line extending on both sides of the Nashville pike and Stones River, which flowed parallel to the road, two miles or more north of Murfreesboro. The opposing forces were so near to each other now that the sounds of their bands could be heard by men on either side. At first, soon after dark on that Tuesday, the federal musicians had played tunes such as "Yankee Doodle" and the Southerners "Dixie" and the like, but when one band started "Home, Sweet Home" the other joined in, and all played as one.

Major General William Rosecrans had seen enough of Bragg's lines on Tuesday to determine that the terrain features favored neither army. Despite recent rains Stones River could still be forded anywhere. There was no really high ground, only a few gently rolling hills of little military importance. This was farmland, much of it cleared and cultivated, with scattered groves of trees left as wood-lots.

Rosecrans may have wondered why Braxton Bragg had chosen to give battle so near Murfreesboro. One reason might be to control the web of roads leading into the town. But Bragg's supply stockpiles were in it, which might be a mistake on the rebel's part but one that could compel him to fight harder.

Supplies were the key here in the west, or so Rosecrans had concluded. He had amassed all he could at Nashville before moving out, enough to reply to General-in-Chief Halleck's "I cannot prevent your removal" wire: "I need no other stimulus to do my duty than the knowledge of what it is. To threats of removal and the like I must be permitted to say that I am insensible."

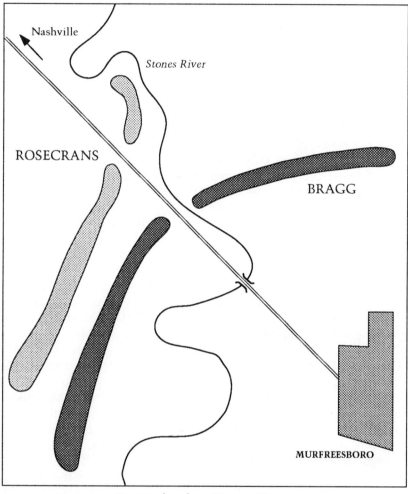

Pre-Murfreesboro/Stones River

Now, though, Rosecrans would have to be insensible to what John Hunt Morgan's cavalry raid was doing to the L & N Railroad and even Wheeler's slashes along his flanks and in his rear. He would have to attack on Wednesday, early. But how?

With him Rosecrans had about 44,000 men in three corps, each commanded by a seasoned major general. He meant to use Thomas Leonidas Crittenden's divisions on the eastern end of his line to launch an attack over the ground east of Stones River. George Thomas's corps would be in the center; on the western end, Alexander McCook's.

"Our right [western wing] must be secure for three hours," Rosecrans told his generals on Tuesday evening, "until we can take Murfreesboro."

"I can hold against anything for three hours," General McCook assured Rosecrans.

Ironically, Braxton Bragg also meant to lead with a left hook, striking the western end of the federal line with his main weight: Lieutenant General William Hardee's corps and a division led by Major General John P. McCown, an officer Bragg considered unreliable but whose position in the line was least critical because it was westernmost. Bishop Polk, now, like Hardee, a three-star general, would be in the center. Across Stones River, Major General John Breckinridge's division would guard the eastern flank. In all, Bragg had roughly 37,000 men—possibly more, maybe fewer.

So Stones River might have been a pinwheel battle, like First Manassas, had Bragg not gotten Hardee's divisions and McCown's in motion while General McCook's federal troops were still enjoying their breakfasts early on Wednesday, New Year's Eve. McCown's westernmost brigades discovered that the Yankee line was (as Shelby Foote has described it) like a huge pocket knife and that they could start the tip of its blade northeastward, and Hardee's troops joined in the effort to push the blade around to close it.

But as often happened, early success bred early distress. McCown allowed his troops to veer too far to the west, creating a gap. To fill it Hardee sent in Pat Cleburne's division, the force he had hoped to hold in reserve until the moment came to break through Rosecrans's reeling line and exploit the victory. And there was another problem: Major General Benjamin Franklin Cheatham's division was not pressing the Yankees as hard as the bishop-general commanding the center corps wished.

Hard-fighting, hard-drinking Ben Cheatham appeared to have gotten too far down the bottle too early that morning. Though his saber was unsheathed and waving and his profanity neared eloquence, Cheatham's leadership was confused in quality, so much so that his failure to keep his brigades advancing allowed the Yankees to pour fire into the flank of Pat Cleburne's troops.

Something more serious than any general's premature desire to wash the old year out, though, was at work. The farther to the northeast and the closer to the Nashville turnpike escape route the Confederates pushed the Yankees' pocket-knife blade, the more difficult it was for Polk's, and especially Hardee's, troops to maintain pressure on it, and the easier it became for Rosecrans to strengthen his forces along it.

That morning, William Rosecrans saw what was happening from his saddle, not from some farmhouse well to the rear of the firing. As soon as it was apparent that McCook's line could not hold at all, much less for three hours, General Rosecrans hurried brigades from Crittenden's force westward to plug gaps. "This battle must be won," Rosecrans said repeatedly.

Many who saw the blood on the army commander's uniform as he rode by thought he had been wounded. No, Rosecrans told someone who asked if he had been hit, "that is the blood of poor Garesché." He meant Colonel Julius P. Garesché, his chief of staff, whose head had been taken off by a cannonball that had narrowly missed Rosecrans.

Phil Sheridan's division was the last in McCook's corps to absorb the rebels' attack. Sheridan had his men, outnumbered ten to one, make a bayonet charge into the oncoming enemy—stunning them by the very audacity of such a thing—while he brought his artillery to the front rank, where it fired at a range of 200 yards. Valor bought time for Rosecrans, which he used to build a line west of the Nashville pike. When Sheridan finally had to withdraw, Rosecrans told him to have his troops replenish their ammunition and gave the bullet-headed Irishman another danger point to hold.

Now Confederate pressure built against the pocket knife's pivot, George Thomas's divisions, in what had been the center at daybreak but was now roughly a horseshoe with its open end to the northeast. If Bragg's forces could break through Thomas's ranks, they could cut Rosecrans's army in two.

When George Thomas rose that morning, he put his relatively new two-star shoulder straps on his finest uniform, the one with gold braid. He wanted to be certain his men knew he was there with them: Why else should generals ever adorn themselves with such gaudy trappings?

And his men did see General Thomas. He stood with them, calming them by being calm, as Bragg's commanders threw three strong assaults against his horseshoe. And so skillfully had Thomas massed his artillery, firing in three directions, when the sun set his troops had held back a final surge to which Braxton Bragg had committed more than half his army.

"This battle must be won," Rosecrans had been saying all day, and he knew it had not been lost, but where did it stand? To get his subordinates' opinions, that evening he called them together. First to speak were those from civilian backgrounds, and their advice was to retreat. Stubborn young professional Phil Sheridan maintained a grim silence. George Thomas, only forty-six but looking sixty that night, sat with his head resting on his arms, which were crossed over his sword's hilt, listening, though some thought he was asleep.

Finally, Thomas heard Rosecrans use the word retreat. He roused suddenly, banged a fist onto Rosecrans', map table, and declared: "This army does not retreat!"

Rosecrans, having gained nothing much by consulting his generals, rode out into the rainy night to inspect his lines. Northward, on ground controlling the Nashville pike, he saw torchbearers lighting campfires—forbidden, by his order—so the rebels must have encircled him. That settled it. This army could not retreat. It would have to fight or die.

That decision and some fragmentary reports of Rosecrans's plight had been about all General-in-Chief Halleck had to go on during his personal struggle with the president on New Year's Day. To lose a position he had never wanted meant far less to Halleck than the apparent destruction of a vital Union field army. And against that background he could never have agreed with Lincoln that settling a dispute within an idle Army of the Potomac deserved priority over rushing support to Rosecrans.

But in the early hours of New Year's Day no one, even on the bloody field near Stones River, knew what was happening. Those campfires Rosecrans had assumed were Confederate were in fact being lighted by his own cavalrymen. And the rumblings of wagons Braxton Bragg heard off to the north were not, as he had assumed, incoming ammunition and supplies for the federals but the evacuation toward Nashville of some of the wounded among Rosecrans's roughly 12,000 casualties.

Bragg's losses that day had been heavy, too—about 9,000. But he possessed the field and the initiative. Rosecrans, he was certain, would have to retreat. So confident was Bragg that he sent a message to Richmond, one ending: "God has granted us a happy New Year."

And so it seemed on the first day of 1863. Rosecrans had moved Thomas's corps back from the horseshoe and straightened his line elsewhere, and Bragg had sent Polk to occupy the ground where so many assaults had been made in vain, but except for some artillery duels neither side seemed anxious to renew the fight.

Again that night Bragg heard the federal wagons on the Nashville pike, and again he hoped that meant the Yankees were pulling out. But at dawn on January 2 he saw that the federal army was still there. Worse, Rosecrans's guns were massed in such a way as to pour heavy fire into the flank of any advance Bragg might try.

But something had to be done, and Bragg's decision was to attack east of Stones River late in the day to seize a hill he considered a threat to his line. John Breckinridge, whose task this would be, protested vehemently. "Sir," Bragg told him, "I have given the order to attack the enemy in your front and expect it to be obeyed."

General Breckinridge tried, but halfheartedly, and as he had feared, the federal guns on his western flank shredded his brigades. When darkness ended the short fight, Bragg had lost another 1,700 men and accomplished nothing.

That night, Cheatham and some of the other generals urged Bragg to retreat. No, the army commander said at first. But the next morning, with Rosecrans still facing him and likely to be getting reinforcements, Bragg changed his mind.

The army would move southeastward thirty-five miles to Tullahoma, he ordered, and on the night of January 3 the retreat began. Rosecrans did not pursue.

So Stones River (in the South, Murfreesboro) would have to be added to the list of indecisive battles, and at a dreadfully heavy cost. Once again both sides' armies had displayed valor in abundance. But neither commander appeared to have had the wit or the will to destroy the other's forces, suggesting that the destructiveness of modern weapons had made clear victories a thing of the past.

Closer to the truth, perhaps, was the theory that by late 1862 morale was the critical factor, especially in battles in which the forces were roughly even in number and experience, as was the case at Stones River. Among the troops the level of discomfort was about the same. But Bragg seemed to have lost his nerve, leaving the field to Rosecrans.

Actually, the weakness was not so much in the Confederate army commander as in his relationship with his subordinates. It was ironic that Bragg could and did attack the problem of desertion by having some of those convicted shot and at the same time be so tolerant of his generals' discontent. At the end of the Kentucky campaign their criticism had almost cost him his command. Now, at Tullahoma, Bragg faced more of it.

Indeed, Bragg invited it, offering to step aside if higher authority found the dissident generals' complaints justified. All the more curious this was, given Breckinridge's protests when given orders to attack, Cheatham's drunkenness, McCown's inability to control his troops' advance, and the unwillingness to fight indicated by the senior commanders' unsolicited advice to withdraw. Moreover, Bragg had retreated only when Wheeler reported that Rosecrans was being reinforced and the rising level of the water in Stones River made his position untenable. Yet Bragg filed no charges, leaving judgment to the president.

Eventually, Davis would order General Johnston to go to Tullahoma, make a personal investigation of the situation, and "do whatever else belongs to the General Commanding." On the surface this appeared to be an echo of Abraham Lincoln's New Year's Day letter to General-in-Chief Halleck. But Johnston was a field commander with no choice but to obey.

Meanwhile, Bragg had few supporters in the South, in part because he had been premature in declaring Rosecrans whipped. As the *Richmond Examiner* complained:

> So far the news has come in what may be called the classical style of the Southwest. When the Southern army fights a battle, we first hear that it has gained one of the most stupendous victories on record; that regiments...have ex-hibited an irresistible and superhuman valor unknown in history this side of Sparta and Rome. As for the generals, they usually get all their clothes shot off and replace them with suits of glory. The enemy, of course, is simply annihilated. Next day more dispatches come, still very good, but not quite as good as the first. The telegrams of the third day are invariably such as to make a mist, a muddle, and a fog of the whole affair.

And Jefferson Davis had a problem with Joe Johnston as well; rather, again. Johnston, it appeared from a letter he sent the president early in January, found that being the commander of all the western forces made him "a distant spectator of the efforts & services of my comrades—a position which would inevitably disgrace me."

In a proliferation of irony, troubles involving generals were plaguing Abraham Lincoln at the same time. Despite his elation over Rosecrans's victory (as the North claimed Stones River to have been), he was still stuck with a general-in-chief who would not command and Burnside, who craved being commanded.

After returning to Falmouth on New Year's Day, Burnside had worked up a plan for taking his forces west of and behind Lee's army. This done, on January 5 he sent messages to Halleck and the president. "I have decided to move the army across the river again," he wrote the general-in-chief, adding that the movement was opposed by nearly all his generals and "involves a greater responsibility than any officer situated as I am ought to incur." He was seeking approval; and he enclosed a letter of resignation to be acted upon if "it is not deemed advisable for me to cross the river." He had no other plan, he admitted, and he was "not disposed to go into winter quarters."

Lincoln left it to Halleck to reply. This the general-in-chief did, and at great length, first reviewing the advice he had given earlier, then he got to the point:

> The great object is to occupy the enemy, to prevent his making large detachments or distant raids, and to injure him all you can with the least injury to yourself. If this can be best accomplished by feints of a general crossing and detached real crossings, take this course; if by an actual general crossing, with feints on other points, adopt that course....It will not do to keep the army inactive. As you yourself admit, it devolves on you to decide upon the time, place, and character of the crossing which you may attempt. I can only advise that an attempt be made, and as early as possible.

And to this the president added on January 7:

> I approve this letter. I deplore the want of concurrence with you in opinion by your general officers, but I do not see the remedy. Be cautious, and do not understand the Government or country is driving you. I do not yet see how I could profit by changing the command of the Army of the Potomac, and if I did, I should not want to do it by accepting the resignation of your commission.

So began what would come to be known as the Army of the Potomac's "mud march." On the morning of Tuesday, January 20, the troops listened as their officers read an order from the commanding general. In part Burnside said: "The auspicious moment seems to have arrived to strike a great and mortal blow to the rebellion, and to gain that decisive victory which is due to the country."

Burnside's men marched westward along the Rappahannock. Their objective was Banks Ford, only six miles or so upstream from their camps, but rain began to fall that afternoon well before they reached the crossing point. It rained all night. By morning the road was a quicksand-like bog, sucking the wheels of wagons and those of gun carriages to their axle hubs. Double- and triple-teaming mule teams failed, and so did regiments of men pulling on ropes. And still the rain poured.

Burnside rode out, only to be greeted by a soldier who teased: "General, the auspicious moment has arrived!" Press on, he ordered, but he authorized sending the men whiskey kegs.

How the kegs got through when artillery pieces were down to their muzzles in mud would never be clear. But they did, and by noon of the next day it was clear even to Burnside—as it had been to jeering Confederates watching the spectacle from the Rappahannock's south bank—that this campaign had been rained out. The general ordered his army back to their camps. But not all of them heeded him, deciding instead that spending the winter at home was the only thing that made any sense.

As the army commander pondered his next move, disturbing reports reached him. Burnside "was fast losing his mind," General Franklin was said to have said. Joseph Hooker told a newspaper reporter that the president was an imbecile for allowing Burnside to remain in command—and otherwise—and that what the country needed was a dictator.

Despairing, Burnside headed for Washington. At noon on Saturday, January 24, he handed the president an order he proposed to issue, one cashiering Hooker and three other officers from the service and relieving six more, among them Franklin. Approve this, he said, or accept my resignation.

Actually, Burnside lacked authority to expel any officer from the service without a trial; only the president could do that. But Lincoln was not inclined to use his powers in this instance, nor did he wish to lose Burnside's services altogether, which meant that he would have to relieve the general and select someone to replace him.

The president's decision was as astonishing as it was fast in coming. On Sunday, January 25, he called Burnside to the Executive Mansion and told him to turn command of the Army of the Potomac over to Major General Joseph Hooker. This was hardly the fate Burnside had intended for Fighting Joe. But he took the blow as a seasoned soldier should, withdrew his resignation, and returned to the command of his old corps.

Lincoln had made up his own mind, consulting no one, and in a private letter to the general who was said to have called him an imbecile he wrote:

> I have placed you at the head of the Army of the Potomac. Of course I have done this upon what appears to me to be sufficient reasons, and yet I think it best for you to know

that there are some things in regard to which I am not quite satisfied with you. I believe you to be a brave and skillful soldier, which, of course, I like. I also believe you do not mix politics with your profession, in which you are right. You have confidence in yourself, which is a valuable, if not an indispensable, quality. You are ambitious, which, within reasonable bounds, does good rather than harm; but I think that during General Burnside's command of the army you have taken counsel of your ambition, and thwarted him as much as you could, in which you did a great wrong to the country and to a most meritorious and honorable brother officer. I have heard, in such a way as to believe it, of your recently saying that both the Army and the Government needed a dictator. Of course, it was not for this, but in spite of it, that I have given you the command. Only those generals who gain successes can set up dictators. What I now ask of you is military success, and I will risk the dictatorship. The Government will support you to the utmost of its ability, which is neither more nor less than it has done and will do for all commanders. I much fear that the spirit which you have aided to infuse into the army, of criticising their commander and withholding confidence from him, will now turn upon you. I shall assist you as far as I can to put it down. Neither you nor Napoleon, if he were alive again, could get any good out of an army while such a spirit prevails in it. And now beware of rashness. Beware of rashness, but with energy and sleepless vigilance go forward and give us victories.

Chapter 21

War Waits for Spring

For General Lee and his Army of Northern Virginia, still holding the high ground west of Fredericksburg, Christmas and New Year had been times for thanksgiving. Along the way from early June to late December 1862 this army had inflicted almost 72,000 casualties while suffering perhaps 48,000. It had been mauled at times, but never had it taken such a whipping as it had given Burnside at Fredericksburg or John Pope at Second Manassas. From all the battlefields it had scavenged something like 75,000 small arms while losing roughly 6,000. And half of Lee's artillery batteries were now equipped with captured Yankee guns: 155 in exchange for 8 given up.

Ambrose Burnside's Mud March had disturbed General Lee not at all, and after it he assumed those people would go into winter quarters across the Rappahannock River near Falmouth. His own men, though, he sent westward and southward along the river's banks to dig trenches and prepare gun positions for use in case the Yankees tried to outflank him in any direction.

Lee seemed to take little notice of Fighting Joe Hooker's rise to command at Falmouth other than to say in a letter to Mrs. Lee: "I owe Mr. F J (sic) Hooker no thanks for keeping me here." Of greater concern was a federal strategic move, down in North Carolina, which might diminish the meager flow of food supplies to his army. In January, Lee had sent Harvey Hill to assume command of Confederate troops in his native state. And lest Yankees approach Richmond from that direction, in mid-February he ordered Major General George E. Pickett's division southward, then John Hood's, and finally James Longstreet to command them under the direction of the War Department in the capital.

Such was General Lee's fear of Mr. F. J. Hooker—for the time being. But he was worried about war-induced inflation in commodity prices and what this meant not only to his army but to the people of the South whose support President Davis must retain. Meat, potatoes, and meal now cost five times as much as they did in May 1861. The price of molasses was up ten times; a yard of calico, eighteen; salt and coffee, thirty. And if the Confederate dollar rotted much more, who could afford to buy the bonds the nation had to sell in order to pay its bills?

Payment was important, for the countryside within wagons' reach of Fredericksburg could provide no more food for the men or fodder for the animals. Everything Lee needed to keep his men alive had to be bought somewhere, somehow, then shipped to him over the single-track R F & P Railroad. He may well have been relieved that it was up to the authorities in Richmond to feed two of his divisions below that city. But Jeb Stuart's cavalry had to be sent westward where mounts could graze, and this limited the flow of information scouts could send Lee.

Preventing the starvation of horses and mules had been of the highest priority to the army commander since early January. In the hope of prolonging the lives of the artillery's animals, he had sent all but a few batteries southward to the North Anna River, where fodder might be more abundant.

Earlier, several times, General Lee had shown audacity by splitting his army in the face of the enemy. Now he had done it again, as secretly as he could, merely so that his army and its essential animals could survive until spring.

General Hooker seemed oblivious to this. His headquarters in Falmouth, wrote Charles Francis Adams, Jr., was "a place no self-respecting man liked to go, and no decent woman could go. It was a combination of barroom and brothel."

Perhaps the son of the Union's ambassador to Great Britain was right. Hooker's fondness for life's pleasures was well known, but some said he shunned John Barleycorn as soon as he took command of the Army of the Potomac. Either way, General Hooker saw to it that his troops had fresh vegetables and soft bread and that they got paid. And, borrowing a morale-boosting idea the late Phil Kearny had planted, Hooker ordered each of his army's corps to identify its troops by distinctive symbols —such as a crescent moon or a Maltese cross—cloth patches sewn onto the soldiers' caps.

Command of the Union's largest and most visible field army may well have sobered Hooker. So might his earlier experiences in tangling with Lee, for he was a veteran of almost all the fights from the Seven Days onward and rainy days may have made his foot wound's aching remind him of Antietam, where Jackson had wrecked his corps in the battle's opening minutes.

General Hooker was not inclined to keep his army in winter quarters, and he did not disagree with anything the general-in-chief had advised Burnside in his letter of January 7, a copy of which Halleck sent the army's new commander. But he wanted no more mud marches, and the weather remained risky. So, with the military situation quiet, during the lull Hooker made some changes in his army's organization.

Out went the grand division scheme. Major General Daniel Butterfield, earlier a corps commander, became Hooker's chief of staff. Given corps to lead were Major Generals George Meade, Daniel Sickles, and John Sedgwick. To increase his cavalry's effectiveness Hooker made a corps of it and selected Major General George Stoneman to command it.

Winter was also a time for planning. This Hooker did secretly. And of one thing he was certain: When next the army moved against Lee, the blow it threw would have to be decisive.

The president appeared willing to let General Hooker get his army in hand, avoiding rashness just as he had advised the Army of the Potomac's commander to do. Now, with little going on anywhere else, Lincoln could concentrate on his duties as president and leave the running of the war to Edwin Stanton and the general-in-chief.

The states of the "Old Northwest"—Minnesota, Wisconsin, Michigan, Ohio, Indiana, and his own Illinois—were much on the president's mind in the opening months of 1863. For the Union it was fortunate that Lincoln understood that region, knew how its citizens' minds worked; had an Easterner been in his place, such a man might well have panicked.

The people in these six states had long since proved their loyalty to the Union, responding generously and repeatedly to Washington's calls for men and everything else required to support the war. But in some ways they were as independent and antifederalist as Southerners.

In politics, northwesterners tended to favor the Democrats' positions, particularly those emphasizing states' and regions' rights. Most of them had come from places where governments had been oppressive or living conditions miserable—Germany, Ireland—or from overcrowded eastern Union states, and they cherished their freedoms and, to some extent, their isolation.

The region's citizens abhorred slavery, but many of them also wished to keep free blacks from entering their states (Illinois had a law to that effect) because whites still at the bottom of the economic ladder feared their jobs and certainly wage levels would be threatened if waves of ex-slaves rushed in. Yet many northwesterners, particularly those with strong commercial ties to the South, were appalled by the abolitionists' demands for coercive action; and when South Carolina led other cotton states out of the Union, few were surprised.

After Fort Sumter the Old Northwest rallied round the Union flag. But by late 1862 perceptions of federal ineptness in prosecuting the rebellion's suppression, together with long casualty lists without commensurate victories, caused leaders in the region to raise disturbing questions.

Governor Oliver P. Morton of Indiana, earlier a strong Lincoln man, wrote that "there was much truth" in some Democrats' claims:

> ...that we of the North-West had no interests or sympathies in common with the people of the Northern and Eastern States; that New England is fattening at our expense; that the people of New England are cold, selfish, money-making, and through the medium of tariffs and railroads are pressing us into the dust; that geographically these States are a part of the Mississippi Valley and in their political association and destiny cannot be separated from the other States of that Valley; that socially and commercially their sympathies and interests are with the people of the Southern States rather than with people of the North and East; that the Mississippi River is the great artery and outlet of all Western Commerce; that the people of the North-West can never consent to be separated politically from the people who control the mouth of that river;...And I give it here as my deliberate judgement, that should the misfortune of arms or other causes, compel us to the abandonment of this war and the concession of the independence of the Rebel States, that Ohio, Indiana, and Illinois can only be prevented, if at all, from a new act of secession and annexation to those States, by a [new] bloody and desolating Civil War....

Some northwesterners joined secret societies such as the Knights of the Golden Circle, partly in opposition to Lincoln's

Emancipation Proclamation. "Copperheads," the dissidents would be called. And by early 1863, Congressman Clement L. Vallandigham, an Ohio Democrat, was telling colleagues:

> Stop fighting. Make an armistice—no formal treaty. Withdraw your army from the seceded States. Reduce both armies to a fair and sufficient peace establishment. Declare absolute free trade between the North and South.

"I am for peace," Vallandigham declared before a New York audience in early March, "because, without peace, permitting this Administration for two years to exercise its tremendous powers, the war still existing, you will not have one remnant of civil liberty left among yourselves."

"Fire in the rear," Abraham Lincoln called all this, and left it to military department commanders to handle. Such, in Ohio, was Ambrose Burnside by April. Burnside ordered the arrest of anyone guilty of seditious utterances likely to obstruct recruiting. Vallandigham's oratory qualified, and he was convicted by a court-martial and sentenced to spend the rest of the war in prison. Lincoln reduced this to expelling Vallandigham, by then a candidate for Ohio's governorship, to the Confederacy, but he fled to Canada.

And soon, in response to movements such as the Knights of the Golden Circle represented, loyal men in the northern cities formed societies of their own, but not in secrecy. Prominent among them were the Union League clubs, of which the one in New York was typical. Its purpose was (and is)

> to promote, encourage, and sustain, by all proper means, absolute and unqualified loyalty to the Government of the United States; to discountenance and rebuke, by moral and social influences, all disloyalty to said Government, and every attempt against the integrity of the Nation.

A critical consideration almost everyone in the North had been overlooking, however, was the inordinate complexity of the geography in the stretch of the Mississippi General Grant was trying to wrest from the rebels. Abraham Lincoln may have recalled it from the two flatboat trips down the Big Muddy he had made decades earlier. But others had much to learn about terrain features and freaks of current the river's long, curling trace on their maps could never convey.

Confederate cavalry raids led by Nathan Bedford Forrest and Earl Van Dorn had convinced Grant that the inland route to Vicksburg was not feasible. His supply route would have to be the Mississippi River itself, and he decided also that he ought to put all of his forces downstream, on the western bank, as near to Vicksburg as he could get them.

Partly in the hope of bypassing Confederate batteries on Vicksburg's bluffs and also to keep his troops busy, he had them try again to dig a canal across a peninsula the river looped around. Earlier attempts had failed, and so did this one, as did others even more ambitious, all for the same reason: the Mississippi's eddies and capricious changes in levels as heavy rains fed it.

But encouragement came in a message from Halleck:

The eyes and hopes of the whole country are now directed to your army. In my opinion, the opening of the Mississippi River will be to us of more advantage than the capture of forty Richmonds. We shall omit nothing which we can do to assist you.

And, mindful perhaps of the heavy pressure being applied on Lincoln by politicians in the Old Northwest, the general-in-chief added: "The President attaches much importance to this."

General Lee was living in a tent south of Fredericksburg, his most frequent visitor a hen who repaid his hospitality by laying an egg under his cot. Not so Spartan was Jackson's corps headquarters. Although he had declined Mrs. Roberta Corbin's invitation to use a wing of her huge house, he accepted a three-room outbuilding her husband (now a private in the Virginia cavalry) had used as the plantation's office.

To it, late in the afternoon, when visitors had departed and the general had finished his paperwork, came the Corbin's five-year-old daughter, Janie, a golden-haired child to whom Jackson was devoted. Staff officers must have rubbed their eyes as they watched her teaching Old Jack how to cut out paper dolls. And one day when Janie was upset because she had lost a favorite comb, the warrior delighted her by trimming the gold braid from his cap and placing it on her head like a coronet.

Otherwise it was a discouraging winter, one in which the troops—scattered for miles along the Rappahannock—had to supplement their thin rations by hunting for sassatras buds and wild onions. Lacking tents, many soldiers lived in huts with chimneys made of mud. Blankets were too few; shoes fell apart. Many of the men kept busy digging entrenchments; others engaged in snowball fights. When a religious revival swept through the army, there were camp meetings and prayer meetings to attend.

Only Stuart's cavalry saw action. On February 24 young Brigadier General Fitzhugh Lee, the army commander's nephew, led 400 of his troopers across Kelly's Ford and attacked Union outposts north of the Rappahannock. At Hartwood Church, about nine miles northwest of Fredericksburg, Fitz Lee's men captured 150 Yankee cavalrymen—horses and all—losing only 14.

Then, in mid-March, came reports that federal cavalrymen were riding from Kelly's Ford toward Culpeper. On the seventeenth, near Brandy Station on the Orange & Alexandria Railroad, Fitz Lee's scouts found the enemy force.

Although Major John Pelham's guns had not yet arrived, Lee ordered a charge. The gallant artilleryman, unable to stay out of the fight, borrowed a horse and spurred it. "Forward!" he shouted, waving his saber, and forward he rode until a federal shell exploded overhead: Pelham fell, a smile on his face.

As Fitz Lee's troopers drove away the Yankees, word spread that Pelham was dead. Stuart, hearing this, leaned against his horse's neck and wept. But someone discovered that Pelham's heart was still beating. Quickly he was taken to the home of his fiancée in Culpeper. But nothing could be done for him and there, without regaining consciousness, only 25, he died.

General Lee, along with much of the Confederacy, mourned the hero's loss. But the federal activity made him wonder if he should call Longstreet back and unite the army before Hooker attacked. And Lee was concerned also over what he might do to prevent "those people" from transferring corps to the war in the west. He was pondering these questions at the end of March when illness struck him down. For days a throat infection had been bothering him, but by March 30 he was experiencing severe pains in his arm, chest, and back. That day, the general had to be moved from his tent to a bedroom at the Yerbys' house.

As the doctors worked on him, "tapping me all over like an old steam boiler before condemning it" as Lee wrote later, his thinking remained focused on the changing military situation. Longstreet, he decided, ought to remain in North Carolina for as long as possible, primarily to gather food and grain and start filled wagon trains northward. His divisions, however, should not get too busy to board rail cars and move northward if Mr. F J Hooker made their presence necessary somewhere along the Rappahannock.

Taking the Army of Northern Virginia back up to Maryland

would be the best way to prevent shifts of Union forces westward, General Lee concluded. But from his window he could see that the early April weather was as bad as any in the winter, so he would have to wait for roads to dry and for Longstreet's troops to finish collecting food and fodder for a long campaign. By the first of May, Lee thought, conditions ought to be favorable —that is, if Hooker remained idle at Falmouth.

General Lee's recovery, and especially his decisions, gave Jackson's spirits a much-needed lift. He had been saddened by the gallant Pelham's death and at almost the same time by the news that scarlet fever had taken the life of his beloved little friend Janie Corbin.

Knowing that the first of May was not far off and anxious to see his own baby daughter, born back in November while he was moving the Second Corps from the Shenandoah Valley eastward to Fredericksburg, Jackson invited his wife to join him for a brief visit. On a rainy April 20, Anna Jackson and the tiny Julia arrived at Guiney's Station. Now, with General Lee once more in his tent, the reunited Jackson family took up residence in the Yerbys' house.

Earlier in April another family, the Lincolns, came down to Falmouth to spend nearly a week with General Hooker's Army of the Potomac. Presumably Fighting Joe had warning in time to remove from the First Lady's sight all traces of whatever had caused young Captain Adams to consider army headquarters unfit for a respectable woman to enter.

For the president the army commander held parades. He allowed any officer who wished to do so to speak with Lincoln privately. Mary Lincoln, on her first trip with her husband, gloried in the attention paid her. Tad followed his father everywhere, even to Stafford Heights, where the president saw a rebel sharpshooter on the Rappahannock's west bank looking at him through field glasses. Lincoln had to be aware that his stovepipe hat made him an especially attractive target. But the Confederate merely lowered his glasses and made a low bow.

Although for the president the trip was something of a vacation, he must have hoped to learn what General Hooker meant to do with his army now that good fighting weather was near. In this Lincoln would be disappointed. Hooker had plans, but not even his staff officers knew what they were. Even so, the commander-in-chief saw enough to agree with Hooker that his was "the finest army on the planet." And in conversations with senior officers Lincoln had the chance to impart some advice: "Next time, put all your men into the fight."

As escort for the Lincolns on the steamer returning them to

Washington, Hooker sent Daniel Sickles, a corps commander now but years earlier a congressman from New York. Sickles found Mrs. Lincoln in a frosty mood. Several nights earlier she had been too fatigued from visiting hospitals to attend a party he had given in the First Family's honor, but young Tad had been there, and from him Mary Lincoln had learned something she most certainly did not like.

Also present at the party was vivacious Agnes Elisabeth Winona Leclerq Joy, Princess Salm-Salm, the pretty twenty-two-year-old wife of a Prussian nobleman serving as a staff officer. When Dan Sickles, rather spirited himself, dared her to go over and give the austere president a kiss, Princess Salm-Salm did—ardently—and so did some of the other young ladies. His father, Tad must have told Mrs. Lincoln, seemed to enjoy it.

So, at dinner in the steamer's wardroom, the First Lady ignored the attempts of her husband and their escort to reduce the distinct chill in the air through charm. Lincoln tried another approach, saying he had not realized how pious Dan Sickles was. How so? "They tell me you're the greatest psalmist in the army. In fact, they say you're more than a psalmist—you're a Salm-Salmist."

For a moment Mrs. Lincoln seemed shocked, then she relaxed into giggles.

There was, in fact, much more to the audacious princess than her skill in kissing. She was also a nurse, and soon she would be busy, for shortly after the then-estranged Lincolns and Sickles left Aquia Landing for Washington, General Hooker began the execution of his secret plan.

Cross the Rappahannock well upstream, the army commander ordered cavalryman George Stoneman, and take the 11,000 sabers in his corps southward to slash Lee's lines of communication. "Let your watchword be," concluded the adjutant who wrote the document, "fight, fight, fight, bearing in mind that time is as valuable to the general as rebel carcasses."

Stoneman led his troopers northwestward from Falmouth on Monday, April 13, but the inclement weather General Lee had watched earlier in the month from his bed in the Yerbys' house persisted, and when the Yankee cavalrymen reached their assigned fords, they found the Rappahannock flooded. And so it remained for two weeks while Stoneman's men and horses consumed the nine days' rations in their 275 wagons, aborting their mission.

In the interval General Hooker revised the plan he had never revealed. Again Stoneman's cavalry corps would sweep far west of Lee's lines at Fredericksburg and plunge southward deep into his rear. Following Stoneman would be three infantry corps destined to cross the Rappahannock at various fords and then concentrate at a clearing called Chancellorsville, in the vast forest known as the Wilderness. Concurrently, Sedgwick would put three corps, via pontoon bridges, on the west bank of the Rappahannock downstream from Fredericksburg, where Franklin's grand division had tangled with Jackson back in December. Lee, his supply lines cut by federal cavalry, his northern flank enveloped and with superior forces west of him, pressed by Sedgwick in front from the east, would be obliged either to retreat toward Richmond or be destroyed.

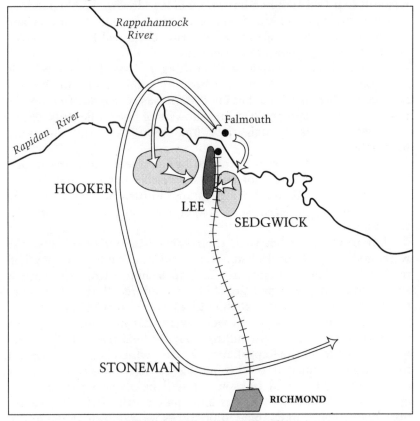

Hooker's Chancellorsville Plan

Hooker had about 135,000 men in his army, about twice as many as Lee unless Longstreet brought his two divisions up in time. Henry Hunt could provide 412 guns but they would not be under his direction; the army commander, who had served in the artillery years earlier, preferred to control the guns himself. Hooker retained few cavalry troopers. But his engineers had pontoon bridging equipment ready for the crossings above and below Fredericksburg, Professor Thaddeus S. C. Lowe had men up in his two observation balloons scanning the Confederate lines, and Fighting Joe appeared to have no qualms when he declared: "My plans are perfect, and when I start to carry them out, may God have mercy on General Lee, for I will have none!"

Miss Julia Jackson would be five months old on April 23, a day her father set aside from all else for her baptism. Into the Yerbys' parlor came the general's staff officers, some of them unaware until recently that Old Jack had known all along, during the Shenandoah Valley campaign and the Seven Days and Second Manassas and Sharpsburg and Fredericksburg, that this child had been conceived and that he might not live to see her.

Certainly Jackson had done nothing to save himself for this occasion. It was remarkable that his only wound so far in this war had been to his raised hand at First Manassas, when so often he had ignored Yankee-fired artillery and showers of hot minié balls whizzing past him as though they had been so many annoying bumblebees.

"Press on!" all present in the parlor could remember him urging his troops, so they were not much surprised when General Jackson lost patience over Anna's delay upstairs. Returning with little Julia in his arms, he ordered Rev. Tucker Lacy to press on with the ceremony.

But if anyone other than their baby daughter could melt the warrior's heart, Anna Jackson could and did. And after they had returned to their bedroom in the Yerbys' house from the church service on Sunday, April 26, Anna would recall that "his conversation was more spiritual than I had ever observed before."

By that time Jackson was well aware that his time with Anna and little Julia was fast dwindling away. Federal troops had already made a feint down the Rappahannock, after which Lee had placed all his troops on combat alert. "I think if a real attempt is made to cross the river," he had told Jackson, "it will be above [west of] Fredericksburg." Jeb Stuart's scouts and spies north of the Rappahannock confirmed rumors that Union forces were indeed on the move.

Monday passed, and Tuesday, with Old Jack spending every moment he could with his wife and their baby daughter. Then, at dawn on Wednesday, April 29, came the dreaded knock on their door: Jubal Early's adjutant, Jackson was told, wished to see him. He said to Anna, "That looks as if Hooker were crossing."

Soon, General Jackson returned. If duty permitted it, he would see Anna and Julia off for Richmond. But as it turned out, the knock on their door had meant what he had feared most.

Jubal Early had good cause to disturb Jackson that morning, Wednesday, April 29, for overnight Joe Hooker's engineers had thrown five pontoon bridges side by side across the Rappahannock down where there had been two back in December. Now, by putting two divisions of his VI Corps on the Confederates' side of the river, Major General John Sedgwick had caught Lee napping. With almost 24,000 men "Uncle John's" corps was the largest in the Army of the Potomac. Waiting on the east bank with his two remaining divisions were John Reynolds's I Corps, with nearly 17,000 troops, and close to 19,000 more in Dan Sickles's III Corps. If Hooker heeded Lincoln's admonition and put all of his men into the next fight, this force of roughly 60,000 and more than 150 guns might well accomplish what George Meade's division almost had on December 13: a breakthrough.

But Sedgwick's powerful wing was the only one Lee could see, which was exactly what Fighting Joe intended. He, too, could split an army in the face of the enemy. And this he had done, two mornings earlier, by starting his other wing—also about 60,000 troops strong and with another 150 guns or more—northwestward up the Rappahannock.

Chapter 22

Chancellorsville:
Audacity Compounded

Oliver O. Howard's troops had led the way on Monday April 27, a rainy morning. Many of the 13,000 men in his XI Corps, earlier led by Pathfinder John Frémont and more recently Franz Sigel, were German-Americans serving under men with names such as von Steinwehr, Schurz, Schimmelpfennig, von Gilsa, Bushbeck, Krzyzanowski. These troops and their new commander were still getting used to each other as the march began; and as it went on and the heavily laden soldiers eased their burdens by throwing away every item they dared, Howard may well have wished Franz Sigel were still their commander.

Following in the wake of Howard's columns were the 13,000 men in Major General Henry W. Slocum's XII Corps. After them came George Meade's V Corps, about 16,000 troops in all, but Hooker split Couch's II corps, telling him to place two of his divisions near Banks Ford, only six miles from Falmouth, and to leave John Gibbon's three brigades nearer Falmouth as a threat to the northern end of Lee's line.

Helping to conceal the enveloping wing's movement from Lee was the four- or five-mile distance between their road and the Rappahannock. Hooker's main risk was that Monday's rain might convert his advance into another mud march, but by Wednesday morning he had no reason to complain.

At about the time Anna Jackson and her baby daughter were boarding the Richmond-bound train at Guiney's Station on April 29, the federal XI, XII, and V Corps were across Kelly's Ford on the upper Rappahannock. They were at least twenty miles west of Fredericksburg, in Lee's rear, still marching, but southeastward now, approaching the Rapidan River's fords. And they were likely to reach the crossroads at Chancellorsville on Thursday the thirtieth before the Confederate army's commander could do anything much but worry about how to deal with Sedgwick's forces on the plain east of him.

If General Lee was surprised by the news that Sedgwick's troops were crossing the Rappahannock, not far from his tent on the morning of the April 29, he gave no sign of it. Tell Jackson, Lee said to an aide, "I am sure he knows what to do."

And as the general commanding may have expected, Jackson ordered his scattered forces south of Fredericksburg back to the same ridgeline the Second Corps had defended on December 13. Lee rode Traveller there for a look at what Sedgwick was doing, saw little, then headed northwestward to see if Hooker might be threatening Banks Ford. Along the way he sent word for his reserve artillery to return from the North Anna River and notified the president that he needed all available troops, especially Longstreet's two bacon-gathering divisions.

Around noon on Wednesday, April 29, from Jeb Stuart came a report that federal infantry and cavalry were crossing the Rappahannock at Kelly's Ford. Later, Stuart telegraphed that his troopers had captured Yankees from three different corps, all headed for the Rapidan south of Kelly's Ford. Near sundown more messages told General Lee that those people were across two of the Rapidan's fords, between him and Stuart.

Lee ordered Stuart to fight his way through and rejoin the army. By nine P.M. he had Richard Anderson's two brigades near Fredericksburg marching westward to join the two already at Chancellorsville. Also, Lee told Lafayette McLaws to get his division ready to follow Anderson.

McLaws's division and Anderson's belonged to Longstreet's corps, which meant that once both were committed, someone would have to replace their absent commander. General Lee intended to perform this duty himself when the time came, knowing that he could trust Jackson to hold Sedgwick.

Early on April 30, though, Lee felt a touch of his recent illness's symptoms; even so, he rode out with Jackson for a look at Sedgwick's force, which was digging in. Jackson wanted to attack. Lee replied that he was not in favor but that he would leave the decision to him; later, Jackson would return from his reconnaissance and agree that attacking was not feasible.

That afternoon, messages from Anderson told Lee that the federals were approaching Chancellorsville and that he had put his division on defensible ground east of that place, which was not a town but merely the name the Chancellor family had given to its large house and outbuildings, set in one of the Wilderness's few clearings where several roads met. Now that Lee was convinced Hooker had split his vastly larger army, so would he: He sent orders to Anderson to entrench and await the reinforcements the division commander had asked for.

Actually, with Longstreet south of Richmond and two of his divisions with him, Lee's army was already divided and had been for over two months. His immediate problem was how many troops to leave behind to oppose Sedgwick's 60,000 east of him. About 10,000 should be enough, he decided: Jubal Early's division and Barksdale's brigade from McLaws's. This would enable him to bring his forces west of Fredericksburg to roughly 40,000 men, far fewer than Hooker's 60,000.

Lafayette McLaws's three brigades marched at midnight to reinforce Anderson. Jackson, who would be in command until General Lee arrived, led the first of his corps' divisions in McLaws's wake several hours later, well before daylight.

"He knows what to do," Lee had said of Jackson, so the army commander spent the foggy morning of Friday, May 1, on the heights overlooking Fredericksburg. For once the misty blanket was an advantage: Jubal Early could spread his men along the six-mile line before federal observers in Professor Lowe's two balloons could see and report the shift in troop strengths Lee was making. Finally, satisfied with Early's deployment and the placement of his artillery, early in the afternoon General Lee turned his back to John Sedgwick's threat and headed Traveller westward to fight Mr. F. J. Hooker.

Everything had happened, and still was developing, exactly as the Army of the Potomac's commander had wished. And this he expressed from Chancellorsville in a message to his men:

> It is with heartfelt satisfaction the commanding general announces to the army that the operations of the last three days have determined that our enemy must either ingloriously fly, or come out from behind his defenses and give us battle on our own ground, where certain destruction awaits him.

There was much truth in Hooker's words. Ignoring the rain as best they could, his troops had marched from Falmouth far to the northwest, crossed the Rappahannock at Kelly's Ford, then spread along several roads through the triangle formed by that river and the Rapidan. Once past Ely's Ford, George Meade's V Corps brushed off Confederate cavalry jabs and plunged into the gloomy thickets of the Wilderness. By noon on April 30, Thursday, Meade led his troops out of the woods and into a clearing from which they could see an imposing two-story brick mansion in its midst: Chancellorsville, such as it was.

Federal cavalrymen had reached there earlier, and their mounts were grazing on the lawn as Meade rode up to the house. Four ladies, dressed in spring dresses, looked down from the second story's porch. "You'd better go back where you came from, Yankee!" one of them shouted. "General Lee's going to be here in a little while!"

It may have been Meade who thanked the lady for her advice and told her she was mistaken, adding that he would be glad to provide escorts to some safer place. "Oh, no!" came her reply. "You'll skedaddle if you know what's good for you—or General Lee'll give you the hospitality of the country!"

Duly warned, General Meade returned his attention to the east. There was a road near the Rappahannock leading past the U.S. Ford to Banks Ford, and he sent a column to find it, sweep eastward along it, and clear it of rebels. This move would make those crossings available to the army commander for bringing in more troops and especially supplies without having to use the roundabout route Meade had been obliged to take.

From Chancellorsville two roads led toward Fredericksburg, the turnpike and, south of it, the Orange Plank Road, and Meade sent forces on both to go as far eastward as they could. Now the ladies were bound to be disappointed: federal bayonets and guns would await Lee no matter which route he chose.

Then up to the Chancellor mansion rode Henry Slocum. "My orders," he told Meade, "are to assume command upon reaching this point and to take up a line of battle here, and not to move forward without further orders." This shocked Meade, who had been executing instructions General Hooker had given the day before. Meade had no choice but to recall his troops.

Why had Hooker changed his mind? No one would know until Fighting Joe arrived. But this was not unusual; seldom did he tell anyone more than he needed to know. Most perplexed of all Hooker's subordinates, perhaps, was John Sedgwick, over on the plain south of Fredericksburg. He had been told to make a demonstration but not an attack, then not to do anything, then to observe Lee's line and attack if he discerned weakness. And while this confusion proliferated, Hooker weakened Sedgwick's wing by taking away Dan Sickles's III Corps.

Utterly bewildered, Sedgwick kept his VI Corps in place and sought guidance from General Butterfield at Falmouth, who was supposed to be the communications link between Uncle John and Hooker. The chief of staff tried to keep things straight. But a mixture of erratic telegraphic contact and couriers' messages left Butterfield in a fog.

Late on that Thursday, April 30, General Hooker reached Chancellorsville. Soon Howard's XI Corps, about three miles west of the Chancellor mansion, was forming a defense line extending southeastward to Slocum's troops, who would hold the southern segment that extended eastward to the place where the roads crossed. Meade's divisions protected the edges of the clearing nearest Fredericksburg.

So matters stood that night when Hooker's congratulatory order reached the men. By then, however, his words seemed too far removed from events to have the intended effect. He spoke of Lee either fleeing "ingloriously" or coming out to "our own ground, where certain destruction awaits him." Did this mean that Fighting Joe was not going to attack the rebels? Would he be content if the army merely held on to Chancellorsville? And as if Hooker were trying to offend everyone, that evening he said, in effect: God Almighty could not prevent him from destroying Lee's army. Men who heard about that remark considered it extreme at best, at worst blasphemy.

Why had Hooker, who had just carried out a movement more brilliant than any executed by a federal commander so far in this war, suddenly done so much to imperil the confidence of so many men in his own army? Had he gone back to drinking? No, Darius Couch wrote later. Had he received news of rebel moves that frightened or confused him? No, none beyond fragmentary reports from signalmen along the north bank of the Rappahannock and from the gondolas of Professor Lowe's balloons. Had he lost confidence in himself?

Moreover, Hooker had said at Chancellorsville on the evening of Thursday, April 30: "The rebel army is now the legitimate property of the Army of the Potomac."

Surely Confederate Major General Richard Anderson had been unaware of the transfer when he withdrew to Tabernacle Church on Wednesday or when, on Thursday, Meade's probes moved toward his thin line and then mysteriously vanished back into the Wilderness. Neither did Lafayette McLaws suspect title had passed when, before dawn on Friday, May 1, he reached Anderson with all but one of his brigades following him, nor did Jackson, who arrived at about eight o'clock that morning.

In accordance with General Lee's orders, Anderson had told his troops to dig in. This Jackson promptly stopped. He ordered McLaws to advance westward toward Chancellorsville along the turnpike. Anderson's division was to take the Orange Plank Road and move abreast of McLaws's troops, south of them. Colonel Porter Alexander's guns were up; these Jackson threw into the force.

Not far behind him, General Jackson knew, were three of his corps' four divisions. They would follow Anderson on the Plank Road, ready for use if there was an opportunity to get around the Yankees' southern flank.

At around eleven o'clock Jackson launched his attack. He knew the ground but nothing about where or in what strength the federals might be. And he had not seen or heard from General Lee since the night before.

Soon after Jackson heard rifle fire from the north, where McLaws's brigades were advancing, a message came in from Stuart. "I will close in on the flank and help all I can when the ball opens," the cavalry commander had written, adding: "May God grant us victory."

On the back of the same piece of paper, Old Jack scribbled a terse reply: "I trust that God will grant us a great victory. Keep closed on Chancellorsville."

At around nine-thirty A.M. on Friday, May 1, General Hooker sent his senior officers a curious message:

> Corps commanders will hold their corps in hand, and, wherever their commands may find themselves night or day, they will keep pickets well thrown out on all the approaches to their positions. The safety of this army depends upon this being rigidly executed.

But by eleven o'clock the light rain had stopped, the sun was out, and so was another order. Meade's corps was to move eastward on the River Road, toward Banks Ford, and along the turnpike; Slocum's divisions would take the Plank Road, with Howard's XI Corps following them; and army headquarters would be at Tabernacle Church after the movement commenced.

In effect, Hooker was telling his corps commanders to do on Friday what he had ordered on Wednesday and George Meade had started to do on Thursday. But nowhere in the directive did the word *attack* appear.

When Major General George Sykes's regulars, leading Meade's V Corps, collided with Lafayette McLaws's Confederate brigades on the turnpike, the ensuing rattle of rifle fire dispelled any notion that this was just another movement. Soon Slocum, on the Plank Road, south of Sykes, ran into Anderson's men. Now the two nations' forces were stabbing at each other, giving up ground, then regaining it, fighting with the same tenacity both sides had displayed up on the Antietam's banks.

Most of the Wilderness was behind the federal commanders; eastward they could see open, rolling country where artillery could make a difference. Given a little more time, with Darius Couch's II Corps divisions coming up, they could fill gaps between the corps. And there was a chance that the booming of guns off to the east meant that John Sedgwick was attacking Lee from the east while they pressed him from the west.

Indeed, in launching his movement Hooker had not forgotten the eastern wing of his army. Back to Butterfield at Falmouth Fighting Joe had telegraphed:

> Direct Major-General Sedgwick to threaten an attack in full force at 1 o'clock, and to continue in that attitude until further orders. Let the demonstration be as severe as can be, but not an attack.

But the noise in the east sounded like an attack, and from a hilltop Darius Couch and Brigadier General Gouverneur Kemble Warren, an engineer on Hooker's staff, were discussing ways of keeping the rebel brigades from swarming around Slocum's southern flank when they learned something they found utterly astonishing: Hooker had called off the movement.

Sykes had it in writing:

> General Sykes will retire to his position of last night, and take up a line connecting his right with General Slocum, making his line as strong as he can by felling trees, etc. General Couch will then retire to his position of last night.

Couch sent a major back to Chancellorsville to protest; and back, in less than an hour the aide returned with the news that the order was to be obeyed. Disobey it, General Warren advised Couch, and he rode back to try to explain the situation to Fighting Joe. Sykes was on commanding terrain. Meade was within sight of Banks Ford. Slocum could handle the problem on his southern flank now that Couch's troops were up. Sickles's III Corps was at Chancellorsville in reserve, ready to surge eastward and link up with Sedgwick to destroy Lee's army. And all the commanders on the scene agreed that it would be madness to withdraw, now that victory was so near.

Withdraw, reiterated Hooker. But he did allow Couch to stay—only until five o'clock.

While all this had been going on, Slocum was pulling his men back as ordered. Couch, on receiving permission to hold, was thoroughly disgusted. "Tell General Hooker," he said to a courier, "he is too late, the enemy are already on my right and rear. I am in full retreat."

General Couch afterward wrote:

> Proceeding to the Chancellor House, I narrated my operations in front to Hooker, which were seemingly satisfactory, as he said: "It is all right, Couch, I have got Lee just where I want him; he must fight me on my own ground." The retrograde movement had prepared me for something of the kind, but to hear from his own lips that the advantages gained by the successful marches of his lieutenants were to culminate in fighting a defensive battle in that nest of thickets was too much, and I retired from his presence with the belief that my commanding general was a whipped man.

Jackson had long since sent waves of brigades westward on the Plank Road and south of it when General Lee arrived from Fredericksburg that Friday afternoon. Pleased by what he saw, the army commander turned Traveller northward to reconnoiter the terrain along the south bank of the Rappahannock.

By so doing, engineer Lee was reverting to the role he had performed in the Mexican War, when twice he had found obscure routes enabling Winfield Scott to outflank Santa Anna. Not so fortunate was he this time. The ground he rode over was cut by ravines; a thrust to sever Mr. F. J. Hooker's supply lifeline at the U.S. Ford was not feasible.

Worse, soon all of Jackson's forces would be within the Wilderness. Roads invited ambush. Now that Hooker had been reinforced by Couch and Sickles, Lee's troops were outnumbered almost two to one. And there was something unsettling about the ease with which Jackson was driving those people toward Chancellorsville. Might this Friday afternoon's fight have been only a feint, one meant to mask a sweep to the southeast, via Spotsylvania, to cut the R F & P Railroad—a trap?

Jackson was with a brigade southwest of the Plank Road, hunting for a trail that might lead northward to the Yankees' defense line. When underbrush too dense for the troops to cut stopped the exploration, Jeb Stuart led Jackson to a knoll from which they could get a rough idea of the roads and terrain farther to the west. Stuart's guns fired enough rounds to give the federals something to think about, drawing a response that shattered the trunks of nearby trees and obliged the generals and the gunners to scurry away.

Near the junction of the Plank Road and the Furnace Road, Jackson found General Lee but they had to hurry into the woods to get beyond the range of a Yankee sniper's rifle. By then the sun was setting. Amid the long shadows they found a fallen log and sat down on it. As the two generals reviewed the first day of May's developments, someone started a campfire, a good idea, because the ground was still wet from the recent rains and the night air would be chilly.

Hooker, said Jackson, would be on the Rappahannock's north side in the morning. Lee disagreed. Having ventured this far westward from Falmouth, he argued, those people would not give up their advantage so easily. They would have to be attacked. But how? Not from the north, from along the Rappahannock's ravine-serrated bank. From the southeast, where they sat?

To find out, Lee sent two officers on a reconnaissance. While he and Jackson waited, their conversation turned to the only alternative remaining: getting around the federals' western flank and then attacking.

Suddenly, up rode General Stuart with heart-stopping news. Hooker's western flank was "in the air"—open, unguarded, all the way from where Howard's XI Corps line ended northward to the Rapidan River.

"How," asked General Lee, "can we get at those people?"

Out of their uniforms' pockets came maps, unreadable now except when held near the campfire. But maps not prepared by Jed Hotchkiss were unreliable. Guides who knew every trail through the Wilderness were needed. Could Stuart find some?

Not long after Stuart departed, the two engineers who had been out seeking nearby approaches to Hooker's lines returned. None worth considering existed, they reported. That settled it: Jackson would sweep past Hooker's defenses and attack from the west. Now it was only a matter of how he would get there.

Outside the Chancellor mansion Union soldiers wounded in Friday's fighting were stretched in rows on the lawn. Moving among them, putting on fresh bandages and doing whatever else they could to ease the Yankees' suffering, were the four ladies who had been so confident that General Lee would come.

Inside the house tension was high. The president wanted to know what was happening now that the Union's largest field army had disappeared into the Wilderness. On Monday Lincoln had telegraphed: "How does it look now?" Hooker replied that he was not ready to give an opinion, that he was busy, and that he would tell the president all he could as soon as he could, "and have it satisfactory." But now it was Friday night.

Fighting Joe decided to leave Washington in the dark a while longer. Perhaps that was just as well, for there was a passive tone to the message he sent Chief-of-Staff Butterfield: "Hope the enemy will be emboldened to attack me. I did feel certain of success. If his communications are cut he must attack me. I have a strong position."

Through the night a courier kept the campfire burning after Jackson and then Lee found places to sleep on the damp ground. First to stir, well before dawn on Saturday morning, was Jackson. At the fire he sat down on a Yankee cracker box and sipped a cup of coffee, ignoring the clatter as his sword —which he had left leaning against a tree—fell over.

Soon Reverend Lacy joined Jackson. Lacy had preached at churches west of Chancellorsville and knew the roads. On the general's map Lacy drew a line, a route around the federal fortifications, one leading to the turnpike west of Howard's corps. No, said Jackson, federal observers might see his movement. Was there another way?

Lacy and mapmaker Jed Hotchkiss rode westward in the dark to find out. General Lee was sitting near Jackson when they returned. Yes, Hotchkiss reported, and he explained the lines he had sketched on the map.

"General Jackson," said Lee, "what do you propose to do?"

"Go around here" came the reply as Jackson pointed to the route on his map Hotchkiss and Lacy had scouted.

"What do you propose to make this movement with?"

"With my whole corps."

"What will you leave me?"

"The divisions of Anderson and McLaws."

Longstreet was far to the south, Jubal Early's 10,000 men ten miles or so away at Fredericksburg, and now Jackson was tempting Lee to split the army again in the face of 72,000 federals—to send 25,000 troops on a fourteen-mile flank march westward to attack Howard while only 14,000 Confederates distracted Hooker from the east: Audacity compounded!

"Well," said General Lee, "go on."

For Oliver O. Howard, a genuinely pious man, Dowdall's Tavern was an unlikely place for his XI Corps' headquarters. But he may have been reluctant to make such profane use of nearby Wilderness

Church, and the tavern was very near the place where—as was the case east of Chancellorsville—the Plank Road branched off from the turnpike, again running south of it as it stretched westward.

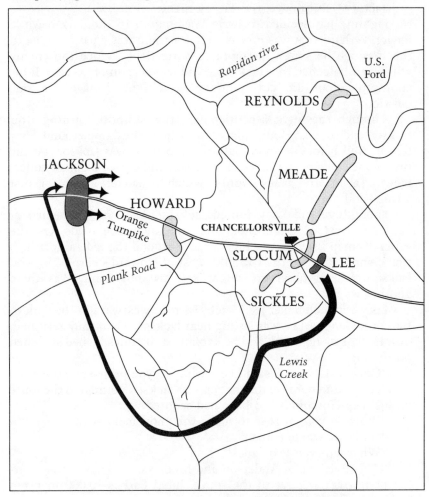

Jackson's Last Flank March

It was hardly a compliment to Howard's troops for the army commander to have placed them three miles or so west of the long federal line's most threatened segment. In fact, his position seemed so distant from danger that Howard did not insist that his men comply with orders to fortify their positions.

Southeast of Dowdall's Tavern the ground was hilly, with Lewis Creek's many ravines and the dense Wilderness thickets making it difficult even for deer to get through. But there was one plateau, called Hazel Grove, that appeared important enough to be defended, and during the night one of Dan Sickles's III Corps's divisions moved down and occupied it.

Soon after sunrise on Saturday, May 2, General Hooker rode southeastward from Chancellorsville, past the artillery massed on the cleared high ground at Fairview, to inspect the bulge in his line at Hazel Grove. Satisfied, Fighting Joe checked on Howard's deployments, then returned to his headquarters to await the arrival of John Reynolds's I Corps from Fredericksburg.

Why Hooker felt he needed Reynolds's divisions more than Sedgwick did was not apparent. He may have wanted to use this additional force to fill the gap between Howard's corps and the Rapidan, recognizing as had Jeb Stuart that the federal western flank was "in the air." As a consequence, though, now Sedgwick would have only his VI Corps for any demonstrations or attacks the Army of the Potomac's commander might order.

With a long march and a fight ahead, Jackson allowed time for his troops to have breakfast before moving out. Another hour or so passed while Lafayette McLaws and Richard Anderson spread their men to cover portions of the line being vacated. Finally, around eight o'clock, the flanking column was ready.

Cavalry led, then came a brigade of Georgians. Old Jack saw General Lee, on Traveller, watching. As Jackson rode by, he pointed to the west: Lee nodded.

Seldom in history had a single army had so many things to do in so many different places during one day. Early's 10,000 would have to keep Sedgwick in place near Fredericksburg. The 14,000 Lee had southeast of Chancellorsville faced the task of making Hooker believe their numbers exceeded 40,000. And now Jackson's three divisions had vanished into the west, swallowed up by the new foliage in the Wilderness's thickets, on their way to a remote place a few men had scouted only the night before.

Failure anywhere could mean disaster everywhere. It would be impossible for Anderson and McLaws to hold their three-mile line if Hooker discovered how thinly manned it was and attacked, yet these two divisions had to attract enough attention to prevent those people from reinforcing Howard. And if Sedgwick got past Early, Lee's force would be caught in the middle.

Could audacity alone offset all these risks?

General Hooker had just returned to the Chancellor mansion from his morning ride when he learned that Sickles's troops at Hazel Grove had spotted a rebel column south of them—troops and wagons moving westward, then southward. This news puzzled Fighting Joe. It was not like Lee to retreat, yet he might be heading for Gordonsville. Or was this a flank march?

To be on the safe side, Hooker sent a warning to Howard. Advance your pickets for purposes of observation, he ordered, and be prepared for an attack from any direction. He told Sickles to advance cautiously and harass the column. But the more Hooker thought about it, the more likely it seemed to him that Lee had decided to "ingloriously fly."

Perhaps it was the warmth of that spring Saturday or his conviction that he had outmaneuvered Lee, but for some reason Hooker seemed curiously complacent. Couch, for one, thought more should be done about that rebel column Sickles's troops were harassing but had not cut. And what of the reports from Howard's officers that enemy troops had been seen south of the turnpike? But apparently Hooker's mind was leaping ahead to the move he ought to make if Lee *was* heading for Gordonsville. Late that afternoon he sent this order to his corps commanders: "The Major-General Com'g desires that you replenish your supplies of forage, provisions, and ammunition and be ready to start at an early hour to-morrow."

And, a little afterward, Hooker wired Butterfield:

> The Major-General commanding directs that General Sedgwick cross the river as soon as indications will permit; capture Fredericksburg with everything in it, and vigorously pursue the enemy. We know that the enemy is fleeing, trying to save his wagon trains. Two of Sickles' divisions are among them.

True, there had been skirmishing where General Jackson's column had turned southward, marching away from Hazel Grove, but brigades left behind as rear guards had held off Yankee probes with scant losses. Like a gray snake the force moved all Saturday morning and into the afternoon, changing from one seldom-used road to another with bewildering frequency. "Press on," Jackson kept urging, keeping the column closed up behind Stuart's cavalry and the guides, until he reached a hilltop from which he could see Wilderness Church and Dowdall's Tavern off to the northeast.

Old Jack could barely suppress his excitement: Howard's troops were completely at ease, their rifles stacked. Cooks were slaughtering beefs. Smoke rose from campfires.

Cavalryman Fitz Lee, the army commander's young nephew, pointed out how the Plank Road, which Jackson had intended to take, led directly to the strongest portion of Howard's line, on Melzi Chancellor's farm, south of Dowdall's Tavern. But if the column continued marching north to the turnpike and turned southeast-ward on it, Jackson could strike the end of Howard's northern flank.

Press on to the turnpike, Jackson told the commander of his leading division; then he took a moment to scribble a terse message for a courier to take to General Lee:

> The enemy has made a stand at Chancellor's which is about 2 miles from Chancellorsville. I hope as soon as practicable to attack. I trust that an ever kind Providence will bless us with great success.

That courier had to gallop the better part of fourteen miles to reach the Confederate army commander, though Lee and Jackson were only about six miles apart as a crow flies, and the trees' shadows on the pine straw were getting long when the messenger arrived. Lee found Jackson's words reassuring. But there was no sound of battle in the west. And Jackson's attack could not be postponed until morning.

All day long General Lee's blessings had been mixed. That morning, Jubal Early had misunderstood the aide Lee had sent, or that officer had gone beyond his instructions; in any case, Early had withdrawn all but one brigade and a few guns from his lines and started westward to join Lee. Now, with Saturday all but gone, Lee still did not know where Early's force was. But there had been no firing in the east, suggesting either that the mistake had been corrected or that Sedgwick had not learned of it. Similarly, Hooker's troops had left Anderson and McLaws alone while Jackson was moving around the federals' western flank. But in midafternoon there had been a few probes, and the next one might be strong enough to break the thin line.

So, as matters stood, not a single thing could General Lee take for granted. His army, scattered as it was, would exist only for as long as Hooker and Sedgwick permitted. And there was no action Lee could take to improve his situation.

At first, hardly anyone in Oliver Howard's corps knew what it meant. Rabbits and squirrels and wild turkeys came running through the underbrush, then white-tailed deer emerged from the thickets—ignoring the startled humans in their paths—and sped past, bounding eastward.

Suddenly the sounds of bugles and demonic yells broke the Wilderness's late-afternoon silence. Artillerymen raced toward their guns. Officers shouted commands to infantrymen, herding them into ranks just as volleys of hot lead stabbed out from the western woods and cut them down. Screams of wounded men—some dropping to the ground, others running to the rear in panic—mixed with the rattles of rifle fire amid the smoke.

Colonel Gustav Schleiter, saber drawn, had just enough time in which to get his Pennsylvanians ready: first rank kneeling, second rank standing, bayonets fixed. But blue-clad men came dashing toward them, most without weapons, yelling frantic warnings. Then came the gray wave. "Fire!" ordered Schleiter just before he was hit in the chest, dropped his sword, and collapsed. A lieutenant urged the Pennsylvanians to stand fast, but they could not; the few not already shot threw away their rifles and fled just as the Confederate tide swept over the bodies.

Near Dowdall's Tavern General Howard's horse reared from the excitement as the mob of fugitives streamed past, oblivious to the sight of their commander, hatless, holding the staff of the U.S. flag with the stump of his arm while he tried to rally his men. "Halt and form!" Howard shouted repeatedly, but in vain. Tears streamed down his face. "Think of your country! Halt and form!"

It had taken less than two hours for Jackson to wreck the Army of the Potomac's XI Corps. At five-fifteen that afternoon he had turned to the division commander whose troops were to lead the attack and asked, "Are you ready, General Rodes?"

"Yes, sir!"

"You can go forward, then."

Robert Rodes's advance had been ragged, but it was powerful enough to sweep through the thickets and clearings and drive the Yankees steadily eastward. With it rode Old Jack, shouting, "Press on! Press on!"

After passing Melzi Chancellor's farm, though, Rodes's men were so disorganized he had to call a halt. "They are running too fast for us!" a young officer had complained. "We can't keep up with them!" But Powell Hill kept the attack going. Up rode Jackson. "Press them!" he ordered. "Cut them off from the United States Ford, Hill! Press them!"

Darkness came early in the Wilderness, and over it a full moon was rising through the battle smoke as if to encourage the Confederates to fight on. But now they would have hard going, for—finally—the Yankees were rallying.

General Lee had feared something of that sort, so at the first sound of gunfire in the west he had ordered Anderson and McLaws to advance near enough to Mr. F. J. Hooker's fortress to keep those people too busy even to think about heading westward to help save Howard. Noise of fierce battle from where Jackson ought to be was all Lee had to go on, yet he pressed his troops on toward the federal lines as though he meant to smash them.

Perhaps because of an acoustic peculiarity, General Hooker had not heard the sounds of Jackson crushing Howard. Fighting Joe was seated on the Chancellor mansion's porch, enjoying Saturday evening's warm breeze and discussing with his aides the firing off to the southeast when—around six-thirty—one of the junior officers went out to the road and looked westward.

"My God!" he cried. "Here they come!"

He meant Oliver Howard's blue-clad mob. Quickly, Hooker and his aides mounted and rode out to try to halt the stampede. "Throw your men into the breech!" shouted Hooker to Hiram G. Berry, the major general commanding the only division nearby. "Receive the enemy on your bayonets!"

But that was no longer necessary, for the Wilderness and darkness and fatigue and the valor of Union troops who stood their ground had at last combined to stop Jackson. Federal artillery firing from Fairview's plateau had much to do with that, as did Dan Sickles, who sent units northwestward from Hazel Grove to threaten Jackson's southern flank.

Even so, confusion compounded near the Chancellor mansion as the leading elements of John Reynolds's I Corps arrived and ran into Howard's demoralized rabble. Inside the headquarters house Joe Hooker's adjutant, Brigadier General James Van Alen, had another problem he knew the general commanding would not welcome. It took the form of a telegram to Hooker from the secretary of war, Edwin Stanton:

> We can not control intelligence in relation to your movements while your generals write letters giving details. A letter from General Van Alen to a person not connected with the War Department describes your position as intrenched at Chancellorsville—can't you give his sword something to do, so that he will have less time for the pen?

Chapter 23

Jackson's Wish Is Fulfilled

W hether it was the bright moonlight or sheer audacity no one would ever know, but one thing was certain: General Jackson was not willing to allow his battle to end where it now stood. Pressing on to the U.S. Ford over the Rappahannock was what he had told Powell Hill to do, and Hill needed a route that would take him north of the throngs of Yankees near Chancellorsville. Unable to wait for anyone else to find such a trail for him, Old Jack pressed on in search of one a cavalryman had said led from the turnpike to the northeast—and in so doing, he rode out several hundred yards east of his own troops.

Sounds of Yankee axes felling trees soon convinced Jackson that the road he was probing was blocked. He turned back, and as he was returning to his line, shots plunged out.

"Cease firing!" Powell Hill shouted, as did Joe Morrison, Anna Jackson's brother. "Who gave that order?" someone yelled back, thinking perhaps the riders were Yankee cavalrymen. "It's a lie! Pour it into them, boys!"

As the volley darted out, Little Sorrel bolted off the road and into the woods, leaving behind the two aides cut down from their saddles. Jackson could no longer control his frightened horse. Captain Robert Wilbourn and another officer galloped after him. Together they halted Little Sorrel and helped Jackson dismount, only to discover that he had been shot through the shoulder, his left arm below the elbow, and his hand.

Powell Hill hurried to the clearing where the officers had placed Old Jack. He held the general's head in his lap for a few minutes, then had to have someone take his place because of a report the Yankees were advancing. With Jackson wounded, Hill was in command of the corps, but only for as long as it took him to reach the turnpike, where both of his legs were numbed suddenly by a federal shellburst's fragments. Hill could find no blood when he felt his boots, but the pain told him he could not ride a horse or do much else.

Now command of Jackson's corps would have to pass again, to Robert Rodes. But, Powell Hill wondered, was Rodes ready for so much responsibility? No, this day had been his first in managing more than a brigade. Jeb Stuart? A cavalryman? An infantryman would be preferable, but Stuart was a leader and a fighter, and every soldier in Jackson's corps knew that.

Hill quickly sent a captain to find Stuart.

General Lee had watched the glow in the western sky and listened to the booming of the federal guns causing it until around midnight, when the noises of fighting gave way to the songs of whippoorwills in nearby trees. Again he stretched out on the ground, covered by a piece of oilcloth to keep away the dew. He had slept less than three hours when he heard voices.

One was Captain Wilbourn's. "Sit down here by me," said the general, "and tell me about the fight last night."

Lee listened carefully as the signal officer told him the whole story, ending with the wounding of Old Jack. At the news Lee moaned, then said, "Ah, Captain, any victory is dearly bought which deprives us of the services of General Jackson, even for a short time!"

Wilbourn gave more details. Lee stopped him: "Don't talk about it; thank God it is no worse!"

Wilbourn changed the subject, to the wounding of Powell Hill. Jeb Stuart had been summoned, he reported, adding that he thought Old Jack's intention had been to continue the attack and cut off Hooker's supply line at the U.S. Ford.

"These people must be pressed today," said General Lee, rising, then, at three o'clock on the morning, Sunday, May 3, he began a message to General Stuart:

> It is necessary that the glorious victory thus far achieved be prosecuted with the utmost vigor, and the enemy given no time to rally. As soon, therefore, as it is possible, they must be pressed, so that we may unite the two wings of the army.

That done, the army commander dipped into a basket a lady had sent him, spread a breakfast for Wilbourn, and advised him to get some sleep. General Lee was on Traveller, about to go and give orders to Anderson and McLaws, when from out of the western darkness rode Jed Hotchkiss.

Lee listened to the mapmaker's report until he mentioned the wounding of Jackson. "I know all about it," he said, "and do not wish to hear any more—it is too painful a subject."

At about the same time, well before dawn, Sandie Pendleton sat beside General Jackson's cot in a tent several miles northwest of Dowdall's Tavern. Scarcely half an hour earlier, surgeon Hunter McGuire had sawed off Old Jack's left arm.

Long and painful had been the general's journey from the place where Wilbourn and another officer had taken Jackson off Little Sorrel's back and watched the battle-crazed horse speed directly into the Yankees' lines. At first, Jackson had tried to walk, but soon someone brought a litter and persuaded him to get on it. Suddenly, one of its bearers was shot; another fled. Lieutenant James Power Smith covered the general's body with his own as federal artillery bombarded the area.

Dorsey Pender, himself wounded, came by and said he feared he would have to fall back. Jackson replied: "You must hold your ground, General Pender, you must hold your ground, sir!"

At the road was an ambulance wagon, its two spaces already filled, one by artilleryman Stapleton Crutchfield. When the officer beside Crutchfield learned it was Jackson who needed to be moved, he told the men outside to remove him.

In a tent at the corps's hospital, surgeon Hunter McGuire told Jackson that his left arm would have to come off and that he would have to be put under the influence of chloroform. Earlier Old Jack had told the surgeon he knew he was dying, and he may have wondered if it would be fitting to appear before God in a drugged condition. But he told Dr. McGuire to go ahead: "Do for me whatever you think best."

And so—Sandie Pendleton could tell by the blanket's sag on the sleeping general's left side—the shattered arm was off. The young staff officer waited patiently until Jackson stirred. "Well, Major," he said to Pendleton, "I am glad to see you; I thought you were killed."

Quickly, remembering that McGuire wanted the general to have more sleep, Pendleton told Jackson that Stuart would be in command of the corps and asked what orders he should take to him.

"I don't know—I can't tell" came a feeble reply. "Say to General Stuart he must do what he thinks best."

Before dawn on that Sunday morning, Major General Gouverneur Warren dismounted at John Sedgwick's headquarters on the plain east of the ridgelines where Jubal Early's men were back in their defensive positions overlooking Fredericksburg. Warren had brought with him an order, one General Hooker had telegraphed to Butterfield late on Saturday night:

> The major-general commanding directs that General Sedgwick cross the Rappahannock on the receipt of this order, and at once take up his line of march on the Chancellorsville road until he connects with us, and he will attack and destroy any force he may fall in with on the road. He will leave all his trains behind, except the pack-train of small ammunition, and march to be in our vicinity at daylight. He will probably fall upon the rear of the forces commanded by General Lee, and between us we will use him up.

Warren told Sedgwick that he had come because he knew the roads west of Marye's Heights and could guide him. Butterfield had wired Sedgwick that everything depended on his carrying out the army commander's order: Fighting Joe's plan gave the VI Corps the opportunity to strike the blow that could destroy Lee's army. But would daylight bring another fog?

Hours earlier, Captain R. H. T. Adams had found Jeb Stuart up near Ely's Ford on the Rapidan and told him that he would have to gallop southward and take command of Jackson's corps. This Stuart did. Rodes gave him all the information he could about the situation, including the plan he had made for going on with the attack at sunrise. Prepare for it, said Stuart; then he sent for young Porter Alexander, the senior artillery officer present, and asked him to get his guns ready.

Alexander spent the rest of the night riding through the thick woods in search of clearings large enough for batteries. At one point he had to get behind a tree to keep from being hit by minié balls: Union forces northwest of Hazel Grove were fighting each other as well as Confederates in the moonlight. But by dawn Alexander had located five positions, one of which would enable him to fire at the federals holding the high ground at Hazel Grove, and he was exhausted.

Later, Alexander described how men in combat renew their energy through brief naps, such as one he took after his long ride, while Colonel R. L. Walker was away on an errand:

> For there is a higher power of sleep, with qualities as

different from the ordinary as light is from heat. I don't think that mere fatigue, or loss of ordinary sleep, produces this higher power of sleep, because I have never been able to obtain it except in connection with a battle & not more than three or four times even then. This was my first experience of it & the recollection of no pleasure of all my life is more vivid & enduring than that of this letting myself, as it were, sink under a dense fluid which penetrated alike eyes & ears & pores until it pervaded the very bones bringing with it, instantly, everywhere a trance of delicious rest & freedom even from dreams. It does not seem possible to dream, but yet the oblivion is half conscious. Could death ever come as that sleep did it would be delicious to die. Walker was not gone ten minutes but when he waked me I came back from a long ways. But I came easily & felt at once refreshed wonderfully, as if by a strong cordial.

Alexander quickly got his guns into their positions. At sunrise they were firing as Jeb Stuart sent his three divisions eastward to attack the log fortifications stretching for a mile and a quarter north to south and blocking the turnpike leading to his goal: Chancellorsville, about a mile away.

Never had there been any question regarding what Stuart had to do; everyone knew the task would be grim. Hooker was in a strong central position with the better part of 80,000 men in six corps, while Stuart was trying to strike from the west with less than 25,000 troops and from the southeast Lee had no more than 14,000 to throw at him. And if Sedgwick obeyed his orders, Lee's force would soon be obliged to fight in two directions at once or "ingloriously fly."

However, Hooker made a colossal mistake early Sunday morning by riding southwestward to Hazel Grove and ordering Dan Sickles to withdraw his two divisions and their guns from that exposed position. Sickles protested, pointing out what surely should have been obvious: Confederate guns on Hazel Grove's plateau could decimate the federal batteries at Fairview and even fire on the Chancellor mansion beyond it. But the army commander wanted Sickles' entire corps up on the turnpike behind the log fortifications, and that is where all but one battery and two regiments were when Stuart launched his attack and Alexander's gunners opened fire on Hazel Grove.

Brigadier General Henry Heth led Powell Hill's division over the Yankees' first defense line, only to encounter more resistance. By then, though, the brigade on the southern end of the Confederate wave was moving up the slope of the Hazel Grove plateau, taking 100 prisoners and capturing four federal guns before running into a rear guard Sickles had posted to protect his divisions' shift to the turnpike.

Porter Alexander rushed guns to Hazel Grove, soon massing about fifty there. Federal batteries at Fairview were the primary targets. From the plateau Alexander's gunners could also shell Yankee defenders in the woods. And now the Confederates had a road that facilitated uniting the wings of the army.

Even so, it was still up to Jeb Stuart's infantrymen on both sides of the turnpike to open the way to Chancellorsville. He sent wave after wave forward, relentlessly, ignoring heavy losses, determined to break through. He threw all three divisions into the struggle, but still the federals fought on, not only in front but from the north, where Hooker had the better part of three corps ready to fall upon Stuart's flank.

During this fierce fighting some of the finest brigades in Jackson's corps had almost ceased to exist, fought out, their survivors mixed with other units. But up rode Stuart, singing "Old Joe Hooker, won't you come out of the Wilderness?" And men who had thought they could do no more got up to show this gallant cavalryman what infantrymen are made of.

At about nine o'clock General Hooker was standing on the Chancellor house's south porch, leaning against a wooden pillar, looking toward Hazel Grove, watching teams of horses pulling guns and caissons northeastward. Suddenly there was a crash. Dust, splinters, and loose brick flew. Half the wooden column hit Hooker's body. An aide clutched him; another sent for an ambulance wagon and a surgeon.

Hooker, insisting he was all right and wanting the troops to see that he was, called for his horse. Aides, eager to get him beyond the range of rebel artillery fire, half-carried him down the rubble-strewn steps, helped him climb into the saddle, and rode with him, guiding him northeastward until second in command Darius Couch caught up with them. But Hooker gave no orders, so Couch returned to his II Corps.

The aides led Hooker on toward Chandler's farm, pausing once when the general seemed to be in pain. For a few minutes he rested on a blanket someone spread. Did he want a sip of stimulant? Yes. Out of a saddlebag came a bottle of whiskey. Moments later, Hooker was back on his horse—just as another solid shot from a rebel artillery piece landed in the middle of the recently abandoned blanket.

At Chandler's farm the army's medical director, Jonathan Letterman, was waiting. Inside a tent Letterman examined the general, emerging to report that his right side was partially paralyzed and that his pain was intense.

Could he continue in command? Letterman declined to take the responsibility for so important a decision, saying that Hooker himself would have to make it.

George Meade arrived, visited with Hooker briefly, asked for permission to attack Stuart's northern flank, and was told not to. Next came Couch. First Hooker told Couch to take over as army commander, then ordered him to move all of the corps inside the tight new defense line north of Chancellorsville. Couch, dismaying Meade and others who wanted to continue the fight, said that Hooker's wishes would have to be carried out —in effect, passing the army's command back to Joe Hooker.

By then the Chancellor house was in flames, and Confederate troops were driving the federal divisions off to the northeast. Protecting the escape route over the Rappahannock at the U.S. Ford was the only thing left for the Army of the Potomac to do: Chancellorsville itself no longer mattered.

Nor did it to General Lee, except as a way point en route to the river into which he meant to drive those people. From well before dawn on that Sunday morning he had been pressing Anderson and McLaws onward. Then he rode to Hazel Grove, and as he watched Porter Alexander's gunners firing, Lee may well have relaxed a little, knowing that the wings of his army were no longer divided. Under heavy federal fire he advanced with Jeb Stuart's southernmost elements, linked now with those of Anderson's division, past Fairview, to the clearing where the infantrymen who had given Stuart that one final critical charge were now mingling with the troops arriving from the southeast.

From their first sight of the erect, immaculate, utterly calm, gray-bearded man riding that unmistakable gray war-horse toward the burning Chancellor house, the soldiers of his Army of Northern Virginia seemed to forget everything they had just endured and broke into wild cheering. Eagerly they thronged around him, brushing Traveller's flanks, ignoring the cries of staff officers to let the general pass so that he could get on with the battle. But the tumultuous and triumphant shouting continued, with General Lee as composed in the midst of it as he had been during the worst moments of any battle.

"It must have been from such a scene," wrote an observer later, "that men in ancient times rose to the dignity of gods."

Soon, though, as officers were trying to get their troops back into ranks, Lee was handed a message from General Jackson. He could not bear to read it, gave it to an aide, listened, and then dictated a reply:

> I have just received your note, informing me that you were wounded. I cannot express my regret at the occurrence. Could I have directed events, I would have chosen for the good of the country to be disabled in your stead. I congratulate you on the victory, which is due to your skill and energy.

Not long afterward, as General Lee was about to attack Hooker's six corps compressed into a strongly fortified defense line, in from Fredericksburg rode one of Jubal Early's staff officers with blood-chilling news.

By noon on that Sunday, May 3, the commander of the Army of the Potomac's right wing had more than 25,000 troops and sixty-six guns fighting the Battle of Fredericksburg repeated.

At dawn a brigade trying to reach the sunken road below Marye's Heights had been thrown back with heavy losses. Next, Gibbon attempted to get around the northern flank, only to be repulsed by fire from the hill and a Confederate force that had just arrived from Banks Ford. Sedgwick decided to try a frontal assault. He sent nearly 5,000 men forward across the plain, and again rebel canister rounds and murderous volleys, fired from the sunken road, littered the ground with blue-clad bodies.

During a lull after the survivors pulled back, Sedgwick and Warren watched as a federal officer took a truce flag toward the sunken road—to ask for a cease-fire so wounded men could be removed, they assumed. Apparently the Confederate commander agreed, for some of the men in gray rose to stretch and look around. Sedgwick was amazed when he saw how few they were and astonished that they had been careless enough to reveal their positions. He quickly ordered another attempt.

Colonel Thomas Scott Allen, commanding the 5th Wisconsin, shouted to his men: "When the signal 'Forward' is given, you will start at the double-quick. You will not fire a gun, and you will not stop until you get the order to halt. You will never get that order!"

Such was the spirit of the federals as they surged across the plain, taking their losses without stopping, advancing until they were in the sunken road, fighting hand to hand, with the rebels defending it, then storming up the slope, driving the graybacks over the ridge. Now only pockets of Confederates remained. Some fought on, using their rifles as clubs, but soon even they were surrendering.

From Marye's Heights a jubilant John Sedgwick sent his divisions westward, guided by Warren. True, by now it was past noon, and Sedgwick was more than six hours late. But nothing seemed in his way. He would, after all, "use up" Lee.

So, more or less, ran the news Jubal Early's staff officer brought to General Lee at Chancellorsville just at the moment the Army of Northern Virginia was about to try to drive Hooker and all his forces into the Rappahannock. "We will attend to Mr. Sedgwick later," said Lee, but he could not postpone that. In fact, he had to improvise, and quickly. Again he split his army, telling Stuart to hold Hooker penned up as best he could with demonstrations and rushing Lafayette McLaws's relatively fresh division back toward Fredericksburg.

Well east of Chancellorsville, Brigadier General Cadmus M. Wilcox, whose brigade had been left behind on Friday afternoon to keep the Yankees from crossing Banks Ford, placed his troops on the Plank Road west of Fredericksburg and forced Sedgwick to slow his divisions' dash westward to a crawl. This gallant delaying action bought the time McLaws needed for his division to reach Salem Church, roughly three miles west of Marye's Heights on the Plank Road. Alexander, still drawing upon the energy gained from his remarkable predawn ten-minute nap, added guns to the line McLaws built.

In the tent miles west of Salem Church, Jackson heard the army commander's message read to him. "General Lee," said Old Jack, "is very kind, but he should give the praise to God."

But Lee already had. From Chancellorsville he had opened his preliminary report to President Jefferson Davis by writing: "We have again to thank Almighty God for a great victory."

In Washington on that Sunday afternoon, the president of the United States was reading long-awaited reports of a very different kind. First, from Butterfield:

> From all reports yet collected, the battle has been most fierce and terrible. Loss heavy on both sides. General Hooker slightly, but not seriously, wounded. He has preferred thus far that nothing should be reported, and does not know of this, but I cannot refrain from saying this much to you. You may expect his dispatch within a few hours, which will give the result.

Then came a relay-delayed message Hooker had sent:

We have had a desperate fight yesterday and to-day, which has resulted in no success to us, having lost a position of two lines, which had been selected for our defense. It is now 1:30 o'clock, and there is still some firing of artillery. We may have another turn at it this p.m. I do not despair of success. If Sedgwick could have gotten up, there could have been but one result. As it is impossible for me to know the exact position of Sedgwick as regards his ability to advance and take part in the engagement, I cannot tell when it will end. We will endeavor to do our best. My troops are in good spirits. We have fought desperately to-day. No general ever commanded a more devoted army.

Surely Abraham Lincoln must have found all these words discouraging. But he may have gotten a few grains of comfort from the difference between these messages and those General McClellan had showered upon him: Hooker was fighting.

The ground near Salem Church was open enough to permit some maneuvering, which General Sedgwick attempted by having one division put most of its pressure on the rebels north of the Plank Road while his other two came up. But at sundown, after a bitterly contested and costly fight, his forces were no nearer Chancellorsville than they had been when they collided with McLaws and Wilcox.

Sedgwick gave up all hope of completing the mission Hooker had given him and turned his thoughts to saving his VI Corps. By sunrise on Monday, May 4, federal engineers had a pontoon bridge in place on the Rappahannock at Scott's Ford, slightly downstream from Banks Ford, and Uncle John was moving his three divisions near the river to ground they could defend while Hooker decided what to do with them.

Now Lee was in a central position, one from which he could attack either Hooker or Sedgwick. Naturally, he chose to strike the weaker federal force. Leaving Stuart's 25,000 men to hold Hooker's 75,000 in place near the U.S. Ford, Lee rode to Salem Church. Anderson's division was following him. When it joined those of McLaws and Early, Lee could commit about 21,000 troops to the destruction of Sedgwick's 19,000.

Obviously, General Lee was gambling that Fighting Joe would keep his six corps inside their V-shaped position near their escape route north of Chancellorsville. And Lee was asking much of troops who had been fighting or marching for days. Porter Alexander noticed that the army commander himself was showing strain. On Monday, May 4, his army's eastern wing threw only one long-belated piecemeal attack, but it at least hastened Sedgwick's withdrawal: By dawn Tuesday the federal VI Corps was safely on the Rappahannock's northern side.

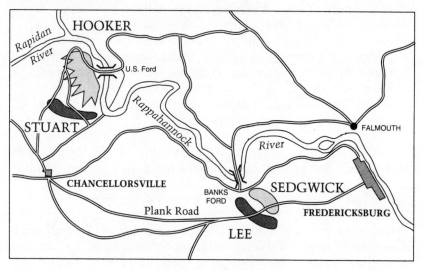

Lee vs. Sedgwick

Lee spent most of that day shifting his forces westward and trying to determine how best to attack Hooker. But long after dark on Tuesday in his tent Fighting Joe held a council of war, after which John Reynolds asked: "What was the use of calling us together at this time of night when he intended to retreat anyhow?"

For so Hooker had decided, and during that rainy night he led the withdrawal to the Rappahannock's northern bank. But there was one brief moment when valor flared anew. When the runoff from rain-filled creeks made the Rappahannock's level rise enough to halt the movement, Darius Couch, second in command, still on the south bank with much of the army, declared: "We will stay where we are and fight it out." Then a peremptory order came from Hooker to bring the rest of the Army of the Potomac across the swollen river as soon as engineers Warren and Comstock had the pontoon bridge ready again.

Within a few days both nations' armies were back in the camps where they had spent the winter, the Confederates near Fredericksburg and the federals around Falmouth. About all that had changed was that roughly 13,000 men were gone from Lee's army and nearly 17,000 from Hooker's. But the Union's losses could be replaced in days, while Southerners' could never be—that of one soldier in particular, Lieutenant General Thomas Jonathan Jackson.

Initially it seemed that Old Jack was out of danger. He was moved to a house near Guiney's Station, where he had met the train nearly a month before when Anna and the baby had come up from Richmond. Now they were back.

On Thursday, the seventh, Reverend Lacy told General Lee that the doctors feared Jackson had pneumonia. The minds of both men may have gone back to Friday night, and the dampness of the ground on which they had all slept, and also to early Saturday morning, when Jackson's sword had fallen to the ground.

Give Jackson his affectionate regards, said Lee to Lacy, "and tell him to make haste and get well, and come back to me as soon as he can. He has lost his left arm, but I have lost my right."

At times the stricken general knew that it was Anna who sat by his bed, and he had words of love for her, but mostly he lingered between sleep and something else, his mutterings suggesting that he thought he was still on the battlefield: "Tell Major Hawks to send forward provisions for the men."

On Saturday, the ninth, Jackson seemed better. He said to Hunter McGuire: "I see from the number of physicians that you think my condition dangerous, but I thank God, if it is His will, that I am ready to go."

On the next day, May 10, he told Sandie Pendleton: "My wish is fulfilled. I have always wished to die on Sunday." For a time, in his delirium, Jackson spoke of Hawks, of Powell Hill. And then, around three o'clock, in a clear voice he said: "Let us cross over the river, and rest under the shade of the trees."

PART THREE

Only the Heroes Are Left

Chapter 24

Vicksburg: *Grant Closes In*

Curiously, among the best comments about Chancellorsville was one made on May 4, well before Fighting Joe Hooker led six of his corps back to the Rappahannock's north bank, and it came in reply to a question: What did General Jackson think of Hooker's plan for the campaign?

"It was, in the main, a good conception, sir," said the man being moved to Guiney's Station in an ambulance wagon, "an excellent plan. But he should not have sent away his cavalry; that was his great blunder. It was that which enabled me to turn him, without his being aware of it, and to take him by his rear. Had he kept his cavalry with him, his plan would have been a very good one."

As it turned out, Major General George Stoneman's 10,000 sabers rode all through the country south of the battle area. But they did it in small, scattered detachments; they were too far to the south to affect General Lee's decisions, and the damage they inflicted was slight.

Hooker not only relieved Stoneman when he returned but blamed him, along with Brigadier General William W. Averell (whose cavalry division Hooker had kept), Oliver Howard, and John Sedgwick, for the Army of the Potomac's defeat. Others, but not President Lincoln, put the responsibility on Fighting Joe. Two main criticisms were that he had lost his nerve too early in the campaign, shifting to the defense without cause to do so, leaving it to Lee to take the initiative; and that he had failed to heed Lincoln's admonition: "Next time, put in all your men." More fault was alleged— much of which the general swept aside later, and privately, when he said: "I was not hurt by a shell, and I was not drunk. For once I lost confidence in Joe Hooker, and that is all there is to it."

Not quite. Opposing Hooker were Robert E. Lee and Thomas J. Jackson at the very time both seemed determined to test the outermost limits of audacity.

They were masters of it. Their men knew it—gloried in it—and gave them and Jeb Stuart, too, their loyalty to the boundaries of their endurance.

Chancellorsville, then, was not so much a battle that Joe Hooker lost as a victory the Army of Northern Virginia *earned*.

"Any victory is dearly bought," Lee had said earlier when Captain Wilbourn had brought him the sad news, "which deprives us of the services of General Jackson, even for a short time." And so felt the entire Confederacy now that Stonewall—as they called Old Jack, though he insisted the name belonged to his old brigade—had crossed over the river.

The warrior was laid to rest with "such ceremonies as a battling people could provide," wrote Douglas Southall Freeman decades afterward, but without the participation of General Lee or the Stonewall Brigade. Hooker's troops were stirring, Lee explained to that unit's disappointed commander. "Jackson," he reminded him, "never neglected a duty while living and he would not rest easier in his grave if his old brigade had left the presence of the enemy to see him buried."

Knowing that his "right arm" could never be replaced, Lee soon reorganized his army into three corps: Longstreet's, with some changes, and the other two commanded by newly promoted lieutenant generals Richard Ewell and Powell Hill. Ewell, with a wooden leg now in place of the one he had lost at Groveton during Second Manassas, had returned as full of fight as ever —which General Lee welcomed, for in the midst of his illness weeks earlier he had decided to take his army away from all the frustrations south of the Rappahannock and lead it northward into Pennsylvania.

"I have Lee's army in one hand and Richmond in the other," Joe Hooker had boasted when he arrived at the Chancellor house, and it was perhaps fortunate that very few heard him say that. On May 8 the *New York World* declared: "Once more the gallant army of the Potomac, controlled by an imbecile department and led by an incompetent general, has been marched to fruitless slaughter." And the condemnation might have been even more vitriolic had it not been for news of a different kind that was beginning to arrive even as both Lee's army and Richmond were slipping from hands that had not, in fact, ever held them.

That compensating news arrived from the west, from below Vicksburg: Ulysses Grant had finally gotten his troops out of the mud on the Mississippi's western bank, and now it looked as though he might have found the solution to his problem.

"Gibraltar of the West," the newspapers called the rebels' fortress at Vicksburg, and for once this was not an exaggeration. Any federal ship's captain who dared to run that lethal four-mile stretch of the river, downstream or up, could expect at least ninety minutes of hell and heavy damage to his vessel if it survived. So Admiral David Farragut had discovered. But he had demonstrated what steady nerves and a willingness to die fighting could accomplish, and his example had given General Grant something new to think about.

Grant needed that. By early April all he had to look back upon was a long string of discouraging failures, none of which had gone unnoticed by Union newspaper reporters. Jesse Grant had been down to the canal-digging site to see what his son was up against, and upon his return home he wrote Elihu Washburne —the Illinois congressman who was perhaps the general's only supporter in Washington other than General-in-Chief Halleck—that maybe Ulysses's West Point classmate William Franklin or Ambrose Burnside ought to be sent to advise him.

Nothing came of that suggestion, but from Washington did come persons who had only thin excuses for staying near enough to General Grant to assess his competence—and possibly to report it if his fondness for whiskey was recurring. Exciting such curiosity may have been the letter flamboyant journalist Murat Halstead wrote to Treasury Secretary Salmon Chase:

> You do once in a while, don't you, say a word to the President, or Stanton, or Halleck, about the conduct of the war? Well, now, for God's sake say that Genl Grant, entrusted with our greatest army, is a jackass in the original package. He is a poor drunken imbecile. He is a poor stick sober, and he is most of the time more than half-drunk, and much of the time idiotically drunk....Grant will fail miserably, hopelessly, eternally. You may look for and calculate his failures, in every position in which he may be placed, as a perfect certainty.

Chase passed Halstead's allegations on to Abraham Lincoln, who found them similar to others he had received. Stale news, the president may have thought, and he put more than this issue in perspective when he stunned a delegation protesting Grant's rumored lapse by remarking: "If I knew what brand of whiskey he drinks, I would send a barrel or so to some other generals."

Ulysses Grant's challenges, then, were not limited to the rebel forces holding Vicksburg or coping with the Mississippi Valley's pro-Confederate geography. He had to demonstrate to everyone that, drunk or sober, he knew what he was doing.

By early April it took the fingers of both hands to count the number of times General Grant had tried to get at the rebel fortress, only to fail. Had he been inclined to, he could have cited the spring's freakish weather and the overflows its rains had caused as excuses. But the future was uppermost in his mind: that, and a plan.

Simply put, Grant's intended path was a fishhook, or the letter J reversed, with Vicksburg on the hook's point and his starting point at the top of the shank, Milliken's Bend, north of his goal and on the Mississippi's western bank. From there he meant to march two of his three corps southward roughly seventy miles along the Louisiana side's chain of lakes and levees to New Carthage. Once enough troops were assembled there, Rear Admiral David Dixon Porter's gunboats would escort transports and barges downriver past Vicksburg's batteries. Next, while Porter's gunners bombarded the Confederates' defenders on the east bank at Grand Gulf, the transports and barges would carry Grant's men from New Carthage down the river and across it to their landing sites. From Grand Gulf he would then advance northward up the hook twenty road miles to its point: Vicksburg.

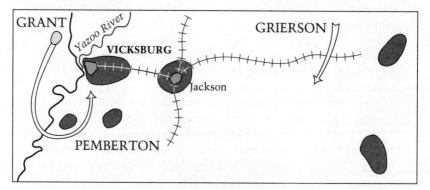

Grant's Final Vicksburg Plan

But General Grant, curiously resembling Fighting Joe in this respect, kept his plan to himself, revealing it only to Admiral Porter, whose cooperation was essential. Porter found it to his liking, but he warned Grant that once past Vicksburg, his vessels could not turn around and move northward against the Mississippi's currents if the venture failed. For a time Grant pondered that risk, then accepted it.

Next to know was the general-in-chief. Fortunately for Grant, Halleck had only one reservation. His purpose was to clear the whole stretch of the Mississippi, a task that would not be completed until Port Hudson, the Confederate strong point 120 or more miles down the river from Vicksburg, was eliminated. Port Hudson was in Louisiana, Nathaniel Banks's department of operations, and Halleck felt it ought to be taken through combined efforts by Grant and Banks. Thereafter, as the general-in-chief saw it, Banks's forces could aid Grant in taking much-stronger Vicksburg. Accordingly, he gave General Grant's river-crossing plan his approval, adding that he wanted Grant to send one corps south, toward Port Hudson, as soon as he reached the Mississippi's eastern bank.

Such was the federal grand strategy. Grant was content to work within it, surely knowing by now that broad plans seldom worked as hoped, and he concentrated on getting his relatively simple one executed. Obviously this required him to share the secret with his three corps commanders. McClernand, whose men would be the first to cross, saw glory and was delighted, while Major General James McPherson and Cump Sherman had misgivings —as well any professional soldier might.

Earlier, Sherman had advised Grant to move the army back to northern Mississippi and revert to the inland route, down the railroad to Jackson, then to Vicksburg. But, Cump added, "whatever plan of action [you] may adopt will receive from me the same zealous cooperation and energetic support as though conceived by myself."

Privately, though, Sherman remained skeptical. "Grant trembles at the approaching thunders of public criticism and must risk anything," he wrote his wife, "and it is my duty to back him." Moreover: "I have no faith in the whole plan."

By contrast, Mississippians were beginning to place more faith in the "galvanized Confederate" who commanded the South's forces in their state: Lieutenant General John C. Pemberton, a native of Pennsylvania with two brothers on the other side. True, Pemberton's wife was a Virginian and he was a believer in state's rights. But South Carolinians had never taken to him during his service there, he had no combat record to speak of, and he had replaced Earl Van Dorn, a Mississippian whose loyalty was unquestioned.

The skill Pemberton had demonstrated in using the few men he had in repelling federal probes, however, had boosted the confidence people in Vicksburg, in particular, had in him. By early April it seemed to his adopted countrymen that the worst was over. From the fortress city's high bluffs anyone could see the Yankees moving northward from the flooded bottoms on the Mississippi's west side, heading for Milliken's Bend and possibly Memphis. Pemberton, too, relaxed. Braxton Bragg's army, he knew, needed men; he started 8,000 northeastward.

Then the euphoria faded. No blue-clad troops were leaving Milliken's Bend. Transports, tugs, and barges were arriving from up the Mississippi. Pemberton quickly recalled his 8,000 and asked western theater commander Joe Johnston for more men.

Pemberton's reversal came not a moment too soon, for after April 17 he began getting reports that a large federal cavalry column was moving southward from La Grange, Tennessee, into eastern Mississippi. Home-guard units alone, it seemed, could not protect the citizens of small towns and farm families from the Yankees' depredations, especially since some of the local defenders were not greatly interested in crossing their own county lines. Such cavalry as he had, Pemberton sent; but he needed more, or at least some threat Johnston or Bragg might generate in the Union raiders' rear.

As April's days sped by, more federal moves distracted John Pemberton. About all he could do, though, was have his men go on digging entrenchments ringing Vicksburg and warn the gunners at Warrenton and Grand Gulf, as well as those in the batteries on the Confederate Gibraltar's bluffs, that Grant was about to start something—that, and hope that help would come in time.

A music teacher and sometime bandleader from Jacksonville, Illinois, particularly a man who had disliked horses since one had kicked him in the face as a boy, was a most unlikely leader for the 1,700-man federal cavalry brigade then plunging steadily southward in eastern Mississippi. Equally improbable was it that any of the men riding under Colonel Benjamin H. Grierson's command had ever expected to find themselves doing what they were in fact engaged in only a year and a half after they had enlisted in the Union army; like the quiet man who led them, they had grown up in little towns in Illinois and Iowa where calm and decency had always prevailed.

Grierson's mission was simple: to cut Pemberton's railroad supply line east of Jackson, severing Vicksburg's linkages with Meridian and Alabama, Georgia, Virginia, and the Carolinas. At first, Grant had thought of it as a strike only volunteers should make, knowing that no federal troopers had ever ridden so deep into Mississippi's heartland before and suspecting, perhaps, that once there, they would have no escape route. But as his overall plan for enveloping Vicksburg evolved, Grant saw the cavalry's deep penetration as a critical element, and he ordered a force sent: Grierson's, as it turned out.

If Colonel Grierson knew his command was to be sacrificed in the event he could not find some way out, the music teacher kept quiet about it. But his men suspected they were going to "play smash with the railroads," and the five days' rations in their haversacks were all they had to count on, so perhaps it was not surprising that whenever they saw an opportunity to live off the land, they seized it, especially in the first few days when Grierson's three regiments were still well over 100 miles north of their objective. A sergeant wrote:

> The column halted for a few moments in front of the dwelling of a poor widow said by all her neighbors to be loyal to our cause, and immediately her yard and house were filled by a crowd of thieves (I cannot call them soldiers, for shame) who instantly appropriated everything they could carry. Some attacked her poultry, chasing the chickens and geese through her very house, and stones and clubs flew in all directions. Others butchered her hogs and splitting them in two, buckled them on their saddles, still warm and dripping with blood. Others took fence rails and burst in the doors of her smokehouse and granary, and in a few moments every morsel of sustenance which a hard year's work had brought her had disappeared as if before a pack of ravenging wolves. The poor lone woman wrung her hands and cried in an agony of despair and terror, and prayed to God to help her, while her children sobbed and screamed in a perfect frenzy of fear.

Yet even so sympathetic an observer added:

> This is the most disagreeable part of a soldier's duty, for taking the all of a defenseless citizen when the women cry and the men turn pale, appropriating the last horse of a poor old woman, and driving off a man's team from before his plow, certainly seems to be tolerably small work for a soldier, but then what is all war but one monstrous evil by the use of which we hope to overcome a much greater, and so long as it tends to subdue the rebellion I suppose the means are justified by the end.

So, now, Ulysses Grant understood war to be, and so did Cump Sherman, who would later say, simply, that war was hell. And so it must have seemed to Julia Dent Grant and Fred, twelve, and

Ulysses, Jr., ten, on the night of April 16 as they sat on the deck of the steamboat *Magnolia*, safely beyond the range of rebel guns on Vicksburg's bluff, watching while Admiral Porter ran seven gunboats, three transports, and a steam ram through plunging fire from the fortress city's batteries.

Porter, hoping to slip by unnoticed, had admonished his captains to steam slowly with no lights showing but—in case stealth failed—to protect pilot houses and boilers by placing wetted bales of hay on decks. Confederates did spot the flotilla, and they set blazes on both banks of the broad river to illuminate targets for gunners on the eastern heights. This silhouetting, vulnerability to eddies because of slow speed, and awkwardness because of coal barges lashed to the gunboats' starboard sides made Porter's vessels seem to be sitting ducks.

Early in the brisk exchange of shells the flashes and booming were enough to send young Ulysses below. But Fred remained, and Grant's wife gripped her husband's hand until the noise eased off. By then, Charles Dana, the observer the authorities in Washington had sent to watch Grant, had counted 525 shots fired at Porter's column. And soon after the gunners high on Vicksburg's bluff ceased firing, from downstream at Warrenton and Grand Gulf came sounds of disturbingly fierce bombardment.

From the landing General Grant galloped southward along the Mississippi's western bank, pressing on through the night until he reached New Carthage near noon on the seventeenth. There he found Porter's ships—all but one a transport. The rest had taken much punishment, yet there had been no fatalities and only thirteen men wounded.

Now, for the first time, Grant had real conviction that the plan on which he was staking everything might just work. McClernand's troops were completing their long march down from Milliken's Bend, Porter was getting a few more ships past Vicksburg's batteries, Colonel Grierson's raid was under way. Soon it would be time to make the crossing to the Mississippi's east bank at Grand Gulf. First, though, Grant wanted to give Pemberton another distraction. To Cump Sherman he wrote:

> The effect of a heavy demonstration [above Vicksburg] would be good as far as the enemy are concerned, but I am loth to order it, because it would be hard to make our own troops understand that only a demonstration was intended and our people at home would characterize it as a repulse. I therefore leave it to you whether to make such a demonstration.

Sherman's quick reply:

> The troops will all understand the purpose and not be hurt by the repulse. The people of the country must find out the truth as best they can; it is none of their business. You are engaged in a hazardous enterprise, and for good reason wish to divert attention; that is sufficient for me, and it shall be done....As to the reports in the newspapers, we must scorn them, else they will ruin us and our country. They are as much enemies to good government as the secesh, and between the two I like the secesh best, because they are a brave, open enemy and not a set of sneaking, croaking scoundrels.

What might have happened if John Pope could have had such a loyal associate at Second Manassas, no one could ever do more than wonder. This Grant-Sherman meeting of the minds resembled that of Lee and Jackson, or at least suggested something of the sort could be developing, for the feint Sherman's men carried out on April 30 and May 1—together with Grierson's cutting of Vicksburg's railroad link to the east, earlier—kept John Pemberton off balance long enough for Grant to change his plan.

Confederate batteries at Grand Gulf, Admiral Porter found out when his gunboats probed them, could not be silenced. Very well, said Grant in effect, we will find another place. It was Bruinsburg, nine miles or so downriver from Grand Gulf, and by noon on April 30 Grant had more than 23,000 troops on the Mississippi's eastern bank. Years afterward, he wrote:

> When this was effected I felt a degree of relief scarcely ever equalled since....I was now in the enemy's country, with a vast river and the stronghold of Vicksburg between me and my base of supplies. But I was on dry ground on the same side of the river with the enemy. All the campaigns, labors, and hardships from the month of December previous to this time that had been made and endured, were for the accomplishment of this one object.

Yet this was only the end of the beginning, the advent of new challenges, the most immediate of which was Grant's lack of a secure supply line. He solved this problem by using every vehicle he could find to carry ammunition; limiting requisition of everything else to hard bread, coffee, and salt; finally, by deciding to "make the country furnish the balance."

General Banks removed another concern by informing Grant that he could not begin a cooperative movement before May 10. Earlier, General-in-Chief Halleck had ended a message by saying that Grant would have to judge circumstances for himself. With that assurance, Grant now considered himself free to commit his entire force to his own goal: Vicksburg.

"Galvanized" Confederate John Pemberton's efforts had not prevented Ben Grierson's cavalry column from ending its sixteen-day, 600-mile ride safely at Baton Rouge, nor had he kept Yankee gunboats and transports from getting past Vicksburg's batteries before that; and with Grant ashore in his rear while Sherman was still near enough to cause trouble, he was running out of ideas. Pemberton was low on troops. From Richmond came promises. General Johnston sent advice.

Pemberton's cavalry was scattered, chasing Grierson's elusive raiders. Brigadier General John S. Bowen had moved his 5,500 men from Grand Gulf to the east, toward Port Gibson, to block the northeastward advance of Grant's 23,000. By May 2, Bowen's force had been brushed aside, and he had evacuated Grand Gulf as well; Grant's columns kept moving northeastward.

President Davis had ordered Pemberton to hold Vicksburg; Johnston continued to urge him to unite his men to whip Grant, implying that Vicksburg mattered little, adding: "Success will give back what was abandoned to win it." Pemberton decided to please both superiors by holding Vicksburg and stopping the federals at the Big Black River. But there was one possibility Pemberton overlooked: that Grant would dare to cut his forces off from any base at all.

Sherman got a shock on May 9 when he reached Grand Gulf and learned that Grant not only meant to live off the land but that he had been doing it for more than a week. But the army commander revealed some anxiety on the eleventh in a message to one of his three corps commanders, Major General James McPherson:

> At [Raymond] you will use your utmost exertions to secure all the subsistence stores that may be there, as well as in the vicinity. We must fight the enemy before our rations fail, and we are equally bound to make our rations last as long as possible. Upon one occasion you made two days' rations last seven. We may have to do the same thing again.

But Raymond, "Jamie" McPherson's objective, was a town on the way to Jackson, not Vicksburg. Had Grant changed his plan again? No, not quite. Ben Grierson's cavalry raiders had cut the railroad east of Jackson, but Grant intended to control it, lest the rebels try to reinforce Pemberton. By the fourteenth he and his forces were in Mississippi's capital, and Sherman's troops were wrecking the railroad facilities and everything else of value to the Confederate war effort.

While Grant was in Jackson, he received two messages, each important, but in different ways. The first was from Secretary of War Edwin Stanton, addressed to Charles Dana, apparently in reply to the reports on Grant the observer had been filing. General Grant "has the full confidence of the Government, is expected to enforce his authority, and will be firmly and heartily supported," wrote Stanton. This surely was enormously reassuring, coming as it did so soon after Murat Halstead and others had done their best to get the supposed drunkard removed from command. But perhaps even more gladdening to Grant was the other message, in which General Johnston told Pemberton:

> I have lately arrived, and learn that General Sherman is between us, with four divisions, at Clinton [west of Jackson]. It is important to re-establish communications, that you may be re-enforced. If practicable, come up in his rear at once. To beat such a detachment would be of immense value. The troops here could co-operate. All the strength you can quickly assemble should be brought. Time is all important.

And time, General Grant realized instantly, was even more important to him. He ordered Sherman to stay at Jackson and finish tearing up the railroad tracks. The rest of his forces he sent westward. Having abandoned his supply line, he was now ignoring the presence of whatever force Johnston might have on his northern flank: Pemberton's destruction was his new goal, and he would have to attain it in a hurry.

One of the copies of Johnston's message reached Pemberton, but it merely added to his perplexity. Earlier, he had moved enough strength east of the Big Black River to strike Grant's supply line if it could be found, delay the federal advance, or cooperate with Johnston. By early morning of May 16 he had three of his divisions on Champion's Hill, just south of the railroad and about halfway between Vicksburg and Jackson, but he remained uncertain about what he should do with those 17,500 troops. Events settled the question: Word came that Grant's forces were headed straight toward his position.

But Pemberton was on the wrong side of the Big Black, not along its western shore, where the Yankees would be easier to kill as they tried to cross. In his rear was a creek with only one bridge over it. And with federals approaching Champion's Hill on three roads, there was nothing he could do but fight.

The northern end of the Confederate defense line proved to be something of a magnet. First to be drawn to it early on the morning of May 16 were troops from Brigadier General Alvin P. Hovey's division, part of John McClernand's corps. Next came General Grant, who could see only that the rugged terrain gave the rebel defenders all the advantages and that the skirmishing was turning into something much more serious.

With Hovey's men stalled, Grant fed more brigades into an effort to get around Pemberton's northern flank. Concurrently, he ordered McClernand, south of there, to attack, but this was one of those days on which the political general was not in a mood to obey orders.

Pemberton, sensing that the federal divisions facing the southern portion of his line were inert, shifted some of his units from there to the northern magnet. He tried repeatedly to get Major General William W. Loring to send more, but Loring proved to be as lethargic as McClernand. Even so, Pemberton massed enough troops to turn the battle into a slugging match on ground that neither side seemed able to control.

General Grant had already demonstrated that he believed in the maxim *Hit Hard, Hit Often, and Keep on Hitting.* That day he employed it again, and by four o'clock that afternoon the federal blows were sending the Confederates pouring toward the bridge over Baker's Creek. Behind them they left eleven guns and Loring's division, which evaded Grant's pursuing forces and eventually joined Joe Johnston up north of Jackson.

Champion's Hill proved a costly fight: Grant's casualties exceeded 2,400, and Pemberton lost more than 3,600 men. On the seventeenth, Grant's forces whipped the Confederates again at the Big Black River, reducing the rebel defenders by another 1,700 at a cost of less than 300 and opening the way to Haines Bluff.

Grant and Cump Sherman got there on the nineteenth. As they looked down at the Union gunboats on the Yazoo River north of Vicksburg, Sherman turned to the army commander and said: "Until this moment I never thought your expedition a success. I never could see the end clearly until now. But this is a campaign. This is a success if we never take the town."

That day, Grant had tried, attacking Vicksburg's defenses on the theory the Confederates might be too demoralized to take another hard smash. In this he was mistaken. On May 22, Grant launched a carefully planned assault coordinated with a two-hour bombardment of Vicksburg delivered by Rear Admiral David Dixon Porter's gunboats on the Mississippi. Again McClernand disappointed Grant at a critical moment; the attempt had to be called off. In these two tries Grant had lost more than 4,100 men. "I now determined," he wrote afterward, "upon a regular siege—to 'out-camp the enemy,' as it were, and to incur no more losses."

This was what General Joseph E. Johnston had been fearing all along. On the day after Champion's Hill he had said so in a message to Pemberton:

> If...you are invested at Vicksburg you must ultimately surrender. Under such circumstances, instead of losing both troops and place, we must, if possible, save the troops. If it is not too late, evacuate Vicksburg and its dependencies, and march them to the northeast.

But on the retreat westward Pemberton's men had gathered all the food and herds of cattle, pigs, and sheep they could take with them into Vicksburg's nine miles of lines. And Grant's columns had closed in too quickly for a breakout to seem feasible. Once again events had settled the question in Pemberton's mind of whether to obey the general commanding in the west or the president in Richmond.

If Johnston wanted the fortress city's garrison saved, he would have to assemble a relief force large enough to reach Vicksburg in time. But he was in a command position he no longer wanted and for which he may not have been strong enough physically. Jefferson Davis had been ill and preoccupied with matters in the east. So, as before, John Pemberton would have to get along as best he could with only the resources he had.

The more General Grant saw of the rebel defense lines and the rippling ridgelines and hollows east of Vicksburg, the more men he realized he would need in order to "out-camp" Pemberton. General-in-Chief Halleck ordered units rushed from Missouri and Ohio and told Rosecrans, still at Murfreesboro: "If you can do nothing [aggressive] yourself, a portion of your troops must be sent to Grant's relief."

Washington had apparently given up hope that Nathaniel Banks could be of any help. Earlier, instead of committing his forces to the capture of Port Hudson and cooperating with Grant in the Vicksburg campaign, Banks had launched a drive to clear the bayous west of

New Orleans of a tiny collection of rebels led by another Shenandoah Valley veteran, Major General Richard Taylor. Emboldened by that success (Banks's first as a general) and supported by Porter's gunboats steaming up the Red River, he chased Taylor all the way to Alexandria in central Louisiana, sending back at least 2,000 wagons filled mostly with bales of cotton before he returned his attention to Port Hudson.

Old Brains was not inclined to give Banks any credit for working the wrong problem. Nor was he pleased when he learned that on May 27 the former governor of Massachusetts had finally tested Port Hudson's defenses: Banks accomplished nothing, but lost nearly 2,000 men in botched assaults.

In this fight were two regiments of free blacks and freed slaves Banks had recruited in southwestern Louisiana and styled the Louisiana Home Guards. At Port Hudson one man in four was a casualty, but that day they won the respect of white federals and the general who had given them their chance to earn it.

Now—just when the general-in-chief was hard-pressed to reinforce Grant—Banks was asking for more men. None were to be had, so he placed Port Hudson under siege.

All along John Pemberton had wanted Edmund Kirby Smith, now commanding forces in the vast Trans-Mississippi Department, to send Dick Taylor eastward to attack Grant's movement along the river's western shore. At about the same time, Kirby Smith was asking Pemberton to assist Taylor in stopping Banks's drive into central Louisiana. Again "cooperation" failed. Once the Yankees had left Alexandria, however, Taylor probed Milliken's Bend; the gesture was noble but weak, and it came too late.

Pemberton also needed cavalry diversions made to disrupt attempts to reinforce Grant. Earl Van Dorn could not respond; a lady in a West Tennessee town where he made his headquarters had given him a welcome warm enough to cause her husband to use a Smith & Wesson to shoot him dead, and his command, in which Texan A. W. Sparks was serving, was being reorganized.

And so it went, with both sides seeking men but only the North able to find any. This left the situation in the west in a stalemate. Rosecrans might have broken it by attacking Bragg in Tennessee, but the federal general was still massing supplies and daring Halleck to relieve him of command. If anything was to be done to bring matters to a decision, the effort would have to be made in the east.

Chapter 25

Stuart Leaves Lee Blind in Pennsylvania

W hat next, General Lee wondered after Chancellorsville. "I considered the problem in every possible phase," he said later, "and to my mind, it resolved itself into a choice of one of two things— either to retire to Richmond and stand a siege, which must ultimately have ended in surrender, or to invade Pennsylvania."

Lee's army had faced starvation all winter. Not until harvest time could Virginia provide more than bare subsistence. Protecting recently planted crops from Yankee devastation was essential; the best way to do that was to draw the federals out of the state, to Pennsylvania, where Northerners could provide food for Southern men and animals. But taking the war North obliged Lee to keep every soldier he had, and for a time it was not clear that he could.

General Longstreet had grown overly fond of independent command during his months of absence from the Army of Northern Virginia, and he suggested to the authorities in Richmond that his corps be sent westward to augment Braxton Bragg's forces facing William Rosecrans's southeast of Nashville. Lee could afford the detachment of two divisions, the Georgian argued; he had whipped Hooker at Chancellorsville without them. No, he was told, invading Pennsylvania as part of Lee's army was a more productive use for his divisions. Longstreet accepted that decision reluctantly, and his glum mood was not brightened by Lee's choice of Virginians Dick Ewell and Powell Hill as corps commanders.

"My old war horse," General Lee had termed Longstreet at Sharpsburg, yet Jackson had seemed closer to the army commander in spirit, both rival and partner in audacity, his "right arm." Into this vacuum the ambitious Longstreet now tried to move. Yes, strategically the Pennsylvania campaign would be offensive, he conceded, but let the tactics employed be defensive; let there be more Fredericksburgs.

General Lee had listened politely, then drawn his plan to meet the circumstances as he saw them. First he would have to slip away from the ridgelines west of Fredericksburg without drawing the attention either of observers in Professor Lowe's balloons or Hooker's scouts. If that could be done, next he would move up the Shenandoah Valley past Winchester, cross the Potomac and western Maryland, then slash northeastward from Chambersburg to the Susquehanna and Pennsylvania's capital city, Harrisburg. This would cut the federals' main railroad connections with the west and also enable Lee to threaten both Baltimore and Philadelphia. Joe Hooker's army? Well, it would have to follow Lee north, away from Richmond and completely out of Virginia. Washington? Not important and to be avoided, for no food or forage could be found near there.

There would surely be a battle somewhere in Pennsylvania. But Lee hoped another victory over Hooker, in the North, would encourage dissidents in the Old Northwest, Copperheads, and others advocating peace to place irresistible pressure on the Union's president and Congress to concede the failure of coercion and accept the independence of the Confederacy. No longer did British or French intervention seem likely, yet the hope might be rekindled. At a minimum, Lee's men and horses might gain a summer living off the land in Pennsylvania's lush Cumberland Valley; that alone made the risks worth taking.

Decisions made, action followed. Jeb Stuart's cavalry was concentrated near Brandy Station. From there he could send his troopers northward, east of the Blue Ridge, and both screen the army's movement down the Shenandoah Valley and hold the gaps. Of the three corps commanders, Dick Ewell knew the Valley best: his corps would lead the advance. Next, Longstreet. Powell Hill's corps Lee would leave at Fredericksburg, stretched to cover the lines as the other units abandoned them, with orders to deceive Hooker to the last moment.

But Fighting Joe knew as early as May 27, a week before the first Confederate departed, that Lee was up to something. Horace Greeley's *New York Tribune* had the story almost that soon: Lee was headed for Pennsylvania. And by June 5, Hooker's balloonists were reporting deserted camps.

That day, the Army of the Potomac's commander sent a long message to the president, one in which he asked for guidance as to what the government wanted him to do with his army. Stay on your side of the Rappahannock, Lincoln advised him, adding:

> I would not take any risk of getting entangled upon the river, like an ox jumped half over a fence and liable to be torn by dogs front and rear, without a fair chance to gore one way or kick the other.

Well, fine, but part of the ox was already over the fence. General Hooker had thrown pontoon bridges across the Rappahannock down near Deep Run, and Sedgwick was back on the Fredericksburg side, where his troops had been a month earlier. Lee's lines were indeed formidable, Uncle John reported, so Hooker left his men in place and turned his attention upriver to Culpeper, where Jeb Stuart's cavalry was said to be getting ready for a raid.

Not quite. Stuart was near Brandy Station, six miles or so to the northeast of Culpeper, and on June 8 he held a review of his nearly 10,000 troopers with the army commander present. Though pleased by the spectacle, however, Lee asked Stuart to abbreviate it lest it tire the horses.

General Lee returned late the next day, for a federal cavalry force almost as large as Stuart's was attacking at the very time the Confederate horsemen were supposed to be riding northward. Traveller was carrying the army commander toward the loudest sounds of firing when the general saw "Rooney," his son, commander of one of Stuart's brigades, being carried to the rear with a serious leg wound.

Union Major General George Stoneman's troopers had struck early and hard on the morning of the ninth, surprising Stuart's widely dispersed units even though the federal horsemen had not expected the Confederates would be where they were. First to recover from the shock had been Stuart. Skillfully, calmly, he drew his forces in to defend Fleetwood Hill, where gray-clad cavalry had passed in review the day before.

For fourteen hours in all there were charges and countercharges aplenty. Brandy Station would be called the greatest cavalry battle ever fought, though Stuart's artillery, firing canister into the flank of a Union division threatening the critical position, made a stunning difference. By sundown the federals were withdrawing, having lost more than 900 men and inflicted perhaps 500 casualties. Both sides claimed victory, neither with validity: Stuart held the battlefield, but for the first time blue-clad troopers had at least matched his in both concentrated force and valor displayed.

Jeb Stuart, however, considered himself humiliated. For such a proud soldier this was only natural, even if unjustified. Yet the feeling would linger past the next day, when he moved northward, and it would not only persist during the next few weeks but cause General Lee more grief than anyone in early June could have foretold.

"Will it not promote the true interests of the cause for me to march to Richmond at once?" Joseph Hooker asked Lincoln in a message sent on the tenth, the day after Brandy Station. Almost at once came the president's response:

> If left to me, I would not go south of Rappahannock upon Lee's moving north of it. If you had Richmond invested today, you would not be able to take it in twenty days; meanwhile your communications, and with them your army, would be ruined. I think Lee's army, and not Richmond, is your sure objective point. If he comes toward the Upper Potomac, follow on his flank and on his inside track, shortening your lines while he lengthens his. Fight him, too, when opportunity offers. If he stays where he is, fret him and fret him.

But Hooker dithered and dithered. Admittedly, abandoning Falmouth was no easy thing: Hooker had 11,000 wounded to move, and as Chancellorsville had proved, Fighting Joe was hardly gifted in reacting once the initiative was Lee's. And, on June 14, a message signed A. Lincoln hardly helped:

> If the head of Lee's army is at Martinsburg and the tail of it on the Plank road between Fredericksburg and Chancellorsville, the animal must be very slim somewhere. Could you not break him?

Hooker replied, in part:

> I do not feel like making a move for an enemy until I am satisfied as to his whereabouts. To proceed to Winchester and have him make his appearance elsewhere would subject me to ridicule.

So might lethargy, though by June 15, Hooker had his headquarters at Fairfax Station, near Washington, and his army was moving up behind him. But his messages continued to have a plaintive tone, as in this one on June 16:

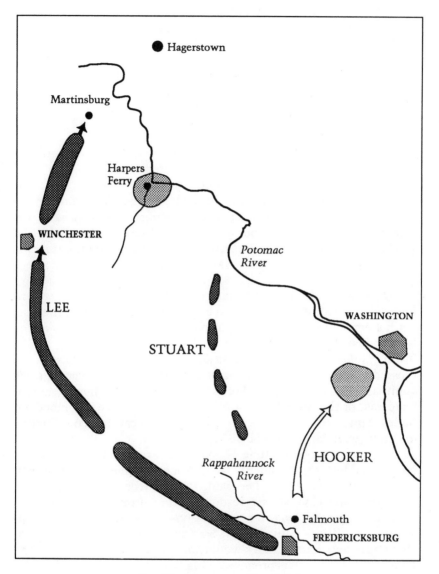

Ewell's Advance to Maryland

You have long been aware, Mr. President, that I have not enjoyed the confidence of the major-general [Halleck] commanding the army, and I can assure you so long as this continues we may look in vain for success, especially as future operations will require our relations to be more dependent upon each other than heretofore.

Lincoln replied quickly and decisively:

> To remove all misunderstanding, I now place you in the strict military relation to General Halleck of a commander of one of the armies to the general-in-chief of all the armies. I have not intended differently, but as it seems to be differently understood, I shall direct him to give you orders and you to obey them.

This was clear enough, or ought to have been, though it bordered on being disingenuous. Lincoln had selected Hooker to command the Army of the Potomac without consulting Secretary of War Stanton or Halleck or anyone; he had surprised everyone by so doing; never had he hesitated to communicate directly with his appointee, nor had he discouraged equally direct replies. Suddenly, what Hooker had taken for granted was gone, and just at the time his need for sympathetic support was peaking.

Dick Ewell often boasted that he had learned all there was to know about leading fifty dragoons but had forgotten everything else, yet his performance during his corps' advance northward down the Shenandoah Valley left little to be desired. After capturing nearly 3,400 Yankee troops and twenty-eight guns at Winchester, he crossed the Potomac and swept into Maryland. But General Lee's "animal" was indeed thin. Longstreet's corps was moving northward east of the Blue Ridge, directed to cross into the Shenandoah Valley if molested, its flank guarded by Stuart's cavalry. Powell Hill's divisions were far to the south.

So matters stood on June 17 when the army commander wrote an unusual letter to President Davis. Peace movements in the North ought to be encouraged, Lee said, for the federals were growing stronger while Confederate resources were diminishing, and "we have no right to look for exemptions from the military consequences." It was a mistake for Southern newspapers to proclaim that under no circumstances would the seceded states return to the Union: "When peace is proposed to us," wrote Lee, "it will be time enough to discuss its terms, and it is not the part of prudence to spurn the proposition in advance."

Having unburdened himself of these thoughts, General Lee, in his other letters to Davis, proposed movements designed to force Grant to abandon the siege of Vicksburg. Fret and fret Washington, Lee seemed to be suggesting. If General Beauregard brought only a skeleton force from Charleston up to Culpeper "those people" might divert divisions from the west to defend their capital's southern approaches while Lee kept Hooker's army well north of the Potomac.

By June 22, however, Fighting Joe was still south of the river. Dick Ewell was gathering food, threats to his corps' safety were minimal, and Lee was thinking of ordering him to advance eastward to the Susquehanna.

At about this time Jeb Stuart told the army commander that he wanted to take the bulk of his cavalry eastward and operate in Hooker's rear as the federals moved northward. For a while, Lee hesitated. Cavalry, he believed, should provide a buffer between Ewell and Hooker—screening, scouting, keeping Ewell and head-quarters informed of whatever moves the Yankees made.

General Lee never wavered from that conviction. In the orders he gave Stuart, however, that primary mission apparently got diluted by attempts to cover contingencies in which the cavalry commander had to be given discretion. Stuart, still nettled by newspapers' criticism of his having been surprised at Brandy Station, was in a mood to smite the Yankees hard enough to make the editors eat their words. And he seemed to assume that Lee was permitting him to operate as he pleased.

Here, on the smallest of scales, was 1860 all over again: emotion overcoming reason. And from this lapse, as had from the host of original sins, much tragic mischief would flow.

Human frailty was already bedeviling the North, though the dispute was not over what to do but real estate. The general-in-chief triggered it, trying to meet Hooker's often expressed cry for more information, by mentioning Harpers Ferry in a message. To that place federal troops driven out of Winchester had retreated. Hooker wanted them. No, Halleck insisted in his wires, never: Harpers Ferry was a thorn in Lee's side, an invaluable threat to his long and vulnerable supply line.

Such squabbling was precisely what Lincoln had sought to eliminate. However, though Hooker's forces were assembling north of the Potomac at Frederick, Maryland, on June 27, Harpers Ferry was still so much on his mind that he wired Halleck:

My original instructions require me to cover Harper's Ferry and Washington. I have now imposed upon me, in addition, an enemy in my front of more than my number. I beg to be understood, respectfully, but firmly, that I am unable to comply with this condition with the means at my disposal, and earnestly request that I may at once be relieved from the position I occupy.

Was this a bluff? Or was the man still too much in awe of Lee? Or was Hooker simply burned out?

None of these, suggested Porter Alexander when he wrote his history of the war he had fought in. Lincoln, Stanton, and Halleck, he asserted, had decided right after Chancellorsville that they would never allow Hooker to fight another battle; for political reasons they felt they could not remove him, so they would fret him and fret him until he quit. Had they?

Well, if the federal authorities lacked confidence in the Army of the Potomac's commander, they had enough sound reasons to relieve him before he asked them to. Yet Lincoln had urged Hooker to consider Lee's army his object, to fight him, even to break him at the weakest point in the length of the "animal."

In any case, Halleck replied to Hooker's wire: "As you were appointed to this command by the President, I have no power to relieve you. Your dispatch has been duly referred for Executive action."

It came swiftly. At three o'clock on the morning of June 28, Colonel James A. Hardie awakened Major General George Gordon Meade and gave him orders appointing him as commander of the Army of the Potomac, together with a letter of instructions from the general-in-chief in which Halleck both assured Meade of full support and made clear his mission and authority:

> You will not be hampered by minute instructions from these headquarters. Your army is free to act as you may deem proper under the circumstances as they arise. You will, however, keep in view the important fact that the Army of the Potomac is the covering army of Washington as well as the army of operation against the invading forces of the rebels. You will, therefore, maneuver and fight in such a manner as to cover the capital and also Baltimore, as far as circumstances will admit. Should General Lee move upon either of these places, it is expected that you will either anticipate him or arrive with him so as to give him battle.

"Well," said General Meade to Hardie, "I've been tried and condemned without a hearing, and I suppose I shall have to go to execution."

Joe Hooker took removal without complaint, never telling anyone whether he had been bluffing. Unlike other generals guillotined—Buell, McClellan, Pope—he would fight again, but not in the east and not as an army commander.

While the career of Fighting Joe wound down, Longstreet brought his men to the banks of the Potomac. Before fording the river they removed their trousers and shoes and were carrying them in bundles over their heads when a bevy of "young and guileless" Maryland ladies turned up to watch the crossing.

Having added a refreshingly different line or two to the history they were making, Longstreet's troops slogged on to the northeast, into Pennsylvania, where Ewell's divisions and Hill's were far ahead of them. On the night of June 28, Ewell was at Carlisle, but Confederate cavalrymen—not Stuart's—were on the west bank of the Susquehanna, about fourteen miles to the east, opposite Harrisburg. Jubal Early's division was at York with a brigade twelve miles or so east of there on the river at Wrightsville.

Could General Jackson have known that the Army of Northern Virginia was attaining the goals he had proposed more than a year earlier, surely he would have been well pleased. General Lee might have been also except for one thing: Stuart's brigades had vanished. Not a word had the cavalryman sent back. Lee was blind, wondering where Hooker's forces were, growing more anxious by the hour.

Stuart had left Salem early on June 25. By the morning of the twenty-seventh his men had covered only thirty-four miles in forty hours, and they were still more than forty miles south of the Potomac. When they did cross it, they had been gone seventy-two hours, and all Stuart learned was that the federal army might be headed for Frederick.

It was time for Stuart to get back into contact with Lee and Ewell, but on June 28 he had no way of knowing where either general might be. That day, his men were on one of the Union army's supply routes; they could not block it for long, but they tarried enough to capture 125 brand-new federal wagons drawn by strong mules and filled with—among other luxuries—hams and bottles of whiskey.

A splendid gift this train of wagons and smartly harnessed mules would make for General Lee, or so Stuart seemed to think, for he kept it with him as he headed northward to cut another federal supply line: the Baltimore & Ohio Railroad. But the cavalryman was stretching discretion to its limits. Worse, he was ignoring the passage of time, letting it get away from him while paroling Yankee prisoners, forgetting that the 125 wagons would slow his pace to that of infantry.

Major General George Gordon Meade's main problem upon his

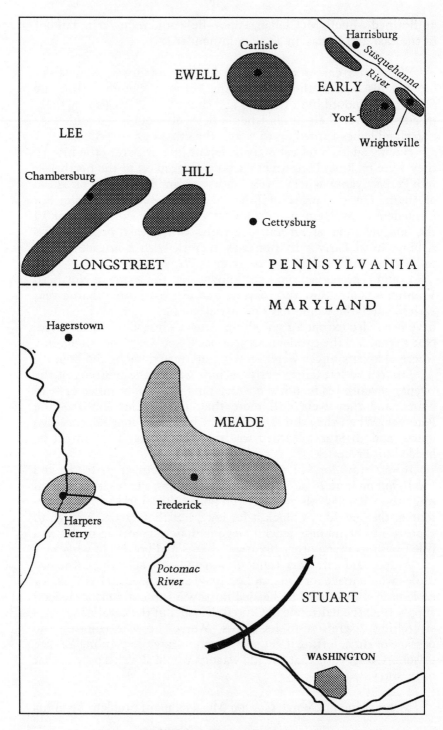

High Tide in Pennsylvania

assumption of command of the Army of the Potomac was that Joe Hooker had not told him or anyone else what his plans were. In talking with Hooker on the morning of June 28, Meade discerned the reason: No plan existed.

When I Corps commander John Reynolds arrived to pay his respects, Meade took out a map and pointed to Emmitsburg, a town just south of the Maryland-Pennsylvania line, and ordered him to march there. Reynolds understood that his mission was merely a probe, that his new army commander was establishing the westernmost end of a line not yet selected, that he was to fall back if he could not find an advantageous position for battle. And, John Reynolds learned, northward behind him Meade was sending Oliver Howard's XI Corps.

Vague though Meade's instructions may have been on the twenty-eighth, by the next day he had all his corps moving. That night, he wrote to his wife Margaret:

> We are marching as fast as we can to relieve Harrisburg but have to keep a sharp lookout that the rebels don't turn around and get at Washington and Baltimore in our rear. They have a cavalry force in our rear, destroying railroads, etc., with a view to getting me to turn back, but I shall not do it. I am going straight at them and will settle this thing one way or the other.

"General Meade," said Lee when told of the command change, "will commit no blunder in my front, and if I make one he will make haste to take advantage of it."

General Lee had learned that Hooker was replaced not from Jeb Stuart but from a spy, one to whom he had listened on the night of June 28 in his tent at Chambersburg only because of Longstreet's assurance that the man known merely as Harrison was reliable. The civilian had revealed much more: Federal forces were at Frederick, north of the Potomac, and near the passes on South Mountain.

Unsettling though this spy's report may have been, it was precisely the kind of information General Lee had been waiting impatiently for Stuart to furnish. Setting aside his concerns as to where his cavalry might be and why its leader had sent him no news, Lee promptly sent out orders changing the entire thrust of the campaign. Ewell was to abandon Carlisle and York and head southward for Cashtown or Gettysburg. And instead of moving eastward behind Ewell, now first Powell Hill and then Longstreet were to hurry their corps toward the same places.

On the next day, the rainy and gloomy twenty-ninth of June, Lee's mood matched the weather. The irony of the situation was cause enough: Jackson had said Hooker lost Chancellorsville because he had no cavalry, and now Lee had none. And even more galling, perhaps, had been the necessity of taking such drastic remedial action merely on the word of a spy. But he went for a walk, and when he returned, he was as calm and composed as ever.

"Tomorrow, gentlemen," Lee told some officers, "we will go over to Gettysburg and see what General Meade is after."

Whether or not the federal high command had been preparing the guillotine for Joe Hooker, Abraham Lincoln had the slanting blade ready to claim William Rosecrans's head. Since the battle of Stones River in early January, Old Rosy had kept his army at Murfreesboro, south of Nashville, though rebel General Bragg's forces were only twenty miles or so away. To General-in-Chief Halleck's repeated proddings Rosecrans had replied that he was accumulating supplies before undertaking a campaign in terrain much too rugged for anyone in Washington to envision.

Now June was half-gone. Halleck, nudged by Lincoln, wired Rosecrans: "Is it your intention to make an immediate movement forward? A definite answer, yes or no, is required."

"If immediate means tonight or tomorrow, no," replied Old Rosy. "If it means as soon as all things are ready, say five days, yes." This meant June 21, but not until the twenty-fourth did he move. When he did, his plan was as complex as his stockpiling had been meticulous.

He employed not one but two feints, left and right of Bragg's positions just north of the Duck River at Shelbyville and Wartrace. But the main federal force was bound for neither place; its mission was to get well to the east of Bragg's forces, obliging him to retreat.

George Thomas's corps was to make the decisive thrust. In it was a brigade led by Colonel John Wilder, the officer who had surrendered Munfordville to the rebels during their drive into Kentucky back in the fall of 1862. Like Stuart, Wilder wanted to redeem his reputation. And though Wilder's troops were infantrymen, he paid for the new Spencer carbines they carried and mounted them on 2,000 of the 43,000-odd horses Rosecrans had accumulated.

Heavy rainfall, beginning as Rosecrans's complicated plan was being set in motion, might have been excuse enough for more delay, but he was indeed ready. So was George Thomas, who let Wilder's improvised mounted infantry lead the way, knowing that horses could get into a key pass infantry could not reach for hours to come; and it would be once-disgraced John Wilder, striking deep in Bragg's rear, who made Rosecrans's campaign a success and may also have saved the army commander's neck.

* * *

In a strict sense, Braxton Bragg had no one but himself to blame for the withdrawal he began from Shelbyville and Wartrace on June 27. For nearly a year he had tolerated the efforts of corps commanders Leonidas Polk and William Hardee to get rid of him, concentrating instead on building the army he led into a highly disciplined, well-fed, and potentially effective field force. And now, with Rosecrans upon him, Bragg could not get Polk or Hardee to obey any order he gave them but one: retreat.

There was, in fact, not much about Braxton Bragg to cause his senior officers to give him the respect a full general was due. Long remembered had been a story, possibly apocryphal but one a person who knew him well might believe true. According to this tale, years earlier Bragg—a company commander—had been given the additional duty of serving as battalion quartermaster. Company commander Bragg submitted a requisition for supplies to Quartermaster Bragg, who by endorsement refused to provide them, whereupon as company commander he protested and as quartermaster still said no. All of this dispute was on paper, which Bragg finally took to his battalion commander for a decision, then got chased from the camp at pistol point. Yet this ugly, often ill, always unpopular man was, like George McClellan, good at getting troops ready for combat and utterly devoted to his wife, whose health in 1863 was worse than his.

Bragg seemed content once more to allow President Davis to judge how much Bishop Pope and Hardee should be blamed for the loss of central Tennessee. Davis, ill at the time, admired all three men too much to make any changes.

And so it was that Confederate weaknesses—not so much in men or guns as in leadership at the highest levels—gave Rosecrans both a reprieve and a rare opportunity to demonstrate the power of maneuver to achieve maximum results at minimal cost, far under 100 federal casualties. Wilder's initiative, too, had contributed greatly. Yet Washington would take little notice of the victory in faraway Tennessee. The reason: Meade had drawn all the attention of the men in the telegraph room.

Ironically, little news was arriving from the Army of the Potomac directly: Stuart had cut the wires. And much of what the Union war managers knew they had learned from a message Meade had written on June 29 but which they had not received until the next day because the courier bringing it had been killed.

Some of what Meade said was confusing—or indicated that he was confused. "My endeavor will be in my movements to hold my force well together, with the hope of falling upon some portion of

Lee's army in detail," he had written, but elsewhere he mentioned that he was scattering his army. Having spoken of falling upon Lee, he also sent engineers to scout *defensible* ground near Pipe Creek, twenty miles or so southeast of Gettysburg.

Army command had stunned Meade, perhaps, falling upon him as it had at such a critical time. Bewildering as well was the multiplicity of interests he had to keep in mind: Baltimore's protection, locations of supply routes, geography, Washington's desires, Lee's audacity—these and more, enough to muddle the clearest of minds.

What the men in the telegraph room could do to help Meade, they did; for instance, near midnight on June 30, Secretary of War Stanton relayed to him a message from railroad expediter Herman Haupt at Harrisburg:

> Lee is falling back suddenly from the vicinity of Harrisburg, and concentrating all his forces. York has been evacuated. Carlisle is being evacuated. The concentration appears to be at or near Chambersburg. The object apparently a sudden movement against Meade, who should be advised by courier immediately.

Chapter 26

Gettysburg

General Lee knew much less than the men at Washington's War Department, with Jeb Stuart vanished and no other cavalry at hand to remedy this most serious loss. All he had to rely upon was a map, but Lee recalled that Isaac Trimble knew the country, and he sent for the Valley campaign veteran.

Trimble told the army commander all he could. Then Lee, pointing on the map to Gettysburg, east of the mountains, the little town resembling the hub of a wagon's wheel, with roads instead of spokes radiating from it, said: "Hereabout we shall probably meet the enemy and fight a great battle, and if God gives us the victory, the war will be over and we shall achieve the recognition of our independence."

Prophesying, however, was not the same thing as planning—something General Lee could not do, absent news from Stuart. And he had still heard nothing from him on the rainy thirtieth of June when he pointed Traveller eastward, leaving Chambersburg, riding with Longstreet's corps, knowing that Powell Hill's men were ahead, near Cashtown, eight miles or so to the northwest of Gettysburg.

Along the way the next morning, Wednesday, July 1, Lee's mood was brightened by the problem of deciding whether to let one of Ewell's divisions or Longstreet's have priority on the road ahead. Ewell's got it, for Lee had learned the corps' other two divisions were southbound more or less toward Gettysburg or Cashtown. Soon he would have his army reunited, provided Stuart ever returned to it from wherever he was.

Wagons the cavalryman meant to give the army commander for

gathering provisions still hampered Stuart, yet he was mindful of his duty to provide a screen enabling Ewell and Lee to know where the Yankees were. But near Hanover, thirteen or so miles east of Gettysburg, on the night of June 30, Stuart read in a Yankee newspaper that Jubal Early was at York. Also, prisoners taken in skirmishes said that Brigadier General Hugh Judson Kilpatrick's cavalry was between Stuart and Gettysburg. Stuart headed for York, moving away from Lee's army, at the pace of the wagons.

Early had long since departed, Stuart discovered at York on the morning of July 1, after an all-night ride, so he pressed on to Carlisle in search of Ewell: again, too late. A rider he had sent to find General Lee returned there with orders for Stuart to hurry to Gettysburg.

Stuart's mounts and men were exhausted, but he started them southward. He had been gone six days or more, and about all he had achieved was the capture of a wagon train.

By then General Lee was having to rely only on what he could see and hear, and on that Wednesday afternoon he heard artillery firing east of him. Leaving Longstreet, nudging the flanks of Traveller, he rode toward the sounds of the guns.

Lee wanted no part of a general engagement or even a meeting engagement capable of leading to something more—not with Ewell's two divisions still to the north, Longstreet's miles to the west, and Stuart nowhere to be found. Whatever Powell Hill had started, he would have to stop. But at Cashtown General Lee found the corps commander sick, so on eastward he rode until he reached Dorsey Pender's division. Henry Heth's, Lee found out, was nearing Gettysburg, fighting, and as best Lee could see through his field glasses, not faring well at all.

Lee may have remembered from a report the night before that Brigadier General J. J. Pettigrew had led his troops toward Gettysburg on Tuesday in search of shoes. On the way, though, they encountered Yankee cavalry and had returned to Cashtown. Now, on Wednesday, Pettigrew's men and the rest of Heth's division were facing blue-clad infantrymen supported by artillery.

Lee was about to order Heth recalled when firing north of Heth's flank broke out. Robert Rodes's division had come down from Carlisle just then and pitched in, forcing the Yankees to split forces away from Heth, and a little later, Jubal Early got east of Rodes and added his division's firepower.

All this was accidental, completely unmanaged. But as the shadows were lengthening on Wednesday, July 1, General Lee could hear the shrill yelling of his troops as he watched them drive the federals to a ridge south of Gettysburg.

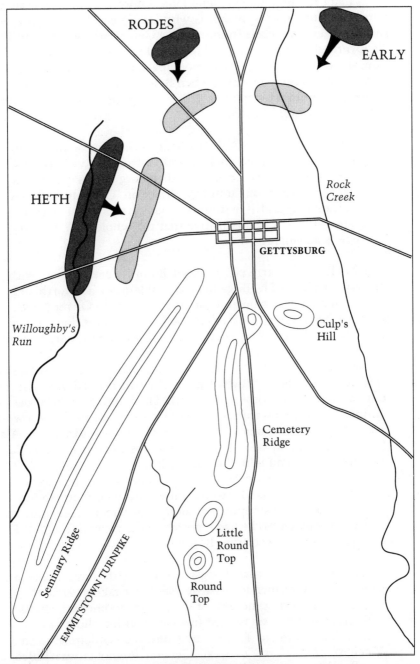

RODES

EARLY

HETH

Rock Creek

GETTYSBURG

Willoughby's Run

Culp's Hill

Cemetery Ridge

Seminary Ridge

EMMITSTOWN TURNPIKE

Little Round Top

Round Top

Gettysburg, First Day

It had been Brigadier General John Buford's task to lead the way northward for I Corps, which is why Union cavalry had prevented the shoes-seeking rebels from reaching Gettysburg on Tuesday, June 30. Overnight Buford deployed his 2,000 troopers along Willoughby Run, west of Seminary Ridge, blocking Cashtown Pike. They were there on Wednesday morning when Buford—from the cupola of the Lutheran Seminary—spotted Heth's division and dashed off a message to General Meade:

> The enemy's force (A. P. Hill's) are advancing on me at this point, and driving my pickets and skirmishers very rapidly. There is also a large force at Heidlersburg that is driving my pickets at that point from that direction. General Reynolds is advancing, and is within 3 miles of this point with his leading division. I am positive that the whole of A. P. Hill's force is advancing.

John Reynolds arrived, replaced Buford's cavalrymen with an infantry division led by Brigadier General James Wadsworth, ordered the rest of his I Corps up and got off a message to Oliver Howard to hurry his XI Corps to Gettysburg. All these things done, Reynolds rode down to the creek where the firing was heaviest, only to be shot in the head.

Now, for a time, Fort Sumter veteran Abner Doubleday was the senior officer present. Toward noon Howard arrived and assumed command. With I Corps troops still blocking the rebels west of Seminary Ridge, Howard sent two of his divisions north of town in case more Confederates came down from that direction. Also, Howard called upon two more nearby corps to rush to Gettysburg: Dan Sickles's III and John Slocum's XII.

In midafternoon on Wednesday, General Meade was still at Taneytown, in Maryland, twelve miles south of Gettysburg, still thinking in terms of stopping Lee along Pipe Creek, a few miles east of his headquarters. So he had reported to the general-in-chief. Then came a message relayed from Buford:

> I am satisfied that Longstreet and Hill have made a junction. A tremendous battle has been raging since 9:30 A.M., with varying success. At the present moment the battle is raging on the road to Cashtown, and within short cannon-range of this town. The enemy's line is a semicircle on the height, from north to west. General Reynolds was killed early this morning. In my opinion, there seems to be no directing person.

"We need help," Buford added. Meade responded by ordering Major General Winfield Scott Hancock northward at once to be the directing person. Why Meade did not go himself just then was not clear. It was as though he had forgotten having said in his dispatch to Halleck: "The enemy are advancing in force on Gettysburg, and I expect the battle will begin to-day."

Oliver Howard had done his best to direct the fight, but by the time Hancock arrived, the Confederates had wrecked his XI Corps, forcing two of its divisions back to the one in reserve on Cemetery Ridge, and Howard was sending Buford's cavalry to stop Powell Hill's men from getting around I Corps' southern flank. Cool was the reception Howard gave Hancock, his junior, a man whose presence he seemed to interpret as lack of Meade's confidence in him. Would that disaster at Chancellorsville never be forgotten?

Hancock, witnessing another rout of the luckless XI Corps, suggested that they share command: an unconventional solution but one that might serve at least for a while. As they stood on Cemetery Ridge, looking around at all the terrain, Hancock turned to Howard. "I think this the strongest position by nature that I ever saw," said Hancock. "If it meets with your approbation, I will select this as the battlefield."

Howard agreed, but he was expecting John Slocum, senior to both generals, to arrive. Some of Slocum's troops came up, but—as if sensing a fiasco and wanting no part of it—the XII Corps commander lagged miles behind. With Sickles's men nearby and the rebels apparently fought out, Howard and Hancock got the elements of four corps ready to defend the long north-south ridgeline until the army commander either took over or ordered a withdrawal to the Pipe Creek defenses.

By seven on that Wednesday evening Slocum had taken charge, as Howard reported in a message to General Meade reflecting more apology than much else, one saying in part:

> I believe I have handled these two corps to-day from a little past 11 until 4, when General [Hancock] assisted me in carrying out orders which I had already issued, as well as any of your corps commanders could have done.

Howard's new position was a strong one, he wrote, then, referring to his having been forced into it, he concluded: "The above has mortified me and will disgrace me. Please inform me frankly if you disapprove of my conduct to-day, that I may know what to do."

Oliver Howard had already lost his right arm to the cause. Now he was offering what remained of his chances to fight on to an army commander who had contributed precisely nothing on that day except confusion.

Late on that Wednesday afternoon General Lee watched the federals' retreat from a vantage point on Seminary Ridge, southwest of Gettysburg, across a shallow valley and the Emmitsburg Road from and parallel to Cemetary Ridge—the high ground to which those people had fled.

As Lee scanned the terrain east of him through his field glasses, up rode General Longstreet. Caution was the corps commander's unsought counsel, though he had seen nothing of that day's fighting. Order the army southward, Longstreet advised, get between Meade's forces and Washington. Select a strong defensive position and wait. "When they attack," he added, "we shall beat them, as we proposed to do before we left Fredericksburg, and the probabilities are that the fruits of our success will be great."

Lee was too much of a gentleman to consider Longstreet's words insubordinate. "If the enemy is there," he replied, meaning those people on Cemetery Ridge, "we must attack him."

Lurking in the minds of both generals must have been the absence of Jeb Stuart and his cavalry. Just as Longstreet did not want Lee to strike a force measurable only through field glasses, the commanding general was reluctant to use infantry alone in a search for another Marye's Heights.

Rebuffed, first Longstreet sulked and then returned to his men, six miles west of there. The army commander rode off toward the town and beyond it. He was hunting for Ewell, wanting to learn for himself why nothing had come of his earlier orders to attack Cemetery Ridge "if practicable."

Those two words amounted to discretion, which General Lee habitually granted corps commanders when they were distant from him. Jackson had always understood that. While serving as a division commander under Old Jack, however, Ewell had received orders that were crisp and explicit no matter how farfetched they may have seemed to him at the time. Lee's manner, Ewell was discovering, was different and somewhat bewildering. And so—to a man who claimed he knew all there was to know about handling fifty dragoons—was having an entire corps to command.

Wednesday afternoon's combat had bothered Ewell not at all personally, even when a bullet hit him: "It don't hurt a bit," he assured an officer near him, "to be shot in a wooden leg." But the fighting had been more costly than General Lee may have thought while he had watched it earlier, or so he learned soon after he reached Ewell's headquarters.

Rodes's division had lost almost 2,500 men. Some leaders new to brigade command had not performed well, causing veteran Isaac Trimble to beg Ewell—in vain—to give him even so small a unit as a regiment so that he could assault the hill overlooking Cemetery Ridge. Jubal Early was reluctant to press beyond the ground his division held. And Ewell seemed stunned.

Sensing that no more could be achieved that day, Lee asked Ewell: "Can't you, with your corps, attack on this flank tomorrow?"

Early, not Ewell, replied, in effect, that it would be better to hold what the corps had while Hill's divisions and Longstreet's drove eastward to Cemetery Ridge, leaving it to Ewell's troops to roll up the Yankees' northern flank. General Lee found this profoundly discouraging. He might well have agreed with a remark Sandie Pendleton had made to Kyd Douglas earlier that day: "Oh, for the presence and inspiration of Old Jack for just one hour!"

Lee rode back to Seminary Ridge. Once there, not content with the way he had left matters, he ran back over his possible courses of action. He ruled out retreat, along with waiting for Meade to mass his forces and attack him. Heed Longstreet's counsel and move southward, cutting off Meade from Washington? No, not without Stuart and his cavalry. What remained? Well, something like Jubal Early had proposed: an attack, somewhere along Cemetery Ridge, by Powell Hill's divisions—at least one of which, Harry Heth's, had taken heavy losses that day—and Longstreet's, which were still off to the west.

First Ewell, then Longstreet, came to General Lee on Seminary Ridge. Ewell now thought he could take Culp's Hill, the one dominating Cemetery Ridge. Fine, said Lee, do it, as soon as practicable after sunrise. Longstreet merely listened, heard no definite time for his troops to arrive, though he must have understood Lee needed them, and departed.

But Lee worked on into the night of Wednesday, July 1, changing his order to Ewell. Now he was to attack Culp's Hill on Thursday only when he heard the sounds of Longstreet's guns.

The moon had been full at Chancellorsville on the night in early May when Old Jack rode too far eastward, and it was full again on the last hour of July 1 when George Meade arrived on Cemetery Ridge. However, even with the moon's help, he could see little of the terrain on which his troops were sleeping.

Until around ten o'clock that evening the commander of the Army of the Potomac had tarried at Taneytown, though he had long been aware that the fighting at Gettysburg was both serious and not going in his forces' favor. If Meade seemed to have been managing instead of leading, however, there were reasons. His 90,000 or so troops outnumbered Lee's by only 20,000, roughly, but he had them in twice as many corps. Meade's roster of corps commanders had changed several times during the day. And he was not satisfied with the performances of some headquarters staff officers he had inherited from Joe Hooker.

Moreover, Meade had been obliged to order all his corps to march to a battlefield whose selection he had left to others—first John Reynolds, whose death had shaken as well as saddened him, then Howard and Hancock—and now the presence of Lee's army at Gettysburg made their choice all but irrevocable. To any army commander this would be a galling circumstance; to one as new to the position as Meade, surely it was most unsettling.

That he expected to fight, though, was clear from part of the message he sent General Halleck that evening:

> A. P. Hill and Ewell are certainly concentrating; Longstreet's whereabouts I do not know. If he is not up tomorrow, I hope with the force I have concentrated to defeat Hill and Ewell. At any rate, I see no other course than to hazard a general battle. Circumstances during the night may alter this decision, of which I will try to advise you.

For General Lee the night had been miserable—something had upset his digestive tract—but he might have been up and looking for signs of activity before dawn, anyway, recalling as he must have that the orders he had given on the evening before called for the fight to be renewed as early as "practicable." Stress, too, may have contributed to his edgy mood on Thursday morning: No one seemed to recognize the importance of *time*.

Ewell had let the hours of daylight get away from him on Wednesday afternoon, stopping his advance too soon and refusing to continue it. Longstreet, as if oblivious to the situation, had shown no sign he recognized how urgently Lee desired him to bring his two nearby divisions eastward to Seminary Ridge.

But a new day, July 2, was at hand. Lee began it by sending aides out to reconnoiter the southern end of the high ground to the east. Soon Longstreet arrived. And Lee came under more stress, for as he had on the afternoon before, again Longstreet advocated moving well south of Meade, finding another Marye's Heights, fighting a tactical-defensive battle.

No one would ever know how General Lee kept his temper from flaring. For at least the third time, though, all he did was hear Longstreet out. And again, patiently, the army commander reminded him of his plan. That was for Longstreet to move his two divisions south of Powell Hill's on Seminary Ridge and then attack eastward, take the high ground where no federals seemed to be, and drive northward along Cemetery Ridge. At the sound of Longstreet's guns, Ewell would strike southward, seize Culp's Hill, and pour artillery fire on Meade's troops in Longstreet's path. And as Longstreet swept northward, Hill's divisions would cross the valley and help push Yankees out of his way.

Nothing here was new. All that had been missing when Lee so directed on the evening before was a definite time for Longstreet to have his troops in place, ready to attack. But it was not Lee's custom to be that specific. From his first campaign, the Seven Days, he had learned that his commanders had to be given some flexibility. Afterward, usually, it had been enough for him to say what he wanted done and roughly when. To Jackson, "as early as is practicable" would have meant as soon as a soldier had daylight enough to get a Yankee in his rifle's sights. Not Longstreet, apparently, for early on Thursday morning John Hood's division was just coming up, McLaws's lagging behind it on the Cashtown road.

It would take time General Lee knew Meade might not allow for Longstreet to move his two divisions south of Hill's men on Seminary Ridge—time Longstreet had wasted by not starting them westward earlier than, obviously, he had. During the night Ewell had forwarded a captured federal message, one that told Lee that Major General George Sykes's V Corps and Slocum's XII were near enough to Gettysburg to make a difference. Unless seized very quickly, Cemetery Ridge would be covered with those people. Was that what Longstreet wanted?

So it seemed, for the disgruntled corps commander called John Hood aside and said: "The General is a little nervous this morning; he wishes me to attack; I do not wish to do so without Pickett. I never like to go into battle with one boot off."

Longstreet meant Major General George E. Pickett, whose division was still many hours' march west of Seminary Ridge. But Longstreet's intent was clear: delay long enough for Lee to call off the attack and move the army far southward.

Worse, when Lee pointed to a spot on the map and ordered McLaws to take his division there, Longstreet told McLaws he wanted it at another location. Quietly the army commander said: "No, General, I wish it placed just opposite."

Longstreet stalked off. Lee waited. After a few minutes he heard his angry lieutenant instructing Porter Alexander to put his artillery where Lee had designated. Apparently taking this to mean Longstreet's tantrum had run its course and that obedience could now be expected, Lee mounted Traveller for a ride north and eastward to see what Dick Ewell was doing.

General Lee may have thought he was making the most of a scrap of time, and surely there was value in seeing Cemetery Ridge from another vantage point. But nothing he learned was reassuring. Culp's Hill, the northeastern barb of the federal fishhook, had been fortified overnight. Ewell had all three of his divisions with him now, but they were not in locations from which they could attack.

"The enemy have the advantage of us," said Lee to Trimble, "in a short and inside line, and we are too much extended. We did not or could not pursue our advantage of yesterday and now the enemy are in a good position."

This he repeated to Ewell, as though he hoped his implied rebuke might spur the corps commander to a higher level of performance this time. Again Lee explained his plan, but he refined it slightly, ordering Ewell to make a demonstration to keep Meade's nearby troops in place while Longstreet struck the federals' southern flank, nearly five miles to the south.

Distances, indeed, may have made a fresh and discouraging impression on General Lee as he rode back toward Seminary Ridge on a morning that had been irritating from its earliest moments and showed no signs of improving. There was not one fishhook, but two, Lee's larger and longer than Meade's, the reverse of the situation at Fredericksburg or Sharpsburg—battles in which Longstreet had been at his best. But as Lee had said to John Hood two hours or so before, "The enemy is here, and if we do not whip him, he will whip us." Why had Longstreet not seen the situation as it truly was?

Had he since Lee had left? Surely he must have, it being close to ten o'clock and with Cemetery Ridge bristling with men and guns. Nearing Powell Hill's lines, however, Lee turned to an aide and asked: "What *can* detain Longstreet? He ought to be in position by now."

George Meade's worries on Thursday morning, July 2, were no less vexing. Some of his corps were slow in coming up: John Sedgwick's VI was still miles away. And though the ground Reynolds and others had selected for giving battle had few deficiencies, Meade was not sure his army should remain on it. The Baltimore Pike seemed much on his mind. It was his line of communications, Sedgwick would be using it, and it was the best route back to Pipe Creek. As though to protect the vital road from one of Lee's audacious sweeps, Meade placed Slocum's XII Corps east of it, in the process drawing northeastward the only division that had been down near the hills known as Round Tops. And, as an added precaution, Meade set Chief-of-Staff Butterfield to work on planning a withdrawal.

Concurrently, however, General Meade had engineer Warren and Slocum out scouting the possibilities of attacking Ewell. Not feasible, they concluded and reported—thus, unknowingly, keeping Gettysburg from turning into a pinwheel battle.

Defending was the immediate thing to do, as troops already settled in proved they understood by digging. But as aides led III Corps' divisions southward along Cemetery Ridge beyond the end of Hancock's line, Dan Sickles saw ground westward he liked much better than the swampy saddle between II Corps and Little Round Top. Ignoring the protests of artilleryman Henry Hunt, Sickles ordered his troops forward and slightly uphill into a peach orchard just east of the Emmitsburg Road. Stone walls made this an arrowhead pointing toward the rebels' lines.

Now, with noon on that Thursday approaching, Longstreet's mood had not so much changed as hardened. Lee, returning, had told him to get on with the attack. Slowly, deliberately, he moved his two divisions southward. And to anyone who raised questions Longstreet's reply was the same: In effect, it is General Lee's battle, so let his orders be carried out to the very last letter.

John Hood's division was southernmost. Elsewhere along the federals' lines the ground was open, gently rolling, much of it under cultivation, with stone walls separating fields and occasional stands of timber. Not so in Hood's sector; he faced outcroppings of rock and huge boulders at the base of Little Round Top, terrain so rugged it could be defended indefinitely by only a few Yankees—and more than a few were visible.

General Hood sent Texan scouts southward in search of an alternative to storming this natural fortress. There was one, they reported: Big Round Top, farther south, was undefended, and Yankee wagon trains were east of its southern slope.

Hood dispatched messengers three times to Longstreet to get permission to bypass Little Round Top and envelop Meade's flank. And three times Longstreet refused: "General Lee's orders are to attack up the Emmitsburg Road."

And so Lee had directed, hours earlier. But during the time Longstreet had frittered away, conditions had changed, worsened. By midafternoon the ridge to the east was bristling with blue-clad troops and guns. And, apparently, only Hood and his men were aware of how drastically different the terrain in their sector was from the easy slopes north of them.

Longstreet did not bother to ride over for a look, nor did he refer any of Hood's thrice-repeated requests to General Lee. Longstreet's sense of time's uses seemed to have reversed. It would take too long to refer the matter to the army commander, though Lee was then not far away. Let his orders be executed, Longstreet reiterated, in effect, *now.*

General Meade knew Dan Sickles was not in his assigned position, but aides could straighten that out, or so he seemed to have assumed as he watched the Baltimore Pike for signs of Sedgwick's VI Corps and waited for Butterfield to finish the withdrawal plan. In fact, the situation on the federal line's southern end was dangerous. Buford's cavalry was supposed to be guarding the Round Tops, but it was not; Meade had neglected to require another outfit to replace him. Rebels were shifting southward. Yes, the Peach Orchard would be an exposed position, but Sickles meant to make the most of it.

Toward the stone wall extending back southeastward from the Emmitsburg Road to the rocky outcropping—literally a Devil's Den, near the base of Little Round Top—he sent Major General David Birney's division. Where the wall angled to the northeast and followed the road, Brigadier General Andrew A. Humphreys's brigades lined it. Between Humphreys's flank and the southernmost unit of Winfield Scott Hancock's II Corps there was a gap. Sickles, his mind on getting his III Corps' into positions suitable to him, neglected to tell Hancock about it.

Dan Sickles's tendency to act first and think later had gotten him into trouble often enough earlier. He would have been convicted of murdering his wife's lover in cold blood on a Washington street in 1859 had his lawyer, Edwin Stanton, not innovated the temporary-insanity defense. At Chancellorsville, however, Sickles had—correctly—resisted Joe Hooker's order to abandon Hazel Grove. And now the former congressman was not so much defying Meade as underweighting the potential consequences of his actions.

Confederate artillery north and south of Sickles's Peach Orchard could concentrate its fire into his arrowhead, and this the rebels did in midafternoon on Thursday, July 2, while the III Corps' commander was at Meade's headquarters. He had been summoned there for a conference, perhaps to hear General Meade explain Butterfield's plan for withdrawal, if it came to that. But sounds of gunfire to the south changed everything. Meade mounted Old Baldy, ordered the just-arrived Sickles to rush back to his Peach Orchard, sent word to Sykes to move his V Corps that way, then—the meeting forgotten—galloped to catch up with Sickles. Engineer Gouverneur

Kemble Warren was galloping, too, along the way finding V Corps's troops that he led straight to Little Round Top just as the Confederates—Hood's men—seemed about to break through.

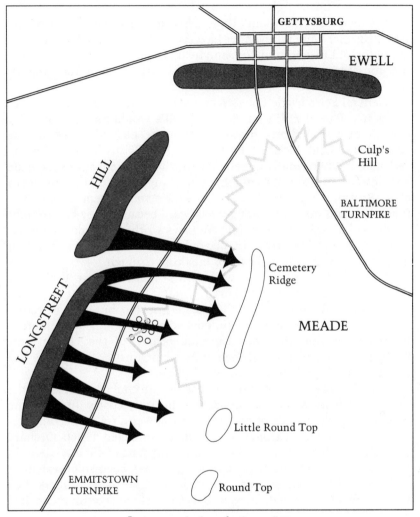

GETTYSBURG

EWELL

Culp's
Hill

BALTIMORE
TURNPIKE

HILL

LONGSTREET

Cemetery
Ridge

MEADE

Little Round Top

EMMITSTOWN
TURNPIKE

Round Top

Longstreet's Attack, Second Day

Birney's troops and those Warren was bringing in were taking the brunt of the rebels' assaults when a shell burst made Old Baldy break eastward, carrying General Meade beyond range. Once the horse was back under control, the army commander began sending orders to Hancock, Howard, all his corps commanders, to rush brigades southward. Suddenly a rebel cannonball all but tore off

Sickles's right leg: Command of the III Corps passed to the embattled Birney.

Earlier, during fighting amid the rocky outcroppings of the Devil's Den and the Round Tops, John Hood had been shot in the arm. Brigadier General Evander Law took over, led Hood's remnants to the top of Little Round Top, and held off Yankee assaults while he sent messages to McLaws, just north of him, begging for support. None came.

General Lee's battle Longstreet had declared it, but once opened, it was his: Powell Hill's corps and Ewell's would join it only after Longstreet began doing his duty. How he elected to do it was curious. He held McLaws back while Hood's division was being decimated. When finally he released McLaws, the advance was made by brigades, from south to north, each unsupported by the one north of it. Brigadier General Joseph Kershaw's men swept toward the Peach Orchard but could not get eastward because they had to fight northward as well. One by one McLaws's other brigades came in, carrying the battle northward, but only after the regiments south of it had come within heartbeats of breaking through.

None had, but then Powell Hill's southernmost division—Anderson's—got engaged. For a time it seemed that Cadmus Wilcox's brigade might crack the federal line. No, but soon Brigadier General Ransome Wright's regiments advanced so far up Cemetery Ridge's slope that they had captured nearly all the Union guns facing them and abandoned them only when, unsupported, they had to retreat lest the Yankees surround them.

This had been the closest, hardest-fought kind of combat for the men on both sides—bitter, unyielding, horribly costly, littering the ground with thousands of bodies from the weird rock outcroppings at the Devil's Den through the artillery-shredded Peach Orchard into wheat fields north of it. Seldom on any battlefield anywhere in this war had such ferocity or so much gallantry been so prevalent or had the sacrifices these warriors made been so tragic, due as they were to the blunders federal as well as Confederate commanders had committed.

Near sundown on Thursday, July 2, Longstreet had done all he would and eyes and ears shifted northward, to Culp's Hill, where Dick Ewell's corps finally seemed to be starting something. More blundering it was, but that Ewell had been doing since Wednesday afternoon.

To seize anything, forces had to be within reach; Ewell's were not, as he might have discovered had he gone out during the day to see for himself. He did join Early in placing some artillery batteries where they could give fire support when the troops assaulted

Cemetery Hill and Culp's Hill east of it. Nothing more: To division commanders Rodes, Early, and Edward Johnson he left the task of deciding how they would cooperate.

They tried, each counting on hasty understandings they had reached with each other, all naturally thinking first of their own units' challenges. Among these was having to move brigades long distances to reach the attack positions. Another was a sharp artillery duel. So much time was lost that it was almost dark when the Confederate infantrymen began climbing the hills they had been looking at all day.

But—lacking any coordination—they went in piecemeal, a brigade or two at a time. Louisianans reached high ground east of Cemetery Hill, only to run out of ammunition during a determined Yankee counterattack. Lacking support, they had to withdraw. Edward Johnson's men clawed their way up Culp's Hill, but one Union brigade left behind was enough to drive the attackers down to trenches abandoned hours earlier when Meade ordered units southward to stop Wright's assault.

Lieutenant General Richard Stoddert Ewell had not worked the wrong problem; he had not even approached the blackboard. And all Jackson's successor had to show for his day's work was the foothold on Culp's Hill Johnson's troops still held in the moonlight after everything else had failed.

Ewell's ineptness, added to Longstreet's nigh-inexplicable conduct, had made that Thursday the Army of Northern Virginia's worst day since Malvern Hill. Nothing had gone as General Lee had said he desired. True, Stuart had arrived, receiving a rebuke instead of congratulations: "Well, General Stuart, you are here at last!" But as July 2 ended, still Lee did not seem to realize that he was not in control of either his army or the battle to which he had committed it.

That night, Longstreet sent an aide to the army commander to give his report. Lee ignored this departure from custom and courtesy. His orders for the next morning, Friday the third, were brief: Ewell and Longstreet would continue their attacks.

George Meade had corrected Sickles's blunder by shifting brigades, weakening his line nearly everywhere. After dark the task was to get units back where they belonged. Not until late on Thursday night could that be done, and as Meade waited for his senior commanders to join him in a conference, he prepared a brief report to General-in-Chief Halleck:

> The enemy attacked me about 4 p.m. this day, and after one of the severest contests of the war, was repulsed at all points. We have suffered considerably in killed and

wounded....I shall remain in my present position to-morrow, but am not prepared to say, until better advised of the condition of the army, whether my operations will be of an offensive or defensive character.

Meade had told Halleck only what he knew, which was not enough to suit him: his reason for the meeting. He opened it by asking his subordinates to answer three questions:

- Under existing circumstances, is it advisable for this army to remain in its present position, or to retire to another nearer its base of supplies?
- It being determined to remain in present position, shall the army attack or wait the attack of the enemy?
- If we await attack, how long?

Stay and fight, wait for Lee to attack, and wait one day and no more were the answers Meade received. That Meade had been doing some thinking for himself, however, he showed when he told General Birney: "If Lee attacks tomorrow it will be in your front. He has made attacks on both our flanks and failed, and if he concludes to try it again it will be in our center."

Chapter 27

The Appalling Cost of Indecision

On the morning of Friday, July 3, two days into a battle neither side had expected to fight there, both armies were on the same ground they controlled late on Wednesday afternoon. About all they had done was fill nearby houses and fields with thousands of wounded men and collect as many of the dead as they could: grim evidence of how determined the troops were to settle something this time. And as the third day dawned, federal as well as Confederate soldiers may well have wondered: If not here, where? If not now, when?

Clearly this scrap at Gettysburg was different, sort of a Fredericksburg with the opposing forces' situations reversed—except for the federals' edge in manpower and artillery. Most of the armies' earlier encounters had been characterized either by successive fights at shifting locations, as during the Seven Days and Chancellorsville, or sharp and climactic battles such as those at Manassas, Antietam Creek, and Fredericksburg. Not until now had the Army of the Potomac and the Army of Northern Virginia gotten locked in a struggle this bitter, at one place, lasting this long, with no end in sight.

And never had the stakes been higher. This was a battle the North absolutely could not afford to lose. If Meade's army were shattered, the roads to Philadelphia and Baltimore would be open, Washington cut off and nearly defenseless, and Abraham Lincoln forced to concede that the Union could not be restored through coercion. Nor could Lee allow his army to be denied this second opportunity to win independence for the Southern states, for there might not be another chance. As he had written Jefferson Davis in

June, the Confederacy's resources were shrinking while those of the federals were increasing.

So, as both George Meade and Robert Lee had decided the night before, both armies would stay and fight. Whether the men agreed, no one would ever know, except by their deeds. For two days their devotion to duty had been superb. All of them were veterans now, inured to horrors unimagined before the war, devoid of every illusion, combat-hardened soldiers, hoping they could endure another day of the deadly work and survive it, wanting most of all to be done with it—one way or the other—and get home again.

For the past two days Lieutenant General James Longstreet had been behaving as though duty, and honor, and country were mere words. And now he seemed as insensitive as before to how utterly dependent on him for high performance the army commander now was.

Early on Friday morning Longstreet again invited relief from command by saying to Lee: "General, I have had my scouts out all night, and I find that you still have an excellent opportunity to move around to the right of Meade's army, and maneuver him into attacking us."

Lee was no more interested in doing any such thing than he had been weeks and days earlier. Then, as though he had issued no orders the night before, Lee told Longstreet he wanted him to attack the federal line. "General," protested Longstreet, "I have been a soldier all my life. I have been with soldiers engaged by couples, by squads, companies, regiments and armies, and I should know, as well as anyone, what soldiers can do. It is my opinion that no 15,000 men ever arrayed for battle can take that position."

Lee did not agree. And he insisted that Longstreet would command the force; Soldier Longstreet would obey, but later he would write of General Lee:

> He knew that I did not believe that success was possible; that care and time should be taken to give the troops the benefit of positions and the grounds; and he should have put an officer in charge who had more confidence in his plan. Two thirds of the troops were of other commands, and there was no reason for putting the assaulting troops under my charge.

But there was: Jackson was dead, Powell Hill was ailing, and Ewell was busy pulling his men back from the trenches on Culp's Hill under heavy fire from Slocum's counterattacking federals.

* * *

Stay and fight was all the Union Army of the Potomac had to do that Friday, and General Meade spent the morning getting ready to do just that. For a time he visited reliable Winfield Scott Hancock, whose corps held the center of Cemetery Ridge. Among matters they may have discussed was what Meade would do if Lee attacked and was repulsed. Sykes's V Corps was already on the southern end of the federal line, west of the Round Tops, facing Longstreet; hardly bloodied in this fight so far was Sedgwick's VI Corps, the Army of the Potomac's reserve. Maybe, if Hancock held, Sykes and Sedgwick could destroy Lee's army.

That was one possibility. But there was another, and that it was on Meade's mind he reflected in a potentially confusing message he sent to Major General William H. French, commanding a division far to the south: "Should the enemy be beaten, reoccupy Harpers Ferry and harass his retreat; should we be forced to withdraw, hasten to Washington to protect the city."

Admittedly, staying and fighting left the initiative to the invader: Lee. Meade seemed content to leave it that way. Toward noon he sat down at Gibbon's mess table and enjoyed a much-belated breakfast—lunch to the other officers present—and waited to see what challenges the afternoon might bring.

Although James Longstreet had seemed pigheaded, some of his objections to General Lee's plan deserved more attention than the Army of Northern Virginia's overwrought commander appeared to have given them. For one, shifting Harry Heth's and part of Pender's divisions southward took time: hours of it. Moreover, the troops' advance would begin with six brigades abreast, but the nearer they approached the attack's focal point, the more open to flanking fire they would be, especially on their northern edge. Could Porter Alexander's artillery both protect against that threat and soften the Yankee defenses in front?

That was asking a lot of the seventy-five guns Alexander was massing well to the east of where the infantry brigades were getting into position for their nearly mile long advance to the center of the Yankee defenses on Cemetery Ridge. The young artilleryman had built his line of batteries almost within the range of federal sharpshooters and given gunners orders for an hour-long bombardment, to commence at one o'clock. But Longstreet wanted more from Alexander. Not long after noon he sent a message to him:

> Colonel: If the artillery fire does not have the effect to drive off the enemy or greatly demoralize him, so as to make

our effort pretty certain, I would prefer that you should advise Pickett not to make the charge. I shall rely a great deal upon your judgment to determine the matter and shall expect you to let General Pickett know when the moment offers.

Until then, as Porter Alexander wrote later, he had been confident that he was carrying out Lee's orders. Now, sharply, he saw that Longstreet had shed the burden of deciding whether the attack should go forward at all—and if so, when—and had passed all the responsibility for the venture down to him.

Indeed, Jackson was dead. And, strangely, Lee was inert.

Colonel Alexander replied:

General: I will only be able to judge the effect of our fire on the enemy by his return fire, as his infantry is little exposed to view and the smoke will obscure the field. If, as I infer from your note, there is any alternative to this attack, it should be carefully considered before opening our fire, for it will take all the artillery ammunition we have left to test this one, and if the result is unfavorable we will have none left for another effort. And even if this is entirely successful, it can only be so at a very bloody cost.

After minutes that must have seemed like hours, back came word from Longstreet: Let the bombardment begin. Alexander turned to General Wright, standing nearby, and asked him: "What do you think of it? Is it as hard to get there as it looks?"

Wright said: "The trouble is not in going there. I went there with my brigade yesterday. There is a place where you can get breath and re-form. The trouble is to stay there after you get there, for the whole Yankee army is there in a bunch."

Alexander found Pickett. Whether the artillery commander reported Wright's comment and expressed all his other concerns would never be clear. But Pickett was "cheerful and sanguine," and Alexander sent a final message to Longstreet: "When our fire is at its best, I will advise General Pickett to advance."

Henry Hunt, now a brigadier general, the artilleryman who had lined his guns hub to hub at Malvern Hill (where two horses had been shot under him), saw what young Alexander was doing. Were the rebels using artillery to protect their center along Seminary Ridge while Lee moved infantry northward?

For that possibility to have occurred to Hunt even briefly was curious. It was as though artillerymen could see openings officers in other branches were unable to spot. As Alexander pointed out later, Cemetery Hill—at the northwestern corner of the federal lines, where their fishhook bent—was the key piece of terrain. From it Confederate artillery fire southward along Cemetery Ridge could force the federal troops to abandon their positions. And Cemetery Hill was Meade's most vulnerable point: Oliver Howard's twice-whipped XI Corps held it. Yet, astonishingly, for two days now Lee and A. P. Hill and Ewell had all but ignored it.

Had Lee finally discovered this opportunity? No, Henry Hunt decided after a closer look at Porter Alexander's guns. Once again the Confederates were going to attack where Meade's advantages were greatest: yesterday the federal army's flanks, today its line's center.

Artilleryman Hunt knew artilleryman Alexander would open the fight with a bombardment, probably a long one. Federal ammunition was abundant in the rear but not nearby, so Hunt instructed his gunners to hold their fire for fifteen or twenty minutes, conserve their rounds, and keep plenty of canister ready to shred the rebel infantry at murderously close range.

Slightly after one o'clock on Friday, July 3, Alexander's guns opened fire. So did some of Powell Hill's and Ewell's, but that was voluntary. For minutes the hot, humid air was filled with hellish noise. Smoke covered the parallel ridgelines. Blasts shook the ground. Seldom if ever had so much firepower been let loose in so confined an area.

West of and behind Alexander's batteries the infantrymen got into their attack formation. Significant, possibly, were the changes in command. Brave Dorsey Pender had been mortally wounded the day before, so his division, borrowed from Ewell's corps, was led by Trimble. Heth, too, had been hit: Johnston Pettigrew had taken his place. Among several brigades it was the same. Pickett's division, southernmost in the line, newly arrived, was intact, but only because several senior officers, such as Richard Garnett, too sick to advance on foot as Pickett had ordered, put duty, honor, and country above all else and insisted on riding at the head of their troops.

Old soldier Brigadier General Lewis Armistead turned to the color-bearer of the 53d Virginia and asked, "Sergeant, are you going to put those colors on the enemy's works today?"

"I'll try, sir," came the reply, "and if mortal man can do it, it shall be done."

In a few more minutes Lew Armistead would draw his saber, stick his battered hat on its point, and lead his men forward, never caring how good a target his bare gray head would be.

Still, even as Alexander's bombardment went on, Longstreet remained hesitant. While he was with Pickett, a courier brought a note from the colonel addressed to the division commander:

> General: If you are coming at all you must come imme-
> diately or I cannot give you proper support; but the enemy's
> fire has not slackened materially, and at least 18 guns are
> firing from the cemetery itself.

Porter Alexander did not know it at the time, but what he referred to as the cemetery was actually the "little clump of trees" he had been told was the focal point for the convergence first of his fire and later the infantry's assault. But that mattered far less than what happened next.

"General," asked Pickett after Longstreet had read the note, "shall I advance?"

Longstreet said nothing, merely dipped his head.

"I shall lead my division forward, sir," said Pickett.

No reply: Longstreet was mounting his horse. Evidently, silence meant approval. Pickett returned to his division.

General Longstreet rode eastward to the Peach Orchard in search of Alexander. It was as though, belatedly, he recalled the key point in the first message the colonel had sent him.

"Go and stop Pickett right where he is," Longstreet told Alexander, "and replenish your ammunition."

"We can't do that, sir!" replied the artilleryman "The [supply] train has but little. It would take an hour to distribute it." And the enemy, he added, would use the time. Longstreet pondered that reality for a moment, then said, "I don't want to make this charge; I don't believe it can succeed. I would stop Pickett now, but that General Lee has ordered it and is expecting it."

Alexander wrote afterward:

> I felt that he was inviting a word of acquiescence on my
> part and that if given he would again order, "Stop Pickett
> where he is." But I was too conscious of my own youth and
> inexperience to express any opinion not directly asked. So I
> remained silent while Longstreet fought his battle out
> alone....

Just then General Garnett rode by, leading his regiments eastward through Alexander's guns, aiming for that little clump of trees. He was one of 15,000 Confederate soldiers in a gray-and-butternut line stretching fully a mile, all battle colors flying proudly, the men in ranks so neatly aligned that it might have been a parade, and now there was nothing James Longstreet could do but wait and watch.

Not much watching could the federal troops along Cemetery Ridge do, sheltered behind stone walls, hugging the ground, as Alexander's rounds searched for them and for Hunt's guns. In the rear it was worse. Many rebel gunners had aimed a little too high or cut fuzes too long, making the Union-held ridge's reverse slope a suburb of hell as their overshots' explosions splintered supply wagons, stampeded crazed livestock, turned artillery caissons into erupting volcanoes, shredded the bodies of stragglers and shirkers, and blew away the house in which Meade and his headquarters' staff were working.

The grim and somewhat perverse sense of humor that combat infantrymen develop to save their sanity must surely have made blue-clad veterans in the line smile as through smoke and flames they glimpsed the often-envied rear echelon getting a sample of war's deadly reality. But when the foot soldiers shifted their eyes from the chaotic scurrying behind them and gazed westward, scanning the long line of Confederates marching steadily toward them, even the stoutest of hearts had cause to skip a beat.

No man in the Army of the Potomac, however seasoned, had ever seen anything quite like it. Something out of old dimly remembered storybooks this seemed, yet it was not. It was all too colorful, with the sun behind the dancing battle flags making them appear blood red; the orange blossoms of federal artillery bursts thinning the gray ranks, but only for a moment before they closed again, the yellowish smoke drifting up into a midafternoon sky blue overhead but not behind Confederate-held Seminary Ridge where— miles west of the green tree-lined horizon—ominous popcorn-white thunderheads were swelling.

Beautiful, glorious, exciting this panorama was—though, every Union soldier knew, embedded within it was sudden death.

Pickett's charge, historians would call it, because some of his division's brigades got beyond the rest. But that was only after almost everything else went wrong.

At first, Pettigrew's four brigades were aligned with two of Pickett's south of them, all moving eastward. Behind them were four more brigades in support. Earlier, some of the Union artillery on Cemetery Ridge had withdrawn. That puzzling but welcome development had drawn all Confederates' eyes straight ahead, to the fences along the Emmitsburg Road, to the upward slope beyond, to stone walls jutting out at odd angles below the skyline. Forgotten about, apparently, was the threat to the advancing line of federal fire from both its flanks.

Brigadier General James L. Kemper's men, southernmost in the formation, were the first to suffer from this lapse when into their midst plunged artillery rounds fired from Little Round Top, the high ground to the south of them that John Hood's division had taken and lost the day before. A single Yankee shell burst might kill and maim as many as ten men. But amid the screams, before the smoke cleared, the ranks closed, and Kemper's troops moved onward, driven leftward by the blasting.

Shortly thereafter, federal guns on Cemetery Hill, at the northwestern corner of Meade's line, began pouring fire along the ranks of Pettigrew's northernmost brigades, shattering them, shredding them. Still the Confederates plodded forward until, suddenly, volleys from Yankee infantrymen stabbed into them. Stunned, some of the men on the northern flank of the advance stood their ground and fought; others began streaming back toward Seminary Ridge.

No Confederate commander meant for it to happen, but the mile-long gray line was being hammered into a wedge. When hit, Kemper's brigade had inclined northeastward; now Pettigrew's survivors, also, were slanting toward the attack's center.

This might have been a powerful wedge. But, compressed by fire from both flanks, Confederate units got mixed. For a time valor seemed about all that powered the advance—valor and the idea that the way home might begin on the far side of Cemetery Ridge.

But the pounding some of Pettigrew's troops had absorbed from guns on Cemetery Hill and Yankee infantrymen had been too much for them to endure. They fled, leaving behind their dead and wounded, throwing away their weapons, deaf to all officers' attempts to rally them, not stopping until they were well past Alexander's guns. Quickly, General Longstreet began thinking about how to defend Seminary Ridge when Meade counterattacked.

George Meade knew next to nothing about what was happening on Cemetery Ridge's western slope. When Alexander's overshots had wrecked his headquarters' cottage and shredded sixteen of the horses tethered to fence rails outside, the army commander led his staff to a barn near the Baltimore Pike. There a rebel shell fragment wounded Chief of Staff Butterfield in the neck, prompting Meade to move on to the headquarters of Slocum's corps—so far in the rear, wrote historian Shelby Foote, he might as well have been "on one of the mountains of the moon."

During Alexander's preparatory barrages Winfield Scott Hancock was riding along his lines as though the rebel rounds exploding near him were so many pesky mosquitoes. To a warning he responded merely: "There are times when a corps commander's life does not count." Infantrymen, connoisseurs of courage though they were crouching behind stone walls as shell bursts shook the ground, cheered as Hancock rode by.

Hancock was on the northern end of his corps' segment when Pettigrew's advancing brigades were approaching, and he watched as the Ohio infantry charged into the rebels' flank. Relishing the result, Hancock galloped southward along Cemetery Ridge to tell Abner Doubleday to do the same thing from the other side.

As he rode past Gibbon's troops General Hancock may well have wondered how fewer than 10,000 men could withstand attack by maybe 15,000. If so, it was fortunate that Colonel Arthur Devereaux halted him long enough to ask permission to place his reserve regiment in the line. "Go in there pretty God-damned quick!" Hancock replied; then he rode on.

When he reached Doubleday, he found that Brigadier General George Stannard had already set his Vermont troops in motion. Now General Hancock had something of a double envelopment in miniature going, one that might pinch off the rebel wedge's point. Suddenly, though, he leaned over his horse's neck and seemed about to fall. Two men caught him and lowered him to the ground. Hancock picked a saddle nail from the wound in his thigh, remarking: "They must be hard up for ammunition."

But a minié ball had done the damage, and to stanch the bleeding, General Stannard used a pistol barrel to tighten the tourniquet he had made from a handkerchief. Soldiers brought a stretcher. Winfield Scott Hancock waved them away. He meant to stay right where he was, to see it all.

Fast approaching now was what matadors in *corridas de toros* know as the moment of truth: when time seems to stand still, when all the strength remaining is focused, when life is most precious, when death is never more clearly the cost of a single wrong move.

Confederates in the wedge's point were very close to the stone walls where Yankees waited when "Fire!" General Garnett shouted, then fell from his saddle, shot dead. Kemper saw this, urged Armistead forward, and dropped—hit in the groin. Pettigrew, a hand already wounded, moved nearer the center. But no longer did what officers wanted done seem to matter. Every soldier understood. With federal guns firing canister and infantry letting loose volleys on both sides and in front of them, the men in gray and butternut charged forward, firing as they advanced, some of them driving away defenders where stone walls made an angle pointing the Confederates' way.

Lewis Armistead saw the chance of breaking through. Still holding his saber with his hat impaled on its point, he got over the stone wall and looked back at maybe 300 men left of the 15,000 or so. "Come on, boys!" the old soldier shouted. "Give them the cold steel! Follow me!"

Follow Armistead they did, seeing amid the smoke his hat up there on the sword ahead of them, charging upslope directly into point-blank canister fire from a battery whose commander was dead, shot through the mouth giving his final order. Lewis Armistead got as far as those guns. Down clattered the gallant general's saber, his hand still grasping it. He died with his other hand gripping the muzzle of a Yankee cannon.

So, at the moment of truth, it was Armistead's charge—in terms of glory, for how better could a soldier die?—yet it would be called Pickett's and remembered ever afterward as a failure. Armistead would be forgotten; Pickett, blamed.

Now the division commander, two of his three generals who had led brigades dead, the other wounded and out of the fight, with bewildered troops milling around him, knew that no more could be asked of the men. Pickett had gotten neither reinforcements nor an answer to his request for them from Longstreet. Yankees to his right and left and in front were stepping up their fire. Gray-clad bodies, some still and others writhing, marked how far the charge had surged, how near to victory.

Pettigrew was trying to rally his few remaining regiments. But he got shot again, this time in his leg. Like Pickett, he saw his men pulling back. "Let them go," he said to an aide, referring to the men starting westward to Seminary Ridge.

There waited General Lee, trusting Longstreet to build a line to stop Meade's inevitable counterattack. "All will come right in the end," he said to the fought-out soldiers streaming past Traveller, "we want all good and true men just now."

Soon came General Pickett. Lee directed him to place his division in the rear and get ready to repel the federals.

"General Lee," replied Pickett, "I have no division now."

"This has been my fight," the army commander told him, "and upon my shoulders rests the blame."

Brigadier General Cadmus Wilcox, going in late, had done well to bring even a fraction of his troops back. He tried to explain to General Lee what had happened, but words failed him. "Never mind, General," said Lee, "all this has been my fault—it is I that have lost this fight, and you must help me out of it the best way you can."

General Meade rode into the II Corps' rear area, learned that Hancock and Gibbon were wounded, saw rebel prisoners being marched off, and asked wounded Lieutenant Frank A. Haskell: "How is it going here?"

"I believe, General, the enemy's attack is repulsed."

It seemed more than Meade could believe. "Thank God," he muttered. For a moment he scanned the confusion there on the reverse slope of Cemetery Ridge; then he gave orders for the line to get ready to resist another assault.

That was an indication both of Meade's respect for Lee as a tenacious fighter and of how little the Army of the Potomac's commander knew of the situation. Perhaps he was too stunned to comprehend a message Hancock sent him:

> I have never seen a more formidable attack, and if the Sixth and Fifth Corps have pressed up, the enemy will be destroyed. The enemy must be short of ammunition, as I was shot with a tenpenny nail.

Now it was past four on Friday afternoon, July 3, and George Meade gave no orders to the VI Corps. Nor, when he joined Gouverneur Warren for a look at the Round Tops, did he seem to have more than securing his southern flank in mind—understandably, for both officers came under rebel infantry fire and both narrowly escaped being hit.

Earlier, Hugh Judson Kilpatrick, only two years out of West Point but now a brigadier general, had launched a cavalry probe aimed at Longstreet's southernmost division. Infantrymen moved out and reclaimed the ruins of the Peach Orchard, but that was on their own initiative—not coordinated with Kilpatrick's thrust—and it was no substitute for the counterattack by V and VI Corps Meade had apparently forgotten to plan.

The general feeling was, wrote General Warren later, "that we had quite saved the country for the time and that we had done enough; that we might jeopardize all that we had done by trying to do too much."

At 8:35 that evening Meade got off a terse message to the general-in-chief, a report from a soldier who did not seem to realize, even four hours afterward, that he had—in Warren's words—"saved the country for the time."

After dark there was a long conference at Powell Hill's headquarters, during which General Lee began giving orders for a retreat. That was inevitable. After three days of fighting, ammunition stocks were low, food sources in the area depleted. Thousands of wounded men had to be evacuated. Federal cavalry had proved surprisingly effective.

"General Meade will commit no blunder in my front," Lee had said a few days earlier on learning of the change in the federal army's command, "and if I make one he will make haste to take advantage of it." That Meade had hesitated to do so that afternoon may well have baffled Lee. But he dared not draw too heavily upon fortune's gift of time. He would keep some forces on Seminary Ridge the next day to cover his army's withdrawal and start the wounded southward at once.

It was one o'clock on the morning of Saturday, July 4, when General Lee reached his headquarters. Wearily, slowly, he dismounted and then leaned against his sturdy gray war-horse, Traveller. "Too bad!" he said. "Too bad! Oh, too bad!"

For days Abraham Lincoln and Secretary of War Stanton had been starved for news. Gettysburg may have been uppermost in their minds, of course, but something of critical importance also seemed to be happening in the west, at Vicksburg.

The two men waited eagerly in the War Department's little telegraph room, growing more anxious by the hour. Such news as they had was stale by the better part of a day. And seldom had so much depended on Meade's ability to prevent a disaster: If he lost, the Union might never be restored.

Then, at some time late on the night of July 3 or in the early hours of the next morning, reassuring words came over the telegraph from Hanover, east of Gettysburg, sent by a reporter named Homer Byington. "Who is Byington?" the understandably cautious president wired back. The reply: "Ask Uncle Gideon."

Gideon Welles, secretary of the navy? Yes. Before the war he had been editor of a Hartford newspaper and knew all the journalists in Connecticut. Byington, he said, was reliable.

Byington had persuaded a telegraph operator in Hanover to go home, get a fresh battery, and try to get a report through. It was impossible, he had been told, the wires were down. But when the new battery was hooked up, the isolation ended—and, presumably, so did much of the tension.

General Meade's message, sent toward Washington at 8:35 P.M. on July 3, reached there at 6:10 A.M. on the fourth. The United States' birthday would be a happy one, after all, but few could imagine, as celebration over Gettysburg broke out, that soon behind this victory's announcement would be another: General Grant had finally captured Vicksburg.

But there was nothing to cheer about along the ridgelines south of Gettysburg. Rain, heavy at times, had made the night a miserable one. Threatening clouds remained at daylight on Saturday as, belatedly, stunned men on both sides began to sense the full magnitude of what had transpired.

Numbers compiled afterward could never give more than a hint of the human costs of those three days of fighting, but they were appalling enough:

	KILLED	WOUNDED	MISSING	TOTALS
Meade	3,155	14,529	5,365	23,049
Lee	3,903	18,735	5,425	28,063
Totals	7,058	33,264	10,790	51,112

If Lee had 75,000 "effectives" at sundown on June 30, now fewer than 47,000 remained. Similarly, in those three bloody days Meade's army had been reduced from roughly 90,000 to less than 67,000. And, by Saturday morning, July 4, the survivors were fought out.

General Lee would withdraw via the Emmitsburg Road, southwestward. Stuart was to send enough troopers to block Yankee cavalry from getting through passes in the ridges to the west and sweeping around the northern flank, others to screen the retreat and protect its rear. The wagons already filled with wounded men would start toward Virginia at once. After them, along a different route, would come Powell Hill's corps, Longstreet's next, finally Ewell's.

That afternoon, amid another heavy rainstorm, Lee sent officers under a truce flag to propose an exchange of able-bodied prisoners. Meade, thinking perhaps of the disadvantages Lee would be obliged to face in feeding 4,000 or so captives from scant supplies, declined.

General Meade had problems of his own. To him was left the grim task of burying the dead, evacuating the thousands of men wounded the day before, collecting weapons and equipment littering the slope of Cemetery Ridge, and getting his troops back into some semblance of order. His losses in officers had been severe; replacements had to be found. And despite signs that Lee might be pulling out, Meade seemed content to stand fast and await reports from cavalry patrols.

On that Saturday afternoon, Confederate cavalryman John Imboden later wrote:

The very windows of heaven seemed to have opened. The

rain fell in blinding sheets, the meadows were soon over-
flowed, and fences gave way before the raging streams.
During the storm, wagons, ambulances, and artillery carriages by hundreds—nay, by thousands—were assembling in
the fields along the road from Gettysburg to Cashtown in
one confused and apparently inextricable mass. As the
afternoon wore on, there was no abatement of the storm.
Canvas was no protection against its fury, and the wounded
men, lying upon the naked boards of the wagon-bodies were
drenched, horses and mules were blinded and maddened by
the wind and water, and became almost unmanageable.

Why had such a rain not fallen the day before, or earlier—in
time, anyway, to break the chain of deadly events? Was it the wrath
of God? Artilleryman Porter Alexander preferred to hope otherwise,
that storms were generated by heavy firing.

The wagons moved westward into the rainy night, bound for
Chambersburg and then southward via Williamsport to the Potomac and across it to Virginia's Shenandoah Valley. Imboden, his
cavalry escorting them, remembered:

I was never out of hearing of the groans and cries of the
wounded and dying. Scarcely one in a hundred had received
adequate surgical aid, owing to the demands on the hard-
working surgeons from still worse cases which had to be left
behind. Many of the wounded in the wagons had been
without food for 36 hours. Their torn and bloody clothing,
matted and hardened, was rasping the tender, inflamed, and
still oozing wounds....
From nearly every wagon as the teams trotted on, urged
by whip and shout, came such cries and shrieks as these:—
"Oh God! Why can't I die?"
"My God! Will no one have mercy and kill me?"...
Some were simply moaning; some were praying, and
others uttering the most fearful oaths and execrations that
despair and agony could wring from them; while a majority,
with a stoicism sustained by sublime devotion to the cause
they fought for, endured without complaint unspeakable
tortures, and even spoke words of cheer and comfort to their
unhappy comrades of less will or more acute nerves. No help
could be rendered to any of the sufferers. No heed could be
given to any of their appeals. Mercy and duty to the many
forbade the loss of a moment in the vain effort then and
there to comply with the prayers of the few. On! On! We

must move on. The storm continued, and the darkness was appalling. There was no time to fill even a canteen of water for a dying man, for, except the drivers and the guards, all were wounded and utterly helpless in that vast procession of misery.

To the end of that gloomy, rain-swept Saturday General Lee had remained facing Cemetery Ridge. Finally, Ewell's men began to withdraw, following Longstreet's southward on the Emmitsburg Road. Lee rode ahead. When he passed John Hood's Texans, they cheered; he raised his hat and nudged Traveller on. Then, when he reached Longstreet's roadside bivouac, he paused.

Not a word of reproach did Lee have for Longstreet. "It's all my fault," he said. "I thought my men were invincible."

Chapter 28

Victory in Front, Fire in the Rear

Near midnight on Independence Day, Brigadier General Herman Haupt and his railroad repair crews were at Oxford, seven miles east of Meade. From there he closed a report to General-in-Chief Halleck with these words:

> Persons just in from Gettysburg report the position of affairs. I fear that while Meade rests to refresh his men and collect supplies, Lee will be off so far that he cannot intercept him. A good force on the line of the Potomac to prevent Lee from crossing would, I think, insure his destruction.

Again Herman Haupt was using his extraordinary ability to view military situations realistically. And apart from the fact that he was among Halleck's few friends, it was habitual for him to say whatever he thought best to anyone, anytime. Haupt could be even more candid with Meade, his West Point classmate, and he was on Sunday morning, July 5, when he reached the army commander's headquarters. The Potomac was only a little more than a day's march away, he pointed out; Meade's army could not be footsore, having fought from behind stone walls; supply was assured with the railroad opening within a few hours. Why not take advantage of Lee's plight now, before he escaped?

> To this General Meade answered [wrote General Haupt afterward] that Lee had no pontoon train and that the river was swollen and not fordable.
> I replied: "Do not place confidence in that. I have men in my Construction Corps who could construct bridges in

forty-eight hours sufficient to pass that army, if they have no other material than such as they could gather from old buildings or from the woods, and it is not safe to assume that the enemy cannot do what we can."

This was sound advice , coming as it did from the man who had built a 400-foot trestle over a deep ravine out of nothing but, in Lincoln's words, "beanpoles and cornstalks." But resting his troops seemed uppermost in General Meade's mind on that Sunday morning. Haupt, discouraged, left. That night, he rode an engine to Washington.

Abraham Lincoln had been careful, even guarded, in wording his announcement of the victory, basing it on the "latest" news from Gettysburg and mentioning the "promise" of further success, as though he either could not quite believe all he knew or considered the battle mainly an encouraging development in what was actually a campaign. And after hearing what General Haupt had to say on July 6, the president seemed more inclined to prod George Meade than to praise him.

At first, the general-in-chief was not so restrained. On the seventh he wired Meade:

> It gives me great pleasure to inform you that you have been appointed a brigadier-general in the Regular Army, to rank from July 3, the date of your brilliant victory at Gettysburg.

By that night, though, Halleck's tone was beginning to change:

> You have given the enemy a stunning blow at Gettysburg. Follow it up, and give him another before he can reach the Potomac....There is strong evidence that he is short of artillery ammunition, and, if vigorously pressed, he must suffer.

"Push forward, and fight Lee before he can cross the Potomac," Halleck urged in still another message on the seventh. As if to underscore that, he sent one more:

> I have received from the President the following note, which I respectfully communicate:
> "We have certain information that Vicksburg surrendered to General Grant on the 4th of July. Now, if General Meade

can complete his work, so gloriously prosecuted thus far, by the literal or substantial destruction of Lee's army, the rebellion will be over."

Ironically, General Meade was getting pressure placed upon him in part because of something he had written in an order to his troops on the fourth, congratulating them:

> Our task is not yet accomplished, and the commanding general looks to the army for greater efforts to drive from our soil every vestige of the presence of the invader.

These words, said Lincoln to John Hay, reminded him of McClellan, who, before Antietam, had declared he meant to clear *Maryland* of rebels. "Will our Generals never get that idea out of their heads? The whole country is our soil."

By then a little more of it was again under the federal flag: Vicksburg. But it had taken seven long weeks of siege to win that critically important strip of high ground overlooking the Mississippi, seven or more months of failures before that.

Only with reluctance, and after Pemberton's well-fortified Confederates had thrown back two of his direct assaults, had General Grant resorted to siege operations. His line had to be more than fifteen miles long in order to contain Pemberton, who was defending Vicksburg's eastern side from trenches stretching only seven miles. The terrain's many ridges and deep ravines were also Confederate advantages. And Grant had no siege guns: Admiral Porter loaned him some large-caliber pieces from his gunboats, though, and these were added to the 220 or so less effective ones his units already had.

In some respects Vicksburg was Fort Sumter with the flags switched. Here the exterior ring of fire was federal. The 20,000 men in the Confederate garrison hoped the forces General Joe Johnston was gathering off to the northeast would rescue them, but they knew better than to count on that. Time was of the essence to the defenders. They had to stretch it out; yet the longer they did, the more dependent the outcome would be on their already-low stocks of food.

Within the Confederate Gibraltar were civilians who for one reason or another had elected to stay. Most of them took care of themselves, some moving into caves dug in the corduroyed ridges east of Vicksburg's fringe—places of refuge whenever Porter's gunboats on the river and Grant's gunners along the eastern crescent opened fire. Soldier's wife Mary Loughborough described how women and children coped:

> Some [cave] families had light bread made in large quantities, and subsisted on it with milk—provided their cows were not killed from one milking to another—without any more cooking until called on to replenish. Though most of us lived on corn bread and bacon, served three times a day, the only luxury in the meal consisting in its warmth, I had some flour, and frequently had some hard, tough biscuit made from it, there being no soda or yeast to be procured....

And there were moments of terror:

> One evening I heard the most heart-rending screams and moans. I was told that a mother had taken a child into a cave about a hundred yards from us; and having laid it on its little bed, as the poor woman believed, in safety, she took her seat near the entrance of the cave. A mortar shell came rushing through the air and fell with much force, entering the earth above the sleeping child—cutting through the cave—oh! most horrible sight to the mother—crushing in the upper part of the little sleeping head and taking away the young innocent life....
>
> A young girl, becoming weary of confinement in the cave, hastily ran to the house in the interval that lapsed between the slowly falling shells. On returning, an explosion sounded near her—one wild scream and she ran into her mother's presence, sinking like a wounded dove, the life blood flowing over the light summer dress in crimson ripples from a death wound in her side....

In the lines east of the cave dwellers the fighting was different from any yet seen in the war. Much of it was done from rifle pits manned by squads of marksmen who seldom had more of an enemy's body than his head for a target. At times there were sorties, small-unit probes of short duration. The federal challenge was to get nearer the Confederates' strong points without resorting to frontal assault, digging approach trenches instead or cutting tunnels under rebel positions and blowing them up with explosive charges: "mines." But gains were measured in a few yards, and victories were limited to momentary satisfactions. Years later, a Confederate engineer, Major Samuel Lockett, described one:

On the 29th of June the enemy had succeeded in getting up close to the parapet of the Third Louisiana redan. We rolled some of their unexploded 13-inch shells down upon them and annoyed them so much as to force them to stop operations. At night they protected themselves against this method of attack by erecting a screen in front of their sap. This screen was made of heavy timbers, which even the shells could not move. I finally determined to try the effect of a barrel of powder. One containing 125 pounds was obtained, a time-fuse set to fifteen seconds was placed in the bunghole, was touched off by myself by a live coal, and the barrel was rolled over the parapet by two of our sappers. The barrel went true to its destination and exploded with terrific force. Timbers, gabions, and fascines were hurled into the air in all directions, and the [federal] sappers once more were compelled to retire.

Occasionally, the troops in some sectors declared impromptu truces, to gather blackberries (thought to be the best cure for diarrhea) or merely to visit. For a few minutes they would swap stories or tobacco or complaints about their generals. Then some officer would come along, order the men back to their trenches, and the siege would go on.

In the end hunger made more difference than anything else. In mid-June, General Pemberton had seized all the cattle inside his lines; the last hog had long since been slaughtered, and soon mules came under the cleaver. Rats might be next. Food, in whatever form, might last until July 5. But would the endurance of a starving garrison?

On June 28 General Pemberton received a letter signed, merely, "Many Soldiers." In part it said:

> If you can't feed us, you had better surrender us....I tell you plainly, men are not going to lie here and perish, if they do love their country dearly. Self-preservation is the first law of nature, and hunger will compel a man to do almost anything.... This army is now ripe for mutiny, unless it can be fed. Just think of one small biscuit and one or two mouthfuls of bacon per day.

Joe Johnston's rescue column was the only hope Pemberton had left. Grant had made certain that such deliverance was not forthcoming by sending Cump Sherman with seven divisions eastward to block the 20,000 or so men Johnston was reported to have assembled. So, on July 3, as gallant Lewis Armistead's hat-tipped saber fell from his dead hand on Cemetery Ridge, John Pemberton began the process of surrendering Vicksburg. Grant wanted the capitulation to be unconditional. Pemberton refused, hoping to keep his men from being held captive in Union prisons. He told his staff: "I am a Northern man, I know my people....I know we can get better terms from them on the Fourth of July than on any other day of the year. We must sacrifice our pride to these considerations."

"Galvanized" Confederate Pemberton was correct; Grant did relent, allowing the garrison to be paroled. To ship that many men, Grant wrote later, would have tied up Union transportation facilities unduly. Moreover, "[Pemberton's army] was largely composed of men whose homes were in the South-west; I knew many of them were tired of the war and would get home just as soon as they could."

Surrender did occur on the Union's Independence Day. But General Grant restrained his men from celebrating that or the victory. The Confederate troops "had behaved so well," wrote Grant, "that I did not want to humiliate them."

Was July 1863 the turning point in this war? Some have said so, thinking mostly of the disasters Confederates suffered in that month's first two weeks.

Gettysburg had cost the South 28,000 troops; at Vicksburg, 31,600 were paroled. Another 6,300 surrendered at Port Hudson on July 9, bringing the total to 65,900 men, most of whom could not be replaced. And as though the Fourth of July had not been calamitous enough, on that day Braxton Bragg's army reached Chattanooga, ending the retreat that had begun on June 26 with William Rosecrans's army sweeping around Bragg's flanks at Shelbyville, leaving the federals in control of nearly all of southeastern Tennessee.

It was more likely that the Southern tide had started to ebb in the fall of 1862, that these defeats were consequences, grim evidence that the new nation was becoming steadily weaker and therefore easier to whip. This was apparent at Gettysburg, where neither the Army of Northern Virginia nor its commanding general performed at the levels attained at Second Manassas, Sharpsburg, Fredericksburg, and Chancellorsville. And in the west, where the Confederacy had never won a major battle or been successful at anything but cavalry raiding, Jefferson Davis's reliance on the patriotism of squabbling generals had resulted in Stones River, Bragg's retreat to Chattanooga, and the loss of Vicksburg and Port Hudson.

Was the North winning in the west entirely because of the South's blunders? No, Grant almost always had advantages in terms of troop strength and firepower, and he was tenacious. Had the

Union stopped losing in the east? Gettysburg suggested that, but it was too soon to make such a claim.

One thing, at least, was clear: Winfield Scott's ridiculed Anaconda strategy was working. The blockade, though far from completely effective, had made it increasingly difficult for the South to get needed supplies from Europe. Regaining full control of the Mississippi's entire length had taken a long time, but General Grant had done it, cutting the Confederacy in two. Now there remained Scott's third element: the squeezing.

Lincoln understood that, and throughout July's second week he applied all the pressure he could on Meade to destroy Lee's army north of the flooded Potomac. Such orders proved easier to give than to execute. Exactly as Herman Haupt had warned Meade on July 5, Lee's men built a bridge out of whatever they could find near Williamsport and crossed over it into Virginia on the night of July 13–14.

Ironically, in July's second half, the Union itself took some heavy squeezing—from the dissidents within its borders. During the spring, Copperhead secession demands seemed less strident, but pro-peace sentiment remained strong at Democratic party conventions held in three of the six states in the Old Northwest. Delegates to the Iowa gathering resolved: "That our Union...can never be perpetuated by force of arms, and that a republican government held together by the sword becomes a military despotism." To prevent that, Illinois Democrats proposed "a National Convention to settle upon terms of peace," with "restoration of the Union as it was" as the goal. And in Connecticut, Democrats took similar positions, as did the crowd at a mass meeting in New York City on June 3.

News of federal victories at Gettysburg and later Vicksburg dampened some of the pro-peace ardor, but by mid-July another antiadministration movement was breaking out. Back in March, Congress had passed a Conscription Act that Lincoln, needing troops, had to accept and apply despite the law's many serious flaws and the Union public's complaints. And this time, fire in the rear would not be a threat but an appalling reality.

By July the draft's complex procedures were being applied throughout the Union. Congress saw the draft as a way to stimulate voluntary enlistments, which had been lagging. But locally the draft was perceived as nationalization of manpower procurement; as coercive; as encouraging bribery, influence peddling, flight to the far west or Canada, and corruption of all sorts; and as discrimination against the poor. A man could be excused from serving if he paid the federal government a $300 "commutation" fee or could afford to hire a substitute. But for many $300 represented a year's wages. And while the fee was supposed to put a cap on what substitutes could charge, demand for them in some places still set higher prices.

"A rich man's war but a poor man's fight" was one of the slogans the law's flaws inspired, and so the "blood money" provisions made it seem. Over time public donations, payment of fees by employers, loans, and other solutions aided enough laborers to dilute the draft's unfairness. But in early July 1863 that was less apparent than the threatening presence of provost marshals in every congressional district.

In New York City application of the draft law triggered a riot like no other in North America before or since. It would get most of the attention, then and afterward, for in New York were concentrated tensions based on race and national origin, economic layering ranging from great wealth to abysmal poverty, and a mix of corruption and inefficiency in government matching the city's preeminence in population.

On Monday, July 13, a mob destroyed the draft's offices at Third Avenue and East Forty-sixth Street, then headed for newspapers' headquarters buildings and attacked police, anyone appearing to be "rich," and—in particular—all colored persons. Blacks were thought to be threats to unskilled and recent immigrant whites' jobs, strikebreakers, the cause of a war the government could not win.

The mob surged over to upper Fifth Avenue, along the way looting stores and bars and clubbing two invalid soldiers to death, and set ablaze the Colored Orphan Asylum. Other rioters broke into the Second Avenue Armory. Soon bodies of blacks were dangling from lampposts; their homes were burning; federal offices were wrecked; Superintendent of Police John A. Kennedy was mauled, his body thrown into a ditch; and all the city's authorities could do was ask Washington to send troops to stop the rampaging.

Washington responded, but this took time because the units had to be moved from Pennsylvania. On Wednesday night, after three days in which Manhattan had been controlled by the mob, several regiments that had turned back Lee's army nearly two weeks earlier arrived and got to work. On Thursday they fired rifle volleys into the crowds, used grapeshot, their bayonets, whatever it took. Estimates of rioters killed ranged from less than 100 to more than 1,000. Eventually, the number of troops sent to New York to keep the peace would rise to 20,000, and the city's government would pay the $300 commutation fee for each of its men drafted, never knowing which of them might have been guilty of crimes that shocked the civilized world.

Ironically, on Saturday, July 18—only a few days after the New York City riots—Colonel Robert Gould Shaw was leading his 54th Massachusetts in an attack on Battery Wagner, a rebel fort at the entrance to Charleston's harbor. That day, Shaw's black soldiers proved that their devotion to the Union cause was second to none. Their assault failed; Colonel Shaw and his orderly sergeant were killed on Battery Wagner's parapet, and nearly half of the rest of the 54th's troops were shot to pieces.

Negro recruits in Grant's army had fought commendably at Port Hudson and Milliken's Bend earlier. But that was all but eclipsed by the circumstances prevailing at Battery Wagner, a strong point thought vital to recapturing Fort Sumter and taking the city where secession's roots were deepest.

Back in April striking at Charleston made sense, or so the planners in the Navy Department seemed to believe. Historian Bruce Catton was referring to Battery Wagner, but his comment may as well have been directed at the entire federal Charleston campaign when he wrote that the fort was "lying at the end of one of those insane chains of war-time logic in which men step from one undeniable truth to another and so come at last to a land of crippling nonsense."

At the beginning of this particular chain of madness was USS *Monitor*, the ugly iron craft with a revolving turret. Impressed by the *Monitor*'s success in driving the ironclad CSS *Virginia* out of the fight at Hampton Roads in March the year before, naval authorities had ordered twenty-seven more ships of this class built, and by early April of 1863 eight were ready to be put to use. But where? Well, what target could be more appealing to discouraged Union citizens than Charleston?

Steam power had enabled Rear Admiral Samuel F. Du Pont to demolish the old notion that ships could not take a fort; he had done that in November 1861 at Port Royal Sound, where he took *two* forts, one named for General Beauregard. Now Du Pont had the very latest products of Union technology, monitors combining the advantages of steam and the protection iron afforded the crews of eleven-inch guns.

At Charleston, however, Beauregard was not a fort's name but—once again—commander of the "ring of fire," batteries lining the shores of the horseshoe-shaped harbor. And on April 7, when Du Pont's flotilla came steaming up the ship channel toward Fort Sumter, General Beauregard's gunners there and everywhere else around three-quarters of a circle gave their counterparts in the federal marvels the smell of hell.

When Admiral Du Pont finally ordered his monitors out of the fight, their captains' damage reports were shocking. Most often hit was the *Keokuk*, ninety times; the least battered was the *Montauk*, fourteen times. Du Pont wanted to try again the next morning. No, advised his ships' commanders, and the *Keokuk* added heavy emphasis to their objections by keeling over and sinking in the shallows seaward of Morris Island. Everything had gone wrong, from designer John Ericcson's drafting tables in New Jersey to the turrets in which Du Pont's sailors' bodies were ripped apart by bolts sent flying through the air by Confederate solid rounds hammering the iron outside. Worse, the sluggish monitors had lacked the power either to hold their places in the battle line or to maneuver once they drifted out of it.

For Admiral Du Pont, at sixty-one, Charleston must have been what Gettysburg would later be to Robert E. Lee, fifty-six. He reluctantly heeded his subordinates' counsel and withdrew.

"Battles," wrote John Rodgers, captain of the USS *Weehawken* (hit fifty-three times) to Navy Secretary Gideon Welles, "are won by two qualities, ability to endure and ability to injure." Rodgers, General McClellan's host aboard the ironclad *Galena*, cruising on the James River near the end of the Seven Days' Battles, was right. The monitors had done little more than add Union-inflicted scars to the masonry walls of Fort Sumter.

But Abraham Lincoln was not willing to let it go at that. He sacked Du Pont and gave the army the major role in the next attempt to take Charleston. When it came, in July, repulse of Robert Shaw's gallant 54th Massachusetts at Battery Wagner led to a siege that would go on and on. But Shaw's men had fought so well that—to cite only one example—the members of New York's Union League Club recruited, equipped, and in March 1864 proudly sent to the war the 20th Regiment United States Colored Troops.

From the Potomac's south bank in July's second half the Army of Northern Virginia moved southward, up the Shenandoah Valley, past Winchester and Front Royal. Meade's forces were east of the Blue Ridge and seemed headed for Gordonsville—far enough to the south to speed Lee's retreat. By early in August the Confederates were holding a line near Culpeper, and Meade's advance was stalled on the Rappahannock north of there.

As Lee's army rested, refitted, and reorganized to adjust for Gettysburg's losses, the commanding general wrote a letter to his president, one suggesting how deeply his defeat had affected him:

> The general remedy for the want of success in a military commander is his removal. This is natural, and, in many

instances, proper. For, no matter what may be the ability of this officer, if he loses the confidence of his troops disaster must sooner or later ensue.

I have been prompted by these reflections more than once since my return from Pennsylvania to propose to Your Excellency the propriety of selecting another commander for this army. I have seen and heard the expression of discontent in the public journals at the result of the expedition. I do not know how far the feeling extends in the army. My brother officers have been too kind to report it, and so far the troops have been too generous to exhibit it. It is fair, however, to suppose that it does exist, and success is so necessary to us that nothing should be risked to secure it. I therefore, in all sincerity, request Your Excellency to take measures to supply my place.

At this point, Jefferson Davis must have groaned, at least inwardly. But General Lee wrote more:

I do this with the more earnestness because no one is more aware than myself of my inability for the duties of my position. I cannot even accomplish what I myself desire. How can I fulfill the expectations of others? In addition I sensibly feel the growing failure of my bodily strength. I have not yet recovered from the attack I experienced last spring. I am becoming more and more incapable of exertion, and am thus prevented from making the personal examinations and giving the personal supervision to the operations in the field which I feel to be necessary. I am so dull in making use of the eyes of others I am frequently misled. Everything, therefore, points to the advantages to be derived from a new commander, and I the more anxiously urge the matter upon Your Excellency from my belief that a younger and abler man than myself can readily be obtained. I know that he will have as gallant and brave an army as ever existed to second his efforts, and it would be the happiest day of my life to see at its head a worthy leader—one that would accomplish more than I ever could perform and all that I have wished.

This was truly astonishing, for it was most unlike Robert Lee to reveal his most private thoughts. He concluded:

I have no complaints to make of any one but myself. I have

received nothing but kindness from those above me, and the most considerate attention from my comrades and companions in arms. To Your Excellency I am specially indebted for uniform kindness and consideration. You have done everything in your power to aid me in the work committed to my charge, without omitting anything to promote the general welfare. I pray that your efforts may at length be crowned with success, and that you may long live to enjoy the thanks of a grateful people.

What a contrast there was between the self-effacing Lee and the hollow vanity of Joseph Eggleston Johnston, who since Vicksburg's fall had been plaguing Davis by having others give anti-administration newspapers information leading editors to praise Johnston and condemn Pemberton and the authorities in Richmond. Of all the Confederacy's full generals only Lee had lived up to Jefferson Davis's hopes. No, the Confederacy could not lose him. So its president replied:

It well became Sidney Johnston when overwhelmed by a senseless clamor to admit the rule that success is the test of merit, and there is nothing which I have found to require a greater effort of patience than to bear the criticisms of the ignorant, who pronounce everything a failure which does not equal their expectations or desires....

As if he had Joe Johnston in mind, Davis wrote on:

Were you capable of stooping to it, you could easily surround yourself with those who would fill the press with your laudations, and seek to exalt you for what you had not done rather than detract from the achievements which will make you and your army the subject of history and object of the world's admiration for generations to come.

That said, now Davis concentrated his fire:

But suppose, my dear friend, that I were to admit, with all their implications, the points which you present, where am I to find that new commander who is to possess the greater ability which you believe to be required? I do not doubt the readiness with which you would give way to one who could accomplish all that you have wished, and you will do me the justice to believe that if Providence should kindly offer such a person for our use, I would not hesitate to avail [myself] of his services.

My sight is not sufficiently penetrating to discover such hidden merit, if it exists, and I have but used the language of sober earnestness when I have impressed upon you the propriety of avoiding all unnecessary exposure to danger, because I have felt our country could not afford to lose you. To ask me to substitute you by some one in my judgment more fit to command, or who would possess more of the confidence of the army, or of the reflecting men of the country, is to demand of me an impossibility.

It only remains for me to hope that you will take all possible care of yourself, that your health and strength may be entirely restored, and that the Lord will preserve you for the important duties devolved upon you in the struggle of our suffering country, for the independence which we have engaged in war to maintain.

The contents of these letters had to be a well-kept secret, for as a Confederate veteran said long after the war: "The army would have arisen in revolt if it had been called upon to give up General Lee." But it did not have to do that. He had done what his sense of honor required, and now he would go on doing his duty as best he could on behalf of his country.

Abraham Lincoln was not as fortunate as Jefferson Davis, at least in terms of the president of the Union's relations with his eastern army's commander. In mid-July, upon learning of Lee's escape across the Potomac, Lincoln vented his anger in a letter to General Meade:

And yet you stood there, and let the flood run down, bridges be built and the enemy move away without attacking him.... Your golden opportunity is lost, and I am distressed immeasurably because of it.

But the president did not send Meade the letter, nor would the general know until years afterward what Lincoln had said to John Hay: "We had them in our grasp. We had only to stretch forth our hands and they were ours. And nothing I could do or say could make the army move."

Commenting on this generations later, British Brigadier General Colin R. Ballard would write in his study of the Union president's generalship: "Lincoln, the amateur strategist, grasped it at the time, while his professional soldiers were congratulating themselves on 'driving the invaders from our soil.'" Well, not quite. Meade had at least pressed southward far enough by July's end to oblige Lee to think first in terms of how best to defend Richmond.

In part that was because the general-in-chief, often the lightning rod for criticism directed at the president, let go the thunderbolt Lincoln had held back. Halleck had wired to the Army of the Potomac's commander:

> I need hardly say to you that the escape of Lee's army without another battle has created great dissatisfaction in the mind of the President, and will require an active and energetic pursuit on your part to remove the impression that it has not been sufficiently active heretofore.

George Meade had gotten active, but he did not like being prodded, and he replied:

> Having performed my duty conscientiously and to the best of my ability, the censure of the President conveyed in your dispatch of 1 p.m. this day is, in my judgment, so undeserved that I feel compelled most respectfully to ask to be relieved from command of this army.

Stimulus, not censure, was intended, or so Halleck told Meade in his next message. No cause existed for his relief.

And so it was that in the war's now-quiet eastern theater one nation's president had used all the eloquence and logic he could conjure up to persuade Gettysburg's loser to remain as the Army of Northern Virginia's commander, while up in Washington Lincoln, through Halleck, had already made it abundantly clear to the battle's winner that the guillotine's blade was raised.

Chapter 29

Chickamauga: *River of Death*

N ow, in 1863's high summer, old faces were reappearing and old ideas and controversies were being resurrected while new proposals were left to simmer in the season's heat.

James Longstreet, for example, had never abandoned his hope of taking his corps out to the west. In August, General Lee gave such a movement his blessing, not because he wanted to be rid of Longstreet but because Braxton Bragg needed help.

At about the same time, the familiar, oddly bewhiskered face of Ambrose Burnside reappeared on the Northern scene. Having survived failure in handling Copperhead civil disobedience to Abraham Lincoln's satisfaction in Ohio earlier, now the loser at Fredericksburg turned up with his IX Corps outside Knoxville in East Tennessee, the pro-Union region the president had long craved having back under the Stars and Stripes.

What tied these two developments together was a railroad, roughly 500 miles of it, from Richmond westward to Knoxville and then to Chattanooga, where Bragg's army sat and watched as Rosecrans's forces approached, snail-like, from the northwest. Using that rail line, Longstreet could have his troops alongside Bragg's in four days. But if Burnside captured Knoxville, the Confederate troop transfer would have to be made via North and South Carolina and Atlanta, a route nearly twice as long, with frequent, time-consuming changes of cars because of differences in track width, among many other disadvantages.

While the Confederates talked, Burnside took Knoxville.

Well to the southwest, Ulysses Grant was waiting for his superiors to make up their minds regarding an idea, seconded surprisingly by Nathaniel Banks: to drive roughly eastward through

Mississippi and Alabama and take Mobile. No, finally came the answer from faraway Washington, Banks's mission was to invade Texas. Grant was to stay at Vicksburg.

Banks, himself one of the Army of the Potomac's discards, sent another, Major General William Franklin, with 4,000 troops westward to attack an unfinished rebel fort on the Texas side of the Sabine River border with Louisiana. This was to be the beginning point for a campaign aimed toward Houston, with Franklin's strength increasing eventually to 15,000 men.

Franklin went by sea, escorted by four gunboats. When his transports neared Sabine Pass on September 8, though, he kept his men on board and left it to the navy to reduce the fort, held by forty-odd Texans led by Lieutenant Richard Dowling.

Seldom, if ever, had so few men with only six guns done so much damage in so short a time to such grandiose federal hopes. "Dick" Dowling's Texans disabled two Union gunboats and drove another one aground; the fourth never got within range, nor did William Franklin take any of his troops ashore. That night, stunned, he ordered his task force to return to New Orleans. Texans' valor apart, an old idea had prevailed: Warships alone could not take a fort.

Within Braxton Bragg's army in Chattanooga the wrangling going on between its commander and his senior generals entered its second year. Into this environment in July came D. Harvey Hill, Jackson's brother-in-law, replacing dissident William Hardee. Hill had fought well in the Army of Northern Virginia, especially at Sharpsburg; yet Lee had not opposed his transfer to command of the North Carolina department, where he was when promoted to lieutenant general. But Hill soon found much about his new leader to dislike, so his presence gave no support to Bragg, who needed it greatly.

Later would come James Longstreet, who would serve Bragg well but sense the western army commander's faults immediately and yearn once more for independent command. Was it that Bragg was so deficient in the admirable qualities Lee possessed or that the newcomers' ambitions fogged their judgments?

Arguments could be built either way, but something about Bragg seemed to invite disobedience to his orders. If a single cause for objection were to be found, his subordinates appeared to consider it justification for doing as they pleased, and this included doing nothing.

Obedience was the oldest idea of them all, fundamental, a soldier's first duty. How important it was would be given new proof in the high summer's battles on terrain more challenging than any yet encountered in more than two years of warfare.

Now William Rosecrans understood how vulnerable Bragg was to flanking movements. When the federal general was satisfied he had amassed enough supplies to sustain him for a while, he sent one corps opposite Chattanooga to shell the town and his other three west and south of it, crossing to Bragg's side of the Tennessee River. That was all it took. Bragg abandoned the city to Rosecrans on September 9 without a fight and slipped southward into a maze of hills and streams and forests in the region drained primarily by a creek called Chickamauga, an Indian word for "river of death."

For Rosecrans it had been so easy he became complacent. He believed rebel deserters who said that Bragg was skedaddling southward along the rail line to Atlanta. And he allowed his four corps to drift out of contact with each other, some by as much as forty miles.

Roughly a year earlier, in Maryland, General Lee had split his army into five parts. But that had been planned and the place and date for reassembly specified; not so in this instance. Rosecrans, with close to 60,000 men, had carelessly exposed three-quarters of them, in three dispersed fragments of maybe 15,000 each, to being chewed up one at a time, and at sundown on September 10, there was nothing much the federal army commander could do to prevent that.

Bragg, with his forces well in hand near Lafayette, was receiving reinforcements. Down from Knoxville had come Simon Bolivar Buckner with 8,000. Joe Johnston had sent him a few brigades. And James Longstreet's two divisions, led by Hood and McLaws, were nearing the end of their long train ride from Virginia via the Carolinas and Atlanta. Soon Bragg would have roughly 70,000 troops, thanks to the Confederacy's central position and what was left of a worn-out railroad net.

General Bragg, too, was in a central position, with three isolated and enormously attractive chunks of Rosecrans's army all but inviting him to destroy them one by one. Opportunities such as this all commanders dream of but few ever have. Here, finally, was Braxton Bragg's chance to erase the past—if only he could grasp it quickly enough.

Union General Thomas gave Bragg an apparently easy morsel to bite by sending a division led by Major General James Scott Negley down and eastward to a pass called Dug Gap on Pigeon Mountain, only five miles or so from Bragg's headquarters at Lafayette. Bragg learned about Negley's presence on Wednesday night, September 9, and ordered Harvey Hill's corps to attack Dug Gap frontally—from the east—while Major General Thomas Hindman's division and Simon Buckner's swept down on the Yankees' flank and rear from

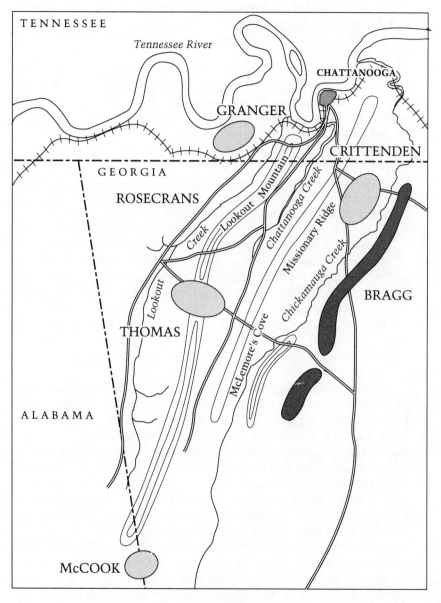

Rosecrans' Dispersal

the north, driving the remnants up McLemore's Cove to its dead end and annihilating them.

All this was meant to happen first thing on Thursday, the tenth. By sundown hardly any of it had. Bragg was infuriated by the excuses, but he tolerated them and told the generals to try again the next morning, Friday, the eleventh. They did, only to find Negley gone; he had retreated to Stevens's Gap, from which word would soon reach General Rosecrans that Bragg's army had by no means skedaddled to Atlanta or anywhere else.

Disappointed, Bragg turned his attention to Crittenden's federal corps. Its leading elements were near Lee & Gordon's Mill and moving toward Bragg's rear. Bishop Polk's divisions were within striking range; Bragg ordered him to attack the Yankees first thing on the morning of Sunday, September 13.

Polk did not: Crittenden, he explained to the furious army commander, was concentrating his divisions and was too strong to be assaulted. Bragg took charge, sent for reinforcements, even got his forces into line for the advance. But hours had slipped by, and Crittenden had backed away. For a second time within a few days Bragg was frustrated.

Now it was too late even to think about smashing McCook's Union corps. But from Lafayette Bragg could counter any moves the federals made, so he drew his forces in closer and waited.

While Braxton Bragg fumed and brooded, William Rosecrans— by Monday, September 14, correctly considering his army in great peril—ordered McCook to bring his corps northeastward to join Thomas's and Crittenden's, and he asked Burnside, up east of Knoxville, to come to his aid. Gone now were all signs of his overconfidence. Bragg's aborted thrust at Crittenden, together with spies' reports that Longstreet was coming by rail, had put the federal army's commander on notice that if the Confederates got around Crittenden's northern flank, they could also drive on westward and cut the Union army's communications line.

Concentration was the first necessity, which for McCook's men made it a question of legs. Terrain made their march one of at least fifty miles. Meanwhile, Rosecrans had to shift Thomas and send for Gordon Granger's corps: Bragg was forcing his decisions now, drawing him to a battleground of the rebel's choosing.

But Bragg's sulking over the earlier fiascoes went on for several days. By Thursday, September 17, Old Rosy's main elements were still separated, but not by much. He had made the most of the yards of time Bragg had given him, but he was still in more trouble than he might be able to survive.

Braxton Bragg snapped out of his stupor on the seventeenth with the intent to give Rosecrans all the trouble he could. Moving northward to consolidate his forces facing Crittenden's federal corps near Lee & Gordon's Mill, confident that Longstreet's men would soon be arriving, accepting cavalry scouts' reports that Rosecrans's corps were nearby and massing but not yet tied in, Bragg seemed determined to destroy Rosecrans's army.

Bishop Polk had a plan for doing that: get around the Yankees' northern flank and cut them off from Chattanooga and their bridges over the Tennessee River west of the city. No, decided Bragg, and his orders for Friday the eighteenth were designed to drive the Union army southwestward up McLemore's Cove and annihilate it there in that cul-de-sac. Nothing of the sort happened. But by sundown John Hood's division had arrived and crossed to Chickamauga Creek's west bank, and several other units were in position to follow Hood during the night, so the day had not been a complete failure.

But Friday night's darkness prevented General Bragg from knowing that Rosecrans, too, was moving troops: Thomas's corps from Pond Spring northward far enough to leapfrog Crittenden; McCooks's up to tie in and protect the federal army's southern flank. By Saturday morning Rosecrans actually had Bragg's army flanked, given Granger's small corps' presence five miles or so north of the nearest Confederate unit.

All this, however, had taken place in wooded terrain where no one could see more than a few yards in any direction except in clearings, which were few and far between. And neither could either commander imagine, or plan for, the challenges Saturday morning would bring.

Nathan Bedford Forrest's Confederate cavalrymen, guarding the northern end of Bragg's line, got the first indication that their army commander was going to be surprised when, soon after sunrise, they were attacked by one of George Thomas's divisions. Forrest pitched into the Yankees and drove them back.

It was a meeting engagement, and it drew more and more of both sides' troops into it, spreading southward through the woods west of Chickamauga Creek's banks. No commander in either army had much control over the shooting going on or the men doing it along the six-mile line. In the forests west of the Chickamauga there was no way to maintain formations. Men in squads or less slugged it out amid battle smoke drifting through the trees, letting go the fury pent up during months of waiting to get it over with. It was a hunter's kind of day except that the game could fire back, making it a simple matter of kill or be killed, and at very close range, which is why so much unplanned slaughtering and maiming took place during that Saturday's hidden combats.

And there were odd moments: Hood and his Texans ran into swarms of yellow jackets just as they were about to make their final breakthrough charge. General Rosecrans stood with the Widow Glenn outside her house, now his headquarters, holding a map and listening to her tell him where she thought the sounds of firing were coming from: "Nigh out about Reed's Bridge—" And a sixty-three-pound boy of twelve, Johnny Clem from Ohio, shot a rebel colonel out of his saddle.

Not until after Saturday's sundown did the fighting stop. Nothing much had changed, except that thousands of men hoping to settle something had died or been wounded. While the tired and thirsty soldiers slept, Rosecrans got his generals together for a council of war: Stay and defend, he decided. At the same time, Bragg was telling his commanders to renew the attack at sunrise Sunday morning.

While these decisions were being made, General Longstreet and his staff got off the last of the trains that had brought them nearly a thousand miles. Surprised and perhaps miffed because neither Bragg nor anyone else had come to meet him, Longstreet rode off into the night in search of his superior's headquarters, only to blunder inside the Yankees' lines; but he got out again, primarily because it was too dark for the guards to get a good look at him.

Before midnight the newcomer found the army commander. Longstreet's fretting over the lack of proper reception at the station may have been eased somewhat when he learned that he would command the army's southern wing; Polk would have the northern one. But except for John Hood's men and a few other brigades, he would be leading troops he knew nothing about in complex terrain he had never seen in daylight. And Longstreet may well have been appalled by the discovery that Bragg was reorganizing his army only a few hours before opening an attack at dawn on a critical battle's second day.

George Thomas, weary from marching all Friday night and fighting all day that Saturday, slept through the council of war at the Widow Glenn's house, stirring when asked for his opinion long enough to say only, "I would strengthen the left," meaning his exposed northern flank. "Old Pap" wanted Negley's division shifted from south of him to where he was sure Bragg would strike at sunrise. Rosecrans assured him Negley would be sent. Even so, Thomas remained uneasy, and so did his troops. They knew they had better have thick log walls between them and rebel lead if Sunday's fighting was going to be anything like Saturday's had been.

All night the sounds of axes cutting and trees falling kept other soldiers from getting much sleep. At dawn, making edgy men even more unsettled, layers of haze gave the sun an ominous blood red color as it rose.

Sunrise was supposed to be the signal for the Confederate attack to begin. An hour afterward, however, Braxton Bragg was still listening in vain for the booming of General Polk's guns. Furious, the army commander jumped into the saddle and rode in search of the bishop. But he found Harvey Hill first, and upon him Bragg vented some of his wrath.

Innocent, the corps commander pleaded. Hill had not been at the campfire where the orders for Sunday were given, and he had received none afterward from Polk; yes, his divisions were neither where Bragg expected nor ready to attack; but how could they have been when he had been left to wonder what to do?

Polk rode up, after having given orders belatedly to two divisions under Hill's command—which had been expanded as part of General Bragg's overnight army reorganization without Hill's knowing it—and the bishop added such emphasis as he could to Bragg's demands that their subordinate get something going. Harvey Hill did, but with the meticulous, time-consuming care Longstreet had first displayed on Gettysburg's second day.

When Hill's divisions attacked (by then four hours late, hours in which the Yankee ax wielders had built more and more fortifications), the blood was gone from the sun, but Southerners by the hundreds were shedding theirs on the ground in front of the barricades. Finally, General Bragg had what he had ordered, an assault hammering westward to break the northern segment of Rosecrans's line and then push the survivors southwestward into McLemore's Cove, where his forces could annihilate them.

"I would strengthen the left," the exhausted George Thomas had advised the night before, and William Rosecrans spent most of the morning on Sunday, September 20, trying to do just that. Had the terrain west of Chickamauga Creek been as unobstructed as the ground along Stones River north of Murfreesboro, the federal army commander might have seen for himself that Negley had not leapfrogged up to Thomas's northern flank. But here, with the waning high summer's lush foliage masking everything, Rosecrans had to rely on aides' reports regarding his troops' locations and movements—and Bragg's.

In these circumstances, in midmorning, General Rosecrans acted on erroneous information and opened a half-mile-wide gap in his line by ordering one division too many northward to heed

Thomas's repeated appeals for reinforcements. Soon, though, and without leaving his headquarters, he would be able to see for himself the result.

General Longstreet had heard nothing at all from his army commander since their parting near midnight. From the sounds of the fighting, though, it seemed as if attacking in echelon from north to south—Bragg's intent—might turn the battle into another costly fiasco. Far better it would be, the newly appointed wing commander decided, to mass enough brigades to throw one solid punch. And that is exactly what Longstreet on his own initiative got ready to do.

At about eleven-fifteen that Sunday morning, with Hood's Texans in the lead, Longstreet sent roughly 16,000 troops westward along a narrow front. Heavy Yankee fire plunged into the attackers from both right and left, but not from straight ahead. Was this a trap? No. Once they jumped over barricades abandoned only moments earlier, Longstreet's punchers saw federal columns marching away to the north; with savage fury, screaming their marrow-chilling yell, the Confederates charged into them.

"Go ahead and keep ahead of everything!" shouted Hood to Brigadier General Bushrod Johnson. And Johnson and the rest of Longstreet's force surged on for a mile, directly into the gap Rosecrans had created by shuffling divisions.

Few federals stayed to fight. By entire brigades they ran, scrambling northward from the woods to Dry Valley Road, which led to McFarland's Gap in Missionary Ridge and beyond to Chattanooga. In only forty-five minutes Longstreet had wrecked McCook's Union corps, sweeping along with it Rosecrans and his staff.

Only seconds after the Roman Catholic general had crossed himself, he told the officers gathered near Widow Glenn's house: "If you care to live any longer, get away from here!" He did not have to say that twice, nor did he wait for news of what had happened to Crittenden's corps. He would learn along the fugitive-thronged road to Chattanooga that Longstreet's punch had destroyed Crittenden, too.

That left solid George Thomas, still holding Polk's wing of the Confederate army east of him while he worked frantically to build a new east-west line to defend his southern flank and rear. To him Rosecrans sent his chief of staff, Major James A. Garfield, with a message giving Thomas discretion to stay and fight till dark or retreat. But during the time it took for Garfield to evade Forrest's rebel cavalrymen swarming north of Thomas's corps, Old Pap made his own decision: to stand fast.

By noon the Confederate drive had stalled, partly from sheer

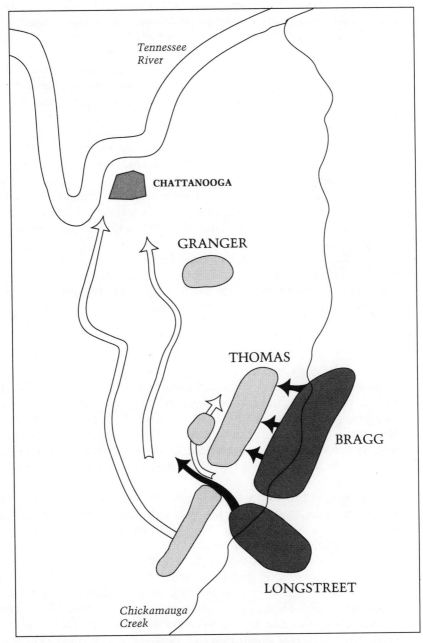

Tennessee River

CHATTANOOGA

GRANGER

THOMAS

BRAGG

LONGSTREET

Chickamauga Creek

Longstreet's Attack, Second Day

fatigue but also because Yankee fire was coming from the north and it was a problem. Earlier, John Hood had not been able to wave his saber as he led his troops forward; his sword arm had been shot at Gettysburg and was in a sling. Now, as he was rallying his Texans for another charge, a minié ball struck his left thigh and shattered the bone. Thinking their leader was dying, his men surged forward to exact revenge. But this alone was no solution, and Longstreet knew it.

After giving orders for his line to swing northward like a gate to face the federals and for his troops to be given their noonday meal and then regroup and replenish their ammunition, the southern wing's commander rode off in response to an order to meet General Bragg for a conference. Longstreet welcomed this chance to report, but he also had a suggestion to make: Let some of Polk's brigades join his for another smash while the rest held Thomas's eastern-facing divisions in place.

At the conference Bragg ignored Longstreet's achievement and turned down the newcomer's proposal. "There is not a man in the right wing," said Bragg, "who has any fight left in him." Then he rode northeastward to Reed's Bridge, leaving it to the astonished Longstreet to continue the fight without orders or support or any sign that the army commander gave a damn about anything.

Union Major General Gordon Granger's 6,000 men amounted to a three-brigade division, though they were called a corps, and so far in this campaign they had been given only guard duty or held as Rosecrans's reserve: their status on this Sunday. All morning Granger had listened to the echoes of heavy fighting south of him. Shortly before noon, convinced that Thomas was in trouble, with no orders to do so, he started two of his brigades on a four-mile march southward.

Granger had to wait while soldiers retreating northward got out of his advancing troops' way, whereupon he sent word for the last of his brigades to follow him. And soon he would find out how desperately Old Pap needed him.

By four o'clock that afternoon Thomas had seven worn-down and nearly fought out divisions facing Bishop Polk's hammering from the west but only two holding back Longstreet's punching from the south. Thomas's main assets were a spur of Missionary Ridge called Snodgrass Hill and the artillery batteries he had placed on it. But Longstreet might move around to the west and get beyond his flank and into his rear, so when Granger arrived, Old Pap sent his troops to the point of greatest danger.

Granger reached it just in time to absorb and deflect one of

Longstreet's heavy blows. Now Thomas could breathe a little easier, but still—as at Stones River—he moved among his men, encouraging them by his presence to stand fast.

They did, almost until dark, until General Thomas began to withdraw them one unit at a time, in the face of attacks, never yielding, never revealing to the rebels what he was doing. In a manner as calm as their commander—who would ever afterward be known as "the Rock of Chickamauga"—the brigades marched away from what the Indians had called the river of death.

"The trouble with us," Jackson had said back on May 2 as he was leading his flank march at Chancellorsville, "has always been to have a reserve to throw in at the critical moment, to reap the advantages gained. We have always had to put in all our troops—and never had enough at the time most needed."

And so it had been once again on this Sunday, September 20. There could be no pursuit of Thomas's retreating columns, though Forrest and a few of his cavalry scouts rode after them, for every one of Braxton Bragg's units had fought, and by sundown most were too exhausted to do anything but take possession of the abandoned Yankee lines—and to cheer.

As soon as the firing ceased, the Confederates' shouting began. It spread from one cluster of men to the next, all along the valley, until it became so loud anyone within five miles could hear it. And it went on and on into the twilight, amid the battle smoke lingering in the woods, in celebration of the first major victory Bragg's army had clearly won.

Curiously, the commanding general's reaction was to get on his cot and go to sleep. Perhaps he was eager to end a day on which nothing much had gone according to his plans and orders. Longstreet's wing, not Polk's, had broken the federal line not by attacking in echelon but by massing and striking with full force. Then Longstreet had driven the fugitives northward instead of in the opposite direction, up McLemore's Cove. How, then, could anyone call it a victory when Rosecrans's army had not only escaped the annihilation Bragg had meant for it but was falling back into the fortified line south of Chattanooga?

All that had happened that Sunday along the Chickamauga was that two armies had given fresh meaning to the name earlier Americans had left for the stream: the river of death. On that Sunday night it was obvious to the celebrants that losses on both sides had been enormous. How high the cost of two days' fighting had been would be apparent afterward:

	KILLED	WOUNDED	MISSING	TOTALS
Bragg	2,312	14,674	1,468	18,454
Rosecrans	1,657	9,756	4,453	15,866
Totals	3,969	24,430	5,921	34,320

Bragg had lost roughly twenty-eight men out of every hundred in the fight; Rosecrans, about twenty-nine. Seldom, if ever, in any campaign had casualty percentages been so high. And they might have been even higher at Chickamauga if dense stands of trees had not restricted the use of artillery fire.

For the Confederate scavengers no battlefield had been as rewarding. From it they took fifty-one federal guns, more than 23,000 small arms, and great quantities of ammunition, wagons, medical supplies, and draft animals.

But there was no way of quantifying the federals' humiliation. Even the soldiers who had fought longest and hardest felt it, some in greater measure when they found out how much earlier so many of their generals had reached Chattanooga. Sadly eroded was the affection they had felt for Old Rosy, a man who had inspired them by his bravery at Stones River but who had never had a chance to display it again on this Sunday, swept along as he had been by surging waves of fugitives. Cocky "Little Phil" Sheridan, too, a tenacious fighter at Shiloh, Perryville, and especially Stones River, seemed to have lost heart. Only one general emerged with enhanced respect—George Henry Thomas, the native Virginian who had become a "galvanized" Yankee—and only because Thomas, with Gordon Granger's timely help, had kept a crushing defeat from turning into a total disaster.

And as Monday's dawn neared, there was nothing the whipped federal soldiers could do but wait for Bragg to move his army up to Chattanooga and give its defenders the chance to redeem at least some of their pride.

Braxton Bragg, unwilling to believe the federals had fled all the way to Chattanooga, asked a Confederate soldier who had described their panic: "Do you know what a retreat looks like?"

"I ought to, General," replied the private. "I've been with you during your whole campaign."

Cavalryman Forrest spent early Monday morning probing and observing. "I think they are evacuating as hard as they can go," he said in a message to Polk and Bragg. "I think we ought to press forward as rapidly as possible." But nothing came of that, or from proddings by anyone else, so several days passed before Bragg got his lines up to Rosecrans's south of the city.

Again Bishop Polk tried to get General Bragg relieved of his command. Both Harvey Hill and Longstreet supported Polk, but Nathan Bedford Forrest took a more direct course of action. Angered by many stings from Bragg, on September 28, Forrest rode to the general's tent.

"I have stood your meanness as long as I intend to," the cavalryman told the army commander. "You have played the part of a damned scoundrel, and are a coward, and if you were any part of a man I would slap your jaws and force you to resent it. You may as well not issue any more orders to me, for I will not obey them, and I will hold you personally responsible for any further indignities you endeavor to inflict upon me. You have threatened to arrest me for not obeying your orders promptly. I dare you to do it, and I say to you that if you ever again try to interfere with me or cross my path it will be at the peril of your life."

Immediately after Forrest left the tent the man with him predicted much trouble, only to be told: "He'll never say a word about it." Bragg did not. But he relieved General Polk, and in early October the bishop's protests drew the president to the west to try to settle the squabbling. And Davis made some changes: He sent Harvey Hill back to North Carolina, and unrepentant dissident William Hardee resumed command of his corps. He left Polk in Atlanta. Later, Longstreet would take his troops northeastward to attempt the recapture of Knoxville. Davis sent Forrest to West Tennessee to operate on his own.

While the Confederates sorted themselves out, the federal war managers recognized that Rosecrans had to be reinforced within a very short time. Lincoln, recalling Longstreet's shift and assuming correctly that General Meade had no apparent plans to strike Lee, ordered the XI and XII Corps of the Army of the Potomac to be rushed by rail from central Virginia all the way northward, westward, then southward to Chattanooga. He put this detached force under the command of Fighting Joe Hooker. Literally overnight, Secretary of War Edwin Stanton mobilized railroad and supply resources to make this transfer. It was completed in a little over a week.

Then began the federal head rolling. General Rosecrans opened it by relieving Crittenden and McCook. And he may not have been surprised when, a month after his apparent desertion of a fight that had gone on for another six hours, Washington's guillotine fell on his neck.

William Starke Rosecrans, the army commander who had been cautious and provident to the point of daring removal earlier, got it for circumstances on September 20 he had not been able to control.

But it could be argued that another factor was involved: General Grant's availability after Vicksburg.

For a time, though, it had seemed that Meade might have to be replaced first. General-in-Chief Halleck had offended him by saying, in his usual to-the-point manner, in a message:

> Lee is unquestionably bullying you. If you cannot ascertain his movements, I certainly cannot. If you pursue and fight him, I think you will find out where he is. I know of no other way.

"Truisms," Meade responded, requesting relief from command, but Halleck, as a gentleman, though general-in-chief, assured him no disparagement had been intended. Meade left it at that. Otherwise, Secretary of War Stanton's plans might have been derailed. But on October 17 Stanton shared a train seat with Grant from Indianapolis to Louisville, along the way offering him two sets of orders and asking him to choose one. In both Grant was designated supreme commander in the west. One draft left the Chattanooga command intact; the other called for Thomas to replace Rosecrans. "I accepted the latter," wrote Grant later. And in so doing, without knowing it, he opened a new phase not only of his own service but of the way in which the rest of the war would be fought.

Chapter 30

Missionary Ridge: *Revenge of the Blue*

"**F**inish the work before you, my dear general," wrote the Army of Northern Virginia's commander to James Longstreet when he learned of the victory at Chickamauga, "and return to me. I want you badly and you cannot get back too soon."

General Lee's army and Meade's federal forces were still menacing each other along the upper Rappahannock near Culpeper. But when Lee discovered that two Union corps had been sent to reinforce Rosecrans, again audacity stirred him. Preventing the authorities in Washington from sending more of Meade's troops to plague Braxton Bragg was the main purpose of the plan Lee made. But his health was not good, and his army was too weak to attack Meade's head-on, so he devised a sweep around the federals' western flank: Stuart's cavalry would screen the advance of Powell Hill's corps and Dick Ewell's to Warrenton. Once there, his army would be within striking distance of—for the third time—Manassas. With Longstreet's corps absent, that was about as far to the north as Lee hoped to get. But if he could hold Meade so near Washington that the people of Virginia might pass the winter free of federal threats, the risks would be worth accepting.

Near Bristoe Station on the Orange & Alexandria Railroad, however—where, in August of the year before, Jackson's men had gleefully derailed federal trains—Powell Hill's corps got hit by withering Yankee fire. There the hopes for Third Manassas fell apart. General Lee had bullied Meade's main force all the way north of Bull Run to Centreville, but the depletion of resources in the nearby Virginia counties made remaining there impossible. So Lee fell back south of both the Rappahannock and the Rapidan, and Meade followed. And after skirmishes along Mine Run in November, troops on both sides prepared to spend a third winter in the field.

Survival was precisely what Braxton Bragg meant to deny Rosecrans's 45,000 troops inside Chattanooga's fortifications. Belatedly, the Confederate commander had placed his men in an arc extending from the Tennessee River crossings west of the city so far upstream that the federals had to rely on a sixty-mile route through desolate country to get any supplies.

It was ironic that Rosecrans, so meticulous about amassing stockpiles of supplies earlier, would leave his men to face exactly the circumstances he had feared most. Inside Chattanooga there was not enough ammunition for one day's fighting. Daily rations were reduced to a fraction of their usual amounts. Nothing could be done to keep artillery horses and mules from starving; too few guns could be moved to attempt a breakout.

Although supplies in abundance were accumulating west of Chattanooga, it took wagon trains eight days to get there via the only safe route. Each wagon had to carry enough grain to keep the team pulling it alive for a round trip, reducing space for rations. Heavy rains made miserable roads impassable. In one quick strike rebel cavalrymen burned 400 wagons and killed their teams. But Grant had ordered Thomas to stay at all hazards, and Old Pap replied: "We will hold the town till we starve."

While Grant was coming southward, however, Thomas told engineer W. F. Smith to carry out an idea he had first offered to Rosecrans. Baldy Smith, banished from the Army of the Potomac after Fredericksburg, built rafts on which troops floated down the Tennessee late one night and surprised the light rebel force holding Brown's Ferry, west of Chattanooga, while resurrected Joe Hooker marched eastward from the supply base and attacked to open the road and secure it.

And so it was that two rejects from the eastern army saved a western one, for by October 29 what Thomas's grateful soldiers called the "Cracker Line" was open. Neither Bragg's guns atop Lookout Mountain nor his feeble probes of Hooker's protective ranks could stop the flow of food and supplies; Old Pap would neither have to hold the city to the last man nor see even one starve; and now General Grant could get on with what he thought had to be done, which was to get the army out of Chattanooga.

Launching an offensive drive took on all the more appeal when Grant learned that Bragg had sent Longstreet's divisions toward Knoxville, but getting ready would take a while, and the newly appointed western commander was not about to turn his armies loose until he had them well in hand. And in early November they were not, except for George Thomas's Army of the Cumberland. Cump Sherman's men were repairing the tracks ahead of the trains carrying them eastward from Memphis; this force, now called the Army of the Tennessee, was still days west of Chattanooga. Castoff Ambrose Burnside's 25,000-man Army of the Ohio had to hold Knoxville. Joe Hooker's two corps, a gift from Washington, would be watched closely by their givers.

And Grant knew Washington would be watching him as well. During a post-Vicksburg visit to New Orleans he had been thrown by a skittish horse, damaging his leg so badly he was still using crutches many weeks later when he got to Chattanooga. This had set off rumors that so able a rider must have been drunk when the fall crippled him. Rumors of this kind were by now part of this soldier's pay. Yes, there was a remarkable letter Abraham Lincoln had written Grant on July 13, after Vicksburg:

> I do not remember that you and I ever met personally. I write this now as a grateful acknowledgment for the almost inestimable service you have done the country. I wish to say a word further.... When you got below, and took Port Gibson, Grand Gulf, and vicinity, I thought you should go down the river and join General Banks; and when you turned northward east of the Big Black, I feared you had made a great mistake. I now wish to make the personal acknowledgment that you were right, and I was wrong.

But Grant would not have been surprised at Indianapolis if Secretary of War Stanton had relieved him instead of giving him such broad new responsibilities, and unless he was careful now, the president's words might be the only satisfaction he would have had when the guillotine blade fell on his neck, too.

Sending Longstreet's corps up to drive Burnside's Army of the Ohio out of Knoxville and East Tennessee was not evidence that General Bragg had gone mad. President Davis wanted this done, Bragg feared Grant might order Burnside to reinforce Chattanooga's garrison, and the venture took away one more dissident general.

Serving under Bragg had made Longstreet crave distance from him. Still, he protested; his force—even with Porter Alexander's artillery and part of Joe Wheeler's cavalry, in all about 15,000 troops—would be too small, and Bragg would be exposing the remainder of his army to defeat if Grant attacked.

But Bragg was adamant, so Longstreet started his corps on the

100-mile trip northeastward to deliver what was supposed to be a quick, hard blow. For the first sixty miles most of the men could be moved by rail. But there were delays, and beyond the tracks' end at the Holston River, Longstreet's spearhead had to skirmish the rest of the way. Instead of one week it took two for the Confederates to reach Knoxville's outer defenses.

They got that far without a battle because General Grant had told Burnside to keep Longstreet's force from being able to return to Chattanooga. If Burnside could gain time for him by so doing, Grant would send columns up to make Longstreet's men "take to the mountain passes by every available road."

Perhaps easier in his mind now that General Grant was in charge of things in the west, Abraham Lincoln took one of his rare trips at about the same time Longstreet and Burnside were squaring off at Knoxville. The president's journey was short, only to Gettysburg, for the dedication on November 19 of a cemetery larger by far than the one that had been there, on Cemetery Hill south of the little town, before the battle.

Educator and orator Edward Everett would deliver the main address. Few of the 12,000 or so people attending, mostly families in mourning for Union soldiers who had died there, could hear him, but Everett's gestures were flamboyant, especially for a man of seventy, classic, grand, suggesting that whatever he was saying was indeed eloquent. Whether merely being polite or stunned by sadness, the crowd remained until the orator finally finished what must have seemed an interminable speech. Then came Abraham Lincoln's turn, which meant the ceremonies were almost over and soon the trip homeward could begin—unless the president had more to say than Everett. He did not. All Lincoln said was this:

> Four score and seven years ago our fathers brought forth on this continent, a new nation, conceived in Liberty, and dedicated to the proposition that all men are created equal.
>
> Now we are engaged in a great civil war, testing whether that nation, or any nation so conceived and so dedicated, can long endure. We are met on a great battle-field of that war. We have come to dedicate a portion of that field, as a final resting place for those who here gave their lives that that nation might live. It is altogether fitting and proper that we should do this.
>
> But, in a larger sense, we can not dedicate—we can not consecrate—we can not hallow—this ground. The brave men, living and dead, who struggled here, have consecrated

it, far above our poor power to add or detract. The world will little note, nor long remember what we say here, but it can never forget what they did here. It is for us the living, rather, to be dedicated here to the unfinished work which they who fought here have thus far so nobly advanced. It is rather for us to be here dedicated to the great task remaining before us—that from these honored dead we take increased devotion to that cause for which they gave the last full measure of devotion—that we here highly resolve that these dead shall not have died in vain—that this nation, under God, shall have a new birth of freedom—and that government of the people, by the people, for the people, shall not perish from the earth.

Then those present could go home, and before many more days they could read what they may not have heard Lincoln say. "I should be glad," Edward Everett wrote him, "if I could flatter myself that I came as near to the central idea of the occasion in two hours as you did in two minutes." Replied Lincoln: "In our respective parts yesterday, you could not have been excused to make a short address, nor I a long one."

Out in the west General Bragg was having second thoughts about the decision to send Longstreet's corps up to Knoxville. Bragg had figured on Longstreet's making a quick round trip, on his finishing off Burnside early enough to be back before Grant could cause trouble. But from what Bragg could see of federal activity in Chattanooga—and the view from the top of Lookout Mountain was excellent—the Yankees were getting much stronger much sooner than he had expected.

Remembering, perhaps, Longstreet's protests and as if to say, "You were right and I was wrong," without using those words, Bragg decided to send two of his eight divisions up to him—the army commander's theory being, apparently, that the more troops Longstreet had, the sooner Burnside would be crushed and the whole force could return. Or maybe it was the arrival of Cump Sherman's divisions from out of the west, soon followed by their disappearance in Knoxville's direction, that triggered Bragg's action. Either way, Bushrod Johnson took a division northeastward by rail on Sunday, November 22, and Pat Cleburne began loading his troops on the cars the next morning.

So mired in mistakes by now was General Bragg that almost anything else he did could only compound the damage. But the proper thing was to notify Longstreet that 11,000 men were on their way, and this Bragg did on Sunday, in a message that told Longstreet he could attack Burnside in the meantime "if practicable" or wait for the reinforcements to reach him.

Longstreet had found no weak spots in Burnside's lines in nearly a week of probing. He would use the discretion General Bragg had granted him; he would wait.

By the time his president was making remarks at Gettysburg, General Grant had formed a plan to take Bragg's army out of the war. It called for Sherman's force to disappear, but only for the purpose of moving east of the rebel containment line and then to drive southward to Chickamauga Station and cut Bragg off from getting any more supplies from Atlanta. Thomas's role was merely to hold the Confederates on Missionary Ridge while Sherman's divisions got around the rebels' flank and deep into their rear; then Hooker's two divisions might climb Lookout Mountain and enjoy the view of Alabama, Georgia, and Tennessee.

Relegation to the position of tourists by General Grant's order may have seemed galling to Fighting Joe and his troops, veterans of Fredericksburg and Chancellorsville, all anxious to redeem their reputations. Revenge for Chickamauga was what the men in George Thomas's army wanted most but seemed least likely to get. It was understandable that newcomer Grant might rely primarily on Sherman, who had been with him in most of his earlier battles, but the plan in its initial form bruised morale in all of Grant's divisions but Cump's.

As it turned out, though, pro-Confederate weather spoiled nearly everything. Heavy rains set the Tennessee River to rampaging and confined Sherman's forces to its north banks. Bragg discovered where Sherman really was on Monday, the twenty-third, just in time for him to cancel the rail movement of Pat Cleburne's division toward Knoxville. And even before then, General Grant had turned to improvising.

On Sunday night a rebel deserter had told Grant that Bragg was withdrawing. To test that, at around noon on Monday, Grant told Thomas to probe the Confederate lines on Orchard Knob, halfway to Bragg's defenses on Missionary Ridge. Instead, Old Pap's 25,000 troops attacked—but only after they had paraded, flags streaming in the wind, bayonets glistening—and by sundown the losers at Chickamauga had driven the victors out of their trenches and all the way southward to Bragg's main line of resistance.

Another change directed Hooker's divisions to assault the Confederates atop Lookout Mountain early on Tuesday morning, November 24. Of all the terrain features near Chattanooga, this rock

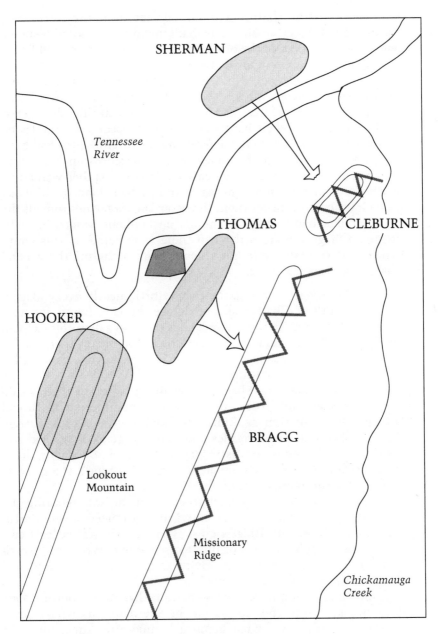

Missionary Ridge

outcropping, rising sharply a thousand feet from the river level, appeared the least attainable. Low-hanging mist layers and distance kept General Grant and the other observers, then on Orchard Knob, well to the east, ignorant of what was happening along the dominant mountain's slopes. And while what equally ignorant newspaper reporters would soon call the "battle above the clouds" was going on, Cump Sherman's forces had been unable to make much progress southward against rebels hardly anyone had expected to find there.

By Tuesday night, then, General Grant's original plan had been turned inside out—not by Bragg, but by circumstances. Cump Sherman's sweep around Bragg's eastern flank was stalled well north of Chickamauga Station. Thomas's troops had done on Monday what Grant had meant for them to try on Tuesday. And from all the signs, Hooker had gotten far enough up Lookout Mountain to be sitting on Bragg's western flank. If there were heroes at this point, Vicksburg's veterans were not among them, including the general Washington was watching.

On Wednesday morning, the twenty-fifth, nearly every man in the lines south of Chattanooga could see the U.S. flag flying atop Lookout Mountain. To the Confederates this was a disturbing omen. But Braxton Bragg could shrug it off, for it also meant that now he had more troops to use in slaughtering Yankees as they came at his defenses on Missionary Ridge.

Curiously, that was what General Bragg expected them to do even after Sherman's forces resumed their hammering at Tunnel Hill, north of Missionary Ridge. To hold Sherman back Patrick Cleburne had only five brigades and fourteen guns. Bragg had five divisions and 112 guns on Missionary Ridge, with no federals closer than the better part of a mile at the time Cleburne's troops were within rock-throwing range of Sherman's attackers.

If Bragg was neglecting Cleburne's fight, he was ignoring the skirmishing going on as Hooker's divisions advanced slowly northward along Missionary Ridge's crest. That trouble was at least two miles away, maybe more, nothing to fret about. What was worth more attention than Bragg was giving it, however, was the federal threat to the northern end of his line.

How Bragg could have been so certain that Pat Cleburne's lone division could stop repeated assaults by Sherman's six would never be clear. But that was what happened, time after time, for eight hours or so on Wednesday. By midafternoon the slopes of Tunnel Hill were almost covered with blue-clad bodies, and Sherman had decided to leave Cleburne alone.

Frustrated by Sherman's inability to advance even after he had been reinforced to the limits, disappointed that Hooker was still too far southward on Missionary Ridge to do any good, and fearing that Bragg might turn his forces northward and strike fought-out Sherman, at about three-thirty General Grant allowed Thomas's four divisions to move near enough to the 400-foot hill to keep Bragg's Confederates in place. That was all Grant wanted; the old plan, calling for Sherman to sweep around the rebel flank might be tried again on Thursday.

What Grant got, late on Wednesday, was a repetition of the surprise Thomas's men had given him on Monday when they had been told merely to threaten Orchard Knob. Once again the veterans of humiliation at Chickamauga put on a parade for the rebels, turning finally into ranks nearly two miles long and advancing steadily toward the rifle pits at the base of Missionary Ridge.

General Grant, angered, demanded to be told who had given orders for what was clearly developing into an attack. Thomas declared his innocence; so did Gordon Granger, adding: "When those fellows get started all hell can't stop them."

Perhaps, but what if Bragg did? Grant had no reserves to use in case the Confederates blunted Thomas's divisions now the way they had been mauling Sherman's all day long, then launched a counterattack. Someone, the theater commander muttered, was going to smell hell if that happened.

And it might. Confederate artillery fire from the crest plunged into the blue masses. So heavy was the barrage that the federals' only alternative to being shredded was to run southward, which they did, charging into the rebel line at the bottom of the ridge, driving the defenders up the slope.

No longer did George Thomas's troops have to worry about the guns. Now it was an infantry fight, a matter of chasing the rebels toward the top, a pursuit by determined men of those whose will to stay and shoot it out seemed to have vanished.

The blue waves surged upward until they rushed over the crest of Missionary Ridge, appearing there so suddenly they almost captured Braxton Bragg. By then, though, some of Old Pap's troops were winded, and others were celebrating. Those who looked southward saw five gray-clad divisions scurrying for such safety as they might find in Atlanta's direction.

Near dark on that Wednesday Pat Cleburne's division was the only Confederate force still fighting, by then as the rear guard for remnants of Bragg's army streaming southward along roads that would eventually lead them to Dalton, Georgia, twenty-five miles south of Chattanooga. During the three days, the broken Army of

Tennessee had lost nearly 6,700 men and forty-one guns, but it was leaving behind not only the glory it had—for the first time—won at Chickamauga but Chattanooga as well, a place with value in strategic terms federal General-in-Chief Halleck had told Lincoln in July 1862 was worth three Richmonds.

Wrecked, too, was Braxton Bragg. From Dalton he sent the president the letter Bishop Polk and nearly every other senior officer who had served under him had hoped for, one that Grant had finally provoked: request to be relieved of his command. There was, wrote Bragg in effect, no excuse for his loss of Missionary Ridge. Sadly, Jefferson Davis agreed.

By then Ulysses Grant was getting congratulations from Washington—mixed with proddings to finish off Longstreet up near Knoxville. To do that, Grant sent Sherman. But he could not quite seem to come to terms with himself about Chattanooga. "Damn the battle!" he said. "I had nothing to do with it."

Such a remark made Grant seem as small as, physically, he was. Worse, by making it, he swept aside the fact that valiant soldiers from Union armies new to him had given him a decisive victory at a cost slightly less than that of the rebels.

Yet, in the months to come, Abraham Lincoln would propose, and the Congress would approve, the reestablishment of the rank of lieutenant general—George Washington's once, Winfield Scott's only by brevet—and appoint Ulysses Grant to it. And by so doing the president placed his hopes of ever restoring the Union on the failure-bent shoulders of a man who had never been thought good at much beyond riding horses.

PART FOUR

Hurry, Hurry, This Is the Last!

Chapter 31

Jackson Whips Banks Again in Louisiana

"Gloom and unspoken despondency," wrote Confederate Mary Chesnut in her diary on December 7, 1863, "hang like a pall everywhere." Members of Congress heard nothing to alleviate it the next day as they listened to President Jefferson Davis's recital of the nation's failures during the year. And soon an editorial in the *Richmond Examiner* summarized the outlook: "Our sole policy and cunningest diplomacy is fighting; our most insinuating negotiator is the Confederate army in line of battle."

Encouraging peace movements in the North had been one of General Lee's hopes in taking the war to central Pennsylvania, but everyone knew what had come of that. Loss of Vicksburg, and with it control of any point along the Mississippi, had all but ended chances for European support in any form. And as the end of 1863 approached, the Confederate army was hardly in a position to negotiate anything.

As if to underscore Davis's somber remarks, Longstreet had to abandon his effort to break through Ambrose Burnside's lines and drive the Yankees out of Knoxville. After waiting for the reinforcements Braxton Bragg had promised, finally finding what seemed a weak spot in the federal defenses, Longstreet had sent his infantry into a predawn attack on the morning of November 29. But in the rainy darkness confusion prevailed, Alexander's artillery could not be used because Longstreet wanted to take advantage of surprise, and too few of his men could climb Fort Sanders's icy parapets in the face of stubborn resistance.

After sunrise the assault might have been pressed, but at the moment of decision a messenger reached Longstreet with orders from the president to withdraw to Dalton. Longstreet broke off the attack, took advantage of a truce to recover the dead and wounded, then learned the next day that Grant had sent Cump Sherman's forces up from Chattanooga toward Knoxville. He waited until December 4, when Sherman was within a day's march, then retreated into northeast Tennessee's mountains in search of a place to get his troops through the winter.

Longstreet's men in particular were glad to see the end of fighting in 1863. Long afterward, artilleryman Porter Alexander wrote:

> We were so deficient in horseshoes that on the advance to Knoxville we stripped the shoes and saved the nails from all dead horses, killing for the purpose all wounded and broken-down animals, both our own and those left behind by the enemy. During the siege, the river brought down a number of dead animals thrown in within the town. We watched for these, took them out, and stripped their feet of shoes and nails. Our men were nearly as badly off for footgear as our animals. I have seen bloody stains left on frozen ground where our infantry had passed. In the artillery we took the shoes from the feet of the drivers to give to the cannoneers who had to march. Our rations were also frequently not even the reduced rations now issued to the whole army. Corn, unground, was often the only ration.

Confederate soldiers had been obliged to be ruthlessly efficient scavengers from First Manassas in mid-1861 onward, but civilians had never had opportunities to plunder Union wealth. Families throughout the South had seen such assets as they had to start with shrink steadily, most painfully in the loss of their irreplaceable and deeply mourned young men but also in every other way anyone could measure.

Those in the path of Yankee invaders, of course, suffered most. Wrote a Union cavalryman to his wife after watching his men loot a house near Brandy Station:

> Bureaus were overhauled, and all they contained stolen or destroyed. Book cases were pillaged or tripped over; furniture smashed or stolen; crockery broken to pieces; mirrors stolen or broken....

By the beginning of 1864 a Confederate paper dollar was worth six cents in coin. Nearly all national and state debts, and many private ones financed by banks, involved the use of bonds or promissory notes, worthless to the holders unless the South won. A soldier's monthly pay, if he received it and could get it home to his family, would not buy a pound of bacon, should one be available. One girl, scolded by her father for wearing a party dress in the middle of the afternoon, told him: "This is all I have."

Southern states' governors were telling the Confederacy's president the same thing. Worse for Davis, some were reminding him in various ways that their states had seceded rather than tolerate coercion from Washington and that they were not about to bow to despotic coercion from Richmond, either.

Davis's own vice president, Alexander Stephens, wrote:

> If the pending proposition before Congress passes, to put the whole country under martial law,...constitutional liberty will go down, never to rise again on this continent, I fear. This is the worst that can befall us. Far better that our country should be over-run by the enemy, our cities sacked and burned and our land laid desolate, than that the people should thus suffer the citadel of their liberties to be entered and taken by their professed friends.

But Stephens, cloaking himself comfortably in principles, was ignored. Nearer the heart of the Confederacy's realities was the young girl whose party dress was all she had left.

In striking contrast, the Union was enjoying an economic boom as 1864 opened. Military matters seemed so well in hand that Abraham Lincoln hardly mentioned them in his address to the Congress, referring its members to the annual reports for 1863 of Secretary of War Stanton and General-in-Chief Halleck.

Lincoln's mind was on settlement of the western lands, immigration, development of mineral resources, amnesty for Southerners other than their rebellion's leaders, on what he called Reconstruction. He proposed that when 10 percent of those who voted in 1860 in states such as Louisiana or Arkansas (where federal forces were again in control) swore loyalty to the Union, they could form new governments and be readmitted and, presumably, vote in the 1864 presidential election.

Down in New Orleans, Nathaniel Banks, politician first and general only of necessity, understood exactly what Lincoln was up to. Moreover, Banks saw his orders to clear central and northern Louisiana of rebels as a means of increasing his own chances of replacing Lincoln as the Republicans' nominee. And if Confederate cotton captured along the way happened to reach mills in Banks's New England political power base—well, it had to go somewhere.

Banks's orders, sent him by General-in-Chief Halleck in the earliest days of 1864, called for another move up the Red River to seize Shreveport while Major General Frederick Steele came south-westward from Little Rock to join him at the gateway to East Texas. Rear Admiral David Dixon Porter's gunboats would escort Banks's columns as they advanced up the river and also protect transports bringing troops borrowed from Cump Sherman's army. But the sooner Banks reached Shreveport, the better: Sherman wanted his men returned in time to launch other drives.

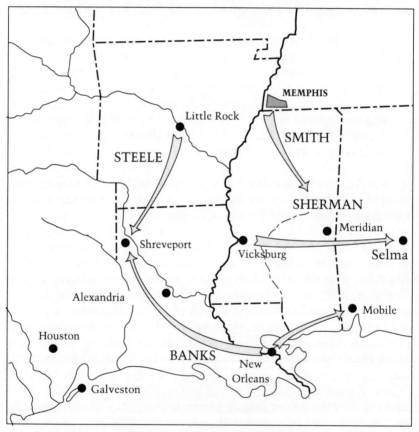

Union Western Campaign Plans

Rather, General Grant wanted them back. Since his victory over Bragg at Chattanooga in November, still commanding Union forces in the west except those under Banks in Louisiana and Major General John Schofield in Missouri, Grant had been busy devising plans for destroying not only the Confederate forces remaining in his theater but their means of support as well.

Cump Sherman's influence was appearing here. Rebels, he thought, should not be coaxed back into the Union. He would "make them so sick of war that generations would pass before they again appeal to it." Sherman was particularly vexed by guerrilla activities. He wrote to a corps commander:

> To secure the safety of the navigation of the Mississippi River I would slay millions. On that point I am not only insane, but mad. Fortunately the great West is with me there. I think I see one or two quick blows that will astonish the natives of the South and will convince them that, though to stand behind a big cottonwood and shoot at a passing boat is good sport and safe, it may still reach and kill their friends and families hundreds of miles off. For every bullet shot at a steamboat, I would shoot a thousand 30-pounder Parrotts into even helpless towns on Red, Ouachita, Yazoo [rivers] or wherever a boat can float or soldier march.

In mid-January, Grant submitted his proposal to Halleck. On a map it would resemble blue snakes slithering across the South from Memphis and Vicksburg to Meridian, then possibly down to Mobile; from Mobile up to Montgomery; from Chattanooga down to Atlanta. Wrecking Confederate railroads was the main purpose. But these moves would be coordinated, timed so that Joe Johnston—appointed reluctantly by Jefferson Davis as commander of what had been Bragg's army—would be caught between converging federal columns and ground to pieces, thus eliminating rebel resistance in the west.

Yes, said the general-in-chief to the Meridian operation. But Halleck knew more than Grant about moves afoot in Congress to bring the victor at Vicksburg and Chattanooga to Washington as a lieutenant general. That would surely happen; and when it did, the new general-in-chief could employ all of the Union's armies as Grant, and the president, desired.

Confederates, too, spent the winter months planning. This effort was coordinated by Braxton Bragg, Jefferson Davis's new military adviser. Bragg was surprisingly effective in such a role; the president was on cordial terms only with General Lee, but Bragg could and did obtain suggestions from Beauregard and Joe Johnston. Through Lee, Longstreet added his ideas, one of which was to convert his entire corps to cavalry and try again to do what Edmund Kirby Smith almost did in 1862: drive through central Kentucky to the Ohio River. Akin to that was Bragg's notion, concentrating for a strike at Nashville, the federal hub for supply movements. But these would be only large-scale raids designed (as General Lee put it) to "alarm and embarrass" the invaders and prevent them from "undertaking anything of magnitude against us." And in the end nothing would come of all this exchanging of proposals and rebuttals. The reason: severe shortages of everything the South needed to wage war.

While Davis's senior generals contemplated impossibilities, a junior one in North Carolina tried a raid of his own. Late in January, George Pickett, left behind when Longstreet took the rest of the First Corps to Chickamauga, marched from Kingston eastward with 4,500 troops, hoping to drive Yankees from the southern end of Pamlico Sound. His objective was New Bern, and once near there, on February 1, he put 300 troops in rowboats and captured the USS *Underwriter*. But Pickett's improvised navy could not move the ship and wound up burning the prize, and his land force had to give up after spending three days in trying to take federal Fort Stevenson.

The siege of Charleston continued down the Atlantic coast. For a time, though, it seemed that a strange new Confederate weapon might drive federal gunboats from the harbor. This was what would later be called a submarine, a cigar-shaped craft powered by men inside turning cranks. Tests during the summer in Mobile Bay seemed promising enough to move the *H. L. Hunley*—named for one of her builders—to Charleston. But accidents drowned two eight-man crews before the crankers could get to a target; Hunley himself died in the second try. On the night of February 17, a third attempt destroyed the USS *Housatonic*. And down with the Yankee ship went the *Hunley*, ending Charlestonians' hopes for deliverance through ingenuity.

Union politics inspired another flare-up south of there. "An effort is being made," wrote Lincoln in mid-January, "by some worthy gentlemen to reconstruct a loyal State government in Florida." This set in motion an 8,000-man force led by Brigadier General Truman Seymour. From Jacksonville westward along the railroad the column advanced for forty miles or so, bound for Tallahassee, only to be defeated and turned back on February 20 by a militia outfit made up mostly of Georgians; Floridians were serving elsewhere.

Some may have been out in central Mississippi among the Confederates Cump Sherman's forces were brushing aside as they swept eastward in the early part of February from Vicksburg toward Meridian, destroying the railroad and anything else of potential value. This was not a "sideshow," as General Grant termed campaigns such as the one in Florida, but an application of his new strategy: deplete and exhaust the South. Sherman's plan called for Brigadier General William Sooy Smith to start with his cavalrymen and reinforcements, about 7,000 men in all, from Memphis southeastward on February 1 and—after wrecking railroads along the 250-mile route—meet Sherman in Meridian on the tenth. From there Grant hoped their combined forces could press directly eastward into Alabama and destroy the Confederate cannon-making facilities at Selma.

But Sooy Smith was late in leaving Memphis, and when he finally got moving, he ran into a Confederate weapon more potent than the *H. L. Hunley* might ever have become: fierce Nathan Bedford Forrest. After calling Bragg a coward to his face back in the fall, Forrest had gone west to recruit and train another force of horsemen; most brought with them whatever mounts and weapons they had; and, green as they were, Forrest put them between Sooy Smith and Meridian.

Smith, far behind the schedule Grant and Sherman had set, may have decided on his own to turn back by the time his scouts neared West Point, Mississippi, on the Mobile & Ohio Railroad. But reverse direction he did, with Forrest's troopers chewing up his rear guard until February 23, when, near Okolona, he decided to make a stand.

He left two regiments behind there to delay the rebels while he took a brigade five miles or so northward to a better position on Ivey's Hill. Forrest's men charged, driving Sooy Smith's troopers up to the main line. Again Forrest charged, pausing briefly to mourn the killing of his youngest brother, then led a furious two-hour fight during which two horses were shot beneath him and he used both pistol and saber in sending three Yankees below. Such an example fired up Forrest's recruits. They drove a force two or three times their own strength ten more miles northward that day. And Sooy Smith kept pulling back until his remnants were once again in Memphis.

Probably without knowing it, by wrecking Smith's command Forrest had saved Selma's cannon works and maybe even Mobile. Sherman, too, had been late, but by February 14 he had reached Meridian. Along the way from Vicksburg his troops had left a streak of devastation twenty-five miles wide, and during the five days he waited for Smith at Meridian, their looting and torching enabled Cump to declare that the town no longer existed. When he was satisfied that Smith would never arrive, Sherman turned back toward Vicksburg. But he took a different route, one far enough north of the railroad for him to boast that he had "made a swath of desolation fifty miles broad across the State of Mississippi which the present generation will not forget."

In fact, Sherman had done more. Now the entire Confederacy was on notice that the nature of this war had changed, that no longer was the Union army in control of generals, such as George Mc-Clellan, who believed civilians and their property ought to be left alone. Two westerners were taking over, both men who in earlier years and months had been failures but who now seemed determined to give the entire South massive doses of it.

By early March 1864, Lieutenant General Ulysses Grant was in a position to do just that. Sherman could in the west, for the new general-in-chief left him in command of that vast region. "War," Cump had said, "is cruelty. There is no use trying to reform it. The crueler it is, the sooner it will be over." And that was the controlling idea Grant took with him when he went to Washington.

Once there, having met Abraham Lincoln and satisfied the president that he was a soldier with no political ambition, Grant asked Henry Halleck to remain as chief of staff and got out of town as quickly as he could, headed for General Meade's headquarters in central Virginia. Halleck took his demotion cheerfully, but Grant was not certain that George Meade would care to have the Union armies' general-in-chief as a permanent guest at his campfires. Indeed, Meade offered to step aside when Grant arrived on March 10. Afterward, Grant wrote: "It is men who wait to be selected, and not those who seek, from whom we may always expect the most efficient results."

The new general-in-chief gave the simplest order possible to Meade: "Where Lee goes, there you will go also." Sherman would strike from Chattanooga and destroy Joe Johnston's army along the way southward to Atlanta. And if Nathaniel Banks could wipe out the rebels in central Louisiana early enough, Grant meant for him to turn eastward and take Mobile.

Perhaps Lieutenant General U. S. Grant remembered from the Vicksburg campaign that depending on Banks to do anything right was to court disappointment. Certainly he wanted nothing to do with the Louisiana operation; he even asked if it could be called off. But, as Halleck explained, the president had his reasons for ordering it, and a wise general-in-chief leaves it at that.

True, Lincoln wanted Louisiana's (and Arkansas') electoral votes cast for the next Republican presidential candidate. But he was also worried about the French presence in Mexico. This he considered a clear, insolent, and intolerable violation of the Monroe Doctrine; Confederates were trading with the French at Mexican ports, which weakened the blockade's effectiveness; and the only solution he could see was Union control of Texas. Banks's earlier attempts along the Gulf coastline to invade the state having failed, it was time to try the Shreveport gateway—and besides, the rebels had factories in East Texas.

Halleck had left it to Banks to work out all the details. Admiral Porter would load the 10,000 troops Sherman was loaning Banks on twenty-one transports at Vicksburg, provide his entire fleet of twenty-two gunboats as escorts down the Mississippi and then up Red River, and deliver them to Alexandria by March 17. There the borrowed force, led by Brigadier General A. J. Smith, would be met by the 15,000-man column William Franklin was to bring up behind a screen of 5,000 cavalrymen. Eventually, Banks expected to have a total of 30,000 troops of all arms, supported by 60 guns on land and 210 on Porter's vessels, all dedicated to the capture of Shreveport by April 15: Sherman's deadline for the return of his units.

General Grant might have felt better about all this had he known how weak the Confederates were west of the Mississippi. General Edmund Kirby Smith had only smatterings of troops and guns scattered throughout his five-state command. That was partly the result of Grant's having isolated the region. But Richmond had never sent much support westward; instead, those authorities had drawn men, horses, food, fodder, cotton—whatever the distant states could provide—eastward. Worse, the Confederate high command had long been exiling troublesome generals and those believed useless because of illness to the Trans-Mississippi Department. Kirby Smith himself was one; another was Richard Taylor, sent west to recover from the partial paralysis that had kept him out of the Seven Days' Battles the campaign after which flamboyant Prince John Magruder found himself in Galveston. And later Sterling Price, the proud Missourian with whom Davis could not come to terms, came to this burial ground of military ambitions.

At least Banks and Frederick Steele (whose forces would be coming southwestward from Little Rock) would not benefit from surprise: Dick Taylor's network of scouts along the Mississippi and in New Orleans were quick to report federal preparations. Kirby Smith called on Magruder to send men, especially Texan cavalry. He appealed to governors for home-guard troops. But at best, he would have next to nothing with which to fight two Yankee columns converging on Shreveport.

In Richard Taylor, though, Kirby Smith had a field general who had learned more than anyone suspected from watching Thomas J. Jackson carefully during the Shenandoah Valley campaign two years earlier. It was Taylor who led the charge that cleared Winchester of federals, sending them fleeing all the way to the Potomac. And the general he had whipped was Nathaniel Banks.

Without knowing it, Kirby Smith had two other assets—politics and weather—and they combined to give him a third: time. In early March, Banks in New Orleans and Steele up in Little Rock tarried to inaugurate governors in compliance with Abraham Lincoln's desire to start reconstructing rebel states dominated by Union forces. Heavy rains first delayed the start of William Franklin's infantry and artillery column and then slowed its advance northward. As a result, Banks began to feel the pressure of Sherman's April 15 deadline build before his invasion could become much of a problem for the Confederates.

Although the terrain in central Louisiana was pool-table flat and laced with bayous instead of compartmented by rugged rock up-thrusts, Dick Taylor employed Jacksonian strategy from the outset. Of necessity, he put up only light resistance as the federals moved up the Red River; after evacuating everything of military use from Alexandria on March 15, he let David Dixon Porter's sailors have the town; and when A. J. Smith's troops came ashore and started overland, Taylor lured them toward Shreveport. By then he had 7,000 men with him, as many as he was likely to have, though a few more Texans might come in, and he could begin to hunt for a place Jackson would have liked—one at which he could smite the Yankees on equal terms.

Not until March 25 did General Banks reach Alexandria, on a steamboat called The *Black Hawk*, with cotton speculators already there to greet him. Neither the civilians, some bearing passes signed by A. Lincoln, nor the army commander were pleased by what they saw happening: Porter's sailors and marines were loading bales of cotton on navy gunboats, explaining that they were entitled to them (and to their shares of the cotton's value when sold) as a "prize of war."

Soldiers enjoyed no such right, and they were bitter about it. So was Banks. He had earlier calculated that if he could capture 200,000 bales and the national Treasury sold them for $500 a bale, his campaign would give the government a windfall of $100 million—$50 million more if the number of bales was 300,000. But Banks could not persuade or order Porter to stop the federal navy's seizures; word of them had spread far beyond Alexandria, and Confederates were burning cotton rather than see it hauled away in Yankee wagons.

General Banks's second day in Alexandria was hardly better. William Franklin's column arrived, over a week late, and so did a message Lieutenant General Grant had written eleven days before. If Banks was not in Shreveport by April 30, the new general-in-chief directed, he should abandon the campaign and return to New Orleans. Sherman's April 15 deadline for sending his units back remained in force even if their departure made getting to Shreveport impossible. What Grant really wanted, he explained, was Mobile, and that would be Banks's objective if he could disentangle himself from northern Louisiana early enough.

Grant's offering Mobile as a carrot while using the loss of A. J. Smith's 10,000 men as a stick focused Nathaniel Banks's attention on nature. The winter of 1863–64 had been so dry that the Red River was low, and that amounted to a very serious problem for Admiral Porter. Shallow rapids at Alexandria extended for nearly a mile; in order to support Banks's advance to Shreveport, Porter would have to get gunboats and transports over that barrier, which would take time. The admiral had earlier boasted that he could take his fleet "wherever the sand was damp." Now he might have to prove it.

Banks had another time-consuming concern: supervising the elections in central Louisiana of delegates to a convention at which a new state constitution would be hammered out. That kept him in Alexandria until April 2. But by then Porter had most of the gunboats and transports he wanted upstream, both A. J. Smith and Franklin had their troops chasing Dick Taylor into the rolling, tree-covered country roughly seventy-five miles south of Shreveport, General Steele was on his way southwestward from Little Rock, and it looked as though Nathaniel Banks might soon be inflicting federal wrath on Mobile, after all.

So optimistic was Banks, in fact, that in a message to Chief of Staff Halleck he wrote:

> Our troops now occupy Natchitoches and we hope to be in Shreveport by the 10th of April. I do not fear concentration of the enemy at that point. My fear is that they may not be willing to meet us.

Days later, when he read those last two McClellanesque sentences, Abraham Lincoln remarked: "I am sorry to see this tone of confidence," and he predicted that "the next news we shall hear from there will be of defeat."

Indeed, General Banks had reached pretty far, not realizing until the next day—at Grand Ecore, a landing on Red River a few miles east of Natchitoches—that no one was certain there *was* a road following the stream northward to Shreveport. Could he risk cutting northwestward, away from the river and Porter's gunboats and troop-laden transports, and send his other columns along the inland route via Mansfield?

Yes, Banks decided, expecting that the waterborne forces and his own could get together again somewhere near Springfield Landing for the last thirty-odd miles into Shreveport. He ordered Porter upriver. And now, on April 3, the general seemed to forget that he was only a week short of his new self-imposed deadline. The next day, he took the time to hold a grand review of the 16,000 men in his cavalry, infantry, and artillery units (and the 1,000 supply-filled wagons that would be going up the road with them), but not until the sixth did they begin to move out. And not until the seventh would Admiral Porter cast off.

Edmund Kirby Smith was not among the men Richard Taylor admired. One reason was the combat soldier's inherent contempt for headquarters personnel; another was the senior general's inability to cope with two enemy threats at the same time.

At first, Kirby Smith considered Banks's advance from the south the greater threat to Shreveport, and he had drawn troops southwest-ward from Sterling Price's forces in Arkansas. But on discovering that Steele's column was small, he seemed tempted to give priority to its destruction, after all. This infuriated Taylor, who wrote him:

> Action, prompt, vigorous action, is required. While we are deliberating the enemy is marching. King James lost three kingdoms for a mass. We may lose three states without a battle.

Kirby Smith did move Brigadier General T. J. Churchill's small division down to Keatchie, halfway between Shreveport and Taylor's base at Mansfield, and he implied that if battle seemed imminent, he would bring Churchill's force southward and direct the fight him-self. Earlier, however, Taylor had decided to end his 200-mile retreat at a clearing south of Mansfield called Sabine Crossroads. There, with such troops as he had, he meant to wreck the advancing federal force. "I will fight Banks," Taylor told one of his officers, "if he has a million men."

Old Jack himself might not have found a better place than the one his disciple had selected. Into the clearing from the south came a road that, because of dense woods on both sides, was more of a miles-long tunnel than anything else. This was now the advancing Yankee column's only route to Mansfield. Once the federals emerged from the forest, the first thing they would see was a low hill in the middle of the open space. On it there would be a line of Confederates, actually a screen for the main force Taylor had concealed in the woods all along the clearing's crescent-shaped northern edge.

Taylor's plan was first to lure as many of Banks's troops as he could onto the killing ground and then to grind them up. On the morning of April 8, one federal commander after another reached the clearing, ran into Taylor's screen, and sent back for reinforcements. Banks was glad to send them; he had to get to Mansfield, for north of there he would have three roads to use in his final thirty-five-mile drive to Shreveport; and Mansfield was only three miles north of this delaying rabble.

Because of that narrow road, however, it took hours for more of the federals to get to Sabine Crossroads. Taylor waited nearly all day, a cigar in his mouth, one leg thrown across the saddle of his black horse. Finally, at around four o'clock on the afternoon of April 8, he gave the signal to charge.

Out of the woods his Louisianans and Texans came, yelling, firing, capturing Union guns and turning them against their previous owners, sweeping around the Yankees' flanks. Fighting at some places was fierce, hand to hand. "Try to think you are dead and buried," said one federal regimental commander to his men, "and you will have no fear."

But the federals were almost encircled, and soon they were running. Up rode General Banks. "Form a line here," he cried to some fugitives, as had Oliver Howard at Chancellorsville. "I know you will not desert me."

Desert him they did, scrambling toward their only escape route: the tunnel-like road, clogged now with northbound wagons and guns that could not be turned around. As a Union survivor of the rout described it:

> Still thicker and denser came the frightened crowd, rushing past in every possible manner. Men without hats or coats, men without guns or accoutrements, cavalrymen without horses, and artillerymen without cannon, wounded men bleeding and crying at every step, men begrimed with smoke and powder—all in a state of fear and frenzy, while they shouted at our boys not to go forward any further, for they would all be slaughtered.

For two miles or so Taylor's men chased Yankees through the woods, driving them finally south of the only creek in a region where water was scarce. But along those two miles of road were at least 156 abandoned wagons laden with food and supplies and twenty artillery pieces. The ground was littered with rifles and equipment. And when the roundup was over, the Confederates had also captured nearly 1,000 horses and mules.

Back at the clearing a courier had arrived from Shreveport with the order General Kirby Smith had written that morning, the one in which he had said he would lead the forces in any fight there might be. "Too late, sir," Richard Taylor told the rider; "the battle is won."

Indeed, it had been. But on the next afternoon there would be another, twenty miles or so south of Mansfield at Pleasant Hill, and it would be on ravine-slashed ground of Banks's choosing. This time Taylor had Thomas Churchill's troops, but they were worn out from the long march southward from Keatchie. Even so, Taylor tried to make a Jacksonian-wide envelopment west of the strong federal line. It failed. When the day's fighting ended, it seemed as though Banks would get to Shreveport, after all.

General Banks thought so; he even told A. J. Smith that he meant to advance northward first thing the next morning, April 10. On the evening of the ninth, however, while the guns along Pleasant Hill's lines were cooling, Banks discovered that some of his other generals—among them, William Franklin—wanted no more mauling from Taylor's rebels. Retreat to Grand Ecore, they advised. Banks so ordered.

Around midnight, A. J. Smith learned of this. He came to Banks, protesting vehemently, offering alternatives. No, Banks insisted. Disgusted, Smith found Franklin, second in command, and urged him to place Banks under arrest. "Don't you know," replied Franklin, "this is mutiny?"

Early on the morning of the tenth—the day Banks had told Washington he "hoped" to be in Shreveport—the federal army's withdrawal began. Whether Richard Taylor had won an incredible victory or Nathaniel Banks had merely lost his nerve and thrown away his considerable advantages, one thing was clear: It was Jackson who had, at least for the time being, saved Shreveport.

Ironically, on the morning of April 10 some of Taylor's troops were moving in the opposite direction, northward, bound for Mansfield. General Kirby Smith had arrived, listened to reports of the fighting at Sabine Crossroads and Pleasant Hill, learned that Banks was retreating to Grand Ecore, and thought about Taylor's plea for permission to pursue the Yankees and bag them—gunboats and all. "Never take counsel of your fears," Old Jack had said, but that is what Kirby Smith did. Frederick Steele's federal column up in Arkansas worried him; if he let Taylor get too many miles south of

Shreveport, there would be no hope of holding the town. That was unthinkable, so he told Taylor to pull back to Mansfield and prepare to go even farther northward to fight Steele.

Dick Taylor, suspecting that Steele could be held by the Confederate forces already in Arkansas blocking him, anxious to finish off Banks, protested to the limits of the commanding general's tolerance. But Kirby Smith had made up his mind, and for once he stuck to his decision.

Indeed, General Steele was having more problems than Kirby Smith seemed to realize. Among them was hunger. On March 24, the Union column's second day out of Little Rock, Steele put his 6,800 troops on half rations. Now, two weeks later, nearly 100 miles southwest of Little Rock (and still about that far from Shreveport), men were breaking ranks to hunt for food at farms along the route— finding little, delaying the march. And by April 9, Steele had another 3,600 men to feed. They had come southward from Fort Smith, their own supplies were all gone, and Steele's wagons were almost empty.

Another of the federal commander's problems was harassment of his flanks by Confederate cavalry. Some of these riders had come eastward from the Indian Territory, bringing the number of Sterling Price's defenders close to half that of Frederick Steele's 10,000-plus invaders. But it was not necessary for Price's men to do more than delay the Yankees. The longer the gray-clads held Steele where he was, the sooner the threat of starvation would send the bluecoats scurrying back to Little Rock.

But at Mansfield, Louisiana, on April 10, General Kirby Smith was either ignorant of all this or lacking Taylor's powers of imagination. Either way, he rejected the opportunity to destroy Banks's force and turned to deal with a foe already whipped by hunger more than a hundred miles to the north.

Whether Kirby Smith had forgotten about Admiral Porter's fleet of gunboats and the federal troops on the transports they were escorting up the Red River or if he dismissed this threat to Shreveport when Taylor reminded him of it, his decision to return priority to Arkansas seemed irrevocable. Taylor gave up the bulk of his infantry in compliance with orders, but he kept enough men behind, cavalry mostly, to strike this now-isolated fragment of Banks's invasion force.

While the flotilla steamed upriver, Porter had stopped only to let army troops go ashore to loot and burn plantations. At the place he was to land the soldiers for their final drive to Shreveport, he learned of the rout at Sabine Crossroads and Banks's decision to retreat to

Grand Ecore. With difficulty—the pro-Confederate Red River's water level had fallen sharply—he got his gunboats and transports turned around for the 100-mile dash (as the river snaked) to rejoin Banks.

Most of it was through damp sand, with Taylor's remaining infantry and guns on the bluffs delivering plunging fire into their abundance of unmissable targets. Federals waiting at Grand Ecore could see the punishment Porter's vessels had absorbed. And by then the Yankees had at least two more things to worry about: Down at Alexandria the Red River's rapids were now only streamlets trickling over nearly a mile of exposed rock, and Taylor's men were encircling Banks's refuge.

Banks was giving Taylor credit for five times the 5,000 or so Confederates penning him in. So were the federal troops. One paused from building log fortifications and told Franklin, who had just said they would not be needed: "We have been defeated once, and we think we will look out for ourselves."

Now it was April 15, General Sherman's deadline for the return of the divisions Banks had borrowed. Off to Cump and General Grant went messages explaining why those men must be kept where they were. Admiral Porter wrote: "[A. J. Smith's] is the only part of the army not demoralized, and if he has to leave there would be a most disastrous retreat."

But it would take days for replies to be received, and two weeks remained before Grant's deadline for abandoning the whole campaign. Banks decided to try once more to reach Shreveport. First, though, he had to get out of Grand Ecore.

Chapter 32

Grant Versus Lee

In mid-April, as David Dixon Porter checked the dampness of Red River sand, Generals Grant and Sherman were refining plans for the destruction of the Confederacy's eastern field armies: Lee's in Virginia, Johnston's in northwestern Georgia. Then came dismaying reports from west of the Mississippi. And at about the same time, Nathan Bedford Forrest's rampaging caught the attention of people throughout the Union.

After whipping Sooy Smith at Okolona and dashing Sherman's hopes for the drive into Alabama, Forrest had moved northward from western Tennessee into Kentucky, recruiting and raiding isolated federal garrisons in search of weapons and horses.

By March 25, Forrest's men were plundering federal supplies at Paducah on the Ohio River. Later, newspaper reports chided him for overlooking 140 concealed horses; he sent a detachment back and got them. Forrest's next target was Fort Pillow, on a bluff above the Mississippi, roughly forty miles north of Memphis. Sherman had ordered Fort Pillow abandoned, but on April 12 it was still occupied by nearly 600 troops—about half of them Unionist West Tennesseeans, the rest blacks who had recently been slaves but were now in blue uniforms—under the command of Major L. F. Booth. Forrest's cavalry also had many West Tennesseeans in it, so the fight was bound to be a bitter one.

It began in an ordinary way, with skirmishing. Forrest placed troopers on both flanks of the fort, where they could fire into its defenders if they tried to flee down ravines to the landing. There the survivors might be rescued by a Union gunboat standing by close to the dock. For about five hours Forrest's guns shelled the fort, and the gunboat fired back. By three o'clock that afternoon the "Wizard of the Saddle" had had three horses shot from under him and wanted the fight ended. To do that, he got a party ready to deliver an ultimatum:

As your gallant defense of the fort has entitled you to the treatment of brave men, I now demand an unconditional surrender of your force, at the same time assuring you that they will be treated as prisoners of war. I have received a fresh supply of ammunition, and can easily take your fort.

Before the officers left, there was some discussion as to whether the former slaves would be treated in the same manner as the whites. Yes, said Forrest.

No Confederate knew it, but Major Booth had been killed six hours before. Another officer signed Booth's name to the reply, which was a request for an hour in which to confer with the gunboat's captain. While Forrest was thinking about that, two facts emerged: Inside the fort, whiskey barrels were open, and the troops were showing the effects of it; and several transports were coming upriver bringing artillery as well as infantry reinforcements.

General Forrest gave the federal commander twenty minutes. He added that so great was the hatred existing between the West Tennesseeans in both commands, he could not be responsible for the consequences if he were obliged to storm the fort. Back came a refusal. Forrest ordered a charge. Soon the federals were running down the ravine, peppered by rebel sharpshooters on its banks, rushing toward a gunboat that not only was not at the landing but was not firing.

The acting commander had left the flag flying over the fort; he had not surrendered, nor did he after the dash down the gully began. It appeared to the Confederates that the Yankees, still carrying their weapons and some firing them as they fled, were merely transferring the fight from one place to another. The battle went on until individual bluecoats threw up their hands. Yet this battle would be known ever afterward by the misleading name Union newspapers promptly gave it: the "Fort Pillow Massacre."

Later, it would be reckoned that out of 557 federals in the fort's garrison, 221 had been killed, and among the 336 taken prisoner, 226 were wounded. What infuriated Northern readers of "atrocity" stories, of course, were the numbers regarding the 262 Negro Union troops. Of them, 204 were killed or wounded; 58 were able to walk into Confederate captivity, along with 168 of the 295 whites. But amid near-hysterical allegations, the facts got lost or were ignored. In Nathan Bedford Forrest the North had a made-to-order villain, beginning with the fact that before the war he had been a trader in slaves. By early 1864 he had gained a reputation as a ruthless and fierce fighter who feared no man on either side. Before restraining himself from slapping Braxton Bragg's face, he had told another superior, Joe Wheeler, "I will be in my coffin before I will serve again under your command." And many a Yankee force's commander had seen, and yielded to, scrawled notes threatening to put his whole garrison to the sword if he did not surrender.

Forrest was a natural soldier, one far removed from the cesspools of politics, and he had dealt with Fort Pillow as a military objective and nothing more. But the Union Congress's Committee on the Conduct of the War and all the rest of the vote cravers in the North (for 1864 was an unusually important election year) went into a highly publicized frenzy. From President Lincoln through Secretary of War Stanton to the new general-in-chief and finally to General Sherman sped orders to investigate. Grant added: "If our men have been murdered after capture, retaliation must be resorted to promptly."

Cump Sherman may have hated Forrest more than anyone else; certainly he was anxious to find him as guilty as the Northern newspapers had proclaimed him to be. But when this seasoned professional soldier reported back to General Grant, he did not recommend any retaliation.

Sure, Army of the Potomac veterans told each other, Grant may have done great things out west, but what was going to happen when he ran into Bobby Lee? Then everybody would find out what kind of stuff this quiet little newcomer was made of.

Eliminating Lee and his vaunted Army of Northern Virginia from the war was central in Grant's strategic planning. George Meade's 100,000-plus troops would make the kill; all the other operations Grant ordered were important mainly in terms of the support they gave Meade. "Wherever Lee's army goes, there you will go also," Grant had told him. And where might Lee go?

From the Confederate camps near Orange, Lee could move northeastward down the Shenandoah Valley and threaten Washington for the fourth time. To remove that possibility and also to deny Lee food and fodder from Virginia's granary, General Grant gave Franz Sigel orders to sweep up the Valley toward Staunton.

Where else might Lee turn? Well, Richmond. Apart from the city's political and symbolic significance, it was the hub through which Georgians and Carolinians sent supplies to Lee's army. Any attempt to cut rail lines entering Richmond from the south, certainly to seize his base, was bound to distract Lee. Grant directed

Ben Butler, then at Fort Monroe, to load his forces on ships, make landings from the James River at a place twenty miles southeast of Richmond called the Bermuda Hundred, and go on from there to take the rebel capital.

All these blows were to be thrown at the rebels at the same time. Said Abraham Lincoln, approving, using words a general who had once been a tanner of hides could understand: "Those not skinning can hold a leg."

As May was about to open, however, Grant had to concede that Nathaniel Banks would be neither skinner nor holder; with his 30,000 troops and many of Admiral Porter's gunboats caught deep in central Louisiana by a tiny rebel force and damp sand, the Mobile operation had to be canceled.

Over the 1863–64 winter General Lee had heard a great deal about the North's new hero and how he operated. Had those people, after so many mistakes, finally found a general who could focus all the Union's enormous advantages?

"We have got to whip them," said Lee to an aide, Colonel Walter Taylor; "we must whip them, and it has already made me better to think of it."

From his headquarters near Orange went messages directing scattered units to reassemble. Longstreet's divisions had the longest march, but in late April they reached Gordonsville, and General Lee was there to welcome them. Recalled one veteran:

> The men hung around him and seemed satisfied to lay their hands on his gray horse or to touch the bridle, or the stirrup, or the old general's leg—anything that Lee had was sacred to us fellows who had just come back.

On Monday, May 2, General Lee stood atop Clark Mountain with Longstreet, Ewell, Powell Hill, and the leaders of eight divisions. Lee's purpose was to be certain they understood the military problem as he saw it. Northward beyond the Rapidan, ten miles away, the generals could see splotches of white—the Army of the Potomac's tents and wagon tops. East of Clark Mountain were Germanna Ford and Ely's, which Mr. F. J. Hooker had used a year before on his way to Chancellorsville. Those people would cross there again, General Lee said. But he made no more predictions and gave no orders, leaving it to the generals to study geographic realities no map could convey.

Below them, south of the fords, stretched the green hell of the Wilderness. Inside it, a year ago that very day, Jackson had made his last flank march. Longstreet and two of his divisions had missed that battle, but most of Lee's men and many of George Meade's knew what to expect once they were back inside those thickets. But how much history would be repeated during the next few days?

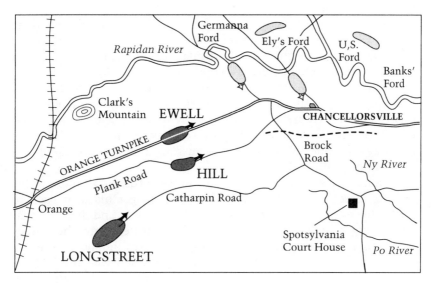

Approaches to the Wilderness

As before, Lee meant to attack. Ewell's corps would move eastward on the turnpike, Hill's on the Orange Plank Road a few miles south of it. Longstreet would come up from Gordonsville on the Catharpin Road, southernmost of the three, roughly parallel to the others near the Wilderness's western edge. These moves were not to begin, however, until Lee was sure Meade's forces were following Hooker's old route.

As he waited, messages confirmed what he had suspected: Federals were moving in the Shenandoah Valley and on the James River below Richmond. But these threats neither distracted him nor made him consider sending units from his army to counter them. Lee had only 65,000 troops to put against George Meade's 100,000 or more; Beauregard had come up from Charleston to block Ben Butler's riverborne invaders; and it was up to John Breckinridge to keep Franz Sigel from getting too far up the Valley. Whipping the two Union generals nearest him was all that seemed to be on Lee's mind as, displaying the calm that was by now legendary, he waited to test Ulysses Grant.

Whether news from Frederick Steele in Arkansas was worse

than messages describing the plights of Nathaniel Banks and the admiral of a fleet that appeared doomed, only Grant could say. But to the men on both sides risking their lives in Louisiana and Arkansas, those fights were the most important ones anywhere—*and* they settled something.

Hunger had plagued Steele's force all along. In mid-April he turned left from the direct route to Shreveport, heading for Camden instead. Once there, the federal commander sent trains out to gather food and fodder. One column was returning with 198 wagonloads of provisions when a strong rebel cavalry force intercepted it near Poison Spring, inflicting 301 casualties on the 1,050-man federal escort before driving it away. Along with corn, bacon, hogs, and geese, the rebels discovered quilts and women's and children's clothing—as one Southerner put it, "all the *et ceteras* of unscrupulous plunder."

Soon after another rebel cavalry unit captured 240 more of his wagons, Steele realized he would do well to get his men back to Little Rock, ordered a withdrawal from Camden, and directed that everything that had to be left behind be burned. Into the flames went tents, cooking utensils, wagons, harnesses (horses and mules were already starving), even bacon and hardtack that might have been issued. This left each man with two crackers and a half pint of cornmeal for the days-long ninety-mile march.

Such, by April 27, was the condition of the Union force Kirby Smith had come northward to whip. When he finally caught up with Steele, roughly halfway between Camden and Little Rock at Jenkins's Ferry on the Saline River, on April 30, Frederick Steele's hungry men stopped Kirby Smith's piecemeal attacks—only to endure three more days of hard marching and fear of starvation before they reached Little Rock and the end of a two-month ordeal hardly anyone else would ever remember.

Kirby Smith's quest for glory in Arkansas may have given Taylor freedom to do what he thought best, but surely to have had the use of those snatched-away troops would have enabled Old Jack's disciple to accomplish a great deal toward smiting Nathaniel Banks hip and thigh. Taylor's force proved too weak to prevent Banks's five-times-larger one from breaking out of Grand Ecore, and all the Confederate commander could do was lash the Yankee hip as the retreating invaders looted and burned plantations, even family farms, as they slogged toward Alexandria. But below the city's now-dry falls Taylor meant to crush Banks's thigh. Splitting his tiny army, he placed men and guns along the Red River's bluffs downstream. From those heights Taylor's infantrymen and artillerymen attacked every steamer that came within range, cutting off Banks's army and Porter's stranded fleet from the outside world.

"We will play the game the Russians played in the retreat from Moscow," wrote the former student of military history to Kirby Smith. Starving Banks's trapped hordes he meant, putting the political general to the challenge Napoleon Bonaparte faced in the winter of 1812 as his Grand Army scurried westward. Ironically, Banks's own soldiers had already made a connection of sorts between the Corsican and their leader. To the tune of "When Johnny Comes Marching Home" they sang:

> In eighteen hundred and sixty-four,
>   Foot balls, foot balls;
> In eighteen hundred and sixty-four,
>   Foot balls, says I;
> In eighteen hundred and sixty-four,
> We all skedaddled to Grand Ecore
> We'll all drink stone blind,
> Johnny, fill up the bowl!

And they ended with a shouted: "Napoleon P. Banks!"

But now it was early May, and at Alexandria to Banks and Porter had come Lieutenant Colonel Joseph Bailey, a former logger from Wisconsin, who offered to build a wing dam 760 feet long across the Red River's exposed rocks. Once enough water had been impounded, Bailey explained, the ten gunboats and an even larger number of transports could run the gap in the dam to safety downstream. Build it, Bailey was told—belatedly, for he had first suggested the project at Pleasant Hill three weeks earlier—and on April 30 the work began.

Richard Taylor could only marvel at this display of Yankee ingenuity, for 30,000 bluecoats were keeping his 6,000 men and the few guns he had too far from Bailey's dam site to disrupt the builders' frantic efforts. But he could take some comfort in knowing that Alexandria was the only place in the central part of his state the Union invaders still controlled.

General-in-Chief Grant could get no comfort at all, however, from any of these developments. Guillotining Nathaniel Banks was about all Grant could think of to do. Impossible, replied Chief of Staff Halleck:

> General Banks is a personal friend of the President, and has strong political supporters in and out of Congress. There will undoubtedly be a very strong opposition to his being removed or superseded....To do an act which will give offense to a large number of his political friends the Presi-

dent will require some evidence in a positive form to show the military necessities of that act. In other words he must have something in a definite shape to fall back upon as his justification. You will perceive that the press in New Orleans and in the Eastern States are already beginning to open in General Banks' favor. The administration would be immediately attacked for his removal. Do not understand me as advocating his retention in command. On the contrary, I expressed to the President months ago my own opinion of General Banks' want of military capacity.

All of which may well have made Ulysses Grant glad he was not mired in Washington but in the field, where most questions were as simple as the difference between life and death.

During the spring Meade had reorganized his army, merging understrength corps with stronger ones, placing the three that remained under commanders he trusted most. Winfield Scott Hancock headed II Corps; Gouverneur Warren, V; John Sedgwick, VI. Like Meade, they were veterans of Chancellorsville; to them the Wilderness's tangles and thickets would present no surprises.

General Grant sent for only one officer from the West: Little Phil Sheridan, who had started the war as a quartermaster but showed such aggressiveness at Perryville and Stones River that by the time he led his troops up Missionary Ridge, he was a major general. Meade, delighted, gave Sheridan command of his 10,000 cavalrymen.

Grant also ordered Ambrose Burnside to bring his IX Corps eastward, but he kept this force under his control. Sparing the loser at Fredericksburg the embarrassment of having to serve under a former subordinate was one reason for this arrangement, although Burnside said it was not necessary. His divisions, however, gave Grant a powerful reserve that he could use either to support Meade or to exploit attractive opportunities.

On May 3, then, in all General Grant had 116,000 or more troops to send against Lee's 65,000. The morale of federal soldiers was high, the weather good, roads were dry, the time had come. At around midnight, Phil Sheridan's cavalrymen were at both Ely's Ford and Germanna Ford, bridges were in place, and by the time the sun rose on May 4 the federal army was crossing the Rapidan and plunging southward, along roads veterans knew well, into the green hell of the Wilderness. Fortunately for General Meade there was no opposition; along with three infantry corps and at least 112 guns he had six miles of wagon trains to get below the river. At sunset on Wednesday, May 4, Warren's V Corps was in camps around Wilderness Tavern on the Orange Turnpike, and Hancock's II Corps was five miles east of there, at Chancellorsville; during the night Uncle John Sedgwick's VI Corps would bivouac between the Rapidan and Warren's position.

General Grant was so pleased with the first day's work that he answered a newspaperman who asked him how long it would take him to reach Richmond: "I will agree to be there in about four days if General Lee becomes a party to the agreement. But if he objects, the trip will undoubtedly be prolonged."

General Lee did indeed object, and he started expressing it on Wednesday morning as soon as he got the message observers on Clark Mountain wigwagged: Meade's army was moving into the Wilderness. Quickly he got his army headed eastward. By sundown Ewell's leading brigades were about five miles west of Wilderness Tavern. Hill's progress had not been that rapid; the point of his advance along the Plank Road lagged Ewell's by three miles. Longstreet's troops were still far to the southwest, pausing to rest along their forty-two-mile march. But Lee was confident that at some time during the next day, Thursday, he would have all of his forces within striking distance.

Lee had felt, and still did, that his best opportunity to attack would come while the federal columns were moving through the forest. Late on Wednesday night word came from Jeb Stuart that the Yankee camps were in the very heart of the Wilderness. Early on Thursday morning Lee told Ewell and Hill to press on eastward. Hill was to set the pace, with Ewell halting and holding his ground until Hill's men caught up. Avoid starting a general engagement, Lee cautioned them; if there was to be one, he wanted Longstreet's corps on hand.

Ewell remembered those admonitions late that morning when he got reports of Yankees moving southward up ahead. He got his lead brigades stopped just before they were surprised by a furious attack: Gouverneur Warren's whole corps meant to drive the Confederates back down the turnpike.

It was a nasty fight, with visibility limited by the dense foliage and formations broken amid the thickets, but soon Ewell had Brigadier General John B. Gordon's troops and Jubal Early's rushing eastward not only to stem the Union assaults but to get on the flanks of the bluecoats. For hours it went on, infantrymen on both sides shooting at sounds, veterans of Chancellorsville remembering that the worst thing that could happen was to be wounded and left behind to burn to death once the woods caught fire—as sooner or later they would.

Now Dick Ewell spurred the digging in earnest. It was all he could do, with no hope of support from Powell Hill's corps, more than two miles south of him. And by midafternoon the federals seemed to be as fought out as his own men were. But just as the firing to his east slackened, Ewell heard more open down on the Plank Road in front of Hill.

While Ewell had been holding his ground, Hill's advance had been blunted by Hancock's II Corps. Stronger even than the one that had almost wrecked Ewell's corps was the attack Hill's two divisions had to contain. And at first the key decisions had to be made by Harry Heth: Powell Hill was sick, which was exactly the way matters had stood on the afternoon of July 1, 1863, west of Gettysburg, Pennsylvania, when Lee arrived.

Again Lee rode up, and again he took charge, telling Heth he wanted him to get up the Plank Road, to its intersection with the Brock Road, the one those people were using to shift forces southward to Todd's Tavern on the Catharpin Road: Longstreet's assigned destination. Harry Heth was willing to try to cut off the flow of Yankees, but he never had the chance. So determined were the Union assaults that Heth and Cadmus Wilcox, whose division was north of the Plank Road, were hard pressed to keep the army commander and Jeb Stuart from being captured. Time and again the Yankees charged—"like the wolf on the fold," as Confederate Porter Alexander wrote later—only to be repulsed and to charge one more time. Darkness ended the savage fight, dooming thousands of wounded men hugging the ground between the lines to wonder whether rescuers could reach them before the flames did.

Two severe beatings were the price General Lee had to pay on that Thursday, May 5, for having waited so long at Orange to make certain Grant was entering the Wilderness. But now he knew that Grant *could* be detained; and the longer he could keep those people in that green hell, the more punishment he might inflict on them— and on the newcomer who may have just made a critical mistake.

Or was it General Meade who had erred? When Warren's men discovered Ewell's advance that morning, the army commander had not consulted the general-in-chief before giving the order to attack. Grant set strategy; Meade, tactics. Such was the split in responsibilities. But was this decision merely tactical?

Either way, Grant let it stand, adding: "If any opportunity presents itself for pitching into a part of Lee's army, do so without giving time for disposition." That was about the only guidance he supplied to Meade that Thursday. Grant sat down on a stump in a meadow, lit a cigar, took out his pocket knife, and spent the rest of the day whittling and smoking.

Messengers came and went, battle sounds swelled and died out, only to roar again, but through it all Grant remained calm to the point of seeming interested only in his carving. Meade did the directing, giving orders, shifting forces, handling the fighting as though his permanent guest had been in Washington. But anyone who thought General Grant had not been paying close attention was mistaken: After sundown he prescribed the attacks Meade's army would launch the next day, beginning at sunrise.

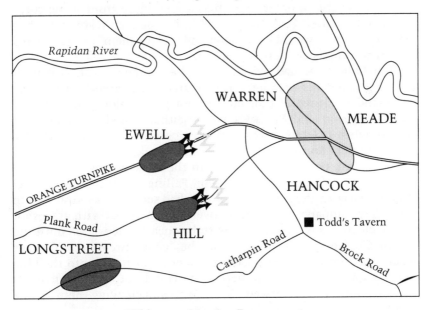

Wilderness Meeting Engagements

Whether the general-in-chief's blurring of the distinction between his role as strategist and Meade's as the Army of the Potomac's commander was intentional or not, from then onward Grant would be either credited or blamed as the maker of major decisions. In effect, he had evolved a new definition of what a general-in-chief's duties were, one completely reversing Henry Halleck's but resembling Lincoln's during the Shenandoah Valley campaign. Ulysses Grant was basically a practical man and a fighter, not a theoretician. But in reverting to the role of a tactician, as he seemed to be doing that Thursday night, he was putting the Union's entire military high command structure—as well as a field army nominally George Meade's—at risk.

General Lee, knowing that Hill's two divisions had drawn heavy federal forces toward them, had sent Longstreet orders to switch from the Catharpin Road north to the Plank Road so that Lee could do two things early Friday morning: have Longstreet continue Hill's attack eastward, and shift Hill's corps into the gap between it and Ewell's men. But unlike Lee, who was inured to the delay the change in routes would cause, Harry Heth expected Longstreet to come up during the night and enable him to take his division (and Cadmus Wilcox's) out of contact and back far enough to entrench.

Heth sought an order to withdraw and dig in from ailing corps commander Powell Hill. No, said Hill, let the men rest where they were; Longstreet would be up soon and replace them. Lee supported Hill in turning back Heth's protests.

But Longstreet had paused to let his marchers rest. Not until morning could his leading brigades arrive. Apparently, the army commander learned of that but did not pass it along; in any case, Heth's division and Wilcox's were neither rested nor dug in at sunrise when federals attacked them frontally and on both flanks. They could do no more than fire and fall back.

Some ran, passing General Lee in the meadow near the Widow Tapp's house. He tried to rally them. Failing, he turned to Colonel William Poague, the artilleryman who had served Jackson so well in the Valley campaign. Poague had twelve guns loaded with grapeshot on the clearing's western edge. With Lee nearby, he waited until the fleeing Confederates sped past; then he opened fire on the Yankees emerging from the woods, sending round after round into the blue mass, knowing that his gunners alone could not stop the federals from driving a wedge between Lee's corps and chewing them up one at a time.

Then, at the most critical moment, from out of the smoke General Lee saw troops coming up the Plank Road from the west. "Who are you?" he cried.

"Texas boys!" Hood's old brigade, they meant, led now by Brigadier General John Gregg. And if they were here, the rest of Longstreet's corps could not be far behind.

"Hurrah for Texas!" shouted the army commander, waving his hat, for once forgetting poise and dignity. "Hurrah for Texas!" The veterans surged toward Traveller, forming a line without a word of command. Then, seeing that he intended to lead their charge, some began yelling, "Go back, General Lee, go back!"

Gregg headed Traveller off, a Texan sergeant grabbed the gray war horse's bridle, but the rider seemed not to hear the shouts of "General Lee to the rear!" Only when he somehow realized that the Texans would not advance unless he withdrew did he ride back to where he was told Longstreet was waiting.

Never had the warrior in Robert Edward Lee—or any other emotion—shattered his near-marble calm. Surely this stunned Longstreet, from whom Lee had concealed every feeling except humility. Now Old Pete, seeking to snap the general out of his trance, said (in effect), Go ahead and command my corps if you want to while I head back to safety.

That had the desired result. While Longstreet threw back the federal onslaught, the army commander reassembled Hill's troops and sent them into the gap south of Ewell's fortified line. By midmorning on Friday, May 6, the Army of Northern Virginia was holding solidly on the turnpike and driving the Yankees back on the Plank Road, spoiling the attacks of Union forces outnumbering them, and raising the question of how best to smash the invaders and prod those who survived homeward.

General Grant had started Friday, May 6, as usual by stuffing twenty or so cigars into his pockets. Soon he was back on the stump where he had spent most of Thursday. And before long, despite the sounds of battle swelling west and northwest of him, out came his pocket knife, and he resumed his whittling.

But he had fresh causes for concern. Part of his plan for this day's work called for Ambrose Burnside to bring his corps southward and then plunge westward, through the gap between the rebel forces, and help Winfield Scott Hancock destroy the one on the Plank Road while Sedgwick and Warren got rid of Ewell's Confederates on the turnpike. But Burnside was late. And Burnside was operating under Grant's command, not Meade's.

Burnside was in fact entangled in the Wilderness, as were some of the troops Hancock was trying to shift. The woods made everything more difficult. Volleys stabbed out from nowhere, pinning men to the ground, and there they preferred to stay, knowing that any fool who stood up was likely to get his belly filled with lead. Warren and Sedgwick, attacking Ewell's lines with no result except mounting casualties, mindful that part of their mission was to prevent Ewell from reinforcing Hill, kept at the task. And when Hancock heard firing from the direction of Todd's Tavern, he knew he could wait no longer for Burnside. He sent reinforcements southward to Brigadier General Francis Barlow's division, weakening his front, making it easier for Longstreet's yelling rebels to fight their way closer up the Plank Road toward the north-south Brock Road.

General Grant's stump in the Lacy farm's clearing was not far east of that intersection of the Wilderness's few key roads, and he was whittling away when fugitives from Hancock's corps ran past, sending some headquarters officers into near panic. Move eastward, Grant was urged. Pausing from his whittling, he replied quietly: "It strikes me it would be better to order up some artillery and defend the present location."

This was done. The gunners could not see far enough ahead to fire, which the general-in-chief may have known would be the case, but he had made his point: Instead of worrying about what the enemy will do to you, think about what you can do to him.

As Longstreet was thinking about what a flank attack might do to the federals, up rode Major General Martin L. Smith, the engineer who had prepared Vicksburg's defenses and who may have had a grudge to settle with Grant. Longstreet sent him in search of a way to break the bloody stalemate in the thickets on both sides of the Plank Road. Soon Smith returned. He had found a stretch of unfinished railroad bed not far south of the Plank Road and parallel to it, he reported; the Yankees were north of the embankment and did not seem to know it was there; and a Confederate force could use this approach to roll up Meade's southern flank.

Longstreet quickly summoned Lieutenant Colonel G. Moxley Sorrell, an aide who had been with him since First Manassas, and told him to collect whatever troops he could and attack from the roadbed northward, and away went maybe 5,000 men, following a twenty-six year-old former Georgia bank clerk who had never taken even a platoon into battle. Was it feasible, James Longstreet wondered, to send his entire corps around the federal flank, beyond the Brock Road, into the Yankees' rear? He sent Smith off to the south on another scouting mission, this time to see how far eastward Meade's line extended. As Longstreet waited, a plan began to develop. Once he began the sweep northward with his divisions, Hill's troops could add their firepower to the advance, and so could Ewell's, and before sundown they might have the whole Army of the Potomac trapped between Confederate bayonets and the Rapidan.

Such were the possibilities when Longstreet heard yells and firing break out southeast of him: Sorrell was attacking. Now the federals blocking the Plank Road were melting back into the green hell. "Press them," Longstreet yelled, riding eastward to congratulate the gallant young colonel. But things had gotten confused, and

one Confederate outfit mistook another for Yankees, and Longstreet
was in the way. He jumped up from his saddle, hit in the neck by a
minié ball; then he slumped. "We're friends!" someone shouted; the
firing stopped. Officers carried the corps commander's body over to
a tree and set him down with his back against its trunk.

Was it history repeated? Even the wounded general seemed to
think so. Blowing bloody foam from his lips, he gave orders for
Major General Charles Field to assume command of the corps. And
when General Lee came, he told him what he had meant to do.

Stretcher-bearers arrived, and a surgeon. Though serious, Longstreet's wound was not mortal. But his body had seemed lifeless to
the men who saw him being evacuated, and word quickly spread that
Old Pete was dead.

Some of the brigades young Sorrell had started northward were
attacking barricades Hancock had ordered erected the day before,
fortifications half ablaze from fires sweeping through the Wilderness. Those Confederates had already done all they could, and when
they heard the sad rumor, they backed away.

Whether the troops' dismay and confusion or his own may have
been the cause, General Lee did not carry out Longstreet's massive
envelopment. Charles Field knew nothing about the plan; moreover,
he would need time in which to get Longstreet's corps in hand again.
Lee lingered for a while, then left it to Field to press Hancock as best
he could. By midafternoon Lee was a mile or so northward, on the
turnpike, there to see how Dick Ewell was faring in his struggle to
keep two Union corps from destroying the divisions Jackson had
once led.

John Gordon had grown tired of pleading with Ewell for permission to take his brigade around the wide-open northern federal flank.
Would the army commander approve? Do it, said Lee, and do it now.

By then the trees' shadows were getting long, but once Lee had
given his blessing, the attack went forward. Surprised, one federal
regiment after another broke and streaked southward. But the blow
came too late to be crushing. "Had the movement been made at an
earlier hour and properly supported," Gordon wrote afterward, "it
would have resulted in a decided disaster to the whole right wing of
General Grant's army, if not in its entire disorganization."

So for General Lee, Friday, May 6, ended in much the same way
as had the day before. Two opportunities there had been to get on
Grant's flanks—both missed, gone now. Lost, too, was Longstreet,
his "old warhorse," in circumstances similar enough to those of a
year earlier to chill the blood.

Meade's men had fought well all day, but nothing had worked

out as General-in-Chief Grant had planned. Whittling and smoking had helped him appear composed, but at sundown his patience snapped. He said to an officer reporting the panic resulting from Gordon's flank attack: "Oh, I am heartily tired of hearing about what Lee is going to do. Some of you always seem to think he is suddenly going to turn a double somersault and land in our rear and on both our flanks at the same time."

Reinforce and attack had been about the only counsel Grant had given Meade. But so far in this campaign the army had suffered roughly 18,000 casualties, and the lines were about where they had been at noon Thursday. The screams of wounded soldiers burning to death had filled the woods the previous night, and that night there would more of it. When, in all the battles fought in the past three years, had 18,000 men been lost before there was any sign of achieving anything?

After sundown, after General Grant had heard the reports and satisfied himself that the Wilderness-entwined army was as secure as his orders could make it, he went into his tent. He was not alone, but that did not seem to matter, for he collapsed on his cot and let loose all the long-repressed emotions of an ordinary man who had known failure and now could see himself whipped again, shedding tears freely, but soon it was as if nothing at all had happened. Casually he asked a departing war correspondent to take a message to Washington for him.

"If you see the President," Grant said, "tell him, from me, that, whatever happens, there will be no turning back."

Chapter 33

Spotsylvania: *Sheer Savagery Reigns*

Abraham Lincoln had been hungry for news. But he recalled something someone had said about Ulysses Grant: that he could be silent in several different languages. Members of Congress wondered what was going on; to one the president replied, "Well, I can't tell much about it. You see, Grant has gone to the Wilderness, crawled in, drawn up the ladder, and pulled in the hole after him, and I guess we'll just have to wait till he comes out before we know just what he's up to."

But reports were coming into the War Department's little telegraph room from other places: Sherman was about to march southeastward from Chattanooga, Franz Sigel was moving up the Shenandoah Valley, and Ben Butler was ashore near Richmond. Then, late on Friday evening, over the wire came a message from Henry Wing, the reporter who had left the Wilderness only a short time before. Could Wing send a story to his newspaper? No, said Secretary of War Stanton, but the president worked out a compromise that brought Wing to Washington shortly after two A.M. on Saturday morning. Lincoln learned only that the slaughter had been terrible on both sides, for the outcome was still uncertain when Wing had left, but there was one more thing: Grant's message to the president that there would be no turning back. Lincoln, overjoyed, hugged the young man.

Wing might not have added much to his story had he stayed in the Wilderness, for on that Saturday, May 7, both sides' commanders seemed willing to give their armies a chance to untangle. Little could be seen in those woods on the best of days, but fog and drifting smoke made this one unrewarding to the eye, and the postbattle stench offended nostrils. Confederates and federals alike

491

pulled back to their entrenchments, making contact only when patrols skirmished.

If precedent meant anything, Grant would recognize that Lee had whipped him and withdraw; the Army of the Potomac's fresh beating was even more severe than Hooker's had been. And not long after sunrise the general-in-chief had started writing orders. He was letting Lee have the Wilderness, shifting the army—carefully, secretly, that night—to a crossroads near a little village called Spotsylvania, between Chancellorsville and Fredericksburg and a little south of both places. But as the day went on, signs of impending retreat accumulated. Guns were pulled out of the line, headed for Chancellorsville and perhaps the ford Hooker had used on his return to Falmouth. Rumors spread. Federal troops' morale plummeted.

It was well after dark when some veterans in the mauled-again Army of the Potomac sensed that they were not headed for the river. The word quickly spread from the head of the column. The road ahead led southward: This was no retreat, it was an *advance*.

Grant, leading it, had to send aides to stop the cheering.

The next morning, Sunday, May 8, federals nearing Spotsylvania found Confederates holding the ground General Grant had hoped to reach first. Had General Lee performed a double somersault to land in their rear?

No, not quite. Lee knew only that Grant was a fighter; he would not retreat, but he might withdraw eastward. That would take him out of the Wilderness and also give him a new and more secure supply line: the Potomac to Aquia Landing and then Fredericksburg. And to protect his new base Grant would try to place his combat forces on the high ground near Spotsylvania.

General Lee had wanted out of the burning forest as much as Grant, but before the Army of Northern Virginia could move, its commander had to designate new leaders for two of his three corps: He chose Richard Anderson to replace Longstreet, Jubal Early for the ailing Powell Hill—which meant that on that Saturday, Lee was about to risk his army in a move from known strength to a distant place by roundabout routes, gambling that his assumptions regarding Grant's thinking were correct, relying on untried subordinates to lead two of his corps.

To Jeb Stuart, Lee gave the tasks of screening the movement from the Yankees and holding Spotsylvania's high ground until Anderson's corps got there. And once the armies were in the open, everything might depend on Stuart to go on doing two things at once, outnumbered two to one by Sheridan's cavalry though he was and as by now Lee's army was by Grant's.

Richard Anderson's gray-clad corps was supposed to rest on the way, but forest fires burning on both sides of the road made that impossible. Anderson pressed southeastward, helping some of Stuart's cavalrymen hold Gouverneur Warren's federal troops out of Spotsylvania. Anderson got there early, but Warren's V Corps infantrymen were late, worn out, and Sheridan's cavalry operations had been a fiasco, mainly because Little Phil's orders never reached some divisions of his 10,000-man force.

By noon on Sunday, the eighth, both armies were concentrating, Lee's on the high ground between the Po and Ny rivers, Grant's in an arc to the northwest of the rebel fortifications. And, at Meade's headquarters, Sheridan was telling the Army of the Potomac's commander he might as well take over the cavalry, for if he (Sheridan) had his way, he would use it to destroy Jeb Stuart.

Angered by Sheridan's insubordination, Meade took the matter to Grant. "He usually knows what he is talking about," said the general-in-chief. "Let him go ahead and do it." That afternoon, Meade ordered Sheridan to ride southward, cut Lee's supply lines, and drive on until he reached Butler's forces threatening Richmond. Ben Grierson had done something like this during the Vicksburg campaign, and it had helped.

This squabble settled, Meade ordered an attack against the lines the rebels were digging with bayonets and tin cups, and Grant wrote a message to Henry Halleck in Washington. Toward the end of it he said: "My exact route to the James River I have not yet definitely marked out."

The next day, Abraham Lincoln read those words. As though he suspected the general-in-chief of putting his shiniest boot forward, he said: "How near we have been to this thing before and failed." Then he added: "I believe if any other general had been at the head of that army it would now have been on this side of the Rapidan."

Grant was out of the Wilderness's burning thickets, but he was not out of the woods. And, ironically, he was trapped by the objective he had given Meade: Destroy Lee's army. It would have been easier by far if he had set Richmond as the primary goal. But by the morning of Monday, May 9, Sheridan's cavalry was headed that way, southward, east of Spotsylvania, so the general-in-chief focused on the question of what to do about the rebel fortifications blocking Meade's army.

Part of General Grant's problem that day was that Lee's forces as well were not out of the woods. To find them, out rode several reconnaissance parties. In one was Uncle John Sedgwick. "They couldn't hit an elephant at this distance," the VI Corps' commander declared, referring to the Confederate sharpshooters peppering his men; then he fell, shot in the face by a minié ball that lodged in his brain and killed him.

Sedgwick had been with the Army of the Potomac from the beginning. He had been wounded twice before in its battles. He had experienced all of the worst, more even than Meade, who would mourn his death as much as any soldier could. So would Robert E. Lee when he learned of it. And though Grant was a newcomer, the news stunned him. "Is he really dead?" he asked his staff officers, adding that if the report was true, it was as if the federal army had lost a division.

Indeed, Sedgwick was dead. Appointed to replace the much beloved leader was Major General Horatio Wright, whose fighting history (as VI Corps veterans may well have reckoned it) had started as recently as Gettysburg.

Then, from Ambrose Burnside, came a report that the rebels seemed to be moving eastward, possibly in a flanking march to cut Grant's ties to his supply base at Fredericksburg. It would later turn out that the oddly bewhiskered Burnside was wrong, but more important was Ulysses Grant's response. Signs of Confederate strength eastward had to mean weakness in the western end of their line. Let Winfield Scott Hancock's II Corps move across the Po River well upstream, Grant told Meade, so that it might sweep southward around Lee's now-enfeebled position, get behind him, and keep him from escaping to Richmond. Hancock's divisions were on the Po River's western banks by sundown.

Earlier that day, May 9, General Lee had reported to Richmond:

> We have succeeded so far in keeping on the front flank of that army [Grant's], and impeding its progress, without a general engagement, which I will not bring on unless a favorable opportunity offers, or as a last resort. Every attack made upon us has been repelled and considerable damage done to the enemy.

Now his challenge was to remain capable of using those words no matter when he sent a message to Jefferson Davis. He could do no more than block. And the defense line his men had built was no masterpiece of military engineering.

Much of the Confederate army's crude fort was concealed by trees, but there were a few clearings, some roughly 200 yards wide,

north of the trace, stretching for three miles between the Po and the
Ny rivers. It zigged and zagged, as unit commanders thought best,
and for a mile near its center it bloomed into a salient. This was not
by design; Ewell's men had simply dug in there after helping Early's
corps beat off a federal attack.

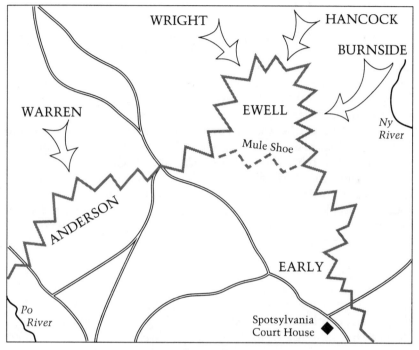

Spotsylvania Positions

With fresh-chopped tree trunks and logs being tugged into place
all along the line—V-shaped, with its point aimed north-northwest-
ward—Spotsylvania could turn into another Fredericksburg. But the
terrain Lee possessed was not much higher than the rest, and he had
used all his troops and guns in covering it, and before the day was
over, he knew that it would not be enough to hold merely the line he
had: Federals seemed determined to get beyond his western flank.
And, worse, Stuart had taken most of his cavalry southward to keep
Little Phil Sheridan's riders from getting too near Richmond.

On Tuesday morning, the tenth, Harry Heth's division began
carrying out orders General Lee had given the night before: to leave
Jubal Early's corps on the eastern end of the line, march westward,
cross the Po, and strike the advancing Yankee force in its flank. Heth
complied. And for a time it seemed he had won a remarkable victory.

No Confederate knew it, but Heth's men were attacking only

the rear guard of Hancock's II Corps. Grant had ordered two of the federal divisions to return; the third was to delay Heth, then follow; and that afternoon, Hancock would take part in an attack the general-in-chief was planning.

Something, in fact, was wrong with Grant's generalship, or at least with his timing. Sending Hancock southward, west of Lee's line, was an excellent idea, one that might have drawn the Confederate army out of its fortified position, giving the federals the chance to fight Lee in the open. But Hancock had paused Monday night; on Tuesday morning, Lee's response seemed formidable; and by then Grant's thinking had reverted to what had worked for him so often in the past: frontal assault.

Warren's V Corps was westernmost, now that Hancock was on his way back, and Warren thought he could break Anderson's segment of the rebel line. Horatio Wright's VI Corps was near the center. And among Wright's officers was Emory Upton, who had graduated from West Point a month after Fort Sumter and at twenty-four was a colonel. Given enough men and strong support, Upton suggested, he could penetrate the western side of the salient some of the Confederates called the Mule Shoe. He proposed to attack in a narrow but powerful column with four waves. The first would advance rapidly, bayonets fixed, not stopping to fire a shot until it reached the rebels' parapet; then it would open a hole and widen it right and left while the second wave dashed in behind it and plunged deeper; the third and fourth would hold the gap open. So pleased was Wright that he built Upton's brigade to twelve regiments, ordered Union artillery to pour enfilade fire on the rebel lines to soften them, and assigned a division to follow Upton's force into the breach.

General Grant's original intent had been to attack Lee's fortress with everything he had west of the Mule Shoe, and with Burnside's IX Corps demonstrating on the line's eastern end, at five P.M. But Warren jumped off earlier than that, got beaten back, and then Hancock tried with nothing but losses to show for his effort. By six it was up to Emory Upton.

In the time given him by his seniors' piecemeal attacks, Upton had taken all the regimental commanders up close to the Mule Shoe's western side and told each officer exactly what he wanted done. They and their men followed the young colonel's instructions precisely. The first wave quickly surged across the open ground. They stormed over the rebels' log barriers, firing, stabbing, driving the surprised defenders back, opening the way for the rest of Upton's force to join them. More than a thousand Confederates, stunned, simply surrendered.

Colonel Upton's troops had done all their commander had asked of them, and now they were holding their astonishing gain, but behind them nothing was happening. The reason: Rebel artillery had caught the supporting federal division while it was moving up, shredding it, scattering clumps of survivors so widely it lost coherence as a fighting unit. Long shadows and the sheer savagery of the Confederates' counterattacks forced Upton to give up all he had won. And behind him he had to leave a thousand or more of his own dead and wounded.

Early the next morning, the Union armies' general-in-chief wrote a message to Washington. In it he said:

> We have now ended the sixth day of heavy fighting [since crossing the Rapidan]. The result to this time is very much in our favor. But our losses have been heavy, as well as those of the enemy. We have lost to this time eleven general officers killed, wounded and missing, and probably twenty thousand men. I think the loss of the enemy must be greater, we having taken over four thousand prisoners, whilst he has taken from us but very few except a few stragglers. I am now sending back to Belle Plain [on the Rappahannock] all my wagons for a fresh supply of ammunition, and purpose to fight it out on this line if it takes all summer.

That Wednesday, May 11, was gloomy and overcast from the start. Back in the woods north and east of the Confederates' ragged lines the federals remained quiet. This was perfectly all right with Lee's army. Every man in it understood that this Union drive was like no other, and they all knew what they had to do: dig, cut more logs for their forts, replenish their ammunition, eat before the rain put out the cookfires.

During that rainy afternoon the army commander rode up to Ewell's salient to inspect the site of Upton's breakthrough. Should the federals strike again, Lee told John Gordon, do not wait for orders, but advance at once and support Major General Edward Johnson's division, the one Ewell had assigned to defend the Mule Shoe's northern tip. This was reassuring to Johnson's infantrymen. But, unaware of Lee's desire that the army get ready to move on short notice, they were disturbed when they learned he had directed the withdrawal of twenty-two of the thirty guns in the Mule Shoe to a road a mile or more to the south. As night fell, Johnson's veterans became even more uneasy: from out of the rain-swept darkness to their north came rumbling sounds mixed with Yankee band music:

why polkas so near midnight?

As had become his habit, General Lee was up again at three o'clock Thursday morning, the twelfth. The sky was just turning from black to dark gray when he heard heavy firing north of him. Soon an officer rode up. "The line is broken," he said, "at the angle in General Johnson's front!"

On the way toward the Mule Shoe's tip, the general learned more. Those twenty-two guns had been returned too late for any of them to fire a round, and twenty of them had been captured by the Yankees pouring over the parapet. Johnson and most of the men in his division were gone, prisoners. John Gordon, remembering Lee's orders, was about to counterattack, but the salient was fast filling with federals.

General Grant's plan had been for Winfield Scott Hancock's II Corps, 15,000 men, to do what Colonel Upton's brigade had almost done on Tuesday: take the Mule Shoe. This time, though, there would be massive support. Burnside's IX Corps would be demonstrating on the salient's eastern side; on its western rim Wright's VI Corps was available to support Hancock's massive assault; and lest Lee try to reinforce Ewell, Warren's V Corps would attack Anderson again.

Grant's admiration of Upton's exploit, however, exceeded his understanding of it. Upton's force had been small enough for him to manage; not until his first wave had widened its breach had he sent in the second, third, and fourth. Now, on Thursday morning, excessive force turned what ought to have been a gap into a barrier.

Hancock's leading elements swept over the rebel parapet easily enough, but there were too many men in the assault wave for its officers to control. This mob blocked units surging up behind it. So dense was the blue-clad throng inside the Mule Shoe, no captured guns could be fired at the retreating rebels. Making prisoners of a whole division had been much easier than getting them to the rear would prove. And amid the heavy rain and confusion no one seemed to know what to do next.

While riding northward, General Lee had tried to rally men running toward safety, removing his hat to make it easier for them to recognize him in the foggy darkness, calling out to them: "Shame on you, go back to your regiments!"

Some did, following the gray man on the gray horse until he met General Gordon. Go ahead, Lee told him, attack—and on he spurred Traveller until he was in the midst of the men who were about to charge.

A bullet zipped through Gordon's coat, missing his spine by an inch. "General Lee," he cried, "this is no place for you." Lee, still bareheaded though the rain was heavy, did not seem to hear Gordon or the shouts of his men: "General Lee to the rear!"

Gordon and a sergeant tugged Traveller's bridle, turning the big horse away from the sounds of firing just ahead; then the Georgians and Virginians advanced, yelling as they plunged into the woods, stopping the federal attack, driving it back. Lee, knowing Gordon had too few troops, rode off in search of more he could send him. Finding an idle brigade, then riding with its commander to speed it forward, he came under long-range Union artillery fire. Traveller reared just as a round passed under his belly. The soldiers who saw it, realizing death had almost claimed their army's leader, cried: "Go back! For God's sake, go back!"

He would, Lee replied, "if you will promise me to drive those people from our works." And the brigade pressed on. It arrived at the Mule Shoe's tip in time to engage in some of the most vicious fighting this war had yet seen.

Now it was midmorning, the rainfall continued, and Gordon, supported by all of Ewell's corps and the brigades Lee had sent him, had nearly cleared the Mule Shoe of Yankees. The ground was littered with bodies, trenches filled with them and bloody rainwater, dead men draped along the carriages and tubes of the unfired guns, and at the barricades the killing went on. And to the north the blue-clad hordes remained, threatening to rush the parapets again at any moment.

John Gordon had given General Lee far more than he had asked of him, but the army commander could not allow him to withdraw: Not until that morning had the work started toward fortifying the wide gap in the line at the Mule Shoe's southern base. As if they sensed Lee's plight, the federal commanders hit from the east and west. Lee managed to strike Burnside's southern flank, slowing his advance. Again Anderson held Warren north of his line. But Wright's VI Corps, within it Upton's revenge-bent brigade, was helping Hancock's divisions renew their assaults where the fighting that Thursday had started. And from then on it was not a battle between armies but a struggle among savages.

In some places ragged lines were only a few yards apart, so close no round could miss, bodies falling on those already slain or maimed or dropping into the blood-drenched mud. At the log barriers soldiers on both sides fired blindly through gaps and probed with their bayonets. If a man tried to cross over, he was grabbed and made a prisoner, unless first he got clubbed or shot or stabbed to death. Elsewhere warriors fired from behind mounds of the dead, protected by bullet-shredded flesh, or threw corpses and even wounded men out of trenches to hang on to life and fight a little longer.

This had been going on for hours, and there seemed no end to it. The fallback line behind them was not ready, so for the Confederates it was kill or be killed. Federal commanders kept as many troops in the Bloody Angle—for that was what the Mule Shoe had become— as the place would hold, feeding men into it to keep the pressure on the rebels. There was no way to evacuate wounded. Usually sundown stopped the fighting, but not on this rain- and blood-soaked Thursday, May 12. Darkness merely made it more difficult for the strugglers in the Bloody Angle to aim and slash and club and stab.

Not until around midnight did the Confederates still alive hear whispered words of deliverance: Withdraw carefully. Too worn out to pursue them, apparently, were the Yankees. By the time skies in the east were brightening, the last remnants of Jackson's old corps were behind the new barricades well south of the place where with unprecedented ferocity Americans had fought each other man to man for sixteen hours.

General Lee went about his duties in his usual calm way on rainy Friday, May 13, but inwardly he was torn by grief. Losing perhaps 3,000 troops was cause enough: Ewell's corps was now hardly more than a division. But at the worst imaginable times on Thursday, Lee had received shattering reports from the south. First he learned that on Wednesday, the eleventh, Sheridan's cavalry and Stuart's had clashed north of Richmond at Yellow Tavern and that Jeb had been taken into the city with a bullet lodged near his liver. Next: Stuart was dead. Then more: Sheridan had torn up miles of the railroad and captured large supplies of food destined for the hungry men at Spotsylvania.

On Tuesday, Stuart, realizing that his force rather than Richmond was Sheridan's objective, said good-bye to his wife, Flora, and their two children at the house near Beaver Dam in which they were staying, then moved his brigades to some hills six miles north of the capital. On Wednesday afternoon Sheridan attacked there, driving back the western end of Stuart's line until Stuart led a countercharge. He was in the thick of it when a Yankee sergeant fired one round from his Colt pistol and ran away. Stuart, reeling, stayed in the saddle until his officers could get him out of range. Fitz Lee arrived. "Go ahead, old fellow," said Stuart, "I know you'll do what is right." Then, annoyed because so many men were clustered near the ambulance wagon waiting to take him away, he said: "Go back! Do your duty as I have done mine, and our country will be safe! Go back! I had rather die than be whipped!"

Stuart was taken to Dr. Brewer's house in Richmond, and on Thursday, Jefferson Davis came to hold his hand. Heros Von Borke was there, Flora on her way. "Fitz Lee will be needing you," he reminded Borke, then he said he would like to hear a song. Those around him began: "Rock of ages, cleft for me..."

Brewer told Stuart he would die very soon. "God's will be done," he replied. "God's will be done."

Virginia's rainy spell stretched on, and so did enough skirmishes and artillery duels to lengthen both sides' casualty lists. News reached Spotsylvania from distant places. Much of it was depressing to General Grant, who may well have wished he were still in the west and Halleck the general-in-chief.

For days it had been obvious that neither Franz Sigel's sweep up the Shenandoah Valley nor Ben Butler's operations near Richmond and Petersburg were forcing Lee to weaken his army. Now Grant learned that both Sigel and Butler had been whipped.

Sigel had moved from near the Potomac southward through the Valley past Winchester and Strasburg to New Market. Near there, west of the Massanutten, on Sunday, May 15, a Confederate force that included the Virginia Military Institute's corps of cadets completely wrecked the attacking federals and sent them scurrying back to the north.

Not so dramatic had been Ben Butler's reduction to abject impotence, and it may have been harder to accept because much of it was self-inflicted. Butler's orders had been to land on the James River's northern bank at the Bermuda Hundred and operate against Petersburg, Richmond, and the rail and turnpike links between the two cities. By May 6, Butler's 25,000 troops and 4,500 cavalry were advancing. That night, however, his force stopped and entrenched. There were probes; one got within sight of Petersburg's church spires and was turned back by nominal resistance, another destroyed a few miles of the Richmond & Petersburg Railroad's track, and a third menaced rebel defenses at Drewry's Bluff on the James.

As Butler wasted days, General Pierre G. T. Beauregard, commanding in that part of Virginia and in the Carolinas, used them, gathering enough regiments, home guards, and War Department clerks to drive the federals back to their original line between the James and the Appomattox rivers. Later, Grant would describe the result: Ben Butler's entire army "was as completely shut off from further operations directly against Richmond as if it had been in a bottle strongly corked."

So instead of three related campaigns in Virginia there would be only one. And at rain-swept Spotsylvania, wherever General Grant sent Meade's army, there also was Lee's.

From the west, though, the general-in-chief got word that another bottle had been uncorked. At April's end, low water in the Red River had trapped ten of Admiral David Dixon Porter's gunboats and even more transports above the almost-dry rapids at Alexandria, immobilizing General Banks's troops, including those Cump Sherman wanted returned for use in his drive toward Atlanta. Then, when it seemed certain that Richard Taylor's vastly outnumbered Confederates' waiting would be rewarded, former Wisconsin logger Joe Bailey had started building a dam across the exposed rocks. "Madness," Admiral Porter had termed the project at first. But as the impounded water rose, so did his hopes: Providence, he declared, had provided "a man equal to the emergency."

As Bailey's dam builders worked night and day, Porter's sailors dumped overboard everything they dared to lighten their craft—and to deny the rebels iron, guns, even food, if the emergency grew into a disaster. One seemed to be occurring on Monday, May 9, when two coal barges Bailey had placed at the dam's center gave way and the precious impounded water cascaded through the breach. Nearest it was Porter's gunboat the *Lexington*, steam up, and she went first. The *Lexington*, caught in the swift current, rolled and bobbed; her bottom grated on the rocks for a moment during which watchers hardly breathed; then she was in the deep water, and cheers shattered the early-morning air.

The *Neosho* made the run, although the backed up water was about gone—and the *Osage*. Would Bailey leave it at that? Well, no. He got his men back to work on wing dams upstream, and by Friday, May 13 (the day after the armies at Spotsylvania had exhausted each other), all of Porter's gunboats and transports were out of the Confederate river's trap.

Now Banks's troops and Porter's sailors seemed to be racing for the safety of the broad Mississippi. Taylor's rebels made the journey as costly for them as he could, ambushing gunboats along the Red River and sinking two, forcing the federal troops to fight a final battle at Mansura, memorable only as the last display of Confederate defiance along Nathaniel P. Banks's way to Washington's guillotine and political oblivion.

The entire Red River campaign had been a fiasco for the North; but none of it had been of Ulysses Grant's making, which may have made it easier for him to put the whole thing behind him. But in so doing, inadvertently he conceded to Jackson, whose disciple Richard Taylor had been, a victory that meant Southerners in central Louisiana and Texas would be free from federal molestation until the end of the war.

Finally, Sherman. Such news as General Grant had from the campaign in northwestern Georgia was as good as anyone familiar with the region's ridgelines and forests could expect. Sherman might seem to be creeping up on Joe Johnston's defenses between Ringgold and Dalton, but the rebels had spent the entire winter fortifying those lines, and Cump was probably hunting for a way to get south of them.

Back to the Virginia campaign: It was time to move on, the general-in-chief decided, and he issued orders for the Army of the Potomac to shift east of Lee's lines and march southward. On Friday, May 20, Hancock's II Corps led the way. Grant must have been glad indeed to be putting the Wilderness and Spotsylvania behind him. Since crossing the Rapidan sixteen days before, in those woods the Confederates had killed, wounded, or captured more than 33,000 of his men.

Chapter 34

Trading Blood for Miles

"T he terrible door of death," William Tecumseh Sherman called Buzzard's Roost, a gap in Confederate-held Rocky Face Ridge, and he decided to find another way to get at Johnston's army and the Western & Atlantic Railroad a few miles east of the long north-south outcropping at Dalton. That was early in May, right after his on-time departure from Chattanooga. And while Cump was as eager as the general-in-chief to remove Johnston's forces from the war, anything seemed preferable to a frontal attack up a sheer cliff the top of which 45,000 rebels with 138 guns had spent months fortifying.

Indeed, for Sherman plenty of alternatives existed. One suggested itself from the very locations of his three armies, their sizes, and the characteristics of their commanders. Due north of Dalton, on the railroad's Knoxville branch line, was John Schofield's Army of the Ohio—with 14,000 troops, hardly a corps, no matter what Washington called it—yet Schofield could threaten Johnston's northern flank. At Ringgold, nearest Buzzard's Roost, George Thomas had 61,000 men in his Army of the Cumberland. And though James McPherson's 25,000 bluecoats in his Army of the Tennessee were back near the Chickamauga battlefield, he could use the roads west of Rocky Face Ridge to get well south of there and strike Resaca, on the W & A thirteen miles south of Dalton, and cut Johnston's supply link to Atlanta.

"I've got Joe Johnston dead!" shouted Sherman, banging his fist on the supper table on the evening of Monday, May 9, when he learned that Jamie McPherson was almost in Resaca. Earlier, Cump had applied Thomas's pressure against Rocky Face Ridge from the west and Schofield's from the north to hold the barrier's defenders in place while McPherson got past Snake Creek Gap and swept

another seven or eight miles eastward into Resaca and trapped the
Confederates.

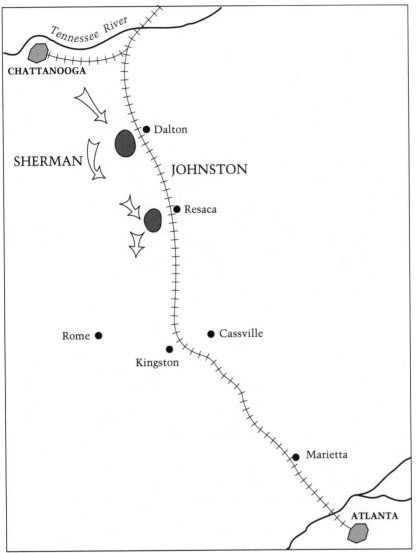

Chattanooga to Atlanta

Celebration, however, proved premature. McPherson found more
rebels in Resaca than he thought it prudent to attack. Using the
discretion granted him in his orders, he withdrew to Snake Creek
Gap for the night. After learning of this, his disappointed commander would say to him: "Well, Mac, you missed the opportunity

of your life."

Nearly a week earlier, as Sherman's forces were moving toward him, Johnston had asked Richmond once more to send him any reinforcements Bishop-General Polk could spare from his command over in Alabama. From nowhere else could help come. And he was inured to his request being rejected; since West Point, Johnston's relations with Davis had been turbulent, and Polk might persuade his friend the president that his troops were needed where they were. He was astonished, then, when Davis told Polk to aid him as much as he could, again when he learned Polk was bringing his whole 19,000-man force with fifty guns and would serve under him as a corps commander. Polk's leading brigade was already at Resaca when McPherson probed. And the bishop's other troops were not far behind.

With Sherman's forces threatening Rocky Face Ridge from the west and north, Johnston withdrew southward. By Friday, May 13, he had his three corps together at Resaca. One was commanded by John Hood, promoted to lieutenant general while convalescing at Richmond from the amputation of the leg that was shattered at Chickamauga. Hood was not used to his new cork leg. The arm shot at Gettysburg was useless; he needed crutches to get around, and when he rode, he had to be helped into the saddle and strapped into it. But he was as full of fight as ever, and Joe Johnston was glad to have him. Welcome, as well, was William Hardee—like Bishop Polk, a dissident under Bragg, but the man who had willingly stepped aside from command of the army so that Johnston might lead it.

Resaca offered no terrain feature as intimidating as Rocky Face Ridge, only some hills north and west of the town, but the former engineer quickly put his troops to work fortifying them. Once again, Johnston had demonstrated his skill in withdrawing. But this, together with Sherman's difficulties in shifting Thomas's army and Schofield's from around Dalton, gave Johnston barely enough time in which to prepare his defenses against attack by more than 100,000 federals.

John Hood prepared himself in another way. While Polk was visiting Johnston's headquarters, Hood asked the bishop to give him baptism and confirmation. For the warrior standing before him— Hood could not kneel and would not sit—Polk gladly performed the rites. And the Episcopal bishop was delighted to perform them again a week or so later for the army's commander, of whom Winfield Scott had said: "Johnston is a great soldier, but he has an unfortunate knack of getting himself shot in nearly every engagement."

On Saturday, May 14, the Union's armies hit everywhere along

Johnston's line, but only at its southern end, where McPherson was hammering, did Sherman's forces gain any ground. Indeed, they lost half a mile of it in Schofield's northern sector when Hood's corps attacked: General Johnston had ordered the probe, suspecting that Sherman might be shifting his strength southward for another flank march.

Again, on May 15, Sunday, the federals struck, and Johnston's lines held. By that night, however, intelligence reports indicated that Sherman *was* beginning another attempt to sever the Confederate army's railroad supply line. Johnston ordered his second withdrawal of the campaign, this time down the W & A toward Kingston, roughly thirty miles from Resaca and forty miles from Dalton.

Typically Johnstonian, his critics in Richmond may well have thought when they learned of the decision. And if Joe Johnston kept withdrawing, if he failed to whip Sherman north of Atlanta, the Confederacy's only remaining East-West railroad line would be lost—and so might be hope for independence.

"Sherman'll never go to hell," one of his admiring troops remarked. "He will flank the devil and make heaven in spite of the guards." Indeed, having twice maneuvered Joe Johnston out of his defensive positions, Cump seemed to have hit upon a combination of capabilities and tactics that could take him all the way to Atlanta. McPherson, young, eager, was to him as Jackson had been to Lee: the enveloper. Thomas, the Rock of Chickamauga, was good to have when the hitting had to be hard. Schofield was useful mainly for keeping pressure on Johnston's northern flank while McPherson got around his southern one.

But Cump (or "Uncle Billy," as the soldiers in his armies now called him) was obliged to keep looking over his shoulder toward the Ohio River. His supply lifeline stretched from Louisville more than 300 railroad miles to his forward base at Chattanooga, and with rebel cavalrymen such as John Morgan and Nathan Bedford Forrest on the loose, every mile was vulnerable. Moreover, he was depending on specially trained repair crews to rush the W & A back into service from Chattanooga southward as he advanced.

Everything Sherman needed he seemed to have. A pontoon bridge over the Oostanaula River southwest of Resaca had been in place in time to help persuade Johnston to abandon Resaca. Cavalry led the way over that crossing for an infantry division, and the combined force headed for Rome, site of an iron works and some factories, fifteen miles or so west of Kingston. Over the pontoon bridge also went McPherson's army, picking up a route west of the W & A's tracks. Thomas's force chased the retreating rebels down the railroad, while Schofield—reinforced by the switch of Joe Hooker's corps from Thomas's army to his—took a road to the east of it. This relieved congestion and gave the armies' commander something else he needed: speed.

General-in-Chief Grant and his commander in the west were conducting military operations to achieve a political goal: the destruction of the Confederate states' abilities to remain in armed rebellion. And in 1864—in the North a presidential election year— what happened on any battlefield would have partisan political consequences as well as those bearing on the national objective. But Grant and Sherman knew from bitter experience that they had no control over how the newspapers might report actions taken for purely military reasons. As to what the public might think, Cump had written Grant back in April 1863: "It is none of their business."

Secretary of War Edwin Stanton thought otherwise. By releasing only selected information about the fighting both in the Wilderness and in northwest Georgia, he set off waves of jubilation throughout the Union. But this worried Abraham Lincoln, who told a friend: "The people are too sanguine; they expect too much at once." And he added, "I shall be satisfied if we are over with the fight in Virginia within a year."

The Union president's instincts were correct. Historian Allan Nevins described the reaction Lincoln feared:

> As Americans thought of two hundred thousand graves of Northern boys staring at the sky, they were aware that another summer of faltering and defeat might be the last. Meanwhile, dwellers in the cities once more opened their newspapers daily to long lists of the slain and maimed; villagers and townspeople bleakly studied the sheets posted on bulletin boards; farm mothers opened War-Department envelopes with trembling fingers.

General Sherman was wrong: What happened on battlefields *was* the public's business, especially in 1864. The men in bereaved families and in those of their friends and neighbors were voters, and they could be expected to vote mindful of the grief of their women and children lingering with their own. That would be in November; first there would be the parties' nominating conventions. And while Lincoln seemed certain to be renominated at Baltimore in early June, there was considerable doubt as to whether he could be reelected in the fall.

"It makes me sick," wrote a Pennsylvanian, "to think what we have lost & the prospect of having nearly five more years of this thing." A Lincoln supporter in Hartford declared that the president's "drifting, conciliatory and temporizing policy," if continued "would ruin us."

The Democrats' alternative to Abraham Lincoln? In mid-May it was too early to predict anything, but advocates of peace at any price were likely to be well represented at their Chicago convention when it opened on August 29. Postponement from July 4 to that high summer date was itself significant. By then the voters would know a lot more about whether Lincoln's generals could whip Lee or Johnston.

"The importance of this campaign to the administration of Mr. Lincoln and to General Grant leaves no doubt that every effort and every sacrifice will be made to secure its success." So wrote General Lee on May 18 to Jefferson Davis, for it was not clear to the Army of Northern Virginia's commander that the president understood how different this federal drive was from earlier ones. Grant would be getting troops from Ben Butler's corked-up army. So far, however, Davis had not sent Lee any of the men Beauregard no longer needed. Lee's dispatch to the president concluded: "The question is whether we shall fight the battle here or around Richmond. If [Beauregard's] troops are obliged to be retained at Richmond I may be forced back."

On Friday, the twentieth, Davis telegraphed Lee that he could expect five brigades. The next day, though, Grant began moving east of Spotsylvania. This meant that Lee would have to keep the forces he had between Grant and Richmond, with no hope of catching part of Grant's army on the march and attacking it. And with Stuart gone forever, cavalry reports told Lee less than he needed to know about where Grant was headed.

Again Lee mentally placed himself in Grant's boots, and again he was able to reduce the federal possibilities to one: Hanover Junction, less than twenty miles north of Richmond. By noon on May 21 he had Ewell's corps marching southward.

After riding twenty-three miles with only a two-hour rest, General Lee reached the North Anna River, a little north of Hanover Junction, early on the morning of Sunday, May 22. With the help of Jed Hotchkiss, Jackson's mapmaker, he started building a defense line. "We wish no more salients," he said, remembering how the Mule Shoe had turned into the Bloody Angle.

By noon the next day the federals were moving into line on the North Anna's northern bank, and artillerymen on both sides got to work. As Lee watched the firing from W. E. Fox's front porch and sipped buttermilk, a Union cannonball hit Fox's doorframe. Calmly,

Lee finished the glass, then thanked Fox and moved on, lest his presence draw more rounds to the house.

That afternoon, federals crossed the North Anna upstream at Jericho Mills, then seized the bridges a mile or so northeast of Lee's line. "Like one closes an umbrella," wrote historian G. F. R. Henderson later, overnight Lee pulled in the divisions on his right and left to form an inverted V with only the point on the North Anna. In effect, Lee's army was now a wedge dividing the Army of the Potomac: Burnside's corps, in the Union center opposite the V's point, could not join Warren's and Wright's to the west or Hancock's east of it without crossing the North Anna. Lee, however, could shift his forces within the angle to fight off attack from any direction. And if he struck Hancock, there was nothing Grant could do without giving Lee an opening in the west or center.

The federal deployment was precisely the kind of mistake General Lee had hoped Grant would make, an absolutely perfect opportunity to wreck the invading army. Yet Lee had to allow the golden moment to pass. Dick Ewell, whose corps was nearest Hancock's and would have to make the assault, was showing signs of a breakdown. Powell Hill was too ill to manage, much less lead, a charge to smash Warren and Wright as the divisions in their corps tried to make the first of two river crossings to go to Hancock's assistance. Anderson had been in command of Longstreet's corps only two weeks. And General Lee's health had broken: He was suffering from an intestinal disorder that left him too weak to mount Traveller.

With Lee's physical stamina went his habitual marble calm. After a stormy conference in the frustrated general's tent, a staff officer emerged and said to another, "I have just told the old man that he is not fit to command this army, and that he had better send for Beauregard." Lee would do nothing of the sort. Nor did he find comfort in Grant's unwillingness to test his defense line. "We must strike them a blow!" Lee told his staff. And to his doctor he said, "If I can get one more pull at [Grant], I will defeat him."

But by Friday, May 27, nearly a week after both armies had left Spotsylvania for the North Anna, Grant's army was on the march again, this time southeastward, suggesting that the federals were headed for the old battlefields along the Chickahominy River, where Lee had driven McClellan's army nearly two years before. Lee could only tell Ewell to lead the way down toward Mechanicsville. Yet despite its disappointments and the Southern weaknesses it had reconfirmed, Lee's stand at the North Anna had preserved Richmond's rail and road access to the Shenandoah Valley. And as Jackson had said, "If this valley is lost, Virginia is lost."

Since Lee had not attacked him at the North Anna, General Grant seemed to think, he could not do it and would not try again— ever. Even so, he kept the river between the Army of the Potomac and Lee's forces as Meade's long columns marched southeastward. Well away from any opposition, they crossed and turned southward on the road to Old Cold Harbor. There, on the first day of June, some of Wright's troops joined Little Phil Sheridan's cavalrymen who had been holding the crossroads.

Old Cold Harbor, about a mile northeast of the Boatswain's Swamp-protected Watt farm's plateau where Fitz-John Porter had been whipped, was on a plateau of its own, with nothing but a few ravines and low hills to the west to keep the terrain from being a plain. But Richmond was only ten crow-flight miles to the southwest, more by the tangled road network north of the Chickahominy, and for a time it seemed that Grant might have beaten Lee to ground both wanted to reach.

There was, however, a problem: No one in a blue uniform knew exactly where Lee's army was until too late on Wednesday, June 1, to do anything about it. Grant ordered an attack the next day, but Meade's army was not in hand, and it had to be called off. The time should be spent by unit commanders, the federal commanding generals directed, in reconnoitering the terrain between them and the Confederate lines.

Orders went out for an advance to begin at four-thirty the next morning, Friday, June 3. On Thursday night some of the Army of the Potomac veterans—guessing what Bobby Lee's men had been doing during the two-day delay—wrote their names and home addresses on slips of paper, then pinned them on the backs of their jackets. This proved a wise precaution. Roughly 7,000 of them were cut down in the opening *minutes* of their frontal attack on the Confederate line.

Apparently, those federal soldiers' generals had failed to do what they had been told to do: reconnoiter the ground west of them during the time available. They did follow orders by telling the survivors to dig in when they recognized that to go forward even a few more yards into the withering rebel volleys and artillery crossfire would be suicidal. And Grant, who had not witnessed the critical half hour or so in which the worst damage was done, came as close as he could to calling the whole thing off near noon when he wrote a message to Meade:

> The opinion of the corps commanders not being sanguine of success in case an assault is ordered, you may direct a suspension of further advance for the present. Hold our most

advanced positions, and strengthen them.

No military art had gone into Cold Harbor unless it was the skill of General Lee in fortifying a position from which his men could deliver such an awesome volume of firepower and inflict such an appalling number of casualties in so short a time. Ulysses Grant would concede this many years afterward when he wrote:

> I have always regretted that the last assault at Cold Harbor was ever made....At Cold Harbor no advantage whatever was gained to compensate for the heavy loss we sustained.

But for those blue-clad soldiers with their names and home addresses pinned on their backs who were still alive, being hit was only the beginning of their ordeal. They would lie on the fire-swept plain, well beyond the reach of their comrades, wondering how many more hours they could endure the pain before both sides agreed on a truce, suffering among the moldering bodies of men to whom death had come suddenly and some who had died only after hours of agony, hoping help would come in time but knowing that they, too, were probably going below.

No truce got worked out until the night of Tuesday, June 7, nearly *four days* after the killing at Cold Harbor had been launched. Federal search parties found 2 men still alive amid 7,000 or more dead Union soldiers.

"We must strike them a blow!" General Lee had said at the North Anna. Now, recovered from his illness, he gave thought in the relatively quiet days of June's second week to attacking Grant's flank. But the federals at Cold Harbor were digging in; Lee left aggressive action to his sharpshooters and turned his mind to what those people were doing elsewhere in Virginia.

Major General David Hunter, picking up where the defeated Sigel had left off, was moving back up the Shenandoah Valley, virtually undefended because Lee had drawn men from there after the battle at New Market in mid-May. Unsettling as well were reports that Grant had sent Sheridan's cavalry riding westward to cut the Virginia Central Railroad and link up with Hunter in the vicinity of Staunton.

Lee understood: Grant was trying once more to force him to split his army. This time, with Richmond almost within sight, Grant succeeded. Sheridan had to be stopped. This mission Lee gave Wade Hampton, retaining only a few cavalry units to watch Grant. Next, Hunter. Lee not only wanted his drive smashed; he meant to try

Jackson's old scheme one more time—to defend Richmond by threatening Washington—and he wanted to do this with the corps Jackson had led. But Dick Ewell's health was not up to such a task. Lee replaced him with Jubal Early and accepted the risk of defending the space left east of Richmond with fewer troops than Grant had in a single federal corps.

From Wade Hampton came the first news. He and Fitz Lee caught up with Sheridan at Trevilian Station, roughly fifty miles northwest of Cold Harbor on the way to Charlottesville, and in a two-day fight that began on June 11 the Confederates wrecked the 9,000-man Yankee cavalry force. But Hunter was sweeping up the Shenandoah Valley, passing Harrisonburg and Port Republic, capturing Staunton, pausing at Lexington to burn the Virginia Military Institute, heading for Lynchburg.

Hardly had the last of Early's men departed when General Lee got reports that Grant's army had disappeared from the trenches near Old Cold Harbor. This was on Monday, June 13. Lee moved quickly across the Chickahominy and southward, forming a new line that extended almost to Malvern Hill.

Now began a period in which Lee was "blind." Earlier, he had suspected that Grant might cross the James and head west to seize Petersburg and try to take Richmond from the south. But with too few cavalrymen still with him and all crossroads to the east guarded by federal detachments, Lee had no reliable information as to where Grant's army was or what it was doing.

In his haste to fortify Petersburg, Beauregard had removed the cork from the Bermuda Hundred bottle. Lee, weakening his line to do so, penned Ben Butler's troops up again. Finally, from Beauregard came enough facts to convince Lee that Grant had shifted Meade's army to the south bank of the James River. Before dawn on Saturday, June 18, Lee started the last of his brigades toward Petersburg. They arrived just in time to help turn back a series of federal attacks, not realizing that the war in the east was entering a new phase.

Getting from the Rapidan to within artillery range of Petersburg had cost Grant roughly 54,000 men—almost as many as Lee ever had to oppose him—and he had neither destroyed Lee's army nor gotten a glimpse of Richmond's church spires. He had not, as he had declared to Halleck on May 11, fought it out on any line if it took "all summer." Not a single battle had he won, yet the Army of the Potomac had suffered losses that would send shudders of grief throughout the Union. And though he had obliged Lee to split his army, on that very day, June 18, at Lynchburg, Jubal Early's Confederates began driving David Hunter's force out of the Shenandoah Valley.

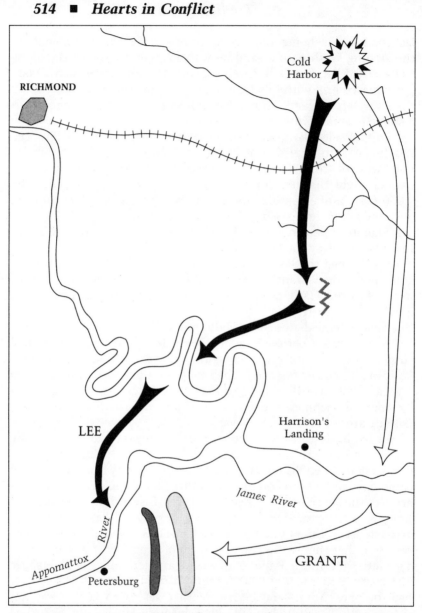

Grant's Marches to Petersburg

The irony was excruciating. All Lieutenant General Grant had actually done was turn the calendar back nearly two years, to July 1862, when George McClellan's final plan had been to move his Army of the Potomac from Harrison's Landing across the James River and try to reach Richmond via Petersburg.

After the fight at Resaca, General Sherman scattered his three armies more widely than before. He could do that because Johnston was obliged to keep his Confederate Army of Tennessee concentrated and to stay near enough to the W & A's tracks to get supplies from Atlanta. Delaying Sherman was about all Johnston could hope to do—when he found ground worth fortifying.

While a federal cavalry column supported by an infantry division took undefended Rome and McPherson's troops marched southward between the Oostanaula River and the W & A's tracks, George Thomas's Army of the Cumberland pressed Johnston down the railroad past Calhoun and Adairsville toward Kingston. There, where the W & A turned eastward, Sherman expected Johnston might make a stand. He may even have hoped Johnston would, for all the elements of the Union armies were converging on Kingston.

Precedents suggested that Sherman had read the situation correctly. But Johnston's thinking had changed on the way from Resaca. Finally, he had found ground he liked. But it was at Cassville, roughly ten miles east of Kingston, and his plans would come as a surprise even to his own men.

A week or so earlier, Johnston had sent a message to Major General Stephen D. Lee, commander of the military department that included Alabama and Mississippi, requesting Lee to order Nathan Bedford Forrest to take his cavalry force up into middle Tennessee and wreck Sherman's railroad supply line. On May 17, before Johnston reached Cassville, Lee replied: Forrest would leave northern Mississippi within three days.

Knowing that when Forrest's men tore up a track it stayed torn up, General Johnston began planning to take the offensive. This course of action became even more attractive when his own cavalry reported Schofield's Union column moving southward far enough east of Thomas's army to make it impossible for Thomas to come to Schofield's assistance. Johnston told Hardee to keep his corps skirmishing with Thomas's federals along the W & A, then he split his forces, sending Polk's corps and Hood's east to Cassville with orders to ambush and destroy Schofield. After that, the Confederate army would reunite and demolish first Thomas and then McPherson.

So elated over the prospects was Johnston that not even another message from Stephen Lee alarmed him. Forrest could not go on the railroad-wrecking campaign, Lee said, because a Union force from Memphis was headed for Confederate positions in northern Mississippi and Forrest would have to block it. Disappointed but undaunted, Johnston issued a general order that was read to his men by their commanders on May 19. It was wordy, much overblown, even McClellanesque, yet embedded in it was the command despairing men had been longing to hear: "You will now turn and march to meet [the enemy's] advancing columns." The effect was electrifying. With the strokes of his pen Johnston restored morale badly eroded by retreating more than forty miles.

Then the whole thing fell apart. John Hood, waiting to strike Schofield, discovered Yankees in his rear: These were Fighting Joe Hooker's men, a force that had missed a turn and gone far astray. Hood had to fall back, and so did Polk, and even when they reached the high ground near Cassville, where Johnston reassembled the army, they advised retreating because Union artillery could pour fire along their positions from the flank. This left Johnston to decide whether to go ahead and attack the federals the next morning or withdraw that night. Reluctantly, Johnston ordered his army to retreat—again.

It was ironic that John Hood, whose reputation as a hard fighter was so firmly established, had become an advocate of pulling back. Moreover, Hood had criticized Johnston earlier for being too willing to retreat—and that he had done so was well understood in Richmond.

General Johnston was bitterly disappointed. But he could take some comfort from the existence, not far to the south of Kingston, of Allatoona Pass on the W & A. He placed his army along this high ground and ordered it to start entrenching.

General Sherman did not have to ride out for a look at Allatoona Pass to know that it was another "terrible door of death" and therefore a place to be bypassed. In 1844, then a lieutenant, Sherman had explored that terrain; twenty years later, he had not forgotten anything he had seen through younger eyes. He gave his armies a few days in which to rest and prepare for the work ahead, which would involve abandoning the railroad, taking twenty days' supplies in wagons and moving all his forces southward well to the west of the W & A's tracks and deep into Johnston's rear. Such an envelopment would maneuver the rebel army out of Allatoona Pass, opening the way for Cump's railroad repairers to extend his lifeline nearer Marietta and Atlanta.

A little crossroads called Dallas, deep in Wilderness-type country, was Sherman's first objective on the way to Marietta. As before, he spread his columns—a necessity, given the poor condition of the roads. He was four miles northeast of Dallas on May 25 when Hooker's troops got into a sharp firefight with a rebel force near New Hope Church.

From a message a captured Confederate courier was carrying Sherman had learned that Johnston was aware of the federals' turning movement, but he may have been surprised by how quickly and by how far the grayclads had moved. Enough of them were in the dense woods to stop the first division Fighting Joe sent to get rid of them, then two more. Darkness and heavy rain ended the first engagement at what Hooker's men would soon be calling the "Hell Hole."

From that beginning a week of federal attacks and repulses followed. Again the fighter in Joseph Eggleston Johnston had emerged; having left the W & A well to the east, he had committed his whole army to the task of punishing the invaders. Wherever Sherman ordered attacks his forces ran into Johnston's defenders firmly entrenched—and Union casualties mounted. This nettled Sherman. Thomas's army, for example, was firing 200,000 rounds of rifle ammunition a day, but it could not advance. And when Sherman rode along his lines, all he saw were "skirmishers dodging from tree to tree, or behind logs on the ground, or who occasionally showed their heads above the hastily constructed but remarkably strong rifle-trenches."

A week of frustration was about all Cump Sherman could endure just then. At about the time he left Kingston, he had wired Chief of Staff Henry Halleck: "We are all in motion like a vast hive of bees and expect to swarm along the Chattahoochee [River, near Atlanta] in five days." Worse, Sherman wanted to get back on the railroad. By the end of May he was nearly ninety miles from Chattanooga, and if Johnston would fight in the woods, there was no telling what his rebel cavalrymen might do.

So General Sherman edged eastward, which proved very easy because Johnston was even more anxious to return to the W & A's tracks. By June 6 both sides' armies were where their commanders wished, deployed across the railroad. Johnston's Confederate line extended ten miles, west to east, and so did Sherman's to the north of it. But the rebels had fortified the high ground. A rainy spell set in. Sherman wrote his brother, a senator from Ohio in Washington, that the campaign was "a big Indian war." Perhaps, but it had cost him more than 9,000 men.

Nothing much happened for another rainy week. Then, while riding his lines with Oliver Howard on June 14, Sherman paused at Hubert Dilger's battery. It was Dilger who had fired into Jackson's troops as they were wrecking Howard's corps at Chancellorsville; since then he had kept his batteries so close to the rebels someone said he ought to place bayonets on the tubes of his artillery pieces.

On Pine Top, a hill within easy range of Dilger's Parrott guns, the two generals saw several Confederates. "Make 'em take cover," Cump said to Howard, who told Dilger to open fire. Sherman rode on. Later that day he was told that observers had deciphered a message rebel signalmen on Pine Top had wigwagged to others. And on the fifteenth, Sherman telegraphed Washington: "We killed Bishop Polk yesterday."

Killing Bedford Forrest had been on Cump Sherman's mind much earlier. To Union commanders at Memphis he had given what amounted to standing orders to prevent Forrest from threatening middle Tennessee's railroads. In late April and early May, Brigadier General Samuel Sturgis made an unsuccessful strike at the Wizard of the Saddle. Afterward, Sturgis wrote Sherman: "I regret very much that I could not have the pleasure of bringing you his hair." Try again, Sherman ordered the man best remembered for having declared, during Second Manassaas, "I don't care for John Pope one pinch of owl dung!"

On the first of June, General Sturgis set out from Memphis with 4,800 infantry, 3,300 cavalrymen, 400 artillerymen with twenty-two guns, and a train of 250 wagons carrying twenty days' provisions. Ben Grierson, the former music teacher, led the cavalry. Among the infantrymen were 1,200 troops in the 55th United States Colored Regiment, who—bent on revenge for the Fort Pillow "massacre"—had vowed that they would show no mercy to any of Forrest's troopers they captured. Sturgis took his force southeastward, in the general direction of Tupelo on the Mobile & Ohio Railroad. Rains made the going miserable.

At first, General Forrest was uncertain as to how he could intercept and then whip Sturgis, but the Wizard had spent his boyhood in the region west of the M & O, and he figured something might happen at a place called Brice's Crossroads, provided the Yankees came down from the northwest. By June 9, Forrest was convinced they would; quickly he sent orders to his then-dispersed units to gather where the roads crossed.

Ben Grierson's cavalry passed flooded bottoms on either side of the road on the way to the bridge over Tishomingo Creek and Brice's Crossroads. Forrest found the federal brigades deployed near the X's center early on the morning of June 10, when he arrived with less than 1,000 men. The Wizard could only guess how many hours it would take the rest of his command to get there. While waiting, he decided, he would attack—in such a way as to persuade the Yankees he outnumbered them.

Thick woods and heavy foliage aided Forrest in deceiving Grierson. By midmorning the Union's line had been dented often enough for Grierson to be sending messengers back to Sturgis with urgent calls for reinforcements. Federal infantrymen rushed southeastward at double-time as they covered the last of five miles. But by ten o'clock on that hot morning Confederate regiments were coming in: Captain John Morton was there with a few guns, and Forrest could hope the small force he had ordered westward from a still-marching unit would ride fast enough to strike deep in Sturgis's rear.

During a lull Forrest ranged his forces in an arc matching in length but not in strength the one Sturgis had formed. At the signal, Forrest told artilleryman Morton, take four guns—each double-shotted with canister—and move up so as to stay abreast of the dismounted cavalrymen as they attacked toward the bridge over Tishomingo Creek. Attack? Attack maybe 8,000 Yankees with less than 2,000 tired troopers? Well, yes. The federal infantrymen had to be exhausted after their sprint, and Grierson's cavalrymen were fought out, so why not attack?

Morton had his four guns up on the line when the bugle sounded. The yelling and rifle volleys confirmed that the advance was beginning, and he blasted away at the Union lines, helping his crews push their guns forward as Forrest's troopers forced the invaders back toward the bridge yard by yard.

Grierson's men, armed with new breech-loading carbines, had no bayonets; they had fired off most of their ammunition earlier. Ammunition gone, they used their weapons as clubs to bash the charging Confederates. Out from holsters came pistols, and often their rounds made the critical difference.

Forrest pressed everywhere until the Yankees broke: Word reached them that grayclads were miles behind them. Morton turned the guns the federals left behind on them, double-shotting their own canister as he fired into the masses surging northwest-ward to the bridge they could not hope to cross, clogged as it was with overturned wagons and dead and dying animals as well as men so panicked they were pushing others into the creek to get even a few more feet nearer what they thought to be safety.

But there was no safety for Sturgis's survivors anywhere that afternoon. Nor would there be any that night or for the next few days. Forrest's troopers kept up a pursuit so utterly relentless that it ended only when their commander fell from his saddle—not shot, from exhaustion.

At Colliersville, Tennessee, some of Sturgis's men had to crawl to reach rail cars that would take them back to Memphis. It had taken the better part of nine days for them to march from Col-liersville to Brice's Crossroads but only two nights and a day to return. Behind them, Forrest's troopers salvaged eighteen federal guns, most of Sturgis's supplies-laden wagons, 1,500 rifles, and possibly 300,000 rounds of ammunition.

Even more important, perhaps, was the effect the Wizard's victory had on Cump Sherman. To Secretary of War Stanton on June 15—the day on which he also reported, "We killed Bishop Polk yesterday"—Sherman wrote:

> I will have the matter of Sturgis critically examined, and if he should be at fault he shall have no mercy at my hands. I cannot but believe he had troops enough. I know I would have been willing to attempt the same task with that force; but Forrest is the devil, and I think he has got some of our troops under cower. I have two officers at Memphis who will fight all the time—A.J. Smith and [Joseph A.] Mower. The latter is a young brigadier of fine promise, and I commend him to your attention. I will order them to make up a force and go out and follow Forrest to the death, if it costs ten thousand lives and breaks the Treasury. There will never be peace in Tennessee until Forrest is dead!

Chapter 35

Early Goes to Washington, Sherman to Atlanta

General Sherman was irritated by more than Samuel Sturgis's failure to scalp the Wizard. Joe Johnston, his army astride the Western & Atlantic south of Big Shanty, was frustrating every attempt the federals made to get around his flanks.

Cump was about to attack head-on when Johnston pulled back another two miles or so and on June 18 formed an even stronger line on Kennesaw Mountain. As before, Sherman poked and probed—in vain, often in fights more costly than he could tolerate. To the Union armies' commander Kennesaw Mountain, rising 700 feet from otherwise flat ground, seemed too heavily fortified to be assaulted. But was it? Johnston had too few men to be able to stretch his lines as far as he had without borrowing some from the center. Was that the place to strike?

Not once in this six-week campaign had Sherman called any of Johnston's bluffs: not up at Buzzard's Roost near Dalton or at Resaca, Cassville, or Allatoona Pass. If the rebel had gotten the idea that Cump was too timid to attack any of his fortification masterpieces, was this the time to show him how wrong he was?

Yes, General Sherman decided, and on June 27, after an hour during which more than 200 federal guns bombarded Kennesaw Mountain, he sent Thomas's army and McPherson's north of it up the steep slopes to assault the Confederates' trenches. After several hours and roughly 3,000 casualties, however, Sherman called it off: Johnston had most certainly *not* been bluffing.

By the end of June, Sherman's casualties for the entire campaign, 17,000 or so, were less than a third of Grant's since the twin drives began in early May. Even so, for the Union to have lost nearly 80,000 of its young men in only two months was shocking. Grant was still twenty miles from Richmond and Sherman about that far from Atlanta, and as July opened, there seemed no end to it. Not in Sherman's mind, at least. To his wife he wrote: "I begin to regard the death and mangling of a couple of thousand men as a small affair, a kind of morning dash—and it may be well that we become hardened."

After holding Kennesaw Mountain for a week after Sherman's assault, General Johnston retreated to a new line near Smyrna on the Western & Atlantic on July 3. By the fifth he was in another one, only two miles north of the Chattahoochee River. Four more days and Johnston was south of it, defending creeks now that there were no more ridgelines or rivers, and Sherman's armies were within sight of Atlanta—because their incessant sweeps northeast and southwest of Johnston's lines had flanked him out of all of them.

By July 10 refugees from north of Atlanta were streaming into the city, and many of its residents were moving out of it. Although politicians seemed stunned, the whole thing had been predictable from the outset, had any of them given thought to how overmatched in troops and matériel Joe Johnston had been. And they would never see how, afterward, Sherman could write: "No officer or soldier who ever served under me will question the generalship of Joseph E. Johnston." Yet the question being asked in Richmond was: Who might replace him?

The probable victim of the Confederate guillotine fought on as best he could, stretching his lines, trying to hold at Peachtree Creek, giving up a place called Buckhead, powerless to stop an eastward federal sweep designed to cut the railroad entering Atlanta from Augusta, the Carolinas, and Virginia. Let the blade fall, Jefferson Davis's cabinet urged him, but the commander-in-chief hesitated.

Would Johnston give the politicians what they seemed to want most, a climactic battle? To find out, Davis sent Braxton Bragg to Atlanta. Johnston gave Bragg the impression that he had no plans at all except to respond to whatever moves Sherman made next. So Bragg telegraphed Davis. A reply came back on July 16 directed to Johnston: "I wish to hear from you as to [your] present situation, and your plan of operations so specifically as will enable me to anticipate events."

Whether Johnston's strong sense of honor precluded his promising more than he knew he could deliver or whether he was merely too exhausted to apply his best efforts to meeting this fresh challenge, the Army of Tennessee's commander sent Davis a message that contained nothing new. Down fell the guillotine.

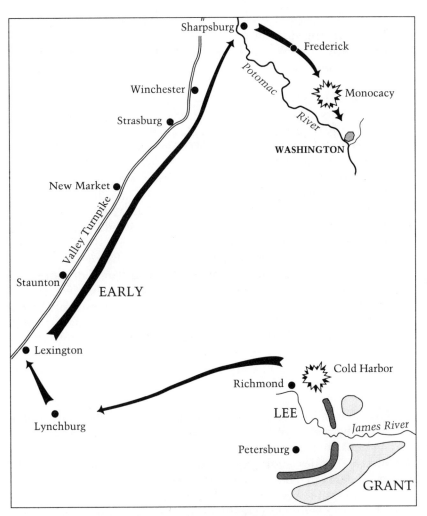

Early's Advance to Washington

Into General Johnston's headquarters early on the morning of July 18 limped John Hood, shaken by the news that he was now a full general and the commander of the Army of Tennessee. To the declarations of Hood and other senior officers that they would protest Davis's decision, Johnston merely replied, "Gentlemen, I am a soldier. A soldier's first duty is to obey."

Ulysses Grant hardly noticed it when in mid-June General Lee sent Jubal Early's corps from Cold Harbor westward to Lynchburg to stop David Hunter's fresh attempt to cut the vital Virginia Central

Railroad. This was a mistake on the general-in-chief's part, one that may have prolonged the war.

Early drove the Hunter-led force that had burned VMI into the Alleghenies and then, using discretion Lee had given him, decided to sweep down the Shenandoah Valley and threaten Washington. But he tarried at Lexington, shrewdly allowing his 14,000 men—some of them survivors of the Stonewall Brigade—to tour the scorched ruins of VMI, finally ordering the band to play a dirge as every man passed by the grave of Lieutenant General Thomas Jonathan Jackson.

Then Early moved northward, down the Valley Turnpike past New Market and the Massanutten, reaching Winchester on July 2. Over the Potomac's fords into federal-held Maryland he pressed, pausing again at the old Sharpsburg battlefield as if to permit that grim day's veterans to rekindle memories they would share with the newcomers as the advance continued.

East of Frederick, on July 9, Early's troops collided with a small Union force that had been assembled hastily in Baltimore and rushed westward to the Monocacy River. In a sharp battle Early got around the Yankees and opened the road to Washington, only thirty miles or so to the southeast. "Press on!" the spirit of Jackson may have prompted. But Early had good reason to stop and think: Some of the federals captured in the fight at the Monocacy River were from Horatio Wright's VI Corps, which belonged to the Petersburg-entrenched Army of the Potomac.

Gratified indeed might Old Jack have been had he known how panicked the people of Washington were by the presence of his old corps almost within sight of the Capitol's unfinished dome. As in Atlanta, 600 miles southwest, refugees were pouring into Washington. Telegraph contact with the rest of the nation had been severed; no trains were moving. Prices for food and everything else soared. On the Potomac a steamer was standing by, ready to remove the president and his family. At the War Department, clerks kept loaded muskets by their desks. General Halleck referred his frantic visitors to the secretary of war and the president, who left it to General-in-Chief Grant to save the Union's capital.

Such trust was rewarded: Grant had shipped one division northward just in time to reach the fight at the Monocacy, and the rest of Wright's VI Corps was on the way. The general-in-chief said that he, too, would come to Washington but changed his mind—which was just as well, for there was no shortage of talent up north. Halleck reflected this in a wire to an idle general in New York City who had offered his services: "We have five times as many generals here as we want but are greatly in need of privates. Anyone volunteering in that capacity will be gratefully received."

Not so welcome on July 11 out at Fort Stevens, northwest of Washington, was Abraham Lincoln: No officer wanted it on his record that the president had been killed while visiting his command. And, anyway, that Monday was a scorcher, and from the fort's parapet about all anyone could see in the distance were dust clouds raised by rebels' columns.

Lincoln may not have even guessed it, but that day's heat and dust, together with the Confederates' accumulated fatigue from marching nearly 250 miles in a little more than two weeks, were doing as much to save Washington as the blue-clad troops disembarking from Petersburg. General Early and a few thousand of his men were within 1,000 yards of the fort, but not enough of the rest would make it through the dust to enable him to launch the attack he knew he must attempt before too many more federals got off their ships.

After sundown on the eleventh, Jubal Early called his generals together at Silver Spring, the summer home of Francis Blair, adviser to presidents since Andrew Jackson's time. First on the Confederate agenda was sampling the vintages from Blair's well-stocked wine cellar. Then Early posed the key question: Should they attack Fort Stevens in the morning and drive on into the city, or withdraw? Attack, counseled Early's subordinates. But almost as quickly as the decision was made, it had to be reversed: On Tuesday morning, July 12, Early was hit by a force Horatio Wright threw at him.

By that time Abraham Lincoln had returned to Fort Stevens for another look. He watched the fighting, ignoring whizzes of rifle rounds and even the fall of an officer hit not three feet away from him, until Captain Oliver Wendell Holmes, Jr., cried: "Get down, you damn fool, before you get shot!"

The Union's president got down, and that night Jubal Early withdrew toward Virginia's Shenandoah Valley. Washington was out of danger. Lincoln's administration, however, was not.

Lincoln had been renominated at the Republican party's early June convention at Baltimore, but nothing much he had done as president had pleased the Radicals, and many of his actions had seemed to encourage such factions as the Copperheads and pro-peace Democrats. So far, though, he had protected the powers of the presidency—as he understood the Founders to have defined them in the Constitution—against the Radicals' attempts to usurp them. Even while Jubal Early had been moving toward Washington he applied a "pocket" veto to the Wade-Davis Bill, which would have overridden his conviction that the states in rebellion were still elements of the Union and should be treated as such when the war was over. Historian J. G. Randall put it this way: "In discussing the future of the Southern states he habitually used the term 'restoration in preference to 'reconstruction,' with its connotations of change drastic, forcible, and delayed."

At the other extreme the number of peace advocates swelled whenever another casualty list was published, causing voters of all political persuasions to wonder if restoration of the Union was worth such appalling sacrifices. *New York Tribune* editor Horace Greeley wrote to Lincoln:

> Confederates everywhere [are] for peace. So much is beyond doubt. And therefore I venture to remind you that our bleeding, bankrupt, almost dying country also longs for peace—shudders at the prospect of fresh conscription, of further wholesale devastations, and of new rivers of blood.

And Greeley had a proposal: Meet Confederate emissaries at Niagara Falls to explore terms. Lincoln sent John Hay with Greeley to the scenic wonder, only to learn, hardly to his surprise, that the whole thing was an empty fiasco. So was another out-of-channels attempt, this one directed by a well-meaning Union amateur who reached Richmond and asked Jefferson Davis how peace could be achieved. "Withdraw your armies from our territory," replied the Confederate president, "and peace will come of itself." And when asked if he could leave any means of achieving peace unexamined, Davis said:

> No, I cannot. I desire peace as much as you do; I deplore bloodshed as much as you do. I tried in all my power to avert this war. I saw it coming, and for twelve years I worked night and day to prevent it, but I could not. And now it must go on till the last man of this generation falls in his tracks, and his children seize his musket and fight his battle, unless you acknowledge our right to self-government.... We are fighting for independence—and that, or extermination, we will have.

Kill that devil Forrest, Sherman had ordered A. J. Smith, and early in July he took a force of 13,000 infantry, 3,000 cavalry, and twenty-four guns toward Tupelo. Near there in mid-month he was stopped in a series of fights. Mississippi Department Commander Stephen Lee led the Confederate resistance, and not with distinction; Nathan Bedford Forrest merely executed his less experienced superior's orders. When Smith withdrew toward Memphis, about all he could report to Sherman, beyond casualties he had inflicted and other damage done, was that someone had shot the Wizard in the foot.

Then, having taken command of the Confederate Army of Tennessee, John Hood apparently felt compelled to demonstrate to the politicians in Richmond his willingness to fight an offensive battle. On July 20 he attacked George Thomas's army along Peachtree Creek with two corps, expecting, after they had mauled Thomas, to shift them eastward to join the third in striking Schofield and McPherson.

Hood's theory was textbook-sound. He had caught Sherman with a two-mile gap separating Thomas and Schofield; he had the advantage of a central position, enabling him to move his troops over shorter distances than Sherman's had to cover; and destroying fragments of an enemy's force one or two at a time was (and is) every combat commander's fondest dream. But there were delays, during which Thomas's men dug in, and that day the Rock of Chickamauga was not to be moved. After dark, Hood had to call it off. He had lost 2,500 men, Sherman, 1,600.

His first effort having failed, John Hood quickly began planning a second. Wrecking McPherson's army, easternmost, was his object. And the plan he made was Jacksonian: a flank march by an entire corps, Hardee's, while the other two—now inside Atlanta's northern and eastern fortifications—kept pressure on Schofield and (northwest of him) Thomas.

Again Hood's scheme had merit. And once more delays would plague its execution. Hardee was supposed to attack at dawn on July 22, but it was after noon before he did. In the interval Union Major General Grenville M. Dodge arrived and placed his troops in the path of the brigades striking McPherson's flank. With Hardee blocked, Hood threw more forces into the battle from the west. And for a time it seemed that this effort might succeed.

General McPherson, rushing from a conference with Sherman to the fighting, rode into a Confederate position. Rather than surrender, he turned his horse and tried to get away, only to be shot in the back and to die minutes afterward. All it took for the word to spread through federal ranks was the return of McPherson's horse without its rider. McPherson's grieving men needed no new orders. They threw back Hood's assaults until he finally stopped them, his vastly outnumbered army thinned that day by 8,000 more losses his nation could not replace, his only achievements the capture of twelve guns and the inflicting of about 3,700 casualties; one was Hood's West Point classmate McPherson.

Even so, by attacking twice, General Hood caused Sherman to

revise his plans. In the days after that fight east of Atlanta the federal armies' commander, having destroyed the Georgia Railroad's link to Savannah and the northeastern Confederacy, started shifting his forces to the west side of the city's lines, his intent now being to cut the tracks entering Atlanta from the south. And along the way, Cump replaced much-mourned James McPherson with Oliver Howard. Hooker, furious at having been passed over, asked to be relieved; Fighting Joe would not serve under the officer he still blamed for his defeat at Chancellorsville; Sherman quickly granted his request.

To command his old corps, Hood drew Stephen Lee over from the Mississippi Department; the first order he gave Lee was to attack the Union army now led by Oliver Howard, Lee's West Point 1854 classmate. On July 28 their forces collided west of Atlanta near Ezra Church. Out Lickskillet Road from the city's defense lines came Stephen Lee, assaulting Howard's federals with all four of his yelling divisions. But, since Chancellorsville, Oliver Howard had become a firm believer in rapid entrenchment, and his orders to dig in were obeyed in time for his army to repel each charge Lee's men made. Hood sent Lieutenant General A. P. Stewart's corps (earlier, Bishop Polk's) to hit the Yankee army's flank. By then, however, the day was ending, and so was Hood's third show of willingness to attack Georgia's invaders. In this one he lost roughly 2,500 men; Howard, perhaps 700.

Total Confederate casualties since Hood assumed command now neared 13,000. He and his army had proved they could and would fight. But Sherman was still able to maneuver his three armies around Atlanta pretty much as he pleased, and after three attempts to strike back, John Hood seemed content to leave it at that for a while. In fact, though, Hood had forced Cump to try something else: a siege.

Now both federal drives were stalled. Grant's had been since mid-June, when Lee slipped his army between Petersburg and Meade's forces. Thereafter, both sides built fortifications stout enough to make frontal assaults too costly. Fighting went on, most of it in the form of exchanges of artillery and mortar fire, which merely motivated infantrymen to dig in deeper.

By early July neither Grant nor Meade could see anything ahead other than siege warfare, but a soldier in a Pennsylvania regiment made up of coal miners had a suggestion: Why not dig a tunnel northward, fill the end of it with tons of gunpowder, and blast a hole in the Confederate line? Ambrose Burnside's corps could then sweep through it, splitting Lee's forces and holding the gap while the rest of

Meade's army poured through.

Impossible, said federal engineers, but General Meade let the Pennsylvanians start digging. By the third week of July their "mine" was finished. Burnside meant to follow up the blast by sending in a fresh and eager colored division. No, said Meade, fearing that if the whole thing failed, the newspapers would say he had committed black soldiers rather than whites to an assault he had known to be highly risky. To replace the rejected outfit Burnside asked his other division commanders to draw straws. The winner, of sorts, was Brigadier General James H. Ledlie. After him would come three waves, each a division in strength, among them the colored troops.

Around dawn on July 30 a gigantic explosion shattered the early-morning calm, making the earth quake and sending up the bodies of gray-clad men into a huge mushroom, creating a crater 150 feet long, more than 90 feet wide, and 30 feet deep. The Pennsylvanian miners had done their work perfectly. But corps commander Burnside had not obeyed Meade's orders to clear away obstacles Confederates had placed south of the blast site, and General Ledlie remained in a shelter far in the rear drinking rum, and his assault troops had to wedge only a few at a time through a gap in the rebel-built entanglements instead of charging in line of battle. Worse, once past the barriers, Ledlie's men—by then leaderless, disorganized, confused—ignored the open ground around the rim of the crater and headed down into it.

Although more than Ledlie's troops soon filled the pit, no division commander was there to lead them out of it. It took Confederates nearest the blast an hour to react, but when they did, they rimmed the huge crater and turned it into a killing ground. So dense were the federals packed, no round fired could miss. At midmorning, Meade ordered Burnside to get his troops out of there. Burnside protested, in vain, then tried. By nightfall he succeeded, having lost 4,000 men.

Seldom in this war had the connection between casualties and inept leadership been so obvious. This ended the war for Ambrose Burnside and James Ledlie. And soon, understandably, the Congressional Committee on the Conduct of the War saw a Lincoln-smiting opportunity in the tragedy. Called to testify, General-in-Chief Grant said:

> I think if I had been a corps commander, and had had that in charge, I would have been down there and would have seen that it was done right; or, if I had been the commander of the division that had to take the lead, I think I would have gone in with my division....I think the cause of the disaster

was simply the leaving the passage of orders from one [level] to another down to an inefficient man.

And then Ulysses Grant added: "I blame his seniors also for not seeing that he did his duty, all the way up to myself."

Federal planners wanted Mobile, the only port on the Gulf of Mexico's coast Confederate blockade runners could still use, shut down. Admiral David Farragut had been waiting for more than a year to do just that. By early August he had enough ships standing off the entrance to Mobile Bay to do the work. The city itself, about thirty miles to the north, was garrisoned by a thin force of rebels, but once federal gunboats controlled the bay, Mobile would lose its significance.

Farragut's first problem was to get his fleet past Fort Morgan, at the west end of Mobile Point, without hitting any of the mines (then called torpedoes) the rebels had placed a few feet beneath the surface of the three-mile-wide stretch of open water separating Fort Morgan and Fort Gaines, at the eastern tip of Dauphin Island. There was a narrow channel, left clear for blockade runners to use, but it was directly under Fort Morgan's forty-seven guns.

Once past Fort Morgan—if Admiral Farragut did not pause to reduce the brick pentagon to rubble on the way northward—he would have to contend with the CSS *Tennessee*, a new ironclad the Confederates had just finished building at Selma, 150 miles up one of the rivers emptying into Mobile Bay. Not wanting to get trapped with the new ram in front, a fort in his rear, and torpedoes west of the 200-yard-wide channel, Farragut decided to destroy Fort Morgan and then the *Tennessee*.

In all, Farragut had eighteen fighting ships, the rebels inside the bay four, the *Tennessee* being the only one that mattered. Of the admiral's eighteen, four were monitors, each with two fifteen-inch guns in a revolving turret. Farragut's plan called for the monitors to approach the cleared channel from the southwest, go east of a red buoy marking the limit of the torpedo field, and blast Fort Morgan out of the war. When the monitors were out of the way, his other ships would steam northward and add their fire. He would command from his flagship, the USS *Hartford*.

By six-twenty on the morning of August 5, the leading monitor, the USS *Tecumseh*, had her heavy guns blazing at Fort Morgan. But her captain ordered a turn to port, west of the red marker buoy, and a torpedo exploded directly under the *Tecumseh's* hull.

Monitors had only one escape hatch, and though several men squeezed through the turret's gun port, it came down to whether the pilot or the captain would use the hatch. "Go on, sir," said the captain; then, as the pilot later wrote; "the vessel seemed to drop from under me." Drop the *Tecumseh* did, plunging to the channel's bottom barely two minutes after running into the torpedo, entombing her captain and ninety-two other men.

By then Admiral Farragut had climbed the *Hartford*'s rigging so that he might see above the gunsmoke on deck. After him came a sailor who secured his body to the ropes lest he be thrown into the water while his wooden flagship lurched and rolled from the hits she was taking from Fort Morgan's remaining guns. Smoke got thicker; freeing himself, Farragut climbed higher.

Much less could anyone below him see, and in the bubbling wake of the *Tecumseh*'s plunge, confusion prevailed as to where the marker buoy was. Someone on the *Hartford*'s deck cried: "Torpedoes ahead!" And from high on the mainmast's rigging David Farragut shouted: "Damn the torpedoes! Full steam ahead!"

Or so millions in the North would read not long afterward, for Mobile Bay meant more in morale boosting than anything else, and its timing was perfect. Candidate Lincoln needed just such a victory more than ever, with Grant and Sherman having lost close to 90,000 troops in getting their armies to places where all they could do was besiege Lee's and Hood's forces.

Audacity had given the Confederate forces enough victories to keep the people of the South hoping that all governments would leave them alone. But with Jackson long dead and General Lee obliged to supervise the digging of miles of trenches, by midsummer of 1864 it may have seemed that never again would bold deeds quicken heartbeats. However, shortly after dawn on Sunday, August 21, Captain William Forrest, the general's brother, rode his horse directly into the lobby of Gayoso House, Memphis's most prominent hotel, and sent his troopers to Union Major General Stephen A. Hurlbut's room with orders to take him captive. Concurrently, cavalrymen led by another brother, Lieutenant Colonel Jesse Forrest, were rampaging through the district's headquarters near Memphis's waterfront with orders to seize the commander, Major General Cadwallader C. Washburn.

Nathan Bedford Forrest's raid on Memphis was what future generations would call a surgical strike, one launched amid strict secrecy, planned and ordered only on the basis of the best reports the Wizard could get outside Memphis as to where all the Union defenders and their generals were, executed by men who knew every alleyway in for what many of them was their hometown. Shock was all the victory he craved, knowing that audacity was his only remaining weapon.

So it mattered little to the Wizard that General Hurlbut had decided to spend that Saturday night somewhere other than in his hotel room or that General Washburn had been obliged to run in his nightclothes half a mile to safety in a nearby fort. Young brother Bill Forrest's ride into Gayoso House's lobby had made the point: Memphis itself was not secure while the Wizard of the Saddle lived.

That much done, General Forrest withdrew, remounting his men on 400 federal horses they had captured. Federal officers left behind would call A. J. Smith's columns back from central Mississippi to defend the city, exactly as Forrest had hoped. But while the Memphis raid was in progress, Smith's men looted homes and businesses in Oxford, then put the torch to them, deaf to the cries of women and children as they inflicted pain and ruin for which there was no military excuse whatsoever.

"Let us destroy Atlanta," said General Sherman to Oliver Howard on August 10, "and make it a desolation." This twist to the war was precisely the opposite of what George McClellan had advised Lincoln two summers earlier in the letter he presented to the president during his visit to Harrison's Landing: Spare Southern civilians the horrors, respect private property, do nothing to embitter the people.

So McClellan had been saying since his relief from command in November 1862. On June 15, 1864, he returned to West Point to dedicate a monument to the regular army's dead and delivered a speech in which he declared that the conflict had been caused by extremists from both sections and that the war was "just and righteous, so long as its purpose is to crush rebellion and save our nation from the infinite evils of dismemberment." But afterward he avoided contact with his fellow Democrats as they prepared to convene at Chicago to nominate a candidate to run against Abraham Lincoln in the November election.

Little Mac was the early favorite, although the party's very strong peace faction had serious problems with McClellan's intention to continue the fighting. As the convention opened on August 29, a split in Democratic ranks appeared imminent over how much more war there should be before peace talks began. But the delegates worked out a compromise: McClellan would be the candidate, running on a platform prepared mostly by the Copperheads. Harmony preserved, the politicians nominated the general on August 31 and adjourned.

Actually, the delegates had merely tossed the bomb with a burning fuse to McClellan. For days he agonized over whether he could accept both the nomination and the extreme pro-peace provisions embedded in the platform document. His plight was rich in irony: Lincoln had set aside the general's now-famous 1862 letter because McClellan appeared to envision a gentle war and a soft peace, yet now the Democrats' candidate was expected to accept language far more beneficial to the South than even he could, with honor, endorse.

Slavery was not even mentioned in the Copperhead-written Democratic platform, nor did their nominee deal with the issue directly in the letter of acceptance he sent to the Democratic Nomination Committee from Orange, New Jersey, on September 8, 1864. In the final draft McClellan wrote: "The preservation of our Union was the sole avowed object for which the war was commenced," and he called for its reestablishment with every state's constitutional rights (including, presumably, rights pertaining to all kinds of property) guaranteed.

Readers would find in McClellan's response whatever they sought, of course. But dissenters had no choice other than to support Little Mac, hoping perhaps that if elected he might prove easy to control.

Curiously, McClellan's rival had all but given up hope. His reelection was impossible, Lincoln's advisers told him; he would be fortunate if the Republicans did not reconvene, change the party's name to "Union," or something like that, and replace him with another candidate.

Henry Raymond, editor of the *New York Times* and chairman of the Republican National Committee, went a long step beyond warning Lincoln that he faced disaster in November. On August 22, Raymond wrote to him:

> Two special causes are assigned for this great reaction in public sentiment—the want of military success, and the impression in some minds, the fear and suspicion in others, that we are not to have peace in any event under this administration until Slavery is abandoned. In some way or other the suspicion is widely diffused that we can have peace with Union if we would.

Confound all enemies, the newspaperman urged, by creating a special commission "to make a distinct proffer of peace to Davis, as head of the rebel armies, on the sole condition of acknowledging the supremacy of the Constitution," with other matters to be settled later by a convention in which statesmen from both North and

South would participate. Well, yes, the president may have thought, this might defang the Copperheads; but what about the Radicals, who again wanted him to replace the moderates in his cabinet with "sound" men?

There was no clever way out, or so Lincoln seemed to have decided by August 23. That day, mysteriously, he wrote a terse memorandum, sealed it, and asked his cabinet members to endorse it sight unseen. In it he declared:

> This morning, as for some days past, it seems exceedingly probable that this Administration will not be re-elected. Then it will be my duty to so co-operate with the President elect [presumably, General McClellan], as to save the Union between the election and the inauguration; as he will have secured his election on such ground that he can not possibly save it afterwards.

So his political fate was still linked to whatever Ulysses Grant and William Tecumseh Sherman might achieve in battle, and it would continue to be, no matter what happened between then and early March 1865. He would appoint no special peace commissions; no changes would he make in the actions he had taken to remove the blight of slavery from the continent.

Even so, even a slight amount of pressure applied by the Copperhead-wrought Democratic platform may have caused Lincoln to correct an error Secretary of War Edwin Stanton had made a year or so earlier. This had to do with exchanges of prisoners, and it was a delicate subject: To negotiate procedures with Confederates was thought to be *de facto* recognition of the new nation. Soldiers commanding field armies and even patrols took less lawyerlike views of the question and swapped prisoners or arranged paroles, anyway, until Stanton shut this down.

That was in June 1863 or thereabouts. In the interval, the number of prisoners of war held in stockades both North and South had increased dramatically. Andersonville, a Confederate prison south of Atlanta built to hold 10,000 men, had 33,000 in it by August 1864. Ironically, Sherman's policy of stripping Georgia's people of food and other resources made conditions worse for those federal captives; eventually, some 13,000 or so would die there of malnutrition, exposure, and disease. And so it was not only at other Southern prisons but at installations in the North where neglect inflicted an appalling toll.

It took a long time and the deaths of uncounted men among both sides' captives for correction to occur. But the North's political campaign accelerated it, which was a welcome fringe benefit of a decision made so quietly that foreign observers were astonished by it: to hold a presidential election in the midst of a civil war unprecedented in its ferocity.

And war-weary though the North was, as sadly depleted as the South's resources were, casualty lists would grow longer as the summer of 1864 advanced. Jubal Early's Confederate "army"— Jackson's old corps—was still in the Shenandoah Valley, and federal forces were gathering to deal with it. Out in Tennessee Nathan Bedford Forrest still had his hair. South of Petersburg the skirmishing between Grant's army and Lee's took a daily toll in lives, though nothing much came of it, and it looked as though that would continue indefinitely. So it was, also, down near Atlanta where Cump Sherman had spent most of August unwillingly conducting a siege.

Suddenly, John Hood changed the situation in Georgia. On August 10 he sent Joe Wheeler, with half of his cavalry, to raid Sherman's railroad supply line. Wheeler's move northward up the Western & Atlantic's track was designed to starve out the Yankees, of course, but along the way he captured horses that could be obtained in no other way, and welcome indeed were the federals' herds of cattle Hood's hungry men saw some of the War Child's troopers driving into Atlanta's lines.

Not even a retaliatory strike Sherman ordered his cavalry to make at Jonesboro, twenty miles or so south of Atlanta on Hood's only remaining rail line, discouraged him. Wheeler's progress reports were coming from places ever northward: Cassville, then Resaca and Dalton. And as the end of August neared, the federal siege guns ceased firing. Returning patrol leaders told Hood that Union trenches were manned only by left-behind skirmishers.

Was this the miracle he needed? Or was it all too good to be true?

When President Davis had asked General Lee if John Hood was capable of replacing Joe Johnston in command of the Army of Tennessee, Lee said he was "very industrious on the battlefield, careless off, and I have had no opportunity of judging of his action when the whole responsibility rested upon him." True enough; but at the time, Jefferson Davis was seeking more industry on battlefields, and he got it in Hood's attacks late in July. Now, though, almost a month later, the quality General Lee had been unable to assess—in effect, John Hood's judgment—became more critical than his aggressiveness.

Hood gave every indication that he had convinced himself that Sherman was retreating. He proclaimed victory in messages to

Richmond. To celebrate it, he ordered a ball held amid the damage Sherman's now-silent siege guns had done in Atlanta. Worse for the Confederacy's future, General Hood did not pay enough attention to the reports his remaining cavalrymen were sending him from points south of Atlanta.

Cump Sherman had been nettled by Joe Wheeler's strikes up the Western & Atlantic but not worried about them, knowing that within a few hours his repair crews along the way would close gaps in the track the rebels made. Moreover, while his siege guns were shelling Atlanta to rubble, he had been squirreling up supply stockpiles ample enough to support an attempt to draw Hood out of his defenses.

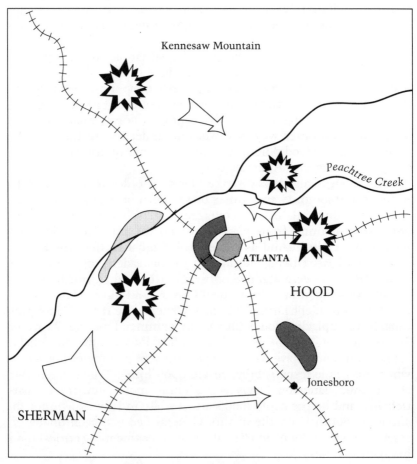

Sherman's Moves Below Atlanta

Destroy the Confederate army opposing him, the general-in chief had ordered Sherman before the campaign opened in early May, and for a time Cump had paid more attention to desolating Atlanta than to his primary mission. But after young Hood had sent away so much of his cavalry and after he had turned into a digger as energetic as Joe Johnston had ever been, Sherman decided to resume the offensive Hood's forces had stalled back on July 28 near Ezra Church.

As before, on August 26, Howard's army led the way as it marched southwestward; once across the West Point Railroad, it would turn southeastward, Jonesboro on the Macon Railroad its destination. After Howard's troops came Thomas's army, then Schofield's, both to make similar but shorter sweeps to the Macon Railroad—the last one available to Hood.

"I have Atlanta as certainly as if it were in my hand!" General Sherman remarked to George Thomas as they rode south of the end of Hood's trenches. This was no idle boast. The fangs of the Union armies' cobra, its tail more than 400 miles to the north at Louisville on the Ohio River, were about to strike a victim transfixed into near immobility: Hood was moving troops southward, but too few and too late to make much difference.

Or so it seemed to Cump, and in the long run he was right, though his armies and Hood's collided near Jonesboro and points northward along the Macon Railroad on September's first day in bitter but inconclusive fighting. On both sides the plans called for detached units to be annihilated by superior ones and then for the victors to chew up the other fragments. But delays plagued the federals and Confederates alike. Confusion prevailed as casualties from heavy skirmishing mounted. Only darkness ended it, leaving Sherman twenty miles south of Atlanta and wondering later during the night of September 1–2 what all those booming sounds he heard in the northern distance meant.

Sherman was hearing Atlanta's fall, though many hours were to pass before the details reached him. He had ordered a mass attack toward Jonesboro and the destruction of Hood's army to be launched at daybreak on September 2, but overnight the rebels disappeared. As the day wore on, Cump got reports that the Confederates had blown up whatever of military value they could not remove from Atlanta, hence, the booming. Not until before sunrise on September 3, however, did General Sherman receive enough hard news to be able to wire Chief of Staff Halleck: "So Atlanta is ours and fairly won."

"Atlanta is ours" was all the Northern people had to be told in order to set off celebrations throughout the Union and effusions of praise from politicians who were quick to overlook the embarrassing fact that former Cadet Sherman had worked the wrong problem: Hood's army, the force the general-in-chief had told him to destroy, had eluded him. And as though Atlanta's capture were enough, even Grant joined the chorus, wiring Cump: "You have accomplished the most gigantic undertaking given to any general in this war, and with a skill and ability that will be acknowledged in history as unsurpassed if not unequalled."

Even earlier, Union newspapers—among them some that had pronounced Sherman hopelessly insane nearly three years before—had termed him preferable to either McClellan or Lincoln as a possible presidential candidate. Cump wrote Halleck: "If forced to choose between the penitentiary and the White House for four years...I would say the penitentiary, thank you." And he added: "We as soldiers best fulfill our parts by minding our own business and I will try to do that."

Chapter 36

Sheridan Torches the Shenandoah Valley

With Atlanta under Sherman's control, Ulysses Grant decided it was time to clear the Shenandoah Valley of Jubal Early's forces. Lincoln had prodded him weeks before, writing:

> I have seen your dispatch in which you say "I want Sheridan put in command of all the troops in the field, with instructions to put himself south of the enemy and follow him to the death. Wherever the enemy goes let our troops go also." This, I think, is exactly right as to how our forces should move, but please look over the dispatches you may have received from [Washington] even since you made that order, and discover, if you can, that there is any idea in the head of anyone [in the War Department] of "putting our army south of the enemy" or of "following him to the death" in any direction. I repeat to you it will neither be done nor attempted unless you watch it every day and hour and force it.

General Grant responded by making a quick trip northward in early August, during which he probably told young Sheridan what he had said in a message to Halleck earlier: Early should be pursued up the Shenandoah Valley by all available troops with instructions to "eat out Virginia clear and clean as far as they go, so that crows flying over it for the balance of the season will have to carry their own provender with them."

But Grant had remained with Sheridan only for long enough to get him started. Early's Confederates blocked Little Phil's drive at Fisher's Hill near Strasburg. Sheridan pulled his 40,000-man force back to camps around Harpers Ferry. There, on August 26, he got a nudge from the distant general-in-chief:

> Give the enemy no rest, and if it is possible to follow to the Virginia Central Railroad, follow that far. Do all the damage to railroads and crops you can. Carry off stock of all descriptions, and Negroes, so as to prevent further planting. If the war is to last another year we want the Shenandoah Valley to remain a barren waste.

By September 14, Grant realized that nothing was going to happen unless he did as Lincoln had suggested: "...watch it every day and hour and force it." Lest the farmers in Virginia's vast granary harvest their crops unmolested, he left Meade in charge at Petersburg and turned up at Little Phil's Harpers Ferry headquarters on September 16 with a plan in his pocket. But Sheridan had a plan of his own. The general-in-chief liked it enough to give him the kind of order usually only company commanders can: "Go in."

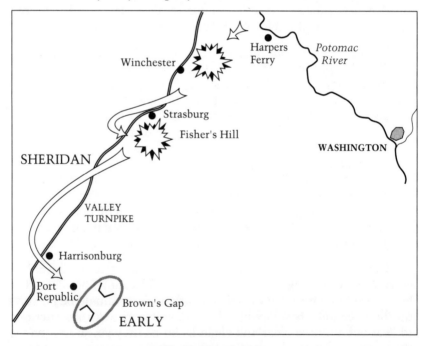

Sheridan's Advance

That Sheridan did, on Monday, September 19, moving from Harpers Ferry southwestward until his 38,000 effectives hit elements of Early's 14,000 a few miles east of Winchester. Little Phil appeared strong enough in troops to do whatever he pleased, and he tried practically everything in the book. But Jubal Early was more experienced in such fights. His divisions had been scattered, but he got them together in time to lengthen the North's casualty lists by roughly 5,000 fresh names before he withdrew slowly through the town, not stopping until his forces—fewer now by nearly 4,000— were beyond Strasburg, twenty miles or so up the Valley Turnpike to the south, back in their old defense lines on Fisher's Hill.

Sheridan was a straight-ahead fighter, but on Thursday, September 22, he employed a touch of military art by getting some of his men around Early's western flank. Inevitably, Early had to withdraw—and to leave behind sixteen guns and nearly 1,400 more casualties, one of them Sandie Pendleton, killed only a few days short of his twenty-fifth birthday; he had declined brigade command and a general's star to serve on Early's staff just as he had on Old Jack's.

"Foot cavalry," the 1862 Valley campaign's victors had been termed, and Early's Confederates proved true to that tradition in this new one. But in 1864 there would be no pausing near Port Republic to fight again, no stopping until they had marched more than eighty miles, from Fisher's Hill to gaps in the Blue Ridge northeast of Staunton, leaving the Valley's ripening crops for Sheridan's men to burn.

While General Grant was waiting for the results Sheridan produced, from his headquarters at City Point (east of Meade's lines south of Petersburg) he sent Lieutenant Colonel Horace Porter to Atlanta to visit Cump Sherman. This followed many exchanges of letters regarding what Sherman ought to do next, studies by Grant's staff, and long debates over possible courses of action. "You know my views thoroughly," Grant told Porter, "and can answer any of Sherman's questions as to what I think."

Uncle Billy was relaxing on the front porch of the house he was using for his headquarters when Colonel Porter arrived on September 16. After lunch, they got to Sherman's ideas. "There ought to be some objective point or points decided upon," he said. "I want to strike out for the sea."

But what about the Confederate force? "There is no telling what Hood will do," replied Sherman. "I don't care much which he does. I would rather have him start north, though; and I would gladly pay his expenses if he would decide to take that horn of the dilemma."

Sherman could split his army, he explained to Porter, the northern wing of it gathering troops to destroy Hood. With the divisions he kept he would cut a swath through Georgia to the Atlantic coast, divide the Confederacy in two, and get ready "to move up in the rear of Lee, or do almost anything else Grant may require of me."

Curiously, a little over a week later, president Jefferson Davis visited Hood at his headquarters at Palmetto, southwest of Atlanta, for the same reason Grant sent Colonel Porter to Sherman: to talk about what to do next.

Hood's objective, Davis told a crowd of soldiers when he arrived, would be Tennessee. And they had shouted, "Johnston! Give us Johnston!" Hood knew about that, and he offered to resign. No, the president decided, approving Hood's plan, which was to place all of his forces between Atlanta and Dalton, where they could cut the Western and Atlantic Railroad. This threat to the long federal supply line would either draw Sherman out of Atlanta, where Hood might have another chance to whip him, or oblige him to move southward to open a new route up from the Gulf Coast—and if he did, Hood would pursue him.

Davis suggested Gadsden, Alabama, as a point from which Hood's army might be supplied from the southwest. Later, he put Beauregard—then reduced to helping Lee defend Petersburg's trenches—in command of Hood and Richard Taylor, who (after refusing to serve under Edmund Kirby Smith any longer) was now in charge of operations in Mississippi. No thought had Davis given, apparently, to restoring Joe Johnston to any position.

So it was that Cump Sherman looked eastward and John Hood took out the maps of the country northward. But, on his way back to Richmond, President Davis went too far toward boosting civilian morale in speeches that told Sherman (who read them in newspapers not long afterward) that Hood's army was headed into his rear and that the Yankees would soon flee "through slaughter" northward to "the beautiful banks of the Ohio."

Sherman sent George Thomas to Nashville with part of his Army of the Cumberland and orders to assemble other forces to help him deal with Hood's approach, explaining to Grant that he wanted to "destroy Atlanta and march across Georgia to Savannah or Charleston, breaking roads and doing irreparable damage. We cannot remain on the defensive." The eccentric Hood's actions, however, he would watch closely: "I cannot guess his movements as I could those of Johnston, who was a sensible man and only did sensible things."

Cavalry sweeps through Sherman's rear had been vexing him all along. John Morgan was on one deep in Tennessee early in September when—surprised by a federal patrol that surrounded the house in which he had been sleeping, and after he had said, "Don't shoot; I surrender"—a Union trooper twenty feet away fired his carbine, then boasted: "I've killed the damned horse thief!" And Joe Wheeler, starting up the W & A's track near Atlanta and moving as far northeastward as Knoxville before turning to the west and south, reached Tuscumbia, Alabama, after six weeks, only to learn that Sherman's repair crews had kept federal supply trains puffing Atlanta-bound the whole time.

And Nathan Bedford Forrest? Well, for perhaps the first time in this war the Wizard was serving under a department commander— Dick Taylor—who was a kindred spirit, one who sent him into central Tennessee to cut the railroads that made Sherman's continued residence in Atlanta possible. Departing from northern Mississippi on September 16, Forrest moved eastward through Alabama to Athens. There he bluffed the Yankee commander into surrendering, then burned railway trestles and tore up miles of track on his way northward into Tennessee.

By September 27, Forrest was burning a bridge 200 feet long near Pulaski. "Press Forrest to the death," Thomas ordered the forces he was sending that way. Too late; the Wizard slipped fifty miles eastward to Sherman's main rail route, the Nashville & Chattanooga, but he had too many Yankees swarming around him to inflict much damage. To confuse his pursuers Forrest split his command, sending part of it southward to Alabama while he rode on toward Nashville. He got as far northward as Spring Hill, maybe thirty miles south of Nashville, on October 1. Now he was back on the Tennessee & Alabama Railroad, the one he had struck along the way to Pulaski, and southward he went, ripping up track, destroying trestles, but knowing that his main problem was to save the fragment of his force still with him.

Blocking Forrest's way was the swollen Tennessee River in northern Alabama. On the second day of a ferrying operation, while poling the last boat to leave the river's north shore, he saw a lieutenant standing idly in the bow. Help pole, Forrest ordered. No, that was beneath an officer's dignity, the major general heard him say just before he slapped the lieutenant so hard his body landed in the water. Forrest extended his pole to retrieve the man, then promised: "If I knock you out of the boat again I'll let you drown."

Dick Taylor must have loved that story when he heard it. The new department commander had to be pleased as well by the results of Forrest's two-week raid. More than 3,000 additional names would appear on Yankee casualty lists, 800 of Forrest's men were riding federal horses, and the captured wagons brought much-needed supplies back to Alabama. Less gratifying were the Wizard's railroad-wrecking efforts, yet soon Sherman would be confessing to General Grant that he could no longer protect his railroads "now that Hood, Forrest, Wheeler, and the whole batch of devils are turned loose without home or habitation."

General Sherman had failed to destroy the rebel army, but by seizing Atlanta he had boosted Lincoln's chances of being reelected enormously. Moreover, possession of this railroad hub and weapons-manufacturing center meshed with his intent to destroy resources that enabled the South to prolong the war. But he yearned to be free of dependence on railroads. "Salt water, salt water," he had told an officer who asked him what was to be done once Atlanta was captured. But before he left for Savannah, he meant to wipe the town off the face of the earth, and to this end he issued orders for removing all its citizens, explaining to Halleck on September 4:

> If the people raise a howl against my barbarity and cruelty, I will answer that war is war, and not popularity-seeking. If they want peace, they and their relatives must stop the war.

Hood protested the evacuation, as did Atlanta's mayor. Sherman replied to Mayor James M. Calhoun on September 12:

> I have your letter of the 11th, in the nature of a petition to revoke my orders removing all the inhabitants from Atlanta. I have read it carefully, and give full credit to your statements of the distress that will be occasioned, and yet shall not revoke my orders, because they were not designed to meet the humanities of the case, but to prepare for the future struggles in which millions of good people outside of Atlanta have a deep interest. We must have peace, not only at Atlanta, but in all America.

Lawyerlike, Sherman built the case for the necessity of eliminating Southern resistance. Then he got specific:

> The use of Atlanta for warlike purposes is inconsistent with its character as a home for families. There will be no manufactures, commerce, or agriculture here, for the maintenance of families, and sooner or later want will compel the inhabitants to go. Why not go now, when all the arrangements are completed for the transfer, instead of waiting till

the plunging shot of contending armies will renew the scenes of the past month?

So much for logic. Now Sherman turned to the overriding questions:

> You cannot qualify war in harsher terms than I will. War is cruelty, and you cannot refine it; and those who brought war into our country deserve all the curses and maledictions a people can pour out. I know I had no hand in making this war, and I know I will make more sacrifices to-day than any of you to secure peace. But you cannot have peace and a division of our country.

Moreover:

> You might as well appeal against the thunder-storm as against these terrible hardships of war. They are inevitable, and the only way the people of Atlanta can hope once more to live in peace and quiet at home, is to stop the war, which can only be done by admitting that it began in error and is perpetuated in pride.
> We don't want your negroes, or your horses, or your houses, or your lands, or any thing you have, but we do want and will have a just obedience to the laws of the United States.

"When peace does come," continued the general, "then will I share with you the last cracker, and watch with you to shield your homes and families against danger from every quarter." And he concluded:

> Now you must go, and take with you the old and feeble, feed and nurse them, and build for them, in more quiet places, proper habitations to shield them against the weather until the mad passions of men cool down, and allow the Union and peace to settle over your old homes in Atlanta.

Poetry was in those words, behind them the compassion of a man three years earlier some newspaper reporters had declared hopelessly insane.

General-in-Chief Grant was not sure Sheridan was doing the best he could. True, Little Phil had driven Jubal Early's Confederates up the Shenandoah Valley to Brown's Gap in the Blue Ridge, but once Sheridan reached Harrisonburg, he had appeared content to stay there. This go-and-stop pattern did not square with Grant's hit-hard, hit-often, keep-on-hitting approach to fighting. Nor was delay in finishing off Early's force acceptable, given Grant's own plan: to isolate Lee's army and Richmond from supplies available via railroads from the southwest and especially from the Shenandoah Valley.

Since mid-June, Lee's skill in fortifying the Petersburg lines and shifting troops quickly from one threatened point to another had enabled him to block Meade's frontal assaults and also attempts to get around western extensions of his defensive positions. Eventually, with enough men, Meade could prevail. But the Army of the Potomac's heavy casualties and enlistment expirations were not being offset by the quantity or quality of replacements, and Early's threat to Washington and continuing presence in the Valley had kept two federal corps up there.

Yet Sheridan might break the deadlock at Petersburg if he destroyed Early, burned the Shenandoah Valley's ripening crops, smashed up the Virginia Central Railroad, and then brought his 40,000-man force back to help Meade whip Lee and take Richmond. Do these things, Grant ordered Little Phil. No, came the reply from Harrisonburg: "I think that the best policy will be to let the burning of the crops in the Valley be the end of this campaign, and let some of this army go elsewhere."

Astonishing as Grant may have found it for a general to suggest *removing* troops from his command, Sheridan's reasons for opposing the general-in-chief's wishes were equally surprising. "I cannot accumulate sufficient stores," wrote Little Phil, to undertake the strike against the railroads, even though he was in a position to burn Virginia's granary. And rather than fight Jubal Early to the death, Sheridan proposed pulling back northeastward nearly a hundred miles to Front Royal and to "operate with the cavalry and infantry."

Withdrawing that far down the Valley amounted to giving Fisher's Hill and nearly everything else back to Early, which made Sheridan's thinking even more difficult to follow. But, like his predecessor as general-in-chief, Ulysses Grant held that a commander on the scene was the best judge of circumstances, and he told Little Phil to do *something*.

That was, as it turned out, to set the torch to every barn and homestead and field his cavalrymen could get to, from Port Republic and Staunton northeastward for ten days, leaving fires that marked the federals' progress every night, making sunlight dim with smoke. "Take all provisions, forage, and stock wanted for the use of your command," Grant had told Sheridan earlier, adding: "Such as cannot be consumed, destroy." Phil Sheridan carried out this order with a ruthlessness not even nature's most devastating forces had ever approached.

"When this is completed," he reported in a message sent to Grant on October 7, "the Valley, from Winchester up [southward] to Staunton, ninety two miles, will have but little in it for man or beast." Early's Confederate cavalrymen confirmed this as they followed the arsonists, finding nothing in their wake but smoldering ruins and grim looks on the faces of refugees.

When Lieutenant General James Longstreet returned to duty in mid-October, he must have been shocked by the changes that had occurred during his five-month convalescence. General Lee he found "worn by past labor," showing signs of his ailments, "troubles multiplying." And the sight of the Army of Northern Virginia in trenches, digging more, had to have been crushing to a soldier who could recall those days when Lee astounded the observing world by leading these forces to places so far north that Longstreet had risked guillotining to restrain his audacity.

Elated as Lee must have been to have his "old warhorse" back, it was unlikely that he told Longstreet that he had been thinking of abandoning Richmond and taking his army westward, where once again he could fight in the open. Holding the lines there at Petersburg was the immediate necessity. Lee assigned a segment to the man who had so often advocated letting Yankees kill themselves by attacking impregnable Confederate defenses; Longstreet turned to the task of repelling federal assaults.

Jubal Early could not remain in Brown's Gap after Yankee burnings made supplies impossible to find, so on October 12 he began following Sheridan's forces down the Valley. Within a few days the Confederates were back into their old positions on Fisher's Hill. There they had to pause: Five miles to the north the federals were holding a line along Cedar Creek to protect their camps. But the Yankees were scattered, resting, and now that Lee had returned Kershaw's division to him, Early could afford to wonder what his 21,000 troops might do to punish the arsonists.

Early was too arthritic to do much scouting, so he sent John Gordon and Jed Hotchkiss up to high ground overlooking the federal camps. Back came the mapmaker with a plan Old Jack would have relished: Make a flank march eastward to places no one in a blue uniform would expect them to try to reach, then attack northward. Some of Early's other generals, however, found this scheme of maneuver too bold. With the Massanutten's northern wall so near the Shenandoah's North Fork, how could an entire corps plus Kershaw's division get from Fisher's Hill to the jump-off points indicated on Hotchkiss's rapidly drawn map? Easily, John Gordon explained, by moving men in a single file through some tight spots, during a moonlit march, in strict silence—by doing the thing the Yankees least expected they would dare attempt. And if it failed? Gordon said he would accept full responsibility.

Let it be done, Jubal Early decided. Gordon would lead the way and make the easternmost strike, Kershaw following and going in west of Gordon, with Brigadier General Gabriel Wharton's division crossing the Valley Turnpike and moving toward Middletown. West of Wharton, who would have the artillery with him, Brigadier General Thomas Rosser was to keep his cavalry guarding the flank of the advance and then pursue. And all troops were to be in their attack positions at five A.M. the next morning, October 19.

Seldom in more than three years of war was any operation carried out with such fidelity to orders. Surprise was of the essence, and first Gordon's men, then Kershaw's, reaped its benefits; they shattered one federal brigade after another as they swept northward, driving the stunned Yankees like so many sheep through camps of units whose commanders had been too slow to believe such a calamity could possibly occur.

Fog had helped initially, and battle smoke, added to it, made the screaming Confederates all but invisible until they were near enough to leave gunpowder burns on the uniforms of Union soldiers who got shot trying to hold back the attackers. At many places the fighting was hand to hand, with rifles used as clubs, but nowhere could even the most gallant stand buy more than minutes, and those minutes could not make much difference. The gray-clads knew what they were doing, and the dazed Yankees' officers could do little more than wonder and watch as their lines dissolved.

By midmorning all of the absent Sheridan's 32,000-man army except Horatio Wright's VI Corps was wrecked. Wright's three divisions were southwest of Middletown, pressed by the Confederates, when Jubal Early and John Gordon met. Briefly Gordon reported the progress made and expressed his intention to continue the attack. Gordon's troops had driven Wright's corps north of Middletown when again Early found the Georgian. "Well, Gordon," he said, "this is glory enough for one day."

"We have but one more blow to strike," replied Gordon, "and then there will not be left an organized company of infantry in Sheridan's army."

"No use in that. They will all go, directly."

"That is the Sixth Corps, General. It will not go unless we drive it from the field."

"Yes," said Early, "it will go too, directly."

Afterward, Gordon wrote, "My heart went into my boots," and generations of historians would agree that General Early's halt was "fatal." But Early had used all the men he had in making first a nightlong, five-mile approach march, then in driving the Yankees another five miles or more, and by late that morning he may well have wanted to ask Gordon whence the forces might come to strike "one more blow." And plundering was keeping many a man beyond the generals' reach. Private John Worsham wrote:

> The world will never know the extreme poverty of the Confederate soldier at this time. Hundreds of men who were in the charge and who captured the enemy's works were barefooted. Every one of them was ragged. Many had on everything they had, and *none* had eaten a square meal for weeks. As they passed through Sheridan's camp, a great temptation was thrown in their way. Many of the tents were open, and in plain sight were rations, shoes, overcoats, and blankets. The fighting continued farther and farther, yet some of the men stopped. They secured well-filled haversacks and, as they investigated the contents, the temptation to stop and eat was too great. Since most of them had had nothing to eat since the evening before, they yielded. While some tried on shoes, others put on warm pants in place of the tattered ones. Still others got overcoats and blankets—articles so much needed for the coming cold.

And there was another factor working, one probably neither Early nor Gordon were aware of when the commanding general said the glory attained was enough for one day: Philip Sheridan had spent the night only fifteen or so miles to the north in Winchester.

This had been Horatio Wright's battle, for Little Phil had left him in command a day or so earlier when he departed for Washington. Wright had been as surprised as any other Union soldier by the audacity of Early's dawn attack; hence, the flight of most of his 32,000 troops before he could rally what remained of his VI Corps north of Middletown.

Word of the disaster reached Sheridan soon after Gordon's corps and Kershaw's division came storming across the fords of the Shenandoah's North Fork. By eight o'clock on the morning of October 19 he was riding Rienzi southward, giving orders to form lines to stop fugitives from the Confederate onslaught. "Boys," he shouted to the stragglers, "if you don't want to fight yourselves, come back and look at others fighting. We will whip them out of their boots before 4 o'clock." And to others he yelled: "Turn back; face the other way. I am going to sleep in that camp tonight or in hell."

By midmorning Little Phil reached Horatio Wright, north of Middletown. "That's all right," he assured the dejected man he had left in charge, and when another general said his troops could cover the withdrawal to Winchester, Sheridan retorted: "Retreat-Hell! We'll be back on our camps tonight." Even so, Little Phil expected the rebels to attack again. As soon as he found out where the federal lines were, he rode Rienzi along them, hatless so the discouraged men could see that he was back with them, and the effect on the troops was galvanizing. As they watched the bullet-headed little man on the big black horse gallop past, they cheered—and cheered all the more when he paused and repeated his promise: "We'll lick them like Hell before night."

Sheridan's men could believe him, for he had set in place a tradition of victories: Winchester, Fisher's Hill, the drive to Harrisonburg. Fugitives who saw him earlier returned. As noon passed, units dispersed during the Confederates' surge got together again.

Gordon probed Sheridan's lines that afternoon, then fell back. Now Little Phil's turn came.

From the eastern end of the federal line to the western one Sheridan shifted young Brigadier General George Armstrong Custer's cavalry division. The rest of his forces would move straight southward, attacking, while Custer got around Early's western flank. This plan had worked at Fisher's Hill nearly a month before— routing Early's defenders, sending them scores of miles southwestward to safe haven in a gap in the Blue Ridge—and Sheridan counted on his troops to remember that.

John Gordon warned Jubal Early, yet the commanding general left roughly half his forces in advanced positions while others south of them sought shelter behind stone walls separating one field from the next. Whether Early still believed enough glory for one day had been won or he was genuinely surprised would never be entirely clear. In any case, when the federal attack came, as Sheridan had promised, at about four o'clock that afternoon, the Yankees poured through the weakest segment of Early's most advanced line—the westernmost, with Custer's cavalrymen near enough to support the federal breakthrough—and began rolling up the Confederate flank.

Now October nineteenth's second battle became the reverse of the first one. Early's units dissolved, pouring southward, leaving it finally to Stephen Dodson Ramseur's division to defend the last of the stone walls. Ramseur, at twenty-seven the youngest graduate of West Point to become a Confederate major general, looking forward to a furlough so he could find out whether the baby his wife had just delivered was a boy or girl and how she was, fell—shot through both lungs. His body had to be left behind as Early's men ran, as if guided by some homing instinct, until they dropped exhausted into the positions on Fisher's Hill they had left less than twenty-four hours before.

Respectful federal soldiers moved Ramseur to Sheridan's headquarters, and surgeons did what they could to save him. To his cot came Custer, the North Carolinian's friend from their years together as cadets. But Ramseur died, and in a way his passing marked the end of the 1864 Shenandoah Valley campaign.

Obviously, Sheridan had won it; why Jubal Early had lost it would be left for historians to debate. But General Lee, whose idea the venture had been back in mid-June, could look upon the results with satisfaction mixed, of course, with sorrow for the men lost. Early had not only given Washington a good scare; he had attracted 40,000 federal troops northward and kept them there, and those achievements may have enabled the rest of the Army of Northern Virginia to survive this long.

"Run! Go after them!" Little Phil had cried to his men as they exploited the breakthrough at Cedar Creek. "We've got the Goddamnedest twist on them you ever saw!"

So, in words a little more presidential, candidate Abraham Lincoln might have urged all speakers campaigning for him. The Union armies' string of victories from Atlanta's seizure early in September through Cedar Creek had "peace" Democrats reeling. And General-in-Chief U. S. Grant added "twist" by deciding to allow soldiers to vote. "They have as much right to demand that their votes shall be counted in the choice of their rulers as those citizens who remain at home," he wrote in reply to a question put to him by Secretary of War Stanton. "Nay, more [right], for they have sacrificed more for their country."

Grant left untouched several other questions Stanton's had prompted. For which candidate would the soldiers vote? How likely was it that granting this privilege would boomerang and provide the margin that defeated Lincoln? And what then?

Through letters and newspapers the men in blue could learn that the nearer election day came, the nastier the political campaign was getting. Some Republicans accused Democrats of treason. The pro-Democrat, pro-peace Columbus, Ohio, *Crisis* engaged in news slanting; it reported Early's morning victory at Cedar Creek and left the story there, and also professed disbelief that Sherman really had control over Atlanta. More direct was another midwestern newspaper's editorial attack on the administration's credibility, one headed: "Abolition Lies—Lincoln's Stock in Trade:

> Lincoln is to be hurrahed through the campaign. The war fervor is to be raised to fever heat and the people to be again fooled into voting for Lincoln, and more war, and more ruin.· Victories are to be shouted over that never were gained, and the telligraph to be used for the purpose of aiding Abolition by magnificent achievements.

The Democrats' desperation increased. "Abe the widow-maker," Lincoln was called, and also "Abraham Africanus the First." Worse, some alleged that Republicans favored miscegenation.

Early November brought an end to demagoguery. Lincoln won 212 electoral votes, McClellan only 21. While the influence of soldiers' absentee ballots was obscured by the fact that only twelve states reported them as such, analyses of their combined popular votes showed that 78 percent of the warriors endorsed Abraham Lincoln, while only 53 percent of the civilians in those states preferred him to Little Mac.

Chapter 37

Liberal Foraging in Georgia

For most of October, Cump Sherman had been waiting for the go-ahead signal for his much-debated march to the Atlantic coast. There was little doubt that General-in-Chief Grant favored such an operation—in the spring he had sent Sherman a map with a jagged line drawn across Georgia from Atlanta to the sea—but, among many other things, Grant was worried about John Hood's army.

After striking the Western & Atlantic Railroad at points as far northward as Dalton, Hood moved westward in mid-October to Gadsden, Alabama. While his troops rested, he worked out a plan for sweeping up into Tennessee, capturing the huge federal supply base at Nashville, then pressing on to central Kentucky. From there he could threaten cities such as Cincinnati on the Ohio River and recruit. All this done, Hood might either send reinforcements to General Lee's army at Petersburg or advance that way and strike Grant's Army of the Potomac in its rear.

And Sherman's armies? Well, Nathan Bedford Forrest was drawing part of George Thomas's command to Nashville. Schofield was on his way back to Knoxville. The 62,000 federals Sherman had at Atlanta, Hood seemed to assume, would operate in Georgia, but his own 40,000 Confederates ought to be able to handle Thomas's or Schofield's fragments.

Hood's army was over near Florence, in northwestern Alabama, by October's close, and this was no secret, which was one reason Grant held Sherman at Atlanta for as long as he did. Was another his concern over the presidential election? This would never be clear, but by November 2 Grant felt easy enough to wire Sherman: "Go on, then, as you propose."

That was to leave Hood for Thomas's army in Nashville to deal with; to abandon the W & A Railroad; to burn Atlanta, and then live off the land all the way eastward across Georgia to salt water—to do what the general-in-chief had specified:

> You will no doubt clean the country where you go of railroad tracks and supplies. I would also move every wagon, horse, mule and hoof of stock as well as the Negroes.

For Hood time was of the essence; anything that delayed his forces' northward advance would enable George Thomas to gather more and more troops at Nashville and to fortify the place. Hood needed Forrest's cavalry to screen the march, but in late October the Wizard was raiding in central Tennessee, and he could not be recalled right away.

Johnsonville, a supply depot on the Tennessee River about sixty miles west of Nashville, was Forrest's objective; but instead of heading for it directly, he decided to isolate it. North of there, upstream, he placed artillery at Fort Heiman (opposite Fort Henry) and Paris Landing, roughly five miles to the south, creating a trap for federal ships using the river.

First to become a victim of Forrest's unusual tactics was the transport *Mazeppa*. After a few rounds from Confederate guns her crew abandoned her. The cavalrymen quickly unloaded the ship's supplies and moved them beyond the range of three Union gunboats attempting a rescue. The *Mazeppa*, damaged in the fight, had to be burned.

That was on October 29. On the thirtieth the transport *Anna* made the five-mile run with light damage, but Forrest's men captured the "tinclad" gunboat *Undine* and the transport *Venus*. Now the Wizard had a navy. After repairs he started his two-ship fleet southward for Johnsonville on November 1, with his mounted troopers moving along muddy roads on the Tennessee's west bank. But Yankee gunboats appeared the next day, and when the smoke cleared, the *Venus* was a federal ship once more.

By November 3 Forrest had artillery going into positions across the Tennessee from Johnsonville, and the *Undine* was taking hits from two Union gunboats sent out from the town's landing. The Confederate sailors decided they had rather continue the fight from horseback, ending Forrest's brief career as a naval commander but opening another one for him as an artillerist.

His target 800 yards across the river was an uncommonly attractive one. Before him on the morning of November 4 he could see three gunboats, eleven transports, and eighteen barges at the wharves. Workers, unaware of the Confederates' proximity, were transferring supplies from the transports to boxcars destined for Nashville. Warehouses were near the landing. Overlooking the scene, meant to protect the activity, was a fort atop a 100-foot hill. But the day was a pleasant one, the first in several, and ladies were coming down from town toward the steamers as if to board them for a trip somewhere.

Forrest changed their plans by timing the fire of all his guns so that their first volley would seem to have come from one enormous one, the rounds hitting the ships concurrently. They did, disabling the gunboats. The women fled back uphill. And despite heavy counterbattery fire from the hilltop fort, the Wizard and his gunners kept at their work until they had destroyed everything of military importance on the river's opposite bank, including a warehouse that went up in a peculiar blue flame, indicating that it had contained whiskey barrels.

Smoke drifting across the Tennessee's waters brought the aroma of burning bacon that night, adding surely to the wishes of Forrest's troopers that the river had been narrow enough to cross. But morning's light on November 5 revealed a supply depot in ruins, and Forrest headed southward. Soon he ran into couriers from Dick Taylor—and more rain. The Wizard hurried as much as he could to reach Hood, helping build rafts to ferry his men over swollen streams, leaving behind another example of military talent and versatility some historians would proclaim as the Confederacy's most overlooked asset.

William Tecumseh Sherman's greatest concern was that Grant or the authorities in Washington might withdraw their approval of his plans, so as soon as he learned that Lincoln had been reelected, he shut down the telegraph. He sent surplus supplies back to Chattanooga. Once everything of value was removed, he would torch the rebel factories and head for salt water.

The army would advance southeastward in two wings, each with two corps. Sherman would control Brigadier General Judson Kilpatrick's cavalry. There would be no general wagon trains, only those carrying ammunition and provisions, and each wing would march about fifteen miles every day. Living off the land required guidelines, so Sherman set them:

> The army will forage liberally on the country during the march. To this end, each brigade commander will organize a good and sufficient foraging party, under the command of one or more discreet officers, who will gather, near the route traveled, corn or forage of any kind, meat of any kind,

vegetables, corn-meal, or whatever needed by the command, aiming at all times to keep in the wagons at least ten days' provisions for his command, and three days' forage. Soldiers must not enter the dwellings of the inhabitants, or commit any trespass; but, during a halt or camp, they may be permitted to gather turnips, potatoes, and other vegetables, and to drive in stock in sight of the camp. To regular foraging parties must be intrusted the gathering of provisions and forage, at any distance from the road traveled.

To corps commanders alone is intrusted the power to destroy mills, houses, cotton-gins, etc.; and for them this general principle is laid down: In districts and neighborhoods where the army is unmolested, no destruction of such property should be permitted; but should guerrillas or bushwhackers molest our march, or should the inhabitants burn bridges, obstruct roads, or otherwise manifest local hostility, then army commanders should order and enforce a devastation more or less relentless, according to the measure of such hostility.

Having covered food and real property, public or private, General Sherman turned to other classes:

As for horses, mules, wagons, etc., belonging to the inhabitants, the cavalry and artillery may appropriate, freely and without limit, discriminating, however, between the rich who are usually hostile, and the poor and industrious, usually neutral or friendly....In all foraging, of whatever kind, the parties engaged will refrain from abusive or threatening language, and may, where the officer in command thinks proper, give written certificates of the facts, but no receipts; and they will endeavor to leave with each family a reasonable portion for their maintenance.

Negroes who are able-bodied and can be of service to the several columns may be taken along; but each army commander will bear in mind that the question of supplies is a very important one, and that his first duty is to see to those who bear arms.

So Sherman directed. And his orders for Atlanta's burning showed similar restraint. Only the industrial district was to be destroyed, and no fire lit until he was present. But on the night of November 15 the flames went their own way, and a smoke plume was rising from the city's ruins early the next morning when Cump

Sherman took a last look from a hill east of Atlanta and set his 62,000 unopposed men in motion toward the sea.

Spurring General Hood was the opportunity he saw in mid-November to whip first John Schofield's 30,000-man force and then maul the one George Thomas was assembling at Nashville. But even to begin to do this Hood had to move northeastward to Columbia, Tennessee, on the Duck River's south bank, roughly halfway between Nashville and Schofield's camps at Pulaski.

Wet and freezing weather swept across the region earlier than usual that November, holding Hood's troops near Florence until the twentieth. Forrest's cavalry, 6,000 sabers strong now, provided a screen for three Confederate columns on that many roads as the Army of Tennessee finally marched northward.

Schofield, at Pulaski, discovered Hood's movement on the twenty-second and saw it for what it was: an attempt to cut his force off from Thomas's growing concentration eighty miles or so to the north. Schofield quickly got his divisions into the race for the two bridges over the Duck River at Columbia. But he had a turnpike and only 35 miles to march, while Hood was obliged to use poor roads and to cover roughly 100 miles. Hood's former West Point roommate won the race, of course, quenching the Confederate general's hope either for a double victory or for keeping the federal elements separated. Schofield held south of the Duck River for a time, then moved to the northern bank and destroyed the bridges.

Blocked now, Hood invoked the spirit of Thomas J. Jackson. On the morning of November 29 he sent Forrest's cavalry around Schofield's eastern flank, herding Union horsemen before him, then Ben Cheatham's corps and A. P. Stewart's behind him to ford the Duck and finish a wide envelopment of Schofield's line while Stephen D. Lee's corps held the federals near Columbia. By mid-afternoon Cheatham's corps was near enough to Forrest's troopers for Hood to try to take Spring Hill. This would give him both the turnpike northward and a second chance to cut Schofield off from Nashville. Seizing Franklin, twelve miles away, would give Hood control of the bridges over the Harpeth River north of the town. And only twenty miles or so north of Franklin was Nashville.

Cavalry skirmishing, however, alerted Schofield to what his classmate was doing early enough for him to send a corps from Columbia via the turnpike twelve miles up to Spring Hill. This force, with the rest of Schofield's army following it, arrived in time to hold both the town and the road against several determined Confederate attacks.

By sunset on November 29 Forrest's troopers had all but run out

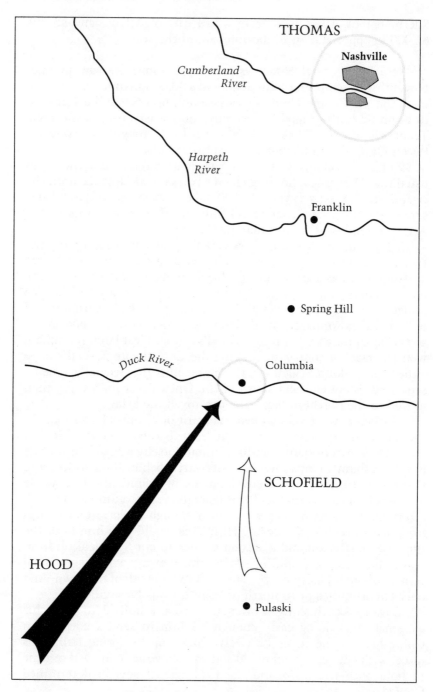

Hood's Advance to Nashville

of ammunition, and Hood's infantry was up and fighting, so the Wizard led his riders a few miles north of Spring Hill on back roads to Thompson's Station, where he replenished his supply by attacking a small federal garrison. Then he moved on, not knowing that he was leaving behind him a development east of Spring Hill that no one would ever fully understand: Hood and the forces with him went to sleep, and Schofield marched his entire army past them, all the way to Franklin.

General Hood was furious the next morning. So were his subordinates, and the bickering eroded the morale of men in the ranks—men who had marched far more than 100 miles. Some were barefoot, yet they would trudge on northward that day through early snow, on the turnpike now, headed for Franklin, only to see when they got there that the federals had spent the time building a line from the western bank of a horseshoe bend in the Harpeth River to the eastern one.

It may have been lingering fury that blinded Hood when he paused a few miles south of Franklin in midafternoon on the thirtieth and scanned Schofield's hastily dug fortifications, for he gave orders for a massive frontal assault. Any of his corps commanders could have pointed out to him that the artillery was not up, the hour was late, the troops exhausted. Ben Cheatham protested and was squelched. "Give me one strong division with my cavalry," Forrest said, "and within two hours I can flank the Federals from their works."

The Wizard's suggestion was Jacksonian, but Hood rejected it. "We will make the fight," he had said when first he saw Schofield's line, and make the fight he was still determined to do. Better here than at Nashville, Hood explained, where the Yankees had been fortifying the ground for three years.

Hood's forces surged straight ahead, yelling, rushing northward with hardly any artillery support, breaking through at one point, holding the gap gallantly but in vain, finally backing off as Schofield's men counterattacked. Hood, having launched his forces, added nothing more to the battle. From his distant vantage point he could not even see it through the low-lying gun smoke. About all he would learn the next day was that he owned a federally deserted burying ground on which he had lost about half his generals and field-grade officers and at least 6,200 men. Among the dead was Patrick Cleburne, shot through the heart after two horses had been killed under him.

Hood could have taken Franklin without the loss of a man or horse if only he had restrained his compulsion to attack. Before he drew near Franklin, Schofield had issued orders for a withdrawal that night, wiring Thomas: "I have no doubt Forrest will be in my rear tomorrow, or doing some greater mischief."

Of course, Hood had no way of knowing that. But he had not listened to those who gave him reasons for waiting: Stephen Lee and two of his divisions were still hours to the south, almost all the guns were with Lee, and Forrest's cavalry could flank Schofield out of his positions. Why, then, had Hood insisted on making the fight? A clue was in his order congratulating the survivors: "While we lament the loss of many gallant officers and brave men, we have shown to our countrymen that we can carry any position occupied by our enemy."

Well, yes. But there were only two differences between Franklin and Cold Harbor. This time Southerners had been cut down in appalling numbers, and the defenders had given up the killing ground after showing that they could hold it.

But John Hood wasted no time on grim comparisons. He sent Forrest northward to screen the Confederate advance to Thomas's lines at Nashville. And there the Wizard beheld fortifications extending for miles, both flanks anchored on the Cumberland's banks, the lines manned by two or possibly three times as many troops as Hood still had.

Now General Hood was trapped by his success in reaching Nashville. If he attacked, he would sacrifice what was left of his army. And if he moved on northeastward, the federal forces he had expected to defeat would be right behind him.

Sherman's burning of Atlanta, decided a British authority on the laws of war half a century later, was fully justified because the city had been "specialized for war." And little fault could posterity find in Cump's orders for the conduct of his troops during their march to the sea. Even so, soon after that movement began, the editor of the *Macon Telegraph* declared:

> It would seem as if in [Sherman] all the attributes of man were merged in the enormities of the demon, as if Heaven intended in him to manifest depths of depravity yet untouched by a fallen race....Unsated still in his demoniac vengeance he sweeps over the country like a simoom of destruction.

No simoom had the march seemed on November 16 when Cump's 62,000 men moved eastward from the plume of smoke rising from Atlanta's lingering fires. As directed, the army split into a wing under Oliver O. Howard's command that would take a route south of the other one, led by Henry W. Slocum and accompanied by

Sherman. Howard would threaten Macon to the south of his wing's course while Slocum menaced Augusta to his north. At times, the outer edges of the army's halves would be eighty miles apart; the forces would converge at Savannah.

But within a few days the officially proclaimed restraints faded from the memories of soldiers sent on foraging parties. By noon, usually, wagons were filled. This left hours that troops spent roaming around the countryside in search of more food—and excitement. There was an air of carnival about it, as though the march were a gigantic game of hide-and-seek. And as more and more families buried valuables, seeking turned into looting, and otherwise decent men degenerated into "bummers."

Years afterward, a major from Indiana described the return of some adventurers:

> At the head of the procession...an ancient family carriage, drawn by a goat, a cow with a bell, and a jackass. Tied behind...a sheep and a calf, the vehicle loaded down with pumpkins, chickens, cabbages, guinea fowls, carrots, turkeys, onions, squashes, a shoat, sorghum, a looking-glass, an Italian harp, sweetmeats, a peacock, a rocking chair, a gourd, a bass viol, sweet potatoes, a cradle, dried peaches, honey, a baby carriage, peach brandy and every other imaginable thing a lot of fool soldiers could take in their heads to bring away.

Whether the peacock, the harp, and a cradle made Georgia's countryside "specialized for war," few officers seemed to care. Nor did it matter that the foragers left tons of fresh food on roadsides to rot while countless women and children were left to endure a winter with nothing to eat.

"War is cruelty," Sherman had declared to Atlanta's mayor, "and you cannot refine it." Some of his bummers added emphasis one day by stopping a funeral procession, taking away the blind mule pulling a wagon in which there was a child's casket and leaving it to a sixteen-year-old girl and women who joined her to tug and push the burden three more miles to the cemetery.

Of course there were many instances of federal soldiers' compassion and pity. But the more shocking an example to the contrary was, the better were its chances of surviving into the Great Remembering. "I don't war on women and children," Cump Sherman would say. But, posterity would ask, was he blind?

"We have five times as many generals here as we want," Chief of

Staff Halleck had declared while Early's divisions were within sight of the Capitol's unfinished dome, and so must Confederate Generals Bragg, Beauregard, Hardee, Taylor, and G. W. Smith have thought when they reached Georgia: Hood had all the troops with him except for Joe Wheeler's 3,500 or so cavalrymen and untrained militia and home-guard units.

Dick Taylor predicted that Macon would be bypassed, and he advised against wasting nigh-nonexistent manpower in any futile attempts to stop the federal cyclone—in vain. G. W. Smith collected about 3,700 males above and below conscription age and put them under the command of militia Brigadier General P. J. Phillips. Avoid battle at all costs, ordered Smith, then he turned his mind to logistics.

Such was the background for the clash that occurred on November 22 near Griswoldville, nine miles northeast of Macon. Phillips, spotting a Yankee force he thought smaller than his own, decided to attack. Whether it was his reputed fondness for the bottle or ignorance or stubbornness that made Phillips do it, three times he ordered his randomly armed, utterly green troops to charge Oliver Howard's véterans, whose only problem was, as it turned out, getting timely resupplies of ammunition for their new Spencer repeating rifles.

There was no military art applied at Griswoldville. For the 1,500 federals it was an unusual kind of target practice. What drove the Confederates can only be imagined: fury at the Yankees' depredations? A chance to follow the examples set by Southerners of military age? Fear of what would happen to more of their women if they failed?

"Old grey haired and weakly looking men and little boys, not over 15 years old, lay dead or writhing in pain," wrote a federal officer who went out to inspect the field where 600 or more Georgians had fallen. And he added: "I hope we will never have to shoot at such men again."

At Milledgeville the next afternoon, troops from Slocum's wing were spreading throughout the city while some officers were staging a mock session in the state's capitol. At the rostrum was cavalry leader Judson Kilpatrick; many of those in the assembly's chamber, suffering from "bourbon fits," passed out before he declared:

> I must confess that my fellows are very inquisitive...if perchance they discover a deserted cellar, believing that it was kindly left for their use by the considerate owner, they take charge of it [and] they look after the plate and other

little matters.

Not so comic was what was happening elsewhere in Georgia's statehouse. Rampaging soldiers amused themselves by throwing books out of windows; outside, the hoofs of a rider's horse pounded volumes looters had not grabbed. A major was tempted to take some law books, but he resisted it. "I should feel ashamed of myself every time I saw one of them in my book case at home," he wrote. "I don't object to stealing horses, mules, niggers and all such *little things*, but I will not engage in plundering and destroying public libraries."

State archives had been moved to the insane asylum a few miles outside Milledgeville before Sherman's men arrived. At the last moment the secretary of state had taken Georgia's great seal home and buried it while his wife wrapped important documents; those they planted in their pigpen, then fled.

Earlier, Governor Joseph Brown had nearly emptied the local penitentiary of male prisoners by offering them pardons if they would join the state's militia. Left-behind women convicts set fire to the building and escaped, one of them finding her way to a federal regiment where (someone reported) she plied "an ancient trade."

Sherman and his officers confined burning in Milledgeville to the arsenal, but its explosion could do little more damage to nearby churches than his soldiers had done. Sunday services at St. Stephen's Episcopal Church, for example, were conducted only in words because the organ had been destroyed by molasses poured over it.

By then, though, Sherman's bummers were gone, looting and burning their way toward Savannah, wrecking the railroad, but accumulating more slaves in their wake than the commanding general desired. "The Angel of the Lord," some adoring blacks called him, the man who "rules the world!"

But Cump remembered the complexities of slavery from his prewar years in the South, and he used every opportunity to urge preachers and other leaders among the blacks to persuade their people to stay behind. While he meant to make Georgia howl, he recognized that his sweep was raising the liberated slaves' expectations excessively. He could not take all 25,000 or so of them along; either they or his men might starve, and his first duty was to his troops. Seldom in a war so ironic in so many instances had there been a situation to equal this one: Cump had made effective the Emancipation Proclamation, but he could not finish what Lincoln—and before him, generations of abolitionists—had started.

Tragedy was inevitable. It began on December 3 when the corps commanded by Major General Jefferson C. Davis approached the pontoon bridge over Ebenezer Creek, swollen by recent rain, roughly thirty-five miles west of Savannah. Davis, once satisfied that the 500 or more former slaves on the west bank were not in the way of his rear guard, rode eastward. Then engineers cut away the pontoon bridge, stranding the wailing blacks, leaving them to the mercy of Confederate cavalrymen chasing the column.

Into the swirling water many of the newly freed surged, only to be swept away to drown. Some crossed on improvised rafts. Union engineers, appalled by the deaths their action was causing, plunged in to save as many blacks as they could.

"War is cruelty," General Sherman had said weeks before. And he did not flinch from ordering Confederate captives to clear the road ahead of "torpedoes," shells buried so near the surface any pressure would explode them. "I don't care a damn if you're blown up," he told a rebel who protested that he had nothing to do with planting the devices. "I'll not have my own men killed like this."

Soon, though, having shown how cruel war could be, General Sherman's wings reached the coastal rice country, a region much less rich in resources available for plunder but one so near Savannah no blue-clad soldier cared greatly. Gone now, in early December, was the holiday spirit. Cump's troops were finally running into real resistance backed by artillery. And there, almost within sight of salt water, the army paused.

Similarly, and only a little earlier, John Hood's forces had come to the end of their march northward from Florence, only to find George Thomas's fortifications blocking them from taking Nashville. During December's first week Hood settled his troops along the hills south of the long federal line and told them to start digging. His only course of action, he saw, was to lure Thomas into attacking him; yet he could not be sure Old Pap would, remembering that it was as a defender the Rock of Chickamauga had won his fame and that a Thomas-led rifleman's skill had cost him a leg.

Hood was crippled in another way now, for more and more deserters were heading home. He had about 24,000 troops left in his four-mile line south of Nashville, down from 38,000 two weeks earlier, when he had left Florence. And back in early May, at Resaca, General Joe Johnston had been issuing rations to an Army of Tennessee numbering more than 64,000.

Numbers had been on George Thomas's mind all along—his counts of horses as well as of troops—but he had also been counting down the days he might have left in command. General-in-Chief Grant had prompted Thomas's anxiety as early as December 2, when he wired:

If Hood is permitted to remain quietly about Nashville, we will lose all the roads back to Chattanooga, and possibly have to abandon the line of the Tennessee river. Should he attack you it is all well, but if he does not, you should attack him before he fortifies.

Old Pap did not know it, but Grant's prod was prompted by one he had received from Secretary of War Edwin Stanton:

The President feels solicitous about the disposition of Thomas to lay in fortifications for an indefinite period, "until Wilson gets equipment." This looks like the McClellan and Rosecrans strategy of do nothing, and let the enemy raid the country. The President wishes you to consider the matter.

By equipment Stanton must have meant horses, aware as he surely was that Brigadier General James Wilson had 12,000 men ready to serve as Thomas's cavalry arm but only 5,000 mounts. Yet this was merely a detail. Far more significant was the coercion being applied from 600 or more miles to the east by men who may have been wondering if the Virginia-born Thomas, a "galvanized Yankee," could be trusted to destroy Hood's army.

Thomas's opinion of his situation was not sought, but he gave it in replying to Grant:

We can get neither reinforcements nor equipments at this great distance from the North very easily, and it must be remembered that my command was made up of the two weakest corps of General Sherman's army, and all the dismounted cavalry except one brigade, and the task of reorganizing and equipping has met with many delays, which enabled Hood to take advantage of my crippled condition. I earnestly hope, however, in a few more days I shall be able to give him a fight.

True, even understated, but not what the Union's war managers wanted to be told. Not a word had they heard from Sherman in nearly three weeks. Hardly a dent could Grant make in Lee's thirty-five miles of fortifications. And not since Sheridan drove Jubal Early away from Cedar Creek in October had readers of Northern newspapers found much to reassure them. And there were fundamental differences between the on-scene commander and the general-in-chief. Slow, methodical, stubborn Thomas was, while Grant had earned his third star by hitting hard, hitting often, and keeping on hitting. This was reflected in the way Grant reacted to Old Pap's reply. On December 5 he directed Thomas to attack at once. The next day he repeated the order, making it peremptory, adding: "There is great danger in delay resulting in a campaign back to the Ohio."

On December 8, Grant wired Chief of Staff Halleck to prepare orders relieving Thomas and replacing him with John Schofield. In Washington, Old Brains balked, warning:

> If you wish General Thomas relieved, give the order. No one here will, I think, interfere. The responsibility, however, will be yours, as no one here, as far as I am concerned, wishes General Thomas removed.

That night, perhaps with reports of Forrest's movements in mind, Grant made a final attempt to budge the Rock:

> It looks to me evidently the enemy are trying to cross the Cumberland, and are scattered. Why not attack at once?...Now is one of the fairest opportunities of destroying one of the three armies of the enemy. If destroyed he can never replace it; use the means at your command, and you can do this, and cause a rejoicing from one end of the land to the other.

In response, George Thomas chose words that seemed to dare Grant to let the guillotine's blade fall on his neck:

> I can only say in further extenuation, why I have not attacked Hood, that I could not concentrate my troops, and get their transportation in order, in shorter time than has been done, and am satisfied that I have made every effort to complete the task.

That done, Thomas turned to young cavalryman James Wilson. "The Washington authorities treat me like a schoolboy," he said, "but if they'll let me alone I'll lick them yet." Old Pap probably meant he would lick Hood's forces, though he could be pardoned if his ambiguity was intentional.

On the next day, December 9, Grant told Halleck to let the angled blade fall. War Department clerks prepared the papers. But again Halleck asked Grant "if you still wish these orders telegraphed to Nashville." Replied the general-in-chief:

I am very unwilling to do injustice to an officer who has done so much good service as General Thomas has, however, and will therefore suspend the order relieving him, until it is seen whether he will do anything.

Now Halleck warned Thomas that only by moving immediately could he save himself from Grant's impatience. To the chief of staff Thomas explained that he had done all within his power in the time spent, ending: "And if he should order me relieved I will submit without a murmur."

And to Grant, Thomas wired:

I have nearly completed my preparations to attack the enemy tomorrow morning, but a terrible storm of freezing rain has come on today, which will make it impossible for our men to fight to any advantage. I am, therefore, compelled to wait for the storm to break and make the attack immediately after.

The general-in-chief, shot back on December 11:

If you delay attacking longer, the mortifying spectacle will be witnessed of a rebel army moving for the Ohio, and you will be forced to act, accepting such weather as you find.

As Thomas read those words, the countryside over which his troops would have to move was sheathed in ice so thick General Hood's troops could not stab through it even with stout knives so that they might continue their digging, which was all they had been doing and all that their commander could order done. Yet the federal lieutenant general had fresh orders prepared for Thomas's relief, and he started Major General John A. Logan toward Nashville to deliver the documents.

Not content with this arrangement, apparently, Grant went to Washington on December 14. He was about to go on out to Nashville on the night of the fifteenth, presumably to supervise Thomas's successor and make certain he obeyed orders to attack Hood, when word reached the War Department's telegraph room that George Thomas had won a great victory.

"I guess," said Grant, "we will not go to Nashville."

Hood—like all infantrymen in any war, knowing that the question of being hit was not *if* but *when*, and whose own wounds begged another: *how seriously*—was not greatly surprised when

Thomas attacked as soon as the fog lifted on the morning of December 15. This was the first half-decent day for a fight in nearly a week. And between ice storms and quick thaws creating seas of mud, the Army of Tennessee's commander may have felt he was as ready as he would ever be.

Erratic weather had prevented Hood from getting as many trenches as he wanted dug to protect his western flank. Most of the cavalry Forrest had left behind, led by Brigadier General James Chalmers, would be operating beyond and north of that end of his four-mile line. A. P. Stewart's corps, like the rest hardly a division in strength, Hood had placed in the uncompleted dugouts on the westernmost hills. Stephen Lee's corps held the center; Ben Cheatham's, the eastern segment.

The first federal blow came against Cheatham and Lee, a demonstration Thomas had ordered that turned into much more than that: Colored regiments and converted quartermaster troops struck the eastern end of Hood's line as if determined to show Old Pap that they were first-rate soldiers. With two of his corps pinned in place, General Hood could only watch as Wilson's Union cavalry beat back Chalmers's and three strong federal corps assaulted A. P. Stewart's men. It was remarkable that Hood's forces could keep fighting until sundown.

But Thomas's victory was not complete. Two miles to the south were the Brentwood Hills, terrain on which Hood could fight again the next day. Overnight Hood redistributed his weaknesses. He shifted Cheatham's corps to the western end of his new, much more compact line. Stewart slid into the center. Stephen Lee had the easternmost portion to defend.

Shy's Hill, Cheatham's on the west, required him to put his divisions in lines forming an angle that proved vulnerable to federal artillery fire that could and did rake both legs of it early on the sixteenth while Wilson's Yankee cavalry swept into the defenders' rear. And again the former quartermasters and the colored regiments went beyond their orders, attacking until they had driven Stephen Lee's troops from Overton Hill.

Now, after more than three years of bitter fighting and thousands of miles of hard marching with few victories to claim and annihilation facing it, many veterans in the Confederate Army of Tennessee surrendered, and the rest simply vanished. The few survivors of the two days' battles streamed southward, leaving it to Nathan Bedford Forrest to hurry westward from Murfreesboro to try to hold back Thomas's pursuit.

"Wilson," the victor shouted that night when he caught up with the cavalryman, "didn't I tell you we could lick 'em?"

For the patient, plodding, immovable Rock to show so much emotion was nigh unprecedented. But he had not merely whipped Hood; he had done something no other Union general had in close to four years of war: destroyed a Confederate army.

Some of the remnants of the Army of Tennessee headed for home. Even those who finally reached Tupelo were too fought out to be of much use, though 5,000 or so would be sent to the Carolinas eventually. General Hood asked to be relieved, and the president granted his request. Forrest's cavalry force—its ranks thinned, its mounts broken down—was about all that remained to carry on the war in the west.

Congratulations poured into Nashville from throughout the jubilant Union, though many had the smell of a secretary's or a staff officer's lamp about them. One exception was a wire from Grant to Thomas, sent on December 18:

> The armies operating against Richmond have fired two hundred guns in honor of your great victory. In all your operations we hear nothing of Forrest. Great precaution should be taken to prevent him crossing the Cumberland or Tennessee rivers below Eastport. After Hood is driven as far as it is possible to follow him, you want to occupy Decatur and all other abandoned points.

Pure Grant, still hectoring. Pure Sherman, too, and more welcome to George Thomas was the letter Cump sent him—from Savannah—on Christmas Day:

> I have heard of your operations on the 17th and I do not believe your own wife was more happy at the results than I was. Had any misfortune befallen you I should have reproached myself for taking away such a large proportion of the army and leaving you too weak to cope with Hood. But as events have turned out my judgment has been sustained, but I am nonetheless grateful to you, and to Schofield, and to all, for the very complete manner in which you have used up Hood....
>
> Here I am now in a magnificent house close by the old barracks around which cluster so many of our old memories of Rankin, and Ridgeley, and Frazer and others. But the old families we used to know are nearly all gone or dead. I will not stay here long, however, but push northwards as the season advances.
>
> The old live oaks are as beautiful as ever, and whilst you

are freezing to death in Tennessee we are basking in a warm
sun, and I fear I did you a personal injustice in leaving you
behind whilst I made my winter excursion. But next time I
will stay home and let you go it.

General Sherman had gotten to the magnificent mansion in
Savannah by waiting until the Confederates abandoned the city,
crossed a hastily constructed bridge into South Carolina, and then
cut it to pieces. By December 21 Sherman's men were in the town,
and their march to the sea was history.

Cump sent a brief message to President Lincoln: "I beg to
present to you as a Christmas gift the city of Savannah, with one
hundred fifty heavy guns and plenty of ammunition, and also about
25,000 bales of cotton."

And a little later, an officer brought a reply:

Many, many thanks for your Christmas gift—the city of
Savannah. When you were about to leave Atlanta for the
Atlantic coast, I was anxious, if not fearful; but feeling you
were the better judge, and remembering that "nothing
risked, nothing gained," I did not interfere. Now the undertaking being a success, the honor is all yours, for I believe
none of us went further than to acquiesce....But what next?
I guess it will be safe if I leave General Grant and yourself to
decide.

Pure Lincoln, this, but "what next" had been a wide-open
question when Sherman first heard from the general-in-chief.
Cump's anger rose as he read:

My idea now is that you establish a base on the sea-coast,
fortify and leave in it all your artillery and cavalry and
enough infantry to protect them....With the balance of your
command come here by water with all dispatch. Select,
yourself, the officer to leave in command, but I want you in
person.

So there it was: Grant saw himself unable to defeat Lee unless he
had his old western forces, led by officers such as Schofield and
Sherman, below Petersburg to help him. "[I] won't do it, goddam it!"
stormed Cump. "I'll not do anything of the kind!"

Scourging the Carolinas as he had Georgia was Sherman's
intention, leaving scars in them comparable to those swaths, some
scores of miles wide, his men had just stripped and burned from

Atlanta southeastward for nearly 300 miles. And this was something he could start right after he took Savannah. Hardee had 9,000 troops, maybe more, but not enough to cause any delay. But moving 50,000 men northward by sea? In Sherman's opinion it would take weeks merely to collect a hundred ships.

"Unless you see objections to this plan, which I cannot see," General Grant had added, "use every vessel coming to you for purposes of transportation." First assuring him that he would obey any orders, Sherman did object. And there the "what next" question rested, unanswered, when an Illinois cavalry unit sat down to its Christmas dinner: oyster soup, oysters on the half shell, roast goose, fried oysters, roast oysters, rice, raisins, coffee. "A little heavy on the oysters," wrote an officer, "but we don't complain."

And how was it in what was left of the Confederacy? Poet Stephen Vincent Benét, in *John Brown's Body*, said it best:

> But this is the last, this is the last,
> The last of the wine and the white corn
>   meal,
> The last high fiddle singing the reel,
> The last of the silk with the Paris label,
> The last blood-thoroughbred safe in the stable
> . . . .
> (This is the last, this is the last,
> Hurry, hurry, this is the last,
> Drink the wine before yours is spilled,
> Kiss the sweetheart before you're killed,
> . . . .
> There is no future, there is no past,
> There is only this hour and it goes fast,
> Hurry, hurry, this is the last,
> This is the last,
> This is the last!

Chapter 38

The Skinning of the Bear

As 1865 opened, Wilmington was not merely the last port on North Carolina's coast still open to blockade runners; it was the *only* one anywhere along the Confederacy's seaward frontier, which is why General-in-Chief Ulysses Grant wanted it taken out of the war. His plans, made mostly before 1864's election, called for the kind of operation that had proved successful at both New Orleans and Mobile: naval bombardment of a coastal fort and a landing by seaborne troops. In this instance, Rear Admiral David Dixon Porter would assemble a fleet to strike Fort Fisher, guarding the Cape Fear River's mouth. Political considerations at the time were such that Grant had to accept Major General Benjamin Butler as leader of the army's units.

"Beast" Butler's involvement nettled Grant, and so did an idea the fumbler advanced: filling an old steamer with tons of gunpowder, moving it against Fort Fisher's mile-long seaward wall, and blowing a gigantic hole through which federal troops could rush and mop up the rebel defenders. But Porter thought the attempt worth making, and Grant's respect for Porter was high, so the skeptical general-in-chief did not object.

Emboldened, Butler directed that the powder ship be modified to resemble a blockade runner. This delay vexed Grant at roughly the same time he was sending Thomas peremptory orders to attack Hood in one wire and trying to get him guillotined in the next. Stormy weather off the Atlantic coast added to his frustration. December's first two weeks, Horace Porter wrote later, were "the most anxious period of Grant's entire military career." Thomas's obliteration of Hood's army eased some of his tension. But unlike Sherman's Christmas present to Lincoln of Savannah, Butler's to

Grant was another fiasco. Fuzes set to ignite the powder ship's 215 tons of explosives hours before daylight on Christmas Eve worked, but Fort Fisher's wall remained untouched: Confederate sentries inside guessed the noise was merely a gunboat's boiler blowing up. Butler landed his 6,500 men, anyway; then he thought better of it and recalled them. Porter covered the withdrawal.

Grant howled for Butler's head, declaring that "the good of the service requires it," and the presidential election being history, down on the Massachusetts political general's neck came the slanted blade. Then, with Butler replaced by competent Major General Alfred H. Terry, Grant sent the task force back to try again. Porter and Terry struck Fort Fisher on January 15, and this time the federal effort succeeded.

Hurry, hurry, Grant had been saying all along. And now, frustrated only by Lee, his urgency was greater than ever, for he was determined that 1865's campaign would be the last.

General Robert Edward Lee recognized that it would have to be the last unless he somehow got replacements for the men he had lost—through casualties and desertions since the six-month stalemate began, and for the corps Jubal Early had taken away but could not return—plus fresh infusions of manpower that would enable him to keep extending his lines as Grant stretched his westward. Duty obliged Lee to request reinforcements; his assessment of the Confederacy's plight told him he would not, indeed could not, ever get them.

President Davis saw this as clearly as General Lee, and in his message to the Confederate Congress in November 1864 he said the unsayable: Black men, slaves, of military age would have to be brought into the army—even if only as cooks and teamsters—to relieve white men needed for combat.

This proposal was not Davis's or Lee's but the echo of one hard fighter Pat Cleburne had advanced in January 1864 after Grant's forces had shattered Braxton Bragg's army and driven it over Missionary Ridge to refuge at Dalton in northwest Georgia. Make soldiers out of slave men, Irish-born Cleburne suggested, and free them and their families. Unthinkable, he was told, and quickly. Davis flatly prohibited any discussion of Cleburne's idea and passed him over by naming the maimed John Hood to fill a then-vacant position as a corps commander.

Well, yes, but that was months in the past and many costly defeats ago. But neither Confederate congressmen nor newspaper editors were anywhere near ready to consider any tampering with the existing relationship between whites and blacks. To do so was to raise too many awkward questions—among them, whether the centralization of effort required for winning independence had become as great a menace to states' rights and individuals' control over their property as the old Union had seemed.

Now, when time was of the essence, with the future of his fast-dissolving nation at stake, Jefferson Davis had to face all of the complexities of the slavery issue his fellow native Kentuckian counterpart in Washington had been agonizing over for many years. What had been, the Confederate president knew, could no longer be. How to lead the embattled country into the most drastic of all internal social changes became his most critical, certainly his most vexing, problem.

Davis must have recognized as his critics tore at him that the Confederacy had been a thin eggshell from the very outset. Being left alone, free from any central government's coercion, had powered the seccession of Southern states. Anticipating invasion from the North, they had ringed their wagons to defend their right to deal with slavery as the people in each state saw fit and to keep from being told what to do by any politicians too distant to horsewhip.

The Southern people had been generous beyond imagining for four years in contributing to the effort to be left alone. For six months, though, the Confederate defense effort had seemed centered on keeping the Yankees out of a city—Richmond—which was fast becoming a meaningless symbol to citizens who would put up with only a minimum of local government.

Southerners would go on making sacrifices, but there was no escaping the irony. Now Jefferson Davis, who had declared Abraham Lincoln's Emancipation Proclamation and the Union's enlistment of black soldiers "the most execrable [actions] recorded in the history of guilty man," was proposing to do almost the very same things.

Yet Abraham Lincoln still had his share of problems with the slavery question, and though they were of a different sort, there was a risk that they could dismember the Union he had tried so hard, for so long, to preserve. At the heart of the matter was an antislavery amendment, the Thirteenth, which he wanted added to the Constitution. But Congress had proved balky, and not merely because of its earlier (and continuing) desire to obtain greater control over the conduct of the war.

All twelve previous amendments had dealt with the powers and functions of the federal government. But this Thirteenth entered new ground, reform of the nation's social fabric, and some legislators raised the very good question of how far the Constitution could be stretched to accommodate any special interests without ceasing to serve the fundamental purposes intended for the document by the Founders. Put briefly, in the opponents' view the proposed amendment might itself be found unconstitutional. And once the Constitution became flawed, where would challenges to its authority end?

What, really, would the Constitution become? The basic law of the land, as it had been understood to be since the Twelfth Amendment was ratified in 1804? Or the Constitution *plus* whatever else might be added to it?

President Lincoln held the moral high ground, and few in Congress opposed the Thirteenth Amendment's intent. It was primarily a dispute over methods. Lincoln had earlier relied on his wartime powers to advance emancipation. But after the war ended and those grants expired, he felt, there should be no turning back: hence, his eagerness to embed emancipation beyond the reach of posterity.

Yet Lincoln's timing made his pressure on Congress a potential mistake. The ratification process was the snag, for it required three-fourths of the states to accept an amendment. Enough of those loyal to the Union all along probably would approve. But what about the states in rebellion? How could he exclude them from the count without reversing his long-held position that they still belonged to the Union?

Preserving—restoring—the Union, Lincoln had declared often and eloquently, was his goal. Emancipation was a measure he had adopted slowly and more of a means to an end than an end in itself. But the war dragged on, and he wanted it won and behind him, and he was too impatient to linger over fine points of Constitutional law, so he used all of his political skills to get the lame-duck Congress to adopt the Thirteenth Amendment and start the ratification process.

By January 31, 1865, both houses had given Lincoln what he wanted. Now he had the full support of the abolitionists, and he could look forward to more of it from the next Congress, one that would be dominated by Republicans. He could do no more to make emancipation a heavy weapon. And, as from the beginning, the soldiers of the Union armies would have to create the conditions in which any political aims whatsoever could be achieved.

While Southerners attempted to think through Jefferson Davis's astonishing proposal regarding turning slaves into soldiers, Secretary of State Judah P. Benjamin launched one more effort to win diplomatic recognition and support. "What is the *policy* and what are the *purposes* of the *western powers of Europe* in relation to this contest?" he asked in a message to his representatives in Paris and London: What more did the Confederacy have to do to win their approval? And he added: "*No sacrifice* is too great, *save that* of honor."

Commissioners James M. Mason and John Slidell understood what "*no sacrifice* is too great" meant, and in diplomatic words they hinted to Napoleon III that ending slavery in the South was not excluded. See what the British think, the emperor of the French suggested. And in London the Confederates were told that they were two years too late.

Discouraging as this outcome may have been, at least two more blows were ahead for Jefferson Davis. One was Congress's enactment of a law making Robert E. Lee general-in-chief—an action amounting to a vote of no confidence in the President's ability to manage military operations: Lee, characteristically, assured his commander-in-chief that he would work with him as he always had. The other disappointment was the failure of a peace conference.

Old Francis Blair, Sr., had made his way through the lines from Washington to Richmond to try out the idea on Davis. The result was a meeting held on February 3 aboard the federal steamer *River Queen* in Hampton Roads. Lincoln was there, with Secretary of State William Seward. Davis sent Confederate vice president Alexander Stephens, president pro tem of the Senate Robert M. T. Hunter, and John A. Campbell from Alabama—back in 1861 a Supreme Court justice and at that time one of those Southern commissioners who had been assured by Premier Seward that Fort Sumter would be abandoned.

Perhaps the most remarkable thing about the Hampton Roads conference was that it occurred. Lincoln held all the winning cards, and the Southerners knew it. Predictably, nothing came of the discussions except a warning to Davis that a negotiated peace was no longer a possibility.

So, for both sides, it was still a matter for their armed forces to settle. General-in-Chief Lee responded by persuading Joe Johnston to assume command of the scant forces opposing the savaging of South Carolina by Sherman's bummers. And Lee went beyond that, committing his enormous prestige to an emphatic endorsement of his president's proposal regarding using slaves to win the war, writing:

> I think we must decide whether slavery shall be extinguished by our enemies and the slaves used against us, or use them ourselves at the risk of the effects which may be produced upon our social institutions. My own opinion is that we should employ them without delay.

And General Lee added that "the best means of securing the

efficiency and fidelity of this auxiliary force would be to accompany the measure with a well-digested plan of gradual and general emancipation."

"Grant has the bear by the hind leg," said Lincoln, "while Sherman takes off its hide." This was as apt a description of the military situation as any as February opened. The Army of the Potomac was holding Lee in his trenches while Cump took his bummers northward from Savannah into South Carolina.

At first, the terrain Sherman's men encountered was pro-Confederate, and once they were north of the swamps, food was hard to find. Soon looting gave way to burning; the Smoky March, it would be called, and arson was the crime bitter South Carolinians would remember longest. Entire villages vanished. General Sherman smiled as he read a message from cavalryman Judson Kilpatrick: "We have changed the name of Barnwell to Burnwell."

Sherman, his army advancing in two wings, left Charleston— bereft of up-country resources—to wither and die. His goal was the state's capital, Columbia, and his troops got there on February 17. Nine rebel generals had done nothing to defend the city. The mayor surrendered, hoping Columbia would be spared destruction. Withdrawing rebel soldiers set fire to some cotton bales and left behind great quantities of whiskey. Arriving federals tried to douse the flames; they were more successful in quenching their thirst.

For generations afterward Sherman would be blamed for what happened next, and he admitted that "several of the men were in liquor." Mainly, though, he claimed that "when night came, the high wind fanned [the cotton flames] again into full blaze, carried it against the frame-houses, which caught like tinder, and soon spread beyond our control."

Perhaps, but by morning of the eighteenth little remained of the city but charred stumps of trees, stark chimneys standing where homes had been, and small clusters of women and children in the streets amid the pitifully few possessions they had been able to bring out, watching smoke rise. "Though I never ordered [Columbia torched] and never wished it," Sherman wrote later, "I have never shed many tears over the event, because I believe it hastened what we all fought for, the end of the war."

Hurry, hurry, Cump seemed to be saying now that Columbia's ruins were behind him and North Carolina was not far away. His objective was Goldsboro; there he meant to link up with the federal corps John Schofield had brought from Nashville and to begin relying upon supplies arriving via salt water.

First on Inauguration Day's list of events was swearing in a new

Union vice president, Andrew Johnson, earlier governor of Tennessee. Johnson was treating a recurring malady with brandy in predecessor Hannibal Hamlin's Capitol office when summoned to the Senate chamber to take his oath of office and deliver a few minutes' remarks. But Andrew Johnson seemed compelled to orate first, and it was only after long-winded and nigh-incoherent harangue that persons near the rostrum shut him down for long enough—finally—to take the oath.

Outside the Capitol a crowd waited, most of them standing in mud, all of them impatient for the president to appear. When he did, applause was scant. So it remained during his uncommonly short address. "Both parties deprecated war," Lincoln said, "but one of them would rather *make* war than let the nation survive; and the other would *accept* war rather than let it perish." Slavery, he continued, was the war's basic cause. Yet he referred to the sufferings of the people North and South as divine punishment for the original sin. Lincoln concluded with these words:

> Fondly do we hope—fervently do we pray—that this mighty scourge of war may speedily pass away. Yet, if God Wills that it continue, until all the wealth piled by the bondsman's two hundred and fifty years of unrequited toil shall be sunk, and until every drop of blood drawn with the lash, shall be paid by another drawn with the sword, as was said three thousand years ago, so still it must be said "the judgments of the Lord are true and righteous altogether."
>
> With malice toward none; with charity for all; with firmness in the right, as God gives us to see the right, let us strive on to finish the work we are in; to bind up the nation's wounds; to care for him who shall have borne the battle, and for his widow, and his orphan—to do all which may achieve and cherish a just, and a lasting peace, among ourselves, and with all nations.

Sunshine brightened the otherwise gloomy scene as Chief Justice Salmon P. Chase administered the oath of office and Abraham Lincoln leaned down to kiss the opened page of the ceremonial Bible. And, on March 3, this may have seemed an entirely auspicious omen.

Auspicious for the North, certainly; but what message had Abraham Lincoln meant to convey to his countrymen in the South? Were "malice toward none" and "charity for all" signals that he would let the erring sisters return fearless of retribution, that caring for the survivors would have no geographic bounds?

If so, they did not seem to have much impact. Uncounted thousands of Southerners had already decided they would have to rely upon themselves and their land to survive. Many families wrote to their soldiers: Bring your rifle and come home.

By early March, as General Lee rode Traveller along the thirty-five miles of trenches stretching from east of Richmond far west of Petersburg, he heard more and more officers tell him about high desertion rates. Perhaps the only comfort he could find in such reports was that if hundreds were leaving, thousands were staying. But beyond taking military measures to discourage the homeward treks, about all he could do was warn the politicians in Richmond that the army defending the seat of government was melting away night by night.

From the recently appointed general-in-chief's viewpoint it was a blessing that the troops remaining were not aware of the overall situation. There in Petersburg's trenches Lee had about 35,000 infantrymen—hardly any mounted cavalry—facing an estimated 150,000 well-equipped, well-fed federals. Grant would have another 20,000 soon, now that Sheridan's riders had broken Jubal Early's last defense at Waynesboro and dispersed the remnants of Jackson's old corps, and Thomas could send 30,000 more east. Down in North Carolina, Joe Johnston was assembling forces from Mississippi and Charleston and all the other places he could call upon. At best, though, he would have only 15,000 men fit to use in trying to delay Sherman's and Schofield's 80,000 sweeping northward to join Grant.

By Lee's most optimistic calculations he might have 65,000 men if he could slip out of the Petersburg trenches and combine his army and Johnston's before Grant could react. But even if President Davis would agree to give up Richmond, which appeared very unlikely, sooner or later this concentrated Confederate army would have to deal with roughly 280,000 federal troops. And as if being outnumbered in some climactic battle by more than four to one were not discouraging enough, General Lee had no assurance his already half starved men could be supplied for much longer no matter what he decided to do.

Jefferson Davis told Lee that Richmond must be held to the last, and that ended consideration of military alternatives. Earlier and briefly there had been a chance that Lee and Grant might meet and work something out. But Abraham Lincoln had squelched that, telling Grant that peace was a political matter reserved for the president alone to handle. And so it was that both native Kentuckians left it to their armies' commanders to fight the war out, wherever it stood, to the very end of it.

This is the last, this is the last, General Joe Johnston seemed to have realized when on the way to Charlotte he wired Lee: "It is too late." But, stout soldier he still was, by the second week in March he began to be more hopeful. His forces were assembling near Raleigh, and Joe Wheeler's cavalrymen were reporting that Sherman's separated columns were being delayed by heavy rains that sent streams out of their banks and reduced roads to quagmires. Something, he decided, might yet be done.

It was to strike Slocum's wing of the federal army as it approached a complex of swollen streams near Averasboro. On March 16, Hardee's 11,000 fought all day in heavy rain, with Yankees outnumbering them two to one. That fight was a costly draw. But, Hardee could report, for the first time since Atlanta, Sherman's advance had been checked—for a day.

Goldsboro was Sherman's objective, Wade Hampton's cavalry scouts told Johnston, and the federal columns were still miles apart. About halfway between Averasboro and Goldsboro was Bentonville. Concentrate there, he ordered, then he devised the kind of trap Forrest might have set. Hampton's riders would lure Slocum's advancing troops into it, then the jaws would close, and the Confederates would charge; and after wrecking Slocum, they would attack Howard's wing of Sherman's army. Joe Johnston's plan was classic. But he had forgotten, certainly he underweighted, the risk inherent in trying to combine his approaching forces on a battlefield.

William Hardee was late, too late for his jaw of the trap to close. But when he got there, he added his troops to the fight, including his sixteen-year-old son, who would be among the dead when it ended. There was no shortage of leaders: Johnston of course, but also Braxton Bragg and Stewart and eclipsed Harvey Hill and Stephen Lee, who had brought the remnants of Hood's army all the way to North Carolina from Mississippi. But on March 19, at Bentonville, Johnston's men had fought with uncommon fury. They were still in place the next morning to protect the evacuation of nearly 1,700 wounded over the last bridge left over a stream to his rear.

Sherman might have smashed Johnston on the twentieth, but his mind was on reaching Goldsboro, where he could link up with Schofield, resupply and refit his men, and give his weary troops some rest. In fifty days or so he had led them northward from Savannah almost 400 miles without breaks except to forage and burn. And in contrast to Johnston, who could think only of defeating pieces of his enemy's army, Sherman was anxious to annihilate the entire Confederate force.

Emancipation of slaves who might serve in the army was a

subject the Confederate Congress proved unable to handle. On March 13 they authorized the formation of armed black units, but added: "Nothing in this act shall be construed to authorize a change in the relation which the said slaves shall bear toward their owners." Jefferson Davis and General Lee, among other Southerners, may have wondered why the lawgivers bothered to do anything at all. But the president, who had nothing to lose at this point, risked justifying charges that he was a dictator by declaring in General Order No. 14:

> No slave will be accepted as a recruit unless with his own consent and with the approbation of his master by a written instrument conferring, as far as he may, the rights of a freedman.

But four months had passed since first Davis suggested the unsuggestable; nine months, since Petersburg's stalemate began. And in those miles and miles of ever-emptying trenches, there was the realization that there was only this hour, and it was going fast. General Lee knew it, and in the third week of March he committed his Army of Northern Virginia's hard core to seizing a federal strong point called Fort Stedman.

He gave the task to John Gordon. Before dawn on March 25, Gordon's men struck, surprising the Yankees, driving them back, opening the kind of gap federal Brigadier General Emory Upton had created months ago up at Spotsylvania's Mule Shoe. But George Meade's Union artillerymen concentrated the fire of their guns on the Confederates making the breakthrough, pounding Gordon's men, obliging General Lee to call his troops back. And that other fighter, Grant, sensed that Lee had stripped his trenches to make the attempt. The federal commander quickly ordered a general assault everywhere along nearly forty miles of lines. At day's end Lee had lost 4,000 men; Grant, 2,000. Nothing at all had changed except for 6,000 or more families North and South left to wonder, as they grieved, why their loved ones had to be victims of this monstrous madness at the very time so many seemed to feel the war was almost over.

So may Abraham Lincoln have wondered the next day as he rode a horse among fresh-killed bodies near Fort Stedman and watched the wounded being carried toward field hospitals near his general-in-chief's headquarters at City Point. He had brought his wife and Tad down from Washington on the steamer *River Queen*, arriving the evening before. During the predawn hours on the twenty-fifth the president had been awakened by sounds of heavy gunfire not far away. Now that he saw in the faces of dead men—some blue-clad and others in butternut rags—what war is meant to do and so recently had done, it would not be at all surprising if so sensitive a man as Lincoln had recalled something Thomas Jefferson had said. That was, more or less, "I tremble for my country when I recall that God is just."

Yet so might Jefferson Davis have thought had he been in that saddle there that morning. Or General Lee, whose fault the Fort Stedman attempt had been, or any of the troop leaders or politicians on both sides whose failures had led so far to the deaths of roughly half a million young American men. There was plenty of guilt, centuries of it. But how much higher must the price go to pay for the original sin?

Lincoln had hoped the war was nearer its end, hoped also he could be there to see it end—which was one reason he had come down. And maybe it was almost over. So General Grant said, and Sherman, too. Sherman's presence at City Point was a surprise; he had come there by steamer from North Carolina to work out the details of joining forces for crushing Lee. Go back, the president had urged Sherman, hurry, hurry, and finish the last of the work.

General Sheridan was there, too; rather, he had passed through City Point after bringing his cavalry eastward from Lynchburg and north of Richmond, moving over the battlefields where Lee had whipped McClellan nearly three years ago. But Grant wanted Sheridan's troopers over on the west end of the miles of trenches, and Little Phil had hurried westward.

Now, at long last, Ulysses Grant seemed to be focusing the full power of the Union's military force on Lee's army. Yet the busy general-in-chief was scheduling troop reviews in the president's honor. That was all right, or it would have been if Mary Todd Lincoln had remained aboard the *River Queen*.

Apparently Mrs. Lincoln had never gotten over the incident during another trip, back in the spring of 1863, when she had stayed behind while her husband attended a party where (son Tad reported) the vivacious young Princess Salm-Salm had kissed the president. Here at City Point she found that several generals' wives were also visiting. Mrs. Lincoln's first display of her intense jealousy came when she heard that her husband may have been alone briefly with Mrs. Charles Griffin. Worse by far was the scene Mary Lincoln created when, riding with Julia Grant in an ambulance wagon approaching a parade's reviewing party, she spotted Mrs. E. O. C. Ord on a horse beside the president's mount. Seeing the other women arriving, Mrs. Ord rode over to join them. There she caught the blast of the First Lady's harshest invective. And afterward, during a dinner party the Lincolns held for the Grants and members of his staff, Mary Lincoln humiliated her husband by attacking him repeatedly in front of their guests. One of them recalled long afterward:

> [Lincoln] called her "mother," with his old-time plainness; he pleaded with eyes and tones, and attempted to palliate the offenses of others, till she turned on him like a tigress; and then he walked away, hiding that noble, ugly face that we might not catch the full expression of its misery.

Reviews over, a frosty truce between Julia Grant and Mary Lincoln prevailing, the general-in-chief got on with the war. With Sherman's army likely to arrive within another two weeks, all Grant needed to do was wait. But he had the capability to whip Lee, and he decided to use it. He quietly issued orders for the kind of maneuver he had employed in May and June: a slide around Lee's western flank, to return the fighting to open country. In so doing, Grant would seize the last of the railroads still supplying Lee's troops and Richmond. And in countering this effort Lee would have to thin his lines, thus making a Union breakthrough inevitable.

While entertaining his distinguished visitor in the last week of March, Grant moved Gouverneur Warren's V Corps and A. A. Humphreys's II out to join Sheridan's cavalry. This maneuvering force alone, 50,000 strong, outnumbered all of the Confederates Lee had in close to forty miles of trenches.

Reports of federal activity did not surprise General Lee. For weeks he had realized that if the war was to continue—and it would have to, for the president had removed surrender from the list of options—the fighting must be on different ground, in country too far west or southwest of Richmond for the city to be protected. The only questions open were whether Lee or Grant initiated that move and when.

Now Grant was answering the first question, forcing Lee to decide when he would begin to withdraw, or put another way, how much more time he could give the quartermasters to transfer rations and fodder for the worn-out animals to points along the escape route and the politicians to ship essential government property (including the treasury) westward. Each hour of delay would have to be paid for by Lee's half-starved men in the long lines of trenches. And there was the possibility that federals would settle the timing question by breaking through.

But Lee had to do something about Sheridan's presence out beyond the western end of the Confederate defenses. On March 27 he added some troops to George Pickett's desertion-depleted division and sent it and about 4,200 cavalry under Fitzhugh Lee to the threatened area. Lee's orders called for this 10,600-man force to protect the flank by attacking.

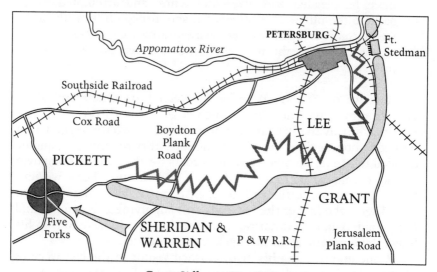

Grant Sidles to Five Forks

Such a response was the best the army's commander could make. Still more feeble was the execution. At first, Fitz Lee and Pickett blundered about in Wilderness-like terrain, but by April 1 they were concentrated at Five Forks, a strategically important point and one General Lee had ordered held "at all hazards." That afternoon, though, Pickett and Fitz Lee took advantage of a lull in federal pressure to ride a few miles over to cavalryman Tom Rosser's camp for a ritual tidewater Virginians relished: a shad bake. And in their absence Phil Sheridan and Warren wrecked the defenders left behind at Five Forks.

On that Saturday evening, General Lee reacted to the few details he had about the disaster by wiring Longstreet to bring Major General Charles Field's 4,600-man division westward from southeast of Richmond. Lee had earlier warned Davis that he might be obliged to save the escape route by weakening the eastern lines. Now he was doing precisely that.

General Longstreet reached Lee's headquarters house at four o'clock the next morning, Sunday, April 2, and soon A. P. Hill joined them. They were talking in the army commander's bedroom when an aide brought news that the federals had broken the lines. Lee rushed from his bed to the front door. He saw a line of troops advancing toward the house, but in the fog and faint light he could not determine whether their uniforms were blue or gray. Blue, they proved.

Powell Hill, realizing his corps was the one penetrated, mounted and galloped away, with Sergeant G. W. Tucker following him. Longstreet rode eastward to hurry Field's most advanced unit, then approaching Petersburg. Lee dressed, strapped on his sword, and called for Traveller.

From a nearby hilltop Lee looked southward at the blue-clad masses. Arriving riders told him what had happened. The Union predawn assault had been general, but Horatio Wright's VI Corps had done the critical damage. Wright lost roughly 1,100 men in fifteen minutes, but he opened a gap, swept westward in the rear of A. P. Hill's trenches and scattered the defenders, then turned to chase some of them toward Petersburg. Federals striking Gordon's corps overran his front initially; now he was counterattacking—successfully, so far. About 1,000 yards southwest of Petersburg Fort Gregg's garrison was holding on.

So matters stood when Sergeant Tucker, the courier who had galloped off with Powell Hill, returned. He was riding Hill's dappled gray horse, leading his own. Hill and the courier had come upon two of Wright's stragglers; refusing the general's order to surrender, they shot him. "He is at rest now," said General Lee, "and we who are left are the ones to suffer."

Mrs. Hill was in Petersburg. Go to her, Lee asked Tucker and an aide, and break the news as gently as possible. They need not have wondered how they might. "The General's dead," she told them. "You would not be here unless he was dead."

The Yankee skirmish line General Lee had seen earlier had backed away from his headquarters. He returned to the house and got orders moving on the telegraph and by courier. Among the last messages he sent was this one, to Secretary of War John C. Breckinridge:

> I see no prospect of doing more than holding our position here till night. I am not certain I can do that. If I can I shall withdraw to-night north of the Appomattox [River], and, if possible, it will be better to withdraw the whole line to-night from James River [southeast of Richmond]....Our only chance, then, of concentrating our forces, is to do so near Danville railroad, which I shall endeavor to do at once. I

advise that all preparation be made for leaving Richmond to-night.

About an hour later Jefferson Davis was sitting alone in his pew at St. Paul's—Varina and the children had left on Friday, after she had sold many of their belongings—when the sexton tiptoed down the aisle and handed the president a note: "General Lee telegraphs that he can hold his position no longer. Come to the office immediately. Breckinridge."

As quietly as possible, Davis left. Before the service ended, the sexton had handed notes to several more key officials, and they, too, departed.

By then General Lee was outside his headquarters directing the fire of some Napoleon guns at the federals massing south of there. As he was leaving the house a Union artillery round had barely missed him; now the building was in flames. A little later, a wounded gunner told the Yankee who had captured him and had asked who the old man on the gray horse was: "General Robert E. Lee, sir, and he was the last man to leave these guns."

Lee had headed Traveller eastward to Petersburg. Once in reach of telegraph lines again, he and Colonel Walter Taylor, the chief of staff, refined the withdrawal orders sent that morning, designating the routes each column should take as it marched westward, setting eight P.M. as the time for the movement to begin, specifying Amelia Court House—forty miles or so to the southwest, on the railroad to Danville—as the next point of concentration. But messages came in as well, one of them in reply to the many warnings he had sent the president:

> To move tonight will involve the loss of many valuables, both for the want of time to pack and of transportation. Arrangements are progressing, and unless you otherwise advise, the start will be made.

For the first time in nearly twenty-four utterly devastating hours, General Lee's poise gave way to anger. He tore the message to pieces. "I am sure," he said, "I gave him sufficient notice."

Yet he replied with restraint:

> I think it is absolutely necessary that we should abandon our position tonight. I have given all necessary orders on the subject to the troops, and the operation, though difficult, I hope will be performed successfully.

Through the midday and early afternoon hours of Sunday, April

2, though, General Lee had kept an anxious eye on Fort Gregg and its smaller neighbor, Fort Whitworth, the only places Confederates were still resisting outside Petersburg's inner defense lines. These outposts were about all that was left of what had been almost forty miles of outer fortifications. When they fell, Lee expected, Grant would launch his massed Army of the Potomac's corps in a crushing, vengeance-seeking assault on what was left of the Army of Northern Virginia.

Inside Fort Gregg it was as though every one of the 214 men there shared the spirit of the man who had been the last to leave the Napoleon guns earlier that Sunday. They had been asked to provide two hours; they gave three, during which shell explosions splintered logs in the fort's barricades, sending sharp wooden spears into gunners' bodies as they fired canister point-blank at the 8,000 blue-clads who were about to sweep over Fort Gregg's pitifully few infantrymen.

The Yankees poured into the fort, some dying as bayonets pierced them, others dodging bricks the Confederates threw at them and rifle butts swung at their skulls. "Shoot and be damned!" a gunner told the federals warning him not to fire. He fired and fell, his body riddled.

Chapter 39

Appomattox

General Grant's advantage was that he was nineteen miles nearer Burkeville, a key point on Lee's escape route, than Lee. There was no point in pursuing the whipped Confederates; it would be far easier to head them off. At a minimum this would prevent Lee from joining his depleted forces with those of Joe Johnston. At best, beating Lee to Burkeville might be all it would take to force Lee to surrender.

Why Burkeville? Well, that was where Lee's Richmond and Danville Railroad and the federally dominated Southside (from Petersburg) crossed. If Lee got southwest of Burkeville first, he would be in a region from which he could draw at least some food supplies. And feeding his army and his animals, Grant may have concluded from what he had seen of the condition of prisoners and dead horses earlier that Sunday, might be more important to Lee than any other consideration.

Ulysses Grant knew he had won and that now it was only a matter of time—which was on his side. That Sunday morning (possibly as Jefferson Davis was leaving his pew at St. Paul's in Richmond), he scribbled a short note to his wife:

> I am now writing from far inside what was the Rebel fortifications this morning but what are ours now. They are exceedingly strong and I wonder at the success of our troops carrying them by storm. But they did do it, and without any great loss. We have captured about 12,000 prisoners and 50 pieces of artillery. As I write this news comes of the capture of 1,000 more prisoners. Altogether this has been one of the greatest victories of the war. Greatest because it is over what the Rebels have always regarded as their most invincible

army and the one used for defence of their Capitol. We may have some more hard work but I hope not. Love and kisses for you and Jess.

Robert E. Lee had no chance to send any message to his wife, doomed to remain in doomed Richmond while her soldier was withdrawing his men from the city's last defensive positions. Yet Mary Anne Randolph Custis Lee might have smiled with approval had she known of another decision her husband made.

Down in Petersburg, and after he had sent all the orders General Lee had to give, young Colonel Walter Taylor asked the army commander for permission to go to Richmond that night and marry Betsy Saunders, with the understanding that he would be back in the morning. What could have been more astonishing to Lee than this request, coming as it did on a day in which he had sent Powell Hill's wife the worst of all possible news, witnessed the loss of an entire corps and all the vital ground it had held, rejected the president's appeal for more time, and—as Taylor knew better than any other staff officer—had ordered the most distasteful of any warrior's courses of actions, a retreat?

Even so, General Lee said to Taylor: "Go on."

Richmond, Walter Taylor discovered, was falling apart. The departures of Davis and other senior government officials from the churches had stunned the congregations. When they gathered outside, one young woman recalled:

There was little discussion of events. People meeting each other on the streets would exchange silent hand clasps and pass on. I saw many pale faces and trembling lips, but I heard no expression of fear. Movement was everywhere, nowhere panic.

By midafternoon the news had spread. An officer on his way from church to rejoin his command wrote:

Bundles, trunks, and boxes were brought out of houses....Vehicles of every sort and description, and a stream of pedestrians with knapsacks or bundles filled the streets which led out from the western side.

Ladies stood in doorways or wandered restlessly about the streets, asking every passerby for the latest news. All formality was laid aside...all felt the more closely drawn together.

Government officials packed their most important papers, preparing to take a train westward late that night. Though it was Sunday, banks opened so that depositors could get their now-worthless money. Gold was all that meant anything; someone offered a thousand dollars in the rare metal for a horse.

But as the hours passed, desperation increased. A man ran down West Main Street shouting that the government commissary was open for anyone wanting food; the crowd responding became a mob. Looting broke out. A girl living across the street from the house where Walter Taylor was soon to be married wrote:

> People were running about everywhere with plunder and provisions. Barrels and boxes were rolled and tumbled about the streets....Barrels of liquor were broken open and the gutters ran with whisky and molasses. There were plenty of straggling soldiers who had had too much whisky. Rough women had it plentifully, and many Negroes were drunk. The air was filled with yells, curses, cries of distress, and horrid songs.

Inevitably, fires dotted the city, some set by order of officials to prevent Yankee seizure of warehoused commodities. Admiral Raphael Semmes destroyed the last of the Confederate navy; the city rocked as powder magazines from gunboats exploded. The house next to Mrs. Lee's was burning, and a church across the street was in flames, but she refused to leave.

At around eleven o'clock that night President Davis and members of his cabinet assembled at the depot and boarded their special train. After it came another carrying the Confederate Treasury's boxes of gold and silver coins and ingots—half a million dollars' worth, the only money the government had for continuing the war after the trains reached Danville.

Midnight came, and shortly thereafter, in a house on West Main, the rector of St. Paul's pronounced Walter Taylor and Betsy Saunders man and wife. The girl living across the street who had witnessed the drunken mob's carousing and heard their "horrid songs" earlier was still at her window a little more than three hours later, sleepless, watching as the bridegroom and his new brother-in-law emerged, mounted their horses, and rode westward to rejoin General Lee.

At about that time—now it was Monday, April 3, though daylight was two hours off—Porter Alexander was in Richmond waiting for the last of his guns to arrive from the lines east of the city. Spotting abandoned goods blockade runners had brought in, he wrote, he helped himself:

First I took a fine English bridle. Next a nice, thick, felt contrivance to put under a saddle in place of a horse blanket. Last I looked over a big pile of beautiful English bacon-sides & picked out the biggest & prettiest....It proved our very salvation in the next two or three days, for we had left camp with very little on hand.

After sunrise, Alexander's forces gathered now and moving westward, he turned for "a last look at the old city for which we had fought so long & so hard." And he added:

I don't know that any moment in the whole war impressed me more deeply with all its stern realities than this. The whole river front seemed to be in flames, amid which occasional heavy explosions were heard, & the black smoke spreading & hanging over the city seemed to be full of dreadful portents. I rode on with a distinctly heavy heart & with a peculiar sort of feeling of orphanage.

"On to Richmond!" Horace Greeley had urged the Union in his *New York Tribune* after Fort Sumter's fall in April 1861, and on to Richmond Abraham Lincoln went on April 4, 1865—and for a time he rested in the chair Jefferson Davis had sat in for nearly four years. Lincoln had walked into the city, as had Union troops the day before, walked with Tad beside him for two miles from the James River landing up the hill. Crowds gathered as the news spread that he was in the city, but his only distress came when a black man knelt before him. And all he wanted, he said as he sat in the Confederate president's chair, was a glass of water.

Forgotten, now, was any weight Lincoln may have given the day before, Monday, April 3, to a message from alarmed Secretary of War Edwin Stanton:

Allow me respectfully to ask you to consider whether you ought to expose the nation to the consequences of any disaster to yourself in the pursuit of a treacherous and dangerous enemy like the rebel army....Commanding Generals are in the line of their duty running such risks. But is the political head of a nation in the same condition?

Survivors in the army that had mauled forces led by Irvin McDowell, George McClellan, John Pope, Ambrose Burnside, Joseph Hooker, and at times by George Meade and Grant seemed glad to be out of their miserable trenches and on the road again as they marched westward on April 3. General Lee, on Traveller, had watched them pass until around eleven o'clock on Sunday night, his *noche triste*, then he followed them into the darkness, away from the flames and explosions in lost Richmond.

At Amelia Court House, Lee expected, the provisions he had ordered sent there would be waiting. But when he arrived early on the morning of Tuesday, April 4, the day Lincoln would enter Richmond, all that Lee and his 30,000 desperately hungry men found stockpiled was artillery ammunition. That day and part of the next foraging parties swept the countryside. Most wagons returned empty. Worse, that day Lee learned that Sheridan's cavalry was entrenched along the Richmond and Danville Railroad roughly eight miles southwest of his camps.

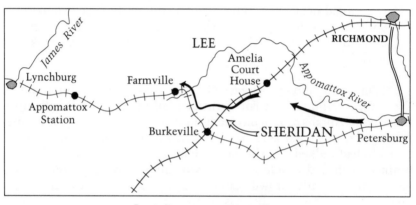

Lee's Retreat to Farmville

Gone now was Lee's hope of being able to follow the tracks southwestward to rations at Burkeville. But some were supposed to be at Farmville, twenty-six miles west of Amelia Court House, and he ordered a night march to reach them. That proved to be more than all his units could do. Trapped by federals in Sayler's Creek valley east of Farmville on Thursday, April 6, the 3,000 troops led by Dick Ewell—earlier, commander of Richmond's militia and home guard units—put up a brief fight and then melted. Again, mistakes had proliferated. Richard Anderson, following Longstreet's leading corps, lost contact with Old Pete's last company when he had to stop and beat off attacking Yankees, and he sent no word forward. This caused a gap, which the federals used in whipping Ewell, who had not communicated with John Gordon, whose brigade-size corps was the rear guard, fighting off Union assaults.

"My God!" said General Lee as from a ridge he gazed down into

Sayler's Creek valley where Ewell's men and Gordon's were, "has the army been dissolved?"

No, not quite. Many of Gordon's men made it up the ridge, as did most of Anderson's who had been engaged; and as tired as they were, they rallied when they saw the gray man on the gray horse holding a flagstaff and waving the Stars and Bars. And Longstreet's corps was safe. But on "Black Thursday," Philip Sheridan and the forces he directed captured Lieutenant General Ewell, two major generals, three brigadier generals—in all, perhaps 8,000 men. This Little Phil reported to Grant, adding: "If the thing is pressed I think Lee will surrender." And not long afterward would come an echo to Grant, a message from Abraham Lincoln: "Let the *thing* be pressed."

The first of Longstreet's troops reached Farmville early the next morning, Friday, the seventh, and this time they found the food they had been marching and fighting to reach since Sunday night. General Lee had thought that—with the Appomattox River behind him and the bridges over it destroyed, his men might have a day in which to draw rations and get some rest before pressing on. Not so. Mouth-watering aromas were just beginning to rise from cookfires when the army commander had to order his starving troops to go out and to block "those people" who had crossed the river despite the burning of High Bridge.

Lee's orders had been to burn both High Bridge *and* a lower wagon bridge near it. But half of anything now seemed about all that any Confederate troops could do. The neglected wagon span and fords had been all the rampaging Yankees needed. Lee was furious when he found out about this failure. Recalled a witness: "He spoke of the blunder with a warmth and impatience which served to show how great a repression he ordinarily exercised over his feelings."

So Lee pressed on from Farmville, doomed to march farther away from any chance of linking his forces with Joe Johnston's, compelled now, as he had been since Sunday night, to keep moving toward food. His axis of advance was the Southside Railroad leading westward to Lynchburg. This was the last railroad of any significant value to the Confederacy, but federals on its tracks south of Farmville obliged Lee to lead his men along country roads toward the Southside's Appomattox Station during Black Thursday's night and Friday morning, April 7.

Sheridan, too, was headed for Appomattox Station, bent on intercepting eight trains bringing rations to General Lee's army. This was the last of the races the Army of Northern Virginia's commander would run, and he would lose it.

To anyone looking at a map of Grant's Appomattox campaign

afterward, it would seem that he had been using Sheridan like a sheepdog to get ahead of Lee and keep turning the Confederates northwestward, away from the railroad to Danville, while Meade and Ord supported Little Phil's cavalrymen and snapped at the rebels' flank and rear guard. And so it may have been. But this was no simple thing to do. Grant was maneuvering 80,000 troops in unfamiliar terrain; weather was often rainy, making mud lakes of roads and filling streams; and supply problems might become serious unless crews converting the Southside's tracks to the slightly narrower federal gauge from Petersburg westward worked faster.

Even so, by Friday afternoon on April 7, Grant was on the front porch of a house in Farmville watching his troops march by. To him the night before had come a doctor related to Dick Ewell, who had been captured at Sayler's Creek. According to staff officer Horace Porter, the visitor told Grant:

> Ewell had said in conversation that their cause was lost when [Grant] crossed the James River, and he considered that it was the duty of the authorities to negotiate for peace then, while they still had a right to claim concessions, adding that now they were not in condition to claim anything. He said that for every man killed after this somebody would be responsible, and it would be little better than murder. He could not tell what General Lee would do, but he hoped he would at once surrender his army.

Grant may have been thinking about that on the Farmville hotel's porch that Friday afternoon. Sending for paper and a pen, Grant wrote Lee:

> The results of the past week must convince you of the hopelessness of further resistance on the part of the Army of Northern Virginia in this struggle. I feel that it is so, and regard it as my duty to shift from myself the responsibility of any further effusion of blood by asking of you the surrender of that portion of the Confederate states army known as the Army of Northern Virginia.

General Lee was at Cumberland Church, three miles or so to the north of Farmville, on the night of April 7 when a courier brought him the message from Grant. Lee read it quietly, then passed it to Longstreet: "Not yet," Old Pete advised.

Lee said nothing. Instead, he wrote a reply to Grant:

I have recd your note of this date. Though not entertaining
the opinion you express of the hopelessness of further
resistance on the part of the Army of N. Va.—I reciprocate
your desire to avoid useless effusion of blood, & therefore
before considering your proposition, ask the terms you will
offer on condition of its surrender

Not bothering to correct punctuation or invite the opinion of
Longstreet or anyone else, General Lee got his response on its way to
Farmville. Not yet, he may have agreed. But he had only to look at
the roadside to realize how little hope still remained: Many of his
men had thrown away their weapons and empty knapsacks and were
likely to stay there until the Yankees came by and took them
prisoner.

Such was the destructiveness of starvation coupled with exhaustion. Lee's troops had been marching for five days and nights, with
hardly a break except for skirmishing or fighting. Since leaving the
Petersburg lines on Sunday night—famished even then—they had
covered more than sixty miles. Hardly any of the men had gotten
anywhere near the rations at Farmville, and none were to be had east
of Appomattox Station, still twenty-eight miles away. Yet on toward
hoped-for rations Lee sent his ammunition wagons and some of the
last of the guns that Friday night. If the men could get enough food
and rest at Appomattox Station, he might still reach Danville and
possibly Joe Johnston's forces; if not, if Grant blocked the way
southwestward, he could only follow the Southside Railroad toward
trains bringing provisions eastward from Lynchburg.

Through Saturday's sunshine the march went on. As Lee was
resting that afternoon, he learned that a number of his generals felt
that further resistance was futile, the implication being that they
would take the responsibility for advising surrender if that would
spare him humiliation. Angrily he rejected the idea. "Evidently,"
wrote Porter Alexander, who was not involved in the proposal, "Lee
preferred to himself take the whole responsibility of surrender, as he
had always taken that of his battles, whatever their issue, entirely
alone."

On Saturday night General Lee received a delayed letter in a
sealed envelope from Ulysses Grant:

Your note of last evening in reply to mine of same date,
asking the condition on which I would accept the surrender
of the Army of Northern Virginia is received. In reply I
would say that peace being my great desire, there is but one
condition I would insist upon, namely, that the men and

officers surrendered shall be disqualified from taking up arms again against the government of the United States until properly exchanged. I will meet you, or will designate officers to meet any officers you may name for the same purpose at any point agreeable to you for the purpose of arranging definitely the terms upon which the surrender of the Army of Northern Virginia will be received.

General Lee had meant to explore peace everywhere when he had written his response to Grant's first message, or so it seemed from the reply he now sent:

I recd at a late hour your note of today. In mine of yesterday I did not intend to propose the surrender of the Army of N. Va.—but to ask the terms of your proposition. To be frank, I do not think the emergency has arisen to call for the surrender of this Army, but as the restoration of peace should be the sole object of all, I desired to know whether your proposals would lead to that and I cannot therefore meet you with a view to surrender the Army of N. Va.—but as far as your proposal may affect the C. S. forces under my command & tend to the restoration of peace, I shall be pleased to meet you at 10 A.M. tomorrow on the old stage road to Richmond between the picket lines of the two armies.

Tomorrow would be Sunday, April 9. But on this Saturday night General Lee's westernmost troops were still a few miles from Appomattox Station, and he was issuing orders to attack and close the distance to rations. Even as he did, though, the men still with the Army of Northern Virginia could look up at the clouds and see in them, to their front and southern flank and rear, the orange reflection of Yankee campfires.

Early on Sunday morning Lee called Porter Alexander to him and said, "Well, we have come to the Junction, and they seem to be here ahead of us. What have we got to do today?"

If Lee saw fit to "try and cut our way out," replied the young artilleryman, "my command would do as well as they have ever done." Too few men left, the army commander pointed out. Then Alexander offered an alternative to surrender: Let each man, with his arms, report to the governor of his state and let the governors decide whether to continue the war.

This appeared to Lee to be guerrilla warfare. Calmly, with his usual courtesy (wrote Alexander later), he explained his views:

We must consider its effect on the country as a whole. Already it is demoralized by four years of war. If I took your advice, the men would be without rations and under no control of officers. They would be compelled to rob and steal in order to live. They would become mere bands of marauders, and the enemy's cavalry would pursue them and overrun many wide sections they may never have occasion to visit. We would bring on a state of affairs it would take the country years to recover from.

"I had not a single word to say in reply," Alexander would recall. "He had answered my suggestion from a plane so far above it, that I was ashamed of having made it."

So everything depended on the attempt to reach the rations. To General Lee came terse news from John Gordon: "I have fought my corps to a frazzle, and I fear I can do nothing unless I am heavily supported by Longstreet's corps."

Impossible: Longstreet was holding back two federal corps in Lee's rear. "Then," said Lee, immaculately dressed in his finest uniform and wearing his best sword, "there is nothing left for me to do but go and see General Grant, and I would rather die a thousand deaths."

General Grant was not at the meeting place at 10:00 A.M. The night before, he had been disappointed by Lee's reply, and he was suffering from a blinding headache, so he had postponed any further action in the matter until Sunday morning. But he did send Lee a message:

Your note of yesterday is received. As I have no authority to treat on the subject of peace the meeting proposed for 10 A.M. today could lead to no good. I will state, however, General, that I am equally anxious for peace with yourself, and the whole North entertains the same feeling. The terms upon which peace can be had are well understood. By the South laying down their arms they will hasten that most desirable event, save thousands of human lives, and hundreds of millions of property not yet destroyed. Seriously hoping that all our difficulties may be settled without loss of another life, I subscribe myself, etc.

That done, Grant got on with the day's work. He was on his way to visit Sheridan when a courier caught up with him and handed him a letter from Lee:

I received your note of this morning on the picket line, whither I had come to meet you and ascertain definitely what terms were embraced in your proposal of yesterday with reference to the surrender of this army. I now ask an interview in accordance with the offer contained in your letter of yesterday for that purpose.

There remained one message to send. Grant wrote to Lee:

Your note of this date is but this moment (11:50 A.M.) received, in consequence of my having passed from the Richmond and Lynchburg roads to the Farmville and Lynchburg road. I am writing this about four miles west of Walker's Church, and will push forward to the front for the purpose of meeting you. Notice sent to me on this road where you wish the interview to take place will meet me.

Colonel Orville Babcock departed to deliver the letter to Lee, but he paused when he saw Sheridan, who was furious because a halt in the fighting had been called. "Damn them," he told Babcock, "I wish they had held out an hour longer and I would have whipped hell out of them." Little Phil raised a clenched fist. "I've got 'em like that!"

Starvation had brought General Lee's remnants so close to Appomattox Station, yet hunger was also on the minds of many of the federal troops who had not had their breakfast when they were ordered up to stem the Confederates' attack on Palm Sunday morning, April 9, 1864. One Union officer, gazing at the rebel line, thought there might be more battle flags out there than soldiers. He had the strange feeling that the rebels' ground had blossomed with a great row of poppies and roses.

Then the federals saw a gray-clad rider bearing a flag of truce toward Sheridan, and firing died away, and the rumor spread that Grant and Lee were going to settle the whole thing. Historian Bruce Catton commented:

Yet the fact of peace and no more killing and an open road home seems to have been too big to grasp, right at the moment, and in the enormous silence that lay upon the field men remembered that they had marched far and were very tired, and they wondered when the wagon trains would come up with the rations.

There was much irony in this, even more in what happened to

Virginian Wilbur McLean. Having allowed Generals Johnston and Beauregard to use his house a few miles east of Manassas as a temporary headquarters back in July 1861 and then having seen it destroyed by federal gunfire on the day of the war's first major battle, McLean had moved his family to a place so far from the fighting he thought danger could not follow, to the little village called Appomattox Court House. Now, almost four years later, the war had caught up with him.

To Wilbur McLean came Colonel Walter Marshall, sent by Lee to select an appropriate place for the dreaded but inevitable meeting with Grant. McLean showed Marshall an empty building first, which the colonel rejected. Curiously, McLean did not suggest either the courthouse or a brick tavern nearby. But he did offer his own house; Marshall accepted, then ordered Sergeant G. W. Tucker, who had seen Powell Hill killed, to bring General Lee and Union Colonel Babcock to McLean's home.

Around midday on that Palm Sunday, General Lee dismounted and handed Traveller's reins to Tucker, who led the gray horse over to graze on McLean's lawn. Inside the house the Army of Northern Virginia's commander found a parlor more comfortably furnished than any he had seen in many a month. Apart from a sofa and other things a war-spared family might be expected to have, there were two chairs, each with a table by it. Lee took the chair farthest from the room's entrance. Marshall, his only aide, and Colonel Babcock sat down and remained silent.

No one would ever know what Robert Edward Lee was thinking as he waited for Grant to arrive. He was fifty-eight now, a soldier for forty of his years, husband, father, a man whose entire life had been driven by duty. This, he may have realized, was the last.

"His specialty," a tutor had said of Lee decades earlier, "was *finishing up.* He imparted a finish and a neatness, as he proceeded, to everything he undertook." Would Lee, could he, get through this afternoon's challenge? Or, waiting, was he wishing he had given in to an earlier temptation? Watching the fight at daybreak, he had said, "How easily I could be rid of this, and be at rest! I have only to ride along that line and all will be over!" Then he added: "But it is our duty to live. What will become of the women and children of the South if we are not here to protect them?"

Finally, after about half an hour, the clatter of riders dismounting outside and the clump of boots on McLean's front steps broke Sunday's calm. General Grant came into the parlor, his plain uniform splattered with mud, feeling ashamed of his appearance because he was "afraid Lee might think I meant to show him studied discourtesy by so coming."

General Lee rose and shook hands with Grant, and soon they were talking about the only other time they had met, in Mexico. "Our conversation grew so pleasant," Grant recalled many years later, "that I almost forgot the object of our meeting."

But Grant gave a signal for other Union officers to enter the room, and he presented them to Lee. After the handshaking the two commanders sat down, each with a small marble-topped table by his chair, and after a little more reminiscing Lee said, "I suppose, General Grant, the object of our present meeting is fully understood."

Discussion of terms followed, leading to Grant's calling for his order book, lighting his pipe, and wondering what to write. Inspiration came. Grant showed the product to Lee, who covered his emotion by taking out his glasses and wiping the lenses with his handkerchief before he read the document that would determine the fate of the army he had led for so long:

> In accordance with the substance of my letter to you of the 8th instant, I propose to receive the surrender of the Army of Northern Virginia on the following terms, to wit: Rolls of all the officers and men to be made in duplicate, one copy to be given to an officer to be designated by me, the other to be retained by such officer or officers as you may designate. The officers to give their individual paroles not to take up arms against the Government of the United States until properly exchanged; and each company or regimental commander to sign a like parole for the men of their commands. The arms, artillery and public property to be parked and stacked, and turned over to the officers appointed by me to receive them. This will not embrace the side-arms of the officers, nor their private horses or baggage. This done, each officer and man will be allowed to return to his home, not to be disturbed by U. S. authority so long as they observe their paroles and the laws in force where they may reside.

"This will have a very happy effect on my army," said Lee as he returned the text to General Grant. And well may he have made such a comment, for Grant's closing sentence was in effect amnesty, assurance that they would not be prosecuted for treason. But there was one problem, and Lee raised it.

Horses used by cavalrymen and artillerymen were soldiers' property, not the Confederate government's. "I will instruct the officers I shall appoint to receive the paroles," said Grant, "to let all the men who claim to own a horse or mule to take the animals home with them to work their little farms."

General Lee was pleased and said so, adding that this would go far "toward conciliating our people." Curious, his choice of words: "our people," not "*my* people" or the South. It was as though he were already accepting the notion that the Union was whole again, though he knew it could not be until all commanders of Confederate forces followed his example.

While Grant's aide made copies of the surrender document and Colonel Marshall prepared Lee's letter of acceptance, talk turned to current conditions. Lee asked if he might return the 1,000 or so federal prisoners he was holding; he could not feed them because the trains he had expected from Lynchburg had not arrived. Yes, replied Grant, tactfully not telling Lee that the trains had been captured and offering to provide rations to Lee's army. Would 25,000 be enough? Lee could only say yes, "and it will be a great relief, I assure you."

General Lee signed his acceptance letter with no sign of emotion, then rose, bowed to the officers standing along the wall, and walked out. On the porch other officers snapped to attention and saluted. Lee saluted in return, walked down the steps, and waited for Sergeant Tucker to replace Traveller's bridle. From the browband Lee pulled out his warhorse's gray forelock, parted it, smoothed it. He mounted. Now he could see General Grant standing on McLean's porch, his hat raised. Lee raised his, then nudged Traveller toward the last of his army's lines, riding out of history into legend.

General Grant and members of his staff departed soon thereafter, leaving behind them Sheridan and other officers, who cavorted for a while and then summoned a very nervous Wilbur McLean. As Colonel Porter described the scene in the parlor:

> Sheridan paid the proprietor twenty dollars in gold for the table on which General Grant wrote the terms of surrender, for the purpose of presenting it to Mrs. Custer, and handed it over to her dashing husband, who galloped off to camp bearing it upon his shoulder. Ord paid forty dollars for the table at which he sat, and afterward presented it to Mrs. Grant, who modestly declined it, and insisted that Mrs. Ord should be the possessor.

Lee's chair was claimed, and Grant's; a pair of brass candlesticks; an inkstand, the sofa, even a child's doll—the "silent witness." Added Porter: "Some mementos were carried off for which no coin of the republic was ever exchanged."

Outside, word spread quickly, and some eager artillerymen

began firing blanks in celebration. This Grant swiftly ordered stopped—in vain. A soldier in Meade's camp wrote:

> The air is black with [tossed-up] hats and boots, coats, knapsacks, shirts and cartridge boxes, blankets and shelter tents, canteens and haversacks. They fall on each other's necks and laugh and cry by turns. Huge, lumbering, bearded men embrace and kiss like schoolgirls, then dance and sing and shout, stand on their heads and play at leap-frog with each other....All the time, from the hills around, the deep-mouthed cannon give their harmless thunders, and at each hollow boom the vast concourse rings out its joy anew that the murderous shot and shell no longer follow the accustomed sound.

Bands played, no two of them the same song, no one caring, for all this noise and outpouring of emotion was powered by an idea so simple it was heartstopping: These men had lived, and they would go on living now, and gone suddenly was all fear.

Confederates expressed their feelings in a very different way. As the erect gray man on the gray horse came in sight, they got up and thronged around him, cheering at first, and then, seeing tears roll down his face, hushed. "General," someone said, "we'll fight 'em yet." But Lee rode on. "Men," he said as they crowded each other to get near enough to touch his legs or Traveller, "we have fought the war together, and I have done the best I could for you. You will all be paroled and go to your homes until exchanged."

His men pressed on until Lee reached a peach orchard, where they were turned away by troops determined to let the general have some privacy. Given it, he paced, restless, angry. Federal officers soon came to his place of refuge for no apparent reason. Lee, surely resenting being stared at like a lion in a cage, was characteristically polite to them. Then, when his tent was ready, he went into it and stayed there alone, perhaps remembering what a private had said to him as the troops were hugging Traveller's neck and stroking the big horse's flanks: "General, I have had the honor of serving in this army since you took command. If I thought I were to blame for what has occurred today I could not look you in the face, but I always try to do my duty. I hope to have the honor of serving under you again. Good-bye, General; God bless you."

Ulysses Grant was no relic hunter: He had left before the stripping of Wilbur McLean's parlor began, so stunned by that Sunday afternoon's event that he had to be reminded to tell anyone in Washington about it. All he wrote at four-thirty P.M. on April 9 to Secretary of War Stanton was:

> General Lee surrendered the Army of Northern Virginia this afternoon upon terms proposed by myself. The accompanying additional correspondence will show the conditions fully.

Blue-clad soldiers bearing ration boxes and herding cattle came into the Confederate camps. The smells of beef roasting soon filled the late-evening air along with the scent of approaching rain. A Union army bugler blew taps—Daniel Butterfield's best-remembered contribution to the war now ended, at least in Virginia—and a federal band played "Home, Sweet Home."

Overnight rain continued into Monday morning, April 10. At General Lee's direction, Colonel Marshall got to work on a farewell order to the troops. Lee met Grant for a visit of maybe half an hour. As Grant recalled it:

> [I] suggested to General Lee that there was not a man in the Confederacy whose influence with the soldiery and the whole people was as great as his, and that if he would now advise the surrender of all the armies I had no doubt his advice would be followed with alacrity. But Lee said, that he could not do that without consulting the President first. I knew there was no use to urge him to do anything against his ideas of what was right.

Then General Grant started for his old headquarters at City Point, Washington his ultimate destination. On Monday, while Grant's train was being delayed by three derailments, the news of his victory at Appomattox was driving people in the federal capital into frenzied celebration. Five hundred guns fired salutes all that rainy day; processions of office workers filled the muddy streets. And so it was throughout the Union. The war was not completely over, but victory seemed near enough to howl about, and howl the war-weary Northerners did.

When the general-in-chief reached the War Department on Thursday morning, April 13, he found that Secretary Stanton was ready to stop all recruiting and drafting and to curtail orders for supplies. Grant agreed; Mobile had been captured the day before, Wilson's cavalry had scattered Nathan Bedford Forrest's riders in Alabama and was now raiding Georgia, and Sherman had stopped the destruction of North Carolina after he learned of Sunday's events at Appomattox.

On Good Friday, the fourteenth, General Grant was a guest at a cabinet meeting. Joe Johnston's army would surrender soon, the president told him, for, he had had, the night before, the same odd dream he always had before some momentous development. And what could this latest dream portend but Sherman's victory?

Grant politely declined an invitation to join the Lincolns that evening to see a play at Ford's Theater. Mrs. Grant, he explained, was anxious to leave for a visit with their children in New Jersey.

Chapter 40

War Gives Way to a Troubled Peace

$\mathbf{N}$ow Robert E. Lee was a paroled prisoner of war, free to depart, but he would not leave until the formalities were completed. One was issuing General Order No. 9:

> After four years of arduous service marked by unsurpassed courage and fortitude, the Army of Northern Virginia has been compelled to yield to overwhelming numbers and resources.... You will take [home] with you the satisfaction that proceeds from the consciousness of duty faithfully performed; and I earnestly pray that a Merciful God will extend to you His mercy and protection.
>
> With an unceasing admiration of your constancy and devotion to your Country, and a grateful remembrance of your kind and generous consideration for myself, I bid you all an affectionate farewell.

George Meade and artillerist Henry Hunt, friends in Old Army days, came to visit Lee. He was pleased that his men were to be given free transportation home on federal military railroads and ships. On Tuesday he wrote a preliminary report to Davis beginning: "It is with pain that I announce to Your Excellency the surrender of the Army of Northern Virginia."

Then came the morning of April 12, the day his men were to lay down their arms and their units' colors for the last time. Federal Major General Joshua L. Chamberlain, whose timely action at Little Round Top on Gettysburg's second day may have saved Meade's army, was designated to carry out this part of the surrender. As John Gordon and the first remnants of his corps arrived, Chamberlain ordered his men to salute: Gordon returned it smartly and passed the word back for the men to do likewise. And so it went, until finally Longstreet's corps had stacked its arms and the Army of Northern Virginia passed out of existence and into the mists of memory.

On Sunday, while Grant and Lee were coming to terms, Abraham Lincoln was on the *River Queen* bound for Washington, entertaining his family and guests by reading aloud from Shakespeare's *Macbeth*. One passage intrigued him so much he repeated it:

> Duncan is in his grave;
> After life's fitful fever he sleeps well;
> Treason has done his worst; nor steel, nor
>   poison,
> Malice domestic, foreign levy, nothing
> Can touch him further.

Once in Washington, Lincoln received disturbing news from Richmond. While he had been near there, Judge John A. Campbell had asked if Virginia's legislature might reassemble to begin the process of Reconstruction. Yes, the president was thought to have said; in any case, such an effort was under way on April 12, when certain members of the Congressional Committee on the Conduct of the War were visiting Richmond and learned of it. Senator Benjamin F. Wade, of all Radicals perhaps the most extreme, was furious. An observer wrote:

> Mr. Wade said in substance, if not in exact words, that there had been much talk of the *assassination* of Lincoln— that if he authorized [the Virginians' gathering]...by God, the sooner he was assassinated the better!

Well, that was politics—which someone, later, would say "ain't beanbag." The issue was whether the peace given the South would be along Lincoln's humane and conciliatory lines or the Radicals' harshly punitive ones. And, curiously, some of the Northern people thought the generals ought to do the peacemaking—not the politicians, whose blunders four, five, even more years earlier had led to the whole appalling catastrophe.

Even so, it was up to the Union's wartime commander-in-chief to lead the reunification effort, and he was talking about that with his cabinet on Good Friday afternoon, the fourteenth. His day's work done, he told his wife that the Grants were leaving for New

Jersey that evening and would not (as handbills and the newspapers were proclaiming) be their guests in the president's box at Ford's Theater. Perhaps Mary Lincoln was relieved: Julia Grant was not one of her favorite people. She invited another couple, then joined her husband for a quiet dinner.

By that time, on that Friday evening, the Grants were in the private car provided them by the railroad's president, and the general knew why Julia had insisted they get out of Washington as soon as possible. During luncheon with friends in a hotel's dining room she had been struck by the rudeness of a man trying to listen to the ladies' conversation. Then, as the Grants were riding in a carriage on the way to the train, Julia had spotted the same man on a horse riding near them. Finally, once she and the Union armies' general-in-chief were aboard the rail car, at both its ends train crewmen locked the doors.

Jefferson Davis and his cabinet left Danville on April 10 amid rumors that Lee had surrendered. The president's arrival in Greensboro was almost ignored by a populace fearing Yankee reprisals; a refugee family gave him an upstairs bedroom in their rented quarters; all but one of his cabinet members found shelter in the train's coaches, now on a siding, or in empty boxcars. Ailing Secretary of the Treasury George Trenholm was taken in by a local banker hoping to exchange worthless Confederate bonds for treasury gold. That resource, however, had already gone down the tracks to Charlotte.

Davis summoned General Johnston to the temporary capital for a conference. Beauregard had already arrived, Secretary of War John Breckinridge was expected. On April 12, the president made it clear to them that he meant to continue the fight no matter what may have happened to Lee and his army. The generals could hardly believe Davis was serious, especially with depressing news pouring in from Alabama. The next day, John Breckinridge arrived and told them Lee had indeed surrendered. President Davis asked for opinions as to what to do next. The people were tired of the war, said Johnston, and the Confederacy was "without money, or credit, or arms, or ammunition, or means of procuring them." His men were deserting. There was no choice but to ask Sherman for terms. Reluctantly, Davis agreed to seek a truce "to permit the civil authorities to enter into the needful arrangements to terminate the existing war."

That done, Davis spent Good Friday in getting ready to go to Charlotte. He and those with him would have to ride, using back roads: Yankee cavalry had torn up the tracks.

Good Friday, 1865, was also the fourth anniversary of Fort Sumter's surrender and the war's beginning. Appropriately, at noon, Major General Robert Anderson stood amid the rubble—all that was left of the fort in Charleston's harbor—and with thousands watching and bands playing, he raised the same battle-torn flag he had lowered on April 14, 1861. With the banner rippling in the breeze, a minister from Brooklyn ended the ceremony with a benediction that included these words:

> Remember those who have been our enemies, and turn their hearts from wrath and war, to love and peace. Let the desolations that have come on them suffice, and unite them with us in ties of a better brotherhood than of old; that the cities, and homes, and happiness they have lost may be more than replaced in the long prosperity they shall hereafter know.

So Abraham Lincoln had been thinking on that Good Friday, and before leaving for Ford's Theater, he talked with Representative Schuyler Colfax of Indiana about calling a special session of Congress to expedite conciliation. Then it was time to go, to pick up young Clara Harris and her fiancé, Major H. R. Rathbone, the couple Mary Lincoln had invited to join them in place of the departed Grants. Earlier, the president had told an aide of his reluctance. "It has been advertised that we will be there, and I cannot disappoint the people. Otherwise I would not go." But he went. And once the play *Our American Cousin*, began, Lincoln seemed to enjoy it.

The British farce in which Laura Keene starred was in its third act at about ten-fifteen, when through the unguarded door and into the presidential box stepped John Wilkes Booth, twenty-six, a sometime actor. He blocked the door behind him. With a one-shot Derringer he fired at the back of the head of the man in the rocking chair. Dropping the pistol, Booth slashed Rathbone's arm with a knife, then rushed to the edge of the box, tried to let himself down to the stage by clinging to bunting, got a spur caught and fell, breaking his left leg. But up he rose and said: *"Sic semper tyrannis!"* And a moment later he was gone, hobbling offstage toward the theater's rear door.

It had happened so suddenly that the people in the audience were stunned. Not Rathbone: "Stop that man!" he cried. "He has shot the President!"

To the box, its door opened by Rathbone, came young Army

surgeon Charles A. Leale and actress Laura Keene. They found Lincoln slumped in his rocking chair as though he had merely gone to sleep. At first, Leale searched the president's body for stab wounds. Only when he put his hand beneath Lincoln's head as they were moving him did he discover a half-inch hole. Booth's single round had entered his victim's brain from the left rear and embedded itself behind Lincoln's right eye.

"His wound is mortal," said the doctor, who had seen many like it on battlefields. Two other surgeons were there by then, and they agreed that the few signs of life remaining in Lincoln would fade if they tried to move him to the Executive Mansion, six blocks away. Their decision was to take him to a house across Tenth Street. There he would linger, in a coma, for the next nine hours or so while Clara Harris and Laura Keene tried to keep nigh-hysterical Mary Lincoln out of the room where her stricken husband lay on a corn-shuck mattress and Senator Charles Sumner sat, sobbing uncontrollably, holding the dying president's hand.

Secretary of War Edwin Stanton rushed to the little house facing Ford's Theater and took charge. With good reason: At about the same time Booth shot Lincoln, another assailant broke into William Seward's home and slashed the Secretary of State and his son before escaping into the rain-swept darkness. For a time it was thought Vice President Andrew Johnson might be a target, but he appeared, unharmed, to look into the room where Abraham Lincoln was barely clinging to life.

Stanton ordered a massive hunt for Booth and alerted the troops in Washington to guard offices against arson and prevent others in the government from being attacked. His first theory was that this whole thing was a huge Confederate plot: How else could such a dreadful calamity have occurred?

General Grant was in Philadelphia when he got a wire from Major Eckert, one ending: "The Secretary of War desires that you return to Washington immediately." He caught the next train south, possibly the only one running because Stanton was freezing all means of movement not directed by him.

Then, at about seven on the morning of April 15, Captain Robert Lincoln led his mother into the little room—briefly, leaving behind Stanton, crying, tears streaming into his beard. A few minutes passed. The army's surgeon general checked vital signs and found none. Said Stanton: "Now he belongs to the ages."

Stunning grief overspread a nation that so recently had been rejoicing. From Maine to California church bells tolled. In Washington thousands of mourners passed the casket in the Capitol's rotunda. More stood outside the Executive Mansion on Wednesday, the nineteenth, as funeral services were held in the East Room: Mrs. Lincoln was too distraught to attend.

Afterward a train carried Abraham Lincoln back home to Illinois, reversing the route another one had taken in bringing him to Washington early in 1861. At each stop, saddened crowds gathered. Not for nearly a month would he reach his grave in Springfield.

Few men then living had known Lincoln as well as Homer Bates and Major Tom Eckert. In the War Department's telegraph room they had watched him, night and day, for four years as he read the messages coming in from battlegrounds as far west as Pea Ridge and as near as Fort Stevens. Bates and Eckert had seen him fight Stonewall Jackson in the Shenandoah Valley—and lose. He always seemed to lose, and there were all those other times when men died by the thousands without settling anything or seeming to bring victory one day nearer. Yet Lincoln had kept at it, as much a soldier as any man in the field in that respect, despite being disappointed by failures of one commander after another, taking the blame for McDowell, McClellan, Banks, Frémont, Buell, Pope, Burnside, Hooker, Rosecrans, Butler, Halleck, even at times Meade and Grant.

To Eckert and Bates he may have seemed the last casualty in a war he had seen approaching but could not prevent. They may have thought back, also, to the times they had seen him place telegraphed warnings into an envelope marked, simply, "Assassinations." Or remembered the days he had sat there drafting the Emancipation Proclamation. Or recalled how this gentlest of men could send an order to kill.

Greatness was what Bates and Eckert had witnessed, and now it was gone with the man they mourned.

Although Secretary Stanton had wired the news to Sherman at noon on Saturday, the general did not receive it until early Monday morning, the seventeenth, as he was on the way to meet General Johnston. Sherman told the telegraph operator not to reveal the contents of Stanton's message to anyone until he returned.

Once at the conference site, midway between Hillsboro and Durham, Sherman asked Johnston to have a few private words with him. Sherman wrote afterward:

> As soon as we were alone together I showed [Johnston] the dispatch announcing Mr. Lincoln's assassination, and watched him closely. The perspiration came out in large drops on his forehead, and he did not attempt to conceal his

distress. He denounced the act as a disgrace to the age, and hoped I did not charge it to the Confederate Government. I told him I could not believe that he or General Lee, or the officers of the Confederate army, could possibly be privy to acts of assassination; but I would not say as much for Jeff. Davis, George Sanders, and men of that stripe....I then told Johnston that he must be convinced that he could not oppose my army, and that, since Lee had surrendered, he could do the same with honor and propriety. He plainly and repeatedly admitted this, and added that any fighting would be "murder;" but he thought that, instead of surrendering piecemeal, we might arrange terms that would embrace all the Confederate armies. I asked him if he could control other armies than his own; he said, not then, but intimated that he could procure authority from Mr. Davis.

They agreed to meet at the same place the next day, and with Joe Johnston on Tuesday came Confederate Secretary of War John Breckinridge. At first Sherman refused to deal with a civil official, but Johnston pointed out that Breckinridge was also a major general, and Cump relented. And when the three men entered a house, Sherman pulled a whiskey bottle and glasses out of a saddlebag and suggested they have a drink. Nothing could have pleased Breckinridge more, for he had long been without his favorite beverage. As the discussions went on, the one-time vice president of the United States made a number of helpful suggestions, so many that Sherman said: "See here, gentlemen, who is doing the surrendering anyhow? If this thing goes on, you'll have me sending an apology to Jeff Davis."

Instead, Sherman wrote terms dealing with a number of non-military matters as well as the surrender of all Confederate armies. But at one point in his drafting he paused, went over to his saddlebag, drew out the bottle, took a drink, then sat down and picked up his pen. The document called for a truce while both governments ratified the agreement. Their work done, at least for the time being, the adversaries parted.

"General Johnston," said Breckinridge as they rode away, "General Sherman is a hog! Yes, sir, a hog! Did you see him take that drink by himself?" Cump was just absentminded, Joe Johnston explained. "Ah, no Kentucky gentleman would ever have taken away that bottle. He knew we needed it."

Indeed, General Sherman had been overly generous. Confederate Postmaster General John Reagan wrote to Davis:

[Sherman's draft] contains no direct reference to the

question of slavery, requires no concession from us in regard to it, and leaves it subject to the Constitution and the laws of the United States and of the several States just as it was before the war.

President Andrew Johnson and the cabinet were incensed by what they saw as a field general's usurpation of powers only his civilian superiors possessed. Grant, present at the stormy meeting, was told to get the thing done right or turn Sherman loose to destroy what was left of Johnston's army. Quietly, the general-in-chief hurried down to Raleigh, arriving on April 24. "I am instructed to limit my operations to your immediate command, and not to attempt civil negotiations," Sherman said in a note to Johnston. "I therefore demand the surrender of your army on the same terms as were given General Lee at Appomattox, April 9th instant, purely and simply."

On April 26, 1865, General Joseph Eggleston Johnston surrendered the 73,260 men on his army's rolls, of which 14,770 or fewer were still with him. Sherman sent ten days' rations to the departing Confederates and loaned animals to them "to insure a crop." Cump wrote to Johnston:

> Now that the war is over, I am as willing to risk my person and reputation as heretofore to heal the wounds made by the past war, and I think my feeling is shared by the whole army.

And the Virginian replied:

> The enlarged patriotism exhibited in your orders reconciles me to what I have previously regarded as the misfortune of my life, that of having to encounter you in the field. The enlightened and humane policy you have adopted will certainly be accepted.

So ended the war in the east, but soon squabbling broke out among the victors. While General Grant was on his way to Raleigh, Edwin Stanton had edited some of the communications pertaining to Sherman's negotiations with Johnston and leaked the maimed versions to the *New York Times*. The implication left in readers' minds was that Cump had not only willfully exceeded his authority and offered the South too soft a peace but that he had also been "bought" by rebel gold to permit Jefferson Davis to escape.

Why Stanton had done such a thing would remain as much a mystery as his other twists and turns. Cump Sherman could take care of himself. Not Henry Halleck: First Stanton shoved Old Brains down to Richmond as commander of the Virginia military district; then he altered one of Halleck's dispatches to make it seem that he was accusing Sherman of accepting Confederate gold. Halleck wrote Cump to set him straight, but Sherman ignored his letters, destroying forever what may have been the most important friendship he had ever had.

Madness, Texan A. W. Sparks had called the mood of the people in the hot summer of 1860 as night after night the ominous comet streaked across the skies; and madness the war had surely been. Yet there had been a certain distorted logic operating during those four years; rather, the substitution of military ways of thought for ordinary decision making. And now, with the fighting all but over, everything everywhere was falling apart.

Malice toward none, charity for all, Lincoln had desired. His generals reflected that spirit in the terms they extended. But before the assassinated president's funeral, his successor was declaring to Radical visitors: "I hold that robbery is a crime; rape is a crime; murder is a crime; *treason* is a crime—and crime must be punished. Treason must be made infamous, and traitors must be impoverished."

And Tennesseean Andrew Johnson went beyond (in effect), indicting all Southerners, centering his wrath on the fugitive Confederate president. "One hundred thousand dollars Reward in Gold will be paid to any person or persons who will apprehend and deliver Jefferson Davis to any of the military authorities of the United States," promised a circular issued by Stanton's War Department. "Several millions of specie reported to be with him will become the property of the captors."

Senator Ben Wade must have been pleased indeed by these changes in policy. Earlier, with Lincoln dead but not yet buried, he had said: "By the gods, there will be no trouble *now* in running the government." Punitive-minded Radicals would be in control, Wade meant, which was a world away from what the man lying in the casket had intended.

Now the government of the Confederate States of America consisted of six men on horseback and one prone in an ambulance wagon, moving first to Charlotte and then down through South Carolina and finally into central Georgia. Their route was more or less governed by the one Varina Davis had taken when she left Charlotte—she always seemed to be a few days ahead of them—for her husband was determined to see her and their children before he started the long ride westward to the Trans-Mississippi, where he hoped to collect the only troops not yet surrendered and continue the struggle.

Riding on back roads as he was, the president had no way of knowing how few men remained, where they were, or how quickly they were dwindling. In the region west of Georgia and east of the Mississippi River Lieutenant General Richard Taylor had fewer than 15,000—including what was left of Forrest's cavalry—and he had no idea what Davis wanted, where he was, or if he was still alive. But Taylor was aware that Lee and Johnston had surrendered, and at a place called Citronelle, north of Mobile, on May 4 he accepted the Appomattox terms.

The thought of being paroled was so abhorrent to Nathan Bedford Forrest that he considered heading for Mexico. In the end, however, he decided to stay and use such influence as he had to make peace work. And so he advised his troopers, writing:

> Civil war, such as you have just passed through, naturally engenders feelings of animosity, hatred, and revenge. It is our duty to divest ourselves of all such feelings; and, as far as in our power to do so, to cultivate friendly feelings toward those with whom we have so long contended, and heretofore so widely, but honestly, differed. Neighborhood feuds, personal animosities, and private differences should be blotted out; and, when you return home, a manly, straightforward course of conduct will secure the respect even of your enemies. Whatever your responsibilities may be to government, meet them like men.

And the Wizard, a lieutenant general now although he had entered the war as a private, many times wounded, a man who had had twenty-nine horses shot from under him, the killer of thirteen Yankees in hand-to-hand combat, concluded:

> I have never, on the field of battle, sent you where I was unwilling to go myself; nor would I now advise you to a course which I felt myself unwilling to pursue. You *have been* good soldiers; you *can be* good citizens. Obey the laws, preserve your honor, and the Government to which you have surrendered can afford to be, and will be, magnanimous.

That was on May 9. Before then one cabinet member after another had dropped out of Jefferson Davis's little cavalcade, heading homeward. But the president of nothing kept riding on in search of his family. On the morning of the seventh he caught up with Varina, and they were camped roughly forty miles south of Macon on the morning of May 10 when federal cavalry captured Jefferson Davis, his wife, Texans John Reagan and Francis R. Lubbock, and the very little that was left of the Confederate treasury—probably less than $10,000 in gold, an amount so small in any case that it could be carried in saddlebags.

Later it would be alleged that Davis had tried to escape wearing his wife's clothes. So newspapers would report. In haste he had picked up Varina's raincoat rather than his own, and she had thrown a shawl around his neck before sending him out of their tent. But a worse fate awaited him. He would spend the next two years in a dungeon at Fort Monroe, in solitary confinement, while the magnanimous federal government agonized over what else should be done to punish him.

Not so hesitant were Andrew Johnson and Edwin Stanton in dealing with the assassination. Stanton, in fact, had launched a massive search for John Wilkes Booth while Abraham Lincoln was still struggling to live. Booth evaded the dragnet, but it snared several people with ties to the fugitive. And in the course of the search, someone found a letter indicating that the murder plot had been designed in Richmond.

"Certainly I have no special regard for Mr. Lincoln," Jefferson Davis had said when told of the assassination, "but there are a great many men of whose end I had rather hear than his. I fear it will be disastrous to our people, and I regret it deeply."

General Lee was just arriving in Richmond on April 15 when news reached the city. He was worn out and in no mood to say anything to anyone outside his family. Not until September did he comment on the sad event. It was a crime, he wrote, "that must be deprecated by every American."

Yet in the days following Lincoln's death, anti-Confederate feelings ran strong. The Northern public's angry mood was not eased by news on April 28 that shortly after leaving Memphis the steamer *Sultana* had exploded with a loss of perhaps 1,800 lives. There was no connection with Booth; the cause was an overstrained boiler; but the *Sultana*, built to carry fewer than 400 passengers, was taking 2,000 Union soldiers toward their homes along the upper Mississippi—men emaciated by long captivity in Andersonville and other Confederate prisons.

Concurrently, to tragic irony was added frustration. John Wilkes Booth's bullet-riddled body was brought to Washington from south of Fredericksburg, where Union cavalrymen had shot him on April

26, as he stood in a burning tobacco barn. Now the full story of how
he came to the point of killing the president would never be known,
and Confederate complicity or innocence was doomed to incessant
debate.

There was one more chance to get at the truth, the trial of
Booth's alleged coconspirators, but Andrew Johnson left it to a
military commission to dispense justice. The main charge was that
the accused had conspired with (among other rebels) Jefferson Davis,
but no proof of that was offered. Instead, the trial record was filled
with unsubstantiated allegations and implications. As a result, Mary
Surratt—proprietor of a boardinghouse where Booth had stayed—
was hanged along with three men who may well have been his
accomplices. Three more were imprisoned for life, including Dr.
Samuel A. Mudd, who had set Booth's broken leg. A fourth man was
sentenced to a six-year term for helping the assassin get out of Ford's
Theater.

Everywhere east of the Mississippi peace was returning to the
land, even in Washington. By May 22 Mary Lincoln's health had
improved enough for her to surrender the Executive Mansion to the
Johnsons, who had waited patiently while she recovered from her
shock. And as if to end the Union-wide mourning for Abraham
Lincoln, General Meade's army and Cump Sherman's were camped
on opposite sides of the Potomac—to keep the unruly westerners
from fighting the much-envied "paper collar" troops—in preparation for a gigantic two-day victory parade.

Technically, this was premature. Out in the unconquered Trans-
Mississippi, Confederate General Edmund Kirby Smith had opened
negotiations but had not yet surrendered, nor would he sign the
now-familiar document until June 2, aboard a federal steamer in
Galveston harbor. Brigadier General Stand Watie held out even
longer. The Cherokee chieftain was the last rebel army leader to
surrender, on June 23, near Fort Towson in the Indian Territory (now
Oklahoma).

But none of this really mattered, except to Little Phil Sheridan,
who was furious because several days before the parade General
Grant sent him to New Orleans to carry out a project Lincoln had
never been able to undertake: placing U.S. forces along the Rio
Grande to show Napoleon III that he wanted the French army out of
Mexico. It was a bluff, of course. But what better man to run one was
there than the fierce Sheridan?

Yet the whole war had come down now to symbols, which for
the North meant that there should be one final, enormous parade.
To Major General George Gordon Meade the general-in-chief gave

the honor of leading it on May 23, and from the Capitol along Pennsylvania Avenue toward the Executive Mansion the men of the Army of the Potomac marched. Along their way buildings were draped with red, white, and blue bunting, and pretty girls not only pelted the soldiers with flowers but ran out to embrace the victors. It was the same the next day, the twenty-fourth, when Cump Sherman rode at the head of his "bummers"—except that the welcome given them may have been even more tumultuous.

This parade was the last, the final glimpse the veterans would have of their proud battle banners, most of them almost shredded by bullet holes, their colors already fading—mute testimony to uncommon valor and devotion to duty the marchers and the ghosts among them had displayed on battlefields whose names were even then forgotten.

For these men there remained only another night or two in camp, then all the good-byes and promises to keep in touch, the trips home, and—finally—the long remembering.

In June 1865, the CSS *Shenandoah*, commanded by Lieutenant James I. Wadell, was cruising the North Pacific near Alaska. It was from the captain of the brig *Susan Abigail* on June 23 that Waddell first learned of the fall of Richmond. On August 2 the master of the British bark *Barracouta* showed Waddell papers reporting Davis's capture. So began the *Shenandoah*'s 17,000-mile voyage down to Cape Horn and around it, ending finally on November 6, 1865, at Liverpool, when Waddell lowered the last official Confederate banner for the final time and turned his ship over to British authorities.

The *Shenandoah* had been the only Confederate vessel to carry the flag all the way around the world, flying it for six months after the war ended. She fired the last shot for the South on June 22 in the Arctic Ocean. "I claim for her officers and men a triumph over their enemies and over every obstacle," wrote Waddell, "and for myself I claim having done my duty."

That Southern veterans had done their duty was about the only satisfaction they brought home with them, and duty well performed would be the keynote during the Great Remembering—the years of memoir writing and unit history preparation that extended into the twentieth century.

Northerners as well would add volumes of reminiscences. But there was a difference: Southerners appeared to feel under pressure to tell their stories in justification of rebellion, to go beyond the fact that they had been whipped and explain why they had fought so long and so hard.

There was a lot to explain, especially to people defeated in war and entering peace saddened and impoverished by all the sacrifices they had made. Most soldier-authors spared their readers details of the war's boredom and horror and filth and cowardice and stupidity and depravity and disease. Instead, they concentrated on events from which a sense of glory and honor and pride could be derived. In the process, the Confederate States of America gained far more stature in print than it ever enjoyed during that government's brief existence.

Veterans such as A. W. Sparks, the Texan comet watcher who had gone to the war because he believed loyalty to his state's laws compelled him to, had spent four hard years soldiering with similarly motivated men from all over the South. As they marched through and fought in parts of it they might never have seen or thought much about otherwise, their narrow parochialism gave way to the realization that they were Southerners as well as Georgians or Arkansans or North Carolinians. Sharing defeat tightened their bonds of respect, leading them to revere even the feebleness of the vanished Confederacy as the "Lost Cause."

Well, why not? There would be no parades for the first Americans ever to experience defeat, only hugs and kisses from their loved ones before they planted crops or went hunting for jobs. Reconstruction proved harsh, embittering. Questions nagged; for example, one raised by Sparks near the end of his book when he asked, referring to the whole experience: "Has it taught us that the court of arms is the highest tribunal on earth and all laws should be subservient thereto?"

Sparks may seem an unreconstructed rebel—yet no more of one was he than Socrates, imprisoned and condemned to die by Greek authorities for disagreeing with them that the opinions of some men only are to be valued while the opinions of other men are not, and tempted by Crito's offer to arrange his escape. More than two thousand years separated the Confederate veteran and the philosopher, but their perplexity was the same: What is a man to do when the laws he has lived under and respected put his heart in conflict with itself?

Now we know what an entire nation did when its laws, more to the point the lack of preventive measures, placed so many of its citizens' hearts and minds and bodies in conflict. Yet the Civil War *did* settle something, as Americans have been reminded since the early 1890s whenever they recite the Pledge of Allegiance.

The Union, once restored, was understood to be a government no longer vulnerable to secession. Yes, indivisibility was reached through coercion; but from it would evolve a mix of loyalties—federal, state, and local, nationwide—which in subsequent wars and peace has reconfirmed the belief Lincoln expressed in his first inaugural address:

> We are not enemies, but friends. We must not be enemies. Though passion may have strained, it must not break our bonds of affection. The mystic chords of memory, stretching from every battlefield and patriot grave to every living heart and hearthstone all over this broad land, will yet swell the chorus of the Union when again touched, as surely they will be, by the better angels of our nature.

Slavery was the second dispute the Civil War settled, even before it ended: However belatedly, as a last resort, Jefferson Davis—not content with the work of the Confederate Congress—accepted emancipation as the price of continuing the fight.

Again, coercion prevailed. So did irony. At one point Lincoln had advocated paying Southerners $400 per slave to give them up. That would have dented the federal treasury by an estimated $1.6 billion; as it turned out, the eventual outlay would be $10 billion greater—apart from disruption, North and South, of the lives of perhaps 4 million young men and their families and the deaths of many more than half a million soldiers and not giving effect to the incalculable value of Southerners' physical property worn out and devastated during four years of resisting invasion.

After the guns cooled, the task of assuring liberty and justice for all reverted to the politicians. Unfortunately, they would bungle it as they had their chances to prevent the war. Ratification of the Thirteenth, Fourteenth, and Fifteenth amendments to the Constitution notwithstanding, blacks would go on suffering from segregation and discrimination nationwide for many generations to come.

But there *is* for all liberty in this land, and in time to come there may be justice for all—and an end, finally to punishment Americans have endured since 1860 for the original sin. Still, not until all the words in our pledge of allegiance are facts rather than hopes can we declare the Civil War truly over and know that its valiant ghosts are resting in peace.

Bibliography

Bibliographical Note:

Readers who find footnotes annoying have been spared 4,620 of these vexations. My sources are listed below, but this does not begin to cover my debt to them—nor can these few words express my appreciation for the inspiration as well as factual inputs they provided.

Aiding me greatly in using Civil War participants' own words were books such as Stephen W. Sears' *The Wartime Papers of George B. McClellan*, the source of the general's letters to his wife. Mere listing in the usual way hardly seems adequate acknowledgement of the enormous value the works of Sears and others added to my effort.

I am grateful also to the libraries and staff members whose gracious assistance made this book possible. Especially helpful were the Desmond/Fish Library in Garrison, New York, which obtained many books for me through inter-library loans, and The Union League Club of New York which made the *Official Records* and many other basic works available.

Special thanks I owe Alan C. Aimone, Assistant Librarian for Special Collections at the U.S. Military Academy Library, for his review of the manuscript and suggestions which saved me from some particularly embarrassing errors.

C. A.

Alexander, E. P. *Military Memoirs of a Confederate*. New York: Scribner's, 1907.

Ambrose, Stephen E. *Halleck: Lincoln's Chief of Staff*. Baton Rouge, La.: Louisiana State University Press, 1962.

Badeau, Adam. *Military History of Ulysses S. Grant*. 3 vols. New

York: D. Appleton, 1881.

Ballard, Colin R. *The Military Genius of Abraham Lincoln*. Cleveland and New York: World, 1952.

Ballard, Michael. *Pemberton: A Biography*. Jackson, Miss.: University Press of Mississippi, 1992.

Barnard, J. G. *The Peninsular Campaign*. New York, Van Nostrand, 1864.

Barron, Samuel B. *The Lone Star Defenders*. Washington, D.C.: Zenger, 1983.

Basler, Roy P., ed. *The Collected Works of Abraham Lincoln*. 9 vols. New Brunswick, N.J.: Rutgers University Press, 1953–1955.

Bates, Homer. *Lincoln in the Telegraph Office*. New York: Century, 1907.

Bauer, K. Jack. *The Mexican War*. New York: Macmillan, 1974.

Beatty, John. *Memoirs of a Volunteer, 1861–1863*. New York: W. W. Norton, 1946.

Benet, Stephen Vincent. *John Brown's Body*. New York: Rinehart, 1927.

Beringer, Richard E., Herman Hattaway, Archer Jones, William N. Still, Jr. *Why the South Lost the Civil War*. Athens, Ga.: University of Georgia Press, 1986.

Bernstein, Iver. *The New York City Draft Riots*. New York: Oxford, 1990.

Bigelow, John Jr. *The Campaign of Chancellorsville*. New Haven: Yale University Press, 1910.

Bill, Alfred Hoyt. *The Beleagured City*. New York: Knopf, 1946.

Boatner, Mark M. III. *The Civil War Dictionary*. New York: McKay, 1959.

Boyd, Belle. *Belle Boyd in Camp and Prison*. 2 vols. London: Saunders, Otley, & Co., 1865.

Brown, D. Alexander. *Grierson's Raid*. Urbana, Ill.: University of Illinois Press, 1962.

Cash, W. J. *The Mind of the South*. New York: Anchor, 1954.

Castel, Albert. *Decision in the West: The Atlanta Campaign of 1864*. Lawrence, Kans.: University Press of Kansas, 1992.

Catton, Bruce. *A Stillness at Appomattox*. Garden City: Doubleday, 1953.

———. *Grant Takes Command*. Boston: Little, Brown, 1968.

———. *Never Call Retreat*. Garden City: Doubleday, 1965.

———. *Terrible Swift Sword*. Garden City: Doubleday, 1963.

———. *The Coming Fury*. Garden City: Doubleday, 1961.

Chesnut, Mary Boykin. *A Diary from Dixie*. Edited by Ben Ames Williams. Boston, Houghton Mifflin, 1949.

Clausewitz, Karl von. *On War*. New York: Modern Library, 1943.

Cleaves, Freeman. *Meade of Gettysburg.* Norman, Okla.: University of Oklahoma Press, 1960.

Coddington, Edwin B. *The Gettysburg Campaign: A Study in Command.* New York, Macmillan, 1984.

Cook, Joel. *The Siege of Richmond.* Philadelphia: G. W. Childs, 1862.

Connelly, Thomas Lawrence. *Army of the Heartland: The Army of Tennessee, 1861–1862.* Baton Rouge, La.: Louisiana State University Press, 1967.

———. *Autumn of Glory: The Army of Tennessee 1862–1865.* Baton Rouge, La.: Louisiana State University Press, 1971.

Cozzens, Peter. *No Better Place to Die.* Urbana and Chicago: University of Illinois Press, 1992.

———. *This Terrible Sound: The Battle of Chickamauga.* Urbanna and Chicago: University of Illinois Press, 1992.

Craven, Avery. *The Coming of the Civil War.* New York: Scribner's, 1942.

Crawford, Samuel Wylie. *The Genesis of the Civil War.* New York: C. L. Webster Co., 1887.

Crippen, Lee F. *Simon Cameron: Ante Bellum Years.* New York: Da Capo, 1972.

Davis, Burke. *Jeb Stuart: The Last Cavalier.* New York: Rinehart, 1957.

———. *Sherman's March.* New York: Random House, 1980.

———. *They Called Him Stonewall.* New York: Rinehart, 1954.

———. *To Appomattox: Nine April Days, 1865.* New York: Rinehart, 1959.

Davis, William C. *Jefferson Davis: The Man and His Hour.* New York: HarperCollins, 1991.

Dennett, Tyler, ed. *Lincoln and the Civil War in the Diaries and Letters of John Hay.* New York: Dodd, Mead, 1939.

Department of Military Art and Engineering, United States Military Academy. *Jomini, Clausewitz and Schlieffen.* West Point, N.Y.: USMA Printing Office, 1948.

Doubleday, Abner. *Reminiscences of Forts Sumter and Moultrie.* New York: Harper & Brothers, , 1876.

Douglas, Henry Kyd. *I Rode With Stonewall.* Chapel Hill, N. C.: University of North Carolina Press, 1940.

Dowdey, Clifford. *Lee.* Boston: Little, Brown, 1965.

———. *Lee's Last Campaign.* Boston: Little, Brown, 1960.

———. *The Land They Fought For.* Garden City: Doubleday, 1956.

———. *The Seven Days.* Boston: Little, Brown, 1964.

Downey, Fairfax. *Storming of the Gateway: Chattanooga, 1863.* New York: McKay, 1960.

Duran, Fray Diego. *The Aztecs*. New York: Orion, 1964.

Early, Jubal A. *War Memoirs*. Bloomington, Ind.: University of Indiana Press, 1960.

Edge, Frederick Milnes. *Major-General McClellan and The Campaign on the Yorktown Peninsula*. London: Trübner & Co., 1865.

Edman, Irwin, ed. *The Works of Plato*. New York: Modern Library, 1928.

Elliott, Charles Winslow. *Winfield Scott: The Soldier and the Man*. New York: Macmillan, 1937.

Esposito, Vincent J., chief ed. *The West Point Atlas of American Wars*. 2 vols. New York: Praeger, 1959.

Euripides, *Phrixus*, Fragment 970, in *Bartlett's Familiar Quotations*, 10th ed. New York: Blue Ribbon, 1919.

Faust, Patricia L., ed. *Historical Times Encyclopedia of the Civil War*. New York: Harper & Row, 1986.

Fehrenbacher, Don E., ed. *Abraham Lincoln: Speeches and Writings 1859–1865*. Second of 2 vols. New York: Library of America, 1989.

Foner, Eric. *Reconstruction: America's Unfinished Revolution, 1863–1877*. New York: Harper & Row, 1988.

Foote, Shelby. *The Civil War*. 3 vols. New York: Random House, 1958, 1963, 1974.

Freehling, William W. *The Road to Disunion: Secessionists at Bay*. New York: Oxford, 1990. First of two volumes projected.

Freeman, Douglas Southall. *Lee's Dispatches*. New York: G. P. Putnam's Sons, 1957.

————. *Lee's Lieutenants*. 3 vols. New York: Scribner's, 1942.

————. *R. E. Lee*. 4 Vols. New York: Scribner's, 1934.

Fuller, J. F. C. *The Generalship of Ulysses S. Grant*. New York: Dodd, Mead, 1929.

Furgurson, Ernest B. *Chancellorsville 1863: The Souls of the Brave*. New York: Knopf, 1992.

Gallagher, Gary W., ed. *Fighting for the Confederacy: The Personal Recollections of General Edward Porter Alexander*. Chapel Hill, N.C. and London: University of North Carolina Press, 1989.

Gordon, George H. *From Brook Farm to Cedar Mountain*. Boston: Osgood, 1883.

Govan, Gilbert E. and James Livingood. *A Different Valor: The Story of General Joseph E. Johnston*. Indianapolis, Ind.: Bobbs Merrill, 1956.

Grant, Ulysses S. *Ulysses S. Grant: Memoirs and Selected Letters*. Compiled by Mary Drake and William S. McFeely. New York:

Library of America, 1990.

Gray, Wood. *The Hidden Civil War: The Story of the Copperheads.* New York: Viking Press, 1942.

Griffith, Paddy. *Rally Once Again: Battle Tactics of the Civil War.* New Haven: Yale University Press, 1989.

Halstead, Murat. *Fire the Salute!* Kingsport, Tenn.: Kingsport Press, 1960.

Hattaway, Herman, and Archer Jones. *How the North Won.* Urbana, Ill.: University of Illinois Press, 1983.

Haupt, Herman. *Reminiscences.* Milwaukee: Wright & Joy, 1901.

Henderson, G. F. R. *Science of War.* London: Longmans, Green, 1912.

_____. *Stonewall Jackson and the American Civil War.* New York: McKay, 1961.

Hendrick, Burton J. *Lincoln's War Cabinet.* Boston: Little, Brown, 1946.

Hennessy, John. *Return to Bull Run: The Campaign and Battle of Second Manassas.* New York: Simon & Schuster, 1992.

Henry, Robert Selph. *The Story of the Confederacy.* New York: Grosset & Dunlap, 1936.

_____. *The Story of Reconstruction.* Indianapolis and New York: Bobbs Merrill, 1938.

Herman, Marguerita Z. *Ramparts: Fortification From the Renaissance to West Point.* Garden City Park, N.Y.: Avery, 1992.

Hoehling, A. A. *Damn the Torpedoes!* Winston-Salem, N.C.: John F. Blair, 1989.

Hood, John B. *Advance and Retreat.* Bloomington, Ind.: University of Indiana Press, 1959.

Hughes, Robert M. *General Johnston.* New York: D. Appleton, 1912.

Johnson, Ludwell H. *Red River Campaign: Politics and Cotton in the Civil War.* Baltimore: Johns Hopkins Press, 1959.

Johnson, Robert U., and C. C. Buel, eds. *Battles and Leaders of the Civil War.* 4 vols. New York: Century, 1887–1888.

Johnston, William Preston. *The Life of Gen. Albert Sidney Johnston.* New York: D. Appleton, 1879.

Jones, Archer. *Civil War Command & Strategy.* New York: Free Press, 1992.

Jones, Terry L. *Lee's Tigers.* Baton Rouge, La.: Louisiana State University Press, 1987.

Jordan, Thomas J. and J. P. Pryor. *The Campaigns of Lieut.-Gen. N. B. Forrest and of Forrest's Cavalry.* Dayton, Ohio: Press of the Morningside Bookshop, 1973.

Josephy, Alvin M. *The Civil War in the American West.* New York: Knopf, 1992.

Kennedy, Frances H., ed. *The Civil War Battlefield Guide.* Boston:

Houghton Mifflin, 1990.

Kerby, Robert L. *Kirby Smith's Confederacy*. New York: Columbia University Press, 1972.

Leech, Margaret. *Reveille in Washington*. New York: Harper, 1941.

Lewis, Lloyd. *Captain Sam Grant*. Boston: Little, Brown, 1950.

———. *Sherman: Fighting Prophet*. New York: Harcourt Brace, 1932.

Livermore, Thomas L. *Numbers and Losses in the Civil War in America, 1861–1865*. Boston: Houghton Mifflin, 1901.

Long, E. B. *The Civil War, Day by Day: An Almanac, 1861–1865*. Garden City: Doubleday, 1971.

Loughborough, Mary. *My Cave Life in Vicksburg*. Little Rock, Ark.: Kellogg Printing Co., 1882.

Luvaas, Jay, and Harold W. Nelson, eds. *The U. S. Army War College Guide to the Battles of Chancellorsville & Fredericksburg*. Carlisle, Pa.: South Mountain Press, 1988.

Macdonald, John. *Great Battles of the Civil War*. New York: Macmillan, 1988.

Mahan, Alfred Thayer. *The Influence of Seapower upon History*. New York: Sagamore, 1957.

Marszalek, John F. *Sherman: A Soldier's Passion for Order*. New York: Free Press, 1992.

Marvel, William. *Burnside*. Chapel Hill, N.C.: University of North Carolina Press, 1991.

McPherson, James M. *Abraham Lincoln and the Second American Revolution*. New York: Oxford, 1990.

———. *Battle Cry of Freedom: The Civil War Era*. New York: Oxford, 1988.

———. *Ordeal By Fire*. New York: Knopf, 1982.

McWhinney, Grady, and Judith Lee Hallock. *Braxton Bragg and Confederate Defeat*. 2 Vols. Tuscaloosa, Ala.: University of Alabama Press, 1969, 1992.

McWhinney, Grady, and Perry D. Jamieson. *Attack and Die: Civil War Tactics and the Southern Heritage*. Tuscaloosa, Ala.: University of Alabama Press, 1982.

Meredith, Roy. *Storm over Sumter*. New York: Simon & Schuster, 1957.

Miers, Earl Schenck and Richard A. Brown, editors. *Gettysburg*. New Brunswick, N.J.: Rutgers University Press, 1948.

Miers, Earl Schenck. *The Web of Victory*. New York: Knopf, 1955.

Montgomery, James Stuart. *The Shaping of a Battle: Gettysburg*. Philadelphia: Chilton, 1959.

Morris, Roy, Jr. *Sheridan: The Life and Wars of General Phil Sheridan*. New York: Crown, 1992.

Myers, William Starr. *General George Brinton McClellan*. New York: Appleton Century, 1934.

Nevins, Allan. *The Emergence of Lincoln*. 2 Vols. New York: Scribner's, 1950.

———. *The War for the Union*. 4 Vols. New York: Scribner's, 1959-1971.

———. *Frémont: The West's Greatest Adventurer*. 2 vols. New York: Harper, 1928.

Nicolay, John G. and John Hay. *Abraham Lincoln: A History*. 10 Vols. New York: Century, 1886–1890.

Niven, John. *Gideon Welles - Lincoln's Secretary of the Navy*. New York: Oxford, 1973.

Nolan, Alan T. *Lee Considered: General Robert E. Lee and Civil War History*. Chapel Hill, N. C.: University of North Carolina Press, 1991.

O'Connor, Richard. *Thomas: Rock of Chickamauga*. New York: Prentice-Hall, 1948.

Palfrey, Francis Winthrop. *The Antietam and Fredericksburg*. New York: Scribner's, 1882.

Parks, Joseph Howard. *General Edmund Kirby Smith, C.S. A.* Baton Rouge, La.: Louisiana State University Press, 1962.

Parrish, T. Michael. *Richard Taylor: Soldier Prince of Dixie*. Chapel Hill, N.C.: University of North Carolina Press, 1992.

Pinchon, Edgcumb. *Dan Sickles*. Garden City: Doubleday, 1945.

Porter, Horace. *Campaigning With Grant*. Edited by Wayne C. Temple. Bloomington, Ind.: University of Indiana Press, 1961.

Potter, David M., and Don E. Fehrenbacher. *The Impending Crisis, 1848–1861*. New York: Harper & Row, 1976.

Randall, J. G. *Lincoln the President*. 4 Vols. New York: Dodd Mead, 1945–1955.

Richardson, Rupert N., Ernest Wallace, and Adrian N. Anderson. *Texas: The Lone Star State*. Englewood Cliffs, N.J.: Prentice-Hall, 1981.

Roland, Charles P. *An American Iliad*. Lexington, Ky.: University Press of Kentucky, 1991.

Ropes, John Cadman. *The Army Under Pope*. New York: Scribner's, 1881.

Rowland, Dunbar, ed. *Jefferson Davis, Constitutionalist: His Letters, Papers, and Speeches*. 10 vols. Jackson, Miss.: University Press of Mississippi, 1923.

Royster, Charles. *The Destructive War*. New York: Knopf, 1991.

Sandburg, Carl. *Abraham Lincoln: The War Years*. 4 vols. New York: Harcourt, Brace, 1939.

Schenck, Martin. *Up Came Hill*. Harrisburg, Pa.: Stackpole Books,

1958.

Sears, Stephen W. *George B. McClellan: The Young Napoleon*. New York: Ticknor & Fields, 1988.

_____. *Landscape Turned Red: The Battle of Antietam*. New Haven and New York: Ticknor & Fields, 1983.

_____. *The Civil War Papers of George B. McClellan*. New York: Ticknor & Fields, 1989.

_____. *To the Gates of Richmond: The Peninsula Campaign*. New York: Ticknor & Fields, 1992.

Sherman, William Tecumseh. *Memoirs of General W. T. Sherman*. With notes by Charles Royster. New York: Library of America, 1990.

Sigaud, Louis A. *Belle Boyd - Confederate Spy*. Richmond, Va.: Dietz, 1944.

Simon, John Y., editor. *The Papers of U. S. Grant*. 14 vols. Carbondale, Ill.: Southern Illinois University Press, 1967–1985.

Sparks, A. W. *Recollections of the Great War*. Tyler, Tex.: Lee & Burnett, 1901.

Stackpole, Edward J. *Chancellorsville*. 2d ed. Harrisburg, Pa.: Stackpole Books, 1988.

Stampp, Kenneth M. *America in 1857*. New York and Oxford: Oxford, 1990.

_____. *The Imperiled Union*. New York: Oxford, 1980.

Starr, Louis M. *Bohemian Brigade: Civil War Newsmen in Action*. Madison, Wisc.: University of Wisconsin Press, 1987.

Steele, Matthew Forney. *American Campaigns*. 2 vols. Washington, D.C.: United States Infantry Association, 1947.

Stern, Philip Van Doren. *An End to Valor*. Boston: Houghton Mifflin, 1958.

Strode, Hudson. *Jefferson Davis: Confederate President*. 3 vols. New York: Harcourt, Brace, 1955–1964.

Swanberg, W. A. First Blood. New York: Scribner's, 1957.

_____. *Sickles the Incredible*. New York: Scribner's, 1956.

Tanner, Robert G. *Stonewall in the Valley*. Garden City: Doubleday, 1976.

Taylor, Richard. *Destruction and Reconstruction*. New York: D. Appleton, 1879.

Thomas, Benjamin P. and Harold M. Hyman. *Stanton: The Life and Times of Lincoln's Secretary of War*. New York: Knopf, 1962.

Thomas, Emory M. *The Confederate Nation*. New York: Harper & Row, 1979.

Thomason, John W. Jr. *Jeb Stuart*. New York: Scribner's, 1930.

Time-Life Books, editors, *The Civil War: Lee Takes Command*. Alexandria, Va.: Time-Life Books, 1984.

U. S. Navy Department. *Official Records of the Union and Confederate Navies in the War of the Rebellion.* 27 vols. Washington, D.C.: Government Printing Office, 1894–1917.

Vandiver, Frank E. *Mighty Stonewall.* New York: McGraw-Hill, 1957.

Villard, Henry. *Lincoln on the Eve of '61.* New York: Knopf, 1951.

War of the Rebellion: Official Records of the Union and Confederate Armies. 70 vols. in 128. Washington, D.C.: Government Printing Office, 1880–1901.

Wert, Jeffry D. *From Winchester to Cedar Creek: The Shenandoah Campaign of 1864.* Carlisle, Pa.: South Mountain Press, 1987.

Wheeler, Richard. *The Siege of Vicksburg.* New York: Crowell, 1978.

Wilbur, Henry W. *President Lincoln's Attitude Towards Slavery and Emancipation.* New York: Biblo & Tannen, 1914, reprinted 1970.

Williams, Kenneth P. *Lincoln Finds a General.* 5 vols. New York: Macmillan, 1949–1959.

Williams, T. Harry. *Lincoln and His Generals.* New York: Knopf, 1952.

―――. *Lincoln and the Radicals.* Madison, Wisc.: University of Wisconsin Press, 1965.

―――. *P. G. T. Beauregard.* Baton Rouge, La.: Louisiana State University Press, 1954.

Wills, Brian Steel. *A Battle From the Start.* New York: HarperCollins, 1992.

Woodworth, Steven E. *Jefferson Davis and His Generals.* Lawrence, Kans.: University Press of Kansas, 1990.

Wyeth, John A. *The Life of General Nathan Bedford Forrest.* New York and London: Harper, 1904.

Index